Introduction to Physical Anthropology

SEVENTH EDITION

Robert Jurmain

Department of Anthropology
San Jose State University
San Jose, California

Harry Nelson

Emeritus
Department of Anthropology
Foothill College
Los Altos, California

Lynn Kilgore

Department of Anthropology
Colorado State University
Fort Collins, Colorado

Wenda Trevathan

Department of Sociology
and Anthropolgy
New Mexico State University
Las Cruces, New Mexico

West / Wadsworth

I(T)P® an International Thomson Publishing Company

Belmont, CA • Albany, NY • Bonn • Boston • Cincinatti • Detroit • Johannesburg
London • Los Angeles • Madrid • Melborne • Mexico City • Minneapolis/St. Paul
New York • Paris • Singapore • Tokyo • Toronto • Washington

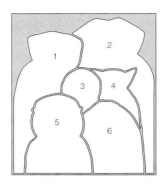

1. Proboscis monkey (*Nasalis larvatus*)
2. Bonobo (*Pan paniscus*)
3. Cottontop tamarin (*Saguinus oedipus*)
4. Golden-crowned or Tattersall's sifaka
   (*Propithecus tattersalli*)
5. Moustached guenon (*Cercopithecus cephus*)
6. Red uakari (*Cacajao calvus rubicundus*)

PRODUCTION CREDITS
Design and production: Hespenheide Design
Copy editor: Janet Greenblatt
Illustrations: Alexander Productions, Paragon 3, Sue Sellars, Cyndie Wooley
Cover illustration: Stephen D. Nash
Photography: see credits on pages 558–560

For more information, contact Wadsworth Publishing Company, 10 Davis Drive, Belmont, CA 94002,
or electronically at http://www.thomson.com/wadsworth.html

International Thomson Publishing Europe
Berkshire House 168-173
High Holborn
London, WC1V7AA, England

International Thomson Editores
Campos Eliseos 385, Piso 7
Col. Polanco
11560 México D.F. México

Thomas Nelson Australia
102 Dodds Street
South Melbourne 3205
Victoria, Australia

International Thomson Publishing Asia
221 Henderson Road
#05-10 Henderson Building
Singapore 0315

Nelson Canada
1120 Birchmount Road
Scarborough, Ontario
Canada M1K5G4

International Thomson Publishing Japan
Hirakawacho Kyowa Building, 3F
2-2-1 Hirakawacho
Chiyoda-ku, Tokyo 102, Japan

International Thomson Publishing GmbH
Königswinterer Strasse 418
53227 Bonn, Germany

International Thomson Publishing Southern Africa
Building 18, Constantia Park
240 Old Pretoria Road
Halfway House, 1685 South Africa

ISBN 0-314-20289-7

Contents

1

Introduction

2

The Development of Evolutionary Theory

3

The Biological Basis of Life

4

Heredity and Evolution

5

Microevolution in Modern Human Populations

6

Approaches to Human Variation and Adaptation

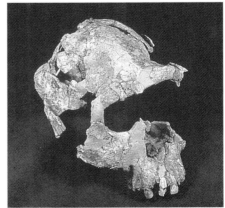

7

Growth and Development

8

Macroevolution: Overview and Principles

9

An Overview of the Living Primates

10

Fundamentals of Primate Behavior

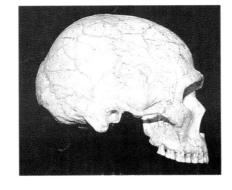

11

Primate Models for Human Evolution

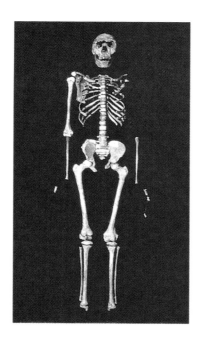

12

Primate Evolution

13

Paleoanthropology

14

Plio-Pleistocene Hominids

15

Plio-Pleistocene Hominids: Organization and Interpretation

16

Homo erectus

17

Neandertals and Other Archaic *Homo sapiens*

18

Homo sapiens sapiens

Preface

In almost two decades of textbook preparation, we have followed the development and expansion of physical anthropology. In this 7th edition of *Introduction to Physical Anthropology*, we attempt to continue to provide a current and accessible synthesis of our field. To this end, we have updated the book throughout and include discussions of new fossil discoveries (e.g., Eocene anthropoids, *Ardipithecus, Australopithecus anamensis*). We also provide photographs and information regarding new Paleolithic cave art from France and an expanded discussion of the interpretation of Paleolithic art. New perspectives on the use of mitochondrial and nuclear DNA to calibrate contemporary population diversity are included in Chapter 5. Finally, the use of the same types of genetic methodologies to assess the emergence and dispersal of modern humans is discussed in Chapter 18.

The most noticeable organizational change to this edition is the inclusion of two new authors, Lynn Kilgore and Wenda Trevathan. Lynn Kilgore has been a co-author on two of our other texts (*Essentials of Physical Anthropology* and *Understanding Physical Anthropology and Archeology*) and has contributed some sections to previous editions of this book. Wenda Trevathan is new to our team, but has had considerable textbook-writing experience and is currently a co-author on *Anthropology: An Applied Perspective* by Ferraro, Trevathan, and Levy, a general anthropology textbook also published by West. As an expert in the field of human growth and development, Dr. Trevathan adds an important new emphasis to our coverage—and this topic in this edition is covered as a new chapter (Ch. 7, Human Growth and Development).

Most introductory survey courses inevitably present significant challenges to both students and instructors. Introductory Physical Anthropology is no exception, and we have thus tried to design the text to provide a variety of pedagogical aids. For example, as in earlier editions, a running glossary (with pronunciation guides), a full glossary at the end of the book, maps, photo layouts (depicting hominid anatomical characteristics), and boxed features are again utilized. To provide further assistance to students while reading the boxed features, we have added a further aid: For technical, more substantive boxes the background is untinted; for more supplementary (e.g., historical or biographical) features, the background is tinted.

We have also added a new pedagogical feature, timelines, to the chapters dealing with fossil evidence of primate/hominid evolution (Chs. 12–18). We think that, in addition to the large-format maps (which assist students in placing sites in space), the new timelines will help them place important discoveries (and evolutionary stages) in time.

Our experience has also taught us that some innovations work better than others. One modification which we tried in the sixth edition has here been returned to its original form. As in earlier editions, the materials on the historical development of evolutionary theory are once again included in a separate chapter (Ch. 2). Accordingly, as compared to the sixth edition, there has been some rearrangement in the ordering of chapters and the placement of some topics relating to evolutionary theory in Chapters 4 and 5. Further, Chapter 6 has been completely rewritten and restructured so that the materials on traditional approaches to human diversity (i.e., "race") are now more coherent and lead immediately to the more contemporary focus on human adaptation.

As in the sixth edition, we have asked some of our colleagues to supply guest essays (in which they discuss how they became anthropologists as well as various aspects about their personal research). We are most grateful to our seven colleagues who have contributed guest essays to this edition: David Begun, Margaret Conkey, Ellen Ingmanson, Kamoya Kimeu, Linda Klepinger, Henry McHenry, and James McKenna.

We have been highly fortunate throughout our earlier editions to benefit from the detailed comments and suggestions of our various reviewers. In this edition we are especially appreciative of the current reviewers: David R. Begun, University of Toronto; Susan Cachel, Rutgers University; Steven Churchill, University of New Mexico; Philip de Barros, Palomar College; Barbara J. King, College of William & Mary; Mary H. Manhein, Louisiana State University; Michael Nunley, Central Michigan University; Janis Silva, Solano Community College; Sam D. Stout, University of Missouri, Columbia; Linda L. Taylor, University of Miami; William Wihr, Portland Community College; and Marcus Young Owl, California State University, Long Beach.

We also wish to acknowledge Pat McGrath, Shirley McGreal, Dieter Steklis, and Thomas Wolfie for invaluable assistance with the Issues for Chapters 8 and 9. And we are particularly indebted to Barbara King for her comprehensive and most helpful editing, and to Marcus Young Owl for developing the study guide that accompanies this book.

We also express our continued great appreciation to the many friends and colleagues who have generously provided photographs: C. K. Brain, Gunter Brauer, Desmond Clark, Jean DeRousseau, Denis Etler, Diane France, David Frayer, David Haring, Ellen Ingmanson, Fred Jacobs, Arlene Kruse, Carol Lofton, Lorna Moore, John Oates, Bonnie Pedersen, Lorna Pierce, David Pilbeam, William Pratt, Judith Regensteiner, Wayne Savage, Rose Sevcik, Elwyn Simons, Meredith Small, Fred Smith, Judy Suchey, Li Tianyuan, Phillip Tobias, Alan Walker, Milford Wolpoff, and Xinzhi Wu.

Finally, we wish to thank those who have assisted directly in the production of this book, Gary Hespenheide (of Hespenheide Design) and most especially our editors at West: Clyde Perlee, Editor-in-Chief; Denise Simon, Executive Editor; and Janine Wilson and Shannon Buckels, Developmental Editors. The professionalism of the editors at West Educational Publishing, led by Clyde Perlee, has not only made our textbooks possible, but has enhanced each of them immeasurably. For their friendship, support, and enduring confidence we will always be grateful.

Robert Jurmain
Harry Nelson
Lynn Kilgore
Wenda Trevathan

Introduction

Introduction

▲ **Hominidae**
The taxonomic family to which humans belong; also includes other, now extinct, bipedal relatives.

▲ **Hominids**
Members of the family Hominidae.

One day, perhaps at the beginning of the rainy season some 3.7 million years ago, two or three individuals walked across a grassland savanna in what is now northern Tanzania. These individuals were early members of the taxonomic family **Hominidae**, the family that also includes ourselves, modern *Homo sapiens*. Fortunately for us (the living descendants of those distant travelers), a record of their passage on that long-forgotten day remains in the form of fossilized footprints, preserved in hardened volcanic deposits.

As chance would have it, shortly after heels and toes were pressed into the dampened soil and volcanic ash of the area, a volcano, some 12 miles distant, erupted. The ensuing ashfall blanketed everything on the ground surface, including the footprints of the **hominids** and those of numerous other species as well. In time, the ash layer hardened into a deposit, which preserved a quite remarkable assortment of tracks and other materials that lay beneath it (Fig. 1–1).

These now-famous Laetoli prints indicate that two hominids, one smaller than the other, perhaps walked side by side, leaving parallel sets of tracks. But

FIGURE 1–1
Early hominid footprints at Laetoli. The tracks to the left were made by one individual, while those to the right appear to have been formed by two individuals, the second stepping in the tracks of the first.

because the prints of the larger individual are obscured, possibly by those of a third, it is unclear how many actually made that journey so long ago. What is clear from the prints is that they were left by an animal that habitually walked **bipedally** (on two feet). It is this critical feature that has led scientists to consider these ancient passersby as hominids.

In addition to the preserved footprints, scientists at Laetoli and elsewhere have discovered numerous fossilized skeletal remains of what most now call *Australopithecus afarensis*. These fossils and prints have volumes to say about the beings they represent, provided we can learn to interpret them.

What, then, have we actually gleaned from the meager evidence we possess of those creatures who beckon to us from an incomprehensibly distant past? Where did their journey take them that far-gone day, and why were they walking in that particular place? Were they foraging for food within the boundaries of their territory? Were they simply walking to a nearby water source? Did the two (or three) indeed travel together at all, or did they simply use the same route within a short period of time?

We could ask myriad questions about these individuals, but we will never be able to answer them all. They walked down a path into what became their future, and their immediate journey has long since ended. It remains for us to sort out what little we can know about them and the **species** they represent. In this sense, their greater journey continues.

From the footprints and from fossilized fragmentary skeletons, we know that these hominids walked in an upright posture. Thus, they were, in some respects, anatomically similar to ourselves, but their brains were only about one-third the size of ours. Although they may have used stones and sticks as tools, much as modern chimpanzees do, there is no current evidence to suggest they manufactured stone tools. In short, these early hominids were very much at the mercy of nature's whims. Compared to many of their contemporaries, they were not strong. They certainly could not outrun most predators, and their lack of large projecting canine teeth rendered them relatively defenseless.

Chimpanzees often serve as living models for our early ancestors, but in fact, the earliest hominids occupied a different habitat, exploited different resources, and probably had more to fear from predators than do chimpanzees. However much we may be tempted to compare early hominids to living species, we must constantly remind ourselves that there is no living form that adequately represents them. Just like every other living thing, they were unique.

On July 20, 1969, a television audience numbering in the hundreds of millions watched as two human beings stepped out of a spacecraft and onto the surface of the moon. To anyone born after that date, this event is taken more or less for granted, even though it has not been repeated often. But the significance of that first moonwalk cannot be overstated, for it represents humankind's presumed mastery over the natural forces that govern our presence on earth. For the first time ever, people actually walked upon the surface of a celestial body that (as far as we know) has never given birth to biological life.

As the astronauts gathered geological specimens and frolicked in near weightlessness, they left traces of their fleeting presence in the form of footprints in the lunar dust (Fig. 1–2). On the atmosphereless surface of the moon, where no rain falls and no wind blows, the footprints remain undisturbed to this day. They survive as mute testimony to a brief visit by a medium-sized, big-brained creature who presumed to challenge the very forces that had created it.

We humans uncovered the Laetoli footprints, and we question the nature of the animal who made them. Perhaps one day, creatures as yet unimagined will

▲ **Bipedally**
On two feet. Walking habitually on two legs is the single most distinctive feature of the Hominidae.

▲ **Species**
A group of organisms that can interbreed to produce fertile offspring. Members of one species are reproductively isolated from members of all other species (i.e., they cannot mate with them to produce fertile offspring).

FIGURE 1–2
Human footprints left on the lunar surface during the Apollo mission.

ponder the essence of the being that made the lunar footprints. What do you suppose they will think?

We humans, who can barely comprehend a century, can only grasp at the enormity of 3.7 million years. We want to understand the essence of those creatures who traveled that day across the savanna. By what route did an insignificant but clever bipedal **primate** give rise to a species that would, in time, walk on the surface of a moon some 230,000 miles from earth? How did it come to be that in the relatively short span (in geological time) of fewer than 4 million years, an inconsequential savanna dweller evolved into the species that has developed the ability to dominate and destroy much (if not all) of life on the planet?

How did it happen that *Homo sapiens*, a result of the same evolutionary forces that produced all other life on this planet, gained the power to control the flow of rivers and alter the very climate in which we live? As tropical animals, how were we able to leave the tropics and disperse over most of the earth's land surfaces, and how did we adjust to local environmental conditions as we so expanded? How could our species, which numbered fewer than 1 billion individuals until the mid-nineteenth century, come to number over 5.6 billion worldwide today and, as we now do, add another billion every 11 years?

These are some of the many questions that physical or biological anthropologists attempt to answer, and these questions are largely the focus of the study of human evolution and adaptation. These issues, and many more, are the topics covered directly or indirectly in this text, for physical anthropology is, in part, human biology seen from an evolutionary perspective. However, physical anthropologists are not exclusively involved in the study of physiological systems and biological phenomena. When such topics are placed within the broader context of human evolution, another factor must also be considered: the role of **culture**.

Culture is an extremely important concept, not only as it pertains to modern human beings, but also in terms of its critical role in human evolution. It has been said that there are as many definitions of culture as there are people who attempt to define it. Quite simply, culture can be said to be the strategy by which humans adapt to the natural environment. In this sense, culture includes technologies that range from stone tools to computers; subsistence patterns ranging from hunting and gathering to agribusiness on a global scale; housing types, from thatched huts to skyscrapers; and clothing, from animal skins to high-tech synthetic fibers (Fig. 1–3). Because religion, values, social organization, language, kinship, marriage rules, gender roles, inheritance of property, and so on, are all aspects of culture, each culture shapes peoples' perceptions of the external environment, or world view, in particular ways that distinguish that culture from all others.

One fundamental point to remember is that culture is *learned* and not biologically determined. Culture is transmitted from generation to generation independent of biological factors (i.e., genes). For example, if a young girl of Vietnamese ancestry is raised in the United States by English-speaking parents, she will acquire English as her native language. She will eat Western foods with Western utensils and will wear Western clothes. In short, she will be a product of Western culture, because that is the culture she will have learned. We are all products of the culture in which we are socialized, and since most human behavior is learned, it clearly is also culturally patterned.

But, as biological organisms, humans are subject to the same evolutionary forces as all other species. On hearing the term *evolution*, most people think of the appearance of new species. Certainly, new species formation is one conse-

▲ **Primate**
A member of the order of mammals Primates (pronounced "pry-may-tees"), which includes prosimians, monkeys, apes, and humans.

▲ **Culture**
All aspects of human adaptation, including technology, traditions, language, and social roles. Culture is learned and transmitted from one generation to the next by nonbiological means.

(a)

(b)

(c)

(d)

quence of evolution; however, biologists see evolution as an ongoing biological process with a precise genetic meaning. Quite simply, evolution is a change in the genetic makeup of a population from one generation to the next. It is the accumulation of such changes, over considerable periods of time, that can result in the appearance of a new species. Thus, evolution can be defined and studied at two different *levels*: that of the population (*microevolution*) and that of the species (*macroevolution*). Evolution as it occurs at both these levels will be addressed in this text.

One critical point to remember is that the human predisposition to assimilate a particular culture and to function within it is influenced by biological factors. In the course of human evolution, as you will see, the role of culture increasingly assumed an added importance. Over time, culture and biology

FIGURE 1–3

(a) An early stone tool from East Africa. This artifact represents the oldest type of stone tools found anywhere. (b) Assortment of implements available today in a modern hardware store. (c) A Samburu woman building a simple, traditional dwelling of stems, plant fibers, and mud. (d) A modern high-rise apartment complex, typical of industrialized cities.

▲ **Biocultural evolution**
The mutual, interactive evolution of human biological structure and human culture. The concept that biology makes culture possible and that developing culture further influences the direction of biological evolution; a basic concept in understanding the unique components of human evolution.

▲ **Adaptation**
Functional response of organisms or populations to the environment. Adaptation results from evolutionary change (specifically, as a result of natural selection).

▲ **Anthropology**
The field of inquiry that studies human culture and evolutionary aspects of human biology; includes cultural anthropology, archeology, linguistics, and physical anthropology.

interacted in such a way that humans are said to be the result of **biocultural evolution**. In this respect, humans are unique among biological organisms.

Biocultural interactions have not only resulted in such anatomical, biological, and behavioral changes as increased brain size, reorganization of neurological structures, decreased tooth size, and development of language in humans, to list a few, but continue to be critical in changing disease patterns as well. As a contemporary example, rapid culture change (particularly in Africa) and changing social and sexual mores may have influenced evolutionary rates of HIV, the virus that causes AIDS. Certainly, these cultural factors influenced the spread of HIV throughout populations in both the developed and developing worlds.

The study of many of the biological aspects of humankind, including **adaptation** and evolution, could certainly be the purview of human biologists, and it frequently is. However, particularly in the United States, when such research also considers the role of cultural factors, it is placed within the discipline of **anthropology**.

What Is Anthropology?

Stated ambitiously but simply, anthropology is the study of humankind. (The term *anthropology* is derived from the Greek words *anthropos*, meaning "human," and *logos*, meaning "word" or "study of.") Anthropologists are not the only scientists who study humans, and the goals of anthropology are shared by other disciplines within the social, behavioral, and biological sciences. For example, psychologists and psychiatrists investigate various aspects of human motivation and behavior while developing theories that have clinical significance. And because historians focus on recorded events in the human past, their research is limited to, at most, a few thousand years. The main difference between anthropology and such related fields is that anthropology integrates the findings of many disciplines, including sociology, economics, history, psychology, and biology.

The focus of anthropology is very broad indeed. Like other disciplines, anthropology is divided into numerous specialized subfields, but fundamentally its concentration is on human biological and cultural evolution. In short, anthropologists explore all aspects of what it means to be human.

In the United States, anthropology comprises three main subfields: cultural, or social anthropology; archeology; and physical, or biological, anthropology. Additionally, some universities include linguistic anthropology as a fourth area. Each of these subdisciplines, in turn, is divided into more specialized areas of interest. Following is a brief discussion of the main subdisciplines of anthropology.

Cultural Anthropology

Cultural anthropology is the study of all aspects of human behavior. It could reasonably be argued that cultural anthropology began with Aristotle, or even earlier. But for practical purposes, the beginnings of cultural anthropology are found in the nineteenth century, when Europeans became increasingly aware of what they termed "primitive societies" in Africa and Asia. Likewise, in the New World, there was much interest in the vanishing cultures of Native Americans.

The interest in traditional societies led numerous early anthropologists to study and record lifeways that unfortunately are now mostly extinct. These studies produced many descriptive **ethnographies** that became the basis for subse-

▲ **Ethnographies**
Detailed descriptive studies of human societies. In cultural anthropology, an ethnography is traditionally the study of a non-Western society.

quent comparisons between groups. Early ethnographies emphasized various phenomena, such as religion, ritual, myth, use of symbols, subsistence strategies, technology, gender roles, child-rearing practices, dietary preferences, taboos, medical practices, and how kinship was reckoned.

Ethnographic accounts, in turn, formed the basis for comparative studies of numerous cultures. Such *cross-cultural* studies, termed *ethnologies*, broadened the context within which cultural anthropologists studied human behavior. By examining the similarities and differences between diverse cultures, anthropologists have been able to formulate many theories about the fundamental aspects of human behavior.

The focus of cultural anthropology has shifted over the course of the twentieth century. But traditional ethnographic techniques, wherein anthropologists spend months or years living in and studying various societies, are still employed, although the nature of the study groups may have changed. For example, in recent decades, ethnographic techniques have been applied to the study of diverse subcultures and their interactions with one another in contemporary metropolitan areas. The subfield of cultural anthropology that deals with issues of inner cities is appropriately called *urban anthropology*. Among the many issues addressed by urban anthropologists are the relationships between ethnic groups, those aspects of traditional cultures maintained by immigrant populations, poverty, labor relations, homelessness, access to health care, and problems facing the elderly.

Medical anthropology is the subfield of cultural anthropology that explores the relationship between various cultural attributes and health and disease. One area of interest is how different groups view disease processes and how these views affect treatment or the willingness to accept treatment. When a medical anthropologist focuses on the social dimensions of disease, physicians and physical anthropologists may also collaborate. Indeed, many medical anthropologists have received much of their training in physical anthropology.

Economic anthropologists are concerned with factors that influence the distribution of goods and resources within and between cultures. Areas of interest include such topics as division of labor (by gender and age), factors that influence who controls resources and wealth, and trade practices and regulations.

Many cultural anthropologists are involved in gender studies. Such studies may focus on gender norms, how such norms are learned, and the specific cultural factors that lead to individual development of gender identity. It is also valuable to explore the social consequences if gender norms are violated.

There is also increasing interest in the social aspects of development and aging. This field is particularly relevant in industrialized nations, where the proportion of elderly individuals is higher than ever before. As populations age, the needs of the elderly, particularly in the area of health care, become social issues that require more and more attention.

Another relevant area for cultural anthropologists today is in the resettlement of refugees in many parts of the world. To develop plans that properly accommodate the needs of displaced peoples, governments can find the special talents of cultural anthropologists of considerable benefit.

Many of the subfields of cultural anthropology have practical applications and are pursued by anthropologists working outside the university setting. This approach is aptly termed *applied anthropology*. While most applied anthropologists regard themselves as cultural anthropologists, the designation is also sometimes used to describe the activities of archeologists and physical anthropologists. Indeed, the various fields of anthropology, as they are practiced in the United States, overlap to a considerable degree, which, after all, was the rationale for combining them under the umbrella of anthropology in the first place.

Archeology

Archeology is the study of earlier cultures and lifeways by anthropologists who specialize in the scientific recovery, analysis, and interpretation of the material remains of past societies. Although archeology often deals with cultures that existed before the invention of writing (the period commonly known as *prehistory*), *historic* archeologists also examine the evidence of later, complex civilizations that produced written records.

Archeologists are concerned with culture, but they differ from cultural anthropologists in that their sources of information are not living people but rather the **artifacts** and other **material culture** left behind by earlier societies. Obviously, no one has ever excavated such aspects of culture as religious belief, spoken language, or a political system. However, archeologists assume that the surviving evidence of human occupation reflects some of those important but less tangible features of the culture that created them. Therefore, the material remains of a given ancient society may serve to inform us about the nature of that society.

The roots of modern archeology are found in the fascination of nineteenth-century Europeans with the classical world (particularly Greece and Egypt). This interest was primarily manifested in the excavation (sometimes controlled, sometimes not) and removal of thousands of treasures and artifacts, destined for the museums and private collections of wealthy Europeans.

New World archeology has long focused on the pre-Columbian civilizations of Mexico and Central and South America (the Aztecs, Maya, and Inca). In North America, archeological interest was sparked particularly by the large earthen burial mounds found throughout much of the southeast. In fact, Thomas Jefferson conducted one of the first controlled excavations of a burial mound on his Virginia plantation in 1784. Importantly, his goal was not simply the recovery of artifacts; he specifically wished to address the question of how the mound was constructed.

Today, archeology is aimed very much at answering specific questions pertaining to human behavior. Patterns of behavior are reflected in the dispersal of human settlements across a landscape and in the distribution of cultural remains within them. Through the identification of these patterns, archeologists can elucidate the commonalities shared by many or all populations as well as those features that differ between groups. Research questions may focus on specific localities or peoples and attempt to identify, for example, various aspects of social organization, subsistence techniques, or the factors that led to the collapse of a particular civilization. Alternatively, inquiry may reflect an interest in broader issues relating to human culture in general, such as the development of agriculture or the rise of cities. But the design of most archeological projects centers around a number of questions that address a wide range of interests, both specific and broad.

Archeology is a discipline that requires precise measurement, description, and excavation techniques, for it must be remembered that when a site is dug, it is also destroyed. Errors in excavation or recording result in the permanent loss or misinterpretation of valuable information. Therefore, contrary to what many people think, the science of archeology is much more than simply digging up artifacts. Rather, archeology is a multidisciplinary approach to the study of human behavior as evidenced by cultural remains.

For many projects, the specialized expertise of many disciplines is needed. Chemists, geologists, physicists, paleontologists, and physical anthropologists

▲ **Artifacts**

Objects or materials made or modified for use by hominids. The earliest artifacts tend to be tools made of stone or, occasionally, bone.

▲ **Material culture**

The physical manifestations of human activities; includes tools, art, and structures. As the most durable aspects of culture, material remains make up the majority of archeological evidence of past societies.

may all be called on. Even the sophisticated satellite technologies of NASA have been called on to locate archeological sites.

In the United States, the greatest expansion in archeology in recent years has been in the important area of *cultural resource management (CRM)*. This applied approach arose from environmental legislation requiring the archeological evaluation and even excavation of sites that may be threatened by construction and other forms of development. Many contract archeologists (so called because their services are contracted out to developers, government agencies, municipalities, and the like) are affiliated with private archeological consulting firms, state or federal agencies, or educational institutions. In fact, an estimated 40 percent of all archeologists in the United States now fill such positions.

Archeological techniques are used to identify and excavate not only remains of human cities and settlements, but also paleontological sites containing remains of extinct species, including everything from dinosaurs to early hominids. Together, prehistoric archeology and physical anthropology form the core of a joint science called *paleoanthropology*, which is described below.

Linguistic Anthropology

Linguistic anthropology is the study of human speech and language, including the origins of language in general as well as specific languages. By examining similarities between contemporary languages, linguists have been able to trace historical ties between languages and groups of languages, thus facilitating the identification of language families and perhaps past relationships between human populations.

There is also much interest in the relationship between language and culture: how language reflects the way members of a society perceive phenomena and how the use of language shapes perceptions in different cultures. For instance, vocabulary provides important clues as to the importance of certain items and concepts in particular cultures. The most famous example is the use of some 50 terms for snow among the Inuit (Eskimos), reflecting their need to convey specific information about the properties of this form of frozen precipitation. (For that matter, downhill skiers also employ many more increasingly precise terms for snow than do nonskiers.)

Because the spontaneous acquisition and use of language is a uniquely human characteristic, it is a topic that holds considerable interest for linguistic anthropologists, who, along with specialists in other fields, study the process of language acquisition in infants. Since insights into the process may well have implications for the development of language skills in human evolution, as well as in growing children, it is also an important subject to physical anthropologists.

Physical Anthropology

Physical anthropology, as has already been stated, is the study of human biology within the framework of evolution, with an emphasis on the interaction between biology and culture. Physical anthropology is composed of several subdisciplines, or areas of specialization, the most significant of which are briefly described in the following paragraphs.

The origins of physical anthropology are to be found in two principal areas of interest among nineteenth-century scholars. First, there was increasing concern among many scientists (at the time called *natural historians*) regarding the mechanisms by which modern species had come to be. In other words, increasing numbers of intellectuals were beginning to doubt the literal, biblical interpretation of creation. This does not mean that all natural historians had abandoned all religious explanations of natural occurrences. But scientific explanations emphasizing natural, rather than supernatural, phenomena were becoming increasingly popular in scientific and intellectual circles. Although few were actually prepared to believe that humans had evolved from earlier forms, discoveries of several Neandertal fossils in the 1800s began to raise questions regarding the origins and antiquity of the human species.

The sparks of interest in biological change over time were fueled into flames by the publication of Charles Darwin's *Origin of Species* in 1859. Today, **paleoanthropology**, or the study of human evolution, particularly as evidenced in the fossil record, is one of the major subfields of physical anthropology (Fig. 1–4). There are now thousands of specimens of human ancestors housed in museum and research collections. Taken together, these fossils cover a span of at least 4 million years of human prehistory, and although incomplete, they provide us with significantly more knowledge than was available even 15 years ago. It is the ultimate goal of paleoanthropological research to identify the various early hominid species, establish a chronological sequence of relationships among them, and gain insights into their adaptation and behavior. Only then will there emerge a clear picture of how and when humankind came into being.

A second nineteenth-century interest that had direct relevance to anthropology was observable physical variation, particularly as seen in skin color.

▲ **Paleoanthropology**
The interdisciplinary approach to the study of earlier hominids—their chronology, physical structure, archeological remains, habitats, etc.

FIGURE 1–4
Paleoanthropological research at Hadar, Ethiopia, during a recent field season in 1993.

Enormous effort was aimed at describing and explaining the biological differences among various human populations. Although many endeavors were misguided, they gave birth to literally thousands of body measurements that could be used to compare people. Physical anthropologists use many of the techniques of **anthropometry** today, not only to study living groups, but also to study skeletal remains from archeological sites (Fig. 1–5). Moreover, anthropometric techniques have considerable application in the design of everything from airplane cockpits to office furniture.

Anthropologists today are concerned with human variation primarily because of its *adaptive significance*. In other words, traits that typify certain populations are seen as having evolved as biological adaptations, or adjustments, to local environmental conditions. Examining biological variation between populations of any species provides valuable information as to the mechanisms of genetic change in groups over time, which is precisely what the evolutionary process is all about.

Modern population studies also examine other important aspects of human variation, including how various groups respond physiologically to different kinds of environmentally induced stress (Fig. 1–6). Such stresses may include high altitude, cold, or heat.

Other physical anthropologists conduct nutritional studies, investigating the relationships between various dietary components, cultural practices, physiology, and certain aspects of health and disease. Closely related to the topic of nutrition are investigations of human fertility, growth, and development. These fields of inquiry are fundamental to studies of adaptation in modern human populations, and they can provide insights into hominid evolution as well.

It would be impossible to study evolutionary processes, and therefore adaptation, without a knowledge of genetic principles. For this reason and others,

▲ **Anthropometry**
Measurement of human body parts. When osteologists measure skeletal elements, the term *osteometry* is often used.

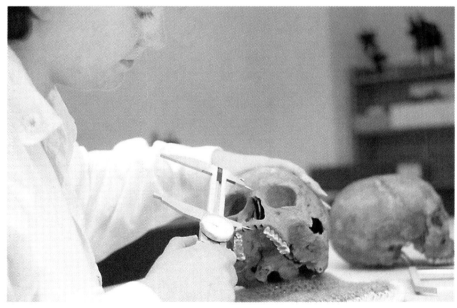

FIGURE 1–5
Anthropology student using sliding calipers to take facial measurements on a human cranium.

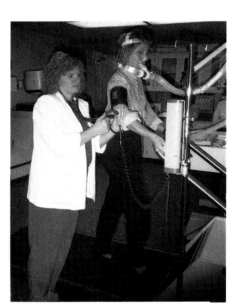

FIGURE 1–6
Researcher using a treadmill test to assess a subject's heart rate, blood pressure, and oxygen consumption.

▲ **Genetics**
The study of gene structure and action and the patterns of inheritance of traits from parent to offspring. Genetic mechanisms are the underlying foundation for evolutionary change.

▲ **Primatology**
The study of the biology and behavior of nonhuman primates (prosimians, monkeys, and apes).

genetics is a crucial field for physical anthropologists. Modern physical anthropology would not exist as an evolutionary science were it not for advances in the understanding of genetic principles.

Not only does genetics allow us to explain how evolutionary processes work, but today's anthropologists use recently developed genetic technologies to investigate evolutionary distances between living primate species (including humans). Moreover, genetic theories have been used (with much debate) to explain, among other things, the origins of modern *Homo sapiens*.

Primatology, the study of nonhuman primates, has become increasingly important since the late 1950s for several reasons (Fig. 1–7). Behavioral studies, especially those conducted on groups in natural environments, have implications for numerous scientific disciplines. Perhaps more importantly, studies of nonhuman animal behavior have assumed a greater urgency in recent decades, owing to the rapidly declining numbers of many species.

The behavioral study of any species provides a wealth of data pertaining to adaptation. Because nonhuman primates are our closest living relatives, the identification of underlying factors related to social behavior, communication, infant care, reproductive behavior, and so on, aids in developing a better understanding of the natural forces that have shaped so many aspects of modern human behavior.

Moreover, nonhuman primates are important to study in their own right (particularly true today because the majority of species are threatened or seriously endangered). Only through study will scientists be able to recommend policies that can better ensure the survival of many nonhuman primates and thousands of other species as well.

Primate paleontology, the study of the primate fossil record, has implications not only for nonhuman primates but also for hominids. Virtually every year, fossil-bearing beds in North America, Africa, Asia, and Europe yield important

FIGURE 1–7
(a) Yahaya Alamasi, a member of the senior field staff at Gombe National Park, Tanzania. Alamasi is recording behaviors in free-ranging chimpanzees. (b) Oakland Zoo docent uses a laptop computer to record behaviors of a captive chimpanzee.

(a)

(b)

new discoveries. Through the study of fossil primates, we are able to learn much about factors such as diet or locomotion in earlier forms. By comparisons with anatomically similar living species, primate paleontologists can make reasoned inferences regarding behavior in earlier groups as well. Moreover, we hope to be able to clarify what we know about evolutionary relationships between extinct and modern species, including ourselves.

Osteology, the study of the skeleton, is central to physical anthropology. Indeed, it is so important that when many people think of physical anthropology, the first thing that comes to mind is bones. The emphasis on osteology exists in part because of the concern with the analysis of fossil material. Certainly, a thorough knowledge of the structure and function of the skeleton is critical to the interpretation of fossil material.

Bone biology and physiology are of major importance to many other aspects of physical anthropology, in addition to paleontology. Many osteologists specialize in metric studies that emphasize various measurements of skeletal elements. This type of research is essential, for example, to the identification of stature and growth patterns in archeological populations.

One subdiscipline of osteology is the study of disease and trauma in archeologically derived skeletal populations. **Paleopathology** is a prominent subfield that investigates the incidence of trauma, certain infectious diseases (including syphilis and tuberculosis), nutritional deficiencies, and numerous other conditions that leave evidence in bone (Fig. 1–8). In this area of research, a precise knowledge of bone physiology and response to insult is required.

A field directly related to osteology and paleopathology is **forensic anthropology**. Technically, this approach is the application of anthropological (usually osteological and sometimes archeological) techniques to the law (Fig. 1–9).

▲ **Osteology**
The study of skeletons. Human osteology focuses on the interpretation of the skeletal remains of past groups. The same techniques are used in paleoanthropology to study early hominids.

▲ **Paleopathology**
The branch of osteology that studies the traces of disease and injury in human skeletal (or, occasionally, mummified) remains.

▲ **Forensic anthropology**
An applied anthropological approach dealing with matters of law. Physical anthropologists use their expertise to assist coroners and others in the analysis and interpretation of human remains.

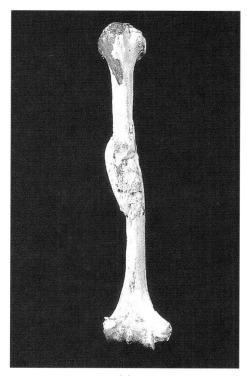

(a)

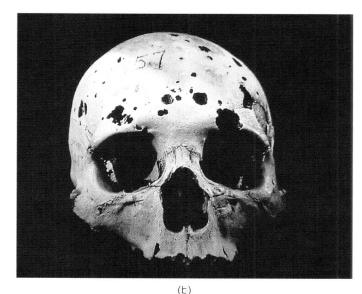

(b)

FIGURE 1–8

(a) Healing fracture of a humerus (upper arm bone) in a skeleton from Nubia (North Africa). (b) Cranial lesions, probably resulting from metasticized cancer.

FIGURE 1–9

Physical anthropologists Lorna Pierce (to left) and Judy Suchey (to right) working as forensic consultants. The dog has just located a concealed human cranium during a training session.

Forensic anthropologists are commonly called on to help identify skeletal remains in cases of disaster or other situations where a human body has been found.

Forensic anthropologists have been instrumental in a number of cases having important legal and historical consequences. They assisted medical examiners in 1993 with the identification of human remains at the Branch Davidian compound in Waco, Texas. They have also been prominent in the identification of remains of missing American soldiers in Southeast Asia and the skeletons of most of the Russian imperial family, executed in 1918. Forensic anthropology is very appealing to many students, but it should be remembered that additional training is important for anyone entering this field, inasmuch as he or she may be called on to provide crucial testimony as expert witnesses in court cases.

Anatomical studies constitute another important area of interest for physical anthropologists. In the living organism, bone and dental structures are intimately linked to the soft tissues surrounding and operating on them. Thus, a thorough knowledge of soft tissue anatomy is essential to the understanding of biomechanical relationships involved in movement. Such relationships are important to the development of conditions, such as arthritis, that are frequently encountered in paleopathology. Moreover, accurate assessment of the structure and function of limbs and other components in fossilized remains requires expertise in anatomical relationships. For these reasons, many physical anthropologists specialize in anatomical studies. In fact, several physical anthropologists hold professorships in anatomy departments at universities and medical schools.

From this brief overview, it can be seen that physical anthropology is the subdiscipline of anthropology that focuses on many varied aspects of the biological and behavioral nature of *Homo sapiens*. Humans are a product of the same forces that produced all life on earth. As such, we represent one contemporary component of a vast biological **continuum** at one point in time, and in this regard, we are not particularly unique. Stating that humans are part of a continuum does not imply that we are at the peak of development on that continuum. Depending on which criteria one uses, humans can be seen to exist at one end of

▲ Continuum

A set of relationships in which all components fall along a single integrated spectrum. All life reflects a single *biological* continuum.

the continuum or the other, or somewhere in between. But humans do not necessarily occupy a position of inherent superiority over other species.

There is, however, one dimension in which human beings are truly unique, and that is intellect. After all, humans are the only species, born of earth, to stir the lunar dust. Humans are the only species to develop language and complex culture as a means of buffering the challenges posed by nature, and, by so doing, eventually gain the power to shape the very destiny of the planet.

It has been said that humans created culture and that culture created humans. This statement is true to the extent that the increased brain size and reorganization of neurological structures that typify much of the course of human evolution would never have occurred if not for the complex interactions between biological and behavioral factors (i.e., biocultural evolution). In this sense, then, it is neither unreasonable nor presumptuous to say that we have created ourselves.

The Anthropological Perspective

Perhaps the most important contribution you will have received from this text—and this course—is a wider appreciation of the human experience. To understand human beings and how our species came to be, it is necessary to broaden our viewpoint, both through time and over space. All branches of anthropology fundamentally seek to do this in what we call *the anthropological perspective*.

Physical anthropologists, for example, are keenly interested in how humans differ from and are similar to other animals, especially nonhuman primates. For example, we have defined *hominids* as bipedal primates, but what are the major components of bipedal locomotion, and how do they differ from, say, those in a quadrupedal ape? To answer these questions, we would need to study human locomotion and compare it with the locomotion seen in various nonhuman primates. Moreover, in addition to observing how humans walk while wearing shoes, we also would be interested in their pattern of locomotion while walking barefoot. Indeed, it would probably be useful to look at the locomotion of people who have never worn shoes, and to obtain these data, we would probably have to leave our own culture and study other quite geographically distant groups.

Through such a wider perspective, we can begin to grasp the contemporary diversity of the human experience and, in so doing, understand more fully both human potentialities and human constraints. And, by extending our breadth of knowledge, it is easier to avoid the **ethnocentric** pitfalls inherent in a more limited view of humanity.

In addition to broadening perspectives over space (i.e., encompassing many cultures and ecological circumstances as well as nonhuman species), an anthropological perspective also extends our horizons *through time*. For example, in Chapter 7 we will discuss human nutrition. However, the vast majority of the kinds of foods currently eaten (coming from domesticated plants and animals) were unavailable prior to 10,000 years ago. Human physiological mechanisms for chewing and digesting foods nevertheless were already well established long before that date. These adaptive complexes go back many hundreds of thousands—perhaps even millions—of years. In addition to the obviously different diets prior to the development of agriculture (approximately 10,000 years ago), earlier hominids might well have differed from humans today in average body size, metabolism, and activity patterns. How, then, does the basic evolutionary

▲ **Ethnocentric**
Viewing other cultures from the inherently biased perspective of one's own culture. Ethnocentrism often results in cultures being seen as inferior to one's own.

"equipment" (i.e., physiology) inherited from our hominid forebears accommodate our modern diets? Clearly, the way to understand such processes is not just by looking at contemporary human responses, but also by placing them in the perspective of evolutionary development through time.

Indeed, most of the topics covered in this book—as most topics considered by all types of anthropologists—are addressed by using a broad application of the anthropological perspective. For physical anthropologists, such an approach usually means extending the perspective both over space as well as through considerable periods of time.

We hope that the ensuing pages will help you develop an increased understanding of the similarities we share with other biological organisms and also of the processes that have shaped the traits that make us unique. We live in what may well be the most crucial period for our planet in the last 65 million years. We are members of the one species that, through the very agency of culture, has wrought such devastating changes in ecological systems that we must now alter our technologies or face potentially unspeakable consequences. In such a time, it is vital that we attempt to gain the best possible understanding of what it means to be human. We believe that the study of physical anthropology is one endeavor that aids in this attempt, and that is indeed the goal of this text.

Summary

In this chapter, we have introduced the field of physical anthropology and have placed it within the overall context of anthropological studies. Anthropology as a major academic area within the social sciences also includes archeology, cultural anthropology, and linguistic anthropology as its major subfields.

Physical anthropology itself includes aspects of human biology (emphasizing evolutionary perspectives), the study of nonhuman primates, and the hominid fossil record. Especially as applied to the study of early hominids (as incorporated within the interdisciplinary field of paleoanthropology), physical anthropologists work in close collaboration with many other scientists from the fields of archeology, geology, chemistry, and so forth.

Questions for Review

1. What is anthropology? What are the major subfields of anthropology?
2. How does physical anthropology differ from other disciplines interested in human biology?
3. What is meant by biocultural evolution, and why is it important in understanding human evolution?
4. What are some of the primary areas of research within physical anthropology? Give two or three examples of the types of research pursued by physical anthropologists.
5. What is meant by the term *hominid?* Be specific.
6. What fields, in addition to physical anthropology, contribute to paleoanthropology?

Suggested Further Reading

Ferraro, Gary, Wenda Trevathan, and Janet Levy. 1994. *Anthropology, an Applied Perspective.* St. Paul: West.

Spencer, Frank, ed. 1982. *A History of Physical Anthropology.* New York:
    Academic Press.

Stiebing, William H., Jr. 1993. *Uncovering the Past: A History of Archaeology.*
    New York: Oxford University Press.

Internet Resources

Nicole's AnthroPage
    http://www.wsu.edu:8000/~i9248809/anthrop.html
    (Links to various anthropologically related subjects, journals, and issues of interest to
    students. Created and maintained by Nicole L. Noonan.)

Evaluation in Science:
Lessons in Critical Thinking

At the end of various chapters throughout this book, you will find a brief discussion on a contemporary topic. Some of these subjects, such as the use of nonhuman primates in biomedical research, are not usually covered in textbooks. However, we feel that it is important to address such issues, because scientists should not simply dismiss those views or ideas of which they are skeptical. Similarly, you should be reluctant to *accept* a view based solely on its personal appeal. Accepting or rejecting an idea based on personal feelings is as good a definition of "bias" as one could devise. Science is an approach—indeed, a *tool*—used to eliminate (or at least minimize) bias.

Scientific approaches of evaluation are, in fact, a part of a broader framework of intellectual rigor that is termed *critical thinking*. The development of critical thinking skills is an important and lasting benefit of a college education. Such skills enable people to evaluate, compare, analyze, critique, and synthesize information so that they will not accept all they hear and read at face value but will be able to reach their own conclusions. Critical thinkers are able to assess the evidence supporting their own beliefs (in a sense, to step outside themselves) and to identify the weaknesses in their own positions. They recognize that knowledge is not merely a collection of facts but an ongoing process of examining information to expand our understanding of the world.

In scientific inquiry, individual "facts" (or better put, *observations*) must be presented clearly, with appropriate documentation. That is the purpose of bibliographical citation, as exemplified throughout this textbook. Once "facts" are established, scientists attempt to develop explanations concerning their relationships. First, a *hypothesis* is formed. A hypothesis is a provisional statement about the relationships between observations. Once a hypothesis receives further confirmation and can be seen to explain a broad array of phenomena, it can be called a *theory*. A theory, then, is a statement of relationships that has some general basis. As such, it not only helps organize current knowledge but, ideally, should also *predict* how new facts may fit into the established pattern. While most dictionaries make a distinction between hypotheses and theories, in practice, most scientists do not emphasize this distinction. Both hypotheses and theories organize information; the latter simply encompass more global, or universal, topics.

A crucial aspect of scientific statements is that they are *falsifiable*; that is, there must be a means of evaluating the validity of hypotheses and theories to demonstrate that the statements may be incorrect. In this way, scientific conclusions are constantly *tested*. Statements such as "Heaven exists" may well be "true" (i.e., describe some actual state), but there is no rational, *empirical* means (based on experience or experiment) by which to test it. Acceptance of such a view is thus based on faith rather than on scientific verification.

We should emphasize that perceived phenomena understood through faith do not necessarily conflict with empirical demonstration. In fact, precisely because there may be areas of knowledge beyond the reach of scientific inquiry, faith-based beliefs provide a powerful influence for many people. Furthermore, these beliefs need not (and for many individuals, scientist and nonscientist alike, do not) conflict with the demonstrable values of scientific thought.

One of the most appealing aspects of perspectives based in faith is that such beliefs are widely and comfortably accepted as true. In science, statements can be tested and falsified (indeed, this is a central component of the scientific approach), but they can never completely be proved "true." Theories can simply be better substantiated and are thus more fully established. However, new evidence can also require modification of hypotheses and theories; and some theories might prove so inadequate as to be rejected altogether. Thus, Newton's theory of gravitation was substantially altered by Einstein's theory of relativity. The old theory of a "missing link" (a kind of halfway compromise between modern humans and modern apes) preceded modern evolutionary thinking and is now seen as simplistic, misleading, and, at a practical level, of no value.

This inherent aspect of scientific inquiry in which theories are always subject to ongoing evaluation is widely misunderstood, frequently with disturbing consequences. For example, as we will note in Chapter 2, claims are often made that evolution is "just a theory." Pronouncements like these, as related to the teaching of evolution in public schools, have found their way into court decisions in California and recent policy statements by the Alabama State Board of Education (see Issue, Chapter 2, for further discussion). In science, knowledge is always proposed, organized, and tested in the form of hypotheses and, more generally, as theories. Our understanding of the action of gravity is just a theory, and so is the sun-centered depiction of the solar system. These two theories have, of course, been supported by an overwhelming amount of highly consistent evidence—but *so has evolutionary theory*. The constraint that science can never establish absolute "truth" should not be confused with an inability to understand the world around us. The human brain is a product of 4 billion years of evolution on this planet, and by using this neurological structure, *Homo sapiens* has the ability to apply rational thought. In the last few hundred years, the scientific method has developed into the most powerful tool invented by our species to utilize these rational capabilities and, in so doing, to come to grips with the universe and how we fit into it.

In scientific inquiry (and everyday life), much of the information we use is assembled in *quantified* (i.e., numerical) form.

Throughout this text, you will be presented with the results of numerous studies that utilize numerical data. For example, it might be stated that female chimps eat more insects than male chimps or that Neandertal males were bigger than females or that the gene for cystic fibrosis is more common in European populations than in other groups. First of all, you should always be cautious of generalizations. What is the specific nature of the argument? What data support it? Can these data be quantified? If so, how is this information presented? (*Note:* Always read the tables in textbooks or articles.)

Regardless of the discipline you ultimately study, at some point in your academic career you should take a course in statistics. Many universities now make statistics a general education requirement (sometimes under the category "quantitative reasoning"). Whether you are required to take such an offering or elect to do so, we strongly encourage it. Statistics often seems a very dry subject, and many students are intimidated by the math it requires. Nevertheless, perhaps more than any other skill you will acquire in your college years, quantitative critical reasoning is a tool you will be able to use every day of your life.

The topics chosen for the chapter closing issues are those that intrigue the authors, and we hope that you will also find them stimulating. Some subjects, such as the Scopes trial (Chapter 2) and the Piltdown hoax (Chapter 13), are of historical interest. In addition, we address several topics that relate to recent advances in science, as exemplified by recombinant DNA research (Chapter 3) and developments in genetic testing (Chapter 4). Here, in addition to challenging you to grasp the basic scientific principles involved, we also ask you to consider the *social implications* of scientific/technological advances.

A responsibility of an educated society is to be both informed and vigilant. The knowledge we possess and attempt to build on is neither "good" nor "bad"; however, the uses to which knowledge may be put have highly charged moral and ethical implications. Thus, a goal of the chapter-closing issues is to stimulate your interest and provide you with a basis to reach your own conclusions. Here are some useful questions to ask in making critical evaluations about these issues or any other controversial scientific topic:

1. What data are presented?
2. What conclusions are presented, and how are they organized (as tentative hypotheses or as more dogmatic assertions)?
3. Are these views the individual opinions of the authors, or are they supported by a larger body of research?
4. What are the research findings? Are they adequately documented?
5. Is the information consistent with information that you already possess? If not, can the inconsistencies be explained?
6. Are the conclusions (hypotheses) testable? How might one go about testing the various hypotheses that are presented?
7. If presentation of new research findings is at odds with previous hypotheses (or theories), must these hypotheses now be modified (or completely rejected)?
8. How do your own personal views bias you in interpreting the results?
9. Once you have identified your own biases, are you able to set them aside so as to evaluate the information objectively?
10. Are you able to discuss both the pros and cons of a scientific topic in an evenhanded manner?

2

The Development of Evolutionary Theory

Introduction

▲ **Evolution**
A change in the genetic structure of a population. The term is also frequently used to refer to the appearance of a new species.

The term **evolution** is sometimes charged with emotion. The concept is often controversial, particularly in the United States, because some religious views hold that evolutionary statements run counter to biblical teachings. In fact, as you are probably aware, there continues to be much opposition to the teaching of evolution in public schools (see Issue, pp. 38–40).

Those who wish to denigrate evolution frequently insist that it is "only a theory"—an attempt, perhaps, to reduce its status to supposition. Actually, to refer to a concept as "theory" is to lend it support. As we noted in Chapter 1, theories are general hypotheses that have been tested and subjected to verification through accumulated evidence. Evolution *is* a theory, one that has increasingly been supported by a mounting body of genetic evidence. It is a theory that has stood the test of time, and today it stands as the most fundamental unifying force in biological science.

Because physical anthropology is concerned with all aspects of how humans came to be and how we adapt physiologically to the external environment, the details of the evolutionary process are crucial to the field. Moreover, given the central importance of evolution to physical anthropology, it is valuable to know how the mechanics of the process came to be discovered. Additionally, to appreciate the nature of the controversy that continues to surround the issue today, it is important to examine the basic evolutionary principles within the social and political context in which the theory emerged.

A Brief History of Evolutionary Thought

▲ **Natural selection**
The mechanism of evolutionary change first articulated by Charles Darwin. Refers to genetic change or changes in the frequencies of certain traits in populations due to differential reproductive success between individuals.

The individual most responsible for the elucidation of the evolutionary process was Charles Darwin. But while Darwin was formulating his theory of **natural selection**, his ideas were being duplicated by another English naturalist, Alfred Russel Wallace.

That natural selection, the single most important mechanism of evolutionary change, should be proposed at more or less the same time by two British men in the mid-nineteenth century may seen highly improbable. But actually, it is not all that surprising. Indeed, if Darwin and Wallace had not made their simultaneous discoveries, someone else would have done so in short order. That is to say, the groundwork had already been laid, and many within the scientific community were prepared to accept explanations of biological change that would have been unacceptable even 25 years before.

Like other human endeavors, scientific knowledge is usually gained through a series of small steps rather than giant leaps. Just as technological innovation is based on past achievements, scientific knowledge builds on previously developed theories. (One does not build a space shuttle without first having invented the airplane.) Given this stepwise aspect of scientific discovery, it is informative to examine the development of ideas that led Darwin and Wallace independently to develop the theory of evolution by natural selection.

▲ **World view**
General cultural orientation or perspective shared by members of a society.

Throughout the Middle Ages, one predominant component of the European **world view** was *stasis*. That is, all aspects of nature, including all forms of life and their relationships to one another, were fixed and unchanging. This view of natural phenomena was shaped in part by a feudal society that was very much a hierarchical arrangement supporting a rigid class system that had changed little for several centuries.

The world view of Europeans during the Middle Ages was also shaped by a powerful religious system. The teachings of Christianity were taken quite literally, and it was generally accepted that all life on earth had been created by God exactly as it existed in the present. Indeed, alterations in plants and animals were seen to be impossible because they would have run counter to God's plan. This belief that life forms could not change eventually came to be known in European intellectual circles as **fixity of species**.

Accompanying the notion of fixity of species was the belief that all God's creations were arranged in a hierarchy that progressed from the simplest organisms to the most complex. At the top of this linear sequence were humans. This concept of a ranked order of living things is termed the *Great Chain of Being* and was first proposed in the fourth century B.C. by the Greek philosopher Aristotle. Although position within the chain was based on physical similarities between species, no evolutionary or biological relationships were implied. Nor did "lower" forms move up the scale to become "superior" ones.

In addition, there was the common notion that the earth was "full" and that nothing new (such as species) could be added. Thus, it was believed that since the creation, no new species had appeared and none had disappeared, or become extinct. And since all of nature and the Great Chain of Being were created by God in a fixed state, change was inconceivable. Questioning the assumptions of fixity was ultimately seen as a challenge to God's perfection and could be considered heresy.

The plan of the entire universe was seen as the Grand Design—that is, God's design. In what is called the "argument from design," anatomical structures were viewed as planned to meet the purpose for which they were required. Wings, arms, eyes—all these structures were interpreted as neatly fitting the functions they performed, and nature was considered to be a deliberate plan of the Grand Designer.

The date the Grand Designer had completed his works was relatively recent—4004 B.C., according to Archbishop James Ussher (1581–1656), an Irish prelate and scholar who worked out the date of creation by analyzing the "begat" chapter of Genesis. The idea of a recent origin of the earth did not begin with Archbishop Ussher, but he was responsible for providing a precise and late date for it.

The prevailing notion of earth's brief existence, together with fixity of species, provided a formidable obstacle to the development of evolutionary theory because evolution requires time. Thus, in addition to overcoming the notion of fixity of species, scientists needed a theory of immense geological time in order to formulate evolutionary principles. In fact, until these prior concepts of fixity and time were fundamentally altered, it would have been unlikely that the idea of natural selection could even have been conceived.

The Scientific Revolution

What, then, upset the medieval belief in a rigid universe of planets, stars, plants, and animals? How did the scientific method as we know it today develop and, with the help of Newton and Galileo in the seventeenth century, demonstrate a moving, not static, universe?

The discovery of the New World and circumnavigation of the globe in the fifteenth century overturned some very fundamental ideas about the planet. For one thing, the earth could no longer be perceived as flat. Also, as Europeans began to

▲ **Fixity of species**
The notion that species, once created, can never change; an idea diametrically opposed to theories of biological evolution.

explore the New World, their awareness of biological diversity was greatly expanded through exposure to plants and animals previously unknown to them.

There were other attacks on the complacency of traditional beliefs. In 1514, a Polish mathematician named Copernicus challenged Aristotle's long-believed assertion that the earth, circled by the sun, moon, and stars, was the center of the universe. Copernicus removed the earth as the center of all things by proposing a *heliocentric* (sun-centered) solar system.

Copernicus' theory did not attract widespread attention at the time, but in the early 1600s, it was restated and further substantiated by an Italian mathematics professor, Galileo Galilei. Galileo came into direct confrontation with the Catholic Church over his publications, to the extent that he spent the last nine years of his life under house arrest. Even so, in intellectual circles, the universe had changed from one of fixity to one of motion, although most scholars still believed that change was impossible for living forms.

Scholars of the sixteenth and seventeenth centuries developed methods and theories that revolutionized scientific thought. The seventeenth century, in particular, was a beehive of scientific activity. The works of such individuals as Keppler, Descartes, and Newton established the laws of physics, motion, and gravity. Other achievements included the discovery of the circulation of blood and the development of numerous scientific instruments, including the telescope, barometer, and microscope. These technological advances permitted investigations of natural phenomena and opened up entire worlds for discoveries such as had never before been imagined.

Scientific achievement increasingly came to direct as well as reflect the changing views of Europeans. Investigations of stars, planets, animals, and plants came to be conducted without significant reference to the supernatural. In other words, nature was seen as a mechanism, functioning according to certain universal physical laws, and it was these laws that scientists were seeking. Yet, most scientists still insisted that a First Cause initiated the entire system. The argument from design was still defended, and support for it continued well into the nineteenth century and persists even today.

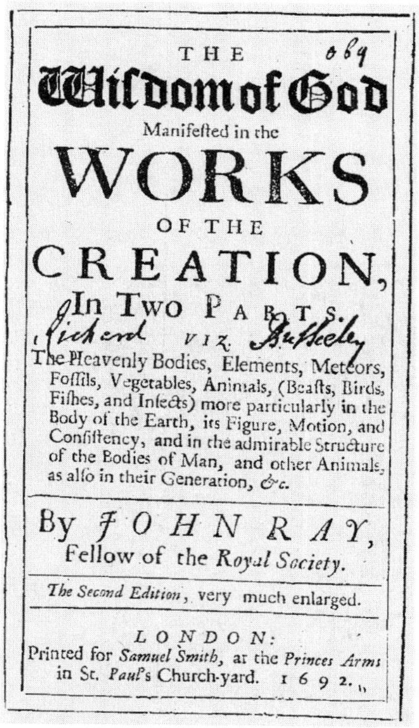

The Path to Natural Selection

Before early naturalists could begin to understand the forms of organic life, it was necessary to list and describe those forms. As attempts in this direction were made, scholars became increasingly impressed with the amount of biological diversity that confronted them.

John Ray   By the sixteenth century, a keen interest in nature's variation had developed, and by the mid-1500s, there were a few descriptive works on plants, birds, fish, and mammals. But it was not until the seventeenth century that the concept of species was clearly defined by Englishman John Ray (1627–1705), an ordained minister trained at Cambridge University.

Ray was the first to recognize that groups of plants and animals could be distinguished from other groups by their ability to reproduce with one another and produce offspring. Such groups of reproductively isolated organisms were placed into a single category he called *species* (*pl.*, species). Thus, by the late 1600s, the biological criterion of reproduction was used to define species much as it is today (Young, 1992), and upon its publication, the concept was enthusiastically received by the scientific community.

Ray also recognized that species frequently shared similarities with other species, and these he grouped together in a second level of classification he

THE
Wisdom of God
Manifested in the
WORKS
OF THE
CREATION,
In Two PARTS.
VIZ.
The Heavenly Bodies, Elements, Meteors,
Fossils, Vegetables, Animals, (Beasts, Birds,
Fishes, and Insects) more particularly in the
Body of the Earth, its Figure, Motion, and
Consistency, and in the admirable Structure
of the Bodies of Man, and other Animals,
as also in their Generation, &c.

By JOHN RAY,
Fellow of the Royal Society.

The Second Edition, very much enlarged.

LONDON:
Printed for *Samuel Smith*, at the *Princes Arms*
in St. *Paul's* Church-yard. 1692.

FIGURE 2–1

Title page from John Ray's publication showing God's plan in nature.

called the *genus* (*pl.*, genera). Ray was the first to use the labels *genus* and *species* in this manner, and they are the terms still in use today. But Ray was very much an adherent of fixity of species. His 1691 publication, *The Wisdom of God Manifested in the Works of Creation* (Fig. 2–1), was intended to demonstrate God's plan in nature, and in this work Ray stressed that nature was a deliberate outcome of a Grand Design.

Carolus Linnaeus   One of the leading naturalists of the eighteenth century was Carolus Linnaeus (1707–1778) of Sweden (Fig. 2–2). He is best known for developing a classification of plants and animals, the *Systema Naturae* (Systems of Nature), first published in 1735.

Linnaeus standardized Ray's more sporadic use of two names (genus and species) for organisms, thus firmly establishing the use of **binomial nomenclature**. Moreover, he added two more categories: class and order. Linnaeus' four-level system of classification became the basis for **taxonomy**, the system of classification still used today.

Another of Linnaeus' innovations was to include humans in his classification of animals, placing them in the genus *Homo* and species *sapiens*. The inclusion of humans in this scheme was controversial because it defied contemporary thought that humans, made in God's image, should be considered separately and outside the animal kingdom.

Linnaeus was also a firm believer in fixity of species, although in later years, faced with mounting evidence to the contrary, he came to question this long-held assumption. Indeed, fixity of species was being challenged on many fronts, especially in France, where voices were being raised in favor of a universe based on change and, more to the point, in favor of the relationship between similar forms based on descent from a common ancestor.

Comte de Buffon   Georges Louis Leclerc (1707–1788), who was raised to the rank of count under the name Buffon, was Keeper of the King's Gardens in Paris (Fig. 2–3). He believed neither in the perfection of nature nor in the idea that nature had a purpose, as declared by the argument from design, but he did recognize the dynamic relationship between the external environment and living forms. In his *Natural History*, first published in 1749, he stressed again and again the importance of change in the universe, and he underlined the changing nature of species.

Buffon believed that when groups migrated to new areas of the world, each group would subsequently be influenced by local climatic conditions and would gradually change as a result of adaptation to the environment. Buffon's recognition of the external environment as an agent of change in species was an important innovation. However, he rejected the idea that one species could give rise to another.

Erasmus Darwin   Erasmus Darwin (1731–1802) is today best known as Charles Darwin's grandfather (Fig. 2–4). However, during his life, this freethinking, high-living physician was well known in literary circles for his poetry and other writings. Chief among the latter was his *Zoonomia*, in which evolutionary concepts were expressed in verse.

More than 50 years before his grandson was to startle the world with his views on natural selection, Erasmus Darwin had expressed similar ideas and had even commented on *human* evolution. From letters and other sources, it is known that Charles Darwin had read and was fond of his grandfather's writings. But the degree to which the grandson's theories were influenced by the grandfather is not known.

FIGURE 2–2
Linnaeus developed a classification system for plants and animals.

▲ **Binomial nomenclature**
(*Binomial* means "two names") In taxonomy, the convention established by Carolus Linnaeus whereby genus and species names are used to refer to species. For example, *Homo sapiens* refers to human beings.

▲ **Taxonomy**
The branch of science concerned with the rules of classifying organisms on the basis of evolutionary relationships.

FIGURE 2–3
Buffon recognized the influence of the environment on life-forms.

FIGURE 2–4

Erasmus Darwin, grandfather of Charles Darwin, believed in species change.

FIGURE 2–5

Lamarck believed that species change was influenced by environmental change. He is known for his theory of the inheritance of acquired characteristics.

▲ **Catastrophism**

The view that the earth's geological landscape is the result of violent cataclysmic events. This view was promoted by Cuvier, especially in opposition to Lamarck.

Jean Baptiste Lamarck   Neither Buffon nor Erasmus Darwin codified his beliefs into a comprehensive system that attempted to *explain* the evolutionary process. The first European scientist to do so was the French scholar Jean Baptiste Pierre Antoine de Monet Chevalier de Lamarck (1744–1829). (Thankfully, most references to Lamarck use only his surname.)

Expanding beyond the views of Buffon, Lamarck (Fig. 2–5) attempted to *explain* evolution. He postulated a dynamic interaction between organic forms and the environment, such that organic forms could become altered in the face of changing environmental circumstances. Thus, as the environment changed, an animal's activity patterns would also change, resulting in increased or decreased use of certain body parts. As a result of this use or disuse, body parts became altered.

Physical alteration occurred as a function of perceived bodily "needs." If a particular part of the body felt a certain need, "fluids and forces" would be directed toward that point and the structure would be modified to satisfy the need. Because the modification would render the animal better suited to its habitat, the new trait would be passed on to offspring. This theory is known as the *inheritance of acquired characteristics*, or the *use-disuse* theory.

One of the most frequently given examples of Lamarck's theory is that of the giraffe, who, having stripped all the leaves from the lower branches of a tree (environmental change), strives to reach those leaves on upper branches. As vital forces progress to tissues of the neck, the neck increases slightly in length, thus enabling the giraffe to obtain more food. The longer neck is subsequently transmitted to offspring, with the eventual result that all giraffes have longer necks than did their predecessors (Fig. 2–6). Thus, according to the theory of acquired characteristics, *a trait acquired by an animal during its lifetime can be passed on.* Today we know this explanation to be inaccurate, for only those traits coded for by genetic information contained within sex cells (eggs and sperm) can be inherited (see Chapters 3 and 4).

Because Lamarck's explanation of species change was not genetically correct, his theories are frequently derided. Actually, Lamarck deserves much credit. He was the first to recognize and stress the importance of interactions between organisms and the environment in the evolutionary process. Moreover, Lamarck was one of the first to acknowledge the need for a distinct branch of science that dealt solely with living things (i.e., separate from geology). For this new science, Lamarck coined the term *biology*, and a central feature of this new science was the notion of evolutionary change.

Georges Cuvier   The most vehement opponent of Lamarck was a young colleague, Georges Cuvier (1769–1832). Cuvier (Fig. 2–7) specialized in vertebrate paleontology, and it was he who introduced the concept of extinction to explain the disappearance of animals represented by fossils. Although a brilliant anatomist, Cuvier never grasped the dynamic concept of nature, and he adamantly insisted on the fixity of species. Just as the abundance of fossils in geological strata was becoming increasingly apparent, it also became more important to explain what they were. But rather than assume that similarities between certain fossil forms and living species indicated evolutionary relationships, Cuvier proposed a variation of a theory known as **catastrophism**.

Catastrophism held that the earth's geological features were the results of sudden, worldwide cataclysmic events. Cuvier's version of catastrophism postulated a series of regional disasters that destroyed most or all of the local plant and animal life. These areas of destruction were subsequently restocked with new forms that migrated in from neighboring, unaffected regions.

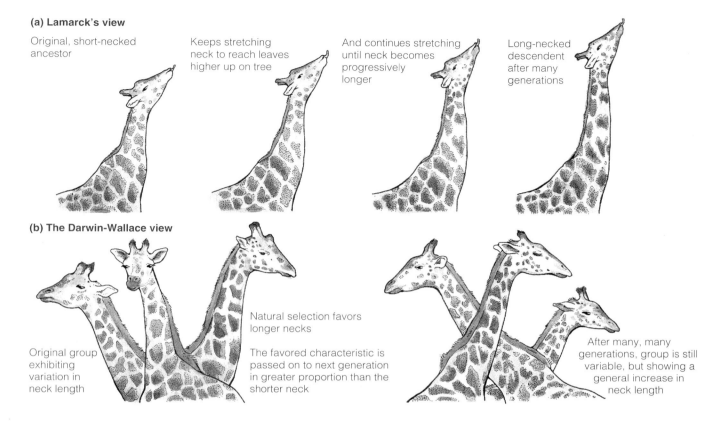

(a) Lamarck's view

Original, short-necked ancestor

Keeps stretching neck to reach leaves higher up on tree

And continues stretching until neck becomes progressively longer

Long-necked descendent after many generations

(b) The Darwin-Wallace view

Natural selection favors longer necks

Original group exhibiting variation in neck length

The favored characteristic is passed on to next generation in greater proportion than the shorter neck

After many, many generations, group is still variable, but showing a general increase in neck length

FIGURE 2–6

Contrasting ideas about the mechanism of evolution. According to Lamarck's theory, acquired characteristics can be passed to subsequent generations. Thus, short-necked giraffes stretched their necks to reach higher into trees for food, and, according to Lamarck, this acquired trait was passed on to offspring, who were born with longer necks. According to the Darwin-Wallace theory of natural selection, among giraffes there is variation in neck length. If having a longer neck provides an advantage for feeding, this trait will be passed on to a greater number of offspring, leading to an increase in the length of giraffe necks over many generations.

To be consistent with the fossil evidence, Cuvier also proposed that destroyed regions were repopulated by new organisms of a more modern appearance and that these forms were the results of more recent creation events. (The last of these creations is the one depicted in Genesis.) Thus, Cuvier's explanation of increased complexity over time avoided any notion of evolution, while still being able to account for the evidence of change as preserved in the fossil record.

Charles Lyell   Charles Lyell (1797–1875), the son of Scottish landowners, is considered the founder of modern geology (Fig. 2–8). He was a barrister by training, a geologist by avocation, and for many years Charles Darwin's friend and mentor. Before he met Darwin in 1836, Lyell had earned wide popular acclaim as well as acceptance in Europe's most prestigious scientific circles, thanks to his highly praised *Principles of Geology*, first published in three volumes in 1830–1833.

In this immensely important work, Lyell argued that the geological processes observed in the present are the same as those that occurred in the past.

FIGURE 2–7

Cuvier explained the fossil record as the result of a succession of catastrophies followed by new creation events.

▲ Uniformitarianism
The theory that the Earth's features are the result of long-term processes that continue to operate in the present as they did in the past. Elaborated on by Lyell, this theory opposed catastrophism and provided for immense geological time.

FIGURE 2–8

Lyell, the Father of Geology, stated the theory of uniformitarianism in his Principles of Geology.

FIGURE 2–9

Thomas Malthus' Essay on the Principle of Population *led both Darwin and Wallace to the principle of natural selection.*

This theory, which has come to be known as **uniformitarianism**, did not originate entirely with Lyell, but had been proposed by James Hutton in the late 1700s. Nevertheless, it was Lyell who demonstrated that such forces as wind, water erosion, local flooding, frost, the decomposition of vegetable matter, volcanoes, earthquakes, and glacial movements all had contributed in the past to produce the geological landscape that exists in the present. Moreover, the fact that these processes could still be observed in operation indicated that geological change continued to occur and that the forces that drove such change were consistent, or *uniform*, over time. In other words, although various aspects of the earth's surface (e.g., climate, flora, fauna, and land surfaces) are variable through time, the underlying *processes* that influence them are constant.

The theory of uniformitarianism flew in the face of Cuvier's catastrophism and did not go unopposed. Additionally, and every bit as controversially, Lyell emphasized the obvious: namely, that for such slow-acting forces to produce momentous change, the earth must indeed be far older than anyone had previously suspected.

By providing an immense timescale and thereby altering perceptions of earth's history from a few thousand to many millions of years, Lyell changed the framework within which scientists viewed the geological past. Thus, the concept of "deep time" (Gould, 1987) remains one of Lyell's most significant contributions to the discovery of evolutionary principles. The immensity of geological time permitted the necessary time depth for the inherently slow process of evolutionary change.

Thomas Malthus   In 1798, Thomas Robert Malthus (1766–1834), an English clergyman and economist, wrote *An Essay on the Principle of Population*, which inspired both Charles Darwin and Alfred Wallace in their separate discoveries of the principle of natural selection (Fig. 2–9). In his essay, Malthus pointed out that if left unchecked by limited food supplies, human populations could double in size every 25 years. That is, population size increases exponentially while food supplies remain relatively stable.

Malthus focused on humans because the ability to increase food supplies artificially reduces constraints on population growth, and he was arguing for population control. However, the same logic could be applied to nonhuman organisms. In nature, the tendency for populations to increase is continuously checked by resource availability. Thus, there is constant competition for food and other resources. In time, the extension of Malthus' principles to all organisms would be made by both Darwin and Wallace.

Charles Darwin   Charles Darwin (1809–1882) was one of six children of Dr. Robert and Susanna Darwin (Fig. 2–10). Being the grandson of wealthy Josiah Wedgwood (of Wedgwood pottery fame) as well as Erasmus Darwin, he grew up enjoying the lifestyle of the landed gentry in rural England.

As a boy, Darwin displayed a keen interest in nature and spent his days fishing and collecting shells, birds' eggs, and rocks. However, this developing interest in natural history did not dispel the generally held view of family and friends that he was not in any way remarkable. In fact, his performance at school was no more than ordinary.

After the death of his mother when he was eight, Darwin's upbringing was guided by his rather stern father and his older sisters. Because he showed little interest in, or aptitude for, anything except hunting, shooting, and perhaps science, his father, fearing Charles would sink into dissipation, sent him to

Edinburgh University to study medicine. It was in Edinburgh that Darwin first became acquainted with the evolutionary theories of Lamarck and others.

During this time (the 1820s), notions of evolution were becoming much feared in England and elsewhere. Certainly, anything identifiable with postrevolutionary France was viewed with grave suspicion by the established order in England. Lamarck especially, was vilified by most English academicians, the majority of whom were also members of the Anglican clergy.

This was also a time of growing political unrest in Britain. The Reform Movement, which sought to undo many of the wrongs of the class system, was under way and, as with most social movements, this one contained a radical faction. Because many of the radicals were atheists and socialists who also supported Lamarck's evolutionary theory, evolution came to be associated, in the minds of many, with atheism and political subversion. Such was the growing fear of evolutionary ideas that many believed that if it were generally accepted that nature evolved unaided by God, "the Church would crash, the moral fabric of society would be torn apart, and civilized man would return to savagery" (Desmond and Moore, 1991, p. 34). It is unfortunate that some of the most outspoken early proponents of **transmutation** were so vehemently anti-Christian, because their rhetoric helped establish the entrenched suspicion and misunderstanding of evolutionary theory that persists even today.

While at Edinburgh, the young Darwin spent endless hours studying marine life with Professor Robert Grant, an outspoken supporter of Lamarck. Darwin's second year in Edinburgh saw him earnestly studying museum collections and attending natural history lectures. Therefore, although he hated medicine and left Edinburgh after two years, his experience there was a formative period in his intellectual development.

Subsequently, Darwin took up residence at Christ's College, Cambridge, to study theology. (Although he was rather indifferent to religion, theology was often seen as a last resort by parents who viewed their sons as having no discernible academic leanings.) It was during his Cambridge years that Darwin seriously cultivated his interests in natural science, and he often joined the field excursions of botany classes. He also was immersed in geology and was a frequent and serious participant in geological expeditions.

It was no wonder that following his graduation in 1831 at age 22, he was recommended to accompany a scientific expedition that would circle the globe. Thus it was, after overcoming his father's objections, that Darwin set sail aboard the *HMS Beagle* on December 17, 1831 (Fig. 2–11). The famous voyage of the *Beagle* was to last for almost five years and would forever change not only the course of Darwin's life, but also the history of biological science.

Darwin went aboard the *Beagle* still believing in fixity of species. But during the voyage, he privately began to have doubts. As early as 1832, for example, he noted in his diary that a snake with rudimentary hind limbs marked "the passage by which Nature joins the lizards to the snakes." He came across fossils of ancient giant animals that looked, except for size, very much like living forms in the same vicinity, and he wondered whether the fossils were the ancestors of those living forms.

During the famous stopover at the Galápagos Islands (see Fig. 2–11), Darwin noted that the flora and fauna of South America showed striking similarities to those of the Galápagos, as well as intriguing differences. Even more surprising, the inhabitants of the various islands differed slightly from one another.

For example, Darwin collected 13 different varieties of Galápagos finches. These varieties shared many structural similarities, and clearly they represented a closely affiliated group. But at the same time, they differed with regard to certain

▲ **Transmutation**
The change of one species to another. The term *evolution* did not assume its current meaning until the late nineteenth century.

FIGURE 2–10
Charles Darwin as a young man.

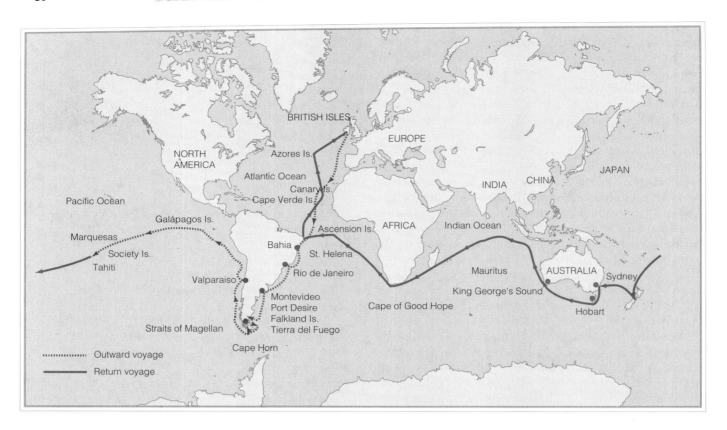

FIGURE 2–11

The route of the HMS Beagle.

physical traits, particularly in the shape and size of their beaks (Fig. 2–12). Darwin also collected finches from the South American mainland, and these appeared to represent only one group, or species.

The insight that Darwin gained from the finches is legendary. He recognized that the various Galápagos finches had all descended from a common, mainland ancestor and had become modified in response to the varying island habitats and to altered dietary preferences. But actually, it was not until *after* he had returned to England that Darwin recognized the significance of the variation in beak structure. In fact, during the voyage, Darwin had paid little attention to his finches. It was only in retrospect that he considered the factors that could lead to the modification of 1 species into 13 (Gould, 1985; Desmond and Moore, 1991).

Darwin returned to England in October 1836 and almost immediately was accepted into the most eminent of scientific circles. He married his cousin Emma Wedgwood and moved to the village of Down, near London, where he spent the rest of his life writing on topics ranging from fossils to orchids (Fig. 2–13). But his overriding concern was the question of species change.

At Down, Darwin began developing his views on what he termed *natural selection*. This concept was borrowed from animal breeders, who "select" as breeding stock those animals that exhibit specific traits they hope to emphasize in offspring. Animals with undesirable traits are "selected against," or prevented from breeding.

Darwin was keenly interested in domestic animals—pigeons, in particular—and how breeders could develop distinctive varieties in just a few generations. (The variations seen in domestic dog breeds may be the best example of the effects of selective breeding.) He applied his knowledge of domesticated species to naturally occurring ones, recognizing that in undomesticated organisms, the selective agent was nature, not humans.

By the late 1830s, Darwin recognized that biological variation within a species was critically important. Furthermore, he acknowledged the importance of sexual reproduction in increasing variation. Then, in 1838, Darwin read Malthus' essay, and in it he found the answer to his question of how new species came to be. He accepted from Malthus that populations increase at a faster rate than resources, and he inferred that in nonhuman animals, increase in population size is continuously checked by limited food supplies. He also accepted Lyell's observation that in nature there is a constant "struggle for existence." These contributions, from Malthus and Lyell respectively, that in each generation more offspring were born than survived to adulthood, coupled with the notions of competition for resources and biological diversity, were all Darwin needed to develop his theory of natural selection. He wrote: "It at once struck me that under these circumstances favourable variations would tend to be preserved, and unfavourable ones to be destroyed. The result of this would be the formation of a new species" (F. Darwin, 1950, pp. 53–54). Basically, this quotation summarizes the whole of natural selection theory.

Darwin wrote a short summary of his views on natural selection in 1842 and revised it in 1844. The 1844 sketch is similar to the argument he presented 15 years later in *On the Origin of Species*, but in 1844 he did not feel he had sufficient data to support his views, so he continued his research without publishing.

Darwin had another reason for not publishing what he knew would be, to say the least, a highly controversial work. As a member of the established order, Darwin knew that many of his friends and associates were concerned with threats to the *status quo*, and evolutionary theory was viewed as a serious threat indeed. In addition, Darwin was a man to whom reputation was of paramount importance, and he was tormented by fears of bringing dishonor and public criticism to those he loved. Thus, it was understandable that he hesitated.

Alfred Russel Wallace   Unlike Darwin, Alfred Russel Wallace (1823–1913) was born into a family of modest means (Fig. 2–14). He went to work at 14, and

(a) Ground finch
Main food: seeds
Beak: heavy

(b) Tree finch
Main food: leaves, buds, blossoms, fruits
Beak: thick, short

(c) Tree finch (called woodpecker finch)
Main food: insects
Beak: stout, straight

(d) Ground finch (known as warbler finch)
Main food: insects
Beak: slender

FIGURE 2–12
Beak variation in Darwin's Galápagos finches.

FIGURE 2–13
The Darwin home, Down House, in the village of Down, as seen from the rear garden. On the Origin of Species *was written here.*

FIGURE 2–14

Alfred Russel Wallace independently uncovered the key to the evolutionary process.

without any special talent and little formal education, he moved from one job to the next. He became interested in collecting plants and animals, and in 1848 he joined an expedition to the Amazon, where he acquired firsthand knowledge of natural phenomena. Then, in 1854, he sailed for Southeast Asia and the Malay Peninsula to continue his study and to collect bird and insect specimens.

In 1855, Wallace wrote a paper to be published in the *Annals and Magazine of Natural History*. The paper suggested that species were descended from other species and that the appearance of new species was influenced by environmental factors (Trinkaus and Shipman, 1992). The Wallace paper spurred Lyell and others to urge Darwin to publish, but still Darwin hesitated. Wallace and Darwin even corresponded briefly.

Then, in 1858, Wallace sent Darwin another paper titled *On the Tendency of Varieties to Depart Indefinitely from the Original Type*. In this paper, Wallace described evolution as a process driven by competition and natural selection. Upon receipt of Wallace's paper, Darwin despaired. He feared that Wallace might be credited for a theory (natural selection) that he himself had formulated. He quickly wrote a paper presenting his ideas, and both the paper by Darwin and the one by Wallace were read before the Linnean Society of London in 1858. Neither author was present. Wallace was not in the country, and Darwin was mourning the very recent death of his young son.

The papers received little notice at the time, but at the urging of Lyell and others, Darwin completed and published his greatest work, *On the Origin of Species*,* in December 1859. Upon publication, the storm broke and has not abated even to this day. While there was much praise for the book, the gist of opinion was negative. Scientific opinion gradually came to Darwin's support, assisted by Darwin's able friend, Thomas Huxley, who for years wrote and spoke in favor of natural selection. The riddle of species was now explained: Species were mutable, not fixed; and they evolved from other species through the mechanism of natural selection.

Natural Selection

Early in his research, Darwin had realized that selection was the key to evolution. With the help of Malthus' ideas, he saw *how* selection in nature could be explained. In the struggle for existence, those *individuals* with favorable variations would survive and reproduce; those with unfavorable variations would not.

For Darwin, the explanation of evolution was simple. The basic processes, as he understood them, are as follows:

1. All species are capable of producing offspring at a faster rate than food supplies increase.
2. There is biological variation within all species; except for identical twins, no two individuals are exactly alike.
3. Because in each generation more individuals are produced than can survive, owing to limited resources, there is competition between individuals. (*Note*: This statement does not imply that there is constant fierce fighting.)
4. Those individuals who possess favorable variations or traits (e.g., speed, disease resistance, protective coloration) have an advantage over individuals

---

*The full title is *On the Origin of Species by Means of Natural Selection, or the Preservation of Favoured Races in the Struggle for Life*.

that do not possess them. By virtue of the favorable trait, these individuals are more likely to survive to produce offspring than are others.

5. The environmental context determines whether or not a trait is beneficial. That is, what is favorable in one setting may be a liability in another. In this way, which traits become most advantageous is the result of a natural process.

6. Traits are inherited and are passed on to the next generation. Because individuals who possess favorable traits contribute more offspring to the next generation than do others, over time, such traits become more common in the population; less favorable traits are not passed on as frequently and become less common. Those individuals who produce more offspring, compared to others, are said to have greater **reproductive success**.

7. Over long periods of geological time, successful variations accumulate in a population, so that later generations may be distinct from ancestral ones. Thus, in time, a new species may appear.

8. Geographical isolation may also lead to the formation of new species. As populations of a species become geographically isolated from one another, for whatever reasons, they begin to adapt to different environments. Over time, as populations continue to respond to different **selective pressures** (i.e., different ecological circumstances), they may become distinct species, descended from a common ancestor. The 13 species of Galápagos finches, presumably all descended from a common ancestor on the South American mainland, are an example of the role of geographical isolation.

Before Darwin, scientists thought of species as entities that could not change. Because individuals within the species did not appear to be significant, they were not the object of study; therefore, it was difficult for many scientists to imagine how change could occur. Darwin, as we have pointed out, saw that variation among individuals could explain how selection occurred. Favorable variations were selected for survival by nature; unfavorable ones were eliminated.

This emphasis on the uniqueness of the individual led Darwin to natural selection as the mechanism that made evolution work. *Natural selection operates on individuals*, favorably or unfavorably, but *it is the population that evolves*. The unit of natural selection is the individual; the unit of evolution is the population.

▲ **Reproductive success**
The number of offspring an individual produces and rears to reproductive age. An individual's genetic contribution to the next generation, as compared to the contributions of other individuals.

▲ **Selective pressures**
Forces in the environment that influence reproductive success in individuals. In the example of the peppered moth, birds applied the selective pressure.

Natural Selection in Action

The best-documented case of natural selection acting in modern populations concerns changes in pigmentation among peppered moths near Manchester, England (Fig. 2–15). Before the nineteenth century, the common variety of moth was a mottled gray color. This light, mottled coloration provided extremely effective camouflage against lichen-covered tree trunks. Also present, though less common, was a dark variety of the same species. While resting on light, lichen-covered trees, the dark, uncamouflaged moths were more visible to birds and were therefore eaten more often. (In this example, birds are the *selective agent*.) Thus, in the end, the dark moths produced fewer offspring than the light, camouflaged moths. Yet, by the end of the nineteenth century, the common gray form had been almost completely replaced by the black variety.

What had brought about this rapid change? The answer lies in the rapidly changing environment of industrialized nineteenth-century England. Coal dust in the area settled on trees, killing the lichen and turning the bark a dark color.

FIGURE 2–15

Variation in the peppered moth. (a) The dark form is more visible on the light, lichen-covered tree. (b) On trees darkened by pollution, the lighter form is more visible.

(a)

(b)

Moths continued to rest on trees, but the gray (light) variety was increasingly conspicuous as the trees became darker. Consequently, they began to be preyed on more frequently by birds and contributed fewer genes to the next generation. In the late twentieth century, increasing control of pollutants has allowed trees to return to their lighter, lichen-covered, preindustrial condition. As would be expected, the black variety of moth is now being supplanted by the gray.

The substance that produces pigmentation is called *melanin*, and the evolutionary shift in the peppered moth, as well as in many other moth species, is termed *industrial melanism*. Such an evolutionary shift in response to environmental change is called *adaptation*.

This example of the peppered moths provides numerous insights into the mechanism of evolutionary change by natural selection:

1. *A trait must be inherited to have importance in natural selection.* A characteristic that is not hereditary (such as a temporary change in hair pigmentation brought about by dye) will not be passed on to succeeding generations. In moths, pigmentation is a demonstrated hereditary trait.
2. *Natural selection cannot occur without variation in inherited characteristics.* If all the moths had initially been gray (you will recall that some dark forms were present) and the trees had become darker, the survival and reproduction of all moths could have been so low that the population might have become extinct. Such an event is not unusual and without variation would nearly always occur. *Selection can work only with variation that already exists.*
3. **Fitness** *is a relative measure that will change as the environment changes.* Fitness is simply differential reproductive success. In the initial stage, the gray moth was the more fit variety because gray moths produced more offspring. But as the environment changed, the black moths became more fit, and a further change reversed the adaptive pattern. It should be obvious that statements regarding the "most fit" life-form mean nothing without reference to specific environments.

▲ Fitness
Pertaining to natural selection, a measure of *relative* reproductive success of individuals. Fitness can be measured by an individual's genetic contribution to the next generation compared to that of others.

The example of the peppered moths shows how different death rates influence natural selection, for moths that die early tend to leave fewer offspring. But mortality is not the entire picture. Another important aspect of natural selection is fertility, for an animal that gives birth to more young would pass its genes on at a faster rate than one that bears fewer offspring. However, fertility is not the whole picture either, for the crucial element is the number of young raised successfully to the point at which they themselves reproduce. We may state this simply as *differential net reproductive success*. The way this mechanism works can be demonstrated through another example.

In a common variety of small birds called swifts, data show that giving birth to more offspring does not necessarily guarantee that more young will be successfully raised. The number of eggs hatched in a breeding season is a measure of fertility. The number of birds that mature and are eventually able to leave the nest is a measure of net reproductive success, or offspring successfully raised. The following tabulation shows the correlation between the number of eggs hatched (fertility) and the number of young that leave the nest (reproductive success) averaged over four breeding seasons (Lack, 1966):

Number of eggs hatched (fertility)	2 eggs	3 eggs	4 eggs
Average number of young raised (reproductive success)	1.92	2.54	1.76
Sample size (number of nests)	72	20	16

As the tabulation shows, the most efficient fertility number is three eggs, for that yields the highest reproductive success. Raising two is less beneficial to the parents, since the end result is not as successful as with three eggs. Trying to raise more than three young is actually detrimental, since the parents may not be able to provide adequate nourishment for any of the offspring. An offspring that dies before reaching reproductive age is, in evolutionary terms, equivalent to never having been born in the first place. Actually, such a result may be an evolutionary minus to the parents, for this offspring will drain their resources and may inhibit their ability to raise other offspring, thereby lowering their reproductive success even further. Selection will favor those genetic traits that yield the maximum net reproductive success. If the number of eggs laid* is a genetic trait in birds (and it seems to be), natural selection in swifts should act to favor the laying of three eggs as opposed to two or four.

Constraints on Nineteenth-Century Evolutionary Theory

Darwin argued eloquently for the notion of evolution in general and the role of natural selection in particular, but he did not entirely comprehend the exact mechanisms of evolutionary change.

As we have seen, natural selection acts on *variation* within species. Neither Darwin nor anyone else in the nineteenth century understood the source of all this variation. Consequently, Darwin speculated about variation arising from "use"—an idea similar to Lamarck's. Darwin, however, was not as dogmatic in his views as Lamarck and most emphatically argued against inner "needs" or "effort." Darwin had to confess that when it came to explaining variation, he simply did not know: "Our ignorance of the laws of variation is profound. Not in one case out of a hundred can we pretend to assign any reason why this or that part differs, more or less, from the same part in the parents" (Darwin, 1859, pp. 167–168).

In addition to his inability to explain the origins of variation, Darwin also did not completely understand the mechanism by which parents transmitted traits to offspring. Almost without exception, nineteenth-century scholars were confused about the laws of heredity, and the popular consensus was that inheritance was

---

*The number of eggs hatched is directly related to the number of eggs laid.

blending by nature. In other words, offspring were expected to express intermediate traits as a result of a blending of their parents' contributions. Given this view, we can see why the actual nature of genes was unimaginable. Without any viable alternatives, Darwin accepted this popular misconception. As it turned out, a contemporary of Darwin's had systematically worked out the rules of heredity. However, the work of this Augustinian monk, Gregor Mendel (whom you will meet in Chapter 4), was not recognized until the beginning of the twentieth century.

Summary

The concept of evolution as we know it today is directly traceable to developments in intellectual thought in western Europe over the last 300 years. In particular, the contributions of Linnaeus, Lamarck, Buffon, Lyell, and Malthus all had significant impact on Darwin. The year 1859 marks a watershed in evolutionary theory, for in that year, the publication of Darwin's *On the Origin of Species* crystallized understanding of the evolutionary process (particularly the crucial role of natural selection) and for the first time thrust evolutionary theory into the consciousness of the common person. Debates both inside and outside the sciences continued for several decades (and in some quarters persist today), but the theory of evolution irrevocably changed the tide of intellectual thought. Gradually, Darwin's formulation of the evolutionary process became accepted almost universally by scientists as the very foundation of all the biological sciences, physical anthropology included. As we approach the twenty-first century, contributions from genetics allow us to demonstrate the mechanics of evolution in a way unknown to Darwin and his contemporaries.

Natural selection is the central determining factor influencing the long-term direction of evolutionary change. How natural selection works can best be explained as differential reproductive success—in other words, how successful individuals are in leaving offspring to succeeding generations.

Questions for Review

1. Trace the history of intellectual thought immediately leading to Darwin's theory.
2. What is *fixity of species?* Why did it pose a problem for the development of evolutionary thinking?
3. What was John Ray's major contribution to biology and the development of evolutionary theories?
4. In what ways did Linnaeus and Buffon differ in their approach to the concept of evolution?
5. What are the bases of Lamarck's theory of acquired characteristics? Why is this theory incorrect?
6. What was Lamarck's contribution to nineteenth-century evolutionary ideas?
7. Explain Cuvier's catastrophism.
8. What did Malthus and Lyell contribute to Darwin's thinking on evolution?
9. Darwin approached the subject of species change by emphasizing individuals within populations. Why was this significant to the development of the concept of natural selection?
10. What evidence did Darwin use to strengthen his argument concerning evolution?
11. How did Darwin's explanation of evolution differ from Lamarck's?

12. What is meant by adaptation? Illustrate through the example of industrial melanism.

13. Define natural selection. What is a selective agent?

14. Explain why the changes in coloration in populations of peppered moths serve as a good example of natural selection.

Suggested Further Reading

Burke, James. 1985. *The Day the Universe Changed.* Boston: Little, Brown.

Desmond, Adrian, and James Moore. 1991. *Darwin.* New York: Warner Books.

Gould, Stephen Jay. 1987. *Time's Arrow, Time's Cycle.* Cambridge, MA: Harvard University Press.

Ridley, Mark. 1993. *Evolution.* Boston: Blackwell Scientific Publications.

Trinkaus, Eric, and Pat Shipman. 1993. *The Neandertals.* New York: Knopf.

Young, David. 1992. *The Discovery of Evolution.* London: Natural History Museum Publications, Cambridge University Press.

Internet Resources

Enter Evolution: Theory and History

http://ucmp1.berkeley.edu/exhibittext/evolution.html

(Good biographical sketches of the "founders of evolution" from Leonardo da Vinci to the twentieth century. Full text of Darwin's *Origin of Species.*)

Evolution on Trial

That it shall be unlawful for any teacher in any of the universities, normals and all other public schools of the State . . . to teach any theory that denies the story of the Divine Creation of man as taught in the Bible, and to teach instead that man has descended from a lower order of animals (Section 1 of the Butler Act, March 21, 1925, State of Tennessee).

In May 1925, several leading citizens from Dayton, Tennessee (population 1,800), were sitting around Doc Robinson's drugstore, the town's social center, discussing various and sundry topics of great import. To settle an argument, they sent for John T. Scopes, a local high school coach and teacher of algebra, physics, and chemistry. Scopes came over from his tennis game, not realizing that he was about to enter the most dramatic period of his life, one he would never forget.

One of the men, a local businessman, said, "John, we've been arguing, and I said that nobody could teach biology without teaching evolution."

"That's right," said Scopes, and showed them the biology textbook that had been adopted by the state of Tennessee.

"Then you've been violating the law," Doc Robinson said.

Although he did not teach biology, Scopes had, one day in April, substituted for the principal, who did. Technically, therefore, it could be said that he had taught biology and had thus violated the newly passed law.

As the discussion continued and it became clear that Scopes felt strongly on the matter of academic freedom, Robinson asked him whether he would stand for a test case. Scopes said he would, whereupon Robinson called the *Chattanooga News* and reported, "This is F. E. Robinson in Dayton. I'm chairman of the school board here. We've just arrested a man for teaching evolution." The man who had been "arrested" finished his soft drink and returned to his tennis game. (Writing 40 years later in 1967, Scopes suggested that the trial was deliberately planned by Dayton businessmen to put that town on the map and bring in business, which is precisely what happened.)

The "arrest" made front-page news across the country. William Jennings Bryan—three times Democratic nominee for president, Secretary of State under Woodrow Wilson, famous for his Cross of Gold speech at the Democratic Convention of 1896, and acknowledged leader of the crusade against Darwinism—offered his services to the prosecution as the representative of the World Christian Fundamentals Association.

With Bryan's entry into the fray, Clarence Darrow, nationally known labor and criminal lawyer, offered his services to the defense without fee or expense. The American Civil Liberties Union was in charge of the case for the defense and provided other well-known lawyers: John Randolph Neal, Arthur Garfield Hayes, and Dudley Field Malone.

In the weeks before the trial, the town of Dayton took on the atmosphere of a circus. The trial was referred to as "the monkey business." Merchants used monkey motifs in their advertising: pins that read "Your Old Man's a Monkey" could be purchased; and at Doc Robinson's drugstore, a monkey fizz was available for refreshment from the summer heat. Hot dog stands, lemonade peddlers, booths selling books on biology or religion, and Bryan's truck, equipped with a loudspeaker touting Florida real estate, all added spice and noise to the carnival.

The trial began on Friday, July 10, 1925, with Judge John T. Raulston on the bench, and ended on Tuesday, July 21. It was clear from the start that Scopes would be convicted. The court, strongly religious, consistently favored the prosecution and forbade the testimony of expert defense witnesses—scientists—who were prepared to prove that evolution was a valid scientific theory. The prosecution insisted that the trial was not about the validity of evolution and that the real issue was simply whether or not Scopes had violated the law.

There were magnificent speeches. On Monday, July 13, in his support of the motion to quash the indictment against Scopes,

Darrow displayed his famous debating skills, and the crowded courthouse hung on every word.

On Thursday, Bryan stood up to speak against the admissibility of scientific testimony. The crowd had been waiting for this moment, but they were to be disappointed. Bryan, by then rather elderly, was not the man he once was; the fire was missing. H. L. Mencken, the acidulous reporter from the *Baltimore Sun*, attended the trial and wrote:

His . . . speech was a grotesque performance and downright touching in its imbecility. Its climax came when he launched into a furious denunciation of the doctrine that man is a mammal. It seemed a sheer impossibility that any literate man should stand up in public and discharge any such nonsense. Yet the poor old fellow did it. . . . To call man mammal, it appeared, was to flout the revelation of God (Tompkins, 1965, p. 48).

Malone replied to Bryan, his former superior officer at the State Department, and his eloquence carried the day even among the spectators who fully supported Bryan. Bryan himself recognized this when he told Malone afterward, "Dudley, that was the greatest speech I have ever heard."

The climax of the trial came on Monday afternoon, July 20, when the defense called Bryan as an expert witness on the Bible. The prosecutors immediately jumped to their feet protesting, aware of the danger inherent in the questions that might be asked and the answers that might be given. However, Bryan himself insisted on testifying, perhaps because he felt compelled

to defend the Bible and "show up" the evolutionists. It was an opportunity not to be missed.

Darrow's strategy was to question Bryan about his literal interpretation of the Bible. The Bible, Bryan held, was true, every word of it, every comma. Every miracle recorded in the Bible actually happened. And it was on these points that Darrow broke Bryan, made him appear foolish, unthinking, and even a "traitor" to the cause of fundamentalism. At one point Darrow asked, "Do you think the earth was made in six days?"

"Not in six days of 24 hours," Bryan replied.

The crowd gasped at this heresy. The Bible read six days, and a day was obviously 24 hours. What was Bryan thinking of? Toward the end of the afternoon, Darrow brought up the Bible story of Adam and Eve and the serpent. Had God punished the serpent by making him crawl on his belly? Bryan said he believed that. Then Darrow asked, "Have you any idea how the snake went before that time?"

"No sir."

"Do you know whether he walked on his tail or not?"

"No, sir, I have no way to know."

The crowd laughed and Bryan's hands nervously trembled and his lips quivered.*

The trial ended the next day. The jury (excused for most of the trial) was called back and charged to decide whether Scopes had violated the law; no other question was to be considered. The jury took but a short time and returned with its ver-

dict—guilty! Judge Raulston fined Scopes $100, and the trial closed.

The case was appealed to the Tennessee Supreme Court, which handed down its decision on January 15, 1927. The court upheld the Butler Act and also recommended that the state drop the indictment against Scopes on the technicality that the judge had imposed the fine, instead of the jury, as Tennessee law required. The court thus made it impossible to appeal the case before the United States Supreme Court.

In the more than 60 years since the Scopes trial, religious fundamentalists have not ceased their attempts to remove the teaching of evolution from the public schools of the nation. Known as "creationists" because they explain the existence of the universe, energy, and life as a result of sudden creation, they are determined either to eliminate the teaching of evolution or to introduce antievolutionary subject matter into public school curricula. In a ploy developed in recent years, creationists have insisted that "creation science" is just as much science as what they term "evolution science." Therefore, they claim, in the interest of fair play, a balanced view should be offered to students: If evolution is taught as science, then creationism should also be taught as science.

So-called "creation science" is not science as we know it.* Far from the spirit of science, creationists assert that their view is absolute and not subject to error. Therefore, it is impossible for any sort of evidence to alter their position, for anything

---

*A diabetic and in ill health, Bryan died on Sunday, July 26, five days after the trial ended.

See Niles Eldredge, "Creationism Isn't Science," *The New Republic*. April 14, 1981, pp. 15–20.

that might modify creationism is automatically rejected.

Consequently, creationism is neither a hypothesis that can be tested nor amenable to falsification (see Issue, Chapter 1). Because such testing is the actual basis of all science, creationism, by its very nature, cannot be considered science. It is religion.

Creationists have been active in state legislatures, promoting the passage of laws mandating the inclusion of creationism in school curricula wherever evolution is taught. To this effect, creationists successfully lobbied the legislature of the state of Arkansas, which passed Act 590 in March 1981.

The law was challenged, and on January 5, 1982, Judge William Ray Overton ruled against the state of Arkansas. He found that "creation science has no scientific merit or education value," that *a theory that is by its own terms dogmatic, absolutist and never subject to revision is not a scientific theory*" (emphasis added), and that "since creation is not science, the conclusion is inescapable that the only real effect of Act 590 is the advancement of religion."

On June 19, 1987, the United States Supreme Court struck down (by a vote of seven to two) a Louisiana law that required the teaching of creationism if the concept of evolution were taught. The Court stated that the Louisiana law

was enacted clearly to advance a religious purpose and was therefore unconstitutional.

Creationists continue their efforts to prevent the teaching of evolution in public schools and to introduce creationism as science. New approaches are being used, however, since the Supreme Court has ruled against laws mandating "equal time" for creation and evolution. One approach is for creationist teachers to claim "academic freedom" to teach creationism as science. These attempts have not been successful thus far. In 1990, a junior high school teacher in northern Illinois sued his superintendent for his "right" to teach creationism and lost. In 1992, a high school biology teacher in California sued his district in an almost identical case and also lost.

Because the Supreme Court decision was decided on the First Amendment grounds of separation of church and state, another tactic being tried is to avoid the use of the term *creationism* and substitute euphemisms that sound less religious. Currently, creationists are fighting evolution by promoting the teaching of "intelligent design theory" or "abrupt appearance theory." Another approach is to teach creationist ideas as "alternatives to evolution" or "evidence against evolution." From a scientific standpoint, there is no dispute about whether evolution occurred, though

there is lively debate over how it occurred and through what mechanisms.

A larger problem than the teaching of "creation science" is the avoidance of evolution by teachers who seek to escape "controversy." In this situation, teachers advance neither theory, and students are left knowing nothing about evolution, one of the most important and influential of all scientific concepts.*

Sources

Ginger, Ray. 1958. *Six Days or Forever?* Boston: Beacon Press.

Scopes, John T., and James Presley. 1967. *Center of the Storm.* New York: Holt, Rinehart, & Winston.

Tompkins, Jerry R., ed. 1965. *D-Days at Dayton.* Baton Rouge: Louisiana State University Press.

Critical Thinking Questions

1. Explain why the courts have consistently ruled against laws that provide for equal treatment of evolution and creationism in public schools.

2. Do you think that creationism should be taught as science in public schools? Why or why not?

---

*For more information about the creation/evolution controversy, contact The National Center for Science Education, Inc., Box 9477, Berkeley, CA 94709-0477.

The Biological Basis of Life

Introduction

This text is about human evolution and adaptation, both of which are intimately linked to life processes that involve cells, the replication and decoding of genetic information, and the transmission of this information between generations. Thus, to present human evolution and adaptation in the broad sense, we must first examine how life is organized at the cellular and molecular levels, and this, in turn, necessitates a brief discussion of the fundamental principles of genetics.

Genetics is the study of how traits are transmitted from one generation to the next. Because physical anthropologists are concerned with human evolution, adaptation, and variation, they must have a thorough understanding of the factors that lie at the very root of these phenomena. Indeed, although many physical anthropologists do not actually specialize in genetics, it is genetics that ultimately links and influences many of the various subdisciplines of biological anthropology.

The discipline of genetics is largely a twentieth-century development, and much of our present knowledge has been acquired within the last 50 years. Today, insights into the numerous aspects of inheritance are increasing at an exponential rate, with new discoveries being made virtually every day. Moreover, as genetic technologies develop and increasingly come into use, they assume an ever greater role in the lives of us all.

It is therefore more important than ever that, as people living at the brink of the twenty-first century, we achieve a basic understanding of the factors that influence our lives. Also, from an anthropological perspective, it is only through the further elucidation of genetic principles that we can hope to really understand the evolutionary mechanisms that have permitted humans to become the species we are today.

The Cell

To discuss genetic and evolutionary principles, we must first have a fundamental understanding of cell function. Cells are the basic units of life in all living organisms. In some forms, such as bacteria, a single cell constitutes the entire organism. However, more complex *multicellular* forms, such as plants, insects, birds, and mammals, are composed of billions of cells. Indeed, an adult human is made up of perhaps as many as 1,000 billion (1,000,000,000,000) cells, all functioning in complex ways to promote the survival of the individual.

Life on earth can be traced back at least 3.7 billion years, in the form of *prokaryotic* cells. Prokaryotes are single-celled organisms, represented today by bacteria and blue-green algae. Structurally more complex cells appeared approximately 1.2 billion years ago, and these are referred to as *eukaryotic* cells. Because eukaryotic cells are found in all multicellular organisms, they are the focus of the remainder of this discussion. In spite of the numerous differences between various life-forms and the cells that constitute them, it is important to understand that the cells of all living organisms share many similarities as a result of their common evolutionary past.

In general, a eukaryotic cell is a three-dimensional entity composed of *carbohydrates*, *lipids*, *nucleic acids*, and *proteins*. It contains a variety of structures called *organelles* within the *cell membrane* (Fig. 3–1). One of these organelles is the **nucleus** (*pl.*, nuclei), a discrete unit surrounded by a thin nuclear mem-

▲ **Nucleus**
A structure (organelle) found in all eukaryotic cells. The nucleus contains chromosomes (nuclear DNA).

brane. Within the nucleus are two nucleic acids that contain the genetic information that controls the cell's functions. These two critically important **molecules** are **deoxyribonucleic acid (DNA)** and **ribonucleic acid (RNA)**. (In prokaryotic cells, genetic information is not contained within a walled nucleus.) Surrounding the nucleus is the **cytoplasm,** which contains numerous other types of organelles involved in various activities, such as breaking down nutrients and converting them to other substances *(metabolism)*, storing and releasing energy, eliminating waste, and manufacturing **proteins (protein synthesis).**

Two of these cytoplasmic organelles—**mitochondria** and **ribosomes**— require further mention. The mitochondria (*sing.*, mitochondrion) are responsible for energy production in the cell and are thus the structural "engines" that drive the cell. Mitochondria have membranes composed partly of proteins, which in turn are produced by coded messages from DNA molecules contained within. This DNA, called mitochondrial DNA (mtDNA), is distinct from that contained inside the nucleus (nuclear DNA). Because these mtDNA molecules are considerably shorter and encode less information than those of nuclear DNA, they have attracted considerable interest in the last few years. (We will return to this topic, especially in Chapter 18, when we discuss the origins of modern *Homo sapiens.*) Ribosomes are roughly spherical in shape and are the most common type of cytoplasmic organelle. They are made up partly of RNA (ribonucleic acid) and are essential to the synthesis of proteins (see p. 48).

There are basically two types of cells: **somatic cells** and **gametes.** Somatic cells are the cellular components of body tissues, such as muscle, bone, skin, nerve, heart, and brain. Gametes, or sex cells, are specifically involved in reproduction and are not important as structural components of the body. In animals, there are two types of gametes: *ova*, or egg cells, produced in the ovaries in females; and *sperm*, which develop in male testes. The sole function of a sex cell

▲ Molecules
Structures made up of two or more atoms. Molecules can combine with other molecules to form more complex structures.

▲ Deoxyribonucleic acid (DNA)
The double-stranded molecule that contains the genetic code. DNA is a main component of chromosomes.

▲ Ribonucleic acid (RNA)
A single-stranded molecule, similar in structure to DNA. The three forms of RNA are essential to protein synthesis.

▲ Cytoplasm
The portion of the cell contained within the cell membrane, excluding the nucleus. The cytoplasm consists of a semifluid material and contains numerous structures involved with cell function.

▲ Proteins
Three-dimensional molecules that serve a wide variety of functions through their ability to bind to other molecules.

▲ Protein synthesis
The assembly of chains of amino acids into functional protein molecules. The process is directed by DNA.

▲ Mitochondria
(*sing.*, mitochondrion) Organelles that are found in the cytoplasm of cells and that are responsible for producing energy for cellular functions.

▲ Ribosomes
Structures that are found in the cytoplasm and that are essential to the manufacture of proteins.

▲ Somatic cells
Basically, all the cells in the body except those involved with reproduction.

▲ Gametes
Reproductive cells (eggs and sperm in animals) developed from precursor cells in ovaries and testes.

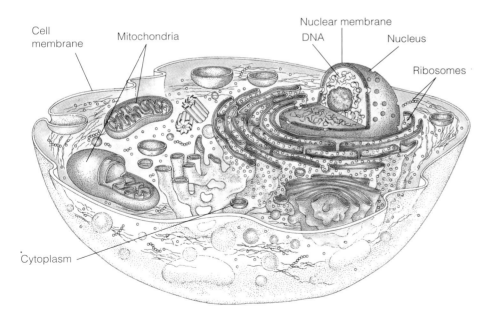

Cell membrane — Mitochondria — Nuclear membrane — DNA — Nucleus — Ribosomes — Cytoplasm

FIGURE 3–1
Structure of a generalized eukaryotic cell, illustrating the cell's three-dimensional nature. Although various organelles are shown, for the sake of simplicity only those we discuss are labeled.

▲ **Zygote**
A cell formed by the union of an egg and a sperm cell. It contains the full complement of chromosomes (in humans, 46) and has the potential of developing into an entire organism.

▲ **Nucleotides**
Basic units of the DNA molecule, composed of a sugar, a phosphate, and one of four DNA bases.

▲ **Complementary**
Referring to the fact that DNA bases form base pairs in a precise manner. For example, adenine can bond only to thymine. These two bases thus are *complementary* because one requires the other to form a complete DNA base pair.

▲ **Replicate**
To duplicate. The DNA molecule is able to make exact copies of itself.

▲ **Enzymes**
Specialized proteins that initiate and direct chemical reactions in the body.

is to unite with a gamete from another individual to form a **zygote,** which has the potential of developing into a new individual. By so doing, gametes transmit genetic information from parent to offspring.

DNA Structure

As already mentioned, cellular functions are directed by DNA. If we are to understand these functions and how characteristics are inherited, we must first know something about the structure and function of DNA.

In 1944, published results of a 10-year study demonstrated that the DNA molecule was the material responsible for the transmission of inherited traits, at least in some bacteria (Avery, MacLeod, and McCarty, 1944). However, the exact physical and chemical properties of DNA were at that time still unknown. In 1953, at Cambridge University, an American researcher named James Watson and three British scientists—Francis Crick, Maurice Wilkins, and Rosalind Franklin—developed a structural and functional model for DNA (Watson and Crick, 1953a, 1953b). For their discovery, Watson, Crick, and Wilkins were awarded the Nobel Prize in medicine and physiology in 1962. (Rosalind Franklin was deceased by 1962, and the Nobel Prize is not awarded posthumously.) The importance of their achievement cannot be overstated, for it completely revolutionized the fields of biology and medicine and forever altered our understanding of biological and evolutionary mechanisms.

The DNA molecule is composed of two chains of even smaller molecules called **nucleotides.** A nucleotide, in turn, is made up of three components: a sugar molecule (deoxyribose), a phosphate, and one of four bases (Fig. 3–2). In DNA, nucleotides are stacked upon one another to form a chain that is bonded along its bases to another **complementary** nucleotide chain. Together the two twist to form a spiral, or helical, shape. The resulting DNA molecule, then, is two-stranded and is described as forming a *double helix* that resembles a twisted ladder. If we follow the twisted ladder analogy, the sugars and phosphates represent the two sides, while the bases and the bonds that join them form the rungs.

The secret of how DNA functions lies within the four bases. These bases are *adenine, guanine, thymine,* and *cytosine,* and they are frequently referred to by their initial letters, A, G, T, and C. In the formation of the double helix, it is possible for one type of base to pair, or bond, with only one other type. Thus, base pairs can form *only* between adenine and thymine and between guanine and cytosine (see Fig. 3–2). This specificity is essential to the DNA molecule's ability to **replicate,** or make an exact copy of itself, and DNA is the only molecule known to have this capacity.

DNA Replication

Cells multiply by dividing in such a way that each new cell receives a full complement of genetic material. This is a crucial point, since a cell cannot function properly without the appropriate amount of DNA. For new cells to receive the essential amount of DNA, it is first necessary for the DNA to replicate.

Prior to cell division, specialized **enzymes** break the bonds between bases in the DNA molecule, leaving the two previously joined strands of nucleotides with

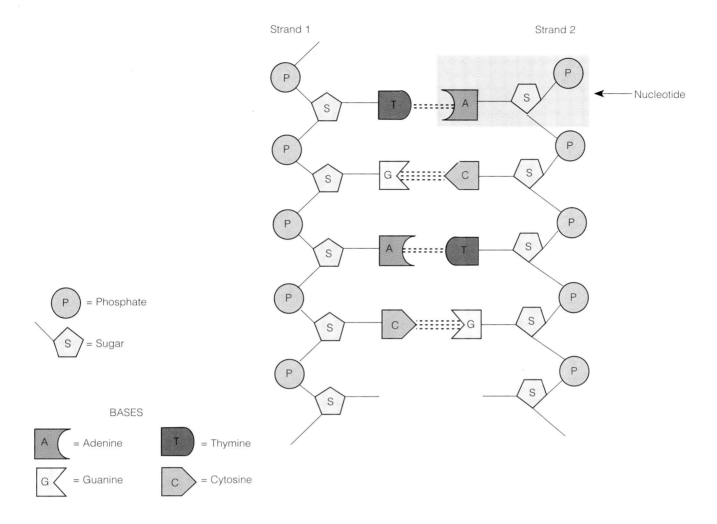

Strand 1   Strand 2

Nucleotide

P = Phosphate

S = Sugar

BASES

A = Adenine   T = Thymine

G = Guanine   C = Cytosine

their bases exposed (Fig. 3–3). The exposed bases attract unattached nucleotides, which are free-floating in the cell nucleus.

Because one base can be joined to only one other, the attraction between bases occurs in a complementary fashion. Thus, the two previously joined parental nucleotide chains serve as models, or *templates*, for the formation of a new strand of nucleotides. As each new strand is formed, its bases are joined to the bases of an original strand. When the process is completed, there are two double-stranded DNA molecules exactly like the original one, and each newly formed molecule consists of one original nucleotide chain joined to a newly formed chain (see Fig. 3–3).

FIGURE 3–2
Part of a DNA molecule. The illustration shows the two DNA strands with the sugar and phosphate backbone and the bases extending toward the center.

Protein Synthesis

One of the most important functions of DNA is that it directs protein synthesis within the cell. Proteins are complex, three-dimensional molecules that function

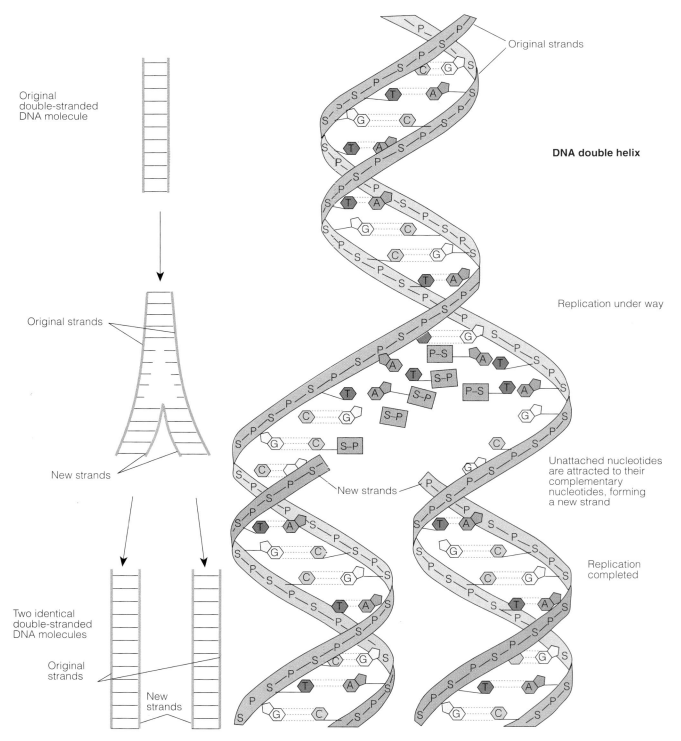

Original double-stranded DNA molecule

Original strands

New strands

Two identical double-stranded DNA molecules

Original strands

New strands

Original strands

DNA double helix

Replication under way

Unattached nucleotides are attracted to their complementary nucleotides, forming a new strand

New strands

Replication completed

FIGURE 3–3

DNA replication. During DNA replication, the two strands of the DNA molecule are separated, and each strand serves as a template for the formation of a new strand. When replication is complete, there are two DNA molecules. Each molecule consists of one new and original DNA strand.

through their ability to bind to other molecules. For example, the protein hemoglobin, found in red blood cells, is able to bind to oxygen and serves to transport oxygen to cells throughout the body.

Proteins function in myriad ways. Some are structural components of tissues. Collagen, for example, is the most common protein in the body and is a major component of all connective tissues. Aside from mineral components, it is the most abundant structural material in bone. Enzymes are also proteins, and their function is to initiate and enhance chemical reactions. An example of a digestive enzyme is *lactase*, which breaks down *lactose*, or milk sugar, into two simpler sugars. Another class of proteins includes many types of **hormones.** Specialized cells produce and release hormones into the bloodstream to circulate to other areas of the body, where they produce specific effects in tissues and organs. A good example of this type of protein is *insulin*, produced by cells in the pancreas. Insulin causes cells in the liver and certain types of muscle tissue to absorb glucose (sugar) from the blood. (Enzymes and hormones will be discussed in more detail in Chapter 7.)

As you can see, proteins make us what we are. Not only are they the major constituents of all body tissues, but they also direct and perform physiological and cellular functions. It is therefore critical that protein synthesis occur accurately, for if it does not, physiological development and activities can be disrupted or even prevented.

Proteins are composed of linear chains of smaller molecules called **amino acids.** In all, there are 20 amino acids, 8 of which must be obtained from dietary sources (see Chapter 7). The remaining 12 are produced in cells. These 20 amino acids are combined in different amounts and sequences to produce potentially millions of proteins. What makes proteins different from one another is the number of amino acids involved and the *sequence* in which they are arranged. For a protein to function properly, its amino acids must be arranged in the proper sequence.

DNA serves as a recipe for making a protein, for it is the sequence of DNA bases that ultimately determines the order of amino acids in a protein molecule. In the DNA instructions, a *triplet*, or group of three bases, specifies a particular amino acid. For example, if a triplet consists of the base sequence, cytosine, guanine, and adenine (CGA), it specifies the amino acid *alanine*. If the next triplet in the chain consists of the sequence guanine, thymine, and cytosine (GTC), it refers to another amino acid—*glutamine*. Therefore, a DNA recipe might look like this: AGA CGA ACA ACC TAC TTT TTC CTT AAG GTC and so on, as it directs the cell in assembling proteins (Table 3–1).

Protein synthesis is a little more complicated than the preceding few sentences would imply. For one thing, protein synthesis occurs outside the nucleus at specialized structures in the cytoplasm called *ribosomes* (see p. 43). A logistics problem arises because the DNA molecule is not capable of traveling outside the cell's nucleus. Thus, the first step in protein synthesis is to copy the DNA message into a form that can pass through the nuclear membrane into the cytoplasm. This process is accomplished through the formation of a molecule similar to DNA called ribonucleic acid, or RNA. RNA is different from DNA in three important ways:

1. It is single-stranded.
2. It contains a different type of sugar.
3. It contains the base uracil as a substitute for the DNA base thymine. (Uracil is attracted to adenine, just as thymine is.)

▲ **Hormones**
Substances (usually proteins) that are produced by specialized cells and that travel to other parts of the body, where they influence chemical reactions and regulate various cellular functions.

▲ **Amino acids**
Small molecules that are the components of proteins.

TABLE 3–1   The Genetic Code

Amino Acid Symbol	Amino Acid	mRNA Codon	DNA Triplet
ALA	Alanine	GCU, GCC, GCA, GCG	CGA, CGG, CGT, CGC
ARG	Arginine	CGU, CGC, CGA, CGG, AGA, AGG	GCA, GCG, GCT, GCC, TCT, TCC
ASN	Asparagine	AAU, AAC	TTA, TTG
ASP	Aspartic acid	GAU, GAC	CTA, CTG
CYS	Cysteine	UGU, UGC	ACA, ACG
GLN	Glutamine	CAA, CAG	GTT, GTC
GLU	Glutamic acid	GAA, GAG	CTT, CTC
GLY	Glycine	GGU, GGC, GGA, GGG	CCA, CCG, CCT, CCC
HIS	Histidine	CAU, CAC	GTA, GTG
ILE	Isoleucine	AUU, AUC, AUA	TAA, TAG, TAT
LEU	Leucine	UUA, UUG, CUU, CUC, CUA, CUG	AAT, AAC, GAA, GAG, GAT, GAC
LYS	Lysine	AAA, AAG	TTT, TTC
MET	Methionine	AUG	TAC
PHE	Phenylalanine	UUU, UUC	AAA, AAG
PRO	Proline	CCU, CCC, CCA, CCG	GGA, GGG, GGT, GGC
SER	Serine	UCU, UCC, UCA, UCG, AGU, AGC	AGA, AGG, AGT, AGC, TCA, TCG
THR	Threonine	ACU, ACC, ACA, ACG	TGA, TGG, TGT, TGC
TRP	Tryptophan	UGG	ACC
TYR	Tyrosine	UAU, UAC	ATA, ATG
VAL	Valine	GUU, GUC, GUA, GUG	CAA, CAG, CAT, CAC
Terminating triplets		UAA, UAG, UGA	ATT, ATC, ACT

▲ **Messenger RNA (mRNA)**
A form of RNA that is assembled on one sequence (one strand) of DNA bases. It carries the DNA code to the ribosome during protein synthesis.

▲ **Codons**
The triplets of messenger RNA bases that refer to a specific amino acid during protein synthesis.

▲ **Transfer RNA (tRNA)**
The type of RNA that binds to specific amino acids and transports them to the ribosome during protein synthesis.

The RNA molecule forms on the DNA template in much the same manner as new strands of DNA are assembled during DNA replication. The new RNA nucleotide chain is a particular type of RNA called **messenger RNA (mRNA)**. During its assembly on the DNA model, mRNA is transcribing the DNA code, and in fact, the formation of mRNA is called *transcription* (Fig. 3–4). Once the appropriate DNA segment has been copied, the mRNA strand (containing from 300 to 10,000 nucleotides) peels away from the DNA model and, after being processed, travels through the nuclear membrane to the ribosome. Meanwhile, the bonds between the DNA bases are reestablished, and the DNA molecule is once more intact.

As the mRNA strand arrives at the ribosome, the message it contains is translated. (This stage of the process is called *translation* because at this point, the genetic instructions are actually being decoded and implemented.) Just as each DNA triplet specifies one amino acid, mRNA triplets—called **codons**—also serve this function. Therefore, the mRNA strand is "read" in codons, or groups of three bases taken together (see Table 3–1).

One other form of RNA—**transfer RNA (tRNA)**—is essential to the actual assembly of a protein. Each molecule of tRNA has the ability to bind to one specific amino acid. A particular tRNA molecule carrying the amino acid matching the mRNA codon being translated arrives at the ribosome and deposits its amino

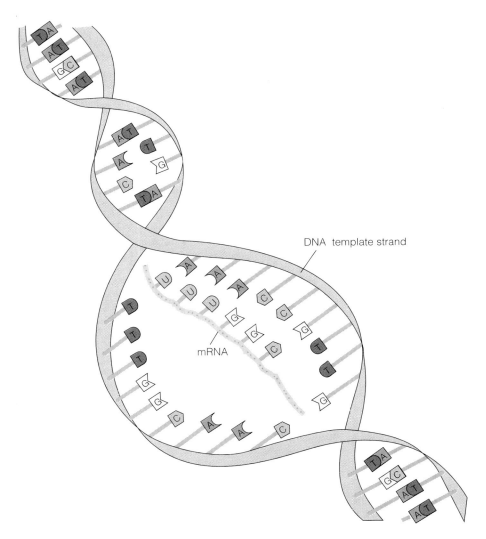

FIGURE 3–4

Transcription. The two DNA strands have partly separated. Free messenger RNA (mRNA) nucleotides have been drawn to the template strand, and a strand of mRNA is being made. Note that the mRNA strand will exactly complement the DNA template strand, except that uracil (U) replaces thymine (T).

DNA template strand

mRNA

acid (Fig. 3–5). As a second amino acid is deposited, the two are joined in the order dictated by the sequence of mRNA codons. In this way, series of amino acids are linked together to form a structure that will eventually function as a protein.

Definition of the Gene

The entire sequence of DNA bases responsible for the synthesis (or manufacture) of a protein or, in some cases, a portion of a protein, is referred to as a **gene.** Or, put another way, a gene is a segment of DNA that specifies the sequence of amino acids in a particular protein. Even more precisely, a gene codes for the production of a **polypeptide chain.** Those proteins composed of only a single polypeptide chain are produced through the action of a single gene. However,

▲ **Gene**
A sequence of DNA bases that specifies the order of amino acids in an entire protein or, in some cases, a portion of a protein. A gene may be made up of hundreds or thousands of DNA bases.

▲ **Polypeptide chain**
A sequence of amino acids that may act alone or in combination as a functional protein.

▲ **Mutation**
A change in DNA. Technically, mutation refers to changes in DNA bases as well as changes in chromosome number and/or structure.

some proteins (collagen and hemoglobin, for example) are made up of two or more polypeptide chains, each of which results from the action of a different gene. Thus, while some proteins result from the action of only one gene, others are produced by two or more.

A gene may comprise only a few hundred bases, or it may be composed of thousands. If the sequence of DNA bases is altered through **mutation** (a change in the DNA sequence), the manufacture of some proteins may not occur, and the cell (or indeed the organism) may not function properly (if it functions at all).

The genetic code is said to be universal in that, at least on earth, DNA is the genetic material in all forms of life (Box 3–1). Moreover, the DNA of all organisms, from bacteria to oak trees to human beings, is composed of the same molecules using the same kinds of instructions. These similarities imply biological relationships among, and ultimately a common ancestry for, all forms of life. What makes oak trees distinct from humans is not differences in the DNA material, but differences in how that material is arranged.

FIGURE 3–5

Assembly of an amino acid chain in protein synthesis.

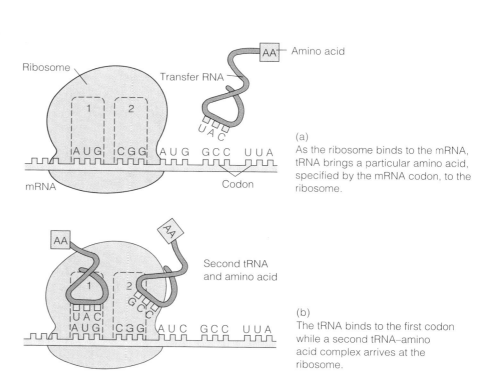

(a)
As the ribosome binds to the mRNA, tRNA brings a particular amino acid, specified by the mRNA codon, to the ribosome.

(b)
The tRNA binds to the first codon while a second tRNA–amino acid complex arrives at the ribosome.

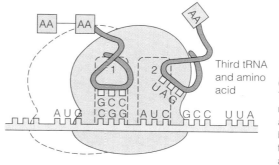

(c)
The ribosome moves down the mRNA, allowing a third amino acid to be brought into position by another tRNA molecule. Note that the first two amino acids are now joined together.

BOX 3–1

Characteristics of the DNA Code

1. **The Code is universal.** In other words, the same basic messages apply to all life forms on the planet, from bacteria to humans. The same triplet code, specifying each amino acid, thus applies to all life on earth. This commonality is the basis for the methods used in recombinant DNA technology.

2. **The Code is triplet.** Each amino acid is specified by a sequence of three bases in the mRNA (the codon), which in turn is coded for by three bases in the DNA.

3. **The Code is continuous—without pauses.** There are no pauses or other delimiters separating one codon from another. Thus, if a base should be deleted, the entire frame would be moved, drastically altering the message downstream for successive codons. Such a gross alteration is termed a *frame-shift mutation.* Note that although the code lacks "commas," it does contain "periods"; that is, three specific codons act to stop translation.

4. **The Code is redundant.** While there are 20 amino acids, there are 4 DNA bases and 64 possible codons. Even considering the three "stop" messages, that still leaves 61 codons specifying the 20 amino acids. Thus, many amino acids are specified by more than one codon (see Table 3–1). For example, leucine and serine are each coded for by six different codons. In fact, only two amino acids (methionine and tryptophan) are coded for by a single codon. Redundancy is useful. For one thing, it serves as a safety net of sorts by helping to reduce the likelihood of severe consequences if there is a change, or *mutation,* in a DNA base. For example, four different DNA triplets—CGA, CGG, CGT, and CGC—code for the amino acid *alanine.* If, in the codon CGA, A mutates to G, the resulting triplet, CGG, will still specify alanine; thus, there will be no functional change.

Mutation: When a Gene Changes

Probably the best way to envision how genetic material is organized and functions is to see what happens when it changes, or mutates. The first clearly elucidated example of a molecular mutation in humans relates to a portion of the hemoglobin molecule. As mentioned, hemoglobin is the component of red blood cells responsible for binding to oxygen molecules and transporting them to body cells and tissues. Normal adult hemoglobin is made up of four polypeptide chains (two *alpha* chains and two *beta* chains) that are direct products of gene action. Each beta chain is, in turn, composed of 146 amino acids.

There are several hemoglobin disorders with genetic origins, and perhaps the best known of these is **sickle-cell anemia,** which results from a defect in the beta chain. Individuals with sickle-cell anemia inherit a variant of a gene from *both* parents that contain the substitution of one amino acid *(valine)* for the normally occurring *glutamic acid.* This single amino acid substitution at the sixth position of the beta chain results in the production of an altered and less efficient form of hemoglobin called hemoglobin S (Hb^S). The normal form is called hemoglobin A (Hb^A). In situations where the availability of oxygen is reduced, such as high altitude, or when oxygen requirements are increased through exercise, red cells bearing Hb^S collapse, roughly assuming a sickle shape. What fol-

▲ **Sickle-cell anemia**
A severe inherited hemoglobin disorder that results from inheriting two copies of a mutant allele. This allele results from a single base substitution at the DNA level.

lows is a cascade of events, all of which result in severe anemia and its conse-quences. Briefly, these events include impaired circulation from blocked capil-laries, red cell destruction, oxygen deprivation to vital organs (including the brain), and, without treatment, death.

Individuals who inherit the altered form of the gene from only one parent have what is termed *sickle-cell trait*; because only about 40 percent of their hemoglobin is abnormal, they are much less severely affected and usually have a normal life span.

The cause of all the serious problems associated with sickle-cell anemia is a minute change in the Hb gene. Remember that both normal hemoglobin and the sickle-cell variety have 146 amino acids, 145 of which are identical. Moreover, to emphasize further the importance of a seemingly minimal alter-ation, consider that triplets of DNA bases are required to specify amino acids. Therefore, it takes 438 bases (146 x 3) to produce the chain of 146 amino acids forming the adult hemoglobin beta chain. But a change in only one of these 438 bases produces the cascade of life-threatening complications seen in sickle-cell anemia.

Figure 3–6 shows a possible DNA base sequence and the resulting amino acid products for both normal and sickling hemoglobin. As can be seen, a single base substitution (from CTC to CAC) can result in an altered amino acid sequence, from

> . . . proline—*glutamic acid*—glutamic acid . . .
> to
> . . . proline—*valine*—glutamic acid . . .

Such a change in the genetic code is referred to as a **point mutation,** and in evolution, it probably is the most common and most important source of new variation in populations. Point mutations, like that for the Hb gene, probably occur relatively frequently during cell division. But a new mutation will have evolutionary significance only if it passed on to offspring through the gametes. Once such a mutation has occurred, its fate in the population will depend on the other evolutionary forces, especially natural selection. In fact, sickle-cell anemia is the best demonstrated example of natural selection acting on human beings, a point that will be considered in more detail in Chapter 4.

Chromosomes

Much of a cell's existence is spent in **interphase,** the portion of its life cycle dur-ing which it is involved with metabolic processes and other activities. During interphase, the cell's DNA exists as an uncoiled, noncondensed, and filamentous substance called **chromatin.** (Incredibly, there are an estimated 6 feet of DNA in the nucleus of every one of your somatic cells!) However, at various times in the life of most types of cells, interphase is interrupted, activities cease, and the cell divides.

Cell division is the process that results in the production of new cells, and it is during this process that the chromatin becomes tightly coiled and is visible under a light microscope as a set of discrete structures called **chromosomes** (Fig. 3–7). A chromosome is composed of a DNA molecule and associated proteins (Fig. 3–8). During normal cell function, if chromosomes were visible, they

▲ **Point mutation**
The change in a single base of a DNA sequence.

▲ **Interphase**
The portion of a cell's cycle during which metabolic processes and other cellular activities occur. Chromosomes are not visible as discrete structures at this time. DNA replication occurs dur-ing interphase.

▲ **Chromatin**
The loose, diffuse form of DNA seen during interphase. When condensed, chromatin forms into chromosomes.

▲ **Chromosomes**
Discrete structures composed of DNA and protein found only in the nuclei of cells. Chromosomes are only visible under magnification during certain phases of cell division.

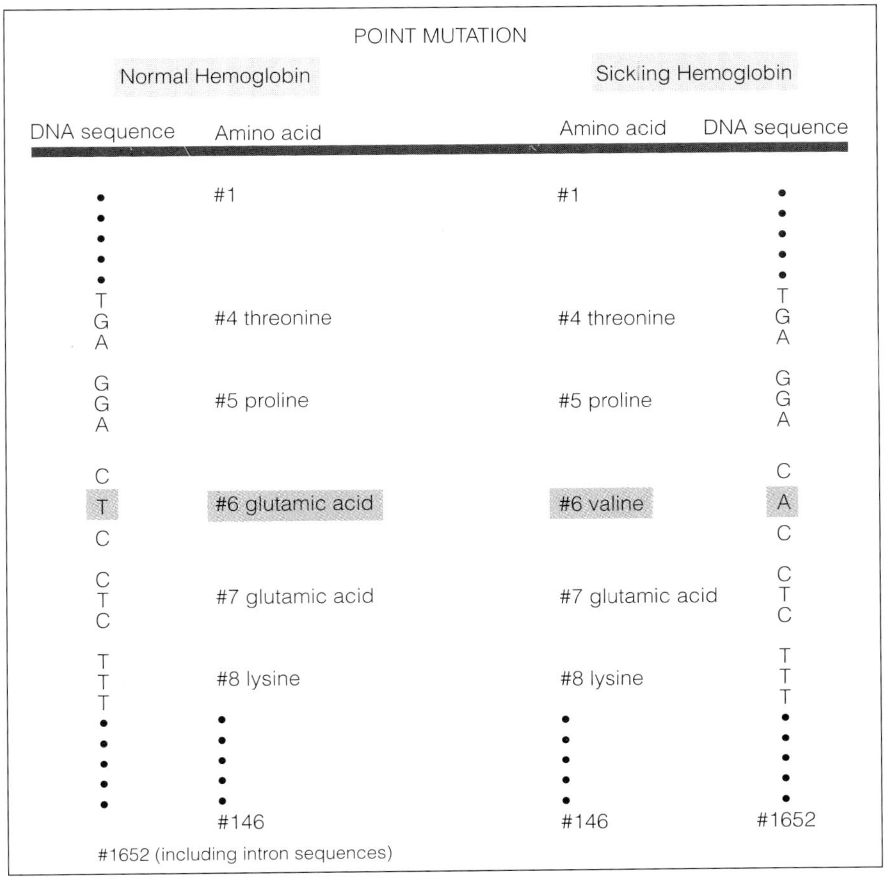

POINT MUTATION

Normal Hemoglobin			Sickling Hemoglobin	
DNA sequence	Amino acid		Amino acid	DNA sequence

• • • • •	#1		#1	• • • • •
T G A	#4 threonine		#4 threonine	T G A
G G A	#5 proline		#5 proline	G G A
C **T** C	#6 glutamic acid		#6 valine	C **A** C
C T C	#7 glutamic acid		#7 glutamic acid	C T C
T T T • • • • •	#8 lysine		#8 lysine	T T T • • • • •
	#146		#146	#1652

#1652 (including intron sequences)

FIGURE 3–6
Substitution of one base at position 6 produces sickling hemoglobin.

would appear as single-stranded structures. However, during the early stages of cell division, they are made up of two strands, or two DNA molecules, joined together at a constricted area called the **centromere**. There are two strands simply because the DNA molecules have *replicated* during interphase, and one strand of a chromosome is an exact copy of the other.

Every species is characterized by a specific number of chromosomes in somatic cells (see Table 3–2). In humans, there are 46. Chimpanzees and gorillas possess 48. This difference in chromosome number does not necessarily indicate that humans possess less DNA than chimpanzees and gorillas. The DNA is simply packaged differently in the three species.

In eukaryotic species, chromosomes generally occur in pairs. Thus, human somatic cells contain 23 pairs. One member of each pair is inherited from the father (paternal), while the other member is inherited from the mother (maternal).

Members of chromosomal pairs are said to be **homologous** in that they are alike in size and position of the centromere and they carry genetic information influencing the same *traits*. This does not imply that homologous chromosomes are genetically identical. It simply means that the characteristics they govern are the same. For example, on both of a person's ninth chromosomes, there is a **locus**, or gene position, that determines which of the four ABO blood types (A, B, AB, or O) he or she will have. However, the two ninth chromosomes might not have identical DNA segments at the ABO locus. In other words, at numerous genetic loci, there may be more than one possible form of a gene, and these molecularly

▲ **Centromere**
The constricted portion of a chromosome. After replication, the two strands of a double-stranded chromosome are joined at the centromere.

▲ **Homologous**
Referring to members of chromosome pairs. Homologous chromosomes carry loci that govern the same traits. During meiosis, homologous chromosomes pair and exchange segments of DNA. They are alike with regard to size, position of centromere, and banding pattern.

▲ **Locus (*pl.*, loci)**
(pronounced lo´-kus and lo-sigh´)
The position on a chromosome where a given gene occurs. The term is used interchangeably with *gene*, and when used in this manner, it refers to the DNA segment that codes for the production of a polypeptide chain.

FIGURE 3–7
Scanning electron micrograph of human chromosomes during cell division. Note that these chromosomes are composed of two strands, or two DNA molecules.

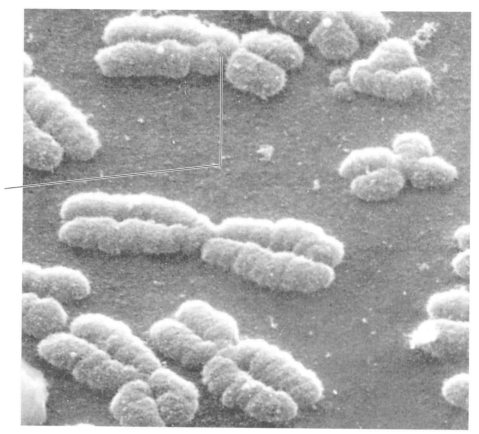

Centromere

▲ Alleles
Alternate forms of a gene. Alleles occur at the same locus on homologous chromosomes and thus govern the same trait. However, because they are different, their action may result in different expressions of that trait. The term is often used synonymously with *gene.*

▲ Autosomes
All chromosomes except the sex chromosomes.

▲ Sex chromosomes
In mammals, the X and Y chromosomes.

different forms are called **alleles.** Thus alleles are alternate forms of a gene that can direct the cell to produce slightly different forms of the same protein and, ultimately, different expressions of traits. At the ABO locus, there are three possible alleles *A, B,* and *O.* (However, since individuals only possesses two ninth chromosomes, only two alleles are present in any one person.) It is the allelic variation at the ABO locus that is responsible for the variation among humans in ABO blood type. Moreover, the potential variation that exists at specific loci in homologous chromosomes (as illustrated by the ABO example) explains how members of a chromosome pair may influence the same traits and yet not be genetically identical. (This point is covered in more detail in Chapter 4.)

There are two basic types of chromosomes: **autosomes** and **sex chromosomes.** Autosomes carry genetic information that governs all physical characteristics except primary sex determination. The two sex chromosomes are the X and Y chromosomes. In mammals, the Y chromosome carries genetic information directly involved with determining maleness. The X chromosome, although termed a "sex chromosome," is larger and functions more like an autosome in that it is not actually involved in primary sex determination but does influence a number of other traits.

Among mammals, all genetically normal females have two X chromosomes (XX); they are female simply because the Y chromosome is not present. All genetically normal males have one X and one Y chromosome (XY). In other classes of animals, such as birds or insects, primary sex determination is governed by differing chromosomal mechanisms.

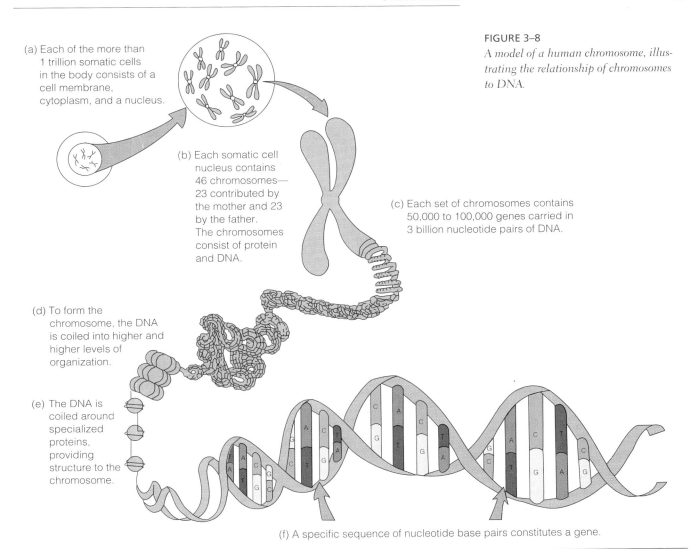

FIGURE 3–8

A model of a human chromosome, illustrating the relationship of chromosomes to DNA.

(a) Each of the more than 1 trillion somatic cells in the body consists of a cell membrane, cytoplasm, and a nucleus.

(b) Each somatic cell nucleus contains 46 chromosomes— 23 contributed by the mother and 23 by the father. The chromosomes consist of protein and DNA.

(c) Each set of chromosomes contains 50,000 to 100,000 genes carried in 3 billion nucleotide pairs of DNA.

(d) To form the chromosome, the DNA is coiled into higher and higher levels of organization.

(e) The DNA is coiled around specialized proteins, providing structure to the chromosome.

(f) A specific sequence of nucleotide base pairs constitutes a gene.

TABLE 3–2 Standard Chromosomal Complement in Various Organisms		
Organism	Chromosome Number in Somatic Cells	Chromosome Number in Gametes
Human (*Homo sapiens*)	46	23
Chimpanzee (*Pan troglodytes*)	48	24
Gorilla (*Gorilla gorilla*)	48	24
Dog (*Canis familiaris*)	78	39
Chicken (*Gallus domesticus*)	78	39
Frog (*Rana pipiens*)	26	13
Housefly (*Musca domestica*)	12	6
Onion (*Allium cepa*)	16	8
Corn (*Zea mays*)	20	10
Tobacco (*Nicotiana tabacum*)	48	24

Source: Cummings, 1991, p. 16.

It is extremely important to note that *all* autosomes occur in pairs. Normal human somatic cells have 22 pairs of autosomes and one pair of sex chromosomes. It should also be noted that abnormal numbers of autosomes are almost always fatal to the individual, usually soon after conception. Although abnormal numbers of sex chromosomes are not usually fatal, they may result in sterility and frequently have other consequences as well (see p. 62 for further discussion). Therefore, to function normally, it is essential for a human cell to possess both members of each chromosomal pair, or a total of 46 chromosomes—no more, no less.

Karyotyping Chromosomes

One method frequently used to examine chromosomes in an individual is to produce what is termed a **karyotype.** (An example of a human karyotype is shown in Fig. 3–9.) Chromosomes used in karyotypes are obtained from dividing cells. (You will remember that chromosomes are visible as discrete entities only during cell division.) For example, white blood cells, because they are easily obtained, may be cultured, chemically treated, and microscopically examined to identify those that are dividing. These cells are then photographed through a microscope to produce *photomicrographs* of intact, double-stranded chromosomes. Homologous chromosomes are then matched up, and the entire set is arranged in descending order by size so that the largest (number 1) appears first.

In addition to overall size, position of the centromere also aids in identification of individual chromosomes, since the position of the centromere is characteristic of each chromosome. Moreover, with the development of special techniques to highlight DNA segments that differentially take up various colored stains, it is now possible to identify every chromosome on the basis of specific *banding patterns.*

▲ **Karyotype**
The chromosomal complement of an individual or that which is typical for a species. Usually displayed in a photomicrograph, the chromosomes are arranged in pairs and according to size and position of the centromere.

FIGURE 3–9

A karyotype of a male, with the chromosomes arranged by size and position of the centromere, as well as by the banding patterns.

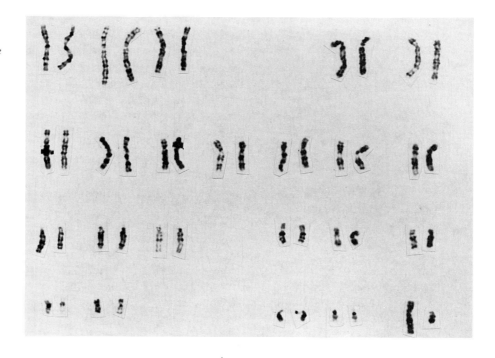

Karyotyping has numerous practical applications. Physicians and genetic counselors routinely use karyotypes to aid in the diagnosis of chromosomal disorders in patients. Moreover, karyotypes are often employed in the prenatal diagnosis of chromosomal abnormalities in developing fetuses.

Karyotypes have also proved extremely useful in comparing the chromosomes of different species. Indeed, karyotype analysis has revealed marked chromosomal similarities shared by different primate species, including humans. The similarities in overall karyotype, as well as the marked biochemical and DNA similarities indicated by banding patterns (discussed in Chapter 9), point to close *genetic* relationships among these three species.

Cell Division

Mitosis

Cell division in somatic cells is called **mitosis.** Mitosis occurs during growth of the individual. It also acts to promote healing of injured tissues and to replace older cells with newer ones. In short, it is the way somatic cells reproduce.

In the early stages of mitosis, a human somatic cell possesses 46 double-stranded chromosomes. As the cell begins to divide, the chromosomes line up in random order along the center of the cell (Fig. 3–10c). The chromosomes then split apart at the centromere, so that the strands are separated from one another. As this separation occurs, the two strands begin to move apart and travel toward opposite ends of the dividing cell (Fig. 3–10d). At this point, each strand is now a separate chromosome, *composed of one DNA molecule.* Once this separation occurs, the cell membrane pinches in and becomes sealed, so that two new cells are formed, each with a full complement of DNA, or 46 chromosomes. Most biology texts subdivide the continuous process of mitotic cell division into four phases: *prophase, metaphase, anaphase,* and *telophase.*

Mitosis is referred to as "simple cell division" because a somatic cell divides one time to produce two daughter cells that are genetically identical to each other and to the original cell. In mitosis, the original cell possesses 46 chromosomes, and each new daughter cell inherits an exact copy of all 46. This arrangement is made possible by the ability of the DNA molecule to replicate. Thus, it is DNA replication that ensures that the quantity and quality of the genetic material remain constant from one generation of cells to the next.

Meiosis

While mitosis produces new cells, **meiosis** may lead to the development of new individuals, since it produces reproductive cells, or gametes. Although meiosis is another form of cell division and is in some ways similar to mitosis, it is a more complicated process.

During meiosis, specialized cells in male testes and female ovaries divide and develop, eventually to become sperm or egg cells. Initially, these cells contain the full complement of chromosomes (46 in humans) and are referred to as **diploid** cells. (The number of chromosomes forming a complete set in a somatic cell is called the diploid number.) Meiosis is characterized by two divisions that result in four daughter cells, each of which contains 23 chromosomes, or half

▲ **Mitosis**
Simple cell division; the process by which somatic cells divide to produce two identical daughter cells.

▲ **Meiosis**
Cell division in specialized cells in ovaries and testes. Meiosis involves two divisions and results in four daughter cells, each containing only half the original number of chromosomes. These cells can develop into gametes.

▲ **Diploid**
Referring to the full complement of chromosomes in a somatic cell—two of each pair.

▲ **Haploid**

Referring to a half set of chromosomes, one member of each pair. Haploid sets are found in gametes.

FIGURE 3–10

Mitosis.

the original number. Because each of these newly formed cells receives only one member of each chromosomal pair, they are said to be **haploid** cells containing a haploid number of chromosomes.

Reduction of chromosome number is a critical feature of meiosis, for the resulting gamete, with its 23 chromosomes, may ultimately unite with another gamete, which also carries 23 chromosomes. The product of this union, the *zygote*, or fertilized egg, reestablishes the diploid number of chromosomes (46). In other words, the zygote inherits the full complement of DNA it needs (half from each parent) to develop and function normally. If it were not for *reduction*

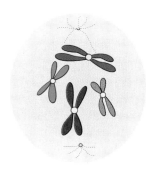

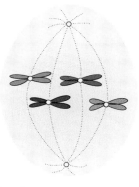

(a) The cell is involved in metabolic activities. DNA replication occurs, but chromosomes are not visible.

(b) The nuclear membrane disappears, and double-stranded chromosomes are visible.

(c) The chromosomes align themselves at the center of the cell.

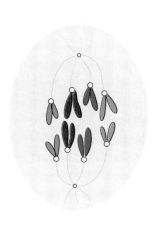

(d) The chromosomes split at the centromere, and the strands separate and move to opposite ends of the dividing cell.

(e) The cell membrane pinches in as the cell continues to divide. The chromosomes begin to uncoil (not shown here).

(f) After mitosis is complete, there are two identical daughter cells. The nuclear membrane is present, and chromosomes are no longer visible.

division (the first division) in meiosis, it would not be possible to maintain the correct number of chromosomes from one generation to the next.

During the first meiotic division all 46 chromosomes line up at the center of the cell as in mitosis, but there is a difference. In this first division, homologous chromosomes come together, forming *pairs* of double-stranded chromosomes. In this way pairs of chromosomes line up along the cell's center (see Fig. 3–11).

FIGURE 3–11
Meiosis.

Chromosomes are not visible as DNA replication occurs in a cell preparing to divide.

Double-stranded chromosomes become visible and homologous chromosomes exchange genetic material in a process called "recombination" or "crossing over."

Chromosome pairs migrate to center of cell.

FIRST DIVISION (REDUCTION DIVISION)

Homologous chromosomes separate, and members of each pair move to opposite ends of the dividing cell. This results in only half the original number of chromosomes in each new daughter cell.

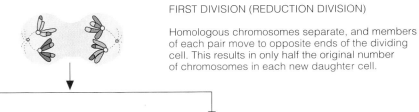

After the first meiotic division, there are two daughter cells, each containing only one member of each original chromosomal pair, or 23 nonhomologous chromosomes.

SECOND DIVISION

In this division, the chromosomes split at the centromere, and the strands move to opposite sides of the cell.

After the second division, meiosis results in four daughter cells. These may mature to become functional gametes, containing only half the DNA in the original cell.

▲ **Recombination (crossing over)**
The exchange of genetic material between homologous chromosomes during meiosis.

FIGURE 3–12

Mitosis and meiosis compared. In mitosis, one division produces two daughter cells, each of which contains 46 chromosomes. Meiosis is characterized by two divisions. After the first, there are two cells, each containing only 23 chromosomes (one member of each original chromosome pair). Each daughter cell divides again, so that the final result is four cells, each with only half the original number of chromosomes.

Pairing of homologous chromosomes is highly significant, for while they are together, members of pairs exchange genetic information in a process called **recombination,** or **crossing over.** Pairing is also important because it facilitates the accurate reduction of chromosome number by ensuring that each new daughter cell will receive only one member of each pair.

As the cell begins to divide, the chromosomes themselves remain intact (i.e., double-stranded), but *members of pairs* separate and migrate to opposite ends of the cell. After the first division, there are two new daughter cells, but they are not identical to each other or to the parental cell because each contains only one member of each chromosome pair and therefore only 23 chromosomes, each of which still has two strands (see Fig. 3–11). Moreover, because of crossing over, each chromosome now contains some genetic variations it did not have previously.

The second meiotic division proceeds in much the same way as in mitosis (see Fig. 3–12). In the two newly formed cells, the 23 double-stranded chromosomes align themselves at the cell's center, and as in mitosis, the strands of each chromosome separate at the centromere and move apart. Once this second division is completed, there are four daughter cells, each with 23 single-stranded chromosomes (i.e., 23 DNA molecules).

Meiosis occurs in all sexually reproducing organisms and is a highly important evolutionary innovation, since it increases genetic variation in populations at a faster rate than mutation alone can do in asexually reproducing species. Individual members of sexually reproducing species are not genetically identical clones of other individuals. Rather, they result from the contribution of genetic information from two parents. From any one human mating, an enormous

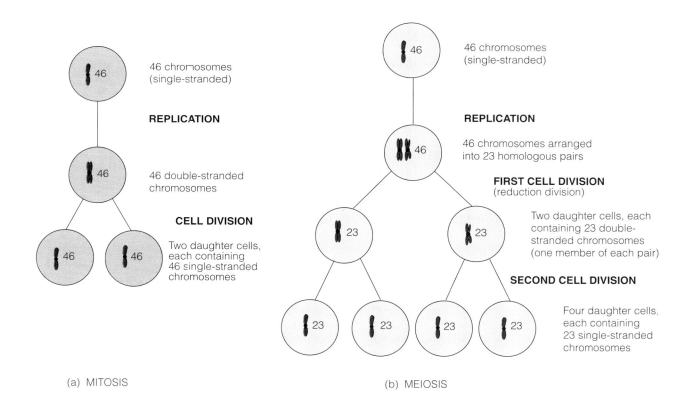

(a) MITOSIS

(b) MEIOSIS

number of possible offspring can result. From just the random arrangements of chromosome pairs lining up along the center of the cell during the first division of meiosis, each parent can produce 8 million genetically different gametes. And given the joint probability accounting for both parents, the total number of possible genetic combinations for any human mating is about 70 trillion. It should be noted that this staggering number is the result solely of the paired arrangements (called **random assortment**) and does not even account for the many more combinations resulting from crossing over.

The genetic uniqueness of individuals is further enhanced by recombination between homologous chromosomes during meiosis, for recombination ensures that chromosomes are not passed on unaltered from one generation to the next. Instead, in every generation, parental contributions are reshuffled in an almost infinite number of combinations, thus altering the genetic composition of chromosomes even before they are passed on. Some estimates suggest that recombination (i.e., crossing over) adds to the number of genetic possibilities by a factor of up to 10 billion (i.e., 10,000,000,000 × 70,000,000,000,000), which produces a number really beyond comprehension. Suffice it to say, with the exception of identical twins, no human being is genetically identical to any other who has ever lived or who ever will live.

Natural selection acts on genetic variation in populations (you will recall that Charles Darwin emphasized this point). In all species, *mutation* is the only source of *new* genetic variation. But in sexually reproducing species, recombination produces new *arrangements* of genetic information, which potentially provide additional material for natural selection to act on.

Genetic variation is essential if species are to adapt to changing selective pressures. If all individuals were genetically identical, natural selection would have nothing to act on and evolution could not occur. It has been argued that this influence on variation is the principal adaptive reason for the evolution of sex. Therefore, although reproduction has been strictly asexual for most of the time life has existed on this planet, sexual reproduction and meiosis are of *major* evolutionary importance because they contribute to the role of natural selection in populations.

▲ **Random assortment**
The random distribution of chromosomes to daughter cells during meiosis; along with recombination, the source of variation resulting from meiosis.

Meiosis in Males and Females

As discussed, meiosis involves two divisions that ultimately produce four daughter cells. However, human females and males differ in the distribution of materials to these cells as well as the *timing* of the process. In females, the process is called oogenesis, and it occurs in the ovaries. The first meiotic division yields one quite large cell, called the *secondary oocyte*, and it contains about 95 percent of the cytoplasm. The other, much smaller cell is called a **polar body.** In the second division, there is again a markedly disproportionate distribution of the cytoplasm, so that one large functional gamete, called the *ovum*, is produced. The other three cells—the polar bodies—receive almost no cytoplasm and cannot function as gametes.

In males, the meiotic process is called *spermatogenesis*, and it occurs in the testes, where primary sex cells divide to produce four haploid cells called *spermatids*. These, in turn, differentiate to yield mature sperm. It should be noted that each haploid sperm cell contains 22 autosomes and either an X *or* Y chromosome. Ova, by contrast, also contain 22 autosomes, but *always* with an X

▲ **Polar body**
A nonviable product of female meiosis, as it contains minimal cytoplasm.

chromosome. Thus, it is the presence of either the X or Y chromosome in the sperm cell that determines the sex of the offspring.

There is also a notable difference in the timing of meiosis in human females and males. In females, meiosis begins in fetal life and is "arrested" before birth early in meiosis. Years later, with sexual maturation, meiosis resumes, producing just one gamete per cycle (about every 28 days). Even then, meiosis does not reach finality to produce a mature ovum unless the gamete is fertilized by a sperm cell. Thus, an ovum that is fertilized when a female is, say, 35 years old actually began meiosis somewhat more than 35 years before. This long-term period of suspended development has been suggested as the main reason for a greater number of meiotic problems accumulating with advanced maternal age (see the following section).

Problems with Meiosis

For meiosis to ensure a reasonably good opportunity for an offspring to complete normal fetal development, the process must be quite exact. The two-stage division must produce a viable gamete with exactly 23 chromosomes—that is, with only one member of each chromosome pair present. Superficially, it appears that the process works quite well, since more than 98 percent of newborns have the correct number of chromosomes. However, this statistic is misleading, for there are many genetic "mistakes" that are not detected among live-born infants. It has been estimated that as many as one of every two pregnancies naturally terminates early as a spontaneous abortion (miscarriage). An estimated 70 percent of these miscarriages are caused by an improper number of chromosomes (Cummings, 1991). Thus, it appears that during meiosis, there are frequent errors with quite serious consequences.

If chromosomes or chromosome strands fail to separate during either of the two meiotic divisions, serious problems can arise. This failure to separate is called **nondisjunction.** The result of nondisjunction is that one of the daughter cells receives two copies of the affected chromosome. The other daughter cell receives none. If such an affected gamete unites with a normal gamete containing 23 chromosomes, the resulting zygote will have either 45 or 47 chromosomes. Having only one member of a chromosome pair is referred to as *monosomy.* The term *trisomy* refers to the presence of three copies of a particular chromosome.

The far-reaching effects of an abnormal number of chromosomes can be appreciated only by remembering that the zygote will faithfully reproduce itself through mitosis. Thus, every cell in the developing body will also have the abnormal chromosomal complement. Most situations of this type involving autosomes are lethal, and the embryo is spontaneously aborted, frequently before the pregnancy is even recognized.

One example of a result of an abnormal number of autosomes is *Down syndrome,* more properly called *trisomy 21,* where there are three copies of the twenty-first chromosome. This is the only example of an abnormal number of autosomes being compatible with life beyond the first few months after birth. Trisomy 21, which occurs in approximately 1 out of every 1,000 live births, is associated with a number of developmental and health problems. These problems include congenital heart defects (seen in about 40 percent of affected newborns), increased susceptibility to respiratory infections, and leukemia.

▲ **Nondisjunction**
The failure of homologous chromosomes or chromosome strands to separate during cell division.

However, the most widely recognized effect of trisomy 21 is mental retardation, which is variably expressed and ranges from mild to severe.

Trisomy 21 is partly associated with advanced maternal age. For example, the risk of a 20-year-old woman giving birth to an affected infant is just 0.05 percent (5 in 10,000). However, 3 percent of babies born to mothers 45 and older are affected (a 60-fold increase). Actually, most affected infants are born to women under the age of 35, but this statistic is due to the fact that the majority of babies are born to women in this age category. The increase in incidence with maternal age is thought to be related to the early initiation of meiosis in females and the presumed age changes in the gametic cell lines, resulting in increased risk of nondisjunction. Indeed, a number of conditions related to nondisjunction of chromosomes are thought to be influenced, in part, by increased maternal age.

Nondisjunctions may also occur in sex chromosomes, producing individuals who, for example, are: XXY (47 chromosomes), XO (45 chromosomes), XXX (47 chromosomes), or XYY (47 chromosomes). While these conditions do not always result in death or mental retardation, some are associated with impaired mental function and/or sterility (Table 3–3). Moreover, still greater numbers of X chromosomes, such as XXXX or XXXY, result in marked mental retardation. And some nondisjunctions of sex chromosomes are lethal. While it is possible to survive without a Y chromosome (roughly half of all humans do), it is not possible to live without an X chromosome. Indeed, the evidence suggests that embryos that possess only a Y chromosome are spontaneously aborted before a pregnancy is even recognized.

Clearly, the importance of accuracy during meiosis cannot be overstated. If normal development is to occur, it is essential that the correct number of both autosomes and sex chromosomes be present.

TABLE 3–3 Examples of Nondisjunction in Sex Chromosomes

Chromosomal Complement	Condition	Estimated Incidence	Manifestations
XXX	Trisomy X	1 per 1,000 female births	Affected women are usually clinically normal, but there is a slight increase in sterility and mental retardation compared to the general population. In cases with more than three X chromosomes, mental retardation can be severe.
XYY	XYY syndrome	1 per 1,000 male births	Affected males are fertile and tend to be taller than average.
XO	Turner syndrome	1 per 10,000 female births	Affected females are short-statured, have broad chests and webbed necks, and are sterile. There is usually no mental retardation, but concepts relating to spatial relationships, including mathematics, can pose difficulties. Between 95 and 99 percent of affected fetuses die before birth.
XXY	Klinefelter syndrome	1 per 1,000 male births	Symptoms are noticeable by puberty: reduced testicular development, reduced facial and body hair, some breast development in about half of all cases, and reduced fertility or sterility. Some individuals exhibit lowered intelligence. Additional X chromosomes (XXXY) are associated with mental retardation.

Summary

This chapter has dealt with several concepts that are fundamental to understanding the processes of biological evolution, especially as related to human adaptation and variation. These are topics that will be discussed in succeeding chapters.

It has been shown that cells are the fundamental units of life and that there are basically two types of cells. Somatic cells make up body tissues, while gametes (eggs and sperm) are reproductive cells that transmit genetic information from parent to offspring.

Genetic information is contained in the DNA molecule, found in the nuclei of cells. The DNA molecule is capable of replication, or making copies of itself, and it is the only molecule known to have this ability. Replication makes it possible for daughter cells to receive a full complement of DNA (contained in chromosomes) during mitosis.

DNA also controls protein synthesis by directing the cell to arrange amino acids in the proper sequence for each particular type of protein. Also involved in the process of protein synthesis is another, similar molecule called RNA. The DNA code for all life is universal and triplet, the latter meaning that amino acids are coded for by DNA bases occurring in groups of three.

Cells multiply by dividing, and during cell division, DNA is visible under a microscope in the form of chromosomes. In humans, there are 46 chromosomes (23 pairs). If the complement is not precisely distributed to succeeding generations of cells, severe consequences will follow.

Somatic cells divide during growth or tissue repair or to replace old, worn-out cells. Somatic cell division is called mitosis. During mitosis, a cell divides one time to produce two daughter cells, each possessing a full and identical (diploid) set of chromosomes.

Sex cells are produced when specialized cells in the ovaries and testes divide in meiosis. Unlike mitosis, meiosis is characterized by two divisions, which produce four nonidentical daughter cells, each containing only half (haploid) the amount of DNA (23 chromosomes) as that carried by the original cell.

Questions for Review

1. Genetics is the study of what?
2. What components of a eukaryotic cell are discussed in this chapter?
3. What are the two basic types of cells in individuals? Give an example of each.
4. What are nucleotides?
5. Name the four DNA bases. Which pairs with which?
6. What is DNA replication, and why is it important?
7. What are proteins? Give two examples.
8. What are enzymes?
9. What are the building blocks of protein? How many different kinds are there?
10. What is the function of DNA in protein synthesis?
11. What is the function of mRNA?
12. What is the function of tRNA?
13. Define gene, allele, and locus.
14. Define chromosome.
15. What are homologous chromosomes?

16. How many cell divisions occur in mitosis? In humans, how many chromosomes does each new cell have?
17. How many cell divisions occur in meiosis? How many daughter cells are produced when meiosis is complete? In humans, how many chromosomes does each new cell contain?
18. Why is reduction division important?
19. What is recombination and why is it important? When does it occur?
20. Why is the genetic code said to be universal? Why is it said to be redundant?
21. What are the two sex chromosomes? Which two do males have? Which two do females have?
22. Why is meiosis important to the process of natural selection?
23. How does meiosis in females differ from meiosis in males?
24. Why is the study of genetics important to physical anthropology?

Suggested Further Reading

Brennan, James R. 1985. *Patterns of Human Heredity*. Englewood Cliffs, NJ: Prentice Hall.

Cummings, Michael R. 1994. *Human Heredity*. 3rd ed. St. Paul: West.

Gribbin, John. 1987. *In Search of the Double Helix*. New York: Bantam Books.

See entire issue of *Scientific American*, vol. 253(4), October 1985, for numerous articles pertaining to molecular genetics and evolution.

Internet Resources

Primer on Molecular Genetics (Department of Energy)
   http://www.gdb.org/dan/doe/intro.html
   (Good basic discussion of DNA, genes, and chromosomes. Has diagrams, illustrations, and a very extensive glossary.)

Genetic Technologies: A Revolution in Science

The basic premise of Michael Crichton's *Jurassic Park* is as follows: A Silicon Valley biotechnology firm develops a method of extracting 150-million-year-old dinosaur DNA from mosquitoes preserved in amber, or fossilized tree sap. Prior to being trapped in tree sap, the mosquitoes had ingested minute quantities of dinosaur blood, a few cells of which remained in the insects' digestive tracts. From the dinosaur DNA, embryos are produced, inserted in genetically engineered plastic eggs. and incubated. The resulting animals, resurrections of several dinosaur species, become the central attraction of an island theme park—*Jurassic Park*.

Far-fetched? Probably. Or is it just possible that someday, science will develop the technology to accomplish at least some of the *Jurassic Park* achievements? Consider that in 1992, a group of scientists at California Polytechnic State University and the University of California at Berkeley cloned (produced copies of) DNA fragments obtained from a bee trapped in amber 25 million years ago. Does this feat mean that scientists will soon be able to produce a bee that has been extinct for 25 million years? Certainly not with today's technology, for the ancient DNA extracted from fossil species represents only a minute sample of the entire DNA sequence of an organism. But by cloning DNA sequences from extinct species and comparing them to the DNA of their presumed descendants, scientists are able to estimate *rates* of genetic change within lineages. This achievement in itself is remarkable; the rest may well remain the stuff of fantasy. However, perhaps we should not completely rule out even some of the more preposterous scenarios, particularly in view of the remarkable developments that have occurred in genetic research since the inception of the biotechnology industry in 1976.

The techniques used in genetic engineering today are highly complex, but the basic principles are fairly straightforward, certainly for those with a grasp of the fundamentals of genetics. Anyone who has ever snipped a cutting off a plant and rooted it has produced a clone (a genetically identical copy of a plant or animal), but current techniques have taken us far beyond the simplicity of "cuttings." Beginning with research in the 1950s, the possibility of using cloning procedures to increase the frequency of desirable traits in domesticated species has approached reality.

Cells from a single plant can be cultured to produce masses of cells, which are then induced to develop roots and shoots, resulting in large numbers of plants, all identical to the original. Variations of these techniques have been applied to a species of pine, the loblolly, with the goal of producing forests of genetically identical, fast-growing trees with high wood content. The result has obvious benefits for the lumber industry and could perhaps also allow for the setting aside of natural forests for preservation.

However, it is important to consider that such cloned forests would not be natural. For one thing, they could possess an unforeseen susceptibility to certain infectious organisms and parasites. Additionally, because they would lack many other types of plants, they would not provide the necessary habitat for most animal species provided by natural forests. These high-tech solutions could be acceptable as long as such tree stands are seen simply as tree farms and providing that sufficient primary and secondary forests are left standing in the interests of species preservation.

But these solutions do challenge traditional views of what constitutes a forest. And we must bear in mind that in terms of biodiversity, such forests of the future run the risk of being little more than sterile wastelands.

The cloning of animals is more complicated, but it is now being practiced (at least to a limited extent) in cattle and other domesticates. The technology was developed in the 1970s and early 1980s and involves the removal of cells from a developing embryo composed of 16 to 32 cells. These cells and the DNA they contain are then inserted into egg cells (harvested from other females) from which nuclei have been removed. The result is several genetically identical fertilized eggs, which are then artificially implanted into hormonally prepared surrogate mothers and allowed to develop.

Such cloning techniques have enormous implications for the livestock industry. Theoretically, breeders will be able to produce quantities of animals all possessing—to the same degree—whatever traits are deemed desirable. This capability could mean that cattle with uniformly higher milk yield or increased muscle mass and sheep

that produce more and better quality wool may be on the horizon. But, again, such genetic homogeneity could certainly render such strains of livestock highly susceptible to the introduction of disease organisms, and with no genetic variation to offer resistance, entire herds could potentially be lost.

Because of the universality of the genetic code, it is possible to transfer DNA from one species to another. For example, recombinant DNA technology permits the insertion of human genes into bacterial cells, which subsequently possess an altered genetic makeup.

Insertion of foreign DNA into bacteria or other organisms was made possible by the discovery of *restriction enzymes* in the mid-1970s. These enzymes (over 300 are currently known) are used to snip out base pair sequences that are then spliced into circular strands of bacterial DNA called *plasmids*. The introduced strand of DNA is sealed into place by other enzymes. The recombinant plasmid then serves as a vector, or carrier, for transferring the foreign DNA into cultured bacterial cells. As these cells divide, the plasmid, including its introduced segment, replicates with the rest of the cell's DNA. Thus, entire

colonies of altered cells serve as manufacturing plants for the gene products (insulin, clotting factor, growth hormone, etc.) specified by the human genes inserted into the plasmid vector.

Genetic engineering has enormous potential for the treatment of disease. Because bacterial cells divide rapidly, ever-increasing numbers are capable of producing commercial quantities of beneficial gene products. For example, insulin for use by patients with insulin-dependent diabetes was formerly derived from nonhuman animals. But since 1982, insulin produced by genetically altered bacteria has helped lower the cost of therapy for the over 2 million Americans who suffer from insulin-dependent diabetes.

In the same manner, numerous other products, such as blood clotting factors (for hemophiliacs), growth hormone, and various other hormones, can now be produced. Previously, these products were derived through blood donations and tissues from human cadavers. Unfortunately, as we are all aware, recipients of products derived in these ways can be exposed to several infectious agents. Therefore, the use of artificially produced substances not only lowers the cost to the patient in many cases, but also greatly reduces the threat of contamination.

By changing the genetic structure of other organisms, we are indeed creating new life-forms and potential new species. (It would certainly seem that such capabilities would put to rest any doubts about the reality of biological evolution.) Following are a few examples of how humans are now capable of manipulating biological processes in other organisms.

Pig embryos have received, and incorporated into their own DNA, genes for human growth hormone, in attempts to produce faster-maturing pigs. Researchers at Harvard University have developed a genetically engineered mouse that carries a gene rendering it highly susceptible to several types of cancer. The resultant strain of mice is now being used in laboratories to test cancer-resistant compounds and also the possible carcinogenic effects of various substances.

Genes conferring resistance to insect pests are now being experi-

mentally introduced into numerous food crops. Plant geneticists are also developing methods of increasing the amino acid content of vegetables and grains normally low in protein. The gene that causes tomatoes to soften when ripe has been manipulated so that this fruit can be allowed to ripen on the vine before being picked and shipped to market. And lastly, genetically altered bacteria, sprayed on strawberries and other crops, can protect such crops from devastating frost buildup even at temperatures some 10–12° F below freezing.

The field of genetic engineering is in its infancy, and we are tempted to believe that these new technologies will offer solutions to many contemporary medical and nutritional problems. Moreover, as we discussed, these genetic technologies can help reveal the mechanisms of biological evolution. With such promise and such tools at our disposal, it is also to be hoped that we use these powerful new techniques wisely.

Critical Thinking Questions

1. What is a clone? How can cloning potentially benefit the agriculture industry? What are some possible problems that might arise from cloning?

2. Do you have doubts or concerns about any of the genetic technologies? If so, what is the basis for your concern? What kinds of information would you require (and from whom) to alleviate these doubts?

3. Do emerging genetic technologies challenge your personal views of life, nature, science, and the role that humans will play in the future? If so, how?

Sources

Crichton, Michael. 1990. *Jurassic Park.* New York: Ballantine Books.

Cummings, Michael R. 1991. *Human Heredity, Principles and Issues.* St. Paul: West.

Ross, Philip E. 1992. "Eloquent Remains," *Scientific American,* 266(5): 114–125.

Heredity and Evolution

Introduction

This chapter is roughly divided into two parts. In the first, we continue with the discussion of genetic principles we began in Chapter 3. That chapter dealt with the structure and function of DNA within the cell. In this chapter, we shift to a somewhat broader perspective and focus on the principles that guide the transmission of traits from parent to offspring. These principles, first elucidated by Gregor Mendel, form much of the basis of modern genetics, and we cover them in some detail because of their relevance to the evolutionary process. The second part of this chapter integrates these basics of DNA function and Mendelian patterns of inheritance into a comprehensive theory of the forces that guide biological evolution.

For at least 10,000 years, beginning with the domestication of plants and animals, people have attempted to explain how traits are passed from parents to offspring. Although most theories have been far from accurate, farmers and herders have known for millennia that they could enhance the frequency and expression of desirable attributes through selective breeding. However, exactly why desirable traits were often seen in the offspring of carefully chosen breeding stock remained a mystery. It was equally curious when offspring did not show the traits their human owners had hoped for.

From the time ancient Greek philosophers considered the problem until well into the nineteenth century, one predominant belief was that characteristics of offspring resulted from the *blending* of parental traits. Blending was supposedly accomplished by means of particles that existed in every part of the body. These *pangenes* contained miniatures of the body part (limbs, organs, etc.) from which the particles derived, and they traveled through the blood to the reproductive organs and blended with particles of another individual during reproduction. There were variations on the theme of *pangenesis*, and numerous scholars, including Charles Darwin, adhered to some aspects of the theory.

There were also questions as to which parent made the greater contribution to the sex and appearance of offspring. One widely accepted explanation, developed in the seventeenth and eighteenth centuries, proposed the existence in sex cells of a miniature, preformed adult called a *homunculus*. Controversy arose, however, over which parent (male or female) contributed the homunculus and which primarily provided nutrition for its development.

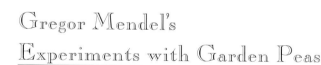

Gregor Mendel's Experiments with Garden Peas

It was not until an Augustinian monk, Gregor Mendel (1822–1884), addressed the question of inheritance that the basic principles of heredity were discovered (Fig. 4–1). Gregor Mendel grew up in a poor peasant family in what is now the Czech Republic. At age 21, he was accepted as a novice in the monastery at Brno, in the Czech Republic.

Mendel was attracted to monastic life, partly because of the security it offered, but also because it presented opportunities for higher education. Moreover, life in Brno did not fit the stereotype of cloistered monasticism. Indeed, at the time, Brno was a center of scientific and cultural endeavor for

FIGURE 4–1
Gregor Mendel.

much of southeastern Europe, and many of the monks there were involved in various areas of scientific research (Hartl, 1983).

After becoming established at Brno, Mendel left for two years to study at the University of Vienna, where he acquired scientific expertise from leading professors in botany, physics, and mathematics. Given this impressive background, it is not so surprising that an obscure monk was able to unravel the mysteries of inheritance and thus achieve one of the most important biological discoveries ever made.

When Mendel returned to Brno, he resumed his work in the monastery garden, where he had been experimenting with the fertilization of flowers, hoping to develop new variations in colors. This activity eventually led him to attempt to elucidate the various ways in which physical traits (such as color or height) could be expressed in plant **hybrids.**

Mendel hoped that by making crosses between two strains of *purebred* plants and examining their progeny, he could determine (and predict) how many different forms of hybrids there were, arrange the forms according to generation, and evaluate the proportion in each generation of each type represented.

▲ **Hybrids**
Offspring of parents who are in some ways genetically dissimilar. The term can also refer to heterozygotes.

Crosses Between Plants: Single Traits

Mendel chose to work with the common garden pea, and he wisely considered one characteristic at a time, rather than what other investigators had done—namely, examining several simultaneously. In all, he focused on seven different traits, each of which could be expressed in two different ways (Table 4–1).

In 1856, Mendel began his experiments by crossing 70 different purebred plants that differed with regard to a specific trait. (In all, Mendel used over 28,000 pea plants before he completed his research.) The plants used in this first cross were designated the parental, or P generation. Using pure lines meant, for example, that if the trait in question was stem length (tall or short), Mendel crossed varieties that produced only tall plants with varieties that produced only short plants. If he was interested in seed color (yellow or green), he crossed plants that produced only yellow seeds with plants that produced all green seeds.

The hybrid offspring of the parental generation were designated the F_1 (first filial) generation. As the F_1 plants matured, all were tall. Not one was short. According to blending theories, height in the F_1 plants should have been

TABLE 4–1 The Seven Garden Pea Characteristics Studied by Mendel		
Characteristic	**Dominant Trait**	**Recessive Trait**
1. Form of ripe seed	Smooth	Wrinkled
2. Color of seed albumen	Yellow	Green
3. Color of seed coat	Gray	White
4. Form of ripe pods	Inflated	Constricted
5. Color of unripe pods	Green	Yellow
6. Position of flowers	Axial	Terminal
7. Length of stem	Tall	Short

intermediate between the heights of the parent plants, but these theories were not confirmed by Mendel's results.

Next, since pea plants have both male and female parts, the F_1 plants were allowed to self-fertilize to produce a second hybrid generation (the F_2 generation). This time all the offspring were not uniformly tall. Instead, approximately 3/4 were tall and the other 1/4 were short. In one experiment, there were 787 tall plants and 277 short plants. This produced an almost exact ratio of three tall plants for every short plant (3:1).

Regardless of the trait he examined, every time the experiment was done, Mendel obtained almost exactly the same results. One expression of the trait disappeared in the F_1 generation and reappeared in the F_2 generation. Moreover, the expression that was present in the F_1 generation was more common in the F_2 plants, occurring in a ratio of approximately 3:1.

These results suggested at least two important facts. First, it appeared that the various expressions of a trait were controlled by discrete *units*, which occurred in pairs, and that offspring inherited one unit from each parent. Mendel correctly reasoned that the members of a pair of units controlling a trait somehow separated into different sex cells and were again united with another member during fertilization of the egg. This is Mendel's *first principle of inheritance*, known as the **principle of segregation.**

Today we know that meiosis explains Mendel's principle of segregation. You will remember that during meiosis, homologous chromosomes (and thus the genes they carry) separate from one another and are distributed to different gametes. However, in the zygote, the full complement of chromosomes is restored, and both members of each chromosome pair (homologous chromosomes) are present in the offspring.

Second, Mendel recognized that the expression that was absent in the F_1 plants had not actually disappeared at all. It had remained present, but somehow it was masked and could not be expressed. To describe the trait that seemed to be lost, Mendel used the term **recessive;** and the expressed trait was said to be **dominant.** Thus, the important principles of *dominance* and *recessiveness* were formulated, and they remain as basic underlying concepts in the field of genetics.

As you already know, a *gene* is a segment of DNA that directs the production of a specific protein or part of a protein, and the location of a gene on a chromosome is its *locus*. You have also learned that at many loci, there are alternate forms of genes called *alleles*, and different alleles can direct the cell to produce slightly different forms of the same protein (see Chapter 3, p. 54).

As it turns out, plant height in garden peas is controlled by two different alleles at one genetic locus. The allele that determines that a plant will be tall is dominant to the allele for short. (It is worth mentioning that height is not governed in this manner in all plants.)

In Mendel's experiments, all the parent (P) plants had two copies of the same allele, either dominant or recessive, depending on whether they were tall or short. When two copies of the same allele are present at the same locus on homologous chromosomes, the individual is said to be **homozygous.** Thus, all the tall P plants were homozygous for the dominant allele, and all the short P plants were homozygous for the recessive allele. (This homozygosity explains why tall plants crossed with tall plants produced only tall offspring, and short plants crossed with short plants produced all short offspring; i.e., they were "pure lines" and lacked genetic variation at this locus.) However, all the F_1 plants (hybrids) had inherited one allele from each parent plant; therefore, they all possessed two different alleles at specific loci. Individuals that possess two different alleles at a locus are **heterozygous.**

▲ **Principle of segregation**
Genes (alleles) occur in pairs (because chromosomes occur in pairs). During gamete production, the members of each pair of alleles separate, so that each gamete contains one member of each pair. During fertilization, the full number of chromosomes is restored, and members of gene or allele pairs are reunited.

▲ **Recessive**
Describing a trait that is not expressed in heterozygotes; also refers to the allele that governs the trait. For a recessive allele to be expressed, there must be two copies of the allele (i.e., the individual must be homozygous).

▲ **Dominant**
Describing a trait governed by an allele that can be expressed in the presence of another, different allele (i.e., in heterozygotes). Dominant alleles prevent the expression of recessive alleles in heterozygotes.

▲ **Homozygous**
Having the same allele at the same locus on both members of a pair of homologous chromosomes.

▲ **Heterozygous**
Having different alleles at the same locus on members of a pair of homologous chromosomes.

Figure 4–2 illustrates the crosses that Mendel initially performed. Geneticists use standard symbols to refer to alleles. Upper case letters refer to dominant alleles (or dominant traits), and lower case letters refer to recessive alleles (or recessive traits). Therefore,

T = the allele for tallness
t = the allele for shortness

FIGURE 4–2
Results of crosses when only one trait at a time is considered.

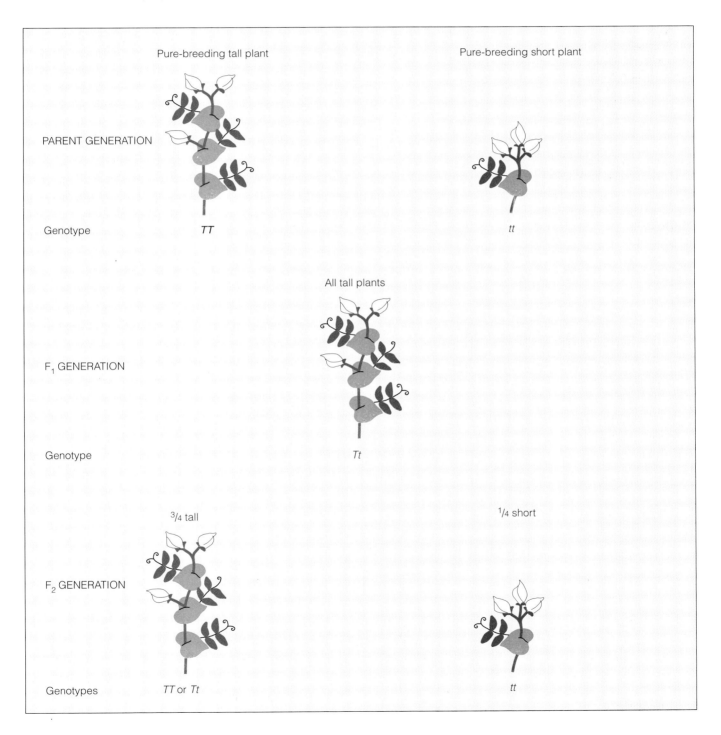

Pure-breeding tall plant

Pure-breeding short plant

PARENT GENERATION

Genotype TT tt

All tall plants

F$_1$ GENERATION

Genotype Tt

$^3/_4$ tall $^1/_4$ short

F$_2$ GENERATION

Genotypes TT or Tt tt

▲ **Genotype**
The genetic makeup of an individual. *Genotype* can refer to an organism's entire genetic makeup or to the alleles at a particular locus.

▲ **Phenotypes**
The observable or detectable physical characteristics of an organism; the detectable expression of the genotype.

▲ **Phenotypic ratio**
The proportion of one phenotype to other phenotypes in a group of organisms. For example, Mendel observed that there were approximately three tall plants for every short plant in the F_2 generation. This is expressed as a phenotypic ratio of 3:1.

▲ **Mendelian traits**
Characteristics that are influenced by alleles at only one genetic locus. Examples include many blood types, such as ABO, and many genetic disorders, including sickle-cell anemia and Tay-Sachs disease.

The same symbols are combined to describe an individual's actual genetic makeup, or **genotype.** The term *genotype* can be used to refer to an organism's entire genetic makeup or to the alleles at a specific genetic locus on homologous chromosomes. Thus, the genotypes of the plants in Mendel's experiments were

$$TT = \text{homozygous tall plants}$$
$$Tt = \text{heterozygous tall plants}$$
$$tt = \text{homozygous short plants}$$

Figure 4–3 is a *Punnett square.* It represents the different ways the alleles can be combined when the F_1 plants are self-fertilized to produce an F_2 generation. In this way, the figure shows the *genotypes* that are possible in the F_2 generation, and it also demonstrates that approximately 1/4 of the F_2 plants are (*TT*) homozygous dominant; 1/4 are heterozygous (*Tt*); and the remaining 1/4 are homozygous recessive *(tt).* It is important to note that the Punnett square does *not* show actual numbers of offspring with specific genotypes. Rather, it demonstrates the proportions of offspring *expected* to have the various possible genotypes.

The Punnett square can also be used to show (and predict) the proportions of F_2 **phenotypes,** or the physical manifestations of genes. Here, the phenotypes are tall and short, and they are directly observable. However, some phenotypes are not directly observable and must be ascertained biochemically, as in blood types. In short, a phenotype is *any* physiological expression of the genotype that we are able, at any level, to detect or measure.

Moreover, the Punnett square illustrates why Mendel observed three tall plants for every short plant in the F_2 generation. By examining the Punnett square, you can see that 1/4 of the F_2 plants are tall because they have the *TT* genotype. Furthermore, an additional 1/2, which are heterozygous (*Tt*), will also be tall because *T* is dominant to *t* and will therefore be expressed in the phenotype. The remaining 1/4 are homozygous recessive *(tt),* and they will be short because no dominant allele is present. It is important to note that the *only* way a recessive allele can be expressed is if it occurs with another recessive allele, that is, if the individual is homozygous recessive at the particular locus in question.

In conclusion, 3/4 of the F_2 generation will express the dominant phenotype, and 1/4 will show the recessive phenotype. This relationship is expressed as a **phenotypic ratio** of 3:1 and typifies all **Mendelian traits** (characteristics governed by only one genetic locus) when only two alleles are involved, one of which is completely dominant to the other.

FIGURE 4–3
Punnett square representing possible genotypes and phenotypes and their proportions in the F_2 generation. The circles across the top and at the left of the Punnett square represent the gametes of the F_1 parents. The four squares illustrate that 1/4 of the F_2 plants will be homozygous tall (TT); another 1/2 also will be tall but will be heterozygous (Tt); and the remaining 1/4 will be short (tt). Thus, 3/4 can be expected to be tall and 1/4 will be short.

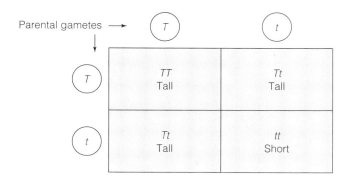

Crosses Between Plants: Two Traits Together

Mendel also made crosses in which two characteristics were considered simultaneously in order to determine if there was a relationship between them. Two such characteristics were plant height and seed color. In peas, seeds are either yellow (dominant) or green (recessive). We use the symbol Y to represent the dominant allele and *y* for the recessive allele.

In the P generation, crosses were made between pure-breeding tall plants with yellow seeds and pure-breeding short plants with green seeds (Fig. 4–4). As expected, the recessive expression of each trait was not seen in the F_1 generation. All the F_1 plants were tall and all produced yellow seeds. However, in the next generation (F_2), both recessive traits reappeared in a small proportion of individuals. The phenotypic ratio for this type of cross is 9:3:3:1, meaning that $9/16$ will be tall with yellow seeds, $3/16$ will be tall with green seeds, $3/16$ will be short with yellow seeds, and $1/16$ will show both recessive traits and be short with green seeds. Although this may seem confusing, it illustrates that there is no relationship between the two traits; that is, there is nothing to dictate that a tall plant must have yellow (or green) seeds. The expression of one trait is not influenced by the expression of the other trait. The allele for tallness *(T)* has the same chance (50–50) of ending up in a zygote with either Y or *y*.

Mendel stated this, his second principle of inheritance, as the **principle of independent assortment.** The principle of independent assortment says that the units (genes) that code for different traits assort independently of each other during gamete formation and recombine in offspring. Today, we know this to be true because we know that the genetic loci controlling these two characteristics are located on different, non-homologous chromosomes, and during meiosis, chromosomes travel to newly forming cells independently of one another. If Mendel had used just *any* two traits, the phenotypic ratios may well not have conformed to those expected by independent assortment (9:3:3:1). The ratios came out as he predicted because the loci governing most of the traits he chose were carried on different chromosomes.

In 1865, Mendel presented his results at a meeting of the local Natural History Society. The following year, the society published his report, but unfortunately, the methodology and statistical nature of the results were beyond the thinking of the time. Indeed, the scientific community was not at all prepared for what they considered to be Mendel's unusual approach; consequently, the significance of his work was unappreciated.

In the latter part of the nineteenth century, several investigators made important contributions to the understanding of chromosomes and cell division. Moreover, the discovery of reduction division in meiosis provided an explanation for Mendel's discoveries. However, Mendel's research remained unknown until 1900, when three different groups of scientists, conducting experiments similar to Mendel's, came across his paper. Unfortunately, Mendel had died 16 years earlier and never saw his work vindicated.

▲ **Principle of independent assortment**
The distribution of one pair of alleles into gametes does not influence the distribution of another pair. The genes controlling different traits are inherited independently of one another.

Mendelian Inheritance in Humans

Mendelian traits (also referred to as *discrete traits* or *traits of simple inheritance*) are controlled by alleles at *one* genetic locus. Currently, more than 4,000 human traits are known to be inherited according to simple Mendelian principles. Examples include several blood group systems, such as ABO.

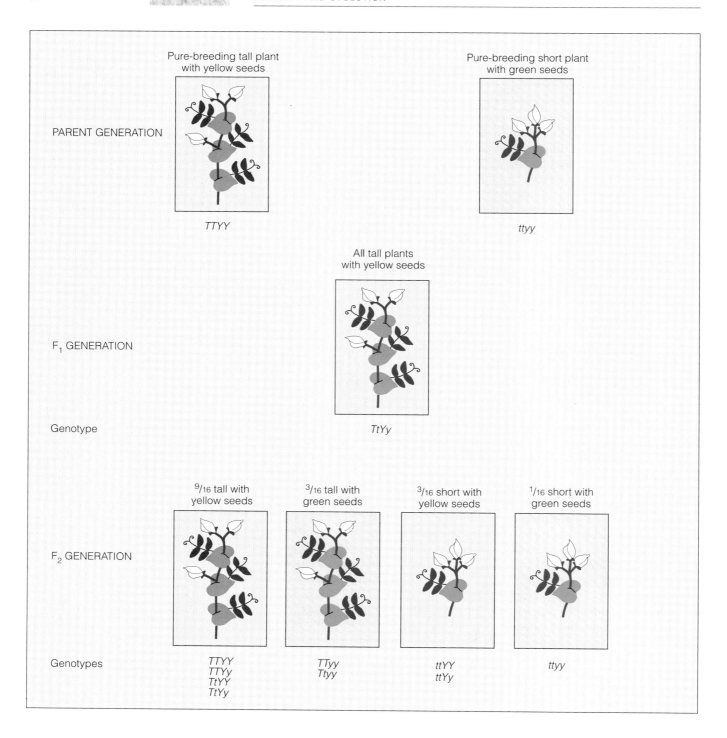

FIGURE 4–4

Results of crosses when two traits are considered simultaneously. Stem length and seed color are independent of each other. Also shown are the genotypes associated with each phenotype. Note that the ratio of tall plants to short plants is ³/4 to ¹/4, or 3:1, the same as in Figure 4–2. The ratio of yellow to green seeds is also 3:1.

In Chapter 3 (p. 54), we stated that the ABO system is governed by three alleles, *A*, *B*, and *O*, found at the ABO locus on the ninth chromosome. These alleles determine which ABO blood type an individual has by coding for the production of special substances called **antigens,** on the surface of red blood cells. If only antigen A is present (i.e., a person is homozygous for the *A* allele), the blood type (phenotype) is A; if only *B* is present, the blood type is B; if both are present, the blood type is AB; and when neither is present, the blood type is said to be O.

Dominance and recessiveness are clearly illustrated by the ABO system. The *O* allele is recessive to both *A* and *B*; therefore, if a person has type O blood, he or she must be homozygous for the *O* allele. Since both *A* and *B* are dominant to *O*, an individual with blood type A can have one of two genotypes: *AA* or *AO*. The same is true of type B, which results from the genotypes *BB* and *BO* (Table 4–2). However, type AB presents a slightly different situation and is an example of **codominance.**

Codominance is seen when two different alleles occur in heterozygous condition, but instead of one having the ability to mask the expression of the other, the products of *both* are fully expressed in the phenotype. Therefore, when both A and B alleles are present, both A and B antigens can be detected on the surface of red blood cells.

A number of genetic disorders are inherited as dominant traits. This means that if a person inherits only one copy of a harmful, dominant allele, the condition it causes will be present (regardless of the existence of a different, recessive allele on the corresponding chromosome). Some conditions inherited as dominant characteristics are *achondroplasia, brachydactyly,* and *familial hypercholesterolemia* (Table 4–3).

Recessive conditions are commonly associated with the lack of a substance, usually an enzyme. For a person actually to have a recessive disorder, he or she must have *two* copies of the recessive allele that causes it. Heterozygotes who have only one copy of a harmful recessive allele are unaffected. Such individuals are frequently called *carriers* (see Box 4–1).

Although carriers do not actually show full-blown manifestations of the recessive allele they carry, they can pass the allele on to their children. (Remember, half their gametes will carry the recessive allele.) If their mate is also a carrier, then it is possible for them to have a child who will be homozygous for the allele, and that child will be affected. In fact, in a mating between two carriers, the risk of having an affected child is 25 percent (refer back to Fig. 4–3). Some recessive disorders that affect humans are *cystic fibrosis, Tay-Sachs disease, sickle-cell anemia* and *phenylketonuria (PKU)* (Table 4–4).

▲ **Antigens**
Large molecules found on the surface of cells. Several different loci governing antigens on red and white blood cells are known. Foreign antigens provoke an immune response in individuals.

▲ **Codominance**
The expression of two alleles in heterozygotes. In this situation, neither allele is dominant or recessive, so that both influence the phenotype.

TABLE 4–2 ABO Genotypes and Associated Phenotypes		
Genotype	Antigens on Red Blood Cells	ABO Blood Type (Phenotype)
AA, AO	A	A
BB, BO	B	B
AB	A and B	AB
OO	None	O

TABLE 4–3	Some Mendelian Disorders Inherited as Autosomal Dominant Traits in Humans
Condition	**Manifestations**
Achondroplasia	Dwarfism due to growth defects involving the long bones of the arms and legs; trunk and head size usually normal.
Brachydactyly	Shortened fingers and toes.
Familial hyper-cholesterolemia	Elevated cholesterol levels and cholesterol plaque deposition; a leading cause of heart disease, with death frequently occurring by middle age.
Neurofibromatosis	Symptoms range from the appearance of abnormal skin pigmentation to large tumors resulting in gross deformities; this so-called *Elephant Man disease* can, in extreme cases, lead to paralysis, blindness, and death.
Marfan syndrome	The eyes and cardiovascular and skeletal systems are affected; symptoms include greater than average height, long arms and legs, eye problems, and enlargement of the aorta; death due to rupture of the aorta is common. Abraham Lincoln may have had Marfan syndrome.

▲ **Pedigree chart**
A diagram showing family relationships in order to trace the hereditary pattern of particular genetic (usually Mendelian) traits.

It is of obvious importance to be able to establish the pattern of inheritance of genetic traits, especially those that result in serious disease. Equally important is the ability to determine an individual's risk of inheriting deleterious alleles, or expressing symptoms, in families with a history of inherited disorders. But because humans cannot be used in experimental breeding programs, as were Mendel's peas, a more indirect approach must be used to demonstrate patterns of inheritance. The principal technique traditionally used in human genetic studies has been the construction of a **pedigree chart,** a diagram of matings and offspring in a family over the span of a few generations.

TABLE 4–4	Some Mendelian Disorders Inherited as Autosomal Recessive Traits in Humans
Condition	**Manifestations**
Cystic fibrosis	Among the most common genetic (Mendelian) disorders among whites in the United States; abnormal secretions of the exocrine glands with pronounced involvement of the pancreas; most patients develop obstructive lung disease, and only about half live to adulthood.
Tay-Sachs disease	Most common among Ashkenazi Jews; degeneration of the nervous system beginning at about 6 months of age; lethal by age 2 or 3 years.
Phenylketonuria (PKU)	Inability to metabolize the amino acid phenylalanine; results in mental retardation if left untreated during childhood; treatment involves strict dietary management and some supplementation.
Albinism	Inability to produce normal amounts of the pigment melanin; results in very fair, untannable skin, light blond hair, and light eyes; may also be associated with vision problems.

BOX 4–1

Recessive and Dominant Alleles Reconsidered

Traditional methods of teaching genetics, based partly upon earlier theories of dominance and recessiveness, have led to a misunderstanding of these basic phenomena. Thus, virtually all introductory students (and most people in general) have the impression that dominance and recessiveness are all-or-nothing situations. This misconception especially pertains to recessive alleles, and the general view is that when these alleles occur in heterozygotes (i.e., carriers), they have absolutely no effect on the phenotype—that is, they are completely inactivated by the presence of another (dominant) allele. Certainly, this is how it appeared to Gregor Mendel and, until the last two or three decades, to most geneticists.

However, the view of inactivated recessive alleles is not as valid as it once seemed. Various biochemical techniques, unavailable in the past but in wide use today, have demonstrated that so-called recessive alleles do indeed exert some influence on phenotype, although these effects are not detectable through simple observation. But even though recessive alleles do not have directly observable effects in heterozygotes, it is clear that our *perception* of recessive alleles greatly depends on whether we examine them at the gross phenotypic level or the biochemical level.

Scientists now know of several recessive alleles that produce some phenotypic effects in heterozygotes. Consider Tay-Sachs disease, a lethal condition that results from the inability to produce the enzyme hexosaminidase A (see Table 4–4). This inability, seen in people who are homozygous for a recessive allele *(ts)* on chromosome 15, invariably results in death by early childhood. Carriers do not have the disease, and practically speaking, they are unaffected. However, in 1979, it was shown that Tay-Sachs carriers, although they are functionally normal, only have about 40 to 60 percent of the amount of the enzyme seen in homozygous dominant normal people. In fact, there are now voluntary serum tests to screen carriers in populations at risk for Tay-Sachs disease.

Similar misconceptions also relate to dominant alleles. The majority of students see dominant alleles as somehow "stronger" or "better," and when dealing with allele frequencies, there is always the mistaken notion that dominant alleles are more common in populations. These misconceptions undoubtedly stem partly from the label "dominant" and the connotations that the term carries. But in genetic usage, those connotations are inappropriate and misleading.

It should be clear from some of the discussion in this chapter that the dominance and recessiveness of various alleles have absolutely nothing to do with the frequency of these alleles. *Dominance and frequency are unrelated phenomena.* Indeed, the various examples of genetic disorders caused by dominant alleles demonstrate that dominant alleles at certain loci are not necessarily more common than their recessive counterparts. If dominant alleles always had higher frequencies the majority of people would express such dominant traits as brachydactyly and achondroplasia (see p. 78).

Likewise, in the ABO system (see p. 54) the *O* allele is recessive to both the *A* and *B* alleles, and yet it is the most common of the three in *all* human populations. Indeed, in some South American Indian populations, the frequency of the *O* allele is virtually 100 percent! Obviously, from this example one cannot argue that the dominant and recessive properties of alleles are related to allele frequency.

As you can see, the relationship between recessive and dominant alleles and their functions are more complicated than they would appear at first glance. (Indeed, most things are.) Previously held views of dominance and recessiveness were guided by available technologies; as genetic technologies continue to change, new theories will emerge, and our perceptions will be further altered. The science of genetics is a relatively new enterprise, and we are still accumulating what will one day be considered basic knowledge. Who knows? It is just possible that one day the concepts of dominance and recessiveness will be obsolete.

Pedigree analysis helps determine if a trait is indeed Mendelian in nature. It also helps establish the mode of inheritance. From considerations of whether the locus that influences a particular trait is located on an autosome or sex chromosome and whether it is dominant or recessive, six different modes of Mendelian inheritance have been recognized in humans: *autosomal dominant, autosomal*

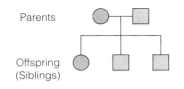

Parents

Offspring
(Siblings)

FIGURE 4–5

Typical symbols used in pedigree charts.

recessive, *X-linked recessive, X-linked dominant, Y-linked,* and *mitochondrial.* We shall discuss the first three of these in some detail.

Standardized symbols are used in the construction of pedigree charts. Squares and circles represent males and females, respectively. Horizontal lines connecting individuals indicate matings, and offspring are connected to horizontal mating lines by vertical lines. Siblings are joined to one another by a horizontal line to which they are connected by vertical lines (Fig. 4–5).

Autosomal Dominant Traits

As the term implies, autosomal dominant traits are governed by loci on autosomes (i.e., any chromosomes except X or Y). One example of an autosomal dominant trait is brachydactyly, a condition characterized by malformed hands and shortened fingers.

Because brachydactyly is caused by a dominant allele, anyone who inherits just one copy will express the trait. (For purposes of this discussion, we will use the symbol *B* to refer to the dominant allele that causes the condition, and *b* for the recessive, normal allele.) Since the allele is rare, virtually everyone who has brachydactyly is a heterozygote (*Bb*). (Generally speaking, individuals who are homozygous dominant for rare, deleterious alleles are uncommon. Mutant alleles that produce abnormalities in heterozygotes cause such extreme defects in homozygotes that affected fetuses frequently abort prior to reaching full term.) Unaffected individuals are homozygous recessive (*bb*).

Figure 4–6 is a partial pedigree for brachydactyly. It is apparent from this pedigree that all affected members have at least one affected parent; thus, the abnormality does not skip generations. This pattern is true of all autosomal dominant traits. Another characteristic of autosomal dominant traits is that there is no sex bias, and males and females are more or less equally affected.

One other fact illustrated by Figure 4–6 is that approximately half the offspring of affected parents are also affected. This proportion is what we would predict for an autosomal dominant trait where only one parent is affected, and it is explained by events in meiosis as well as by Mendel's principle of segregation. (See Figure 4–7.)

Autosomal Recessive Traits

Autosomal recessive traits are also influenced by loci on autosomes but show a different pattern of inheritance. A good example of such a trait is shown in Fig. 4–8,

FIGURE 4–6

Inheritance of an autosomal dominant trait: a human pedigree for brachydactyly.

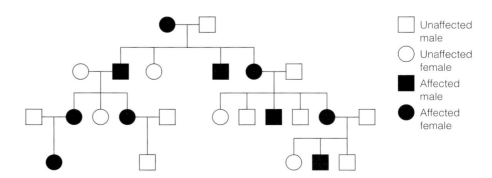

☐ Unaffected male

◯ Unaffected female

■ Affected male

● Affected female

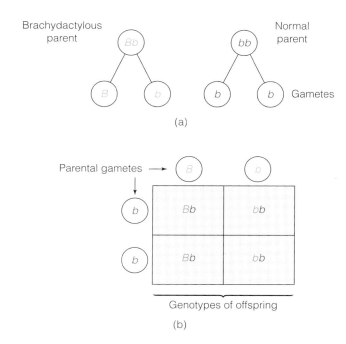

Brachydactylous parent

Normal parent

Gametes

(a)

Parental gametes

Genotypes of offspring

(b)

FIGURE 4–7

The pattern of inheritance of autosomal dominant traits is the direct result of the distribution of chromosomes, and the alleles they carry, into gametes during meiosis.

(a) Diagrammatic representation of possible gametes produced by two parents: one with brachydactyly and another with normal hands and fingers. The brachydactylous individual can produce two types of gametes: half with the dominant allele (B), and half with the recessive allele (b). All the gametes produced by the normal parent will carry the recessive allele.

(b) A Punnett square depicting the possible genotypes in the offspring of one parent with brachydactyly (Bb) and one with normal hands and fingers (bb). Statistically speaking, half the offspring would be expected to have the Bb genotype and thus, brachydactyly. The other half would be homozygous recessive (bb) and would be normal.

a pedigree for albinism, a metabolic disorder causing deficient production of a skin pigment called melanin (see Chapter 6). This disorder is phenotypically expressed as very light skin, hair, and iris of the eyes.

Actually, albinism is a group of genetic disorders, each influenced by different loci. Some forms affect only the eyes, while others also involve skin and hair. The most widely known variety of albinism does influence eye, skin, and hair pigmentation and is caused by an autosomal recessive allele. The frequency of this particular form of albinism varies widely among populations, with an incidence of about 1 in 37,000 in American whites but a much higher frequency, approaching 1 in 200, among Hopi Indians. How populations have come to be so different in the frequencies of various alleles (such as those for albinism) will be a major focus of the next chapter.

Pedigrees for autosomal recessive traits show obvious differences from those for autosomal dominant characteristics. For one thing, recessive traits often appear to skip generations, so that an affected offspring is produced by two phenotypically normal parents. In fact, most affected individuals have unaffected

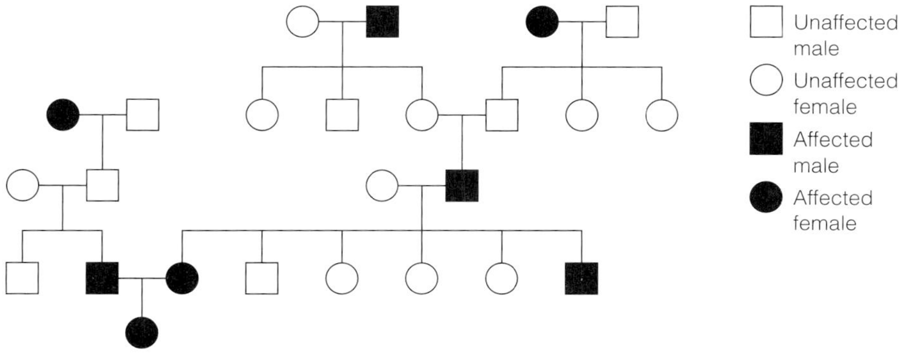

□ Unaffected male

○ Unaffected female

■ Affected male

● Affected female

FIGURE 4–8

Partial pedigree for albinism, an autosomal recessive trait.

parents. In addition, the proportion of affected offspring from most matings is less than the 50 percent so frequently seen in pedigrees for autosomal dominant traits. As in the pattern for autosomal dominant traits, males and females are equally affected. However, when both parents have the trait, all the offspring will be affected.

As Figure 4–9 illustrates, the Mendelian principle of segregation explains the pattern of inheritance of autosomal recessive traits. In fact, this pattern is the very one first elucidated by Mendel in his pea experiments (refer back to Fig. 4–3). Unaffected parents who produce an albino child *must* both be carriers, and their child is homozygous for the recessive allele that causes the abnormality. The Punnett square in Figure 4–9 shows how such a mating produces both affected and unaffected offspring in predictable proportions—the typical phenotypic ratio of 3:1.

Sex-Linked Traits

Sex-linked traits are controlled by loci on sex chromosomes; the term *sex-linked* simply refers to the fact that these loci are located on the X or Y chromosome. (Almost all such loci have no role in primary sex determination.) Of the more than 240 traits suspected to result from this form of inheritance, almost all are controlled by loci on the X chromosome (Table 4–5). Only recently have any traits been traced to regions on the Y chromosome, where at least four loci have been identified. One is involved in determining maleness (the TDF locus), and one other may be involved with sperm production (the H-Y locus). Because of the scarcity of known Y-linked traits, they are not dealt with here.

The best known of the sex-linked traits is hemophilia, caused by a recessive allele at a locus on the X chromosome. This type of condition is thus said to be *X-linked recessive.* Hemophilia results from the lack of a clotting factor in the blood (Factor VIII), and affected individuals suffer bleeding episodes and may hemorrhage to death from incidents that most of us would consider trivial.

The most famous pedigree documenting this malady is that of Queen Victoria and her descendants (shown in Fig. 4–10). The most striking feature shown by this pattern of inheritance is that usually only males are affected. To understand this pattern, once again we must refer to the principle of segregation, but with one additional stipulation: We are now dealing with *sex chromosomes.*

FIGURE 4–9

A cross between two phenotypically normal parents, both of whom are carriers of the albinism allele. From a mating such as this between two carriers, we would expect the following possible proportions of genotypes and phenotypes in the offspring. Homozygous dominants (AA) with normal phenotype, 25 percent; heterozygotes, or carriers (Aa), with normal phenotype, 50 percent; and homozygous recessives (aa) with albinism, 25 percent. This yields the phenotypic ratio of three normal to one albino.

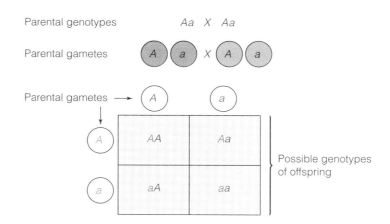

TABLE 4–5 Some Mendelian Disorders Inherited as X-Linked Recessive Traits in Humans

Condition	Manifestations
G6PD (glucose-6-phosphate dehydrogenase) deficiency	Lack of an enzyme (G6PD) in red blood cells; produces severe, sometimes fatal anemia in the presence of certain foods (e.g., fava beans) and/or drugs (e.g., the antimalarial drug primaquin). (See p. 120 for further discussion relating to a possible link with malaria as a selective agent.)
Muscular Dystrophy	One form; other forms can be inherited as autosomal recessives. Progressive weakness and atrophy of muscles beginning in early childhood; continues to progress throughout life; some female carriers may develop heart problems.
Red-green color-blindness	Actually there are two separate forms, one involving the perception of red and the other affecting only the perception of green. About 8 percent of European males have an impaired ability to distinguish green.
Lesch-Nyhan disease	Impaired motor development noticeable by 5 months; progressive motor impairment, diminished kidney function, self-mutilation, and early death.
Hemophilia	There are three forms; two (hemophilia A and B) are X-linked. In hemophilia A, a clotting factor is missing; hemophilia B is caused by a defective clotting factor. Both produce abnormal internal and external bleeding from minor injuries; severe pain is a frequent accompaniment; without treatment, death usually occurs before adulthood.
Ichthyosis	There are several forms; one is X-linked. A skin condition due to lack of an enzyme; characterized by scaly, brown lesions on the extremities and trunk. In the past, people with this condition sometimes were exhibited in circuses and sideshows as "the alligator man."

Because they possess two X chromosomes, females show the same pattern of expression of X-linked traits as for autosomal traits. That is, the only way an X-linked recessive allele can be phenotypically expressed in a female is when she is homozygous for it. Therefore, heterozygous females are unaffected. In cases where female heterozygotes express an X-linked trait, it is an X-linked dominant.

On the other hand, since males are XY and have only one X chromosome, they possess only one copy of an X-linked gene. With only one X chromosome, males can never be homozygous or heterozygous for X-linked loci and are thus referred to as **hemizygous.** Moreover, males do not exhibit dominance or recessiveness for X-linked traits because *any* allele located on their X chromosome, even a recessive one, will be expressed. In fact, any time a recessive allele occurs in a hemizygous state, it is expressed.

The difference between males and females in number of X chromosomes is directly related to the incidence of hemophilia seen in Figure 4–10. Females who have one copy of the hemophilia allele are carriers for the trait. Although they may have some tendency toward bleeding, they are not severely affected. On the other hand, males who have the allele in single dose (on their *only* X chromosome) are severely afflicted, and prior to the availability of recent therapy, they faced short and painful lives.

▲ **Hemizygous**
(*Hemi* means "half") Having only one member of a pair of alleles. Because males have only one X chromosome, all their X-linked alleles are hemizygous. All recessive alleles on a male's X chromosome are expressed in the phenotype.

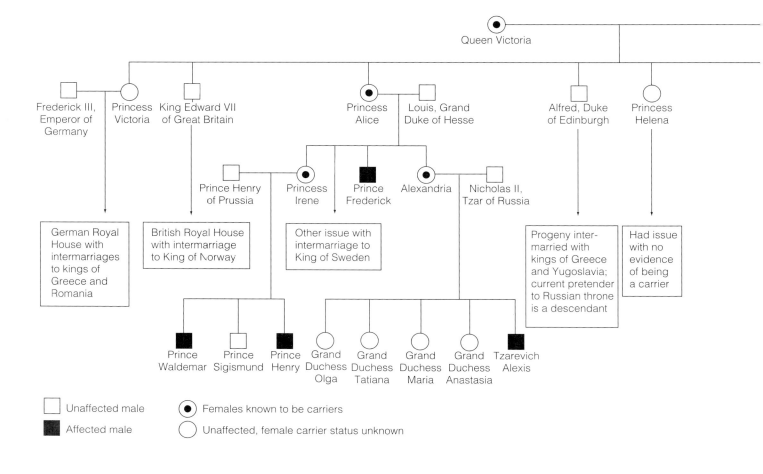

Unaffected male
Affected male
Females known to be carriers
Unaffected, female carrier status unknown

FIGURE 4–10

Pedigree for Queen Victoria and some of her descendants, showing inheritance of hemophilia, an X-linked recessive trait in humans.

▲ **Polygenic**

Referring to traits that are influenced by genes at two or more loci. Examples of such traits are stature, skin color, and eye color. Many polygenic traits are also influenced by environmental factors.

Polygenic Inheritance

Mendelian traits are said to be *discrete*, or *discontinuous*, because their phenotypic expressions do not overlap; rather, they fall into clearly defined categories. For example, Mendel's pea plants were either short or tall, but none was intermediate in height. In the ABO system, the four phenotypes are completely distinct from one another; that is, there is no intermediate form between type A and type B to represent a gradation between the two. In other words, Mendelian traits do not show *continuous* variation.

However, many traits do have a wide range of phenotypic expressions that form a graded series. These are called **polygenic**, or *continuous* traits. While Mendelian traits are governed by only one genetic locus, polygenic characteristics are influenced by alleles at *several* loci, with each locus making a contribution to the phenotype. For example, one of the most frequently cited instances of polygenic inheritance in humans is skin color. The single most important factor influencing skin color is the amount of the pigment melanin present.

Melanin production is believed to be influenced by between three and six genetic loci, with each locus having at least two alleles, neither of which is dominant. Individuals having only alleles for more melanin production (i.e., they are homozygous at all loci) have the darkest skin. Those having only alleles that code for reduced melanin production have very fair skin.

As there are perhaps six loci and at least 12 alleles, there are numerous ways in which these alleles can combine in individuals. If an individual inherits 11

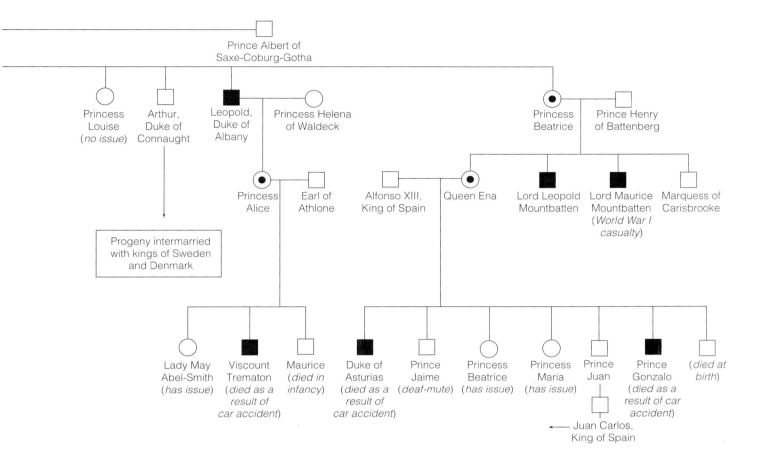

alleles coding for maximum pigmentation and only one for reduced melanin production, skin color will be very dark. As the proportion of reduced pigmentation alleles increases, skin color becomes lighter. That is because in this system, as in some other polygenic systems, there is an *additive effect*. This means that each allele that codes for melanin production makes a contribution to increased melanization. Likewise, each allele coding for reduced melanin production contributes to reduced pigmentation. Therefore, the effect of multiple alleles at several loci, each making a contribution to individual phenotypes, is to produce continuous variation from very dark to very fair skin within the species. (Skin color is also discussed in Chapter 6.)

Polygenic traits actually account for most of the readily observable phenotypic variation seen in humans, and they have traditionally served as a basis for "racial" classification (see Chapter 6). In addition to skin color, polygenic inheritance in humans is seen in hair color, weight, stature, eye color, shape of face, shape of nose, and fingerprint pattern. Because they exhibit continuous variation, most polygenic traits can be measured on a scale composed of equal increments. For example, height (stature) is measured in feet and inches (or meters and centimeters). If one were to measure height in a large number of individuals, the distribution of measurements would continue uninterrupted from the shortest extreme to the tallest. That is what is meant by *continuous traits*.

Because polygenic traits usually lend themselves to metric analysis, biologists, geneticists, and physical anthropologists treat them statistically. Although statistical analysis can be complicated, the use of simple summary statistics, such as the *mean* (average) or *standard deviation* (a measure of within-group variation), permits basic descriptions of, and comparisons between, populations. For example, one might be interested in average height in two different populations and whether or not differences between the two are significant, and if so, why. Or a researcher might determine that in the same geographical area, one group shows significantly more variation in skin color than another, and it would be useful to explain this variability. (You should also note that *all* physical traits measured and statistically treated in fossils are polygenic in nature.)

However, these particular statistical manipulations are not possible with Mendelian traits simply because those traits cannot be measured in the same manner. They are either present or they are not; they are expressed one way or another. But just because Mendelian traits are not amenable to statistical analysis in the same manner of polygenic characters does not mean that Mendelian traits are less worthy of study or less informative of genetic processes. It simply means that scientists must approach the study of these two types of inheritance from different perspectives.

Mendelian characteristics can be described in terms of frequency within populations, yielding between-group comparisons regarding incidence. Moreover, these characteristics can also be analyzed for mode of inheritance (dominant or recessive) from pedigree data. Finally, for many Mendelian traits, the approximate or exact position of genetic loci has been identified, thus making it possible to examine the mechanisms and patterns of inheritance at these loci. Because polygenic characters are influenced by several loci, they cannot as yet be traced to specific loci, and therefore, such analysis is currently not possible.

Genetic and Environmental Factors

From the preceding discussion, it might appear that phenotype is solely the expression of the genotype, but this is not true. (Here we use the terms *genotype* and *phenotype* in a broader sense to refer to an individual's *entire* genetic makeup and *all* observable or detectable characteristics.) The genotype sets limits and potentials for development, but it also interacts with the environment, and many aspects of phenotype are influenced by this genetic/environmental interaction. For many traits, scientists have developed statistical methods for calculating what proportion of phenotypic variation is due to genetic or environmental components. However, it is usually not possible to identify the *specific* environmental factors affecting the phenotype.

Many polygenic traits are quite obviously influenced by environmental conditions. Adult stature is strongly affected by the individual's nutritional status during growth and development. One study showed that children of Japanese immigrants to Hawaii were, on average, 3 to 4 inches taller than their parents. This dramatic difference, seen in one generation, was attributed to environmental alteration—specifically to a change in diet (Froelich, 1970).

Other important environmental factors include exposure to sunlight, altitude, temperature, and unfortunately, increasing levels of exposure to toxic waste and airborne pollutants. All these and many more contribute in complex ways to the continuous phenotypic variation seen in characteristics governed by multiple loci.

Mendelian traits are less likely to be influenced by environmental factors. For example, ABO blood type is determined at fertilization and remains fixed throughout the individual's lifetime, regardless of diet, exposure to ultraviolet radiation, temperature, and so forth.

Mendelian and polygenic inheritance produce different kinds of phenotypic variation. In the former, variation occurs in discrete categories, while in the latter, it is continuous. However, it is important to understand that even for polygenic characteristics, Mendelian principles still apply at individual loci. In other words, if a trait is influenced by seven loci, each one of those loci may have two or more alleles, with one perhaps being dominant to the other or with the alleles being codominant. It is the combined action of the alleles at all seven loci, interacting with the environment, that results in observable phenotypic expression.

Modern Theory of Evolution

By the start of the twentieth century, the essential foundations for evolutionary theory had already been developed. Darwin and Wallace had articulated the key principle of natural selection 40 years earlier, and the rediscovery of Mendelian genetics in 1900 contributed the other major component—a mechanism for inheritance. We might expect that these two basic contributions would have been joined rather quickly into a consistent theory of evolution. However, such was not the case. For the first 30 years of the twentieth century, geneticists (working with experimental animals, such as fruit flies) emphasized sharp contrasts within particular characteristics of organisms such as presence or absence of body parts (e.g., antennae or body segments). As such, evolution was seen as a process of fairly large radical "jumps," and this "mutationist" view came to be seen as an alternative to the "selectionist" tradition.

A *synthesis* of these two views was not achieved until the mid-1930s, and we owe much of our current view of the evolutionary process to this intellectual development (see Box 4–2).

The Modern Synthesis

Biologists working on mathematical models of evolutionary change in the late 1920s and early 1930s came to realize that genetic and selective processes were not opposing themes, but that a comprehensive explanation of organic evolution required *both*. Small new changes in the genetic material—transmitted from parent to offspring by strict Mendelian principles—are, in fact, the fuel for natural selection. The two major foundations of the biological sciences had thus been brought together in what Julian Huxley termed the "modern synthesis."

From such a "modern" (i.e., the middle of the twentieth century onward) perspective, we define evolution as a two-stage process:

1. Production and redistribution of **variation** (inherited differences between individuals)
2. *Natural selection* acting on this variation (whereby inherited differences, or variation, among individuals differentially affect their ability to reproduce successfully)

▲ **Variation (genetic)**
Inherited differences between individuals; the basis of all evolutionary change.

Definition of Evolution

As discussed in Chapter 2, Darwin saw evolution as the gradual unfolding of new varieties of life from previous forms over long periods of time. This depiction is

BOX 4–2

Development of Modern Evolutionary Theory

Our modern understanding of the evolutionary process came about through contributions of biologists in the United States, Great Britain, and Russia.

While "mutationists" were arguing with "selectionists" about the single primary mechanism in evolution, several population geneticists began to realize that both small genetic changes and natural selection were necessary ingredients in the evolutionary formula.

These population geneticists were largely concerned with mathematical reconstructions of evolution—in particular, measuring those small accumulations of genetic changes in populations over just a few generations. Central figures in these early theoretical developments include Ronald Fisher and J.B.S. Haldane in Great Britain, Sewall Wright in the United States, and Sergei Chetverikov in Russia.

While the work of these scientists often produced brilliant insights (see particularly Fisher's *The Genetical Theory of Natural Selection,* 1930), their conclusions were largely unknown to most evolutionary biologists, especially in North America. It remained, therefore, for an individual to transcend these two worlds: the mathematical jargon of the population geneticists and the general constructs of theoretical evolutionary biologists. The scientist who performed this task (and who is credited as the first true synthesizer) was Theodosius Dobzhansky. In his *Genetics and the Origin of Species* (1937), Dobzhansky skillfully integrated the mathematics of population genetics with overall evolutionary theory. His insights then became the basis for a period of tremendous activity in evolutionary thinking that directly led to major contributions by George Gaylord Simpson (who brought paleontology into the synthesis), Ernst Mayr,* and others. In fact, the "modern synthesis" produced by these scientists stood basically unchallenged for an entire generation as *the* explanation of the evolutionary process. In recent years, however, some aspects of this theory have been brought under serious question (see Chapter 8).

---

*For an interesting discussion of the intellectual developments concerning the formulation of modern evolutionary theory, see Ernst Mayr and William B. Provine (eds.), *The Evolutionary Synthesis* (Cambridge, Mass.: Harvard University Press, 1980).

▲ **Evolution**
(modern genetic definition) A change in the frequency of alleles from one generation to the next.

▲ **Allele frequency**
The proportion of one allele among all the alleles that occur at a given locus in a population.

▲ **Population**
Within a species, a community of individuals where mates are usually found.

what most of us think of as evolution, and it is indeed the end result of the evolutionary process. But these long-term effects can come about only by the accumulation of many small evolutionary changes occurring every generation. To understand how the process of evolution works, we must study these short-term events. Darwin attempted this kind of study in his breeding experiments, but because the science of genetics was still in its infancy, he was not able to comprehend fully the mechanics of evolutionary change. Today, we study evolutionary changes occurring between generations in various organisms (including humans) and are able to demonstrate how evolution works. From such a modern genetics perspective, we define **evolution** as *a change in **allele frequency** from one generation to the next.*

Allele frequencies are indicators of the genetic makeup of an interbreeding group of individuals known as a **population.** (We will return to this topic in more detail in Chapter 5.) Let us illustrate the way allele frequencies change (i.e., how evolution occurs) through a simplified example. First of all, we must look at a physical trait that is inherited—in this case, human blood type (discussed on p. 77). The best known of the human blood types is ABO. There are, however, many similar blood type systems controlled by different loci that determine genetically transmitted properties of the red blood cells.

Let us assume that your present class represents a population, an interbreeding group of individuals, and that we have ascertained the ABO blood type of each member. (To be a population, individuals must choose mates more often from *within* the group than from outside it. Of course, the individuals in your class will not meet this requirement, but for the sake of our example, we will overlook this stipulation.) The proportions of each of the A, B, and O alleles are the allele frequencies for this trait. For example, suppose we find that the proportion of alleles in your class (population) is as follows: A = .50; B = .40; O = .10.*

Since the frequencies for these genes represent only proportions of a total, it is obvious that allele frequencies can refer only to groups of individuals, that is, populations. Individuals do not have an allele frequency; they have either A, B, or O (or a combination of these). Nor can individuals change alleles. From conception onward, the genetic composition of an individual is fixed. If you start out with blood type A, you will remain type A. Therefore, an individual cannot evolve: Only a group of individuals—a population—can evolve over time.

What happens when a population evolves? Evolution is not an unusual or mysterious process. In fact, it is incredibly commonplace and may occur between every generation for every group of organisms in the world, including humans. Assume that 25 years from now, we calculate the frequencies of the ABO alleles for the children (offspring) of our classroom population and find the following: A = .30; B = .40; O = .30.

We can see that the relative proportions have changed: A has decreased, O has increased, while B has remained the same in frequency. Such a simple, apparently minor change is what we call evolution. Over the short run of just a few generations, such changes in inherited traits may be only very small, but if further continued and elaborated, the results can and do produce spectacular kinds of adaptation and whole new varieties of life.

Whether we are talking about such short-term effects as in our classroom population from one generation to the next, which is sometimes called **microevolution,** or the long-term effects through fossil history, sometimes called **macroevolution,** the basic evolutionary mechanisms are similar. As we will discuss in Chapter 8, however, they are not identical.

The question may be asked: How do allele frequencies change? Or, to put it another way, what causes evolution? The modern theory of evolution isolates general factors that can produce alterations in allele frequencies. As we have noted, evolution is a two-stage process. Genetic variation must first be produced and distributed before it can be acted on by natural selection.

▲ **Microevolution**

Small changes occurring within species, such as a change in allele frequencies.

▲ **Macroevolution**

Changes produced only after many generations, such as the appearance of a new species.

Factors that Produce and Redistribute Variation

Mutation

You have already learned that an actual molecular alteration in genetic material is called mutation. A genetic locus may take one of several alternative forms,

---

*This simplified example shows only the allele frequencies themselves; in fact, the situation is more complex, especially for ABO, which has three alleles. The way allele frequencies are calculated for a simple two-allele locus will be shown in Chapter 5.

which we have defined as alleles (*A*, *B*, or *O* for example). If one allele changes to another—that is, if the gene itself is altered—a mutation has occurred. (In fact, alleles are the results of mutation.) For such changes to have evolutionary significance, they must occur in the sex cells, which are passed between generations. Evolution is a change in allele frequencies *between* generations. If mutations do not occur in gametes (either the egg or sperm), they will not be transmitted to the next generation, and no evolutionary change can result. If, however, a genetic change does occur in the sperm or egg of one of the individuals in our classroom (*A* mutates to *B* for instance), the offspring's blood type also will be altered, causing a minute shift in allele frequencies of that generation. In Chapter 3, we showed how the change in a single DNA base, a *point mutation*, could cause a change in hemoglobin structure (from normal to sickle-cell). Other mutations that produce phenotypic effects (as discussed earlier in this chapter) include the albinism allele, the allele producing brachydactyly, and the alteration causing Tay-Sachs disease.

Actually, it would be rare to see evolution occurring by mutation alone. Mutation rates for any given trait are quite low, and thus mutations would rarely be seen in such a small population as our class. In larger populations, mutations might be observed (1 individual in 10,000, say), but would, by themselves, have very little impact on shifting allele frequencies. However, when mutation is coupled with natural selection, evolutionary changes are quite possible.

It is important to remember that mutation is the basic creative force in evolution, because it is the *only* way to produce "new" variation. Its key role in the production of variation represents the first stage of the evolutionary process. Darwin was not aware of the nature of mutation. Only in the twentieth century, with the spectacular development of molecular biology, have the secrets of genetic structure been revealed.

Gene Flow

▲ **Gene flow**
Movement of genes between populations.

The movement of genes from one population to another is called **gene flow.** The term *migration* is frequently used instead, but strictly speaking, migration means movement of people, whereas gene flow refers to the exchange of *genes*, which can occur only if the migrants interbreed. Moreover, it should be remembered that even if individuals move temporarily and interbreed within the new population (thus leaving a genetic contribution), they need not remain as part of the population. For example, the offspring of U.S. soldiers and Vietnamese women are the result of gene flow, even though their fathers may have returned to their native population. Even more exotic avenues for gene flow are possible with the advent of new genetic technologies. For generations, frozen sperm (and more recently, frozen eggs) have been routinely transported long distances in commercial farming (e.g., dairy cattle). The same technologies could be used to further disseminate human genes, although this potential hardly seems necessary.

In humans, social rules more than any other factor determine mating patterns, and cultural anthropologists must work closely with physical anthropologists to isolate and measure this aspect of evolutionary change. Population movements (particularly in the last 500 years) have reached enormous proportions, and few breeding isolates remain. It should not, however, be assumed that significant population movements did not occur prior to modern times. Our hunting and gathering ancestors probably lived in small groups that were both mobile and flexible in membership. Early farmers also were probably mobile, expanding into new areas as land wore out and human population size increased. Intensive, highly sedentary agricultural communities came later, but even then, significant migration was still possible. From the Near East, one of the early farming centers, populations spread very gradually in a "creeping occupation of Europe, India, and northern and eastern Africa" (Bodmer and Cavalli-Sforza, 1976, p. 563).

Migration between populations has been a consistent feature of hominid evolution since the first dispersal of our genus and helps explain why in the last million years, speciation has been rare. Of course, migration patterns are a manifestation of human cultural behavior, once again emphasizing the essential biocultural nature of human evolution.

An interesting example of how gene flow influences microevolutionary changes in modern human populations is seen in genetic admixture among African Americans. African Americans in the United States are largely of West African descent, but there has also been considerable genetic admixture with Europeans. By measuring allele frequencies for specific genetic loci (e.g., Rh and Duffy blood groups, discussed in Chapter 5), we can estimate the amount of migration of European alleles into the African American gene pool. Estimates of the amount of gene flow have varied considerably, but one of the most comprehensive studies has suggested for northern cities a figure close to 20 percent (22 percent in Oakland, California, but much lower in the deep South: 4 percent in Charleston, South Carolina, and 11 percent in rural Georgia) (Bodmer and Cavelli-Sforza, 1976).

It would be a misconception to think that gene flow can occur only through such large-scale movements of whole groups. In fact, significant alterations in allele frequencies can come about through long-term patterns of mate selection. If exchange of mates consistently moved in one direction over a long period of time, allele frequencies would ultimately be altered. Due to demographic, economic, and social pressures, individuals must often choose mates from outside the immediate vicinity.

Transportation factors play a crucial role in determining the potential radius for finding mates. Today, highly efficient mechanized forms of transportation make the potential radius of mate choice worldwide, but actual patterns are obviously somewhat more restricted. For example, data from Ann Arbor, Michigan, indicate mean marital distance (the average distance between birthplaces of partners) of about 160 miles, which obviously includes a tremendous number of potential marriage partners.

Genetic Drift

The random factor in evolution is called **genetic drift** and is due primarily to sampling phenomena (i.e., the size of the population). Since evolution occurs in populations, it is directly tied not only to the nature of the initial allele freqencies of the population, but to the size of the group as well. If, in a population of 100 individuals, five type O individuals had been killed in an auto accident before they reproduced, they would not have made a genetic contribution to the next generation. The frequency of the O allele would have been reduced in the next generation, and evolution would have occurred. In this case, with only 100 individuals in the population, the change due to the accident would have altered the O frequency in a noticeable way. If, however, our initial population had been very large (10,000 people), then the evolutionary effect of removing a few individuals would be very small indeed. In fact, in a population of large size, random effects, such as traffic accidents, would be balanced out by the likelihood of such

▲ **Genetic drift**
Evolutionary changes—that is, changes in allele frequencies—produced by random factors. Genetic drift is a result of small population size.

events also affecting individuals with different genetic combinations (i.e., different genotypes). As you can see, evolutionary change due to genetic drift is directly and inversely related to population size. To put it simply, the smaller the population, the larger the effect of genetic drift.

When considering genetic drift, we must remember that the genetic makeup of individuals is in no way related to the chance happenings that affect their lives. In our example, the genetic makeup of individuals has absolutely nothing to do with their being involved in automobile accidents. The accidents are random events, which is why this factor is usually called *random genetic drift.* If, however, a person had died in an auto accident caused by hereditary poor eyesight, such an event would not be genetic drift. If this individual, because of a hereditary trait, dies early and produces fewer offspring than other individuals, this is an example of natural selection.

A particular kind of drift seen in modern human populations is called **founder effect,** or, after its formulator, the *Sewall Wright effect.* Founder effect operates when an exceedingly small group of individuals contributes exclusively to the gene pool of the next generation. This situation leads to what is termed a *genetic bottleneck,* since the "founding" group and its descendants carry only a small proportion of all the alleles (and all the variation) that were present in the original population. This phenomenon can occur when a small migrant band of "founders" colonizes a new and separate area away from the parent group. Small founding populations may also be left as remnants when famine, plague, or war ravage a normally larger group. Actually, each generation is the founder of all succeeding generations in any population.

The cases of founder effect producing noticeable microevolutionary changes are necessarily in small groups. For example, several small and isolated Alpine villages have unusually high frequencies of albinism, and an island in the South Atlantic, Tristan da Cunha, has unusually high frequencies of a hereditary eye disorder. First settled in 1817 by one Scottish family, this isolated island's native inhabitants include only descendants of this one family and a few other individuals, such as shipwrecked sailors. All in all, only about two dozen individuals constituted the founding population of this island. In 1961, the 294 inhabitants were evacuated because of an impending volcanic eruption and removed to England. Extensive medical tests were performed, which revealed four individuals with the very rare recessive disease retinitis pigmentosa. The frequency for the allele causing this disease was abnormally high in this population, and a considerable portion of the group were no doubt carriers.

How did this circumstance come about? Apparently, just by chance, one of the initial founders carried the gene in heterozygous form and later passed it on to offspring who, through inbreeding, occasionally produced affected individuals. The fact that so few individuals founded the Tristan da Cunha population made it possible for one individual (who carried the allele for this disease) to make a disproportionate genetic contribution to succeeding generations (Bodmer and Cavalli-Sforza, 1976).

Genetic drift has probably played an important role in human evolution, influencing genetic changes in small isolated groups. From studies of recent hunter-gatherers in Australia, we know that the range of potential mates is limited to the linguistic tribe usually consisting of around 500 members. Given this small population size, drift could act significantly, particularly if drought or disease should reduce the population even further.

Much insight concerning the evolutionary factors that have acted in the past can be gained by understanding how such mechanisms continue to operate on human populations today. In small populations like Tristan da Cunha, drift plays

▲ **Founder effect**
Also called the *Sewall Wright effect,* a type of genetic drift in which allele frequencies are altered in small populations that are taken from, or are remnants of, larger populations.

a major evolutionary role. Fairly sudden fluctuations in allele frequency can and do occur owing to the small population size. Likewise, throughout a good deal of human evolution (at least the last 4–5 m.y.*), hominids probably lived in small groups, and drift would have had significant impact.

Joseph Birdsell, a physical anthropologist who has worked extensively in Australia, has postulated general models for human evolution from his Australian data. He suggests that population size during most of the Pleistocene was comparable to the 500 figure seen in Australia. Moreover, when agriculturalists became sedentary and isolated in small villages, the effects of drift may have been even greater. Indications of such a phenomenon are still operative in Melanesia, where individuals often spend their entire lives within just a few miles of their birthplace.

While drift has been a factor in human evolution from the start, the effects have been irregular and nondirectional (for drift is *random* in nature). In other words, there is no preexisting factor such as natural selection that determines which alleles will increase or decrease in frequency. Certainly, the pace of evolution could have been accelerated if many small populations became isolated and thus subject to drift. However, by producing populations with varying evolutionary potential, drift only provides fodder for the truly directional force of evolution: natural selection.

Recombination

Since in any sexually reproducing species both parents contribute genes to offspring, the genetic information is inevitably reshuffled every generation. Such recombination does not in itself change allele frequencies (i.e., cause evolution). However, it does produce the whole array of genetic combinations, which natural selection can then act upon. In fact, we have shown how the reshuffling of chromosomes during meiosis can produce literally trillions of gene combinations, making every human being genetically unique.

Natural Selection Acts on Variation

The evolutionary factors just discussed—mutation, gene flow, genetic drift, and recombination—interact to produce variation and to distribute genes within and between populations. But there is no long-term *direction* to any of these factors. How, then, do populations adapt? The answer to that question is: Natural selection provides directional change in allele frequency relative to *specific environmental factors*. If the environment changes, then the selection pressures change as well. Such a functional shift in allele frequencies is what we mean by *adaptation*. If there are long-term environmental changes in a consistent direction, then allele frequencies should also shift gradually each generation. If sustained for many generations, the results may be quite dramatic.

In Chapter 2, we discussed the general principles underlying natural selection and gave two examples in nonhuman animals (peppered moths and swifts). Physical anthropology is, of course, centrally concerned with human evolution, and it is thus most relevant to show how natural selection operates in *human* populations. However, demonstrating clear-cut examples in our species is not an

---

*The abbreviation *m.y.* stands for "million years."

TABLE 4–6   Sickle-Cell Terminology

Sickle-cell allele in heterozygotes:

= carrier, called the sickle-cell trait (not much affected; functions normally in most environments)

Sickle-cell allele in homozygotes:

= sickle-cell anemia or sicklemia (very severe effects, reduced life expectancy)

easy task. Compared to most other animals, humans do not reproduce as rapidly nor are they as amenable to controlled laboratory manipulations. Certainly, everyone is aware of specific instances of natural selection among humans, especially where a severe genetic disease is involved. As a case in point, all individuals who are born with Tay-Sachs disease die in childhood and therefore leave no off-spring. This is an obvious example of natural selection. However, Tay-Sachs disease is a rare condition that is always lethal; thus, no environmental influence comes into play differentially affecting one genotype relative to others. What we want is unambiguous data gathered in human populations that not only conclusively establish differential reproductive success among various genotypes, but also tie it to specific environments. So, while we can see all around us the end results of natural selection affecting humans, obtaining *rigorous* scientific data comparable to that established for other species has proved extremely difficult.

Indeed, the only well-documented case of natural selection in humans deals with the *sickle-cell trait*, which is the result of a point mutation within the gene producing the hemoglobin beta chain (see p. 51). If inherited from both parents, this allele causes severe problems of anemia, circulatory disturbances, and usually early death (see Table 4–6). Even with aggressive medical intervention, life expectancy in the United States today is less than 45 years for victims of sickle-cell anemia. Worldwide, sickle-cell anemia causes an estimated 100,000 deaths per year, and in the United States an estimated 40,000 to 50,000 individuals, mostly of African descent, suffer from this disease.

With such obviously harmful effects, it might seem surprising that the sickle-cell allele (Hb^S) is so frequent in some populations. The highest allele frequencies are found in western and central African populations, reaching levels close to 20 percent; values are also moderately high in some Greek and Asiatic Indian populations (see Fig. 4–11). How do we explain such a phenomenon? Obviously, the allele originated from a point mutation, but why did it spread?

The answer lies in yet another disease that produces enormous selective pressure: malaria. In those areas of the world where Hb^S is found in unusually high frequencies, malaria is also found (compare Figs. 4–11 and 4–12). Caused by a protozoan parasite *(Plasmodium)*, this debilitating infectious disease is transmitted to humans by mosquitoes. In populations where the infection persists, many individuals suffer sharp declines in reproductive success due to high infant mortality or lowered vitality as adults.

Such a geographical correlation between the incidence of malaria and distribution of the sickle-cell allele is indirect evidence of a biological correlation. Further confirmation was provided by British biologist A. C. Allison in the 1950s. Volunteers from the Luo tribe of eastern Africa with known genotypes were injected with the malarial parasite. It goes without saying that the ethics concerning human subjects would preclude such experimentation today. A short time following infection, results showed that carriers, or subjects with one copy of the Hb^S allele (those with *sickle-cell trait*), were much more resistant to malarial infection than the homozygous "normals." Heterozygotes resist infection because their red blood cells provide a less conducive environment for the malarial parasite to reproduce itself. As a result, the parasite often expires before widely infecting the body of a carrier. Conversely, in homozygous "normals," the infection usually persists. It would thus appear that the carriers have higher reproductive success than the so-called "normals," at least in certain environments. Those afflicted with sickle-cell anemia, of course, have the lowest reproductive success of any of the genotypes. Given the field data, experimental evidence, and especially the established link with an environmental factor (malaria), this constitutes our best demonstration of natural selection in contemporary humans.

Review of Genetics and Evolutionary Factors

Starting in Chapter 3 with a discussion of the molecular and cellular bases of heredity, we proceeded in this chapter to show how such genetic information is passed from individuals in one generation to those in the next. In this chapter we also have reviewed evolutionary theory and its current applications, emphasizing the crucial role of natural selection. It may seem that these different levels—molecular, cellular, individual, and populational—are different aspects of evolution, but they are all related and highly integrated in a way that can eventually produce evolutionary change. A step-by-step example will make this clear.

From our discussion of sickle-cell hemoglobin in Chapter 3, you will recall that the actual genetic information is coded in the sequence of bases in the DNA molecule. We start out with a situation in which everyone in the population has the same hemoglobin type; therefore, initially no variation for this trait exists, and without some source of new variation, evolution is not possible. How does this gene change? We have seen that a substitution of a single base in the DNA sequence can alter the code significantly enough to alter the protein product and ultimately the whole phenotype of the individual. Imagine that several generations ago, just such an "accident" occurred in a single individual. For this mutated allele to be passed on to succeeding offspring, the gametes must carry the alteration. Any new mutation, therefore, must be transmitted during sex cell formation.

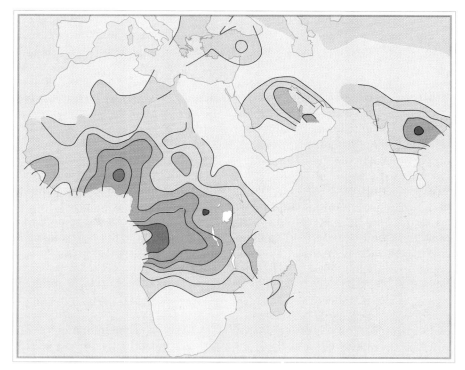

FIGURE 4–11

A frequency map of the sickle-cell distribution in the Old World.

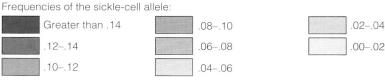

Frequencies of the sickle-cell allele:

Greater than .14	.08–.10	.02–.04
.12–.14	.06–.08	.00–.02
.10–.12	.04–.06	

FIGURE 4–12

Malaria distribution in the Old World.

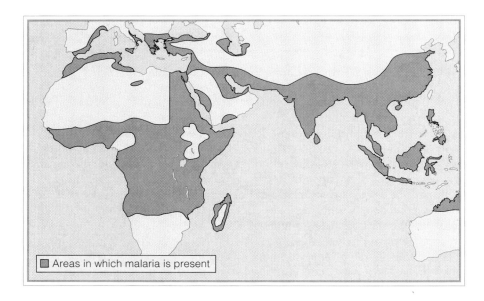

Areas in which malaria is present

Once the mutation has occurred in the DNA, it will be packaged into chromosomes, and these chromosomes in turn will assort during meiosis to be passed to offspring. The results of this process are seen by looking at phenotypes (traits) in individuals, and the mode of inheritance is described simply by Mendel's principle of segregation. In other words, if our initial individual has a mutation in only one paired allele on a set of homologous chromosomes, there will be a 50 percent chance of passing this chromosome (with the new mutation) to an offspring.

Thus far, we have seen what a gene is, how it can change, and how it is passed on to offspring. But what does all this activity have to do with *evolution*? To repeat an earlier definition, evolution is a change in allele frequency in a *population* from one generation to the next. The key point here is that we are now looking at a whole group of individuals, a population, and it is the population that will or will not change over time.

We know whether allele frequencies have changed in a population where sickle-cell hemoglobin is found by ascertaining the percentage of individuals with the sickling allele (Hb^S) versus those with the normal allele (Hb^A). If the relative proportions of these alleles alter with time, evolution has occurred. In addition to discovering that evolution has occurred, it is important to know why. Several possibilities arise. First, we know that the only way the new allele Hb^S could have arisen is by mutation, and we have shown how this process might happen in a single individual. This change, however, is not yet really an evolutionary one, for in a relatively large population, the alteration of one individual's genes will not significantly alter allele frequencies of the entire population. Somehow, this new allele must *spread* in the population.

One way this could happen is in a small population, where mutations in one or just a few individuals and their offspring may indeed alter the overall frequency quite quickly. This case would be representative of genetic drift. As discussed, drift acts in small populations where random factors may cause significant changes in allele frequency. With a small population size, there is not likely to be a balance of factors affecting individual survival or reproduction. Consequently, some alleles may be completely removed from the population,

TABLE 4–7   Levels of Organization in the Evolutionary Process

Evolutionary Factor	Level	Evolutionary Process	Technique of Study
Mutation	DNA	Storage of genetic information; ability to replicate; influences phenotype by production of proteins	Biochemistry, electron microscopy, recombinant DNA
Mutation	Chromosomes	A vehicle for packaging and transmitting genetic material (DNA)	Light, electron microscope
Recombination (sex cells only)	Cell	The basic unit of life that contains the chromosomes and divides for growth and for production of sex cells	Light, electron microscope
Natural selection	Organism	The unit, composed of cells, that reproduces and which we observe for phenotypic traits	Visual, biochemical
Drift, gene flow	Population	A group of interbreeding organisms. We look at changes in allele frequencies between generations; it is the population that evolves	Statistical

while others may become established as the only allele present at that particular locus (and are said to be "fixed" in the population).

In the course of human evolution, drift may have played a significant role at times, and it is important to remember that at this microevolutionary level, drift and/or gene flow can (and will) produce evolutionary change, even in the absence of natural selection. However, long-term evolutionary trends could only have been sustained by *natural selection.* The way this has worked in the past and still operates today (as in sickle-cell) is through differential reproduction. That is, individuals who carry a particular allele or combination of alleles produce more offspring. By producing more offspring than other individuals with alternative alleles, such individuals cause the frequency of the new allele in the population to increase slowly in proportion from generation to generation. When this process is compounded over hundreds of generations for numerous loci, the result is significant evolutionary change. The levels of organization in the evolutionary process are summarized in Table 4–7.

Summary

We have seen how Gregor Mendel discovered the principles of segregation, independent assortment, and dominance and recessiveness by conducting experiments on garden peas. Although the field of genetics has progressed dramatically in the twentieth century, the concepts first put forth by Gregor Mendel remain the basis of our current knowledge on how traits are inherited.

Basic Mendelian principles are applied to the study of the various modes of inheritance we are familiar with today. We have presented three of these in some detail: autosomal dominants, autosomal recessives, and X-linked recessives. The most important factor in all the Mendelian modes of inheritance is the role of segregation of chromosomes, and the alleles they carry, during meiosis. Although our understanding of human inheritance has virtually exploded in the last 50 years, the very foundation of our knowledge rests in the basic rules as set forth by Gregor Mendel almost 150 years ago.

Building on fundamental nineteenth-century contributions by Charles Darwin and his contemporaries and the rediscovery in 1900 of Mendel's work, further refinements later in the twentieth century have been added to contemporary evolutionary thought. In particular, the combination of natural selection with Mendel's principles of inheritance and experimental evidence concerning the nature of mutation have all been synthesized into a modern understanding of evolutionary change, appropriately termed the *modern synthesis*. In this, the central contemporary theory of evolution, evolutionary change is seen as a two-stage process. The first stage is the production and redistribution of variation. The second stage is the process whereby natural selection acts on the accumulated genetic variation.

Crucial to all evolutionary change is mutation, the only source of completely new genetic variation. In addition, the factors of gene flow, genetic drift, and recombination function to redistribute variation within individuals (recombination), within populations (genetic drift), and between populations (gene flow).

Natural selection is the central determining factor influencing the long-term direction of evolutionary change. How natural selection works can best be explained as differential reproductive success—in other words, how successful individuals are in leaving offspring to succeeding generations. To more fully illustrate the mechanics of evolutionary change through natural selection, comprehensive and well-understood examples from other organisms are most helpful. The detailed history of the evolutionary spread of the sickle-cell allele provides the best-documented example of natural selection among recent human populations. It must be remembered that evolution is an integrated process, and this chapter concludes with a discussion of how the various evolutionary factors can be integrated into a single, comprehensive view of evolutionary change.

Questions for Review

1. What is Mendel's principle of segregation?
2. How does meiosis explain the principle of segregation?
3. What is Mendel's principle of independent assortment?
4. Explain dominance and recessiveness.
5. Define *allele*.
6. What is a *phenotype*, and what is its relationship to a genotype?
7. Why were all of Mendel's F_1 pea plants phenotypically the same?
8. Explain what is meant by a phenotypic ratio of 3:1 in the F_2 generation.
9. What is codominance? Give an example.
10. If two people who have blood type A (both with the AO genotype) have children, what proportion of their children would be expected to have O blood? Why?
11. Can the two parents in question 10 have a child with AB blood? Why or why not?
12. Explain why X-linked recessive traits are more common in males than in females.
13. In a cross between two carriers for a recessive trait, why would ¾ of the offspring be expected *not* to show the recessive characteristic?
14. Explain how natural selection works. Illustrate through an example in humans.
15. What is the modern synthesis? Explain how the major components of this theory explain evolutionary change.

16. What is genetic drift? Illustrate through an example for human populations.
17. Define gene flow. Give an example in human populations.
18. What role does variation play in the evolutionary process? Where does variation come from? (*Hint:* You may wish to discuss the source of variation as completely new to a species or as it is introduced into a population *within* a species.)
19. Discuss how evolutionary change occurs as an integrated process. Illustrate through an example.

Suggested Further Reading

Cummings, Michael R. 1994. *Human Heredity.* 3rd ed. St. Paul: West.
Heim, Werner G. 1991. "What is a Recessive Allele?" In *The American Biology Teacher* 53(2): 94–97.
Ridley, Mark. 1993. *Evolution.* Cambridge, MA: Blackwell Scientific.

Internet Resources

Online Mendelian Inheritance in Man (OMIM)
   http://gdbwww.gdb.org/omimdoc/omimtop.html
   (Probably the most up-to-date and comprehensive resource on Mendelian traits in humans available. Excellent discussions of characteristics, history of relevant research and current, extensive bibliographies [useful for term papers].)

Genetic Screening:
A Double-Edged Sword?

Genetic screening is used to identify individuals who possess deleterious genes that may eventually lead to debilitating illness and, perhaps, death. Screening can also identify carriers for certain recessive disorders who, though not affected themselves, can nevertheless pass a defective gene on to their offspring. The applications of genetic screening are numerous, but primarily all are aimed at decreasing the incidence of genetic disorders.

For a number of reasons, chief among which are reducing human suffering and cutting health costs, genetic screening has become a powerful diagnostic tool since the 1970s. Moreover, as new technologies are developed and as more genetic markers for disease are identified, use of such technologies in assessing individual risk will certainly continue to increase.

An estimated 10 percent of Americans at some point experience symptoms of an illness that is at least partly caused by genetic factors. Clearly, the benefits of genetic screening both to the individual and to society are enormous, but as with most things, they carry a price tag. The ability to identify individuals at risk for potentially fatal conditions raises numerous difficult questions never before asked. Currently, advances in genetic technology are proceeding at a rate that has far outpaced our legal and ethical systems.

The purpose of this Issue is to explore some of the beneficial applications of genetic screening as well as some of the difficult choices such screening may pose.

Detection of an individual's carrier status in adults is possible for many conditions through blood testing combined with genetic counseling. Clearly, this ability is of enormous benefit for those individuals who have a family history of some recessive disorder, and who are making family planning decisions of their own.

The same techniques are also increasingly used today to identify persons with a genetic *predisposition* to problems associated with exposure to certain environmental agents. These results permit avoidance of potentially harmful substances when possible. Moreover, employers are increasingly screening employees to identify those who might potentially suffer from contact with particular materials in the workplace. At least 50 genetic traits have been shown to be influenced by such work-related environmental substances as lead, ozone, and nitrogen dioxide.

Newborn infants can be tested for several metabolic disorders to aid in early diagnosis and treatment. The most widespread use of newborn testing is for *phenylketonuria (PKU)*, a recessive disorder that prevents production of the enzyme phenylalanine hydroxylase. Without this enzyme, the body cannot properly metabolize the amino acid phenylalanine, common in meat and dairy products. The accumulation of phenylalanine eventually leads to brain damage and severe mental retardation (see p. 78).

PKU testing is mandatory in most states and involves a simple blood test to detect abnormal levels of phenylalanine. For those infants who test positive, the severe consequences of PKU are avoidable by strict adherence to a low-phenylalanine diet maintained throughout childhood and adolescence. The important point here is that treatment depends on early detection made available through widespread screening practices.

But diagnosis of such conditions as PKU does not have to occur after birth. *Prenatal testing* permits detection of over 200 genetically determined metabolic disorders and all chromosomal abnormalities in a developing fetus. Currently, the two most commonly used methods of detecting metabolic and chromosomal defects in fetuses are *amniocentesis* and *chorionic villus sampling (CVS)*. For any given pregnancy, testing is done only to detect those disorders for which the fetus may be predisposed as a result of family background (i.e., not every detectable condition is tested for in all pregnancies).

Prenatal testing is controversial for the obvious reason that test results may lead to termination of a pregnancy. Although therapeutic abortion may be the outcome, the notion that amniocentesis and chorionic villus sampling are aimed at the elimination of all abnormal fetuses is inaccurate. Not all negative findings result in abortion, and in fact, prenatal testing can be highly beneficial in preparing physicians and parents for the birth of an infant requiring special care and treatment.

Individuals must make personal decisions as to where to draw the line if they are told their fetus has a genetic disorder. Tay-Sachs (see p. 78) carriers can be identified through screening prior to beginning a pregnancy. But if both prospective parents are carriers and they choose to conceive, they face a 25 percent risk of having an affected fetus. Because Tay-Sachs is such a devastating condition with no chance of survival beyond childhood, 80 to 90 percent of diagnosed pregnancies are terminated.

Likewise, the majority (but not all) of pregnancies *with a diagnosis* of trisomy 21 also end in abortion. This fact does not mean, however, that the majority of all trisomy 21 pregnancies are terminated. Most pregnant women over age 35 are not screened. Moreover, the majority (at least 65 percent) of trisomy 21 infants are born to younger women who are not tested unless there are other known risk factors. Since tri-

somy 21 is variably expressed, with many affected persons leading fairly normal, and in some cases productive lives, the certainty of outcome is not as clear as with Tay-Sachs. Because of this uncertainty, some parents who would terminate a Tay-Sachs pregnancy would not do so in the case of a trisomy 21 diagnosis.

Other situations are even more ambiguous. Does one choose abortion if a fetus has PKU, cystic fibrosis, or sickle-cell anemia? All three are treatable to some extent, though at considerable costs (financial and otherwise).

Another serious question is faced by individuals who learn that they themselves possess a gene that will eventually cause illness and death. What does one do with such knowledge? For example, it is now possible to identify people at risk for *Huntington disease*, a fatal, degenerative disorder of the central nervous system. Huntington disease is inherited as an autosomal dominant trait and usually produces no symptoms until middle age. Symptoms include progressive degeneration of the central nervous system, involuntary twitching, mental deterioration, and eventually, after 5 to 15 years, death.

Because Huntington disease is a dominant trait, all affected people (barring new mutations) will have an affected parent (see p. 80). Moreover, anyone who has a parent with Huntington disease has a 50

percent chance of inheriting the gene and thus of developing symptoms by middle age. However, until the development of reliable methods of detecting genetic markers, children of affected parents could not know for certain if they had the defective gene or not. Such a test exists today, and it is possible to know if, in later life, one will succumb to this tragic condition.

Persons with a parent afflicted with Huntington disease face a most terrible dilemma. They can go untested and continue hoping, but not knowing, that they do not have the gene. Or they can be tested and either be tremendously relieved or plan the rest of their lives in anticipation of catastrophic debilitating disease and early death. Unless one has faced such a horrific decision, one cannot adequately comprehend the uncertainty and fear that must surely accompany it. Unfortunately, our technology has given us the tools with which to answer many painful questions, but it has not prepared us for how to cope with what we may learn.

The fact that many genetic disorders are treatable (but, as yet, not curable) raises another issue: cost. With medical costs soaring out of reach for millions today, financial considerations must be addressed, and this obviously raises many deeply painful questions.

How does an individual or the state place a monetary value on a human life? Can we morally establish limits on public expenditures for the treatment of genetic diseases when those diseases can be prevented by prenatal testing and selective abortion? On the other hand, is society obligated to bear the costs of preventable hereditary conditions?

Do people have a fundamental right to have children regardless of circumstances? Or do they have an obligation to society to be personally responsible for the financial costs of medical treatment? Does a fetus have a right to be born free of disease? If so, can an afflicted child later sue the parents for having given birth? Is it indeed desirable for society to be free of "imperfect" people? If so, who defines "perfect," and what does such a policy say about our tolerance of diversity? (One should note that a goal of the Nazi regime in Germany was to rid society of imperfection, as it was defined by the Nazis, and create a "master race.")

These are only a few of the many discomforting ethical questions that have accompanied advances in genetic screening and prenatal testing. There are numerous other questions and potentials for abuse as well. For example, after federal screening programs for the sickle-cell trait were instituted in 1972, individuals testing positive as heterozygotes were, in some cases, reportedly denied health insurance

or employment opportunities. Do employers or insurance companies have the right to refuse opportunities to people because, due to potential health problems, they ostensibly constitute an economic risk? This issue raises the question of whether or not individual rights (including rights to privacy) are violated by government mandates to institute genetic screening programs.

These examples illustrate the conflicts between technology, ethical standards, and the legal system. The questions raised are disturbing because they challenge traditionally held views about fundamental aspects of life. In the past, people with hereditary disorders frequently died. They still do. But now, there are treatments, however costly, for some conditions. Moreover, we now have the means to detect genetic defects or determine their risk of occurrence. How we come to terms with the ethical and legal issues surrounding our new technologies will increasingly become social, religious, and, ultimately, political concerns. Solutions will not come easily and—most assuredly—they will not please everyone.

Sources

Cummings, Michael R. 1991. *Human Heredity* (2nd ed.), St. Paul: West.
Edlin, Gordon. 1984. *Genetic Principles.* Boston: Jones and Bartlett.

Critical Thinking Questions

1. Do you approve of technologies that permit a person to learn if he or she has inherited a lethal allele, as in Huntington disease? Why or why not? If one of your parents developed Huntington disease, would you be tested to see if you had inherited the allele that causes it?

2. What do you see as the most disconcerting aspect of genetic screening? Which do you think is the most positive? Explain.

3. If you were an employer providing health benefits to employees, would you hire someone who carried the allele for Huntington disease? Since appropriate genetic tests are available, do you think you would have a right to such information? Explain your answer.

4. Do you think it is desirable for society to attempt to eliminate all or some genetic diseases? If your answer is "all" explain why. If your answer is "some," where do you draw the line and why? If your answer is "no" to any elimination, explain.

Microevolution in Modern Human Populations

Introduction

How is evolution evaluated and measured in contemporary species? In the last chapter, we discussed the mechanisms of inheritance and the manner in which such heritable characteristics influence evolutionary change. In this chapter, we will demonstrate how these genetic principles lie at the very foundation of the evolutionary process. Moreover, we will show how these factors interact to produce evolutionary change in contemporary human populations. As with all other organisms, the variation exhibited by *Homo sapiens* can be understood within this contemporary evolutionary framework. Evolutionary change not only characterizes the human past, but also continues as a major factor shaping human beings today. In this explicit evolutionary context, physical anthropologists are able to assess larger patterns of human population diversity. We conclude this chapter with a discussion of population diversity and thus prepare the foundation for a further examination of this issue in Chapter 6.

Human Populations

As we defined it in Chapter 4, a *population* is a group of interbreeding individuals. More precisely, a population is the group within which one is most likely to find a mate. As such, a population is marked by a degree of genetic relatedness and shares a common **gene pool**.

▲ **Gene pool**
The total complement of genes shared by reproductive members of a population.

In theory, this is a straightforward concept. In every generation, the genes (alleles) are mixed by recombination and rejoined through mating. What emerges in the next generation is a direct product of the genes going into the pool, which in turn is a product of who is mating with whom.

In practice, however, defining and describing human populations is difficult. The largest population of *Homo sapiens* that could be described is the entire species. All members of a species are *potentially* capable of interbreeding, but are incapable of fertile interbreeding with members of other species. Our species is thus a *genetically closed system*. The problem arises not in describing who potentially can interbreed, but in isolating exactly the pattern of those individuals who are doing so.

Factors that determine mate choice are geographical, ecological, and social. If individuals are isolated on a remote island in the middle of the Pacific, there is not much chance of their finding a mate outside the immediate vicinity. Such **breeding isolates** are fairly easily defined and are a favorite target of microevolutionary studies. Geography plays a dominant role in producing these isolates by rather strictly determining the range of available mates. But even within these limits, cultural rules can easily play a deciding role by prescribing who is most appropriate among those who are potentially available.

▲ **Breeding isolates**
Populations that are clearly isolated geographically and/or socially from other breeding groups.

Human population segments within the species are defined as groups with relative degrees of **endogamy** (marrying/mating within the group). These are, however, not totally closed systems. Gene flow often occurs between groups, and individuals may choose mates from distant localities. With the modern advent of rapid transportation, greatly accelerated rates of **exogamy** (marrying/mating outside the group) have emerged.

▲ **Endogamy**
Mating with individuals from the same group.

▲ **Exogamy**
Mating with individuals from other groups.

It is obvious that most humans today are not clearly members of particular populations as they would be if they belonged to a breeding isolate. Inhabitants of large cities may appear to be members of a single population, but within the city borders, social, ethnic, and religious boundaries crosscut in a complex fashion to form smaller population segments. In addition to being members of these highly open local population groupings, we are simultaneously members of overlapping gradations of larger populations—the immediate geographical region (a metropolitan area or perhaps an entire state), a section of the country, the whole nation, and, ultimately, the whole species.

Population Genetics

Once specific human populations have been identified, the next step is to ascertain what evolutionary forces, if any, are operating on this group. To determine whether evolution is taking place at a given locus, we measure allele frequencies for specific traits and compare these observed frequencies with a set predicted by a mathematical model: the **Hardy-Weinberg theory of genetic equilibrium**. This model provides us with a baseline set of evolutionary expectations under *known* conditions.

The Hardy-Weinberg theory of genetic equilibrium postulates a set of conditions in a population where *no* evolution occurs. In other words, none of the forces of evolution are acting, and all genes have an equal chance of recombining in each generation (i.e., there is random mating of individuals). More precisely, the hypothetical conditions that such a population would be *assumed* to meet are as follows:

▲ **Hardy-Weinberg theory of genetic equilibrium**
The mathematical relationship expressing—under ideal conditions—the predicted distribution of genes in populations; the central theorem of population genetics.

1. The population is infinitely large. This condition eliminates the possibility of random genetic drift or changes in allele frequencies due to chance.
2. There is no mutation. Thus, no new alleles are being added by molecular changes in gametes.
3. There is no gene flow. There is no exchange of genes with other populations that can alter allele frequencies.
4. Natural selection is not operating. Specific alleles confer no advantage over others that might influence reproductive success.
5. Mating is random. There are no factors that influence who mates with whom. Thus, any female is assumed to have an equal chance of mating with any male.

If all these conditions are satisfied, allele frequencies will not change from one generation to the next (i.e., no evolution will take place), and a permanent equilibrium will be maintained as long as these conditions prevail. An evolutionary "barometer" is thus provided that may be used as a standard against which actual circumstances are compared. Similar to the way a typical barometer is standardized under known temperature and altitude conditions, the Hardy-Weinberg equilibrium is standardized under known evolutionary conditions.

Note that the idealized conditions that define the Hardy-Weinberg equilibrium are just that: an idealized, *hypothetical* state. In the real world, no actual population would fully meet any of these conditions. But do not be confused by this distinction. By explicitly defining the genetic distribution that would be *expected* if *no* evolutionary change were occurring (i.e., in equilibrium), we can compare the *observed* genetic distribution obtained from actual human populations. The evolutionary barometer is thus evaluated through comparison of these observed allele and genotype frequencies with those expected in the predefined equilibrium situation.

If the observed frequencies differ from those of the expected model, then we can say that evolution is taking place at the locus in question. The alternative, of course, is that the observed and expected frequencies do not differ sufficiently to state unambiguously that evolution is occurring at a locus in a population. Indeed, frequently this is the result that is obtained, and in such cases, population geneticists are unable to delineate evolutionary changes at the particular locus under study. Put another way, geneticists are unable to reject what statisticians call the *null hypothesis* (where "null" means nothing, a statistical condition of randomness).

The simplest situation applicable to a microevolutionary study is a genetic trait that follows a simple Mendelian pattern and has only two alleles (A, a). As you recall from earlier discussions, there are then only three possible genotypes: AA, Aa, aa. Proportions of these genotypes (AA:Aa:aa) are a function of the *allele frequencies* themselves (percentage of A and percentage of a). To provide uniformity for all genetic loci, a standard notation is employed to refer to these frequencies:

Frequency of dominant allele $(A) = p$
Frequency of recessive allele $(a) = q$

Since in this case there are only two alleles, their combined total frequency must represent all possibilities. In other words, the sum of their separate frequencies must be 1:

$$p \quad + \quad q = 1 \text{ (100\% of alleles at the locus in question)}$$
(Frequency   Frequency
of A alleles)   of a alleles)

To ascertain the expected proportions of genotypes, we compute the chances of the alleles combining with one another into all possible combinations. Remember, they all have an equal chance of combining, and no new alleles are being added.

These probabilities are a direct function of the frequency of the two alleles. The chances of all possible combinations occurring randomly can be simply shown as

$$
\begin{array}{r}
p + q \\
\times \quad p + q \\
\hline
pq + q^2 \\
p^2 + pq \quad\quad \\
\hline
p^2 + 2pq + q^2
\end{array}
$$

Mathematically, this is known as a binomial expansion and can also be shown as

$$(p + q)(p + q) = p^2 + 2pq + q^2$$

What we have just calculated is simply:

Allele Combination	Genotype Produced	Expected Proportion in Population
Chances of A combining with A	AA	$p \times p = p^2$
Chances of A combining with a;	Aa	$p \times q$
a combining with A	aA	$p \times q$ $= 2pq$
Chances of a combining with a	aa	$q \times q = q^2$

Thus, p^2 is the frequency of the *AA* genotype, $2pq$ is the frequency of the *Aa* genotype, and q^2 is the frequency of the *aa* genotype, where p is the frequency of the dominant allele and q is the frequency of the recessive allele in a population.

Calculating Allele Frequencies: An Example

How geneticists use the Hardy-Weinberg formula is best demonstrated through an example. Let us assume that a population contains 200 individuals, and we will use the MN blood group locus as the gene to be measured. This gene produces a blood group antigen—similar to ABO—located on red blood cells. Because the M and N alleles are codominant, we can ascertain everyone's phenotype by taking blood samples and observing reactions with specially prepared antisera. From the phenotypes, we can then directly calculate the *observed* allele frequencies. So let us proceed.

All 200 individuals are tested, and the results are shown in Box 5–1. Although the match between observed and expected frequencies is not perfect, it is close enough statistically to satisfy equilibrium conditions. Since our population is not a large one, sampling may easily account for the small observed deviations. Our population is therefore probably in equilibrium (i.e., at this locus, it is not evolving). At the minimum, what we can say scientifically is that we cannot reject the *null hypothesis*.

Evolution in Action: Modern Human Populations

Once a population has been defined, a population geneticist will ascertain whether allele frequencies are stable (i.e., in genetic equilibrium) or whether they are changing. As we have seen, the Hardy-Weinberg formula provides the tool to establish whether allele frequencies are indeed changing. What factors initiate changes in allele frequencies? There are a number of factors, including those that:

1. Produce new variation (i.e., *mutation*)
2. Redistribute variation through *gene flow* or *genetic drift*
3. Select "advantageous" allele combinations that promote reproductive success—that is, *natural selection*

Note that factors 1 and 2 constitute the first stage of the evolutionary process, as first emphasized by the modern synthesis, while factor 3 is the second stage (i.e., natural selection). There is yet another factor, as implied by the condition of genetic equilibrium (p. 105) that under idealized conditions all matings are random. Thus, the evolutionary alteration (i.e., deviation from equilibrium) is called **nonrandom mating**.

▲ **Nonrandom mating**
Patterns of mating in a population in which individuals choose mates preferentially.

Nonrandom Mating

Although sexual recombination does not itself alter *allele frequencies*, any consistent bias in mating patterns can alter the *genotypic proportions*. By affecting the frequencies of genotypes, nonrandom mating causes deviations from Hardy-

BOX 5–1

Calculating Allele Frequencies in a Hypothetical Population

Observed Data:

Genotype	Number of individuals*	Percent	Number of Alleles M	N			
MM	80	(40%)	160	0			
MN	80	(40%)	80	80			
NN	40	(20%)	0	80			
Totals	200	(100%)	240	+ 160	=	400	
		Proportion:	.6	+ .4	=	1	

Observed Allele Frequencies:

$M = .6 (p)$
$N = .4 (q)$ ($p + q$ should equal 1, and they do)

Expected Frequencies: What are the predicted genotypic proportions if genetic equilibrium (no evolution) applies to our population? We simply apply the Hardy-Weinberg formula: $p^2 + 2pq + q^2$.

p^2	=	(.6)(.6)	= .36
$2pq$	=	2(.6)(.4) = 2(.24)	= .48
q^2	=	(.4)(.4)	= .16
Total			1.00

There are only three possible genotypes (*MM:MN:NN*), so the total of the relative proportions should equal 1; as you can see, they do.

Comparing Frequencies: How do the expected frequencies compare with the observed frequencies in our population?

	Expected Frequency	Expected Number of Individuals	Observed Frequency	Actual Number of Individuals with Each Genotype
MM	.36	72	.40	80
MN	.48	96	.40	80
NN	.16	32	.20	40

*Each individual has two alleles; thus a person who is *MM* contributes two *M* alleles to the total gene pool. A person who is *MN* contributes one *M* and one *N*. One hundred individuals, then, have 200 alleles for the *MN* locus.

Weinberg expectations of the proportions p^2, $2pq$, and q^2. It therefore sets the stage for the action of other evolutionary factors, particularly natural selection.

One variety of nonrandom mating, called **positive assortative mating**, occurs when individuals of like phenotype mate more often than expected by random mating predictions. Because individuals with like phenotypes are also similar to some degree in genotype, the result of positive assortative mating

▲ **Positive assortative mating**
A type of nonrandom mating in which individuals of like phenotype mate more often than predicted under random mating conditions.

increases the amount of homozygosity in the population and reduces heterozygosity (p^2 and q^2 greater than expected; $2pq$ less than expected).

The most consistent mating biases documented in the United States deal with stature and IQ. Of course, both these traits are influenced by environment as well as heredity (see p. 86), and observed correlations also reflect socioeconomic status (generating like environments). Eye color in a Swedish population and hair color in a Lapp group have shown significant degrees of correlation among married couples. Moreover, several studies in the United States and Britain have shown significant correlations for several other phenotypic traits (see Table 5–1).

The opposite of positive assortative mating is **negative assortative mating**, or mating with an individual who is phenotypically dissimilar. Theoretically, if this occurs more than expected by random mating predictions, it should increase the amount of heterozygosity in the population while reducing homozygosity. Curt Stern (1973) suggested that redheaded persons marry each other less often than would be expected, but this has not been substantiated; nor has any other instance of negative assortative mating been conclusively demonstrated in human populations.

A third type of nonrandom mating in humans that can disrupt expected genotypic proportions occurs when relatives mate more often than expected. Called **inbreeding** or consanguinity, such mating will increase the amount of homozygosity, since relatives who share close ancestors will more than likely also share more alleles than would two nonrelated individuals. In reality, inbreeding is just an extreme form of positive assortative mating.

All living societies have some sort of incest taboo banning matings between very close relatives such as between parent and child or brother and sister. Therefore, such matings usually occur less frequently than predicted under random mating conditions (which postulates that these matings, like all others, have a certain probability of occurring).

Whether incest is strictly prohibited by social proscriptions or whether biological factors also interact to condition against such behavior has long been a topic of heated debate among anthropologists. For numerous social, economic, and ecological reasons, exogamy is an advantageous strategy for hunting and gathering bands. Moreover, selective pressures may also play a part, since highly

▲ **Negative assortative mating**
A type of nonrandom mating in which individuals of unlike phenotype mate more often than predicted under random mating conditions.

▲ **Inbreeding**
A type of nonrandom mating in which relatives mate more often than predicted under random mating conditions.

TABLE 5–1 Positive Correlations Between Husbands and Wives in the United States and Britain	
IQ	.47
Ear lobe length*	.40
Waist circumference	.38
Stature	.28
Hip circumference	.22
Weight	.21
Neck circumference	.20

*This is not to say that prospective mates go around measuring or even paying particular attention to each other's ear lobes. Correlation for this trait may be residual of assortative mating for overall size or for certain head dimensions. It also may mean absolutely nothing. If one measures enough traits, statistically some will appear associated strictly on the basis of chance.

Source: Lerner and Libby, 1976, p. 369.

inbred offspring have a greater chance of expressing a genetic disorder and thereby lowering their reproductive fitness. In addition, inbreeding reduces variability among offspring, potentially reducing reproductive success (Murray, 1980). In this regard, an interesting note is that incest avoidance is widespread among vertebrates (Parker, 1976). Moreover, detailed studies of free-ranging chimpanzees indicate that they avoid incestuous matings within their family group (Goodall, 1968); in fact, adults of most primate species consistently establish themselves and then mate within groups other than the one in which they were reared. Apparently, both biological factors (in common with other primates) and uniquely human cultural factors have interacted during hominid evolution to produce this universal behavior pattern among contemporary societies.

Conversely, in certain societies inbreeding among fairly close relations such as cousins is actively encouraged or is unavoidable owing to the small number of potential mates available. A famous case of the latter situation occurred on Pitcairn Island among descendants of the mutineers of the *Bounty* and their Tahitian wives. Only a small founding population (23 or 24) initially settled this tiny island, and this group was still further reduced by intragroup violence. As a result, young men and women of the ensuing generations usually chose spouses with whom they shared several common ancestors. On Pitcairn there was no choice but to partake in considerable inbreeding.

On the other hand, there are some areas where inbreeding, although avoidable, is still actively encouraged. In some parts of Japan, among certain social classes, first-cousin marriages make up almost 10 percent of all marriages, and in the Andhra Pradesh area of India, among certain castes, uncle-niece unions also make up about 10 percent of marriages.

It must be kept in mind, however, that such considerable inbreeding is the exception rather than the rule among human populations. In fact, most groups seem to work very hard at maintaining exogamy, actively promoting exchange of marriage partners between groups. For example, many polar Inuit (Eskimo) groups live in small geographically separate isolates. Despite this, through socially established rules, very little inbreeding occurs. As a general rule, then, most human populations do not inbreed if they can help it.

Inbreeding has important medical consequences in addition to its influence on genetic equilibrium. When relatives mate, their offspring have an increased probability of inheriting two copies of potentially harmful recessive alleles from a relative, such as a grandparent that they share in common. Many potentially deleterious genes normally "masked" in heterozygous carriers may be expressed in offspring of consanguineous matings and thereby "exposed" to the action of natural selection. Among offspring of first-cousin matings in the United States, the risk of congenital disorders is 2.3 times greater than it is for the overall population. Matings between especially close relatives—incest—often lead to multiple genetic defects.

▲ **Racial**
In biology, pertaining to populations of a species that differ from other populations of the same species with regard to some aspects of outwardly expressed phenotype. Such phenotypic variation within a species is usually associated with differences in geographical location.

Human Polymorphisms

The ABO and MN blood groups, as well as the traits discussed in Chapter 4, are *Mendelian* traits. That is, the phenotype of each of these traits can unambiguously be linked to the action of a single locus. These simple genetic mechanisms are much more straightforward than the polygenic traits usually associated with studies of human **racial** variation (discussed in Chapter 6). In fact, the difficulty in tracing the genetic influence on such characteristics as skin color or face shape has led some human biologists to avoid investigations of such polygenic traits. Although physical anthropologists, by tradition, have been keenly interested in explaining such variation, we have seen a trend toward greater concentration on those traits with a clearly demonstrated genetic mechanism (i.e., Mendelian characteristics).

Of greatest use in contemporary studies of human variation are those traits that can be used to document genetic differences among various populations. Such genetic traits are called **polymorphisms**. A genetic trait is a polymorphism "when two or more alleles at a given genetic locus occur with appreciable frequencies in a population" (Bodmer and Cavalli-Sforza, 1976, p. 308). How much is "appreciable" is a fairly arbitrary judgment, but it is usually placed at 1 percent. In other words, if a population is sampled for a particular trait, and frequencies for more than one allele are higher than 1 percent, the trait (more precisely, the locus that governs the trait) is polymorphic. The limit of 1 percent is an attempt by population geneticists to control for mutation effects, which normally add new alleles at rates far below our 1 percent level. To explain this pattern of variation, beyond mutation, some *additional* evolutionary factor (gene flow, drift, natural selection) must also have been at work.

Clearly, then, the understanding of human genetic polymorphisms demands evolutionary explanations. As students of human evolution, physical anthropologists use these polymorphisms as their principal tool to understand the dynamics of evolution in modern populations. Moreover, by utilizing these polymorphisms and comparing allele frequencies in different populations, we can begin to reconstruct the evolutionary events that link human populations with one another. Several polymorphisms are now well known in humans, including those determined from analysis of blood.

▲ **Polymorphism**
A genetic trait governed by a locus with more than one allele in appreciable frequency. That is, the locus has two or more alleles, each with a frequency of at least 1 percent.

ABO

With the first use of transfusions as a medical practice around the turn of the century, serious problems were immediately recognized. Some patients had severe reactions, such as agglutination (clumping) of their blood cells, kidney failure, and even death. In the year 1900, Karl Landsteiner showed that the underlying cause of these incompatibilities was a genetic trait. As you know, this trait, called the ABO blood system, is expressed phenotypically in individuals as antigens located on the surface of their red blood cells (see p. 77). The blood group (i.e., what antigens a person has) is directly determined by his or her genotype for the ABO locus. The complications sometimes resulting from transfusions are due to *antigen-antibody* reactions. In a highly specific fashion, the body can recognize foreign antigens (proteins) and combat their invasion by producing specific antibodies that deactivate the foreign substances. Such an *immune response* is normally beneficial, for it is the basis of fighting infections caused by bacteria or viruses.

Usually, antibodies must be produced when foreign antigens are introduced. However, in the case of ABO, naturally occurring antibodies are already present in the blood serum at birth. Actually, no antibodies are probably "natural," although they may be (as in ABO) stimulated early in fetal life. The genotypes, phenotypes, and antibodies in the ABO system are shown in Table 4–2 (p. 77).

The ABO system is most interesting from an anthropological perspective because the frequencies of the three alleles (A, B, O) vary tremendously among human populations. As the distribution maps indicate (Fig. 5–1), A or B rarely approaches a frequency of 50 percent; frequencies for these two alleles are usually considerably below this figure. Most human groups, however, are polymorphic

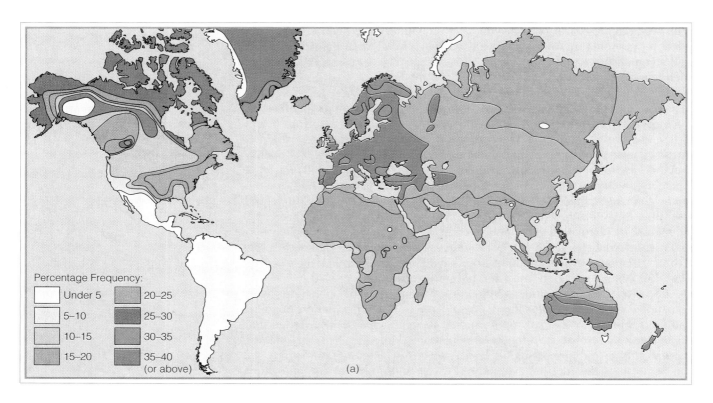

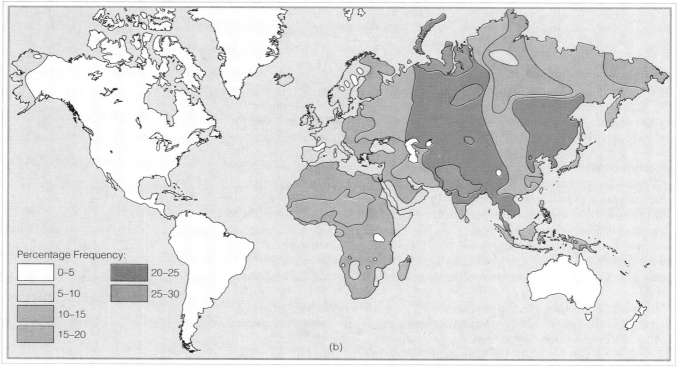

FIGURE 5–1

ABO blood group system. (a) Distribution of the A allele in the indigenous populations of the world. (b) Distribution of the B allele in the indigenous populations of the world. (After Mourant et al., 1976.)

for all three alleles. Occasionally, as in native South American Indians, frequencies of O reach 100 percent, and this allele is said to be "fixed" in this population. Indeed, in most native New World populations, O is at least 80 percent and is usually considerably higher. Unusually high frequencies of O are also found in northern Australia, and some islands off the coast show frequencies of 90 percent and higher. Since these frequencies are considerably greater than for presumably closely related mainland populations, founder effect is probably the evolutionary agent responsible.

In general, the lowest values for O found in the world are in eastern Europe and central Asia. As you might expect, frequencies for A and B can be relatively higher only where O tends to be lower. Generally, B is the rarest of the three alleles, and except among the Inuit, it appears to have been completely absent in the pre-Columbian New World. Moreover, the allele has apparently been introduced into Australia only in recent times.

The B allele reaches its highest peak in Eurasia, where its distribution is the inverse of O. Values up to 20 percent and occasionally slightly higher are found in a broad area in central Asia, western Siberia, and central Mongolia. The highest reported frequencies for B are found in the Himalaya area, reaching a peak of 25 to 30 percent. Generally, the frequency of B declines gradually in populations the farther westward they are in Eurasia.

The A allele has two interesting peaks, one among Blackfoot Indians and surrounding groups in North America and the other distributed over almost the entire Australian continent. With frequencies greater than 50 percent, the Blackfoot display the highest frequencies of A anywhere in the world. Certainly, they are divergent from other North American groups, who all have very high frequencies of O (and therefore low frequencies of A). How did A increase so much among this one tribe and its close neighbors compared to surrounding populations? Possibly drift (founder effect) is the answer, possibly some unknown selective factor. No one knows.

In Australia, except for the northern part, frequencies of A are generally high—particularly in central Australia, where they are 40 percent or higher. One tribe has especially high frequencies of A (53 percent), significantly higher than any surrounding group. Once again, is founder effect responsible? Over the rest of Australia, frequencies of A are fairly even in distribution and gradually decrease as populations become further removed from the center of the continent.

We must point out that distributions of alleles for a single genetic trait like ABO do not conclusively demonstrate genetic relationships between populations. For example, the North American Blackfoot and central Australian Mandjiljara have similar frequencies of A, but are obviously not closely related. On the other hand, in South Africa, the San have lower B frequencies than some of their close neighbors, with whom they share fairly close genetic ties. To understand *patterns* of population relationships, it is absolutely necessary to consider allele frequency distributions for several traits simultaneously (see p. 124).

Why do frequencies of the ABO alleles vary so much in different populations? In some cases, as with the islands off northern Australia and perhaps with the Blackfoot, drift may be the key factor. However, the even distribution of alleles (as B in Eurasia, A in Australia) indicates that selection may also be playing an important role, for the regularity in the frequency distributions is thought to mirror gradual changes in environments.

If, in fact, selection is operating, what are the specific factors involved? Unfortunately, unlike sickle-cell, there is not as yet any proven association between ABO frequencies and *any* selective agent (such as various diseases). There are, however, some clues. For example, A individuals have significantly more stomach cancer and pernicious anemia, while O individuals have more gastric and duodenal ulcers (Vogel, 1970). Such chronic diseases as these are not that common; indeed, they probably do not affect reproductive success very much, since they occur so late in life.

On the other hand, infectious diseases (as already shown for malaria) are potentially selective factors of enormous significance. Some interesting associations between ABO frequencies and incidence of smallpox, tuberculosis, syphilis, bubonic plague, cholera, and leprosy have been suggested. Moreover, it has also been suggested that *O* individuals are more attractive to mosquitoes and are thus bitten more often than *A*, *B*, or *AB* individuals (Wood et al., 1972). Here, too, could be an important contributing factor for infectious disease, since many—including malaria, yellow fever, and typhus—are transmitted by insects (Brues, 1990). As yet, none of these associations is well substantiated. Consequently, the evolutionary factors influencing the distribution of ABO alleles are still largely a mystery.

Rh

Another group of antigens found on red blood cells is the *Rh system*, named after the rhesus monkeys that initially provided the blood cells with which to make antiserum. Developed in 1940 by Wiener and Landsteiner (a full 40 years after the latter's discovery of ABO!), this antiserum was then tested in a large sample of white Americans, in which 85 percent reacted positively.

The individuals showing such a positive agglutination reaction are usually called Rh-positive (Rh⁺), and those whose blood does not agglutinate with the antiserum are called Rh-negative (Rh⁻). These standardized designations refer to an apparently simple two-allele system, with *DD* and *Dd* resulting in Rh⁺ and the recessive *dd* resulting in Rh⁻.

Clinically, the Rh factor—like ABO—can lead to serious complications. However, the greatest problem is not so much incompatibilities following transfusions as those between a mother and her developing fetus (see Box 5–2). For most significant medical applications, Rh⁺ compared to Rh⁻ is accounted for by the three genotypes already noted (*DD*, *Dd*, *dd*). However, the actual genetics of the Rh system are a good deal more complex than explained by just two alleles at one locus. The famous English population geneticist Sir R. A. Fisher suggested that the Rh system is actually three closely linked loci with at least two alleles each.

The distribution of the various allele combinations within the Rh system (which may be pictured as large genes) varies considerably among human populations. Generally, Rh⁻ (*d*) is quite high in European groups, averaging around 40 percent. African populations also have a fair amount of polymorphism at the *D* locus, with frequencies of Rh⁻ centering around 25 percent. Native Americans and Australians, on the other hand, are almost 100 percent Rh⁺.

Other Red Blood Cell Antigen Systems

MN   The pattern of inheritance of the MN blood group that we have referred to previously is very straightforward and is thus a favorite tool in population genetics research. There are three genotypes—*MM*, *MN*, *NN*—all clearly ascertainable at the phenotypic level using antisera obtained from rabbits. Clinically, no observable complications arise as a result of transfusions or mother-fetus incompatibilities; the MN system is anthropologically important because of its variable distribution among human populations.

Almost all human populations are polymorphic (i.e., having both *M* and *N* in "appreciable" frequencies), but the relative frequency of the two alleles varies tremendously. In some areas of Australia, *M* is as low as 2 percent, contrasted with many areas of the New World, where frequencies exceed 90 percent and even reach 100 percent in some areas. The allele *M* is also found in quite high frequency in Arabia, Siberia, and portions of Southeast Asia.

In addition to ABO, Rh, and MN, there are several other polymorphic red blood cell antigen systems. While not clinically significant like ABO or Rh, many of these are important for anthropological studies of population variation. Table 5–2 lists the major antigen systems of human red blood cells.

Polymorphisms in White Blood Cells

An important polymorphic trait called the HLA (human lymphocyte antigen) system has been discovered on some white blood cells (lymphocytes). Of great medical importance, HLA loci affect histocompatibility, or recognition and rejection of foreign tissues—the reason skin grafts and organ transplants are usually rejected. Genetically, the HLA system is exceedingly complex, and researchers are still discovering further subtleties within it. There are at least seven closely linked loci on chromosome 6, making up the HLA system. Taken together, there are already well over 100 antigens known within the system, with a potential of at least 30 million different genotypes (Williams, 1985). By far, this is the most polymorphic of any known human genetic system.

The component loci of the HLA system function together as a kind of "supergene." In addition to the components of the HLA loci themselves, many other factors affecting immune response are known to exist in the same region of chromosome 6. Altogether, the whole system is called the *major histocompatibility complex* (MHC).

The geographical distribution of the various MHC alleles is not yet well known. Some interesting patterns, however, are apparent. For example, Lapps, Sardinians, and Basques show deviations from frequencies of HLA alleles in other European populations, paralleling evidence for ABO, Rh, and MN. In addition, many areas in New Guinea and Australia are quite divergent, possibly suggesting the effects of drift. It is imperative, however, that care be taken in postulating genetic relatedness from restricted polymorphic information. Otherwise, such obviously ridiculous links as some proposed from HLA data (e.g., Tibetans and Australians; Inuit with some New Guineans) would obscure the evolutionary process in human populations (Livingstone, 1980). Since HLA is involved in the superfine detection and deactivation of foreign antigens, selection relative to infectious diseases (particularly those caused by viruses) may also play a significant role in the distribution of HLA alleles.

Evidence is still exceedingly tentative, but some HLA antigens are apparently associated with susceptibility to certain diseases. A disease of the spine called ankylosing spondylitis, as well as multiple sclerosis and some varieties of hay fever, may all result from individuals developing an autoimmune response to their own HLA antigens.

Miscellaneous Polymorphisms

An interesting genetically controlled variation in human populations was discovered by accident in 1931. When the artificially synthesized chemical phenyl-thiocarbamide (PTC) was dropped in a laboratory, some researchers were able to

TABLE 5–2 Other Blood Group Systems Used in Human Microevolutionary Studies

Major Systems	Number of Known Antigens
P	3
Lutheran	2
Kell-Cellano	5
Lewis	2
Duffy	2
Kidd	2
Diego	1
Auberger	1
Xg (sex-linked)	1
Dombrock	1
Stolzfus	1

Source: Lerner and Libby, 1976, p. 354.

BOX 5–2

Mother-Fetus Incompatibilities

A mother-fetus incompatibility occurs when the system of the mother is immunized by cells from a fetus and forms antibodies that then raise problems for that fetus or future ones.

For the Rh trait, complications occur only when the mother is Rh⁻ (*dd*) and the father Rh⁺ (*DD* or *Dd*). Actually, the other loci can also cause incompatibilities, but 95 percent of the problems are due to the D locus.

European populations are the most polymorphic for Rh, and around 13 percent of all matings are at risk. Not all those at risk, however, run into problems. Only about 6 percent of those potentially in danger have any complications. With new preventive treatment, this figure can be expected to decline even further.

The problem of incompatibility arises only if the mother is Rh⁻ and her fetus is Rh⁺. Usually, there are no serious effects in the first pregnancy, for the mother's system has not been immunized. Transfer along the placental boundary does not generally include blood cells, except in the case of rupture. Ruptures, however, do occur normally at birth, so that fetal blood enters the mother's system, stimulating the production of antibodies. Such antibodies do not occur naturally, as in the ABO system, but are produced "on the spot" quite quickly. About 70 percent of all Rh⁻ people have the capability of producing significant amounts of these antibodies, and it requires only one drop of blood to stimulate the process!

When the next pregnancy occurs, transfer of the antibodies from the mother's system takes place across the placental boundary into the fetus. Here is the real problem: The anti-Rh⁺ antibodies react with the fetal blood, causing cell destruction. Consequently, the fetus will be born with a severe malady called *hemolytic disease of the newborn*, which produces severe anemia with accompanying "oxygen starvation." Because of the lack of oxygen, such newborns are sometimes called "blue babies." In recent decades, doctors, prepared in advance for such complications, administered massive transfusions and often saved the infant. However, previous to modern medical treatment, this disease was probably nearly always fatal. Such incompatibilities were thus fairly common in polymorphic populations and should have exerted a powerful selection pressure.

More recently, physicians have sought to prevent incompatibilities by administering serum containing anti-Rh⁺ antibodies to women at risk after their first birth. These antibodies quickly destroy any fetal red blood cells as they enter the mother's circulation, thereby preventing her from forming her own antibodies. Since the serum given the mother is a passive form of immunization (to her), it will shortly leave her bloodstream. Thus, she does not produce any long-acting antibodies, and the quite low risk of first pregnancies should not be increased in the future.

It should also be mentioned that mother-fetus incompatibilities result from ABO as well. However, these are considerably rarer than Rh complications, with less than 0.1 percent of newborns affected. It is possible, though, that some ABO incompatibilities go undetected owing to early fetal death.

A very interesting relationship appears to exist between Rh and ABO incompatibilities. Surprisingly, if the fetus is *both* ABO and Rh incompatible with the mother, the effects are less than if the incompatibility were for only one trait. ABO

smell it, while others could not. It was later established that there is a dichotomy among humans regarding those who can versus those who cannot taste PTC. Although tasters vary considerably in sensitivity, most report a very bitter, unpleasant sensation. The pattern of inheritance follows a Mendelian model, with the inability to taste behaving as a simple recessive. In most populations, a majority of individuals are tasters, but the frequency of nontasters varies dramatically—from as low as 5 percent in Africa to as high as 40 percent in India.

The evolutionary function of this polymorphism is not known, although the fact that it is also seen in some other primates argues that it has a long history. Obviously, evolution has not acted to produce discrimination for an artificial

FIRST PREGNANCY

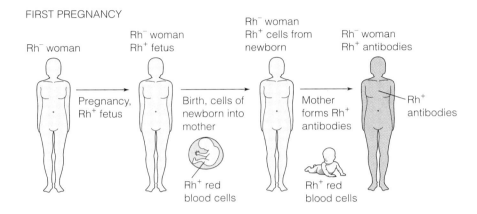

FIGURE 1
Rh incompatibility and hemolytic disease of the newborn: the series of events during first and later pregnancies. (After Novitski, 1977.)

SUBSEQUENT PREGNANCIES

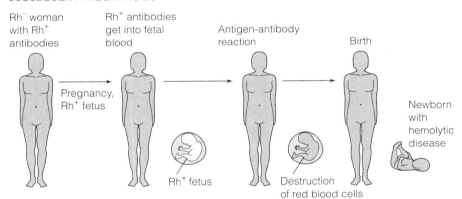

incompatibility seems to buffer the potentially very serious effects of Rh immunization. How this occurs is still unknown, but possibly the naturally occurring anti-A and/or anti-B antibodies coat and inactivate incoming cells, thus preventing them from stimulating the Rh immune response in the mother's system.

substance recently concocted by humans. The observed variation *may* reflect selection for taste discrimination of other, more significant substances. Indeed, taste discrimination, which may allow the avoidance of many toxic plants (which frequently are bitter), may well be an important evolutionary consideration (see p. 165 for a further discussion).

Another puzzling human polymorphism is the variability seen in earwax, or cerumen. Earwax is found in human groups in two basic varieties: (1) yellow and sticky with a good deal of lipids (fats and fatlike substances) and (2) gray and dry with fewer lipids. Cerumen variation appears also to be inherited as a simple Mendelian trait with two alleles (sticky is dominant; dry is recessive).

Interestingly, frequencies of the two varieties of earwax vary considerably among human populations. In European populations, about 90 percent of individuals typically have the sticky variety, while in northern China, only about 4 percent are of this type.

How do we explain these differences? Even between very large groups there are consistent differences in cerumen type, arguing that drift is an unlikely causal mechanism. However, it is difficult to imagine what kind of selective pressure would act directly on earwax. Perhaps, like that previously suggested for PTC discrimination, earwax variation is an incidental expression of a gene controlling something more adaptively significant. Suggestions along these lines have pointed to the relation of cerumen to other body secretions, especially those affecting odor. Certainly, other mammals, including nonhuman primates, pay considerable attention to smell stimuli. Although the sense of smell is not as well developed in humans as in other mammals, humans still process and utilize olfactory (smell) stimuli. Thus, it is not impossible that during the course of human evolution, genes affecting bodily secretions (including earwax) came under selective influence.

Polymorphisms at the DNA Level

Geneticists and physical anthropologists over the last 50 years have used somewhat indirect techniques to study human polymorphisms, observing some *phenotypic* products. For example, the ABO antigens are phenotypic products (quite immediate ones) of the DNA locus coding for them. In the last decade, with the revolution in DNA technology, much more *direct* means have become available by which to study human genetic variation.

mtDNA   In addition to the DNA found in the nucleus (nuclear DNA), human (and other eukaryotic) cells contain another kind of DNA. This DNA, found in the cytoplasm, is contained within the organelles called mitochondria—and is thus called **mitochondrial DNA (mtDNA)**. While nuclear DNA is extraordinarily long, containing an estimated 3 billion nucleotides, mtDNA is much shorter, containing only 16,500 nucleotides. Using special enzymes (restriction enzymes, derived from bacteria) that cut the DNA in specific locations, researchers have been able to sequence much of the mtDNA **genome**. Thus, it has become possible to compare variation among individuals and among populations. Ongoing work is establishing that some mtDNA regions are more variable than others but that for the *total* mtDNA genome, variation within *Homo sapiens* is apparently much less pronounced than in other species (e.g., chimpanzees). The possible evolutionary reasons for this surprising finding might relate to a quite recent origin of all modern *Homo sapiens* from a restricted ancestral population base (thus producing genetic drift/founder effect). We will return to this topic in our discussion of the evolutionary origin of modern humans in Chapter 16.

Nuclear DNA   As with mtDNA analysis, the use of restriction enzymes has permitted much greater precision in direct study of the DNA contained within human chromosomes, that is, nuclear DNA. This work has been greatly facilitated as part of the continuing intense research of the **Human Genome Project**. Untangling the entire human genetic complement is obviously an enormous undertaking, but to date, considerable insight has been gained regarding human variation *directly at the DNA level*. By cutting the DNA of different individuals and comparing the results, researchers have observed great variation in the

▲ **Mitochondrial DNA (mtDNA)**
DNA found in the mitochondria (structures found within the cytoplasm of the cell) and inherited through the maternal line.

▲ **Genome**
The full genetic complement of an individual (or of a species). In humans, it is estimated that each individual possesses approximately 3 billion nucleotides in his or her nuclear DNA.

▲ **Human Genome Project**
A multinational effort designed to map (and ultimately sequence) the complete genetic complement of *Homo sapiens*.

length of the DNA fragments at numerous DNA sites. Accordingly, these genetic differences (caused by variable DNA sequences) are referred to as **restriction fragment length polymorphisms (RFLPs)**. In addition to providing direct evidence of human genetic variation, the RFLPs are also of vital importance in mapping other loci (e.g., that for cystic fibrosis) to specific regions of specific chromosomes.

▲ **Restriction fragment length polymorphisms (RFLPs)**
Variation among individuals in the length of DNA fragments produced by enzymes that break the DNA at specific sites.

Human Biocultural Evolution

We have defined culture as the human strategy of adaptation. Human beings live in cultural environments that are continually modified by human activity; thus, evolutionary processes are understandable only within this *cultural* context. You will recall that natural selection pressures operate within specific environmental settings. For humans and many of our hominid ancestors, this means an environment dominated by culture. For example, the sickle-cell allele has not always been an important genetic factor in human populations. In fact, human cultural modification of environments apparently provided the initial stimulus. Before the development of agriculture, humans rarely, if ever, lived close to mosquito breeding areas. With the development and spread to Africa of **slash-and-burn agriculture**, perhaps in just the last 2,000 years, penetration and clearing of tropical rain forests occurred. As a result of deforestation, open, stagnant pools provided prime mosquito breeding areas in close proximity to human settlements.

Malaria, for the first time, struck human populations with its full impact, and as a selective force it was powerful indeed. No doubt, humans attempted to adjust culturally to these circumstances, and numerous biological adaptations also probably came into play. The sickle-cell trait is one of these biological adaptations. However, there is a definite cost involved with such an adaptation. Carriers have increased resistance to malaria and presumably higher reproductive success, but some of their offspring may be lost through the genetic disease sickle-cell anemia. So there is a counterbalancing of selective forces with an advantage for carriers *only* in malarial environments. The genetic patterns of recessive traits such as sickle-cell anemia are discussed in Chapter 4 (see p. 77).

Following World War II, extensive DDT spraying by the World Health Organization began systematically to wipe out mosquito breeding areas in the tropics. As would be expected, malaria decreased sharply, and also as would be expected, the frequency of the sickle-cell allele also seemed on the decline. The intertwined story of human cultural practices, mosquitoes, malarial parasites, and the sickle-cell allele is still not finished. Forty years of DDT spraying killed many mosquitoes, but, at the same time, natural selection has been acting on these insect populations. Because of the tremendous amount of genetic diversity among insects, as well as their short generation span, several DDT-resistant strains have arisen and spread in the last few years (Fig. 5–2). Accordingly, malaria is again on the rise, with several hundred thousand new cases reported in India, Africa, and Central America.

A genetic trait (such as sickle-cell trait) that provides a reproductive advantage to the heterozygote in certain environments is a clear example of natural selection in action among human populations. The precise evolutionary mechanism in the sickle-cell example is termed a **balanced polymorphism**. A *polymorphism*, as we have defined it, is a trait with more than one allele in appreciable frequency. So when an allele like that for sickle-cell is found in a population in frequencies approaching 10 percent, this is clearly polymorphic. It is higher than

▲ **Slash-and-burn agriculture**
A traditional land-clearing practice whereby trees and vegetation are cut and burned. In many areas, fields were abandoned after a few years and clearing occurred elsewhere.

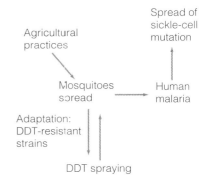

FIGURE 5–2
Evolutionary interactions affecting the frequency of the sickle-cell allele.

▲ **Balanced polymorphism**
The maintenance of two or more alleles in a population due to the selective advantage of the heterozygote.

BOX 5–3

Other Genetic Traits Possibly Associated with Malaria

In many parts of the world, malaria has been an extremely important selective factor over the last several thousand years. Sickle-cell is probably only one of several inherited traits that have spread because they provide resistance. It must be noted, however, that none of these other traits has been documented as well as sickle-cell, nor has there been conclusive experimental evidence comparable to the work of A. C. Allison (see p. 94). Concordance between higher incidence of these genetic traits with geographical areas exhibiting high malarial infection provides *indirect* evidence of possible association in the following:

1. Hemoglobin C—an allele of the same gene producing Hb^A and Hb^S; distributed in Africa mainly in the west but with a few pockets of high incidence in the south. Hb^c is found in many populations where Hb^S is also present. Possibly this allele provides resistance to another strain of malaria and *both* alleles occur in populations exposed to multiple varieties of malaria (Weiss and Mann, 1981).

2. Thalassemia—a general term for several inherited disorders. Rather than a defect in the hemoglobin molecule itself, thalassemias involve a block in hemoglobin production (absence of, or deficient production of, the alpha or beta globin molecules). There are probably a variety of genetic mechanisms (mutations) that can lead to thalassemia, including point mutations, deletions, and disruption of gene regulation. For example, one variety of thalassemia (β^+) is caused by inadequate production of mRNA; consequently, protein synthesis of the beta hemoglobin chain is disrupted. The most harmful expression of this disease syndrome is seen in homozygotes, producing severe anemia. In heterozygotes, there are lit-

tle, if any, harmful effects. Geographical evidence suggests a possible connection between thalassemia and malaria, with the highest frequencies of the disease found among populations around the Mediterranean. The severe form of beta-thalassemia affects as many as 1 percent of newborns in some parts of southern Europe. Tentative experimental evidence suggests that in heterozygotes, thalassemia—like sickle-cell—provides an inadequate environment for malarial infestation and proliferation (Friedman and Trager, 1981).

3. G-6-PD—glucose-6-phosphate dehydrogenase—an enzyme in red blood cells; individuals with a genetically caused deficiency do not produce this enzyme. The gene for this trait is on the X chromosome (i.e., X-linked), and some populations are up to 60 percent deficient (Bodmer and Cavalli-Sforza, 1976). First discovered by adverse reactions with severe anemia when individuals were given certain antimalarial drugs, anemia can also result from exposure to some foods (fava beans, for example). Distribution is again correlated with malarial areas, but apparently the alleles that cause the deficiency in southern Europe are different from those in sub-Saharan Africa. At the biochemical level, G-6-PD deficiency may act like thalassemia, producing a cellular environment not conducive to malarial infection. When exposed to certain drugs or foods (particularly fava beans), individuals with G-6-PD deficiency may have a severe anemic reaction. It is possible, however, that heterozygous carriers may actually increase malarial resistance by eating such foods—potentially an extremely important biocultural interaction (Friedman and Trager, 1981).

can be accounted for by mutation *alone* and thus demands a fuller evolutionary explanation. In this case, the additional mechanism is natural selection.

This brings us back to the other part of the term *balanced polymorphism.* By "balanced," we are referring to the interaction of selective pressures operating in a malarial environment. Some individuals (mainly homozygous normals) will be removed by the infectious disease malaria and some (homozygous recessives) will die of the inherited disease sickle-cell anemia. Those with the highest reproductive success are the heterozygous carriers. But what alleles do they carry? Clearly, they are passing *both* the "normal" allele as well as the sickle-cell allele to offspring, thus maintaining both alleles at fairly high frequencies (*above* the minimum level for polymorphism). Since one allele in this population will not significantly increase in frequency over the other allele, this situation will reach a balance and persist, at least as long as malaria continues to be a selective factor.

Two other traits that may also be influenced by the selective agent of malaria are G-6-PD deficiency and the thalessemias (results of several different mutations that act to block hemoglobin production). However, in both these cases, evidence of natural selection is not as strong as with the sickle-cell allele. The primary evidence suggesting a link with malaria is the geographical concordance of increased frequency of these traits with areas (especially around the Mediterranean) that historically have had a high incidence of malarial infection (see Box 5–3).

Another example of human biocultural evolution concerns the ability to digest milk. In all human populations, infants and young children can digest milk, an obvious necessity for any young mammal. A major ingredient of milk is the sugar *lactose*, which is broken down by humans and other mammals by the enzyme *lactase*. (The action of digestive enzymes and their role in human nutrition will be discussed in more detail in Chapter 7). In most mammals, including humans, the gene coding for lactase production "switches off" by adolescence. If too much milk is then ingested, it ferments in the large intestine, leading to diarrhea and severe gastrointestinal upset. Among many African and Asian populations—a majority of humankind today—most adults are intolerant of milk (Table 5–3).

Recent evidence has suggested a simple dominant mode of inheritance for **lactose intolerance**. The environment also plays a role in expression of the trait—that is, whether a person will be lactose-intolerant—since intestinal bacteria can somewhat buffer the adverse effects. Because these bacteria will increase with previous exposure, some tolerance can be acquired, even in individuals who genetically have become lactase-deficient.

Why do we see variation in lactose tolerance among human populations? Throughout most of hominid evolution, no milk was available after weaning. Perhaps, in such circumstances, continued action of an unnecessary enzyme might inhibit digestion of other foods. Therefore, there *may* be a selective advantage for the gene coding for lactase production to switch off. The question can then be asked: Why can some adults (the majority in some populations) tolerate milk? The distribution of lactose-tolerant populations is very interesting, revealing the probable influence of cultural factors on this trait.

European groups, who are generally lactose-tolerant, are partially descended from groups of the Middle East. Often economically dependent on pastoralism, these groups raised cows and/or goats and no doubt drank considerable quantities of milk. In such a cultural environment, strong selection pressures would act to shift allele frequencies in the direction of more lactose tolerance. Modern European descendants of these populations apparently retain this ancient ability.

Even more informative is the distribution of lactose tolerance in Africa. For example, groups such as the Fulani and Tutsi, who have been pastoralists probably for thousands of years, have much higher rates of lactose tolerance than non-pastoralists.

As we have seen, the geographical distribution of lactose tolerance is related to a history of cultural dependence on milk products. There are, however, some populations that rely on dairying, but are not characterized by high rates of lactose tolerance. It has been suggested that such populations traditionally have consumed their milk produce as cheese and other derivatives in which the lactose has been broken down by bacterial action (Durham, 1981).

▲ Lactose intolerance

The inability to digest fresh milk products; caused by the discontinued production of *lactase*, the enzyme that breaks down lactose, or milk sugar.

TABLE 5–3 Frequencies of Lactose Intolerance

Population Group	Percent
U.S. whites	2–19
Finnish	18
Swiss	12
Swedish	4
U.S. blacks	70–77
Ibos	99
Bantu	90
Fulani	22
Thais	99
Asian Americans	95–100
Native Australians	85

(Lerner and Libby, 1976, p. 327.)

The interaction of human cultural environments and changes in lactose tolerance among human populations is another example of biocultural evolution. In the last few thousand years, cultural factors have initiated specific evolutionary changes in human groups. Such cultural factors have probably influenced the course of human evolution for at least 3 million years, and today they are of paramount importance.

Patterns of Human Population Diversity

A fairly simple approach to help understand human genetic diversity is to look at the pattern of allele frequencies over space for *one* polymorphic trait at a time. Here, allele frequencies are shown geographically on a map in what is called a **cline**. Although we did not label it as such earlier, the distribution of the *B* allele in Eurasia (see Fig. 5–1b) is a good example of a cline. Another well-known example is the distribution of tawny (blond, depigmented) hair in Australia (Fig. 5–3).

Clinal distributions are generally thought to reflect microevolutionary influences of natural selection and/or gene flow. Thus, interpretation is usually explicitly framed in evolutionary terms. Regarding the tawny hair trait in Australia, Joseph Birdsell, of the University of California, Los Angeles, writes:

> The evolutionary significance of this clinal distribution [Fig. 5–4] seems apparent, even though the exact genetic basis for its inheritance has not yet been unraveled. The trait acts as though it was determined by a single codominant gene. It would appear that somewhere in the central region of high frequency, mutations, and probably repeated mutations, occurred from normal dark brown hair to this depigmented variety. The pattern of distribution indicates that it was favored by selection in some totally unknown fashion. Over considerable periods of time, through gene exchange between adjacent tribes,

▲ **Cline**

A gradient of genotypes (usually measured as allele frequencies) over geographical space; more exactly, the depiction of allele distribution produced by connecting points of equal frequency (as on a temperature map).

FIGURE 5–3

A native Australian with tawny hair.

the new mutant gene prospered and spread outward. It seems unlikely that lightly pigmented hair in childhood should in itself have any selective advantage. Rather, it is much more probable that certain effects of this mutant gene have somehow biochemically heightened the fitness of these [native Australians] in their generally desert environment (Birdsell, 1981, pp. 352–353).

Utilizing single traits can be informative regarding potential influences of natural selection or gene flow, but this approach has limitations when we try to sort out population relationships. As noted in our discussion of the HLA polymorphisms, single traits *by themselves* often can yield confusing interpretations regarding likely population relationships. What is needed, then, is a method to analyze a larger, more consistent body of data—that is, to look at several traits simultaneously. Such a *multivariate* approach makes ready use of digital computers. (In the next chapter, we will discuss the more traditional approach using polygenic characteristics and some of the controversies surrounding "racial" classification.)

An excellent example of the contemporary multivariate approach to human diversity was undertaken by Harvard population geneticist R. D. Lewontin (1972), and his results are most informative. Lewontin calculated population differences in allele frequency for 17 polymorphic traits. In his analysis, Lewontin immediately faced a dilemma: Which groups (populations) should he contrast, and how should they be weighted? That is, should larger population segments,

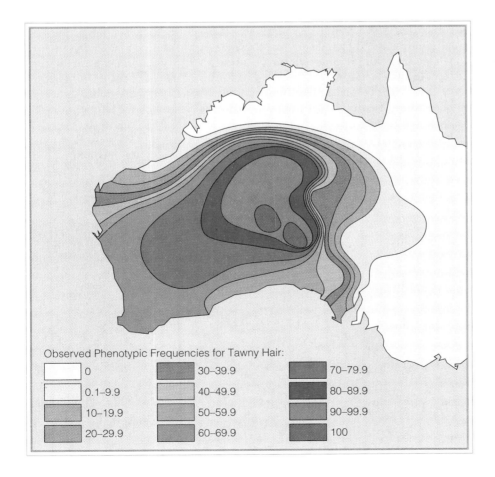

Observed Phenotypic Frequencies for Tawny Hair:

0	30–39.9	70–79.9
0.1–9.9	40–49.9	80–89.9
10–19.9	50–59.9	90–99.9
20–29.9	60–69.9	100

FIGURE 5–4

Phenotypic distribution of tawny hair in Australia. Note the concentration of tawny hair in the center of the distribution, which can be traced by clines in a decreasing gradient.

such as Arabs, carry the same weight in the analysis as small populations, such as the one from the island Tristan da Cunha? After considerable deliberation, Lewontin decided to break down his sample into seven geographical areas, and he included several equally weighted population samples within each (Table 5–4). He then calculated how much of the total genetic variability within our species could be accounted for by these population subdivisions.

The results are surprising. Only 6.3 percent of the total genetic variation is explained by differences among major populations (Lewontin's seven geographical units). In other words, close to 94 percent of human genetic diversity occurs *within* these very large groups. The larger population subdivisions, within the geographical clusters (e.g., within Caucasians: Arabs, Basques, Welsh) account for another 8.3 percent. Thus, geographical and local "races" together account for just 15 percent of all human genetic variation, leaving the remaining 85 percent unaccounted for.

The vast majority of genetic differences among human beings is explicable in terms of differences from one village to another, one family to another, and, to a very significant degree, one person to another—even within the same family. Of course, when you recall the high degree of genetic polymorphism (discussed in this chapter) combined with the vast number of combinations resulting from recombination during meiosis (discussed in Chapter 3), all this individual variation should not be that surprising.

Our superficial visual perceptions tell us that race does exist. But the visible phenotypic traits most frequently used to make racial distinctions (skin color, hair form, nose shape, etc.) may very well produce a highly biased sample, not giving an accurate picture of the actual pattern of *genetic variation*. The simple polymorphic traits discussed in this chapter (many of the same used by Lewontin) are a more objective basis for accurate biological comparisons of human groups, and they indicate that the traditional concept of race is very limited. Indeed, Lewontin concludes his analysis with a ringing condemnation of traditional studies: "Human racial classification is of no social value and is positively destructive of social and human relations. Since such racial classification is now seen to be of virtually no genetic or taxonomic significance either, no justification can be offered for its continuance" (Lewontin, 1972, p. 397).

However, not all population geneticists are this critical. After all, Lewontin did find that about 6 percent of human variation is accounted for by the large geographical population segments traditionally called major "races." Whereas

TABLE 5–4   Population Groupings Used by Lewontin in Population Genetics Study (1972)

Geographical Group	Examples of Populations Included
Caucasians	Arabs, Armenians, Tristan da Cunhans
Black Africans	Bantu, San, U.S. blacks
Asians	Ainu, Chinese, Turks
South Asians	Andamanese, Tamils
Amerinds	Aleuts, Navaho, Yanomama
Oceanians	Easter Islanders, Micronesians
Australians	All treated as a single group

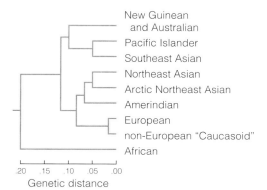

New Guinean
  and Australian
Pacific Islander
Southeast Asian
Northeast Asian
Arctic Northeast Asian
Amerindian
European
non-European "Caucasoid"
African

.20   .15   .10   .05   .00
Genetic distance

FIGURE 5–4

Genetic tree (dendrogram) showing population relationships. This dendrogram was constructed by population geneticists (Cavalli-Sforza et al., 1988) using 44 polymorphic traits.

this is certainly a minority of all human genetic variation, it is not necessarily biologically insignificant.

If one feels compelled to continue to classify humankind into large geographical segments, population genetics offers some aid in isolating consistent patterns of genetic variation. Following and expanding on the approach used by Lewontin, population geneticist L. L. Cavalli-Sforza, of Stanford University, and colleagues evaluated 44 different polymorphic traits ascertained in 42 different human sample populations. From the results, these researchers constructed a "tree" (technically called a dendrogram) depicting the relationships of these samples as part of larger populations (Cavalli-Sforza et al., 1988) (Fig. 5–4). Analysis of mitochondrial DNA has produced similar results, especially showing greater genetic diversity among African populations than among other groups (Stoneking, 1993). Because mtDNA is passed solely through the maternal line (and thus does not undergo recombination), it has certain advantages in reconstructing population relationships. Nevertheless, as a single genetic component, it acts like one large locus; thus, mtDNA results must be supplemented by other genetic data.

Comparative data from nuclear DNA studies (RFLPs) in conjunction with the studies discussed here are thus potentially illuminating. Initial analysis comparing 80 RFLPs in eight different groups (Mountain et al., 1993) again produced patterns quite similar to those established for the traditional polymorphisms and for mtDNA. However, another recent large-scale study (Jia and Chakraborty, 1993) of DNA markers among 59 different groups (and including about 12,000 individuals) found the vast majority of variation (up to 98.5 percent) occurring *within* populations at the *individual* level. These latest data dramatize even further the results obtained by Lewontin, leading one geneticist to conclude, "These results indicate that individual variation in DNA profiles overwhelm any interpopulational differences, no matter how the populations are ethnically or racially classified" (Cummings, 1994, p. 500). And while not quite as overwhelming, *all* the genetically based studies cited here support Lewontin's initial results, strongly indicating that the great majority of human variation does occur within human populations—not between them. How, then, do these genetic data compare and articulate with the traditional concept of race? We turn to this topic in the next chapter.

Summary

In this chapter, we have discussed human variation from an evolutionary perspective. We have focused on the contemporary trend to describe simple genetic polymorphisms that can be measured for allele frequencies as well as emphasizing genetic data obtained directly from analysis of mitochondrial and nuclear DNA.

Moreover, we have reviewed the theoretical basis of the *population genetics* approach, the subdiscipline of physical anthropology that seeks to *measure* genetic diversity among humans. Data on polymorphic traits can be used to understand aspects of human microevolution. For humans, of course, culture also plays a crucial evolutionary role, and the sickle-cell trait and lactose intolerance are thus discussed from an explicit biocultural perspective.

Finally, data derived from population genetics analysis of genetic polymorphisms and DNA variation are employed to evaluate major patterns of human population diversity. From such studies, large population groups (analogous to race) are shown to be of limited utility, but potentially may be used from a population genetics perspective—if these limitations are recognized.

Questions for Review

1. How is a population defined? Discuss why, in human groups, defining particular populations can be very difficult.
2. What is meant by genetic equilibrium?
3. What is meant by nonrandom mating? Give two examples, and discuss how relevant such factors are in human evolution.
4. How has the sickle-cell allele come to be common in some parts of the world? Why is it thought to be a good example of natural selection?
5. What biocultural interactions have occurred that help explain the distribution of lactose intolerance?
6. Discuss how genetic drift may have influenced the geographical distribution of the *A*, *B*, and *O* alleles.
7. Discuss how population genetics data can be used to assess the genetic diversity among different populations. How well do the varied data from simple polymorphisms, mtDNA, and nuclear DNA agree with one another?

Suggested Further Reading

Bodmer, W. F., and L. L. Cavalli-Sforza. 1976. *Genetics, Evolution and Man.* San Francisco: Freeman.

Cummings, Michael R. 1994. *Human Heredity: Principles and Issues.* 3rd ed. St. Paul: West.

Durham, W. 1991. *Coevolution: Genes, Culture and Human Diversity.* Stanford: Stanford University Press.

Lewontin, R. 1974. *The Genetic Basis of Evolutionary Change.* New York: Columbia University Press.

Internet Resources

Cavalli Lab

http://lorka.stanford.edu

(Contains information regarding the Human Genome Diversity Project.)

Quantitative Genetics Resources

http://nitro.biosci.arizona.edu/zbook/book.html

(An electronic supplement for the textbook *Fundamentals of Quantitative Genetics* by Mike Lynch and Bruce Walsh; Walsh maintains the Web site.)

Linda L. Klepinger

Linda L. Klepinger holds a Ph.D. in anthropology from the University of Kansas. She is currently Professor of Anthropology at the University of Illinois at Urbana-Champaign. Her research focuses on skeletal biology and chemistry, forensic anthropology and paleopathology. She is a member of the American Association of Physical Anthropologists, the American Association for the Advancement of Science, Paleopathology Association, a Fellow of the American Academy of Forensic Sciences, and a Diplomate of the American Board of Forensic Anthropology.

In retrospective statements about his life, Heinrich Schliemann claimed that when he was eight years old he had decided that he would discover and excavate Troy. My career decision was not nearly so precocious. In fact, I did not really know what anthropology was until I was about 24 years old. At that time, I was a graduate student in inorganic chemistry investigating the subtleties of isotopic exchange in borohydrides, a topic of considerable interest at the time not only for theoretical considerations about chemical bonding, but also because many of these compounds were so explosive on contact with air that they were believed to have some potential as rocket fuel. This latter trait I found to be the source of some anxiety.

Then two events worked in concert to redirect my academic focus. First, I sat in on a class entitled Comparative Psychology that my husband, a psychology graduate student, was taking. This course explored, among other topics, the evolutionary roots of human behavior, including laboratory and field studies of nonhuman primate behavior and cognition, and inferences about the behavior of departed hominid forebears. I had to abashedly admit that I found this subject a good deal more interesting than boron chemistry and wondered if it were psychologists who usually studied this sort of thing. At that time the answer was "no"; it was more in the realm of ethology and anthropology. Anthropology? (I should point out that currently some psychologists and anthropolo-

gists work cooperatively in investigating evolutionary aspects of human behavior.)

About the same time I became good friends with a neighbor who had introduced himself as a graduate student in anthropology. Anthropology? He was studying skeletal remains from archaeological sites in order to assess biological distances and paleopathology. During several evening forays into his lab, he pointed out to me some techniques for determining age and sex and markers of certain diseases that could be read from the skeletons. I was completely amazed that so much information could be derived from bones (without the necessity of wearing a pointy hat with stars on it). I wound up spending more time in his laboratory than in my own, and decided to check out anthropology in a more formal manner, i.e., I began taking courses. These courses were not just in physical anthropology, but included archeology and sociocultural anthropology. I was not disappointed. My increasing interest in anthropology was matched by an increasingly flagging interest in chemistry. This trend culminated one day at my lab when I realized that I did not really care whether those boron isotopes exchanged or not.

Although I flirted with archeology and cultural anthropology, the study of archeological skeletal material attracted me the most. By a fortunate twist of fate (well, . . . perhaps manipulation), my husband decided to accept a job at the University of Kansas, a school that boasted three faculty members (Professors Bass, Kerley, and McKern) who specialized in various aspects of human osteology. I applied to graduate school in anthropology and was accepted. It was during my studies at KU that I was introduced to forensic anthropology, the application of physical anthropology to the realm of medico-legal investigation, although bioarcheology and paleopathology dominated my doctoral and early postdoctoral research.

So were the years I spent studying chemistry a waste of societal, parental, and personal resources? As it turned out, not at all. My first application of chemistry in the service of bioarcheology came during my study of skeletal material from the Formative period of Ecuador. A museum collection of skulls from the Late Formative exhibited what appeared to be an excessive buildup of dental calculus (tartar) that was not apparent on teeth from the Early Formative. Was this really dental calculus or some sort of concretion deposited on the dentition after burial? Analyses run by two chemists whose aid I had enlisted established that the material was indeed calculus, leaving only the question of cause (probably habitual chewing of coca leaves with lime). The success of that project

encouraged me to attempt again to employ chemistry as a handmaiden to anthropology, specifically to probe further the usefulness of the elemental composition of archeological bone as a direct measure of certain aspects of prehistoric diet. Some earlier reports had offered promise that the concentrations of certain elements in the inorganic phase of bone might reflect such dietary features as the relative proportions of meat and vegetable resources consumed in the past. Unfortunately, many of the previously made assumptions did not hold up well under the closer scrutiny of more controlled tests. For instance, postmortem chemical alteration (diagenesis) was often unpredictable, and even the correlation of dietary consumption to various bone clinical concentrations was often questionable or outright false. The good news was that bone was amenable to chemical analysis; the bad news was that it didn't always give interpretable answers.

In the meantime I was gradually becoming more involved in the forensic aspects of anthropology. Along with several of my colleagues in the field, I began to scrutinize and test methodologies and assumptions. I also found that the lessons of paleopathology have great

crossover value in case work. Recently, I have been amazed at the extent to which forensic cases and related research can inform us about basic functional anatomy and other skeletal phenomena that have application to studies of prehistory. The passage of information between bioarcheology and forensics is a two-way path.

Does skeletal biology have a future in an era of DNA analysis? Does the potential for DNA extraction and amplification from skeletons of the recently and long dead threaten to relegate osteology to the curiosity cabinet of the quaint and obsolete? If I may don the pointy hat with stars on it and try to gaze into the future, I would say no. There will be too many cases in which no useful DNA remains. In the forensic situation, basic skeletal analysis to establish a short list of possible identifications is needed before trying to match the remains with living relatives; time and resources for DNA matching are not unlimited. In the bioarcheological context basic skeletal and archeological data are prerequisite to formulating the questions to be asked of the DNA data. Somehow, we need to ensure that hands-on training of future skeletal biologists will continue.

6

Approaches to Human Variation and Adaptation

Introduction

In Chapters 3 and 4, we saw how physical characteristics are influenced by the DNA in our cells. Furthermore, we discussed how individuals inherit genes from parents and how variations in genes (alleles) can produce different expressions of phenotypic traits. In Chapter 5, we emphasized the study of Mendelian traits in our discussion of evolutionary factors in human populations.

In this chapter, our focus shifts to polygenic traits, or traits that express continuous variation. In particular, we examine how these traits have been used as a basis for traditional *racial* classification, and we look at some of the issues that currently surround the topic of race in physical anthropology.

Following our discussion of historical attempts at racial classification, we look at more recent explanations of certain polygenic traits; instead of emphasizing their utility as "racial markers," we focus on their adaptive value in specific environmental contexts. We also examine how populations and individuals differ in their adaptive responses to such environmental factors as heat, cold, and high altitude. Finally, we consider the role of infectious disease in human evolution and adaptation.

The Concept of Race

▲ **Polytypic**

Referring to species composed of populations that differ with regard to the expression of one or more traits.

All contemporary humans are members of the same **polytypic** species, *Homo sapiens.* A polytypic species is one composed of local populations that differ from one another with regard to the expression of one or more traits. Moreover, *within* local populations there is a great deal of phenotypic (and genotypic) variation between individuals. Most species are polytypic, and consequently, there is no species "type" to which all members exactly conform.

In discussions of human variation, people have traditionally clumped together various attributes such as skin color, shape of the face, shape of the nose, hair color, hair form (curly or straight), and eye color. People possessing particular *combinations* of these and other traits have been placed together into categories associated with specific geographical localities. Such categories are called *races.*

Although we all think we know what we mean by the word *race*, in reality race is an elusive concept. Furthermore, ever since the term gained common usage in English in the 1500s, it has had a wide assortment of definitions, generally referring to groups of organisms that are descended from a common ancestor. Also, since the late 1500s, while most definitions of "race" have had biological implications, some have carried cultural and social connotations.

"Race" has been used synonymously with *species*, as in "the human race," or to refer to a more limited grouping of individuals all descended from a single individual (e.g., "the race of Abraham"). One also hears phrases such as "the English race" or "the Japanese race," where the reference is to nationality. Another often-heard phrase is "the Jewish race," when the speaker is talking about a particular ethnic and religious identity.

Thus, while "race" is usually used as a biological term, or at least one with biological connotations, it is also one with enormous social significance. Moreover, there is still a widespread perception that there is an association between certain physical traits (skin color, in particular) and numerous cultural attributes (such as language, occupational preferences, or even morality). Thus, in many cultural contexts, a person's *social identity* is strongly influenced by the manner in which he or she expresses those physical traits traditionally used to define "racial groups." Characteristics such as skin color are highly visible, and they facilitate an immediate and superficial designation of individuals into socially defined categories. However, so-called racial traits are not the only phenotypic expressions that contribute to social identity. Sex and age are also critically important. But aside from these two variables, an individual's biological and/or *ethnic* background is still inevitably a factor that influences how he or she is initially perceived and judged by others, especially in diverse societies.

The use of expressions of national origin (e.g., African, Asian) or the terms "ethnic" or "ethnicity" as substitutes for racial labels and "race" has become more common in recent years, both within and outside anthropology. Within anthropology, "ethnicity" was proposed in the early 1950s as a means of avoiding the use of "race," which was seen as a more emotionally charged term. Strictly speaking, "ethnicity" refers to cultural factors, and for this reason, some have objected to its use in discussions that also include biological characteristics. However, the fact that "ethnicity" and "race" are used interchangeably reflects the social importance of phenotypic expression and demonstrates once again how phenotype is associated with culturally defined variables.

In its most common biological usage, "race" refers to geographically patterned phenotypic variation within a species. By the seventeenth century, naturalists began to describe races in plants and nonhuman animals, because they recognized that when populations of a species occupied different regions, they sometimes differed from one another in the expression of one or more traits. But even today, there are no established criteria by which races of plants and animals are to be assessed. To a biologist studying nonhuman forms, the degree of genetic difference necessary for racial distinctions is a subjective issue, determined in part by the investigator and in part by the species in question. However, if we are to apply the term to humans, we must elucidate very precisely the degree of genetic difference that exists between individuals *within* populations as well as *between* populations.

In Chapter 5, you learned that the *genetic* perspective is a contemporary view of human variation. Prior to World War II, most scientific studies of human diversity focused on phenotypic variation between large, geographically defined populations, and these studies were largely descriptive. Since that time, the emphasis has shifted to the examination of differences in allele frequencies within and between populations as well as the adaptive significance of phenotypic and genotypic variation. This shift in focus occurred partly as the outcome of historical trends in biological science in general and physical anthropology in particular. Especially crucial to this shift was the emergence of the modern synthesis in biology (see p. 87), which was based on the recognition of the fundamental importance of the *interaction* of natural selection and genetic factors to the process of evolution.

Application of evolutionary principles to the study of modern human variation replaced the nineteenth-century view of race *based solely on observed phenotype*. Additionally, the genetic emphasis dispelled previously held misconceptions that races were fixed biological units that did not change over time, and that were composed of individuals who all conformed to a particular *type*.

Clearly, there are phenotypic differences between humans, and these differences roughly correspond to particular geographical locations. It is unlikely that anyone would mistake a person of Asian descent for one of northern European ancestry. But certain questions must be asked: What is the adaptive significance attached to observed phenotypic variation? What is the degree of underlying genetic variation that influences it? And how important is that genetic variation? These questions place considerations of human variation within a contemporary evolutionary framework.

Although, in part, physical anthropology has its roots in attempts to explain human diversity, anthropologists have never been quite comfortable with the controversial topic of race. Even attempts to reach a consensus in defining the term have consistently failed. Among physical anthropologists there is still sometimes heated debate over whether it is justifiable to apply racial concepts to humans at all.

Today, some anthropologists recognize population patterning corresponding to at least three major racial groups, each composed of several subgroupings. However, no contemporary scholar subscribes to pre-Darwinian and pre-modern synthesis concepts of races (human and nonhuman) as fixed biological entities, the members of which all conform to specific types. Among those who accept the validity of the race concept, there are various viewpoints. Many who continue to use broad racial categories do not view them as particularly important, especially from a genetic perspective, because the amount of genetic variation accounted for by differences *between* groups is vastly exceeded by the variation that exists *within* groups (see Chapter 5, p. 124). But given these considerations, there are scholars who see variation in outwardly expressed phenotype, because of its potential adaptive value, as worthy of investigation and explanation within the framework of evolutionary principles (Brues, 1991).

Forensic anthropologists in particular find the phenotypic criteria associated with race to have practical applications because they are frequently called on by law enforcement agencies to assist in the identification of human skeletal remains. Inasmuch as unidentified human remains are often those of crime victims, and their analysis may lead to courtroom testimony, identification must be as accurate as possible. The most important variables in such identification are the individual's sex, age, stature, and "racial" or "ethnic" background. Using metric and nonmetric criteria, forensic anthropologists employ a number of techniques for establishing broad population affinity, and they are generally able to do so with about 80 percent accuracy.

On the other side of the issue, there are numerous physical anthropologists who argue that race is a meaningless concept when applied to humans. Race is seen as an outdated creation of the human mind that attempts to simplify biological complexity by organizing it into categories. Thus, human races are a product of the human tendency to superimpose order on complex natural phenomena. While classification may have been an acceptable approach some 150 years ago, it is viewed as no longer valid given the current state of genetic and evolutionary science.

Objections to racial taxonomies have also been raised because classification schemes are *typological* in nature, meaning that categories are discrete and based on stereotypes or ideals that comprise a specific set of traits. Thus, in general, typologies are inherently misleading, because there are always many individuals in any grouping who do not conform to all aspects of a particular type.

In any so-called racial group, there will be individuals who fall into the normal range of variation for another group with regard to one or several characteristics. For example, two people of different ancestry might vary with regard to skin color, but they could share any number of other traits, such as height, shape of head, hair color, eye color, or ABO blood type. In fact, they could easily share more similarities with each other than they do with many members of their own populations. (Remember, at most, only about 6 percent of genetic difference among humans has been shown to be due to differences between *large* geographical groups.)

Moreover, as we have stressed, because the characteristics that have traditionally been used to define races are polygenic, they exhibit a continuous range of expression. It thus becomes difficult, if not impossible, to draw discrete boundaries between populations with regard to many traits. This limitation becomes clear if you ask yourself, "At what point is hair color no longer dark brown but medium brown; or no longer light brown but blond?"

The scientific controversy over race is not likely to disappear. It has received considerable attention outside academia in popular publications such as *Newsweek* and *Discover*. But in spite of all the scientific discussion that has ensued, among the general public, variations on the theme of race will undoubtedly continue to be the most common view of human biological and cultural variation. Given this fact, it falls to anthropologists and biologists to continue to explore the issue so that, to the best of our abilities, accurate information regarding human variation is available for anyone who seeks informed explanations of complex phenomena.

Historical Views of Human Variation

The first step toward human understanding of natural phenomena is the ordering of variation into categories that can then be named, discussed, and perhaps studied. Historically, when different groups of people came into contact with one another, they offered explanations for the phenotypic variations they saw, and because skin color was so noticeable, it was one of the more frequently explained traits and most systems of racial classification came to be based on it.

As early as 1350 B.C., the ancient Egyptians had classified humans on the basis of skin color: red for Egyptian, yellow for people to the east, white for those to the north, and black for Africans from the south (Gossett, 1963, p. 4).

The ancient Greeks referred to all black Africans as "Ethiopians," meaning "scorched ones" (Brues, 1990), implying a response to exposure to the sun. Ovid, a first-century A.D. Roman poet, presents us with a Greek myth that offers an environmental explanation for the deeply pigmented skin of sub-Saharan Africans (Book Two of Ovid's *Metamorphoses*). The sun god, Apollo, ill-advisedly allowed his adolescent son Phaeton to drive the chariot of the sun through its daily round across the sky. Feeling an unfamiliar hand upon the reins, the fiery chariot horses bolted, and in their frenzy, they plummeted toward earth. In the end, Apollo was forced to kill Phaeton to keep earth from burning, and as Ovid tells us:

> . . . that was when, or so men think, the people
> Of Africa turned black, since the blood was driven
> By that fierce heat to the surface of their bodies
> (Humphries, 1973, p. 35)

In the sixteenth century, after the discovery of the New World, Europe embarked on a period of intense exploration and colonization in both the New and Old Worlds. Resulting from this contact was an increased awareness of human diversity.

As you learned in Chapter 2, the discovery of the New World was of major importance in altering the views of Europeans, who had perceived the world as static and nonchanging. One of the most influential discoveries of the early European explorers was that the Americas were inhabited by people, some of whom were dark-skinned (compared to most Europeans). Furthermore, these people were not Christian, and they were not considered "civilized" by Europeans. At first, Native Americans were thought to be Asian, and since Columbus believed that he had discovered a new route to India, he called them

▲ **Monogenism**
The theory that all human populations are descended from one pair (Adam and Eve), but they differ from one another because they have occupied different habitats. This concept was an attempt to explain phenotypic variation between groups, but did not imply evolutionary change.

▲ **Polygenism**
A theory, opposed to monogenism, that stated that human "races" were not all descended from Adam and Eve. Instead, there had been several original human pairs, each giving rise to a different racial group. Thus, human "races" were considered to be separate species.

▲ **Plasticity**
The capacity to change; in a physiological context, the ability of systems or organisms to make alterations in order to respond to differing conditions.

"Indians." (This term was later applied to indigenous, dark-skinned populations of Australia as well.)

By the late eighteenth century, Europeans and European Americans were asking questions that challenged traditional Christian beliefs. They wanted to know if other groups belonged to the same species as themselves; that is, were Native Americans and other indigenous peoples indeed human? Were they descendants of Adam and Eve, or had there been later creations of non-Europeans? If the latter were true, then Native Americans had to represent a different species, or else the Genesis account of creation could not be taken literally.

Two schools of thought, known as **monogenism** and **polygenism**, devised responses. In the monogenist view, all humans were descended from a single, original pair (Adam and Eve). Insisting on the **plasticity** of human structure, monogenists contended that local environmental conditions, such as climate and terrain, could modify the original form, resulting in observable phenotypic differences between populations. Monogenist views were initially attractive to many, for they did not conflict with the Genesis version of creation.

The polygenist view, on the other hand, argued that all populations did not descend from a single, original pair, but from a number of pairs. Also, polygenists saw such a wide gap in the physical, mental, and moral attributes between themselves and other peoples that they were sure that outsiders belonged to different species. Furthermore, polygenists did not accept the monogenist notion of plasticity of physical traits, and they rejected the proposition that climate and environment were modifying influences.

Throughout the eighteenth and nineteenth centuries, European and American scientists concentrated primarily on describing and classifying biological diversity as observed in humans as well as in nonhuman species. The first scientific attempt to categorize the newly discovered variation between human populations was Linnaeus' taxonomic classification, which placed humans into four separate groupings (Linnaeus, 1758) (Table 6–1). Linnaeus assigned behavioral and intellectual qualities to each group, with the least complimentary descriptions going to African blacks. This ranking was typical of the period and reflected the almost universal European view that Europeans were superior to all other peoples. (To be fair, we should note that the Europeans were not—and are not—the only people guilty of *ethnocentrism*. Most, if not all, human societies participate in the belief that their own culture is superior to others.)

Johann Friedrich Blumenbach (1752–1840), a German anatomist, classified humans into five categories or races (See Table 6–1). Although Blumenbach's categories came to be described simply as white, yellow, red, black, and brown, he also used criteria other than skin color. Moreover, Blumenbach emphasized that divisions based on skin color were arbitrary and that many traits, including skin color, were not discrete phenomena. Blumenbach pointed out that to attempt to classify all humans using such a system would be to omit completely all those who did not neatly fall into a specific category. Furthermore, it was recognized by Blumenbach and others that traits such as skin color showed overlapping expression between groups. At the time, it was thought that racial taxonomies should be based on characteristics unique to particular groups and uniformly expressed within them. Some scientists, taking the polygenist view, attempted to identify certain physical traits that were thought to be stable or that did not appear to be influenced by external environmental factors. Therefore, these so-called *nonadaptive* traits should exhibit only minimal within-group variation and could thus be used to typify entire populations. Shape of the skull was incorrectly believed to be one such characteristic, and the fallacy of this assumption was not demonstrated until the early twentieth century (Boas, 1912).

TABLE 6–1   Racial Classification Schemes

Linnaeus, 1758

Homo europaeus	Homo afer (Africans)
Homo asiaticus	Homo americanus (Native Americans)

Blumenbach, 1781

Caucasoid	Ethiopian
Mongoloid	American
Malay	

E. A. Hooton, 1926

PRIMARY RACE	PRIMARY SUBRACE
White	Mediterranean
	Ainu
	Keltic
	Nordic
	Alpine
	East Baltic
Negroid	African Negro
	Nilotic Negro
	Negrito
Mongoloid	Classic Mongoloid
	Arctic Mongoloid
	SECONDARY SUBRACE
	Malay-Mongoloid
	Indonesian

Stanley M. Garn, 1965

GEOGRAPHICAL RACES: "a collection of race populations, separated from other such collections by major geographical barriers."

Amerindian	Melanesian-Papuan	Indian
Polynesian	Australian	European
Micronesian	Asiatic	African

LOCAL RACE: "a breeding population adapted to local selection pressures and maintained by either natural or social barriers to gene interchange."

These are examples of local races; there are many, many more:

Northwest European	East African	North Chinese
Northeast European	Bantu	Extreme Mongoloid
Alpine	Tibetan	Hindu
Mediterranean		

MICRORACES: Not well defined but apparently refers to neighborhoods within a city or a city itself, since "marriage or mating is a mathematical function of distance."

▲ **Dolichocephalic**
Having a long, narrow head in which the width measures less than 75 percent of the length.

▲ **Brachycephalic**
Having a broad head in which the width measures more than 80 percent of the length.

▲ **Biological determinism**
The concept that phenomena, including various aspects of behavior (e.g., intelligence, values, morals) are governed by biological (genetic) factors; the inaccurate association of various behavioral attributes with certain biological traits, such as skin color.

▲ **Eugenics**
The philosophy of "race improvement" through forced sterilization of members of some groups and encouraged reproduction among others; an overly simplified, often racist view that is now discredited.

In 1842, Anders Retzius, a Swedish anatomist, developed the *cephalic index* as a method of describing the shape of the head. The cephalic index, derived by dividing maximum head breadth by maximum length and multiplying by 100, gives the ratio of head breadth to length. (It is important to note that the cephalic index does not measure head size.) Compared to the statistical methods in use today, the cephalic index is simplistic and typological, but in the nineteenth century, it was seen as a sophisticated scientific tool. Furthermore, because people could be neatly categorized by a single number, it provided an extremely efficient method for describing and ordering phenotypic variation. Individuals with an index of less than 75 had long, narrow heads and were termed **dolichocephalic**. **Brachycephalic** individuals, with broad heads, had an index of over 80; and those whose indices were between 75 and 80 were *mesocephalic*.

Northern Europeans tended to be dolichocephalic, while southern Europeans were brachycephalic. Not surprisingly, these results led to heated and nationalistic debate over whether one group was superior to the other. Furthermore, when it was shown that northern Europeans shared their tendency to long, narrow heads with several African populations, the cephalic index ceased to be considered such a reliable indicator of race.

By the mid-nineteenth century, monogenists were beginning to reject their somewhat egalitarian concept of race in favor of a more hierarchical view. Populations were ranked essentially on a scale based on skin color (along with size and shape of the head), with Africans at the bottom. Moreover, Europeans themselves were ranked so that northern, light-skinned populations were considered superior to their southern, more olive-skinned neighbors.

The fact that non-Europeans were not Christian and were seen as "uncivilized" implied an inferiority of character and intellect. This view was based in a concept now termed **biological determinism**, which in part, holds that there is an association between physical characteristics and such attributes as intelligence, morals, values, abilities, and even social and economic differences between groups. In other words, cultural variations are *inherited* in the same manner as biological variations. It follows then, that there are inherent behavioral and cognitive differences between groups and that some groups are *by nature* superior to others. Following this logic, it is a simple matter to justify the persecution and even enslavement of other peoples, simply because their appearance differs from what is familiar.

After 1850, biological determinism was a constant theme underlying common thinking as well as scientific research in Europe and the United States. Deterministic (and what we today would call racist) views were held to some extent by most people, including such notable figures as Thomas Jefferson, Georges Cuvier, Benjamin Franklin, Charles Lyell, Abraham Lincoln, Charles Darwin, and Oliver Wendell Holmes. Commenting on this usually deemphasized characteristic of notable historical figures, Stephen J. Gould (1981, p. 32) emphasizes that "all American culture heroes embraced racial attitudes that would embarrass public-school mythmakers."

Francis Galton (1822–1911), a cousin of Charles Darwin, shared the increasingly common fear among Europeans that "civilized society" was being weakened by the failure of natural selection to eliminate unfit and inferior individuals (Greene, 1981, p. 107). Galton wrote and lectured on the necessity of "race improvement" and suggested governmental regulation of marriage and family size, an approach he called **eugenics**.

Although eugenics had its share of critics, its popularity flourished throughout the 1930s. After World War I, the movement was increasingly popular in Europe and the United States, but nowhere was it more popular than in

Germany, where the viewpoint took a disastrous turn. The idea of a "pure race" (see Issue, this chapter) was increasingly extolled as a means of reestablishing a strong and prosperous state. Eugenics was seen as scientific rationale for purging Germany of its "unfit," and many of Germany's scientists continued to support the policies of racial purity and eugenics during the Nazi period (Proctor, 1988, p. 143), when they served as justification for condemning millions of people to death.

But by the close of World War I, while some scientists continued to pursue eugenics policies, others were turning away from racial typologies and classification in favor of a more evolutionary approach. No doubt for some, this shift in direction was motivated by their growing concerns over the goals of the eugenics movement. Probably more important, however, was the synthesis of Mendelian genetics and Darwin's theories of natural selection during the 1930s (see p. 87). This breakthrough influenced all the biological sciences, and many physical anthropologists began to apply evolutionary principles to the study of human variation.

Racism

The most detrimental outcome of biological determinism is racism. Racism is based on the false belief that such factors as intellect and various cultural attributes are inherited along with physical characteristics. Such beliefs also rest on the assumption that one's own group is superior to other groups.

Because we have already alluded to certain aspects of racism, such as the eugenics movement, notions of racial purity, and persecution of people based on racial or ethnic misconceptions, we will not belabor the point here. However, it is important to point out that racism is hardly a thing of the past, nor is it restricted to European and American whites. Racism is a cultural, not a biological, phenomenon, and it is found worldwide.

Ultimately, racism is one of the more dangerous aspects of human behavior because it frequently leads to violence, warfare, terrorism, and genocide. We have seen recent manifestations of racism in many cities in the United States. The rioting that occurred in Los Angeles in 1992 after the acquittal of white police officers accused of beating Rodney King, a black suspect, was a clear example of the tensions among the diverse populations of large urban centers. In the past few years, there has been an increase in racial slurs and hate speech on radio talk shows and, perhaps especially, on the Internet. Sadly, the twentieth century has provided numerous examples of ethnic/racial conflict, and it is crucial to mention that virtually all these conflicts were due to *ethnic* differences between the participants. The unspeakable genocide of the Holocaust during World War II, in Cambodia in the 1970s, in Rwanda in 1994, and the tragedy of Bosnia and Croatia all bespeak the tragic outcomes of intolerance of groups we call "others," however we define the term.

What we observe when we see biological variations between populations (and individuals) are the traces of our evolutionary past. Different expressions of traits such as skin color, eye color, and shape of the face are the results of biological adaptations that human ancestors made to local environmental conditions in a process that began perhaps several hundred thousand years ago. Instead of using these differences as a basis for prejudice and persecution, we should recognize them for what they are: a preserved record of how natural selection shaped our species to meet the varied environmental challenges it faced while expanding its geographical range over most of the planet.

We end this brief discussion of racism with an excerpt from an article, "The Study of Race," by Sherwood Washburn, a well-known physical anthropologist at the University of California, Berkeley. Although written some years ago, the statement is as fresh and applicable today as it was when it was written:

> Races are products of the past. They are relics of times and conditions which have long ceased to exist.
>
> Racism is equally a relic supported by no phase of modern science. We may not know how to interpret the form of the Mongoloid face, or why Rh is of high incidence in Africa, but we do know the benefits of education and of economic progress. We . . . know that the roots of happiness lie in the biology of the whole species and that the potential of the species can only be realized in a culture, in a social system. It is knowledge and the social system which give life or take it away, and in so doing change the gene frequencies and continue the million-year-old interaction of culture and biology. Human biology finds its realization in a culturally determined way of life, and the infinite variety of genetic combinations can only express themselves efficiently in a free and open society. (Washburn, 1963, p. 531)

Intelligence

▲ Intelligence
Mental capacity; ability to learn, reason, or comprehend and interpret information, facts, relationships, meanings, etc.; the capacity to solve problems, whether through the application of previously acquired knowledge or through insight.

As we have shown, belief in the relationship between phenotype and specific behavioral attributes is popular even today, but evidence is lacking that personality or any other behavioral trait differs genetically *between* human groups. Most scientists would agree with this last statement, but one question that has produced controversy both inside scientific circles and among laypeople is whether race (however defined) and **intelligence** are associated.

Both genetic and environmental factors contribute to intelligence, although it is not yet possible to measure accurately the percentage each contributes. What can be said is that IQ scores and intelligence are not the same thing; IQ scores can change during a person's lifetime, and average IQ scores of different populations overlap. Such differences in IQ scores as do exist between groups are difficult to interpret, given the problems inherent in the design of the IQ tests. Moreover, complex cognitive abilities, however measured, are influenced by multiple loci and are thus strikingly polygenic.

Innate factors set limits and define potentials for behavior and cognitive ability in any species. In humans, the limits are broad and the potentials are not fully known. Individual abilities result from complex interactions between genetic and environmental factors. One product of this interaction is learning, and the ability to learn has genetic or biological components. Undeniably, there are differences between *individuals* regarding these biological components. However, elucidating what proportion of the variation in test scores is due to biological factors probably is not possible. Moreover, innate differences in abilities reflect individual variation *within* populations, not inherent differences *between* groups. Comparing populations on the basis of IQ test results is a misuse of testing procedures, and there is no convincing evidence *whatsoever* that populations vary with regard to cognitive abilities, regardless of the assertions in some best-selling books.

The Adaptive Significance
of Human Variation

Today, physical anthropologists view human variation as the result of adaptations to environmental conditions, both past and present. Although cultural adaptations have certainly played an important role in the evolution of *Homo sapiens*, in this discussion we are primarily concerned with biological factors.

All organisms must maintain the normal functions of internal organs, tissues, and cells in order to survive, and this task must be accomplished within the context of an ever-changing environment. Even during the course of a single, seemingly uneventful day, there are numerous fluctuations in temperature, wind, solar radiation, humidity, and so on. Physical activity also places **stress** on physiological mechanisms. The body must accommodate all these changes by compensating in some manner to maintain internal constancy, or **homeostasis**, and all life-forms have evolved physiological mechanisms that, within limits, achieve this goal.

Physiological response to environmental change is, to some degree, influenced by genetic factors. We have already defined adaptation as a functional response to environmental conditions in populations and individuals. In a narrower sense, adaptation refers to *long-term* evolutionary (i.e., genetic) changes that characterize all individuals within a population or species.

Examples of long-term adaptations in *Homo sapiens* include some physiological responses to heat (sweating) and deeply pigmented skin in tropical regions. Such characteristics are the results of evolutionary change in species or populations and they do not vary as the result of short-term environmental change. For example, the ability to sweat is not lost in people who spend their lives in predominantly cool areas. Likewise, individuals born with deeply pigmented skin will not become pale, even if never exposed to intense sunlight.

Short-term physiological response to environmental change, which is also genetically influenced, is called **acclimatization**. Tanning, which occurs in all people, is a form of acclimatization. Another example is the very rapid increase in hemoglobin production that occurs when lowland natives travel to higher elevations. This increase provides the body with more oxygen in an environment where oxygen is less available. In both these examples, the physiological change is temporary. Tans fade once exposure to sunlight is reduced; and hemoglobin production drops to original levels on return to lower altitudes.

In the following discussion, we present some examples of how humans respond to environmental challenges. Some of these examples illustrate adaptations that characterize the entire species. Others illustrate adaptations seen in only some populations. And still others illustrate the process of acclimatization.

▲ **Stress**
In a physiological context, any factor that acts to disrupt homeostasis; more precisely, the body's response to any factor that threatens its ability to maintain homeostasis.

▲ **Homeostasis**
A condition of balance, or stability, within a biological system, maintained by the interaction of physiological mechanisms that compensate for changes (both external and internal).

▲ **Acclimatization**
Physiological response to changes in the environment that occurs during an individual's lifetime. Such responses may be short term. The capacity for acclimatization may typify an entire population or species. This capacity is under genetic influence and thus is subject to evolutionary factors such as natural selection.

Solar Radiation, Vitamin D, and Skin Color

Skin color is often-cited as an example of adaptation and natural selection in human populations. In general, skin color in populations, especially prior to about 1500, follows a particular geographical distribution, especially in the Old World. Figure 6–1 illustrates that populations with the greatest amount of pigmentation are found in the tropics, while lighter skin color is associated with more northern latitudes, particularly the inhabitants of northwestern Europe.

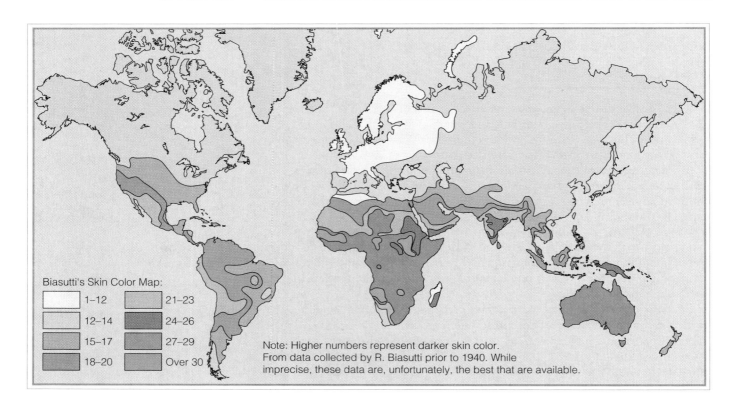

FIGURE 6–1

Geographical distribution of skin color among the indigenous populations of the world. (After Biasutti, 1959.)

Biasutti's Skin Color Map:

1–12	21–23
12–14	24–26
15–17	27–29
18–20	Over 30

Note: Higher numbers represent darker skin color.
From data collected by R. Biasutti prior to 1940. While imprecise, these data are, unfortunately, the best that are available.

Skin color is influenced by three substances: hemoglobin, carotene, and, most important, the pigment *melanin*. Melanin is a granular substance produced by specialized cells in the epidermis called *melanocytes*. All humans appear to have approximately the same number of melanocytes. It is the amount of melanin and the size of melanin granules that vary.

Melanin has the capacity to absorb potentially dangerous ultraviolet (UV) rays that are present (although not visible) in sunlight. Because of this ability, melanin provides protection from overexposure to ultraviolet radiation, which can cause genetic mutations in skin cells. These mutations may ultimately lead to skin cancer, which, if left untreated, can eventually spread to other organs and result in death.

As already mentioned, exposure to sunlight triggers a protective mechanism in the form of temporarily increased melanin production (acclimatization). (The visible manifestation of this increase is a tan.) This protective response occurs in all humans except albinos, who carry a genetic mutation that prevents their melanocytes from producing melanin (Fig. 6–2). Moreover, tanning is limited in many fair-complexioned people of northern European descent who do produce small amounts of melanin, but have a reduced capacity for temporary increases in melanin production.

Natural selection appears to have favored dark skin in areas nearest the equator, where the sun's rays are most direct and thus, where exposure to UV light is most intense. In considering the potentially harmful effects of ultraviolet radiation from an *evolutionary* perspective, three points must be kept in mind: (1) Early hominids lived mostly in the tropics, where solar radiation is more intense than in temperate areas like northwestern Europe; (2) unlike modern city dwellers, most earlier hominids spent the majority of time outdoors; (3) early hominids did not wear clothing that would have provided some protection from the sun. Given these conditions, ultraviolet radiation could indeed have been a powerful agent selecting for optimum levels of melanin production in early human ancestors.

As hominids migrated out of Africa into Europe and Asia, selective pressures changed. In particular, those populations that eventually occupied northern Europe encountered cold temperatures and cloudy skies sometimes during the summer as well as in winter. Winter also meant fewer hours of daylight, and with the sun well to the south, solar radiation was indirect. Moreover, since physiological adaptations were not sufficient to meet the demands of living in colder climates, these populations had undoubtedly adopted certain cultural practices, such as using fire and wearing animal skins and other types of clothing. As a consequence of reduced exposure to sunlight, the advantages provided by deeply pigmented skin in the tropics were no longer important, and selection for melanin production may have been relaxed (Brace and Montagu, 1977).

However, relaxed selection for dark skin is probably not adequate to explain the very depigmented skin seen especially in some northern Europeans. More than likely, another factor, the need for adequate amounts of vitamin D, was also critical. The theory concerning the possible role of vitamin D, known as the *vitamin D hypothesis*, offers the following explanation.

Vitamin D plays a vital role in the mineralization and normal growth of bone during infancy and childhood and is available in a few foods, including fish oils, egg yolk, butter, cream, and liver. But the body's primary source of vitamin D is its own ability to synthesize it through the interaction of UV light and a cholesterol-like substance found in skin cells. Therefore, if normal bone growth is to occur, adequate exposure to sunlight is essential. Insufficient amounts of vitamin D during childhood result in *rickets*, which leads to bone deformities throughout the skeleton, especially the weight-bearing bones of the lower extremity and pelvis. Thus, people with rickets frequently have bowed legs and pelvic deformities. Pelvic deformities are of particular concern for women, for they can lead to a narrowing of the birth canal, which, in the absence of surgical intervention, frequently results in the death of both mother and fetus during childbirth. This example illustrates the potential for rickets as a significant selective factor favoring less pigmented skin in regions where climate and other factors operate to reduce exposure to UV radiation.

In the past, reduced exposure to sunlight would have been detrimental to darker-skinned individuals in more northern latitudes. In these individuals, higher concentrations of melanin filtered out much of the UV radiation that was available. If, in addition, the diets of groups that came to inhabit northern Europe did not provide adequate amounts of vitamin D, selective pressures would have shifted even further over time to favor less pigmented skin. There is substantial evidence, both historically and in contemporary populations to support this vitamin D hypothesis.

During the latter decades of the nineteenth century, black inhabitants of northern U.S. cities suffered a higher incidence of rickets than whites. Northern blacks were also more commonly affected than blacks living in the South, where exposure to sunlight is greater. (The supplementation of milk with vitamin D was initiated to alleviate this problem.) Another example is seen in Britain, where darker-skinned East Indians and Pakistanis show a higher incidence of rickets than whites (Molnar, 1983).

Perhaps more social importance has been attached to variation in skin color than to any other single human biological trait. In point of fact, there is no reason this should be so. Aside from its probable adaptive significance relative to UV

FIGURE 6–2
An African albino.

radiation, skin color is no more important physiologically than many other biological characteristics. But from an evolutionary perspective, skin color provides an outstanding example of how the forces of natural selection have produced geographically patterned variation as the consequence of two conflicting selective forces: the need for protection from overexposure to UV radiation, on the one hand, and the need for adequate UV exposure for vitamin D synthesis on the other.

The Thermal Environment

Mammals and birds have evolved complex mechanisms to maintain a constant internal body temperature. While reptiles must rely on exposure to external heat sources to raise body temperature and energy levels, mammals and birds possess physiological mechanisms that, within certain limits, increase or reduce the loss of body heat. The optimum body temperature for normal cellular functions is species-specific, and for humans it is approximately 98.6° F.

Homo sapiens is found in a wide variety of habitats, with thermal environments ranging from exceedingly hot (in excess of 120° F) to bitter cold (less than −60° F). In such extremes, particularly cold, human life would not be possible without cultural innovations. But even accounting for the artificial environments in which we live, such external conditions place the human body under enormous stress.

Response to Heat   All available evidence suggests that the earliest hominids evolved in the warm-to-hot savannas of East Africa. The fact that humans cope better with heat than they do with cold is testimony to the long-term adaptations to heat that evolved in our ancestors.

In humans, as well as certain other species, such as horses, sweat glands are distributed throughout the skin. This wide distribution of sweat glands makes possible the loss of heat at the body surface through evaporative cooling, a mechanism that has evolved to the greatest degree in humans.

The capacity to dissipate heat by sweating is seen in all human populations to an almost equal degree, with the average number of sweat glands per individual (approximately 1.6 million) being fairly constant. However, there is variation in that persons not generally exposed to hot conditions do experience a period of acclimatization that initially involves significantly increased perspiration rates (Frisancho, 1993). An additional factor that enhances the cooling effects of sweating is increased exposure of the skin through reduced amounts of body hair. We do not know when in our evolutionary history loss of body hair began, but it represents a species-wide adaptation.

Heat reduction through evaporation can be expensive and indeed dangerous, in terms of water and sodium loss. Up to 3 liters of water can be lost by an average human engaged in heavy work in high heat. The importance of this fact can be appreciated if you consider that the loss of 1 liter of water is approximately equivalent to losing 1.5 percent of total body weight, and loss of 10 percent of body weight can be life threatening.

Another mechanism for radiating body heat is **vasodilation**, whereby capillaries near the skin's surface widen to permit increased blood flow to the skin. The visible effect of vasodilation is flushing, or increased redness of the skin, particularly of the face, accompanied by warmth. But the physiological effect is to permit heat, carried by the blood from the interior of the body, to be emitted from the skin's surface to the surrounding air. (Some drugs, including alcohol,

▲ **Vasodilation**
Expansion of blood vessels, permitting increased blood flow to the skin. Vasodilation permits warming of the skin and also facilitates radiation of warmth as a means of cooling. Vasodilation is an involuntary response to warm temperatures, various drugs, and even emotional states (blushing).

also produce vasodilation, which accounts for the increased redness and warmth of the face in some people.)

Body size and proportions are also important in regulating body temperature. In fact, there seems to be a general relationship between climate and body size and shape in birds and mammals. In general, within a species, body size (weight) increases as distance from the equator increases. In humans, this relationship holds up fairly well, but there are numerous exceptions.

Two rules that pertain to the relationship between body size, body proportions, and climate are *Bergmann's rule* and *Allen's rule.*

1. *Bergmann's rule (concerns the relationship of body mass or volume to surface area)*: Among mammals, body size tends to be greater in populations that live in colder climates. This is because as mass increases, the relative amount of surface area decreases proportionately. Because heat is lost at the surface, it follows that increased mass allows for greater heat retention and reduced heat loss.
2. *Allen's rule (concerns shape of body, especially appendages)*: In colder climates, shorter appendages, with increased mass-to-surface ratios, are adaptive because they are more effective at preventing heat loss. Conversely, longer appendages, with increased surface area relative to mass, are more adaptive in warmer climates because they promote heat loss.

According to these rules, the most suitable body shape in hot climates is linear with long arms and legs. In a cold climate, a more suitable body type is stocky with shorter limbs. Considerable data gathered from several human populations generally conform to these principles. In colder climates, body mass tends, on average, to be greater and characterized by a larger trunk relative to arms and legs (Roberts, 1973). People living in the Arctic tend to be short and stocky, while many sub-Saharan Africans, especially the East African pastoralists, are tall and linear (Fig. 6–3). But there is much human variability regarding

(a)

(b)

FIGURE 6–3

(a) This African woman has the linear proportions characteristic of many inhabitants of sub-Saharan Africa. (b) By comparison, the Inuit woman is short and stocky. These two individuals serve as good examples of Bergmann's and Allen's rules.

body proportions, and not all populations conform so obviously to Bergmann's and Allen's rules.

Response to Cold   Human physiological responses to cold increase heat production and enhance heat retention. Of the two, heat retention is more efficient because less energy is required. This is an important point because energy is derived from dietary sources. Unless food resources are abundant, and in winter they frequently are not, any factor that conserves energy can have adaptive value.

Short-term responses to cold include increased metabolic rate and shivering, both of which generate body heat, at least for a short time. **Vasoconstriction**, another short-term response, restricts heat loss and conserves energy. In addition, humans possess a subcutaneous (beneath the skin) fat layer that serves as insulation throughout the body. Behavioral modifications include increased activity, increased food consumption, and assuming a curled-up position.

Increases in metabolic rate (the rate at which cells break up nutrients into their components) release energy in the form of heat. Shivering also generates muscle heat, as does voluntary exercise. But these methods of heat production are expensive because they require an increased intake of nutrients to provide needed energy. (Perhaps this explains why we tend to have a heartier appetite during the winter and why we also tend to increase our intake of fats and carbohydrates, the very sources of energy our bodies require.)

In general, people exposed to chronic cold (meaning much or most of the year) maintain higher metabolic rates than those living in warmer climates. The Inuit (Eskimo) people living in the Arctic maintain metabolic rates between 13 and 45 percent higher than observed in non-Inuit control subjects (Frisancho, 1993). Moreover, the highest metabolic rates are seen in inland Inuit, who are exposed to even greater cold stress than coastal populations. Traditionally, the Inuit had the highest animal protein and fat diet of any population in the world. Such a diet, necessitated by the available resource base, served to maintain the high metabolic rates required by exposure to chronic cold.

Vasoconstriction restricts capillary blood flow to the surface of the skin, thus reducing heat loss at the body surface. Because retaining body heat is more economical than creating it, vasoconstriction is very efficient, provided temperatures do not drop below freezing. However, if temperatures do fall below freezing, continued vasoconstriction can allow the skin temperature to decrease to the point of frostbite or worse.

Long-term responses to cold vary among human groups. For example, in the past desert-dwelling native Australian populations were subjected to wide temperature fluctuations from day to night. As they wore no clothing and did not build shelters, their only protection from nighttime temperatures that hovered only a few degrees above freezing was provided by sleeping fires. They experienced continuous vasoconstriction throughout the night that permitted a degree of skin cooling most people would find extremely uncomfortable. But there was no threat of frostbite, and continued vasoconstriction helped prevent excessive internal heat loss.

By contrast, the Inuit experience intermittent periods of vasoconstriction and vasodilation. This compromise provides periodic warmth to the skin that helps prevent frostbite in below-freezing temperatures. At the same time, because vasodilation is intermittent, energy loss is restricted, with more heat retained at the body's core.

The preceding examples illustrate but two of the many ways in which human populations vary with regard to adaptation to cold. Although all humans

▲ **Vasoconstriction**
Narrowing of blood vessels to reduce blood flow to the skin. Vasoconstriction is an involuntary response to cold and reduces heat loss at the skin's surface.

respond to cold stress in much the same manner, there is variation in how adaptation and acclimatization are manifested.

High Altitude

Today, perhaps as many as 25 million people live at altitudes above 10,000 feet. In Tibet, permanent settlements exist above 15,000 feet, and in the Andes, they can be found as high as 17,000 feet (Fig. 6–4).

At such altitudes, multiple factors produce stress on the human body. These include **hypoxia** (reduced available oxygen), more intense solar radiation, cold, low humidity, wind (which amplifies cold stress), a reduced nutritional base, and rough terrain. Of these, hypoxia exerts the greatest amount of stress on human physiological systems, especially the heart, lungs, and brain.

▲ **Hypoxia**
Lack of oxygen. Hypoxia can refer to reduced amounts of available oxygen in the atmosphere (due to lowered barometric pressure) or to insufficient amounts of oxygen in the body.

Hypoxia results from reduced barometric pressure. It is not that there is less oxygen in the atmosphere at high altitudes; rather, it is less concentrated. Therefore, to obtain the same amount of oxygen at 9,000 feet as at sea level, people must make certain physiological alterations aimed at increasing the body's ability to transport and utilize efficiently the oxygen that is available.

People who reside at higher elevations, especially recent immigrants, display a number of manifestations of their hypoxic environment. Reproduction, in particular, is affected through increased rates of infant mortality, miscarriage, and prematurity. In Colorado, for example, infant deaths are nearly twice as common above 8,200 feet (2,500 m) as at lower elevations. Low birth weight is also more common and is attributed to decreased fetal growth due to impaired maternal-fetal transport of oxygen (Moore and Regensteiner, 1983).

Compared to populations at lower elevations, lifelong residents of high altitude display slowed growth and maturation. Other differences include larger chest size, associated, in turn, with greater lung volume and larger hearts.

High-altitude natives and nonnatives exhibit certain differences in acclimatization and adaptation to hypoxia. Frisancho (1993) calls these different responses "adult acclimatization" and "developmental acclimatization." *Adult acclimatizations* occurs upon exposure to high altitude in people born at low elevation. The responses may be short-term modifications, depending on duration of stay, but they begin within hours of the altitude change. These changes include an increase in respiration rate, heart rate, and production of red blood cells. (Red blood cells contain hemoglobin, the protein responsible for transporting oxygen to organs and tissues.)

Developmental acclimatizations are acquired by high-altitude natives during growth and development. (Note that this type of acclimatization is present only in people who grow up in high altitude areas, not in those who moved there as adults.) In addition to greater lung capacity, people born at high altitudes are more efficient than migrants at diffusing oxygen from blood to body tissues. Hence, they do not rely as heavily on increased red cell formation as do newcomers. Developmental acclimatization serves as a good example of physiological plasticity by illustrating how, within the limits set by genetic factors, development can be influenced by environment.

There is evidence that some *populations* have also adapted to high altitudes. Indigenous peoples of Tibet who have inhabited regions higher than 12,000 feet for around 25,000 years may have made genetic (i.e., evolutionary) accommodations to hypoxia. Altitude does not appear to affect reproduction in these people to the degree it does in other populations. Infants have birth weights as high as those

(a)

(b)

FIGURE 6–4

(a) La Paz, Bolivia at just over 12,000 ft. above sea level is home to 1,000,000 people. (b) A household in northern Tibet, situated at an elevation of over 15,000 feet above sea level.

of lowland Tibetan groups and higher than those of recent (20 to 30 years) Chinese immigrants. This fact may be the result of alterations in maternal blood flow to the uterus during pregnancy (Moore et al., 1994).

Another line of evidence concerns the utilization of glucose (blood sugar). Glucose is critical in that it is the only source of energy used by the brain, and it is also utilized, although not exclusively, by the heart. Both highland Tibetans and the Quechua (inhabitants of high-altitude regions of the Peruvian Andes) burn glucose in a way that permits more efficient use of oxygen. This implies the presence of genetic mutations in the mitochondrial DNA that directs how cells use glucose. It also implies that natural selection has acted to increase the frequency of these advantageous mutations in these groups.

There is no certain evidence that Tibetans and Quechua have made evolutionary changes to accommodate high-altitude hypoxia. Moreover, the genetic mechanisms that underlie these populations' unique abilities have not been identified. The new data are intriguing, however, and strongly suggest that selection has operated to produce evolutionary change in these two groups. If further study supports these findings, we have an excellent example of evolution in action producing long-term adaptation at the population level.

Infectious Disease

Infection, as opposed to other disease categories, such as degenerative or genetic disease, is a category that includes those pathological conditions caused by microorganisms (viruses, bacteria, and fungi). Throughout the course of human evolution, infectious disease has exerted enormous selective pressures on populations and thus has influenced the frequency of certain alleles that affect the immune response. Indeed, it would be difficult to overemphasize the importance of infectious disease as an agent of natural selection in human populations.

Malaria provides perhaps the best single example of the evolutionary role of disease. In Chapter 5, you saw how malaria has operated in some African and Mediterranean populations to alter allele frequencies at the locus governing hemoglobin formation. In spite of extensive long-term eradication programs, malaria still poses a serious threat to human health. Indeed, the World Health Organization estimates the number of people currently infected with malaria to be between 300 and 500 million worldwide. This number is increasing, too, as drug-resistant strains of the disease-causing microorganism become more common (Olliaro et al., 1995).

During the eighteenth century, smallpox accounted for approximately 10 to 15 percent of all deaths in parts of Europe. This viral disease, once a killer of staggering proportions, is the only condition, so far, to have been successfully eliminated by modern medical technology. By 1977, through massive vaccination programs, the World Health Organization was able to declare the disease organism to be extinct.

The best-known epidemic in history was that of the Black Death (bubonic plague) in the mid-fourteenth century. Bubonic plague is caused by a bacterium and is transmitted from rodents to humans by fleas. In just a few years, this deadly disease had spread (following trade routes and facilitated by rodent-infested ship cargoes) from the Caspian Sea throughout the Mediterranean area to northern Europe. During the initial exposure to this disease, as many as one-third of the inhabitants of Europe died.

A less well known but even more devastating example was the influenza **pandemic** that broke out in 1918 at the end of World War I. This was actually one of a series of influenza outbreaks, but it has remained notable for its still unexplained virulence and the fact that it accounted for the death of over 21 million people worldwide.

▲ **Pandemic**
An extensive outbreak of disease affecting large numbers of people over a wide area; potentially, a worldwide phenomenon.

The effects of infectious disease on humans are mediated culturally as well as biologically. Innumerable cultural factors, such as architectural styles, subsistence techniques, exposure to domesticated animals, even religious practices, all affect how infectious disease develops and persists within and between populations.

Until about 10,000 to 12,000 years ago, all humans lived in small nomadic gathering and hunting groups. As these groups rarely remained in one location more than a few days at a time, they had minimal contact with refuse heaps that house disease **vectors**. But with the domestication of plants and animals, people became more sedentary and began living in small villages. Gradually, villages became towns, and towns, in turn, developed into densely crowded, unsanitary cities.

▲ **Vectors**
Agents that serve to transmit disease from one carrier to another. Mosquitoes are vectors for malaria, just as fleas are vectors for bubonic plague.

As long as humans lived in small bands, there was little opportunity for infectious disease to have much of an impact at the population level. Even if an entire local group or band were wiped out, the effect on the overall population in a given area would have been negligible. Moreover, for a disease to become **endemic** in a population, sufficient numbers of people must be present. Therefore, small bands of hunter-gatherers were not faced with continuous exposure to endemic disease.

But with the advent of settled living and close association with domesticated animals, opportunities for disease increased. As sedentary life permitted larger group size, it became possible for some diseases to become permanently established in some populations. Living in settled communities that were completely lacking in garbage and sewage disposal meant that human inhabitants were continuously exposed to refuse, untreated human and nonhuman animal waste, and unsafe drinking water with its threat of typhoid and cholera. Refuse heaps

▲ **Endemic**
Continuously present in a population. In regard to disease, refers to populations in which there will always be some infected individuals.

attracted mosquitoes that in some areas carried malaria and yellow fever; rodents with fleas (known for their role in transmitting plague and typhus); and other potential carriers of microbial disease. Moreover, the close association with cattle and the consumption of milk (in some cultures) provided an opportunity for the spread of such maladies as tuberculosis. Thus, the crowded, unsanitary conditions that characterized parts of all cities until the late nineteenth century, and that still persist in much of the world today, have greatly added to the disease burden borne by human inhabitants.

Humans and **pathogens** exert selective pressures on each other, creating a dynamic relationship between disease organisms and their human (and nonhuman) hosts. Just as disease exerts selective pressures on host populations to adapt, microorganisms also evolve and adapt to various pressures exerted upon them by their hosts.

Evolutionarily speaking, it is to the advantage of any pathogen not to be so virulent as to kill its host too quickly. If an individual host dies immediately upon infection, the viral or bacterial agent may not have time to reproduce and infect other hosts. Selection frequently acts to produce resistance in host populations and, at the same time, to reduce the virulence of disease organisms, to the benefit of both in a process of *coevolution*. However, populations exposed for the first time to a new disease frequently die in huge numbers. In fact, it was just such a situation that accounted for the decimation of indigenous New World populations after contact with Europeans exposed them for the first time to smallpox. This also appears to be the case with the current worldwide spread of HIV, the virus that causes AIDS.

AIDS In the United States, the first cases of AIDS (acquired immune deficiency syndrome) were reported in 1981. It was during that year that health officials first recognized that a new and very deadly infectious disease had emerged, one that would eventually reach pandemic proportions. Since that time, an estimated 20 million people worldwide have been infected with HIV (human immunodeficiency virus), the agent that causes HIV disease, or AIDS. In the United States, at least 500,000 people, and perhaps as many as 1.5 million, have been infected with HIV, and by July 1996, almost 320,000 had died of AIDS complications.

A few words about viral infection are warranted here. Unlike bacteria, viruses are not living cells. Most viruses are composed of strands of DNA encased within a protein shell. Once a virus enters a host's body, it invades target cells and inserts its own DNA into the cell's cytoplasm. By thus gaining control of some cellular functions, the viral DNA directs the cell to produce virus particles. These new viruses eventually spill out to invade other cells, frequently killing the original host cell in the process. In response to viral assault, the host's immune system mounts various defenses, which, if successful, keep the infection under control and the host symptom free. In fact, immune response is the basis for vaccination (more accurately called "immunization"). Because viruses do not respond to antibiotic treatment, vaccination is the only effective method of fighting viral disease.

HIV was first identified and described in 1985, at which time it was assigned to a family of viruses called *retroviruses*. Retroviruses contain RNA instead of DNA, and they are unique in their ability to convert their RNA to DNA once they have entered a target cell. They are also unique in that the newly formed viral DNA becomes incorporated directly into the host cell's nuclear or chromosomal DNA. Since the 1970s when retroviruses were first identified, a number of species-specific forms have been identified, including those that cause disease in cats, sheep, horses, cattle, monkeys, and humans. In general, retroviruses cause

▲ **Pathogens**
Substances or microorganisms, such as bacteria or viruses, that cause disease.

various forms of leukemia or, as in the case of HIV, they directly attack immune cells and cause immune deficiencies. The reason that HIV is so lethal, is that it attacks the very cells capable of combating the virus.

HIV is transmitted from person to person through the exchange of bodily fluids, usually blood or semen. It is not spread through casual contact with an infected person. Within six months of infection, most persons test positive for anti-HIV antibodies, meaning that their immune system has recognized the presence of foreign antigens and has responded by producing antibodies. However, serious HIV-related symptoms may not appear for years. HIV is a "slow virus" in that it may persist in a host's body for years before the onset of severe illness. This asymptomatic state is called a "latency period," and the average latency period in the United States is over 11 years.

HIV can attack a variety of types of cells, but it especially targets the so-called T4 helper cells, a key component of the immune system. When a person's T cell count drops below minimum levels, that person will begin to exhibit symptoms caused by various "opportunistic" infections. Opportunistic infections are caused by various bacteria, fungi, and viruses that are commonly present in the environment or the body, but are continuously suppressed by a healthy immune system. However, when the immune system begins to fail, these infections emerge. A diagnosis of AIDS is given when an HIV-infected person's T cell count drops to the point that indicates immune suppression and when symptoms of opportunistic infection appear.

While it was once thought that everyone infected with HIV would eventually die of AIDS, this opinion has been cautiously revised. Many patients are now known to have lived with HIV for up to 15 years with few symptoms, and in a very small number, the virus has dropped to undetectable levels.

The fact that some infected individuals appear to be less susceptible than others to HIV may partly be explained by the recently reported discovery of a genetic mutation that appears to confer resistence to some strains of HIV-1 (Samson et al., 1996; Dean et al., 1996). This mutation relates to a major protein "receptor site" on the surface of certain immune cells. (Receptor sites are protein molecules that enable certain forms of HIV-1, and other viruses, to invade cells.) In this particular case, a mutant allele results in a malfunctioning receptor site. Evidence now suggests that individuals who are homozygous for this allele may be completely resistant to many types of HIV-1 infection. In heterozygotes, resistance is increased and the course of HIV disease is slowed. Interestingly, the presence of the mutant allele has been demonstrated only in people of European descent among whom the frequency of the allele approaches 10 percent (Samson et al., 1996). However, current evidence indicates that the mutation is absent in other groups so far tested (Japanese and various sub-Saharan groups). Thus, while the locus is polymorphic in Europeans, it apparently is not in some other populations. The degree of interpopulational variation regarding this locus remains to be determined, and it also remains to be shown why the mutant allele is as frequent as it seems to be in Europeans.

The origins of HIV have not been definitely ascertained, but it is generally believed that it first appeared in Africa. HIV is genetically similar to another retrovirus, SIV (simian immunodeficiency virus), which is found in species of African monkeys. SIV produces no symptoms in the African monkeys that are its traditional hosts, but when injected into Asian monkeys (macaques), it eventually causes immune suppression, AIDS-like symptoms, and death. These facts imply that SIV has a long evolutionary history in African monkey populations and that the latter have adapted to accommodate a virus that is deadly to their Asian relatives.

Although it has not been proved, it is possible that HIV evolved from the genetically similar SIV, perhaps within the last few decades. If not, the two are at least closely related. One scenario is that humans may initially have been exposed through contact with monkeys, perhaps while skinning or preparing a carcass as food. Evidence to support this theory comes from the fact that one strain of HIV (HIV-2) that is common in West Africa, but rare in the United States, is almost genetically identical to SIV. Regardless of how HIV evolved and first infected humans, its rapid spread fits the pattern expected when populations are first exposed to "new" pathogens. Apparently, African monkeys and SIV have shared a sufficiently long evolutionary history that they have adapted to one another. Humans and HIV have not yet done so, and the deadly consequences are borne by humans, not the virus.

HIV is the most mutable virus known. In addition to HIV-2, there are two other types: HIV-1, by far the most common, and group O (or "outlyers"). Furthermore, within the HIV-1 grouping, there are at least nine subtypes (Hu et al., 1996). Furthermore, the virus mutates rapidly once it enters a host's body, so that in a single infected person, there are many distinct variants of HIV. Given this degree of variation, it is not surprising that developing a vaccine for this virus has been an extremely elusive goal. Many therapies have been developed, mainly to combat different infections as they arise. Antiviral agents have also been helpful. Unfortunately, all these therapies produce potentially serious side effects, and most are not effective for long periods in any case. Still, recent strategies using a combination of treatments have produced extremely promising results and appear to have virtually eliminated HIV from the bloodstream of most patients involved in preliminary testing.

At this point there is no cure for AIDS, and there is nothing definite on the horizon. However, rates of new infection have leveled off in the United States, so that currently there are more deaths per year (of people who were exposed to the virus 10 to 15 years ago) than there are new reported cases. This leveling off has been due in no small measure to public education and subsequent changes in behavior.

The Continuing Impact of Infectious Disease There is a growing concern in the biomedical community over the effects of antibiotic and pesticide use, practices that have flourished since the 1950s. Antibiotics have exerted selective pressures on bacterial species that have, over time, developed antibiotic-resistant strains. Consequently, the past few years have seen the *reemergence* of many bacterial diseases, including influenza, tuberculosis, pneumonia, and cholera, in forms that are less responsive to treatment. What is more, various treatments for nonbacterial conditions have also become ineffective. One such example is the appearance of chloroquin-resistant malaria, which has rendered chloroquin (the traditional preventive medication) virtually useless in some parts of Africa. And many insect species have developed resistance to commonly used pesticides. (See p. 119 for a discussion of DDT and malaria.)

It remains to be seen what the long-term consequences of twentieth-century antibiotic therapy and pesticide-based eradication programs will be on disease patterns. But there are many scientists who fear that we may not be able to develop new antibiotics and treatments fast enough to keep pace with the appearance of potentially deadly new bacteria and other pathogens. Thus, we have radically altered the course of evolution in some microbial species, just as they have altered our own evolutionary course in the past and clearly continue to do so in the present.

In addition to threats posed by antibiotic-resistant bacteria, there are other factors that may contribute to the emergence (or reemergence) of infectious disease. Scientists are becoming increasingly concerned over the potential for global warming to expand the geographical range of numerous tropical disease vectors such as mosquitoes. And, the destruction of natural environments may not only contribute to global warming, but it also has the potential of causing disease vectors, formerly restricted to local areas, to spread to new habitats.

Fundamental to all these factors is human population size which, as it continues to soar, causes more environmental disturbance and through additional human activity, adds further to global warming. Moreover, in developing countries where as much as 50 percent of mortality is due to infectious disease (as compared to about 10 percent in the United States), overcrowding and unsanitary conditions increasingly contribute to increased rates of communicable illness.

One other factor associated with the rapid spread of disease, and directly related to technological change, is the mixing of people at an unprecedented rate. Indeed, an estimated one million people per day cross national borders by air (Lederberg, 1996)! In addition, new road construction and wider availability of motor-driven vehicles allow more people (armies, refugees, truck drivers, etc.) to travel farther and faster than ever before. One could scarcely conceive of a better set of circumstances for the appearance and spread of communicable disease, and it remains to be seen if scientific innovation and medical technology are able to meet the challenge.

Summary

In this chapter, we have investigated some of the ways in which humans differ from one another, both within and between populations. We explored how this variation has been approached historically in terms of racial typologies and as a function of adaptation to a number of environmental factors, including solar radiation, heat, cold, and high altitude. We have also considered infectious disease, with particular emphasis on AIDS, and the dynamic relationship between pathogens and human hosts.

The topic of human variation is very complicated, and the biological and cultural factors that have contributed to that variation and that continue to influence it are manifold. But from an explicitly evolutionary perspective, it is through the investigation of changes in allele frequencies in response to environmental conditions that we will continue to elucidate the diverse adaptive potential that characterizes our species.

Questions for Review

1. What is a polytypic species?
2. What is a biological definition of "race"? Why is race socially important?
3. How would you define the term *race*? Why do anthropologists have difficulty defining race?
4. What is biological determinism?
5. What was the eugenics movement, and what were its goals?
6. What are some of the objections to applying racial concepts to humans?
7. What are racial typologies?
8. How did eighteenth- and nineteenth-century European scientists deal with human phenotypic variation?
9. What is homeostasis?

10. Under what conditions might light skin color be adaptive? Under what conditions might dark skin color be adaptive?
11. What physiological adjustments do humans show in coping with cold stress?
12. What is a physiological definition of stress?
13. What are the principal sources of stress at high altitude? Of these, which is most important? What are some of the ways humans respond to high-altitude stress?
14. What cultural factors have changed the patterns of infectious disease in humans?
15. Define infectious disease.
16. What causes AIDS?
17. Discuss an evolutionary scenario for HIV.

Suggested Further Reading

Bodmer, W. F., and L. L. Cavalli-Sforza. 1976. *Genetics, Evolution, and Man.* San Francisco: Freeman.

Chiras, Daniel D. 1991. *Human Biology.* St. Paul: West.

Frisancho, A. Roberto. 1993. *Human Adaptation and Accommodation.* Ann Arbor: University of Michigan Press.

Gould, Stephen Jay. 1981. *The Mismeasure of Man.* New York: Norton.

Jacoby, R., and N. Glauberman (eds). 1995. *The Bell Curve Debate.* New York: Times Books.

Ramenofsky, Ann F. 1992. "Death by Disease." *Archaeology* 45(2): 47–49.

Discover. 1994. Special issue: The Science of Race. 15 (November).

Journal of the American Medical Association, 1966. Entire issue, 275 (January 17). (Numerous articles pertaining to climate change and reemergence of infectious diseases.)

Internet Resources

How is AIDS Transmitted?
http://www.cmpharm.ucsf.edu/%7Etroyer/safesex/howisaidstransmitted.html
(Excellent discussion of HIV and modes of transmission by the Centers for Disease Control National AIDS Clearinghouse.)

Racial Purity:
A False and Dangerous Ideology

During the late nineteenth and early twentieth centuries, a growing sense of nationalism was sweeping Europe and the United States. At the same time, an increased emphasis on racial purity had been coupled with the more dangerous aspects of what is termed "biological determinism" (see page 136). The concept of pure races is based, in part, on the notion that in the past, races were composed of individuals who conformed to idealized types and who were similar in appearance and intellect. Over time, some variation had been introduced into these pure races through interbreeding with other groups, and increasingly, this type of "contamination" was seen as a threat to be avoided.

In today's terminology, pure races would be said to be genetically homogenous, or to possess little genetic variation. Everyone would have the same alleles at most of their loci. Actually, we do see this situation in "pure breeds" of domesticated animals and plants, developed *deliberately* by humans through selective breeding. We also see many of the detrimental consequences of such genetic uniformity in various congenital abnormalities, such as hip dysplasia in some breeds of dogs.

With our current understanding of genetic principles, we are able to appreciate the potentially negative outcomes of matings between genetically similar individuals. For example, we know that inbreeding increases the likelihood of offspring who are homozygous for certain deleterious recessive alleles. We also know that decreased genetic variation in a species diminishes the potential for natural selection to act, thus compromising that species' ability to adapt to certain environmental fluctuations. Furthermore, in genetically uniform populations, individual fertility can be seriously reduced, potentially with disastrous consequences for the entire species. Thus, even if pure human races did exist at one time (and they did not), theirs would not have been a desirable condition genetically, and they most certainly would have been at an evolutionary disadvantage.

During the latter half of the nineteenth century, many Americans and Europeans had come to believe that nations could be ranked according to technological achievement. It followed that the industrial societies of the United States and Europe were considered to be the most advanced and to have attained a "higher level of civilization" owing to the "biological superiority" of their northern European forebears. This concept arose in part from the writings of Herbert Spencer, a British philosopher who misapplied the principles of natural selection to societies in a doctrine termed "social Darwinism." Spencer believed that societies evolved and,

through competition, "less endowed" cultures and the "unfit" people in them would be weeded out. Indeed, it was Spencer who coined the much misused (and almost always abused) phrase, "survival of the fittest," and his philosophy became widely accepted on both sides of the Atlantic, where its principles accorded well with notions of racial purity.

In northern Europe, particularly Germany, and in the United States, "racial superiority" was increasingly embodied in the so-called "aryan race." *Aryan* is a term that is still widely used, albeit erroneously, with biological connotations. Actually, "aryan" does not refer to a biological unit or Mendelian population, as the majority of people who use the term intend it. Rather, it is a linguistic term that refers to an ancient language group that was ancestral to the Indo-European family of languages. (Among the many and varied modern Indo-European languages are Hindi, Persian, Greek, Polish, German, and English.)

By the early twentieth century, the "aryans" had been transformed into a mythical super race of people whose noble traits were embodied in an extremely idealized "nordic type." The true "aryan" was held to be tall, blond, blue-eyed, strong, industrious, and "pure in spirit." "Nordics" were extolled as the developers of all ancient "high" civilizations and as the founders of modern industrialized nations. In Europe, there was growing emphasis on the superiority of northwestern Europeans as the modern representatives of "true nordic stock," while southern and eastern Europeans were viewed as inferior.

In the United States, there prevailed the strongly held opinion that America was originally settled by Christian "nordics." Prior to about 1890, the majority of newcomers to the United States had come from Germany, Scandinavia, and Britain (including Ireland). But by the 1890s, the pattern of immigration had changed. The arrival of increasing numbers of Italians, Turks, Greeks, and Jews among the thousands of newcomers raised fears that society was being contaminated by immigration from southern and eastern Europe.

Moreover, in the United States, there were additional concerns about the large population of former black slaves and their descendants. As African Americans left the South in increasing numbers to work in the factories of the North, many unskilled white workers felt economically threatened by new competition. It was no coincidence that the Ku Klux Klan, which had been inactive for a number of years, was revived in 1915 and by the 1920s was preaching vehement opposition to blacks, Jews, and Catholics in support of the supremacy of the white, Protestant, "nordic race." These sentiments were widespread in the general population, although they did not always take the extreme form extolled by the Klan. One result of these views was the Immigration Restriction Act of 1924, which was aimed at curtailing the immigration of "non-nordics," including Italians, Jews, and eastern Europeans, in order to preserve America's "nordic" heritage.

To avoid the further "decline of the superior race," many states practiced policies of racial segregation until the mid-1950s. Particularly in the South, segregation laws resulted in an almost total separation of whites and blacks, except where blacks were employed as servants or laborers. Moreover, *antimiscegenation* laws prohibited marriage between whites and blacks in over half the states, and unions between whites and Asians were frequently illegal as well. In several states, marriage between whites and blacks was punishable either as a misdemeanor or a felony, and astonishingly, some of these laws were not repealed until the late 1950s or early 1960s. Likewise, in Germany by 1935, the newly instituted Nuremberg Laws forbade marriage or sexual intercourse between so-called "aryan" Germans and Jews.

The fact that belief in racial purity and superiority led ultimately to the Nazi death camps in World War II is undisputed (except for continuing efforts by certain white supremacist and neo-Nazi organizations). It is one of the great tragedies of the twentieth century that some of history's most glaring examples of discrimination and viciousness were perpetrated by people who believed that their actions were based in scientific principles. In reality, such beliefs constitute nothing more than myth. There is absolutely no evidence to suggest that pure human races ever existed. Indeed, such an idea flies in the face of everything we know about natural selection, recombination, and gene flow. The degree of genetic uniformity throughout our species (compared to some other species), as evidenced by mounting data from mitochondrial and nuclear DNA analysis, argues strongly that there has always been gene flow between human populations and that genetically homogenous races are nothing more than fabrication.

The numerous abuses committed in the name of racial purity in the twentieth century were, in part, outgrowths of the rise of nationalism in Europe and the United States during the late nineteenth century. Unfortunately, however, prejudice based on a belief in racial purity and superiority is alive and well. The dogma preached by such white supremacist groups as *White Aryan Resistance* is no different from that espoused by the Nazi leadership in pre-World War II Germany. The dangers of such thinking have been manifested in incalculable human suffering. As we stand at the threshold of the twenty-first century, we can but wonder if the generations who will see it to its conclusion will have learned from the mistakes of their predecessors.

Critical Thinking Questions

1. Given what you know about evolutionary factors, discuss why the notion of "pure races" is inaccurate. Also discuss why you think the concept of racial purity has been (and remains) so prevalent.

2. What is the concept of an "aryan race," and why is it incorrect? Is this concept dead today?

Growth and Development

Introduction

As noted in Chapter 1 and elsewhere, modern human beings are the result of *biocultural evolution*. In other words, human biology and behavior today have been shaped by the biological and cultural forces that operated on our ancestors. In fact, it would be fruitless to attempt an understanding of modern human biology and diversity without considering that humans have evolved in the context of culture. It would be like trying to understand the biology of fish without considering that they live in water.

A good place to explore the interaction of culture and biology is human growth and development. There is, of course, much variation in the extent to which cultural factors interact with genetically based biological characteristics, and this influences how the latter are expressed in individuals. Some genetically based characteristics will be exhibited no matter what the cultural context of growth and development happen to be. If a person inherits two alleles for albinism, for example (see Chapter 4), he or she will be deficient in production of the pigment melanin, resulting in lightly colored skin, hair, and eyes. This phenotype will emerge regardless of the cultural environment in which the person lives. Likewise, the sex-linked trait for color blindness (also described in Chapter 4) will be exhibited by all males who inherit it, no matter where they live.

Other characteristics, such as intelligence, body shape, and growth will reflect the interaction of environment and genes. We know, for example, that each of us is born with a genetic makeup that influences the maximum stature we can achieve in adulthood. But to reach that maximum stature, we must be properly nourished during our growing years and avoid many childhood diseases and other stresses that inhibit growth. What factors determine whether we are well fed and receive good medical care? In the United States, socioeconomic status is probably the primary determinant of nutrition and health. Thus, socioeconomic status is an example of a cultural factor that affects growth.

In another culture, diet and health status might be influenced by whether the individual is male or female. In some cultures, males receive preferential care in childhood and are thus often larger and healthier as adults than are females (Fig. 7–1). If a culture values thinness in women, young girls may try to restrict their food intake in ways that affect their growth. But if plumpness is valued, the effect on diet in adolescence will likely be different. These are all examples of how cultural values affect growth and development.

Fundamentals of Growth and Development

▲ **Growth**
Increase in mass or number of cells.

▲ **Development**
Differentiation of cells into different types of tissues and their maturation.

The terms *growth* and *development* are often used interchangeably, but they actually refer to different processes. **Growth** refers to an increase in mass or number of cells, whereas **development** refers to the differentiation of cells into different types of tissues and their maturation. Increase in cell number is referred to as *hyperplasia*, and increase in cell size, or mass, is called *hypertrophy*. Some cells are manufactured only once and can never be replaced if damaged (e.g., nerve and muscle cells); some cells are continuously dying and being replaced (skin and red blood cells); and some can be regenerated if damaged (cells in the liver, kidneys, and most glands). (See Chapter 3 for discussions of cell division.)

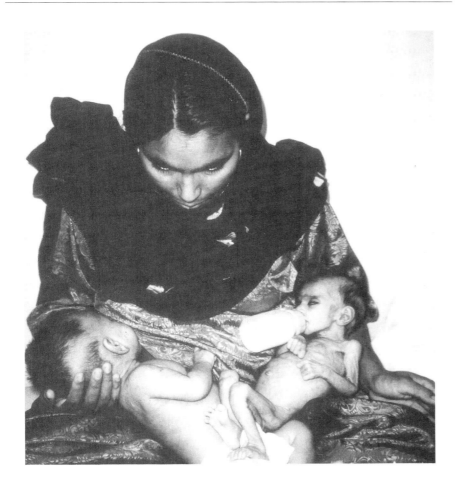

FIGURE 7–1

This is a mother with her twin children. The one on the left is a boy and is breast-fed. The girl, on the right is bottle-fed. This illustrates both differential treatment of boys and girls in many societies and the potential negative effects of bottle-feeding. Dr. Mushtag A. Khan, Pakistan Institute of Medical Sciences, Islamabad

Bone Growth

The first "skeleton" of the human fetus is made entirely of cartilage. This cartilage skeleton is sometimes referred to as a "model" of what the bony skeleton will look like. During growth, the cartilage cells are gradually broken down and replaced by bone cells in a process known as **ossification.** A newborn infant has more than 600 centers of bone growth in the body. During childhood, many segments of bones are connected to each other by cartilage, which decays more rapidly than bone deteriorates after death. As the child grows and the cartilage is replaced by bone, segments fuse to form adult bones, thus reducing the number of separate pieces. By the time growth is completed, there are approximately 206 bones.

Figure 7–2 shows an example of the process of ossification of the humerus, or upper arm bone. The shaft is referred to as the *diaphysis,* and the ends are called the *epiphyses* (*sing.,* epiphysis). Growth in one end is completed when the epiphyses unite with the diaphysis. There are two types of cells responsible for bone growth. The *osteoclasts* remove or destroy bone or cartilage cells, while the *osteoblasts* deposit new bone cells. Growth of a bone occurs not only in length, as we have been discussing, but also in width. The shaft of the femur of an infant is much thinner than that of an adult, and the hollow interior is also much

▲ **Ossification**

Process by which cartilage cells are broken down and replaced by bone cells.

FIGURE 7–2

Skeletal age: epiphyseal union in the humerus. Some regions of the humerus exhibit some of the earliest fusion centers in the body, while others are among the latest to complete fusion (not until late adolescence).

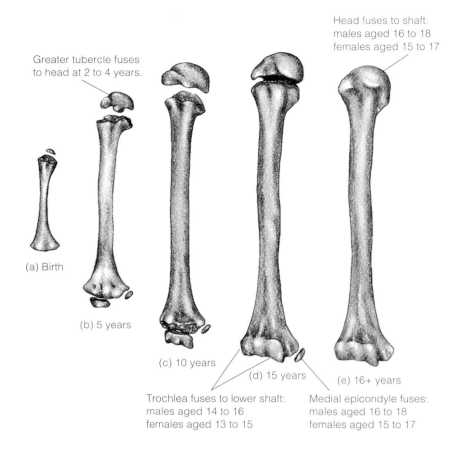

Greater tubercle fuses to head at 2 to 4 years.

Head fuses to shaft: males aged 16 to 18 females aged 15 to 17

(a) Birth

(b) 5 years

(c) 10 years

(d) 15 years

(e) 16+ years

Trochlea fuses to lower shaft: males aged 14 to 16 females aged 13 to 15

Medial epicondyle fuses: males aged 16 to 18 females aged 15 to 17

▲ **Distal**

The end of a bone that is farthest from the point at which the bone attaches to the body. For example, the elbow is at the distal end of the humerus.

▲ **Proximal**

The end of a bone that is closest to the point at which the bone attaches to the body. For example, the head of the humerus is on the proximal end.

smaller. For the shaft to widen and for the interior to increase in size, osteoclasts must destroy bone in the inner part of the shaft while osteoblasts are continually depositing bone on the outer surface (Fig. 7–3). Such "appositional" growth continues throughout life, well after growth in length has been completed.

The epiphyses at the ends of long bones unite with their shafts in fairly predictable patterns, enabling an anthropologist to estimate the age at death of young individuals from skeletal remains. For example, growth is completed in the elbow region in most people by approximately age 19 (a bit earlier in girls than in boys). What this means is that the epiphyses on the **distal** end of the humerus have united with the humeral shaft and the epiphyses at the **proximal** ends of the radius and ulna (lower arm bones) have united with their shafts (Fig. 7–4). By age 20 (again with some sex difference), the epiphyses have united in the hip and ankle regions. The epiphyses in the shoulder region do not unite until age 23, and the very last epiphyses to unite are in the medial clavicle, the projecting parts of the collarbone near the base of the throat.

Stature

Increased stature is a common indicator of health status in children because it is easy to assess under most circumstances. There are two ways in which increases in height are typically plotted on a graph. One way is to plot a *distance curve*, showing the height obtained in a given year. (Fig. 7–5a is a typical distance curve for height in an American girl.) Obvious growth spurts can be seen in early infancy and at puberty. Typically, well-nourished humans grow fairly rapidly during the first two trimesters (6 months) of fetal development, but growth slows during the third trimester. After birth, the rate of development increases and remains fairly rapid for about four years, at which time it decreases again to a relatively slow, steady level that is maintained until puberty. At puberty, there is a very pronounced increase in growth. During this so-called **adolescent growth spurt,** Western teenagers typically grow 9–10 cm per year. Subsequent to the adolescent growth spurt, the rate of development declines again and remains slower until adult stature is achieved by the late teens.

Another way to describe growth is to plot the amount of increase in height gained each year. This produces *a velocity curve* and depicts the growth spurts even more clearly (Fig. 7–5 b). If we were to plot the height distance and velocity curves for a chimpanzee, a baboon, and a dog, we would see that the curves are different for each species. Some have argued that the human growth curve, with its characteristic spurt at adolescence is unique to our species. Others argue that chimpanzees show small but significant spurts at puberty, making their curves similar to those of humans and suggesting that the adolescent growth spurt may be a characteristic that predates the separation of the chimpanzee and human evolutionary paths, approximately 5 to 7 million years ago. Nevertheless, no other mammal shows this characteristic to the same degree as do modern humans. In addition to total height, parts of the body (e.g., limbs, organs) also show similar growth curves, with rapid increases in the first trimester of gestation, during the first four years of life, and again at puberty.

Growth curves for boys and girls are significantly different, with the adolescent growth spurt occurring approximately two years earlier in girls than in boys (reflected in the fact that the ends of long bones unite earlier in girls than in boys). At birth, there is slight **sexual dimorphism** in many body measures (e.g., height, weight, head circumference, and body fat), but the major divergence in these characteristics does not occur until puberty. Table 7–1 shows the differences between these measure for boys and girls at birth and at age 18. Boys are slightly larger than girls at birth and are even more so at age 18, except in the last two measures, triceps skinfold and subscapular skinfold. These two measurements give information on body fat content and are determined by a special skinfold measuring caliper. The triceps skinfold measure is taken by gently pinching the skin and fat underneath the upper arm, and the subscapular measurement is taken by gently pinching the skin and fat below the shoulder blade. These measures reflect differences not only in the more obvious characteristics of height and weight, but also in body composition, with girls generally having more body fat than boys at all ages.

Brain Growth

The head is a relatively large part of the body at birth. The continued growth of the brain after birth occurs at a rate far greater than that of any other part of the body, with the exception of the eyeball. At birth, the human brain is about 25 percent of its adult size. By 6 months of age, the brain has doubled in size, reaching 50 percent of adult size. It reaches 75 percent of adult size at age 2^1/2 years, 90 percent at age 5 years, and 95 percent by age 10 years. There is only a very small spurt at adolescence, making the brain an exception to the growth curves characteristic of most other parts of the body. As we will see later in this chapter, this pattern of brain growth, including the relatively small amount of growth before birth, is unusual among primates and other mammals. By contrast, the typical picture for most mammalian species is that at least 50 percent of adult brain size has been

▲ **Adolescent growth spurt**

The period during adolescence in which well-nourished teens typically increase in stature at greater rates than at other points in the life cycle.

▲ **Sexual dimorphism**

Differences in physical characteristics between males and females of the same species. For example, humans are slightly sexually dimorphic for body size, with males being taller, on average, than females of the same population.

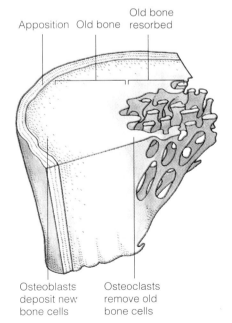

FIGURE 7–3

Bone cells are deposited on the outer portion of a bone by osteoblasts. In the interior of the shaft of the bone, osteoclasts remove bone, enlarging the marrow cavity.

obtained prior to birth. For humans, however, the narrow pelvis necessary for walking bipedally provides limits on the size of the fetal head that can be delivered through it. That limitation, in addition to the value of having most brain growth occur in the more stimulating environment outside the womb, has resulted in human infants being born with far less of their total adult brain size than most other mammals. (As we will see in Chapter 14, this pattern of delayed maturation was probably already established in hominid evolution by 1.5 m.y.a.)

Nutritional Effects on Growth and Development

The function of the digestive system is to take in nutrients and break them down into components that provide the basic materials needed for growth and development (even more basically, to provide energy for cellular functions). Diet has an impact on human growth at every stage of the life cycle. During pregnancy,

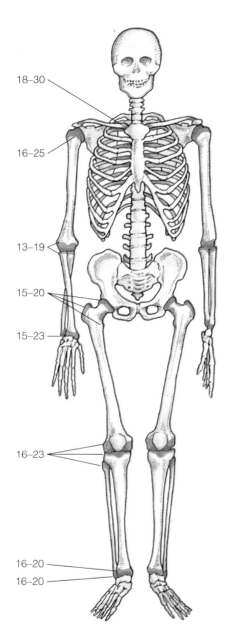

FIGURE 7–4

Ages of epiphyseal union. For example, the epiphyses unite in the elbow between ages 13 and 19.

FIGURE 7–5

Distance and velocity curves of growth in height for a healthy American girl.

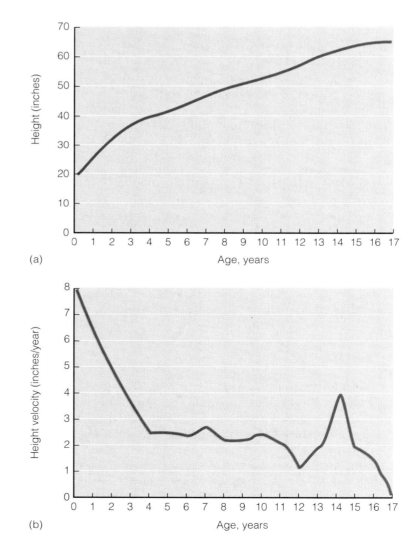

	Boys		Girls	
	Birth	**18**	**Birth**	**18**
Recumbent length (cm)*	49.9	181.1	49.3	166.7
Weight (kg)*	3.4	69.9	3.3	55.6
Head circumference (cm)[†]	34.8	55.9	34.1	54.9
Triceps skinfold (mm)	3.8[††]	8.5[§]	4.1[††]	17.5[§]
Subscapular skinfold (mm)	3.5[††]	10.0[§]	3.8[††]	12.0[§]

TABLE 7–1 Some Measurements of Size at Birth and at Age 18 for Children Born in the United States

* Hamill et al., 1977
† Nellhaus, 1968.
†† Johnston and Beller, 1976.
§ Johnson et al., 1981.

Source: From Boqin, 1988:22.

for example, a woman's diet can have a profound effect on the development of her fetus and the eventual health of the child. Moreover, the effects are transgenerational, because a woman's own supply of eggs is developed while she herself is *in utero* (see Chapter 3). Thus, if a woman is malnourished during pregnancy, the eggs that develop in her female fetus may be damaged in a way that will impact the health of her future grandchildren.

Basic Nutrients for Growth and Development

Nutrients needed for growth, development, and body maintenance are organized into five major categories: proteins, carbohydrates, lipids (fats), vitamins, and minerals. *Proteins*, composed of amino acids (see p. 47), are important for maintaining cell structure in muscles, skin, hair, organs, and bones. Antibodies and enzymes are proteins, as are most hormones. When you eat a meal, stomach and pancreatic enzymes break the protein down into the 20 amino acids described in Chapter 3. The amino acids are then absorbed into the bloodstream through the walls of the small intestine and are transported to other cells in the body, where they will be used in the synthesis of new proteins (the process by which this occurs is described in Chapter 3). Excess amino acids not needed for protein synthesis enter the mitochondria of the cells (see Chapter 3), where they are converted to *ATP* (adenosine triphosphate), the energy used to run your body.

Carbohydrates are important sources of energy needed to run the body. Good sources of carbohydrates are potatoes, beans, and grains. Carbohydrate digestion begins in the mouth, where the salivary enzymes begin to break down complex carbohydrates (*polysaccharides*) into simple ones, known as sugars. Enzymes in the small intestine further break down *disaccharides* (two sugars linked together) into *monosaccharides* (single sugars). Table sugar, for example, is a disaccharide known as *sucrose*. The enzyme *sucrase* breaks it down into the monosaccharides *glucose* and *fructose*. Another example of a disaccharide is *lactose*, which is broken down by the enzyme lactase into the monosaccharides glucose and *galactose*. As noted in Chapter 5, many adults are unable to produce the enzyme lactase and have problems consuming dairy products, which have high lactose content.

Monosaccharides are absorbed into the bloodstream through the walls of the small intestine in a manner similar to that for amino acids. From there they are transported to the liver, where all are converted into glucose, the primary source of energy for the body. Indeed, glucose is the only source of energy utilized by the brain. The hormone insulin is responsible for regulating glucose levels in the blood and tissues. The condition in which insufficient amounts of insulin are produced, or the cells are unable to respond to the insulin that is available, is referred to as *diabetes*. We shall see later that diabetes, the eighth leading cause of death in the United States, is a disorder of relatively recent origin (Eaton, Shostak, and Konner, 1988). Glucose not needed for other functions is either converted into *glycogen*, a polysaccharide stored in the liver and muscles, or converted into fat. When levels of glucose fall too low, the glycogen can then be reconverted into glucose. Glucose provides fuel for the body through its conversion into ATP (in the mitochondria of the cells) in a process similar to that of amino acid conversion. One enzyme on the pathway of conversion of glucose to ATP is G-6-PD. Deficiency in this important enzyme is an example of an X-linked recessive trait in humans (see Table 4–5); people who lack this enzyme often develop a severe form of anemia when they eat certain foods.

Lipids comprise the third major nutrient category and include fats and oils. Fats are broken down into fatty acids and are absorbed into the bloodstream through the walls of the small intestine with the assistance of lipoproteins and bile salts. Fatty acids are further broken down into glucose and converted into ATP in the cell mitochondria, where they are stored until needed for energy.

Vitamins are another category of nutrients needed for growth and for a healthy, functioning body. Unlike the other organic compounds (proteins, carbohydrates, and lipids), vitamins do not contribute energy to run our bodies. But they do function in important ways, making vitamin deficiencies detrimental to health. Vitamins serve as components of enzymes that speed up chemical reactions. There are two categories of vitamins: those that are water-soluble (the B vitamins and vitamin C) and those that, like fats, are not soluble in water but are soluble in fat (vitamins A, D, E, and K). The fat-soluble vitamins can be stored, so a deficiency of any of them is slow to develop. Because water-soluble vitamins are excreted in urine, very little is stored; these vitamins must be consumed almost daily in order to maintain health.

Unlike other nutrients, minerals are not organic, but they too contribute to normal functioning and health. The minerals needed in the greatest quantity include calcium (this mineral alone makes up 2 percent of our body weight, mostly in the skeleton and teeth), phosphorus, potassium, sulfur, sodium, chlorine, and magnesium. Our needs for iron are comparatively low, but this mineral plays a critical role in oxygen transport. Iron-deficiency anemia is one of the most common nutritional deficiency diseases worldwide, especially in women of reproductive age, whose iron needs are greater than those of men. Other essential minerals include iodine, zinc, manganese, copper, cobalt, fluoride, molybdenum, selenium, and chromium.

Evolution of Nutritional Needs

Our nutritional needs have coevolved with the types of food that were available to human ancestors throughout our evolutionary history. Because the earliest mammals and the first primates were probably insect eaters, humans have inherited the ability to digest and process animal protein. Early primates also evolved the ability to process most vegetable material. Our more immediate apelike ancestors were primarily fruit eaters, so we are able to process fruits. Furthermore, human needs for specific vitamins and minerals reflect these ancestral nutritional adaptations. A good example is our need for vitamin C, also known as ascorbic acid. Vitamin C plays an important role in the metabolism of all foods and in the production of energy, which we use to stay alive. It is a crucial organic compound for all animals—so crucial, in fact, that most animals are able to manufacture, or *synthesize*, it internally and need not depend on dietary sources. It is likely that most of the early primates were able to make their own vitamin C. As the monkeys evolved, however, they began to eat more leaves and fruits and less animal protein; thus, they were getting plenty of vitamin C in their diets. At some point in early primate evolution (about 35 m.y.a.; see Chapter 12), it is hypothesized that some individuals "lost" the ability to synthesize vitamin C, perhaps through a genetic mutation. This loss would not have been disadvantageous as long as dietary sources of vitamin C were regularly available. In fact, it may have been selectively advantageous to conserve the energy required for the manufacture of vitamin C, so that natural selection favored those individuals in a species who were unable to synthesize it. Eventually, all descendants of these early higher primates (i.e., modern monkeys, apes, and humans) were unable to synthesize vitamin C and became dependent entirely on external (food) sources.

Through much of the course of human evolution, the inability to manufacture vitamin C was never a problem because of the abundance of the vitamin in the human diet. It has been estimated that the average daily intake of vitamin C for preagricultural people was 440 mg, compared to an approximate 90 mg in the current American diet (Eaton and Konner, 1985). When people get insufficient amounts of vitamin C, they often develop **scurvy,** a disease that was probably extremely rare or absent in preagricultural populations (agriculture arose approximately 10,000 to 12,000 years ago). Symptoms of scurvy include abnormal bleeding of gums, slowed healing of wounds, loss of energy, anemia, and abnormal formation of bones and teeth. Scurvy was probably not very common until humans developed the technological ability to remain at sea for extended periods, requiring sailors to make do for several weeks after all fresh food reserves were exhausted. Today, the condition occasionally appears in infants who are fed exclusively on powdered or canned milk that does not have added vitamin C.

Humans also lack the ability to synthesize some of the amino acids that are necessary for growth and maintenance of the body. As noted in Chapter 3, there are 20 amino acids that make up the proteins of all living things. Plants synthesize all the amino acids, but animals must get some or all from the foods they consume. *Lactobacillus*, for example, is a bacterium that lives in milk; since it can get all 20 amino acids from the milk it consumes, it is unable to synthesize any of them. Because adult humans cannot synthesize eight of the amino acids in sufficient quantities, we must get them from the foods we eat ; they are thus referred to as the eight **essential amino acids** (for infants, there are nine). Interestingly, the amounts of each of the amino acids we need parallel the amounts present in animal protein (Table 7–2), suggesting that food from animal sources may have been an important component of ancestral hominid diets when our specific nutrient needs were evolving (see Chapter 13). Biologically, most humans can best meet their needs for protein from animal sources, but meat consumption is expensive, in both ecological and economic terms. By combining vegetables such as legumes and grains, humans can obtain the eight essential amino acids in the correct proportions (Fig. 7–6). Thus, most contemporary

▲ **Scurvy**
Disease resulting from a dietary deficiency of vitamin C. It may result in anemia, poor bone growth, abnormal bleeding and bruising, and muscle pain.

▲ **Essential amino acids**
The eight (nine for infants) amino acids that must be ingested by humans for normal growth and body maintenance; includes tryptophan, leucine, lysine, methionine, phenylalanine, isoleucine, valine, and threonine (histidine for infants).

TABLE 7–2   Essential Amino Acid Content of Some Foods (mg amino acid per 100 g food)

FOOD	TRP	LEU	LYS	MET	PHA	ISL	VAL	THR	Protein Score
"Ideal"	180	612	540	288	360	540	540	360	100
Egg	198	1092	794	384	720	818	918	620	100
Beef	150	1030	1080	308	512	664	690	550	83
Milk (cow)	180	1260	992	308	622	814	880	584	78
Milk (human)	180	980	700	220	470	590	670	480	
Oats	148	872	424	168	618	604	696	384	79
Whole wheat flour	160	891	359	200	652	572	612	386	47
Rice	130	1070	472	284	614	644	830	482	72
Cassava	262	368	620	44	266	236	288	272	22

populations meet their needs for protein by eating enough variety of vegetable foods that adequate proportions of amino acids are achieved. Examples of familiar cuisines that reflect these combinations include beans and corn in Mexico, beans and rice in Caribbean cultures, rice and lentils in India, and black-eyed peas and cornbread in the southern United States. These are all examples of how cultural processes interact with biological processes to produce successful adaptations.

Another example of biological and cultural interaction in meeting nutritional needs is seen in the traditional methods for processing corn into tortillas or hominy. Wherever corn is a major part of the diet, it is associated with a high incidence of the disease **pellagra,** which results from a deficiency of the vitamin

▲ **Pellegra**

Disease resulting from a dietary deficiency of niacin (vitamin B_3). Symptoms include dermatitis, diarrhea, dementia, and death (the "four Ds").

FIGURE 7–6

Complementarity of beans and wheat. (Adapted from Scientific American.*)*

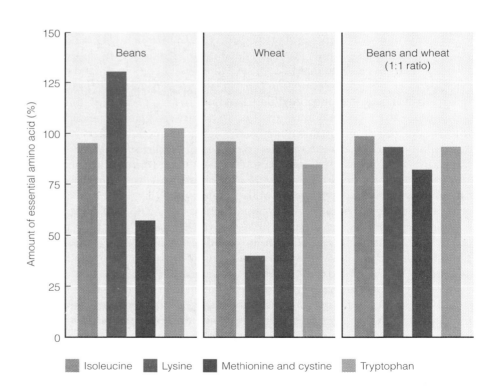

■ Isoleucine   ■ Lysine   ■ Methionine and cystine   ■ Tryptophan

niacin (vitamin B₃). The exception to this pattern is the Americas, where corn was originally domesticated and where pellagra is not common. The reason for this appears to be the practice of adding lime or ashes to the cornmeal when making tortillas or hominy. These additives increase the availability of niacin in the corn so that it can be absorbed by the body (Katz et al., 1974). Unfortunately, when corn was exported to the rest of the world, this particular technology was not exported with it.

Because humans can use cultural responses to adapt to environmental challenges, does that mean that culture has enabled us as a species to transcend the limitations placed on us by our biology? At this stage of human history, it seems that we are still constrained by our evolved nutritional needs. These needs reflect adaptation to a food base that included a great deal of variety. Not only did we evolve against a background of variety, we are now "stuck with" requirements for variety. As agriculture has evolved and population size expanded, however, the human food base has become narrower, leading to the appearance of nutritional deficiency disease, which, like scurvy and pellagra, probably did not exist in the evolutionary past (i.e., prior to the development of agriculture).

Diets of Humans Before Agriculture

The preagricultural diet, while perhaps high in animal protein, was low in fats, particularly saturated fats (Table 7–3). This is because the fat of wild animals is highly unsaturated (Table 7–4). The diet was also high in complex carbohydrates (including fiber), low in salt, and high in calcium. We do not need to be reminded that the contemporary American diet has the opposite configuration of the one just described. It is high in saturated fats and salt and low in complex carbohydrates, fiber, and calcium (Table 7–5). There is very good evidence that many of today's diseases in the industrialized countries are related to the lack of fit between our diet today and the one with which we evolved (Eaton, Shostak, and Konner, 1988).

Many of our biological and behavioral characteristics evolved because in the past they contributed to adaptation; but today they may be maladaptive. An example is our ability to store fat. This capability was an advantage in the past, when food availability often alternated between abundance and scarcity. Those who could store fat during the times of abundance could draw on those stores during times of scarcity and remain healthy, resist disease, and, for women, maintain the ability to reproduce. Today, people with adequate economic resources spend much of their lives with a relative abundance of foods. Considering the number of disorders associated with obesity, that formerly positive ability to store extra fat has now turned into a liability. Our "feast or famine" biology is now incompatible with the constant feast many of us face today.

The ability to store fat during periods of food shortage may be due in part to past selection, as suggested by geneticist James V. Neel in reference to the recent incidence of one type of diabetes, non–insulin-dependent diabetes (NIDDM). He proposes that the genes for fat storage and the genes that predispose people to diabetes may be closely associated and terms the combination a "thrifty genotype" (Neel, 1962). In the past, the negative consequences of the genotype (i.e., diabetes) were rarely manifested because of recurring periods of food shortage. More recently, however, high-carbohydrate diets and a steady "feast" have resulted in dramatic increases in the disorder. In 1900, diabetes ranked twenty-seventh among the leading causes of death in the United States; today it ranks eighth. Moreover, the highest incidence in the world is found among Piman-speaking peoples of southern Arizona and northern Mexico, whose modern diets are high in fat and sugar. Recent research suggests that if Piman peoples were to add more of their traditional foods back into their diets and reduce fat and sugar intake, their susceptibility to diabetes would decrease (Nabhan, 1991).

It is clear that both deficiencies and excesses of nutrients can cause health problems and interfere with growth and development. Certainly, many people in all parts of the world, both industrialized and developing, suffer from inadequate supplies of food of any quality. We read daily of thousands dying from starvation due to drought, warfare, or political instability. We have noted that the agricultural revolution is partly responsible for some of the problems with food and health we see today. The blame must be placed not only on the narrowed food base that resulted from the emergence of agriculture, but also on the

TABLE 7–3 Selected Meats in Agricultural and Preagricultural Diets			
	Meat (100 g portion)	Protein (g)	Fat (g)
Domestic meat	Prime lamb loin	14.7	32.0
	Ham	15.2	29.1
	Regular hamburger	17.9	21.2
	Choice sirloin steak	16.9	26.7
	Pork loin	16.4	28.0
Wild game	Goat	20.6	3.8
	Cape buffalo	—	2.8
	Warthog	—	4.2
	Horse	20.5	3.7
	Wild boar	16.8	8.3
	Beaver	30.0	5.1
	Muskrat	27.2	4.1
	Caribou	—	2.4
	Moose	—	1.5
	Kangaroo	—	1.2
	Turtle	26.8	3.9
	Opossum	33.6	4.5
	Wildebeest	—	5.4
	Thomson's gazelle	—	1.6
	Kob (waterbuck)	—	3.1
	Pheasant	24.3	5.2
	Rabbit	21.0	5.0
	Impala	—	2.6
	Topi	—	2.2
	Deer	21.0	4.0
	Bison	25.0	3.8

Note: Dashes indicate that data are not available.
Source: From Eaton, Shostak, and Konner, 1988.

increase in human population that occurred when people began to settle in permanent villages and have more children. Today, the crush of billions of humans almost completely dependent on cereal grains means that millions face undernutrition, malnutrition, and even starvation.

TABLE 7–4 Percentage of Polyunsaturated Fats in Selected Meats

		Polyunsaturated Fatty Acids as % of all Fatty Acids
Domestic meat	Beef	2.0
	Pork	9.6
	Lamb	2.7
	Veal	4.2
	Chicken	17.0
Wild game	Cape buffalo	30.0
	Eland	35.0
	Hartebeest	32.0
	Giraffe	39.0
	Kangaroo	36.0
	Warthog	43.0
	Caribou	22.0
	Grouse	60.0

Sources: Domestic Meat section of Table XII from B. K. Watt, and A. L. Merrill, *Composition of Foods.* Agriculture Handbook No. 8, U.S. Dept. of Agriculture, Washington, D.C., 1975. From Eaton, Shostak, and Konner, 1988.

TABLE 7–5 Pre-agricultural, Contemporary American, and Recently Recommended Dietary Composition

	Pre-agricultural Diet	Contemporary Diet	Recent Recommendations
Total dietary energy (%)			
Protein	33	12	12
Carbohydrate	46	46	58
Fat	21	42	30
Alcohol	~0	(7–10)	—
P:S ratio*	1.41	0.44	1
Cholesterol (mg)	520	300–500	300
Fiber (g)	100–150	19.7	30–60
Sodium (mg)	690	2,300–6.900	1,000–3.300
Calcium (mg)	1,500–2,000	740	800–1,500
Ascorbic acid (mg)	440	90	60

* Polyunsaturated: Saturated fat ratio.

Undernutrition and Malnutrition

▲ **Undernutrition**
A diet insufficient in quantity (calories) to support normal health.

▲ **Malnutrition**
A diet insufficient in quality (i.e., lacking some essential component) to support normal health.

▲ **Fertility**
Production of offspring; distinguished from *fecundity*, which is the ability to produce children. For example, a woman in her early 20s is probably fecund, but she is not actually fertile unless she has had children.

▲ **Lactation**
The production of milk in mammals.

▲ **Catch-up period**
A period of time during which a child who has experienced delayed growth because of malnutrition, undernutrition, or disease can increase in height to the point of his or her genetic potential.

▲ **Beriberi**
Disease resulting from a dietary deficiency of thiamine (vitamin B_1). Symptoms include nerve damage and cardiovascular problems.

▲ **Goiter**
Enlargement of the thyroid gland resulting from a dietary deficiency of iodine.

▲ **Cretinism**
Mental and growth retardation in infants resulting from iodine deficiency in the mother during pregnancy.

By **undernutrition,** we mean an inadequate quantity of food; in other words, not enough calories are consumed to support normal health. There is, of course, a great deal of variation in what constitutes an "adequate" diet (factors such as age, health, and activity levels all affect this determination), but it has been estimated that between 16 and 63 percent of the world's population are undernourished.

Malnutrition refers to an inadequate amount of some key element in the diet, such as proteins, minerals, or vitamins. In underdeveloped countries, protein malnutrition is the most common variety. The hallmark of severe protein malnutrition is *kwashiorkor*, a disease manifested by tissue swelling (especially in the abdominal area, giving its victims the typical "swollen belly" profile), anemia, loss or discoloration of hair, and apathy. A related syndrome, *marasmus*, is caused by the combined effects of protein *and* calorie deficiency.

More than causing discomfort, malnutrition greatly affects reproduction and infant survival. Malnourished mothers have difficult labor, more premature births, more children born with birth defects, higher prenatal mortality, and generally lower birth weights of newborns. Given all these potential physiological difficulties, it is surprising that overall **fertility** among malnourished mothers is not disrupted more than it is. Moderate chronic malnutrition (unless malnutrition becomes exceedingly severe, approaching starvation) has only a small effect on the number of live births (Bongaarts, 1980).

Children born to malnourished mothers are at a disadvantage even at birth. They are smaller and behind in most aspects of physical development. After birth, if malnutrition persists, such children fall further behind because of their mothers' generally poor **lactation.** Growth processes often slow down greatly when environmental insults are severe (malnutrition and/or disease). Later on, a period of accelerated growth (called the **catch-up period**) can make up some of the deficit. There are certain critical periods, however, in which growth in certain tissues is normally very rapid. If a severe interruption occurs during one of these periods, the individual may never catch up completely. For example, malnutrition during the last trimester of fetal life or during the first year of infancy can have marked effects on brain development. Autopsies of children who have died from complications of severe malnutrition have shown reduced brain size and weight, as well as fewer numbers of brain cells (Frisancho, 1978).

Deficiencies of specific nutrients are common in some parts of the world. **Beriberi,** caused by a deficiency of the vitamin thiamine (vitamin B_1), is the fourth leading cause of death in the Philippines. It is associated with the refined rice commonly eaten in the Philippines. Ironically, unrefined rice is an excellent source of thiamine, but it is removed during processing. This is an example of how cultural values may undermine biological adaptations. That is, refined white rice is seen as more pure and of higher social value than the more nutritious unrefined rice. Similarly, refined white bread was once more valued in the United States than the unrefined whole wheat bread.

Mineral deficiencies are also common today. Iron-deficiency anemia is a leading cause of pregnancy complications in many parts of the world, including the United States. Insufficient iodine causes **goiter** in adults and **cretinism** (a form of mental retardation) in infants whose mothers were deprived during pregnancy. Goiters form in the neck area when the thyroid gland enlarges as it tries to compensate for a lack of iodine in the diet. Goiters are most common in inland areas of the world, where soils are low in iodine; people living near the sea normally get sufficient iodine in their diets. In modern times, however, iodine is routinely added to salt, dramatically reducing the incidence of iodine deficiency worldwide. An interesting relationship between the ability to taste PTC (see

p. 115) and certain foods that are known to interfere with iodine absorption (they are said to be *goitrogenic*) suggests that this polymorphism may be subject to natural selection. These foods include members of the cabbage family (e.g., broccoli, cauliflower, and Brussels sprouts) and peanuts. They contain chemicals similar to PTC, so that the tasters are more likely to avoid these foods than nontasters. In areas of iodine-deficient soils, it is adaptive to restrict consumption of goitrogenic foods. Thus, PTC tasting may be favorably selected over nontasting in those areas.

In summary, our nutritional adaptations were shaped in an environment that included times of scarcity alternating with times of abundance. The variety of foods consumed was so great that nutritional deficiency diseases were rare. Small amounts of animal foods were probably an important part of the diet in many parts of the world. In northern latitudes, subsequent to approximately 1 million years ago, meat was an important part of the diet, but because meat was low in fats, the negative effects of high meat intake that we see today did not occur. Our diet today is often incompatible with the adaptations that evolved in the millions of years preceding the development of agriculture. The consequences of that incompatibility include both starvation and obesity.

Other Factors Influencing Growth and Development

Genetics

No matter how much you eat in your lifetime or how excellent your health, you will not be able to exceed your genetic potential for stature and a number of other physiological parameters. Genetic factors set the underlying limitations and potentialities for growth and development, but the life experience and environment of the organism determines how the body grows within those parameters. How do we assess the relative contributions of genes and the environment in their effects on growth? One of the most common sources of information comes from studies of monozygotic and dizygotic twins. Monozygotic ("identical") twins come from the union of a single sperm and ovum and share 100 percent of their genes. Dizygotic ("fraternal") twins come from separate ova and sperm and share only 50 percent of their genes, just as any other siblings from the same parents. If monozygotic twins with identical genes but different growth environments are exactly the same in stature at various ages (i.e., show perfect correlation or concordance for stature), then we can conclude that genes are the primary, if not the only, determinants of stature. Most studies of twins reveal that under normal circumstances, stature is "highly correlated" for monozygotic twins, leading to the conclusion that stature is under fairly strong genetic control (Table 7–6). Weight, on the other hand, seems to be more strongly influenced by diet, environment, and individual experiences than by genes.

Hormones

Hormones are substances produced in one cell that have an effect on another cell (see p. 47). Most hormones are produced by *endocrine* glands; they are transported in the bloodstream, and almost all have an effect on growth. The

			DZ	
Age	**Total *n***	**MZ**	**Same sex**	**Different Sex**
Birth	629	0.62	0.79	0.67
3 months	764	0.78	0.72	0.65
6 months	819	0.80	0.67	0.62
12 months	827	0.86	0.66	0.58
24 months	687	0.89	0.54	0.61
3 years	699	0.93	0.56	0.60
5 years	606	0.94	0.51	.068
8 years	444	0.94	0.49	0.65

TABLE 7–6　Correlation Coefficients for Height Between Monozygotic (MZ) and Dizygotic (DZ) Twin Pairs from Birth to Age 8.

Source: From Wilson, 1979,. after Boqin, 1988:163.

hypothalamus (located at the base of the forebrain) can be considered the relay station, control center, or central clearinghouse for most hormonal action. This control center receives messages from the brain and other glands and sends out messages that simulate hormonal action. Most of the hormonal messages transmitted from the hypothalamus result in the inhibition or release of other hormones. Thus, hormones have names like luteinizing-hormone-releasing hormone (LHRH), prolactin-inhibiting hormone (PIH), and growth-hormone-releasing hormone (GHRH, also called somatostatin).

One of the primary targets of the inhibiting and releasing hormones of the hypothalamus is the pituitary gland, located in a pocket of bone, just behind the eyes. It has two parts, the anterior pituitary and the posterior pituitary. The anterior pituitary produces hormones that regulate reproduction (FSH and LH), milk production (prolactin), metabolism (ACTH), and growth (GH). The posterior pituitary produces hormones that control water balance (vasopressin) and uterine and breast involvement in labor and nursing (oxytocin) (other hormones and their functions are listed in Table 7–7).

We can use the hormone thyroxine, produced by the thyroid glands in the neck, to illustrate the action of hormones and the communication system among the endocrine glands (Fig. 7–7) (Crapo, 1985). Thyroxine regulates metabolism and aids in body heat production. When thyroxine levels fall too low for normal metabolism, the brain senses this and sends a message to the hypothalamus. The hypothalamus reacts by releasing TRH, or thyrotropin-releasing hormone. TRH goes to the anterior pituitary, where it stimulates the release of TSH, or thyroid-stimulating hormone. TSH then goes to the thyroid gland, stimulating it to release thyroxine. When the brain senses that the levels of thyroxine are adequate, it sends signals that inhibit the further release of TRH and TSH. In many ways, this process is similar to what your household thermostat does: When it senses that the temperature has dropped too low for comfort, it sends a message to the furnace to begin producing more heat; when the temperature reaches or exceeds the preset level, the thermostat sends another message to turn the furnace off.

TABLE 7–7	Hormones and Their Effects	
Endocrine Gland	**Hormones Produced**	**Role In**
Anterior Pituitary	FSH (Follicle Stimulating Hormone)	reproduction
	LH (Luteinizing Hormone)	reproduction
	Prolactin	milk production
	ACTH (Adrenocorticotropic Hormone)	metabolism
	GH (Growth Hormone)	
Posterior Pituitary	Vasopressin	water balance
	Oxytocin	labor and nursing
Thyroid	Thyroxin	metabolism and growth
Parathyroids	PTH (Parathyroid Hormone)	calcium metabolism
Pancreas	Insulin	glucose metabolism
	Glucagon	glucose metabolism
Adrenals	Cortisol	metabolism, blood pressure
	Aldosterone	salt regulation
	Epinephrine	energy mobilization
Ovaries	Estrogen	reproduction
	Progesterone	reproduction
Testes	Testosterone	reproduction

Environmental Factors

Environmental factors, such as altitude and climate, have effects on growth and development. Perhaps the primary influence of such external factors comes from their effects on nutrition, but there is evidence of independent effects as well. For example, as noted in Chapter 6, infant birth weight is lower at high altitude, even when such factors as nutrition, smoking, and socioeconomic status are taken into consideration. In the United States, the percentage of low-birth-rate (LBW) infants (those weighing less than 2,500 g or 5.7 pounds) is about 6.5 percent at sea level, rising to 10.4 percent at 5,000 feet and almost 24 percent above 10,000 feet. In a Bolivian study, the mean birth weight was 3,415 g (7.8 pounds) at low elevations and 3,133 g (7.1 pounds) at high elevations (Hass et al., 1980). Most studies of children have found that those at high elevations are shorter and lighter than those at low elevations.

In general, populations in cold climates tend to be heavier and have longer trunks and shorter extremities than populations in tropical areas. This reflects Bergmann's and Allen's rules, discussed in Chapter 6. Exposure to sunlight also appears to have an effect on growth, most likely through its effects on vitamin D production. Children tend to grow more rapidly in times of high sunlight concentration (i.e., in the summer in temperate regions and in the dry season in monsoonal tropical regions). Vitamin D, necessary for skeletal growth, requires sunlight for its synthesis (see p. 141).

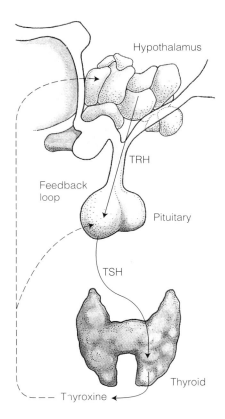

FIGURE 7–7

Example of a feedback loop. When thyroxin levels in the blood fall too low, the hypothalamus releases TRH (thyrotropin-releasing hormone), which goes to the anterior pituitary, triggering the release of TSH (thyroid-stimulating hormone). TSH causes thyroxine to be released from the thyroid gland. Release of TRH and TSH is then inhibited.

The Human Life Cycle

Not all animals have clearly demarcated phases in their lives; moreover, among mammals, humans have more such phases than do other species (Fig. 7–8). Protozoa, among the simplest of animals, have only one phase; many invertebrates have two: larval and adult. Almost all mammals have at least three phases (gestation, infancy, and adulthood). Most primates have four phases: gestation, infancy, juvenile (usually called childhood in humans), and adult. Monkeys, apes, and humans add a phase between the juvenile phase and adulthood that is referred to as the subadult period (adolescence, or teenage, in humans). Finally, for humans there is the addition of a sixth phase in women, the postreproductive years following menopause. One could argue that during the course of primate evolution, more recently evolved forms have longer life spans and more divisions of the life span into phases, or stages.

Most of these life cycle stages are well marked by biological transitions. Gestation begins with conception and ends with birth; infancy is the period of nursing; childhood, or the juvenile phase, is the period from weaning to sexual maturity (puberty in humans); adolescence is the period from puberty to the end of growth; adulthood is marked by the birth of the first child and/or the completion of growth; and menopause is recognized as having occurred one full year after the last menstrual cycle. These biological markers are similar among higher primates, but for humans, there is an added complexity: They occur in cultural contexts that define and characterize them. Puberty, for example, has very different meanings in different cultures. A girl's first menstruation (menarche) is often marked with ritual and celebration, and a change in social status typically occurs with this biological transition. Likewise, menopause is often associated with a rise in status for women in non-Western societies, whereas it is commonly seen as a negative transition for women in many Western societies. As we shall see, collective and individual attitudes toward these life cycle transitions have an effect on growth and development.

Conception and Pregnancy

The biological aspects of conception and gestation can be discussed in a fairly straightforward way, drawing information from what is known about reproduc-

FIGURE 7–8

Life cycle stages for various animal species.

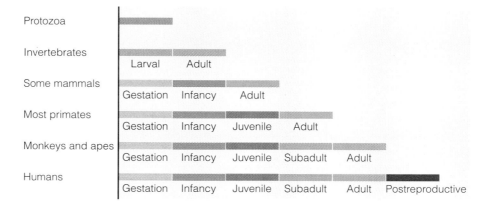

tive biology at the present time: A sperm fertilizes an egg; the resulting zygote travels through a uterine (fallopian) tube to become implanted in the uterine lining; and the embryo develops until it is mature enough to survive outside the womb, at which time birth occurs. But this is clearly not all there is to human pregnancy and birth. Female biology may be somewhat similar the world over, but cultural rules and practices are the primary determinants of who will get pregnant, as well as when, where, how, and by whom.

Once pregnancy has occurred, there is much variation in how the woman should behave, what she should eat, where she should and should not go, and how she should interact with other people. Almost every culture known, including our own, imposes dietary restrictions on pregnant women. Many of these appear to serve an important biological function, particularly that of keeping the woman from ingesting toxins that would be dangerous for the fetus. (Alcohol is a good example of a potential toxin whose consumption in pregnancy is discouraged in the United States.) Food aversions to coffee, alcohol, and other bitter substances that many women experience during pregnancy may be evolved adaptations to protect the embryo from toxins. The nausea of early pregnancy may also function to limit the intake of foods potentially harmful to the embryo at a critical stage of development (Profet, 1988; Williams and Nesse 1991).

Thus, it appears that our biological heritage includes adaptations that improve pregnancy outcome, but we reinforce these with cultural restrictions that improve it even more (or, in some cases make it worse). This is not to say that every food restriction or aversion of pregnancy is adaptive; but many are likely to prove advantageous if evaluated carefully. For example, many of the foods forbidden to women during pregnancy are proteins, such as eggs and chicken. Restriction of these items may at first seem maladaptive, since proteins are important for fetal growth and development. But they also cause stress on the mother's kidneys, which are already under great strain during pregnancy. Thus, physicians in the United States often advise against consumption of excess protein.

Gestation length in humans and in our closest relatives, chimpanzees and gorillas, are very similar, although for other life cycle stages, human spans are almost twice those of chimpanzees and gorillas. Ashley Montagu (1961), Stephen Jay Gould (1977), and others have suggested that the human gestation period may actually be about 15 to 18 months, but we are delivered "early" in order to be born at all—a necessity considering the large size of the fetal human head compared to the relatively narrow maternal pelvis. Extending the gestation period by another 6 to 9 months would bring it more in line with what would be expected from looking at other life cycle stages (Fig. 7–9).

Perhaps the most obvious difference between human and other primate infants at birth is the degree of brain development (Table 7–8). The human brain at birth is about 25 percent as large as it will be in adulthood, measuring approximately 350 cm^3. By 1 year, it will have more than doubled in size, tripling by age 3. In contrast, nonhuman primate infants are born with brains averaging one-half the size of adults of their species.

An undeveloped brain seems necessary for birth to occur through a narrow pelvis, but it may also be advantageous for other reasons. For a species as dependent on learning as we are for survival, it may be adaptive for most of our brain growth to take place in the presence of environmental stimuli rather than in the relatively unstimulating uterus. This may be particularly true for a species dependent on language. The language centers of the brain develop in the first three years of life, when the brain is undergoing its rapid expansion; these three years are considered a critical period for the development of language in the human child.

FIGURE 7–9
Primate age spans.

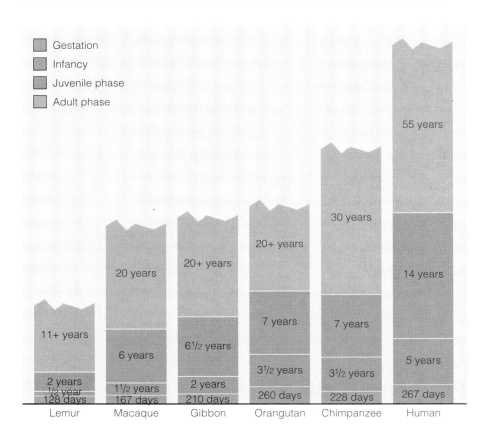

TABLE 7–8 Neonatal Brain Weight as a Percentage of Adult Brain Weight for Selected Mammalian Species	
Mammal	**Neonatal Brain Weight (%)**
Harbor porpoise	38
California seal	50
Horse	52
Llama	76
Cow	44
Galago	40
Howler	57
Spider monkey	58
Rhesus macaque	68
Hamadryas baboon	40
Common chimpanzee	36
Gorilla	56
Human	26

Birth

Birth is an event that is celebrated with ritual in almost every culture studied. In fact, the relatively little fanfare associated with childbirth in the United States is unusual by world standards. Because risk of death for both mother and child is so great at birth, it is not surprising that it is surrounded with ritual significance. Perhaps because of the high risk of death, we tend to think that birth is far more difficult in humans than it is in other mammals. But since almost all primate infants have large heads relative to body size, birth is challenging to many primates (Fig. 7–10).

Most primates infants are born facing their mothers, which facilitates reaching down and guiding the infant out of the birth canal. Because the human pelvis is designed for walking on two legs (bipedalism), the relatively larger *back* of the infant's head fits best against the relatively larger *front* of the mother's pelvis. This means that human infants are born facing toward the back of the mother's birth canal. This neonatal orientation provides a greater challenge to the mother, who must reach behind her to pull the infant from the birth canal. Such added difficulty might explain why humans routinely seek assistance at the time of birth rather than seek isolation, as do other mammals. Simply having someone else there to guide the baby out, to wipe its face so it can begin breathing, and to keep the umbilical cord from choking it can significantly reduce mortality associated with birth (Trevathan, 1987). A survey of world cultures reveals that it is very unusual to give birth alone, particularly to a first child. Even in cultures where the ideal may be to give birth alone, it rarely happens that way (Eaton, Shostak, and Konner, 1988).

The relation between the average diameter of the birth canal of adult females and average head length and breadth of newborns of the same species.

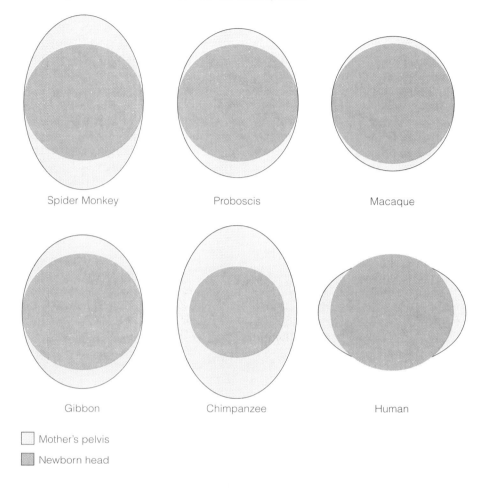

Spider Monkey   Proboscis   Macaque

Gibbon   Chimpanzee   Human

☐ Mother's pelvis
▨ Newborn head

FIGURE 7–10

The relation between the average diameter of the birth canal of adult females and average head length and breadth of newborns of the same species. (After Jolly, 1985.)

Infancy

Infancy is defined as the period during which nursing takes place, typically lasting about four years in humans. When we consider how unusual it is for a mother to nurse her child for even a year in the United States or Canada, this figure may surprise us. But considering that four or five years of nursing is the norm for chimpanzees, gorillas, orangutans, and for women in foraging societies, most anthropologists conclude that four years was the norm for most humans in the evolutionary past (Eaton, Shostak, and Konner, 1988). Other lines of evidence confirm this pattern, including the lack of other foods that infants could consume until the origin of agriculture and the domestication of milk-producing animals. In fact, if the mother died during childbirth in the preagricultural past, it is very likely that the child died also, unless there was another woman available who could nurse the child. Jane Goodall has noted that this is also true for chimpanzees: Infants who are orphaned before they are weaned do not usually survive. Even those orphaned after weaning are still emotionally dependent on their mothers and exhibit clinical signs of depression for a few months or years after the mother's death, assuming they survive the trauma (Goodall, 1986).

Human milk, like that of other primates, is extremely low in fats and protein (Fig. 7–11). Such a low nutrient content is typical for species in which mothers are seldom or never separated from their infants and nurse in short, frequent bouts. Not coincidentally, prolonged, frequent nursing suppresses ovulation (Konner and Worthman, 1980); this helps to maintain a four-year birth interval, during which infants have no nutritional competition from siblings. Thus, nursing served as a natural birth control mechanism in the evolutionary past, as it does in some populations today.

Breast milk also provides important antibodies that contribute to infant survival. Throughout the world, breast-fed infants have far greater survival rates than those who are not breast-fed or who are weaned too early (see Fig. 7–1). The only exception to this is in societies where scientifically developed milk substitutes are readily available and appropriately used. The importance of adequate nutrients during this period of rapid brain growth cannot be overestimated. Thus, it is not surprising that there are many cultural practices designed to ensure successful nursing.

Childhood

Humans have unusually long childhoods, reflecting the importance of learning for our species. *Childhood* is that time between weaning and puberty when the brain is completing its growth and acquisition of technical and social skills is taking place. For most other mammals, once weaning has occurred, getting food is

FIGURE 7–11

Carbohydrate, protein, and fat composition of milk of selected mammals (indicated in percent). (From Ben Shaul, 1962.)

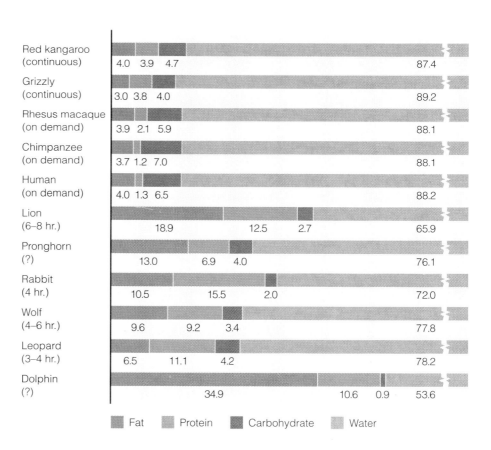

	Fat	Protein	Carbohydrate	Water
Red kangaroo (continuous)	4.0	3.9	4.7	87.4
Grizzly (continuous)	3.0	3.8	4.0	89.2
Rhesus macaque (on demand)	3.9	2.1	5.9	88.1
Chimpanzee (on demand)	3.7	1.2	7.0	88.1
Human (on demand)	4.0	1.3	6.5	88.2
Lion (6–8 hr.)	18.9	12.5	2.7	65.9
Pronghorn (?)	13.0	6.9	4.0	76.1
Rabbit (4 hr.)	10.5	15.5	2.0	72.0
Wolf (4–6 hr.)	9.6	9.2	3.4	77.8
Leopard (3–4 hr.)	6.5	11.1	4.2	78.2
Dolphin (?)	34.9	10.6	0.9	53.6

left to individual effort. Humans may be unique in the practice of providing food for children or juveniles (Lancaster and Lancaster, 1983). Such sustained care requires much extra effort by parents, but the survival rate of offspring is a great deal higher than in other primates (Table 7–9). During childhood, the roles of fathers and older siblings become very significant. While mothers are highly involved with caring for new infants, the socialization and child care of other children often fall to other family or community members.

Adolescence

A number of biological events mark the transition to adulthood for both males and females. These include increase in body size, change in body shape, and the development of testes and penes in boys, and breasts in girls. Hormonal changes are the driving forces behind all these physical changes, especially increased testosterone production in boys and increased estrogen production in girls. As already noted, menarche (the first menstruation) is a clear sign of puberty in girls and is usually the marker of this transition in cultures where the event is ritually celebrated.

In humans and other primates, females reach sexual maturity before males do, although they are not usually capable of becoming pregnant until several years after the first menstruation. A number of factors affect the onset of puberty in humans, including genetic patterns (children tend to become mature at about the same age as their parents), nutrition, disease, and stress.

For girls, it appears that a certain amount of body fat is necessary for menarche and the maintenance of ovulation (Frisch, 1988). Both diet and activity levels affect the accumulation of body fat. This may explain the trend toward the lower age of menarche that has been noted in human populations in the last

TABLE 7–9 Providing for Juveniles

	Percent of Those Who Survive	
	Weaning	Adolescence
Lion	28	15
Baboon	45	33
Macaque	42	13
Chimpanzee	48	38
Provisioned macaques	82	58
Human Populations		
!Kung*	80	58
Yanomamo †	73	50
Paleoindian ††	86	50

* A hunting and gathering population of southern Africa.
† Horticultural population of South America.
†† Preagricultural people of the Americas.
Source: Adapted from Lancaster and Lancaster, 1983.

hundred years and the tendency for girls who are very active and thin to mature later than those who are heavier and less active. High activity and low body fat also characterize many ballet dancers and marathon runners, who often cease to menstruate during periods of intense training.

Since pregnancy and nursing require an increase in caloric consumption, body fat may serve as a signal to the body that there is enough caloric reserve to support a pregnancy. When the levels of body fat fall too low, ovulation may cease temporarily to prevent initiation of a pregnancy that is likely to fail. A *Homo sapiens* girl in the time prior to agriculture probably reached puberty at about age 16 and had her first child at about age 20. Like girls today, she probably had several years of menstrual cycles following menarche during which ovulation was rare.

Adolescence is the time between puberty and the completion of physical growth or the social recognition of adulthood. This social recognition may result from marriage, bearing a child, or a particular accomplishment. In nonhuman primates, the equivalent stage is defined in males as the time from which they are capable of fertilization to the time when physical growth is complete. At this point, they have male-specific features and size and are recognized as adults by other members of the social group. Females begin to engage in sexual behavior, exhibiting signs of sexual receptivity before they are capable of bearing young. These early cycles are usually not ovulatory and define the period of adolescence for them. Adulthood comes with the first pregnancy.

Adulthood and Aging

Pregnancy and child care occupy much of a woman's adult life in most cultures, as they likely did in the evolutionary past. For most women who use contraception, the years from menarche to menopause are marked monthly by menstruation, except when they are pregnant or nursing. A normal menstrual cycle has two phases: the follicular phase, in which the egg is preparing for ovulation, marked by high estrogen production; and the luteal phase, during which the uterus is preparing for implantation, marked by high progesterone production. If the egg is not fertilized, progesterone production drops off and menstruation, the shedding of the uterine lining, occurs. A woman who never becomes pregnant may have as many as 400 cycles between menarche and menopause. Because reliable contraceptives were unavailable in the preagricultural past, this high number of menstrual cycles is probably a relatively recent phenomenon. It has been suggested, in fact, that highly frequent menstrual cycling may be implicated in several cancers of female reproductive organs, especially of the breast, uterus, and ovaries (Eaton et al., 1994). During the course of human evolution, females may have had as few as 60 menstrual cycles in their entire lives, unless they were sterile or not sexually active.

In addition to caring for children, women in the majority of world cultures also participate in economic activities. Adulthood for men typically includes activities related to subsistence, religion, politics, and family. Women may be equally or less involved in these activities, depending on the culture.

During adulthood, the status of an individual may change as new skills are acquired or new achievements made. Where such records are kept, status may be defined by chronological age, as seen in the common pattern of retirement at age 65 or 70 in the United States.

For women, menopause, or the end of menstruation, is a sign of entry into a new phase of the life cycle. Estrogen and progesterone production begin to decline toward the end of the reproductive years until ovulation (and thus menstruation) ceases altogether. This occurs at approximately age 50 in all parts of the world. Throughout human evolution, the majority of females (and males) did not survive to age 50; thus, few women lived much past menopause. But today, this event occurs when women have as much as one-third of their active and healthy lives ahead of them. As already noted, such a long period of postreproductive time is not found in other primates. Female chimpanzees and monkeys experience decreased fertility in their later years, but most continue to have monthly cycles until their deaths. Occasional reports of menopause in apes and monkeys have been noted, but it is far from a routine and expected event.

Why do human females have such a long period during which they can no longer reproduce? One theory relates to parenting. Since it takes about 12 to 15 years before a child becomes independent, it has been argued that females are biologically "programmed" to live 12 to 15 years beyond the birth of their last child (Mayer, 1982). This suggests that the maximum human life span for preagricultural humans was about 65 years, a figure that corresponds to what is known for contemporary hunter-gatherers and for prehistoric populations. Another theory regarding menopause suggests that it was not the subject of natural selection itself; rather it is an artifact of the extension of the human life span. Some have suggested that the maximum life span of the mammalian egg is 50 years (you will recall that all the ova are already present before birth; see p. 62). Thus, although the human life span has increased in the last several hundred years, the reproductive life span has not.

Postreproductive years are somewhat well defined for women, but "old age" is a very ambiguous concept. In the United States, we tend to associate old age with physical ailments and decreased activity. Thus, a person who is vigorous and active at age 70 might not be regarded as "old," whereas another who is frail and debilitated at age 55 may be considered old.

One reason we are concerned with this definition is that old age is generally regarded negatively and is typically unwelcome in the United States, a culture noted for its emphasis on youth. This attitude is quite different from many other societies, where old age brings with it wealth, higher status, and new freedoms, particularly for women. This is because high status is often correlated with knowledge, experience, and wisdom, which are themselves associated with greater age in most societies. Such has been the case throughout most of history, but today, in technologically developed countries, knowledge is changing so rapidly that the old may no longer control the most relevant knowledge.

By and large, people today are living longer than they did in the past because, in part, they are not dying from infectious diseases. The top five killers in the United States, for example, are heart disease, cancer, stroke, accidents, and chronic obstructive lung disease. Together these account for 75 percent of deaths (Eaton, Shostak, and Konner, 1988). All these conditions are considered "diseases of civilization" in that most can be accounted for by conditions in the modern environment that were not present in the past. Examples include cigarette smoke, air and water pollution, alcohol, automobiles, high-fat diets, and environmental carcinogens. It should be noted, however, that the high incidence of these diseases is also a result of people living to older ages because of factors such as improved hygiene, regular medical care, and new medical technologies.

The final phase of the life cycle, if we can call it that, is death. Humans all over the world celebrate this transition, often with great fanfare and expense. Some people interpret evidence from Neandertal remains to mean that ritual treatment of the dead may go back as far as 100,000 years in human history (see

Chapter 17). Death is a less ambiguous transition than any of the others previously described, although there is great variation in what is believed to happen to the individual after death. There is also variability in mortuary practices surrounding the disposal of the physical remains. Most common are cremation and burial.

Summary

This chapter has reviewed the fundamental concepts of growth and development and how those processes occur within the contexts of both biology and culture. Diet has an important effect on growth, and human nutritional needs themselves result from biocultural evolution. The preagricultural human diet was reviewed, with the suggestion that many of our contemporary ills may result from incompatibilities between our evolved nutritional needs and the foods that are currently consumed. In particular, the preagricultural diet was probably high in complex carbohydrates and fiber and low in fat and sodium. Diets for many contemporary people are low in complex carbohydrates and fiber and high in fat and sodium. This type of diet has been implicated in many current health problems.

The human life cycle can be divided into six phases: gestation, infancy, juvenile, subadult, adult, and postreproductive. Each is fairly well defined by biological markers. Pregnancy lasts about nine months in humans, and infants are born with only about 25 percent of their adult brain size. This means that human infants are helpless at birth and therefore dependent on their parents for a long time. Birth is a bit more challenging for humans than for other mammals because of the very close correspondence between maternal pelvic size (narrow because of bipedalism) and fetal head size (large, even though the brain is relatively undeveloped). Infancy is the period of nursing, approximately four years for most humans and apes. The unusually long period of childhood in humans is important as the time in which social and technological skills are acquired. Sexual maturation is apparent at puberty, but full adult status is not achieved until growth has been completed and childbearing capabilities are reached. The last phase of the human life cycle, the postreproductive period, is marked in women by menopause, the cessation of menstruation and ovulation.

Questions for Review

1. What is meant by the analogy "Water is to fish as culture is to humans"?
2. Describe how a bone grows.
3. What is sexual dimorphism? List some examples in humans.
4. Briefly describe human brain growth.
5. What are essential amino acids? Develop a scenario for how our need for these amino acids might have evolved.
6. Give two examples of ways in which culture and biology interact in meeting human nutritional needs.
7. What were the characteristics of the preagricultural human diet? What are the major differences today?
8. Briefly discuss the source and effects of the major hormones involved in growth and development.
9. How does gestation length compare in humans and apes? Why is it shorter in humans than might be expected?
10. Why is nursing important for infant health? What is the proposed relationship between nursing and ovulation?

11. What is the proposed significance of providing food for children beyond the age of weaning?
12. What biological changes occur in males and females at puberty? What role does body fat appear to play in females?
13. What are some of the proposed explanations for menopause in human females?

Suggested Further Reading

Bogin, Barry. 1988. *Patterns of Human Growth*. Cambridge: Cambridge University Press.

Cohen, Mark Nathan. 1989. *Health and the Rise of Civilization*. New Haven: Yale University Press.

Diamond, Jared. 1992. *The Third Chimpanzee: The Evolution and Future of the Human Animal*. New York: Harper Collins.

Eaton, S. Boyd, Marjorie Shostak, and Melvin Konner. 1988. *The Paleolithic Prescription*. New York: Harper & Row.

Shipman, Pat, Alan Walker, and David Bichell. 1985. *The Human Skeleton*. Cambridge, MA: Harvard University Press.

Sinclair, D. 1989. *Human Growth after Birth*. New York: Oxford University Press.

Tanner, James M. 1990. *Foetus into Man: Physical Growth from Conception to Maturity*. 2d ed., Cambridge, MA: Harvard University Press.

Trevathan, Wenda R. 1987. *Human Birth: An Evolutionary Perspective*. Hawthorne, NY: Aldine de Gruyter.

Internet Resources

Aeiveos Science Group
  http://www.aeiveos.com/
  (Excellent source for topics related to aging. Information on theories related to diet, nutrition, genetics, disease, and other factors associated with aging processes. Includes current bibliographies and links to numerous related sites.)

James J. McKenna

James J. McKenna, Professor of Anthropology, Pomona College, and Senior Researcher, Department of Neurology, University of California, Irvine, School of Medicine (SIDS Project)

Anthropology in a Sleep Laboratory Maketh a Career? What Physical Anthropology, SIDS, Watching Monkeys, and Having a Baby Have in Common.

"It's something about human evolution . . . you know, human bones and artifacts," said one of my friends about a course called "Introduction to Physical Anthropology." I needed a course to fulfill my social sciences requirement as a premed at UC Berkeley in the late sixties. I decided to take a chance. I was curious about how anybody could think that humans actually *"evolved."* Of course, bacteria and algae evolved, but people? I was a devout Catholic, and Catholics did not evolve!

From the first lecture to the last I was truly amazed; you might say *inspired.* So fascinated was I that I couldn't bring myself to believe that anything that I was learning was actually true! As I encountered evolutionary theory, fossil monkeys, primate behavior, and both human fossil and archeological evidence for human cultural and biological origins, I knew I was a goner. My medical career was out. I was an anthro major! But what do you do with it, my parents asked?

I had no idea. But I could worry about *that* later. For now, I would just love it! I developed a strong interest in nonhuman primate behavior and its physiological correlates—especially how social contact, proximity, grooming, and mother-infant separation affected health and development. I wanted to learn more about whether or not human cultural patterns (child care, kin-ship, subsistence, aggression, reconciliation, love, etc.) emerged from biological needs or were simply random or strictly learned, or both. Most especially, I was interested in how principles of behavior documented among nonhuman primate parents and infants could be applied to human beings to explain contemporary patterns of birth, parenting and infancy. Under the guidance of a brilliant teacher (Professor Phyllis Dolhinow) my career began to take some general form. But still, I thought, anthropology? What will I do with it?

Throughout graduate school I focused on all the subfields of anthropology finding that each one supported and enriched the meaning and purposes of the others. Gaining familiarity with all of them was the best thing I ever did, because years later I felt reasonably comfortable about crossing discipline boundaries to enter the world of pediatric sleep, SIDS (Sudden Infant Death Syndrome); as a result, my biomedical research is in no small measure due to the early insights and practice gained in weaving ideas and concepts together from diverse anthropological evidence! The integration of the past and the present, the biological and the cultural, the "scientific" and humanistic became the beauty, the fun, the power, and uniqueness of anthropology.

After completing a dissertation on ecological aspects of infancy and parenting among Indian langur monkeys, I finally discovered one of the things that you do with an anthro major—and that is to share and explore it! I began my college research and teaching career. I found myself enjoying the excitement of sharing anthropology with undergraduates in the same way that my teachers enjoyed sharing it with me. For the first time in my anthropological career, I actually talked in class! All was well. My life direction was set. I was known as a primatologist. And then everything began to change. I became a parent!

Jeff was born with colic—which means that he (like many other infants) cried and cried and cried and nobody knew why. Of course, all the monkey and ape infants I had read about or studied couldn't help me now; and, yet, I did know that monkey and ape infants are carried, handled, and given breast milk and affection continuously—they were never separated from their mothers. It's a primate thing. And what I began to appreciate was that if my son slept with us, and if I held and rocked my son in my arms, he stopped crying. He especially appreciated me dancing Saturday Night Fever disco with him (John Travolta and the Bee Gees style) which was the rage. It was almost the only thing that would work to calm him. The only other thing that would work was if I lay down next to him and breathed closely into his face. My little infant son would relax and respond to the speed and form of my breathing. I learned I could manipulate his breathing speed to compliment my own and we both would fall asleep!

Then what struck me changed my career. This little one-month-old seemed to be sensitive to my breathing and chest movement cues! But why should I be surprised? Almost

all nonwestern, nonindustrial, contemporary human infants sleep next to their parents and "expect" to be regulated physiologically especially by their breast feeding mothers after birth. In fact, their bodies are designed for it. After all, human infants are the least neurologically mature primate of all and subject to the most external regulation and support for the longest period of time! I began to realize that sleeping apart from our infants is a cultural idea, and has nothing to do with their three-million-year-old biology—or the needs of their primate bodies. I began to wonder: might not separation from the caregiver deprive infants of optimal breast feeding rates and potentially important sensory exchanges with the caregiver—exchanges that may regulate something as fundamental as infant breathing and safe infant sleep? Cosleeping might be life affirming and, possibly, lifesaving. Might safe forms of cosleeping help to prevent SIDS?

This was my entree into a new field. Evolutionary concepts validated by cross-cultural ethnographic and monkey-ape studies, suddenly and strangely seemed highly relevant to creating more accurate models of "normal" infant sleep and, potentially, some insights into an enigmatic infant killer known as the sudden infant death syndrome or SIDS, a malady for which no current medical models were adequate to explain or understand. I realized that whatever the causes of SIDS, the research will be constrained until we understand that infants sleeping alone is not biologically normal!

Almost seventeen years later I am known as a biological anthropologist who specializes in infant sleep, SIDS, and evolutionary medicine. With support from the National Institutes of Health my sleep research colleagues (Drs. Sarah Mosko and Chris Richard) and I have completed several major studies conducted in a sleep laboratory showing that infants who regularly sleep with their mothers, who bedshare, exhibit remarkably different sleep patterns, breast feeding behavior, arousal patterns, and breathing from solitary sleeping infants. Whether or not cosleeping can truly help to prevent SIDS among some infants needs to be tested further. But already the combination of these diverse fields has produced results which have forever changed attitudes about what constitutes "normal" infant sleep. Moreover, we have helped to expand the possible types of sleeping arrangements that parents can elect and feel good about. Infant-parent cosleeping can no longer be thought of as abnormal, bizarre, or inherently dangerous.

I never could have predicted that a class in anthropology would change my life—or that personal insights borne from personal experiences could give rise to new scientific ideas, or how professional activities and personal experiences could become so entwined and interdependent. And it's still true as my friend once described it, that physical anthropology is "something about human evolution." But be forewarned: it's also about a whole lot more!

Macroevolution: Overview and Principles

Introduction

In the preceding chapters, we surveyed the genetic mechanisms that are the foundation of the evolutionary process. Moreover, Chapters 5 and 6 have shown in detail how *microevolutionary* changes are investigated in contemporary human populations. In this chapter, we turn to the *macroevolutionary* process. We will review aspects of vertebrate (and specifically mammalian) evolution over the great time depth of these major groups. The fundamental perspectives reviewed here concerning geological history, principles of classification, and modes of evolutionary change will serve as a basis for topics covered throughout the remainder of this text.

The Human Place in the Organic World

Some estimates suggest that there are more than 10 million species living today; of these, perhaps 1.5 million have been named and described. When you add to this number all those species that are now *extinct*, the total that may have existed is staggering, certainly exceeding tens of millions.

How do biologists cope with all this diversity? As is typical for *Homo sapiens*, scientists approach complexity through simplification and generalization. Thus, biologists group life-forms together; in other words, they construct a **classification** system.

Even with the tens of thousands of species that biologists do know something about, there is still too much variety to handle conveniently. The solution is to organize this diversity into groupings to (1) reduce the complexity and (2) to indicate evolutionary relationships.

All life on earth is part of an organic continuum. From the beginnings of life, more than 4 billion years ago, all life-forms have shared in a common ancestry. Our contemporary attempts to organize the bewildering array of organisms that have evolved make relative interpretations of relationships. Since all organisms fall *somewhere* on the biological continuum, our conclusions simply place humans, for example, within this continuous framework and then judge which other organisms are evolutionarily closer to our lineage and which are more distant.

Organisms that move about and ingest food (but do not photosynthesize, as in plants) are called *animals*. More precisely, the multicelled animals are placed within the group called the **Metazoa**. Within the Metazoa there are more than 20 major groups termed *phyla* (*sing.*, phylum). One of these phyla is the **Chordata**, animals with a nerve cord, gill slits (at some stage of development), and a stiff supporting cord along the back called a *notochord*. Most chordates today are **vertebrates**, in which the notochord has become a vertebral column (which gives its name to the group); in addition, vertebrates have a developed brain and paired sensory structures for sight, smell, and balance.

The vertebrates themselves are traditionally subdivided into six classes: bony fishes, cartilaginous fishes, amphibians, reptiles, birds, and mammals. We will discuss mammalian classification later in the chapter.

Taxonomy

Before we go any further, it would be useful to discuss the bases of animal classification. The field that specializes in delineating the rules of classification is

▲ **Classification**
In biology, the ordering of organisms into categories, such as phyla, orders, and families, to show evolutionary relationship.

▲ **Metazoa**
Multicellular animals; a major division of the animal kingdom.

▲ **Chordata (Chordates)**
The phylum of the animal kingdom that includes vertebrates.

▲ **Vertebrates**
Animals with bony backbones. Includes fishes, amphibians, reptiles, birds, and mammals.

called *taxonomy*. Organisms are classified first, and most traditionally, on the basis of physical similarities. Such was the basis of the first systematic classification devised by Linnaeus in the eighteenth century (see Chapter 2).

Today, basic physical similarities are still considered a good starting point in postulating schemes of organic relationships. For similarities to be useful, however, they *must* reflect evolutionary descent. For example, the bones of the forelimb of all terrestrial air-breathing vertebrates (tetrapods) are so similar in number and form (Fig. 8–1) that the obvious explanation for the striking resemblances is that all four kinds of air-breathing vertebrates ultimately derived their forelimb structure from a common ancestor.

Structures that are shared by species on the basis of descent from a common ancestor are called **homologies**. Homologies alone are reliable indicators of evolutionary relationship. But we must be careful not to draw hasty conclusions from superficial similarities. For example, both bats and birds have wings, but bats and birds should not be grouped together solely because they share this one trait. In many other respects bats and birds are *not* closely related (e.g., only birds have feathers; only mammals have fur). Such structural features as the wing of a bird and the wing of a bat that superficially appear to be similar and have evolved through common function are called **analogies**. You should be aware that when comparing two different organisms—for example, bats and birds—some of the shared structures may result from homology while others are the result of analogy (the wing structures are analogous, but as you will see, the basic bone confirmation is homologous). If, however, we compare the wing of a bat with that of a butterfly, then almost no homology exists, and whatever similarities we do perceive are almost entirely the product of analogy. The separate development of analogous structures comes about in evolution through related processes termed *parallelism* and *convergence*—what experts now prefer to call **homoplasy**.

In making consistent evolutionary interpretations and devising classifications that reflect these interpretations, evolutionary biologists must concentrate on the homologies and treat the analogies as extraneous "noise." Nor is it sufficient simply to isolate the homologies. For certain purposes, some structural homologies are much more informative than others. The forelimbs of air-breathing vertebrates are all similar in overall structure. Some may be adapted

▲ **Homologies**
Similarities between organisms based on descent from a common ancestor.

▲ **Analogies**
Similarities between organisms based strictly on common function with no assumed common evolutionary descent.

▲ **Homoplasy** (*homo*, meaning "same," and *plasy*, meaning "growth"). The separate evolutionary development of similar characteristics in different groups of organisms.

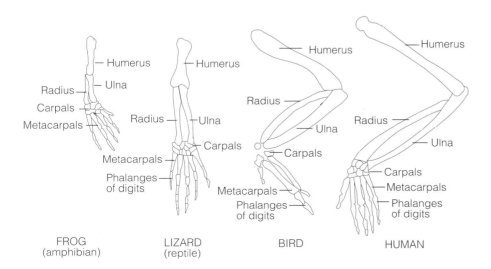

FIGURE 8–1
Homologies. The similarities in the bones of these animals can be easily explained by descent from a common ancestor.

▲ **Primitive**

Relating to a character state that reflects an ancestral condition and thus not diagnostic of those derived lineages usually branching later.

▲ **Derived**

Relating to a character state that is modified from the ancestral condition and reflects a more specific evolutionary line and thus is more informative of precise evolutionary relationships.

▲ **Shared derived**

Relating to specific character states shared in common between two forms and considered the most useful for making evolutionary interpretations.

▲ **Cladistics**

The approach to taxonomy that groups species (as well as other levels of classification) on the basis of shared derived characteristics. In this way, organisms are classified solely on the basis of presumed closeness of evolutionary relationship.

▲ **Geological timescale**

The organization of earth history into eras, periods, and epochs commonly used by geologists and paleoanthropologists.

into wings, others into legs. If we were to group birds and bats on the basis of a functional (derived) modification into a wing, we would be assuming that the common ancestor of both possessed wings. From fossil evidence, this clearly was *not* the case.

Nor can we sort birds from bats or frogs from lizards on the basis of the number of bones in the forelimb. They all possess *generally* similar structures (presumably which they all *did* inherit from a common vertebrate ancestor). We would say, therefore, that the basic forelimb structure for all tetrapods is **primitive**. The term *primitive* is not used to indicate a characteristic or type of organism that is in any way inferior. Perhaps a less confusing term would be *ancestral*. Among mammals, for example, human (and other primate) hands retain the ancestral condition of five digits, while the hooves of cattle with only two digits are much more **derived** (i.e., modified from the ancestral condition). Few people—perhaps because we are so *anthropocentric*—would be willing to concede that hooves are superior to hands. Of course, hooves function better to support a large grazing animal, while hands serve other functions in animals that spend time in trees (see Chapter 9). As you can see, concepts like "inferior" and "superior" are meaningless when we are comparing organisms.

As noted, *only* birds have feathers and *only* mammals have fur. In comparing mammals with other vertebrates, presence of fur is a *derived* characteristic. Similarly, in describing birds, feathers are derived only in this group.

So, how do we know which kinds of characteristics to use? The answer is determined by which group one is describing and with what it is being compared. For the most part, it is best to use those characteristics that reflect more specific evolutionary adaptations; in other words, derived characteristics are the most informative. Moreover, when grouping two forms together (say, a bat with a mouse, both as mammals), this should be done *only* when they show **shared derived** characteristics (here, both possessing fur). (See Fig. 8–2 for an example of a classification of animals.)

The current emphasis on identification and application of shared derived characteristics underscores a contemporary school of taxonomy called **cladistics**. Now widely used in physical anthropology and other disciplines, practitioners of this approach, called cladists, have sought to add more rigor to interpretations of evolutionary relationships. An important scientific aspect of cladistic methods is that the proposed hypothesis must be explicitly stated, detailing derived traits as contrasted to primitive traits. In this way, the scientific validity of evolutionary schemes is more easily tested, since the basic tenets are clearly presented in a falsifiable form.

Timescale

In addition to the staggering array of living and extinct life-forms, biologists must also contend with the vast amount of time that life has been evolving on earth. Scientists have devised several schemes—but in this case to organize *time*, not organic diversity.

Geologists in particular have formulated the **geological timescale** (Fig. 8–3). Very large time spans are organized into eras and periods. Periods, in turn, can be broken down into epochs (as we will do later in our discussion of primate evolution).

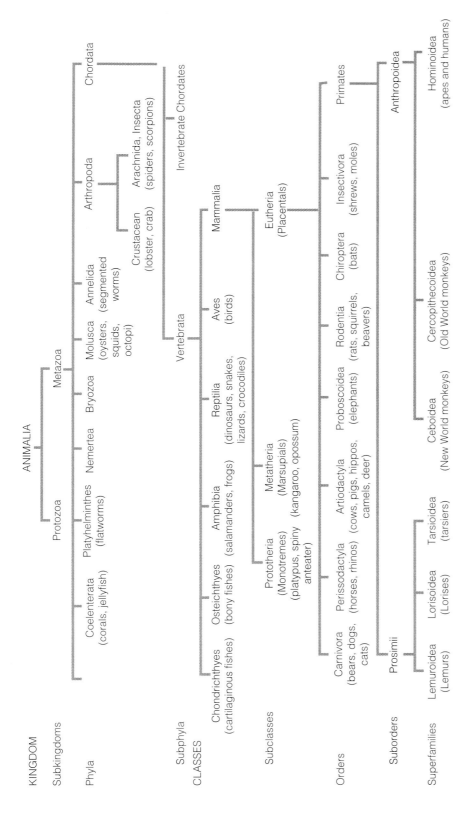

FIGURE 8–2
Classification chart, modified from Linnaeus. All animals are placed in certain categories based on structural similarities. Not all members of categories are shown. For example, there are up to 20 orders of placental mammals (8 are depicted). A comprehensive classification of the primate order is presented in Chapter 9.

FIGURE 8–3
Geological time scale.

ERA	PERIOD	(Began m.y.a.)	EPOCH	(Began m.y.a.)
CENOZOIC	Quaternary	1.8	Holocene Pleistocene	0.01 1.8
CENOZOIC	Tertiary	65	Pliocene Miocene Oligocene Eocene Paleocene	5 22.5 34 55 65
MESOZOIC	Cretaceous	136		
MESOZOIC	Jurassic	190		
MESOZOIC	Triassic	225		
PALEOZOIC	Permian	280		
PALEOZOIC	Carboniferous	345		
PALEOZOIC	Devonian	395		
PALEOZOIC	Silurian	430		
PALEOZOIC	Ordovician	500		
PALEOZOIC	Cambrian	570		
PRE-CAMBRIAN				

Vertebrate Evolutionary History—
A Brief Summary

For the time span encompassing vertebrate evolution, there are three eras: the Paleozoic, the Mesozoic, and the Cenozoic. The first vertebrates are present in the fossil record dating to early in the Paleozoic 500 million years ago (m.y.a.) and probably go back considerably further. It is the vertebrate capacity to form bone that accounts for their more complete fossil record *after* 500 m.y.a.

During the Paleozoic, several varieties of fishes (including the ancestors of modern sharks and bony fishes), amphibians, and reptiles appeared. In addition, at the end of the Paleozoic, close to 250 m.y.a., several varieties of mammal-like reptiles were also diversifying. It is widely thought that some of these forms gave rise to the mammals.

The evolutionary history of vertebrates and other organisms during the Paleozoic and Mesozoic was profoundly influenced by geographical events. We know that the positions of the earth's continents have dramatically shifted during the last several hundred million years. This process, called **continental drift**, is explained by the geological theory of *plate tectonics*, which views the earth's crust as a series of gigantic moving and colliding plates. Such massive geological movements can induce volcanic activity (as, for example, all around the Pacific rim), mountain building (e.g., the Himalayas), and earthquakes. Living on the edge of the Pacific and North American plates, residents of the Pacific coast of the United States are acutely aware of some of these consequences, as illustrated by the explosive volcanic eruption of Mt. St. Helens or the frequent earthquakes in Alaska and California.

Geologists, in reconstructing the earth's physical history, have established the prior (significantly altered) positioning of major continental landmasses. During the late Paleozoic, the continents came together to form a single colossal landmass called *Pangea* (Fig 8–4). In actuality, the continents had been drifting on plates, coming together and separating, long before the end of the Paleozoic (*c.* 225 m.y.a.), and to be more precise, the large landmass at this time should be called Pangea II. During the early Mesozoic, the southern continents (South America, Africa, Antarctica, Australia, and India) began to split off from Pangea, forming a large southern continent called *Gondwanaland*. Similarly, the northern continents (North America, Greenland, Europe, and Asia) were consolidated into a northern landmass called *Laurasia*. During the Mesozoic, Gondwanaland and Laurasia continued to drift apart and to break up into smaller segments. By the end of the Mesozoic (*c.* 65 m.y.a.), the continents were beginning to assume their current positions (Fig. 8–4b).

The evolutionary ramifications of this long-term continental drift were profound. Groups of land animals became effectively isolated from each other by large water boundaries, and the distribution of reptiles and mammals was significantly influenced by continental movements. Although not producing such dramatic continental realignments, the process continued through the Mesozoic and into the Cenozoic. The more specific consequences of continental drift on early primate evolution are discussed in Chapter 12.

During most of the Mesozoic, reptiles were the dominant land vertebrates, and they exhibited a broad expansion into a variety of **ecological niches**, which included aerial and marine habitats. Such a fairly rapid expansion, marked by diversification of many new species, is called an **adaptive radiation** (see Box 8–1). No doubt, the most famous of these highly successful Mesozoic reptiles are the dinosaurs, which themselves evolved into a wide array of sizes and lifestyles. Dinosaur paleontology, never a boring field, has advanced several startling notions in recent years: that many dinosaurs were warm-blooded; that some varieties were quite social and probably also showed considerable parental care; that many forms became extinct as the result of major climactic changes to the earth's atmosphere from collisions with comets or asteroids; and finally that not all dinosaurs became entirely extinct, with many descendants still living today (i.e., all modern birds).

The first mammals are known from fossil traces fairly early in the Mesozoic, but the first *placental* mammals cannot be positively identified until quite late in the Mesozoic, approximately 70 m.y.a. This highly successful mammalian adaptive radiation is thus almost entirely within the most recent era of geological history, the Cenozoic.

The Cenozoic is divided into two periods, the Tertiary (about 63 million years duration) and the Quaternary, from about 1.8 m.y.a. up to and including

▲ **Continental drift**
The movement of continents on sliding plates of the earth's surface. As a result, the position of large landmasses has shifted dramatically during earth's history.

▲ **Ecological niches**
The positions of species within their physical and biological environments, together making up the *ecosystem*. A species' ecological niche is defined by such components as diet, terrain, vegetation, type of predators, relationships with other species, and activity patterns, and each niche is unique to a given species.

▲ **Adaptive radiation**
The relatively rapid expansion and diversification of an evolving group of organisms as they adapt to new niches.

▲ **Epochs**

Categories of the geological timescale; subdivisions of periods. In the Cenozoic, epochs include Paleocene, Eocene, Oligocene, Miocene, Pliocene (from the Tertiary), and the Pleistocene and Holocene (from the Quaternary).

the present. Because this division is rather imprecise, paleontologists more frequently refer to the next level of subdivision within the Cenozoic, the **epochs**. There are seven epochs within the Cenozoic: the Paleocene, Eocene, Oligocene, Miocene, Pliocene, Pleistocene, and Holocene (the last often referred to as the Recent [See Fig 8–3]).

Mammalian Evolution

Following the extinction of dinosaurs and many other Mesozoic forms (at the beginning of the Cenozoic), there was a wide array of ecological niches open for the rapid expansion and diversification of mammals. The Cenozoic was an opportunistic time for mammals, and it is known as the Age of Mammals. Mesozoic mammals were small animals, about the size of mice, which they resembled superficially (Fig 8–5). The mammalian adaptive radiation of the Cenozoic saw the rise of the major lineages of all modern mammals. Indeed, mammals, along with birds, replaced reptiles as the dominant terrestrial vertebrates.

How do we account for the rapid success of the mammals? Several characteristics relating to learning and general flexibility of behavior are of prime importance. To process more information, mammals were selected for larger brains than those typically found in reptiles. In particular, the cerebrum became generally enlarged, especially the outer covering, the neocortex, which controls higher brain functions (Fig. 8–6). In some mammals, the cerebrum expanded so much that it came to comprise the majority of brain volume; moreover, the number of surface convolutions increased, creating more surface area and thus providing space for even more nerve cells (neurons).

For such a large and complex organ as the mammalian brain to develop, a longer, more intense period of growth is required. Slower development can occur internally (*in utero*) as well as after birth. While internal fertilization, and especially internal development, are not unique to mammals, the latter is a major innovation among terrestrial vertebrates. Other forms (birds, most fish,

FIGURE 8–4

Continental drift. Changes in positions of the continental plates from late Paleozoic to late Eocene. (a) The position of the continents during the Mesozoic (c. 125 m.y.a.) Pangea is breaking up into a northern landmass (Laurasia) and a southern landmass (Gondwanaland). (b) The position of the continents at the beginning of the Cenozoic (c. 65 m.y.a.).

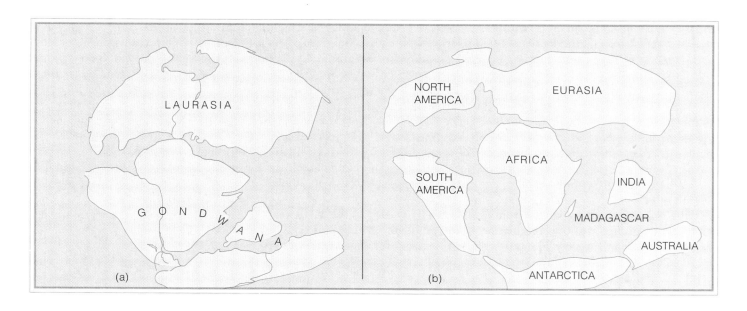

BOX 8–1

Evolutionary Processes

Adaptive Radiation

The potential capacity of a group of organisms to multiply is practically unlimited; its ability to increase its numbers, however, is regulated largely by the available resources of food, shelter, and space. As the size of a population increases, its food supply, shelter, and space decrease, and the environment will ultimately prove inadequate. Depleted resources engender pressures that will very likely induce some members of the population to seek an environment in which competition is considerably reduced and the opportunity for survival and reproductive success increased. This evolutionary tendency to exploit unoccupied habitats may eventually produce an abundance of diverse species.

An instructive example of the evolutionary process known as *adaptive radiation* may be seen in the divergence of the stem reptiles into the profusion of different forms of the late Paleozoic and especially those of the Mesozoic. It is a process that has taken place many times in evolutionary history when a life-form has rapidly taken advantage, so to speak, of the many newly available ecological niches.

The principle of evolution illustrated by adaptive radiation is fairly simple, but important. It may be stated thus: *A species, or group of species, will diverge into as many variations as two factors allow: (1) its adaptive potential and (2) the adaptive opportunities of the available zones.*

In the case of reptiles, there was little divergence in the very early stages of evolution, when the ancestral form was little more than one among a variety of amphibian water-dwellers. In reptiles, a more efficient egg than that of amphibians (i.e., one that could incubate out of water) had developed, but although it had great adaptive potential, there were few zones to invade. However, once reptiles became fully terrestrial, there was a sudden opening of available zones—ecological niches—accessible to them.

This new kind of egg provided the primary adaptive trait that freed reptiles from their attachment to water. The adaptive zones for reptiles were not limitless; nevertheless, conti-

nents were now open to them with no serious competition from any other animal. The reptiles moved into the many different ecological niches on land (and to some extent in the air and sea), and as they adapted to these areas, they diversified into a large number of species. This spectacular radiation burst forth with such evolutionary rapidity, it may well be termed an adaptive explosion.

Generalized and Specialized Characteristics

Another aspect of evolution closely related to adaptive radiation involves the transition from *generalized characteristics* to *specialized characteristics*. These two terms refer to the adaptive potential of a particular trait: a trait that is adapted for many functions is called generalized, whereas a trait that is limited to a narrow set of ecological functions is called specialized.

For example, a generalized mammalian limb has five fairly flexible digits adapted for many possible functions (grasping, weight support, digging). In this respect, our hands are still quite generalized. On the other hand (or foot), there have been many structural modifications in our feet suited for the ecologically specialized function of stable weight support in an upright posture.

The terms *generalized* and *specialized* are also sometimes used when speaking of the adaptive potential of whole organisms. For example, the aye-aye (an unusual primate living in Madagascar) is a highly specialized animal structurally adapted in its dentition for an ecologically narrow rodent/woodpecker-like niche—digging holes with prominent incisors and removing insect larvae with an elongated finger.

The notion of adaptive potential is a relative judgment and can estimate only crudely the likelihood of one form evolving into one or more other forms. Adaptive radiation is a related concept, for only a generalized ancestor can provide the flexible evolutionary basis for such rapid diversification. Only a generalized species with potential for adaptation into varied ecological niches can lead to all the later diversification and specialization of forms into particular ecological niches.

FIGURE 8–5

Mesozoic mammal. A speculative reconstruction of what a Mesozoic mammal might have looked like.

▲ **Viviparous**

Giving birth to live young.

▲ **Heterodont**

Having different kinds of teeth; characteristic of mammals, whose teeth consist of incisors, canines, premolars, and molars.

and reptiles) incubate their young externally by laying eggs (i.e., they are oviparous), while mammals, with very few exceptions, give birth to live young and are thus said to be **viviparous**. Even among mammals, however, there is considerable variation among the major groups in how mature the young are at birth. As you will see, it is in mammals like ourselves, the *placental* forms, where development *in utero* goes the furthest.

Another distinctive feature of mammals is seen in the dentition. While living reptiles consistently have similarly shaped teeth (called a *homodont* dentition), mammals have differently shaped teeth (Fig. 8–7). This varied pattern, termed a **heterodont** dentition, is reflected in the primitive mammalian array of dental elements, which includes 3 incisors, 1 canine, 4 premolars, and 3 molars for each quarter of the mouth. Since the upper and lower jaws are usually the same and are symmetrical for both sides, this "dental formula" is conventionally illustrated by dental quarter (see Box 9–2, p. 213, for a more complete discussion of

FIGURE 8–6

Lateral view of the brain. The illustration shows the increase in the cerebral cortex of the brain. The cerebral cortex integrates sensory information and selects responses.

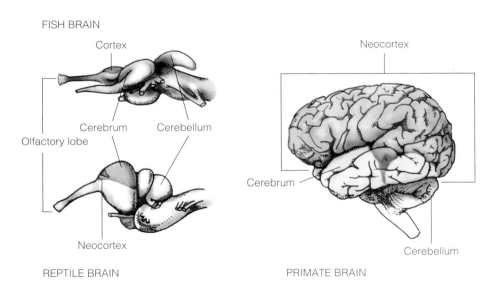

dental patterns as they apply to primates). Thus, with 11 teeth per quarter segment, the primitive mammalian dental complement includes a total of 44 teeth. Such a heterodont arrangement allows mammals to process a wide variety of foods. Incisors can be used for cutting, canines for grasping and piercing, and premolars and molars for crushing and grinding.

A final point regarding teeth relates to their disproportionate representation in the fossil record. As the hardest, most durable portion of a vertebrate skeleton, teeth have the greatest likelihood of becoming fossilized (i.e., mineralized). As a result, the vast majority of the available fossil data for most vertebrates, including primates, consists of teeth.

Another major adaptive complex that distinguishes contemporary mammals from reptiles is the maintenance of a constant internal body temperature. Also colloquially (and incorrectly) called warmbloodedness, this central physiological adaptation is also seen in contemporary birds (and was also probably characteristic of many dinosaurs as well). In fact, many contemporary reptiles are able to approximate a constant internal body temperature through behavioral means (especially by regulating activity and exposing the body to the sun). In this sense, reptiles (along with birds and mammals) could be said to be *homeothermic*. Thus, the most important distinction in contrasting mammals (and birds) with reptiles is how the energy to maintain body temperature is produced and channeled. In reptiles, this energy is obtained directly from exposure (externally) to the sun; reptiles are thus said to be *ectothermic*. In mammals and birds, however, the energy is generated *internally* through metabolic activity (by processing food or by muscle action); mammals and birds are hence referred to as **endothermic**.

Major Mammalian Groups

There are three major subgroups of living mammals: the egg-laying mammals, or monotremes (Fig. 8–8), the pouched mammals, or marsupials (Fig. 8–9), and

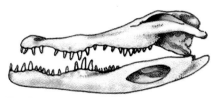

REPTILIAN (alligator): homodont

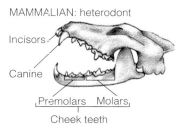

MAMMALIAN: heterodont

Incisors
Canine
Premolars Molars
Cheek teeth

FIGURE 8–7
Reptilian and mammalian teeth.

▲ **Endothermic** (*endo*, meaning "within" or "internal").
Able to maintain internal body temperature through the production of energy by means of metabolic processes within cells; characteristic feature of mammals, birds, and probably some dinosaurs.

FIGURE 8–8
The spiny anteater (a monotreme).

FIGURE 8–9
A wallaby with an infant in the pouch (marsupials).

BOX 8–2

Convergent and Parallel Evolution*

Convergent Evolution

The discussion of marsupials offers an opportunity to present another evolutionary process, *convergent evolution*. We pointed out in Box 8–1 that in the early stages of development, there is a tendency for newly evolved forms to become highly diversified when they invade varied environments. The diversification results from modifications of the descendants and the ancestral form as they adapt to new ecological niches.

Convergent evolution is the process in which two *unrelated* groups of organisms, living in similar environmental conditions, develop a similar appearance and lifestyle. That is, similar environmental demands make for similar phenotypic responses (Mayr, 1970, p. 365). Two similar environments could therefore result in similar adaptive characters.

Striking examples of convergence are the pouched (marsupial) mammals of Australia and placental mammals. Australia was isolated from South America before the great placental mammalian radiation of the Cenozoic, and marsupials survived because they were free from the competition of the more efficient placentals. When placental mammals become prominent in the Cenozoic, only a few were able to invade Australia (via island hopping) from Southeast Asia.

Without competition, the pouched mammals spread into the varied environments of the isolated continent. There were marsupials that resembled, to a lesser or greater degree, a wolf, cat, flying squirrel, groundhog, anteater, mole, and mouse. And each of these marsupials occupied ecological niches generally similar to the placental mammals they most closely resembled (Simpson et al., 1957, p. 470).

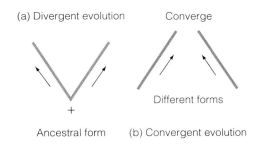

(a) Divergent evolution   Converge

Ancestral form   (b) Convergent evolution

Different forms

FIGURE 1

Parallel Evolution

A process similar to convergent evolution is *parallel evolution*. However, in parallel evolution, the ancestral form is less remote; thus, descendant lines share a greater degree of relatedness than is the case in convergent evolution. For example, the muriqui (a New World monkey) and the gibbon (an Old World small-bodied ape) both possess elongated arms. These two forms are members of independent primate lineages that diverged from each other more than 30 m.y.a. Dating to this time, the last common ancestor of these lines did *not* possess this trait. Thus, it was acquired (as a derived feature) separately in both lineages, presumably as a result of similar adaptive pressures in a tree-living setting. The fact that these lines retain significant shared descent, setting common limits on evolutionary direction, defines this process as parallel evolution (rather than convergence).

---

* As we discussed on p. 187, both convergent and parallel evolution are now frequently subsumed under the term *homoplasy*.

---

the placental mammals. The monotremes are extremely primitive and are considered more distinct from marsupials or placentals than these latter are from each other.

The most notable distinction differentiating the marsupials (Box 8–2) from the placentals is the form and intensity of fetal development. In marsupials, the young are born extremely immature and must complete development in an external pouch. It has been suggested (Carrol, 1988) that such a reproductive strategy is more energetically costly than retaining the young for a longer period *in utero*. In fact, the latter is exactly what placental mammals have done through a more advanced placental connection (from which the group gets its popular name). But perhaps even more basic than fetal nourishment is the means to

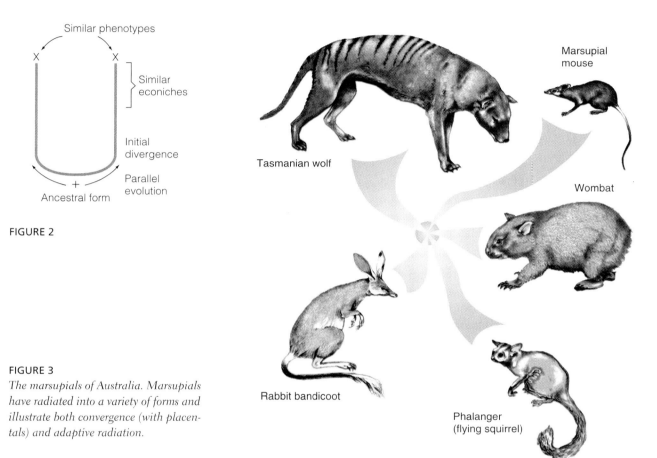

FIGURE 2

FIGURE 3

The marsupials of Australia. Marsupials have radiated into a variety of forms and illustrate both convergence (with placentals) and adaptive radiation.

allow the mother to *tolerate* her young internally over an extended period. Marsupial young are born so quickly after conception that there is little chance for the mother's system to recognize and have an immune rejection of the fetal "foreign" tissue. But in placental mammals, such an immune response would occur were it not for the development of a specialized tissue that isolates the fetus from the mother's immune detection, thus preventing tissue rejection. Quite possibly, this innovation is the central factor in the origin and initial rapid success of placental mammals (Carroll, 1988).

In any case, with a longer gestation period, the central nervous system could develop more completely in the fetus. Moreover, after birth, the "bond of milk" between mother and young also would allow more time for complex neural structures to form. It should also be emphasized that from a *biosocial* perspective, this dependency period not only allows for adequate physiological development, but also provides for a wider range of learning stimuli. That is, the young mammalian brain receives a vast amount of information channeled to it through observation of the mother's behavior and through play with age-mates. It is not sufficient to have evolved a brain capable of learning. Collateral evolution of mammalian social systems has ensured that young mammal brains are provided with ample learning opportunities and are thus put to good use.

Modes of Evolutionary Change

We have discussed evolution from both a *microevolutionary* perspective in Chapters 5 and 6 and from a *macroevolutionary* one in this chapter. The major evolutionary factor underlying macroevolutionary change is **speciation**, the process whereby new species first arise. As you will recall, we have defined a species as a group of *reproductively isolated* organisms, a characterization that follows the biological species concept (Mayr, 1970). According to this same view, the way new species are first produced involves some form of isolation. Picture a single species of organisms (baboons, for example) composed of several populations distributed over a wide geographical area. Gene exchange (gene flow) will be limited if a geographical barrier such as an ocean, mountain range, or sufficient distance effectively separates these populations. This extremely important form of isolating mechanism is termed *geographical isolation*.

If one population of baboons (A) is separated from another population (B) by a mountain range, individual baboons of population A will not be able to mate with individuals from B (Fig. 8–10). As time passes (several generations), genetic differences will accumulate in both populations. If population size is small, we can predict that genetic drift (see p. 91) will cause allele frequencies to change in both populations. Moreover, since drift is *random* in nature, we would not expect the effects to be the same. Consequently, the two populations will begin to diverge.

As long as gene exchange is limited, the populations can only become more genetically different with time. Moreover, greater difference would be expected if the baboon groups are occupying slightly different habitats. These additional genetic differences would be incorporated through the process of natural selection. Certain individuals in population A may be most reproductively fit in their

▲ **Speciation**
The process by which new species are produced from earlier ones; the most important mechanism of macroevolutionary change.

FIGURE 8–10
A speciation model.

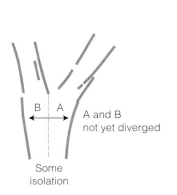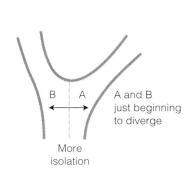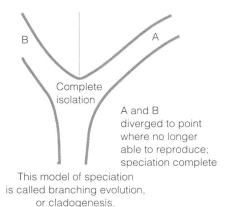

B A   A and B not yet diverged

Some isolation

B A   A and B just beginning to diverge

More isolation

B   A

Complete isolation

A and B diverged to point where no longer able to reproduce; speciation complete

This model of speciation is called branching evolution, or cladogenesis.

own environment, but would show less reproductive success in the environment occupied by population B. Thus, allele frequencies will shift further, and the results will be different in the two groups.

With the cumulative effects of genetic drift and natural selection acting over many generations, the result will be two populations that—even if they were to come back into geographical contact—could no longer interbreed and produce fertile offspring. More than just geographical isolation might now apply. There may, for instance, be behavioral differences interfering with courtship—what we call *behavioral isolation*. Using our *biological* definition of species, we now would recognize two distinct species, where initially only one existed.

Until recently, the general consensus among evolutionary biologists was that microevolutionary mechanisms could be translated directly into the larger-scale macroevolutionary changes, especially speciation. A smooth gradation of change was assumed to run directly from microevolution into macroevolution. A representative view was expressed by a leading evolutionary biologist, Ernst Mayr: "The proponents of the synthetic theory maintain that all evolution is due to accumulation of small genetic changes, guided by natural selection, and that transspecific evolution [speciation] is nothing but an extrapolation and magnification of events that take place within populations and species" (Mayr, 1970, p. 351).

In the last two decades, this view has been seriously challenged. Many theorists now believe that macroevolution cannot be explained solely in terms of accumulated microevolutionary changes. Many current researchers are convinced that macroevolution is only partly understandable through microevolutionary models.

Gradualism vs. Punctuated Equilibrium

The traditional view of evolution has emphasized that change accumulates gradually in evolving lineages—the idea of phyletic gradualism. Accordingly, the complete fossil record of an evolving group (if it could be recovered) would display a series of forms with finely graded transitional differences between each ancestor and its descendant. The fact that such transitional forms are only rarely found is attributed to the incompleteness of the fossil record, or, as Darwin called it, "a history of the world, imperfectly kept, and written in changing dialect."

For more than a century, this perspective dominated evolutionary biology; but current opinion holds that evolutionary mechanisms operating on species over the long run are often not continuously gradual. In some cases, species persist for thousands of generations basically unchanged. Then, rather suddenly, at least in evolutionary terms, a "spurt" of speciation occurs. This uneven, nongradual process of long stasis and quick spurts has been termed **punctuated equilibrium** (Gould and Eldredge, 1977).

What the advocates of punctuated equilibrium are disputing concerns the "tempo" and "mode" of evolutionary change commonly understood since Darwin's time. Rather than a slow, steady tempo, this alternate view postulates long periods of no change punctuated only occasionally by sudden bursts. From this observation, punctuated equilibrium further suggests that the mode of evolution, too, must be different from that suggested by classical Darwinists. Rather than the gradual accumulation of small changes in a single lineage, punctuated equilibrium theory argues that an *additional* evolutionary mechanism is required to push the process along. Followers of this theory thus hypothesize *speciation* as

▲ **Punctuated equilibrium**
The concept that evolutionary change proceeds through long periods of stasis, punctuated by rapid periods of change.

the major influence in bringing about rapid evolutionary change. Speciation can result from microevolutionary factors, especially genetic drift and natural selection. However, the theory of punctuated equilibrium suggests that once speciation occurs, particularly when accelerated rapidly, it directs *macroevolution* in a way quite distinct from what microevolution *alone* would do.

How well does the paleontological record agree with the predictions of punctuated equilibrium? Indeed, considerable fossil data show long periods of stasis punctuated by occasional quite rapid changes (on the order of 10,000 to 50,000 years). Intermediate forms are rare, not so much because the fossil record is poor, but because the speciation events and longevity of these transitional species were so short that we should not expect to find them very often.

The best supporting evidence for punctuated equilibrium has come from the fossilized remains of marine invertebrates. How well, then, does the vertebrate and especially the primate fossil record fit the punctuated equilibrium model? In studies of Eocene primates, rates of evolutionary change were shown to be quite gradual (Gingerich, 1985; Brown and Rose, 1987; Rose, 1991). In another study, of Paleocene plesiadapiforms, evolutionary changes were also quite gradual. Although no longer considered primates, these forms show a gradual rate of change in another, closely related group of mammals. The predictions postulated by punctuated equilibrium have thus far not been substantiated in those evolving lineages of primates for which we have adequate data to test the theory.

It would, however, be a fallacy to assume that evolutionary change in primates or in any other group must therefore be of a completely gradual tempo. Such is clearly not the case. In all lineages, the pace assuredly speeds up and slows down as a result of factors that influence the size and relative isolation of populations. In addition, environmental changes that influence the rapidity and long-term direction of natural selection must also be considered. Still, as postulated by the modern synthesis, microevolution and macroevolution need not be "decoupled" as some evolutionary biologists have recently suggested.

Summary

This chapter has surveyed background information concerning vertebrate and, more specifically, mammalian evolution. Perspectives on organic diversity and the geological timescale were discussed. Early vertebrate evolution was briefly reviewed, with emphasis placed on the origin and diversification of mammals, especially placental mammals. Two fundamental features shared by all mammals are *heterodontism* and *endothermy*. In addition, the crucial role of continental drift as it influenced mammalian evolution was highlighted. Finally, the contemporary debate concerning the tempo and mode of evolutionary change (i.e., the gradualist versus punctuated equilibrium models) was also discussed.

Questions for Review

1. What are the two primary goals of organic classification?
2. What are the major groups of vertebrates?
3. What are the major eras of geological time over which vertebrates have evolved?
4. What primary features distinguish mammals—especially placental mammals—from other vertebrates?
5. What is meant by homology? Contrast with analogy, using examples.

6. Why do biologists, in making interpretations of evolutionary relationships, concentrate on derived features as opposed to primitive ones? Give an example of each.

7. What is meant by continental drift? How might continental drift have influenced the evolution and diversification of mammals during the Mesozoic?

8. What is heterodontism? What is one major functional ramification of this feature?

9. What are homeothermy and endothermy? How do modern placental mammals differ from contemporary reptiles in terms of temperature regulation?

10. Contrast the gradualist view of evolutionary change with that suggested by punctuated equilibrium theory. Give an example from mammalian (primate) evolution that supports one view or the other.

Suggested Further Reading

Carroll, Robert L. 1988. *Vertebrate Paleontology and Evolution*. New York: Freeman.
Ridley, Mark. 1993. *Evolution*. Boston: Blackwell Scientific Publications.

Internet Resources

Dinosauria.
http://ucmp1.berkeley.edu/exhibittext/dinosaur.html
(An internet version of a paleontology exhibit from University of California, Berkeley. Excellent text with definitions, topical discussions, and some graphics.)

The Tree of Life.
http://phylogeny.arizona.edu/tree/phylogeny.html

(A very complete classification of organisms following cladistic methodology.)

Earth Sciences.
http://www.gold.net/users/dt89/sites.html

(A central listing of earth sciences Web sites worldwide, excellent for geology and paleontology.)

Deep Time

The vast expanse of time during which evolution has occurred on earth staggers the imagination. Indeed, this fundamental notion of what John McPhee has termed "deep time" is not really understood or, in fact, widely believed. Of course, as we have emphasized beginning in Chapter 1 (see Issue, pp. 18–20), *belief*, as such, is not part of science. But observation, theory building, and testing are. Nevertheless, in a world populated mostly by nonscientists, the concept of deep time, crucial as it is to geology and anthropology, is resisted by many people. This situation is really not surprising; as an idea that can be truly understood (i.e., internalized and given some personal meaning), deep time is in many ways counterintuitive. As individuals, human beings measure their existence in months, years, or in the span of human lifetimes.

But what are these durations, measured against geological or galactic phenomena? In a real sense, these vast time expanses are beyond human comprehension. We can reasonably fathom the reaches of human history, stretching to about 5,000 years ago. In a leap of imagination, we can perhaps even begin to grasp the stretch of time back to the cave painters of France and Spain, approximately 17,000 to 25,000 years ago. How do we relate, then, to a temporal span 10 times this, back to 250,000 years ago (about the time of the earliest modern *Homo sapiens*)—or to 10 times this span to 2,500,000 years ago (about the time of the appearance of our genus, *Homo*)? We surely can respond that any of these time blocks are vast—and then *more* vast. But multiply this last duration another 1,000 times (to 2,500,000,000), and we are back to a time of fairly early life-forms. And we would still have to reach further into earth's past another 1.5 billion years to approach the *earliest* documented life.

The dimensions of these intervals are humbling, to say the least. The discovery in the nineteenth century of deep time (as we documented in Chapter 2) in what Stephen Jay Gould of Harvard University calls "geology's greatest contribution to human thought" plunged one more dagger into humanity's long-cherished special view of itself. Astronomers had previously established how puny our world was in the physical expanse of space, and then geologists showed that even on our own small planet, we were but residues dwarfed within a river of time "without a vestige of a beginning or prospect of an end" (from James Hutton, a founder of modern geology and one of the discoverers of deep time). It is no wonder that there is resistance to the concept of deep time; it not only stupefies our reason, but implies a sense of collective meaninglessness and reinforces our individual mortality.

Geologists, astronomers, and other scholars have struggled for over a century, with modest success, to translate the tales told in rocks and hurtling stars in terms that can be understood by everyone. Various analogies have been attempted—metaphors, really—drawn from common experience. Among the most successful of these attempts is a "cosmic calendar" devised by eminent astronomer Carl Sagan in his book *Dragons of Eden* (1977). In this version of time's immensity, Sagan likens the passage of geological time to that of one calendar year. The year begins on January 1 with the "Big Bang," the cosmic explosion marking the beginning of the universe and the beginning of time. In this version, the Big Bang is set at 15 billion years ago,* with some of the major events in the geological past as follows:

Time unit conversions using the Cosmic Calendar:

1 year = 15,000,000,000 years
1 month = 1,250,000,000 years
1 day = 41,000,000 years
1 hour = 1,740,000 years
1 minute = 29,000 years
1 second = 475 years

Big Bang	January 1
Formation of the earth	September 14
Orgin of life on earth (approx.)	September 25
Significant oxygen atmosphere begins to develop	December 1
Precambrian ends; Paleozoic begins; invertebrates flourish	December 17
Paleozoic ends and Mesozoic begins	December 25
Cretaceous period; first flowers; dinosaurs become extinct	December 28
Mesozoic ends; Cenozoic begins; adaptive radiation of placental mammals	December 29
	December 31 Events
Appearance of early hominoids (ancestors of apes and humans)	12:30 P.M.
First Hominids	9:30 P.M.
Extensive cave painting in Europe	11:59 P.M.
Invention of agriculture	11:59:20 P.M.
Renaissance in Europe; Ming Dynasty in China; emergence of scientific method	11:59:59 P.M.
Widespread development of science and technology; emergence of a global culture; first steps in space exploration	NOW; the first second of the New Year

---

* Recent evidence gathered by the Hubble Space Telescope has questioned the established date for the Big Bang. However, even the most recent data are somewhat contradictory, suggesting a date from as early as 16 billion years ago (indicated by the age of the oldest stars) to as recent as 8 billion years ago (indicated by the rate of expansion of the universe). Here, we will follow the conventional dating of 15 billion years; if you apply the most conservative approximation (8 billion years) the calibrations shift as follows: 1 day = 22,000,000 years; 1 hour = 913,000 years; 1 minute = 15,000 years. Using these calculations, for example, the first hominids appear on Dec. 31 at 7:37 P.M., and modern *Homo sapiens* are on the scene at 11:42 P.M.

Sources

Finkbeiner, Ann. 1995. "Closing in on Cosmic Expansion" Research News. *Science*, 270:1295–1296.

Gould, Stephen Jay. 1987. *Time's Arrow, Time's Cycle*. Cambridge, MA: Harvard University Press.

McPhee, J. 1980. *Basin and Range*. New York: Farrar, Straus, and Giraux.

Sagan, Carl. 1977. *Dragons of Eden*. New York: Random House.

Critical Thinking Questions

1. What types of evidence are used to establish deep time?
2. Why do many people have trouble with the concept of deep time?
3. What is your opinion of the validity of deep time for the universe and earth history? What types of evidence would you require to alter your position?
4. From a scientific perspective, identify what is wrong with the following statements:
   a. Deep time for the age of the earth is true.
   b. I believe in deep time.

9

An Overview of the Living Primates

Introduction

Thus far, we have presented the basic biological background for understanding human evolution, and we have also shown how these evolutionary mechanisms operate on contemporary human populations. The remainder of this textbook is devoted to the very formidable task of explaining what it is to be human.

Evolution has produced a continuum of life-forms, as demonstrated genetically, anatomically, and behaviorally. To gain an understanding of any organism, it is necessary, whenever possible, to compare its anatomy and behavior with those of other, closely related forms. This comparative approach helps elucidate the significance of physiological and behavioral systems as adaptive responses to various selective pressures throughout the course of evolution. This statement applies to *Homo sapiens* just as surely as to any other species, and if we are to identify the components that have shaped hominid evolution, the starting point must be a systematic comparison between humans and our closest living relatives, the approximately 190 species of nonhuman **primates** (prosimians, monkeys, and apes). This chapter describes the *physical* characteristics that define the order Primates, gives a brief overview of the major groups of living nonhuman primates, and introduces some methods of comparing living primates through genetic data. (For a detailed comparison of human and nonhuman skeletons, see Appendix A.) The following two chapters concentrate on various *behavioral* features that characterize nonhuman primates.

Before proceeding further, we once again must call attention to a few common misunderstandings about evolutionary processes. As we have previously emphasized, evolution is not a goal-directed process. The fact that **prosimians** evolved before **anthropoids** does not mean that prosimians "progressed" or "advanced," to become anthropoids. Extant primate species are in no way "superior" to their evolutionary predecessors or to one another. Consequently, in discussions of major groupings of contemporary nonhuman primates, there is no implied superiority or inferiority of any of these groups. Each grouping (lineage, or species) has come to possess unique qualities that make it better suited than others to a particular habitat and lifestyle. Given that all contemporary organisms are "successful" results of the evolutionary process, it is best to avoid altogether the use of such loaded terms as "superior" and "inferior."

Finally, you should not make the mistake of thinking that contemporary primates (including humans) necessarily represent the final stage or apex of a primate lineage. Remember, the only species that represent final evolutionary stages of particular lineages are those that become extinct.

Primate Evolutionary Trends

All primates possess numerous characteristics they share in common with other placental mammals. Such traits include body hair; a relatively long gestation period followed by live birth; different types of teeth (heterodontism); the ability to maintain a constant internal body temperature through physiological means (*endothermy*); increased brain size; and a considerable capacity for learning and behavioral flexibility. Therefore, to differentiate primates as a group from other mammals, we must describe those characteristics or combinations of traits that define the primate order.

This is not a simple task, for among mammals, primates have remained quite *generalized*. That is, primates have retained many primitive mammalian traits that other mammalian species have lost over time. In response to particular

---

▲ **Primates**

Members of the mammalian order Primates (pronounced "pry-may´-tees"), which includes prosimians, monkeys, apes, and humans. When the term is used colloquially, it is pronounced "pry´-mates."

▲ **Prosimians**

Members of a suborder of Primates, the *Prosimii* (pronounced "pro-sim´-ee-eye"). Traditionally, the suborder includes lemurs, lorises, and tarsiers.

▲ **Anthropoids**

Members of a suborder of Primates, the *Anthropoidea* (pronounced "ann-throw-poid´-ee-uh"). Traditionally, the suborder includes monkeys, apes, and humans.

selective pressures, many mammalian groups have become increasingly **specialized.** For example, through the course of evolution, horses and cattle have undergone a reduction of the number of digits (fingers and toes) from the primitive pattern of five, to one and two, respectively. Moreover, these species have developed hard, protective coverings over their feet in the form of hooves. While this type of limb structure is adaptive in prey species, whose survival depends on speed and stability, it restricts the animal to only one type of locomotion. Moreover, limb function is limited entirely to support and locomotion, while the ability to manipulate objects is completely lost.

Primates, precisely because they are *not* so specialized, cannot be simply defined by one or even two common traits. As a result, biologists (Napier and Napier, 1967; Clark, 1971) have pointed to a group of **evolutionary trends** that, to a greater or lesser degree, characterize the entire order. Keep in mind that these are a set of *general* tendencies and are not all equally expressed in all primates. Indeed, this is the situation we would expect in a diverse group of generalized animals. Moreover, while some of the trends are unique features found in primates, many others are retained primitive mammalian characteristics. These latter are useful in contrasting the generalized primates with the more specialized varieties of other placental mammals.

Thus, the following list is intended to give an overall structural and behavioral picture of that kind of animal we call "primate," focusing on those evolutionary trends that tend to set primates apart from other mammals. Using certain retained (primitive) mammalian traits along with more specific ones to accomplish this task has been the traditional approach of **primatologists**. Some contemporary primatologists (Fleagle, 1988) feel that it is highly useful to enumerate all these features to better illustrate primate adaptations. Thus, a common evolutionary history with adaptations to similar environmental challenges is seen to be reflected in the limbs and locomotion, teeth and diet, senses, brain, and behaviors of those animals that make up the primate order.

A. *Limbs and locomotion*
1. *A tendency toward erect posture (especially in the upper body).* Shown to some degree in all primates, this tendency is variously associated with sitting, leaping, standing, and occasionally, bipedal walking.
2. *A flexible, generalized limb structure, permitting most primates to engage in a number of locomotory behaviors.* Primates have retained some bones (e.g., the clavicle, or collarbone) and certain abilities, (e.g., rotation of the forearm) that have been lost in other, more specialized mammals. Various aspects of hip and shoulder **morphology** also provide primates with a wide range of limb movement and function. Thus, by maintaining a generalized locomotor anatomy, primates are not restricted to one form of movement, as are many other mammals. Primate limbs are also used for activities other than locomotion.
3. *Hands and feet with a high degree of **prehensility** (grasping ability).* All primates use the hands, and frequently the feet, to grasp and manipulate objects (Fig. 9–1). This capability is variably expressed and is enhanced by a number of characteristics, including:
   a. *Retention of five digits on hands and feet.* This varies somewhat throughout the order, with some species showing marked reduction of the thumb or of the second digit.
   b. *An opposable thumb and, in most species, a divergent and partially opposable big toe.* Most primates are capable of moving the thumb so that it comes in contact (in some fashion) with the second digit or the palm of the hand.

▲ **Specialized**
Evolved for a particular function. The term *specialized* usually refers to a specific trait (e.g., incisor teeth), but may also refer to the entire way of life of an organism.

▲ **Evolutionary trends**
Overall characteristics of an evolving lineage, such as the primates. Such trends are useful in helping categorize the lineage as compared to other lineages (i.e., other placental mammals).

▲ **Primatologists**
Scientists who study the evolution, anatomy, and behavior of nonhuman primates. Those who study primate behavior in noncaptive animals are usually trained as anthropologists.

▲ **Morphology**
The form (shape, size) of anatomical structures; can also refer to the entire organism.

▲ **Prehensility**
Grasping, as by the hands and feet of primates.

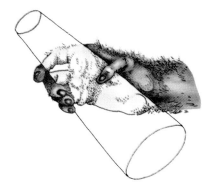

FIGURE 9–1
Primate (macaque) hand.

▲ **Diurnal**
Active during the day.

▲ **Nocturnal**
Active during the night.

▲ **Stereoscopic vision**
The condition whereby visual images are, to varying degrees, superimposed on one another. This provides for depth perception, or the perception of the external environment in three dimensions. Stereoscopic vision is partly a function of structures in the brain.

▲ **Binocular vision**
Vision characterized by overlapping visual fields provided by forward-facing eyes; essential to depth perception.

   c. *Nails instead of claws.* This characteristic is seen in all primates except some New World monkeys. Some prosimians also possess a claw on one digit.
   d. *Tactile pads enriched with sensory nerve fibers at the ends of digits.* This trend serves to enhance the sense of touch.
B. *Diet and teeth*
  1. *Lack of dietary specialization.* This is typical of most primates, who tend to eat a wide assortment of food items.
  2. *A generalized dentition.* The teeth are not specialized for processing only one type of food, a pattern correlated with the lack of dietary specialization.
C. *The senses and the brain*
  All primates (**diurnal** ones in particular) rely heavily on the visual sense and less so on the sense of smell, especially compared to many other mammals. This emphasis is reflected in evolutionary changes in the skull, eyes, and brain.
  1. *Color vision.* This is characteristic of all diurnal primates. **Nocturnal** primates lack color vision.
  2. *Depth perception.* **Stereoscopic vision**, or the ability to perceive objects in three dimensions, is made possible through a variety of mechanisms, including:
   a. *Eyes positioned toward the front of the face (not to the sides).* This configuration provides for overlapping visual fields, or **binocular vision** (Fig. 9–2).
   b. *Visual information from each eye transmitted to visual centers in both hemispheres of the brain.* In nonprimate mammals, most optic nerve fibers cross to the opposite hemisphere through a structure at the base of the brain. In primates, about 40 percent of the fibers remain on the same side (Fig. 9–2).
   c. *Visual information organized into three-dimensional images by specialized structures in the brain itself.* This capacity for stereoscopic vision is dependent on each hemisphere of the brain having received visual information from both eyes and from overlapping visual fields.
  3. *Decreased reliance on the sense of smell (olfaction).* This trend is seen in an overall reduction in the size of olfactory structures in the brain. Corresponding reduction of the entire olfactory apparatus has also resulted in decreased size of the snout. (In some species, such as baboons, the large muzzle is not related to olfaction, but to the presence of large teeth, especially the canines) (see Box 9–1).
  4. *Expansion and increasing complexity of the brain.* This is a general trend among placental mammals, but is especially true of primates. In primates, this expansion is most evident in the visual and association areas of the neocortex (portions of the brain where information from different sensory modalities is integrated). Expansion in regions involved with the hand (both sensory and motor) is seen in many species, particularly humans (see Box 9–1).
D. *Maturation, learning, and behavior*
  1. *A more efficient means of fetal nourishment, longer periods of gestation, reduced numbers of offspring (with single births the norm), delayed maturation, and extension of the entire life span.*
  2. *A greater dependence on flexible, learned behavior.* This trend is correlated with delayed maturation and consequently longer periods of infant and child dependency on the parent. As a result of both these

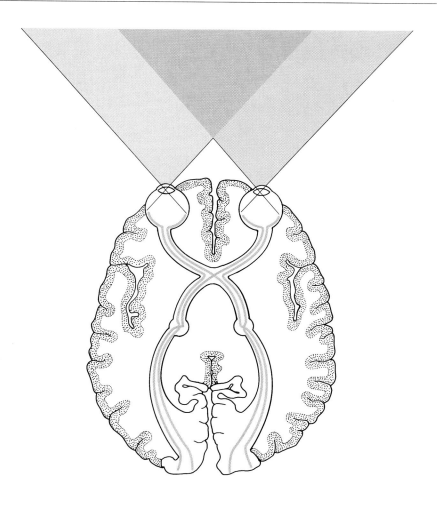

FIGURE 9–2
Simplified diagram showing overlapping visual fields (binocular vision) in primates (and some predators) with eyes positioned at the front of the face. Stereoscopic vision (three-dimensional vision) is provided in part by binocular vision and in part by the transmission of visual stimuli from each eye to both hemispheres of the brain. (In nonprimate mammals, all visual information crosses over to the hemisphere opposite the eye in which it was initially received.) Depth perception is also enormously facilitated by specialized structures in the visual cortex, the region at the back of the brain that receives and integrates visual stimuli.

trends, parental investment in each offspring is increased, so that although fewer offspring are born, they receive more intense and efficient rearing.

3. *The tendency to live in social groups and the permanent association of adult males with the group.* Except for some nocturnal forms, primates tend to associate with others, at least with offspring. The permanent association of adult males with the group is uncommon in mammals but widespread in primates.

4. *The tendency to diurnal activity patterns.* This is seen in most primates; only one monkey species and some prosimians are nocturnal.

The Arboreal Adaptation

The single most important factor influencing the evolutionary divergence of the primates was the adaptation to **arboreal** living. While other placental mammals were adapting to grasslands or to subterranean or even marine environments, primates found their **adaptive niche** in the trees. This environment—with its myriad challenges and opportunities—was the one in which primate ancestors established themselves as a unique kind of animal.

▲ **Arboreal**
Tree-living; adapted to life in the trees.

▲ **Adaptive niche**
The entire way of life of an organism: where it lives, what it eats, how it gets food, etc.

Primate Cranial Anatomy

Several significant anatomical features of the primate cranium help us distinguish primates from other mammals. The mammalian trend toward increased brain development has been further emphasized in primates, as shown by a relatively enlarged braincase. In addition, the primate emphasis on vision is reflected in generally large eye sockets; and the decreased dependence on olfaction is indicated by reduction of the snout and corresponding flattening of the face (Fig. 1).

Here are some of the specific anatomical details seen in modern and most fossil primate crania:

1. The primate face is shortened, and the size of the brain case, relative to that of the face, is enlarged compared to other mammals (Fig. 1).

2. Eye sockets are enclosed at the sides by a ring of bone called the *postorbital bar* (Fig. 1). In most other mammals, there is no postorbital bar. In addition, in anthropoids and tarsiers, there is a plate of bone at the back of the eye orbit called the *postorbital plate*. The postorbital plate is not present in prosimians. The functional significance of these structures has not been thoroughly explained, but it may be related to stresses on the eye orbits imposed by chewing (Fleagle, 1988).

3. The region of the skull that contains the structures of the middle ear is completely encircled by a bony structure called the *auditory bulla*. In primates, the floor of the auditory bulla is derived from a segment of the temporal bone (Fig. 2). Of the skeletal structures, most primate paleontologists consider the postorbital bar and the derivation of the auditory bulla to be the two best diagnostic traits of the primate order.

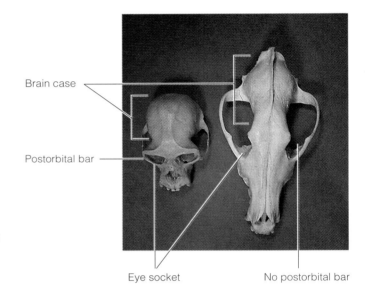

Brain case

Postorbital bar

Eye socket   No postorbital bar

FIGURE 1
The skull of a gibbon (left) compared to that of a red wolf (right). Note that the absolute size of the brain case in the gibbon (approximately 15 pounds) is slightly larger than that of the wolf (about 60 pounds).

4. The base of the skull in primates is somewhat flexed so that the muzzle (mouth and nose) is positioned lower relative to the brain case (Fig. 3). This arrangement provides for the exertion of greater force during chewing, particularly as needed for the crushing and grinding of tough vegetable fibers, seeds, and hard-shelled fruits.

Primates became primates largely as a result of their adaptation to arboreal living. We can see this process at work in their reliance on vision for survival. In a complex, three-dimensional environment with uncertain footholds, acute vision with depth perception is a necessity. Climbing can be accomplished by either digging in with claws (as in squirrels and raccoons) or grasping around branches with prehensile hands and feet. Primates adopted this latter strategy, which allowed a means of progressing on the most tenuous of surfaces. Thus, in

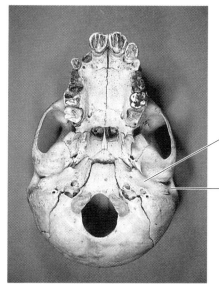

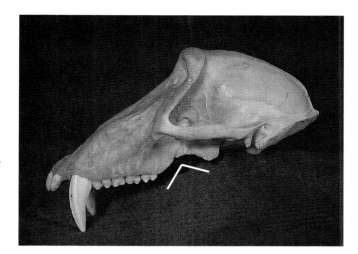

Portion of temporal
bone enclosing
auditory buila

External opening to
ear (external auditory
meatus)

FIGURE 2

*The base of an adolescent chimpanzee skull. Note that in an adult
animal, the bones of the skull would be fused together and would
not appear as separate elements as shown here.*

FIGURE 3

*The skull of a male baboon (a) compared to that of a red wolf (b).
The angle at the base of the baboon skull is due to flexion. The corresponding area of the wolf skull is flat. Note the forward facing
position of the eye orbits above the snout in the baboon. Also, be
aware that in the baboon, the enlarged muzzle does not reflect a
heavy reliance on the sense of smell. Rather, it serves to support very
large canine teeth, the roots of which curve back through the bone
for as much as 1½ inches.*

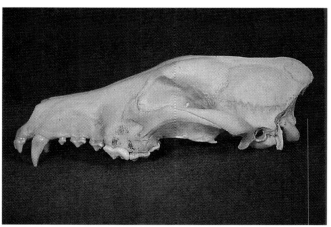

primates we also see pentadactyly (5 digits), prehensility, and flattened nails. In
addition, the varied foods found in a tropical arboreal environment (such as fruit,
leaves, insects, and small mammals) led to the primates' omnivorous adaptation
and hence to retention of a generalized dentition.

Finally, the elongated life span, increased intelligence, and more elaborate
social system are primate solutions to coping with the manifold complexities of
an arboreal habitat. In such an environment, there are varied and seasonal food

▲ **Arboreal hypothesis**
The traditional view that primate characteristics can be explained as a consequence of primate diversification into arboreal habitats.

resources, and predators (eagles) can appear from above, in the trees (snakes), or from below (leopards). This crucial development of increased behavioral flexibility may have been further stimulated by a shift from nocturnal to diurnal activity patterns (Jerison, 1973).

A critique of this traditional **arboreal hypothesis** for the origin of primate structure has been proposed by Matt Cartmill (1972; 1992) of Duke University. Cartmill points out that the most significant primate trends—forward-facing eyes and grasping hands and feet—may *not* have arisen from adaptive advantages in a purely arboreal environment. According to this alternative theory, called the *visual predation hypothesis*, primates may first have adapted to the bushy forest undergrowth and only the lowest tiers of the forest canopy. Here, early primates could have exploited insects, which they may have preyed upon primarily by stealth. Thus, we could envision a small, primitive, largely insectivorous primate ancestor clinging to small branches with partially grasping hands while judging distances with forward-facing close-set eyes.

The visual predation hypothesis and the arboreal theory are not mutually exclusive explanations. The complex of primate characteristics might have begun in nonarboreal settings, but could have become even more adaptive once insect hunting was done in the trees.

One thing is certain, at some point, the primates did take to the trees in earnest, and that is where the vast majority of nonhuman primates still live today. Whereas the basic primate structural complexes may have been adapted for visual predation, they became ideally suited for the arboreal adaptation that followed. We would say, then, that primates were "preadapted" for arboreal living.

The Living Primates

Habitats

With just a couple of exceptions, contemporary nonhuman primates are found in tropical or semitropical areas of the New and Old Worlds. In the New World, these areas include southern Mexico, Central America, and parts of South America. Old World primates are found in Africa, India, Southeast Asia (including numerous islands), and Japan (Fig. 9–3).

The majority of primates are, as we have mentioned, mostly arboreal and live in forest or woodland habitats. However, some Old World monkeys (e.g., baboons) have, to varying degrees, adapted to life on the ground in areas where trees are sparsely distributed. Moreover, among the apes, gorillas and chimpanzees spend a considerable amount of time on the ground in forested and wooded habitats. However, no nonhuman primate is adapted to a fully terrestrial lifestyle, and all spend some time in the trees.

Teeth

As noted, primates are generally *omnivorous*. Indeed, the tendency toward omnivory is an example of the overall lack of specialization in primates. The fact that primates are not restricted to one or a few dietary items is important and has contributed to their enormous success during the last 50 million years.

BOX 9–2

Tale of the Teeth

The number and kinds of teeth present are extremely important for interpreting the relationships of *both* living and fossil forms. There are four different kinds of teeth found in a generalized placental mammal, and primates have almost universally retained all four types: incisors, canines, premolars, and molars. A shorthand device for showing the number of each kind of tooth is called a *dental formula* (Fig. 1). This formula indicates the teeth in one-quarter of the mouth (since the arrangement of teeth is symmetrical and usually the same in upper and lower jaws). For example, in many New World monkeys the dental formula is 2-1-3-3 (2 incisors, 1 canine, 3 premolars, and 3 molars in each quarter of the mouth—a total of 36 teeth). The formula in *all* Old World monkeys, apes, and humans is 2-1-2-3—a total of 32 teeth. Most lemur and loris dental formulae are 2-1-3-3 (total of 36), but the highly specialized aye-aye shows (for a primate) remarkable reduction in numbers of teeth:

$$\frac{1\text{-}0\text{-}1\text{-}3^*}{1\text{-}0\text{-}0\text{-}3}$$

for a total of only 18 teeth.

Dental formulae are extremely useful indicators of evolutionary relationships because they are normally under tight genotypic control. In other words, environmental influence usually will not alter the dental formula. In making studies of primate dental phenotypes, we are

*When the formula in the lower jaw differs from that of the upper jaw, both are shown. For example, the aye-aye has 1 incisor, 1 premolar, and 3 molars in the upper jaw. In the lower jaw there are 1 incisor and 3 molars. There are no canine teeth.

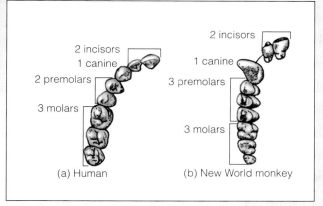

FIGURE 1
Dental formulae. The number of each kind of tooth is given for one-quarter of the mouth.

quite certain, therefore, that our comparisons are based on structural homologies. Thus, similarities in structure (relative numbers of teeth) can be used as indicators of evolutionary similarity.

Dental evidence is extremely important in the interpretation of fossils, since teeth—the hardest component of the body—are the most commonly fossilized part and comprise the vast majority of fossil primate discoveries. In addition, cusp pattern and functional wear can be used to help reconstruct dietary behavior in fossil animals. The identification of diet is of central importance in any attempt to reconstruct the nature of the ecological niche and ultimately the entire way of life of a fossil form.

We also mentioned earlier that most primates possess fairly generalized teeth. For example, the cheek teeth have low, rounded **cusps**. Equipped with this type of premolar and molar morphology, most primates are capable of processing a wide variety of foods ranging from tough or hard items, such as leaves and seeds, to more easily processed fruits, insects, and even meat.

Although the majority of primate species tend to emphasize some food items over others, most eat a combination of fruit, leaves, and insects. Many obtain animal protein from birds and amphibians as well. Some (baboons and, especially, chimpanzees) occasionally kill and eat small mammals, including other primates. Others, such as African colobus monkeys and the leaf-eating monkeys

▲ Cusps
The elevated portions (bumps) on the chewing surfaces of premolar and molar teeth.

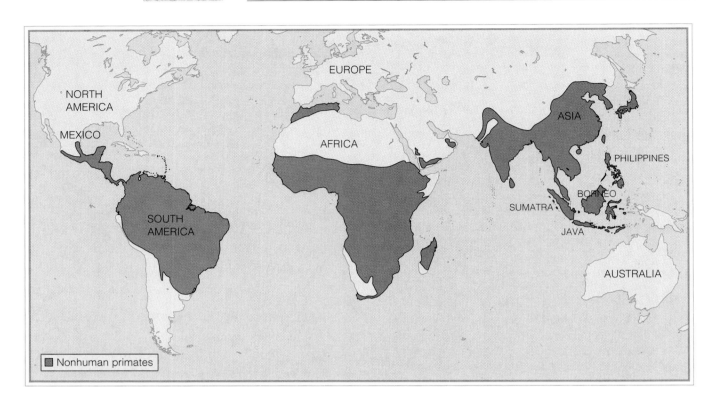

FIGURE 9–3

Geographical distribution of living non-human primates.

▲ **Quadrupedal**

Using all four limbs to support the body during locomotion. The basic mammalian (and primate) form of locomotion.

▲ **Macaques**

(muh-kaks´) Group of Old World monkeys made up of several species, including the rhesus monkey.

(langurs) of Southeast Asia, have become more specialized and subsist primarily on leaves.

Locomotion

A basic way to understand the variety of living primates is through comparison of their locomotor behavior. Since so much of the body, especially the musculoskeletal system, is involved in locomotion, we can gain an understanding of comparative primate anatomy through a structural-functional approach that emphasizes locomotor behavior.

Almost all primates are, at least to some degree, **quadrupedal**, meaning they use all four limbs to support the body during locomotion. However, to describe most primate species in terms of only one or even two forms of locomotion would be to overlook the wide variety of methods they may use to move about. Many primates employ more than one form of locomotion, and they owe this important ability to their generalized structure.

Although the majority of quadrupedal primates are arboreal, terrestrial quadrupedalism is fairly common and is displayed by some lemurs, baboons, and **macaques**. Typically, the limbs of terrestrial quadrupeds are approximately of equal length, with forelimbs being 90 percent (or more) as long as hind limbs (Fig. 9–4a). In arboreal quadrupeds, forelimbs are proportionately shorter and may be only 70 to 80 percent as long as hind limbs (Fig. 9–4b).

Quadrupeds are also characterized by a relatively long and flexible *lumbar spine* (lower back). This lumbar flexibility permits the animal to bend the body during running, thus positioning the hind limbs and feet well forward under the

(a)

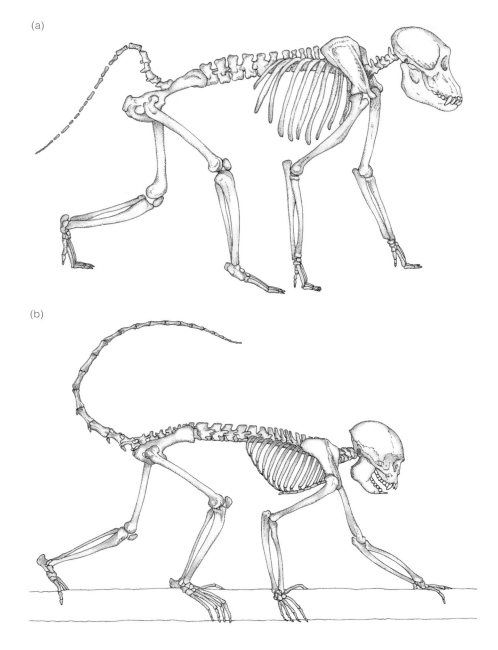

(b)

FIGURE 9–4
*Skeletons of quadrupedal monkeys. (a)
Savanna baboon, an Old World terres-
trial quadruped. (b) Bearded saki, a New
World arboreal quadruped. (Redrawn
from original art by Stephen Nash. In
Fleagle, John G.,* Primate Adaptation
and Evolution, *1988. New York:
Academic Press.)*

body and enhancing their ability to propel the animal forward. (Watch for this
the next time you see slow-motion footage of cheetahs or lions on television.)

Another form of locomotion is *vertical clinging and leaping*, seen in many
prosimians. As the term implies, vertical clingers and leapers support themselves
vertically by grasping onto trunks of trees while their knees and ankles are tightly
flexed (Fig. 9–5). Forceful extension of their long hind limbs allows them to
spring powerfully away in either a forward or backward direction. Once in
midair, the body rotates so that the animal lands feet first on the next vertical
support.

Yet another type of primate locomotion is **brachiation**, or arm swinging,
where the body is alternatively supported under either forelimb. Because of
anatomical modifications at the shoulder joint, all apes and humans are capable

▲ **Brachiation**
A form of suspensory locomotion in
which the support is alternated from
one forelimb to the other.

of true brachiation. However, only the small gibbons and siamangs of Southeast Asia use this form of locomotion almost exclusively.

Brachiation is seen in species characterized by arms longer than legs, a short stable lumbar spine, long curved fingers, and reduced thumbs (Fig. 9–6). Because these are traits seen in all the apes, it is believed that although none of the great apes (orangutans, gorillas, chimpanzees, and bonobos) habitually brachiates today, they most likely inherited these characteristics from brachiating or perhaps climbing ancestors.

Some monkeys, particularly New World monkeys, are termed *semibrachiators*, as they practice a combination of leaping with some arm swinging. In some New World species, arm swinging and other suspensory behaviors are enhanced by use of a *prehensile tail*, which, in effect, serves as a marvelously effective grasping fifth "hand." It should be noted that prehensile tails are strictly a New World phenomenon and are not seen in any Old World primate species.

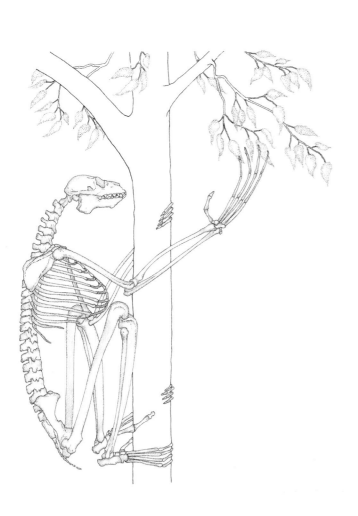

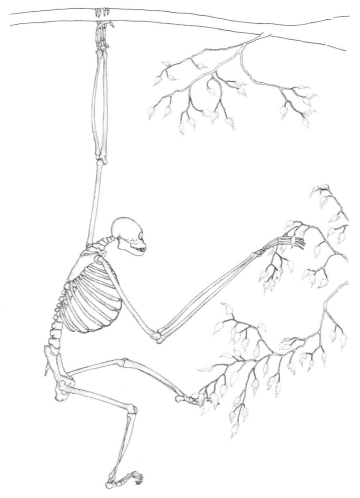

FIGURE 9–5

Skeleton of a vertical clinger and leaper (indri). (Redrawn from original art by Stephen Nash. In Fleagle, John G., Primate Adaptation and Evolution, 1988. New York, Academic Press.)

FIGURE 9–6

Skeleton of a brachiator (gibbon). (Redrawn from original art by Stephen Nash. In Fleagle, John G., Primate Adaptation and Evolution, 1988. New York: Academic Press.)

Primate Classification

In Chapter 8, we reviewed some of the principles of taxonomic classification. Consequently, you know that organisms have traditionally been categorized on the basis of morphological similarities, using many of the same categories originally established by Linnaeus in the eighteenth century. You also know that a major objective of any modern classification is to show evolutionary relationships between categories.

Traditionally, the living primates have been classified as shown in Fig. 9–7. In this, as in any taxonomic system, organisms are organized into increasingly narrow categories. For example, the order Primates includes *all* primates. However, at the next level down, the suborder, the primates have conventionally been divided into two large categories: *Prosimii* (all the prosimians: lemurs and lorises and, customarily, the tarsier) and *Anthropoidea* (all the monkeys, apes, and humans). Therefore, the suborder is less inclusive than the order. At the level of the suborder, the prosimians are grouped separately from all other primates, and this classification makes the biological and evolutionary statement that prosimians are more closely related to one another than they are to any of the anthropoids. Likewise, all anthropoid species are more closely related to one another than to the prosimians.

At each succeeding level (infraorder, superfamily, family, genus, and species), finer distinctions are made between categories until, at the species level (at least theoretically), only those animals that can interbreed and produce viable offspring are included. In this manner, classifications not only organize diversity into categories, but also illustrate evolutionary and genetic relationships between species and groups of species.

However, the traditional manner of classification, based on morphological traits, has inherent shortcomings. As more detailed data relating to primate relationships have accumulated, some long-held conclusions have been altered and some revisions to traditional classifications have been proposed. The two areas that have stimulated the greatest interest are the reclassification of the tarsier and the evolutionary relationships of the great apes (orangutans, gorillas, chimpanzees, and bonobos), to each other and to humans.

Tarsiers (see p. 220) are highly derived animals that display several unique physical characteristics. Traditionally, they have been classified as prosimians (with lemurs and lorises) because they possess a number of prosimian traits, but they also share certain anthropoid features (see p. 222). Moreover, biochemically, tarsiers are more closely related to anthropoids than to prosimians (Dene et al., 1976); however, with regard to chromosomes, they are distinct from both.

Today, many primatologists classify tarsiers closer to anthropoids than to prosimians. One alternate scheme places lemurs and lorises in a different suborder, Strepsirhini; and includes tarsiers with monkeys, apes, and humans in another suborder, Haplorhini (Szalay and Delson, 1979) (Fig. 9–8). In this scheme, the traditional suborders Prosimii and Anthropoidea have been replaced. Other similar systems have also been proposed, but so far, none has been agreed on.

The second area where modifications have been suggested involves the **hominoids**, with the problem being how to classify the great apes. Traditionally, all four species were placed in one family (Pongidae), separate from humans (Hominidae). But from genetic data, we now know that the closest relationships actually exist among the African forms (chimpanzees, bonobos, gorillas, and humans) and that these are all more closely allied to each other than any is to the Asian orangutan (see p. 233 for further discussion). Thus, the traditional term *pongid* has a limited evolutionary meaning. The pongids, or great apes, as

▲ **Hominoids**
Members of the superfamily Hominoidea. The group includes apes and humans.

FIGURE 9–7
Traditional primate taxonomic classification. This abbreviated taxonomy illustrates how primates are grouped into increasingly specific categories. Only the more general categories are shown, except for the great apes and humans.

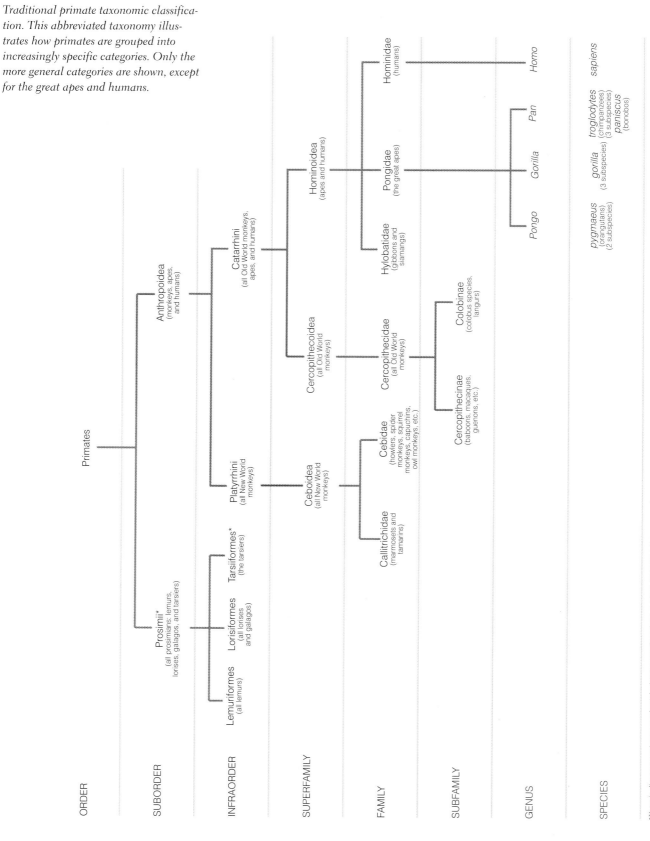

*There is disagreement among primatologists concerning where to place the tarsier. Many researchers suggest that they more properly belong closer to the anthropoids and thus revise the primate classification to reflect this view. Here, for simplicity, we continue to use the traditional classifications.

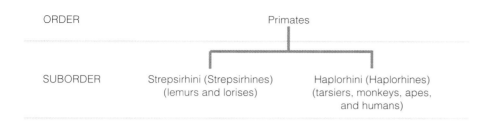

ORDER		Primates	
SUBORDER	Strepsirhini (Strepsirhines) (lemurs and lorises)		Haplorhini (Haplorhines) (tarsiers, monkeys, apes, and humans)

FIGURE 9–8

Revised partial classification of the primates. In this system, the terms Prosimii *and* Anthropoidea *have been replaced by* Strepsirhini *and* Haplorhini, *respectively. The tarsier is included in the same suborder with monkeys, apes, and humans to reflect a closer relationship with these forms than with lemurs and lorises. (Compare with Figure 9–7.)*

traditionally defined, are not a single, closely related group, but represent two evolutionarily distinct, albeit morphologically similar groups (African and Asian).

Furthermore, and perhaps more controversial, because it hits so close to home, DNA data indicate that humans and chimpanzees are closer to each other genetically than either is to the gorilla (Sibley and Ahlquist, 1984). For that matter, chimpanzees (including bonobos) and humans share more genetic similarities than do zebras and horses, or goats and sheep. On the basis of these results, it would be entirely appropriate to classify humans and chimpanzees (and perhaps gorillas as well) within the same family and perhaps the same genus. Humans would continue to be called *Homo sapiens*, whereas chimpanzees would be classed as *Homo troglodytes*. While many people are not prepared to accept the new terminology at this time, it certainly is a more accurate reflection of basic genetic and evolutionary facts.

We have included the traditional system of primate classification here, even though we acknowledge the need for modification. At present, not all anthropologists and biologists have completely accepted the revised terminology. Until consensus is reached and new designations are formally adopted, we think it appropriate to use the standard taxonomy along with discussion of some proposed changes. It is also important to point out that while specific details and names have not yet been worked out, the vast majority of experts do accept the evolutionary implications of the revised groupings.

An Overview of Contemporary Primates

Prosimians

The most primitive of the primates are the true prosimians, the lemurs and lorises (we do not include the tarsier here). By "primitive" or "least derived," we mean that these prosimians, taken as a group, are more similar anatomically to their earlier mammalian ancestors than are the other primates (monkeys and apes). Therefore, they tend to exhibit certain more primitive characteristics, such as a more pronounced reliance on *olfaction* (sense of smell). Their greater olfactory capabilities (compared to other primates) are reflected in the presence of a moist, fleshy pad (**rhinarium**) at the end of the nose and in the relatively long snout, which gives prosimians a somewhat doglike appearance. Moreover, prosimians mark territories with scent in a manner not seen in many other primates.

There are numerous other distinctions that set prosimians apart from the anthropoids, including somewhat more laterally placed eyes, differences in reproductive physiology, and shorter gestation and maturation periods. Prosimians also possess a dental specialization known as the "dental comb." The dental comb is formed by forward-projecting lower incisors and canines, and together these modified teeth are used in both grooming and feeding (Fig. 9–9).

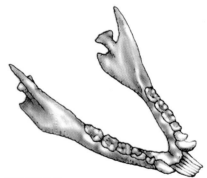

FIGURE 9–9

Prosimian dental comb, formed by forward-projecting incisors and canines. The first lower premolar has become modified to be more caninelike in shape, size, and function.

▲ **Rhinarium**

(rine-air´-ee-um) The moist, hairless pad at the end of the nose seen in most mammalian species. The rhinarium enhances an animal's sense of smell.

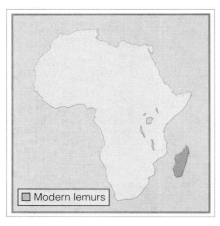

☐ Modern lemurs

FIGURE 9–10
Geographical distribution of modern lemurs.

Lemurs and Lorises   There are two groupings of prosimians: lemurs and lorises. Lemurs are found only on the island of Madagascar and adjacent islands off the east coast of Africa (Fig. 9–10). As the only nonhuman primates on Madagascar, which comprises some 227,000 square miles, lemurs diversified into numerous and varied ecological niches without competition from the higher primates (i.e., monkeys and apes). Thus, while lemurs became extinct elsewhere, the 22 surviving species on Madagascar represent an evolutionary pattern that has vanished elsewhere.

Lemurs range in size from the small mouse lemur, with a body length (head and trunk) of only 5 inches, to the indri, with a body length of a little over 2 feet (Napier and Napier, 1985). While the larger lemurs are diurnal and exploit a wide variety of dietary items such as leaves, fruit, buds, bark, and shoots, the smaller forms (mouse and dwarf lemurs) are nocturnal and are insectivorous.

Lemurs display considerable variation regarding numerous other aspects of behavior. While many are primarily arboreal, others, such as the ring-tailed lemur (Fig. 9–11), are more terrestrial. Some arboreal species are quadrupeds, and others (sifakas and indris) are vertical clingers and leapers (Fig 9–12). Socially, several species (e.g., ring-tailed lemurs and sifakas) are gregarious and live in groups of 10 to 25 animals composed of males and females of all ages. Others (the indris) live in monogamous family units, and several nocturnal forms are mostly solitary.

Lorises (Fig 9–13), which are very similar in appearance to lemurs, were able to survive in continental areas by adopting a nocturnal activity pattern at a time when most other prosimians became extinct. In this way, they were (and are) able to avoid competition with more recently evolved primates (the diurnal monkeys).

The five loris species (loris in the strict sense) are found in tropical forest and woodland habitats of India, Sri Lanka, Southeast Asia, and Africa. Also included in the same general category are six to nine species (Bearder, 1987) of galago (Fig. 9–14), which are widely distributed throughout most of the forested and woodland savanna areas of sub-Saharan Africa (Fig. 9–15).

Locomotion in lorises is a slow, cautious climbing form of quadrupedalism, and flexible hip joints permit suspension by hind limbs while the hands are used in feeding. All galagos, however, are highly agile and active vertical clingers and leapers. Some lorises and galagos are almost entirely insectivorous; others supplement their diet with various combinations of fruits, leaves, gums, and slugs. Lorises and galagos frequently forage for food alone (females leave infants behind in nests until they are older). However, ranges overlap, and two or more females occasionally forage together or share the same sleeping nest.

Both lemurs and lorises represent the same general adaptive level. They both have good grasping and climbing abilities and a fairly well-developed visual apparatus, although stereoscopic vision is not as well developed as in anthropoids. Color vision also may not be as well developed as in higher primates, and is not present in nocturnal species. Most retain a claw, commonly called a "grooming claw," only on the second toe. Most lemurs and lorises also have prolonged life spans as compared to most other small-bodied mammals, averaging about 14 years for lorises and 19 years for lemurs.

Tarsiers

There are three recognized species of tarsier (Fig. 9–16), all restricted to island areas in Southeast Asia (Fig. 9–17), where they inhabit a wide range of habitats,

FIGURE 9–11
Ring-tailed lemur.

FIGURE 9–12
Sifakas in their native habitat in Madagascar.

FIGURE 9–13
Slow loris.

FIGURE 9–14
Galago, or "bush baby."

FIGURE 9–15
Geographical distribution of modern lorises and galagos.

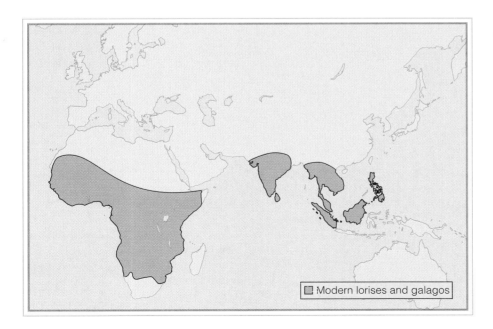

Modern lorises and galagos

FIGURE 9–16
Tarsier.

FIGURE 9–17
Geographical distribution of tarsiers.

from tropical forest to backyard gardens. Tarsiers are nocturnal insectivores, leaping onto prey (which may also include small vertebrates) from lower branches and shrubs. They appear to form stable pair bonds, and the basic tarsier social unit probably is a mated pair and its young offspring (MacKinnon and MacKinnon, 1980).

As stated previously, tarsiers exhibit a combination of anatomical traits not seen in any other primate and they have been classified traditionally as prosimians (along with lemurs and lorises). This designation was due to a number of factors, including small body size, large ears, the presence of grooming claws, and an unfused mandible.

However, tarsiers also exhibit a number of anthropoid characteristics, such as lack of a rhinarium and eye sockets that are enclosed in bone both at the back and at the sides. Tarsiers are also more similar biochemically to anthropoids than they are to prosimians.

Finally, tarsiers are unique among primates in that their particularly enormous eyes, which dominate much of the face, are immobile within their sockets. To compensate for the inability to move their eyes, they are able to rotate their heads 180° in a decidedly owl-like manner.

As you can see, tarsiers do indeed present an intriguing combination of prosimian and anthropoid traits, along with a few of their own. It is therefore not at all surprising that they represent a puzzle for taxonomists.

Anthropoids

A number of features distinguish the anthropoids from the prosimians, including the following:

1. Generally larger body size
2. Larger brain (in absolute terms and relative to body weight)
3. More rounded skull
4. Complete rotation of eyes to front of face to permit full binocular vision
5. Bony plate at back of eye orbit
6. No rhinarium (implying reduced reliance on the sense of smell)
7. Increased parental care
8. Increased gestation and maturation periods
9. More mutual grooming

Monkeys represent approximately 70 percent (about 130 species) of all primates, and as a group, they are the most varied. It is frequently impossible to give precise numbers of species because the taxonomic status of some primates remains in doubt and primatologists are still making new discoveries. (In fact, two "new" marmoset species were identified in 1996.) Monkeys are divided into two groups based on geographical area (New World and Old World), as well as several million years of distinct evolutionary history.

New World Monkeys The New World monkeys exhibit a wide range of size, diet, and ecological adaptation. In size, they vary from the tiny marmosets and tamarins (about 12 ounces) to the 20-pound howler (Figs. 9–18 and 9–19). New World monkeys are almost exclusively arboreal, and some never come to the ground. Like Old World monkeys, all except one species (the douroucouli, or owl monkey) are diurnal. Although confined to the trees, New World monkeys

FIGURE 9–18
A pair of golden lion tamarins.

FIGURE 9–19
Howler monkeys.

can be found in a wide range of arboreal environments throughout most forested areas in southern Mexico and Central and South America (Fig. 9–20).

One of the characteristics distinguishing New World monkeys from those found in the Old World is shape of the nose. New World forms have broad, widely flaring noses with outward-facing nostrils. Conversely, Old World monkeys have narrower noses with downward-facing nostrils. This difference in nose form has given rise to the terms *platyrrhine* (flat-nosed) and *catarrhine* (downward-facing nose) to refer to New and Old World anthropoids, respectively.

New World monkeys are divided into two families: **Callitrichidae** and **Cebidae**. Some scientists include spider monkeys (Fig. 9–21), muriquis (woolly spider monkeys), and howlers in a third family, the Atelidae (Fleagle, 1988).

The callitrichids (marmosets and tamarins) are the most primitive of monkeys, retaining claws instead of nails and usually giving birth to twins instead of one infant. Marmosets and tamarins are mostly insectivorous, although marmoset diet includes gums from trees, and tamarins also rely heavily on fruits. Locomotion is quadrupedal, and their claws aid in climbing vertical tree trunks, much in the manner of squirrels. Moreover, some tamarins employ vertical clinging and leaping as a form of travel. Socially, callitrichids live in family groups composed usually of a mated pair, or a female and two adult males, and their offspring. Indeed, marmosets and tamarins are among the few primate species in which males are heavily involved in infant care.

There are at least 30 cebid species ranging in size from the squirrel monkey (body length 12 inches) to the howler (body length 24 inches). Diet varies, with most relying on a combination of fruit and leaves supplemented, to varying degrees, by insects. Most cebids are quadrupedal, but some—for example, the spider monkeys—are semibrachiators. Some cebids, including the spider monkey and howler, also possess powerful prehensile tails that are used not only in locomotion but also for suspension under branches while feeding on leaves and fruit (Fig. 9–21). Socially, most cebids are found either in groups of both sexes and all age categories or in monogamous pairs with subadult offspring.

▲ **Callitrichidae**
(kal-eh-trick´-eh-dee)

▲ **Cebidae**
(see´-bid-ee)

FIGURE 9–20
Geographical distribution of modern New World monkeys.

FIGURE 9–21
Spider monkey. Note the prehensile tail.

Old World Monkeys   The monkeys of the Old World display much more morphological and behavioral diversity than is seen in New World monkeys. Except for humans, Old World monkeys are the most widely distributed of all living primates. They are found throughout sub-Saharan Africa and southern Asia, ranging from tropical jungle habitats to semiarid desert and even to seasonally snow-covered areas in northern Japan (Fig. 9–22).

FIGURE 9–22
Geographical distribution of extant Old World monkeys.

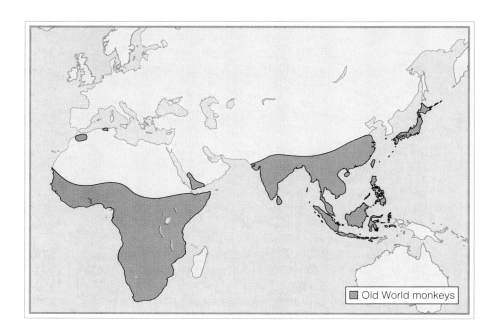

Old World monkeys

Most Old World monkeys are quadrupedal and primarily arboreal, but some (e.g., baboons) are also adapted to life on the ground. Whether in trees or on the ground, these monkeys spend a good deal of time sleeping, feeding, and grooming while sitting with their upper bodies held erect. Usually associated with this universal sitting posture are areas of hardened skin on the buttocks (**ischial callosities**) that serve as sitting pads. Old World monkeys also have a good deal of manual dexterity, and most have tails that serve in communication and balance.

Within the entire group of Old World monkeys there is only one taxonomically recognized family: **Cercopithecidae**. This family, in turn, is divided into two subfamilies: the **cercopithecines** and **colobines**.

The cercopithecines are the more generalized of the two groups, showing a more omnivorous dietary adaptation and distinctive cheek pouches for storing food. As a group, the cercopithecines eat almost anything, including fruits, seeds, leaves, grasses, roots, insects, birds' eggs, small reptiles, and small mammals (the last seen in baboons).

The majority of cercopithecine species, such as the arboreal and sometimes colorful guenons (Fig. 9–23) and the more terrestrial savanna and hamadryas baboons (Fig. 9–24), are found in Africa. However, the several species of macaque, which include the well-known rhesus monkey, are widely distributed in southern Asia and India.

Colobine species are more limited dietarily, specializing on mature leaves, a behavior that has led to their designation as "leaf-eating monkeys." The colobines are found mainly in Asia, but both the red colobus and black-and-white colobus are exclusively African (Fig. 9–25). Other colobines include several species of Asian langur and the proboscis monkey of Borneo.

Locomotor behavior among Old World monkeys includes arboreal quadrupedalism in guenons, macaques, and langurs; terrestrial quadrupedalism in baboons, patas, and macaques; and semibrachiation and acrobatic leaping in colobus monkeys.

A marked difference in body size or shape between the sexes, referred to as **sexual dimorphism**, is typical of some terrestrial species and is particularly

▲ **Ischial callosities**
Patches of tough, hard skin on the buttocks of Old World monkeys and chimpanzees.

▲ **Cercopithecidae**
(serk-oh-pith´-eh-sid-ee)

▲ **Cercopithecines**
(serk-oh-pith´-eh-seens) The subfamily of Old World monkeys that includes baboons, macaques, and guenons.

▲ **Colobines**
(kole´-uh-beans) The subfamily of Old World monkeys that includes the African colobus monkeys and Asian langurs.

▲ **Sexual dimorphism**
Differences in physical characteristics between males and females of the same species. For example, humans are slightly sexually dimorphic for body size, with males being taller, on average, than females of the same population.

FIGURE 9–23
Adult male Sykes monkey, one of several species of guenon.

(a)

FIGURE 9–24
Savanna baboons. (a) Male. (b) Female.

(b)

▲ **Estrus**

(ess´-truss) Period of sexual receptivity in female mammals (except humans) correlated with ovulation. When used as an adjective, the word is spelled "estrous."

FIGURE 9–25
Black-and-white colobus monkey.

pronounced in baboons and patas. In these species, male body weight (up to 80 pounds in baboons) may be twice that of females.

Females of several species (especially baboons and some macaques) exhibit pronounced cyclical changes of the external genitalia. These changes, including swelling and redness, are associated with **estrus**, a hormonally initiated period of sexual receptivity in female mammals correlated with ovulation.

Several types of social organization characterize Old World monkeys, and there are uncertainties among primatologists regarding some species. In general, colobines tend to live in small groups, with only one or two adult males. Savanna baboons and most macaque species are found in large social units comprising

several adults of both sexes and offspring of all ages. Monogamous pairing is not common in Old World monkeys, but is seen in a few langurs and possibly one or two guenon species.

Monkeys, Old and New World: A Striking Case of Parallel Evolution We have mentioned several differences between Old World monkeys and New World monkeys, but the fact remains that they are all monkeys. That is, they all are adapted to a similar (primarily arboreal) way of life. With the exception of the South American owl monkey, they are diurnal, and all are social, usually fairly omnivorous, and quadrupedal, though with variations of this general locomotor pattern.

These similarities are all the more striking when we consider that Old and New World monkeys have gone their separate evolutionary paths for tens of millions of years. In fact, a noted primate paleontologist, E. L. Simons (1969), suggests that the split may have occurred more than 50 m.y.a. Both lineages would then have evolved independently from separate prosimian ancestors. The current consensus among researchers, however, disputes this claim (Hoffstetter, 1972; Ciochon and Chiarelli, 1980) and postulates that both Old and New World monkeys arose in Africa from a common monkey ancestor and later reached South America by "rafting" over on chunks of land that had broken away from mainland areas. (It should be mentioned that large "floating islands," complete with trees, have occasionally been observed on the open ocean.) A number of conditions that existed 50–30 m.y.a. could have facilitated such a crossing. South America and Africa were somewhat closer than they are today, and it is believed that prevailing ocean currents would have been favorable. In fact, it is believed that a voyage of around 600 miles could have been accomplished in less than three weeks. In addition, a series of large volcanic islands that existed in the Caribbean and South Atlantic may have served as "stepping stones" for would-be immigrants.

Whether the last common ancestor shared by New and Old World monkeys was a prosimian or a monkey-like animal, what is most remarkable is that the two forms have not diverged more than they have over the last 30 million years or so. The diverse arboreal adaptations we see in the living monkeys of both hemispheres is the result of **parallel evolution** that has occurred in geographically distinct populations responding to similar selective pressures in tropical arboreal environments. The result is that the primates we recognize as monkeys evolved in both the New and Old Worlds.

Hominoids

Traditionally, the superfamily **Hominoidea** includes the "lesser" apes placed in the family **Hylobatidae** (gibbons and siamangs); the great apes in the family **Pongidae** (orangutans, gorillas, chimpanzees and bonobos); and humans in the family Hominidae.

Apes (and humans) differ from monkeys in numerous ways:

1. Generally larger body size, except for the gibbons and siamangs
2. Absence of a tail
3. Shortened trunk (lumbar area relatively shorter and more stable)
4. Differences in position and musculature of the shoulder joint (adapted for suspensory locomotion)
5. More complex behavior

▲ **Parallel evolution**
The independent evolution of similarities in structure in distantly related (or nonrelated) lineages. Morphological similarities result from adaptation to similar selective pressures.

▲ **Hominoidea**
The formal designation for the superfamily of anthropoids that includes apes and humans.

▲ **Hylobatidea**
(high-lo-baht´-id-ee)

▲ **Pongidae**
(ponj´-id-ee)

FIGURE 9–26

Geographical distribution of modern Asian apes.

6. More complex brain and enhanced cognitive abilities
7. Lengthened period of infant development and dependency

Gibbons and Siamangs   The eight gibbon species and the closely related siamang are today found in the southeastern tropical areas of Asia (Fig. 9–26). These animals are the smallest of the apes, with a long, slender body weighing 13 pounds in the gibbon (Fig. 9–27) and 25 pounds in the larger siamang.

The most distinctive structural feature of gibbons and siamangs is related to their functional adaptation for brachiation. They have extremely long arms, long, permanently curved fingers and short thumbs, and powerful shoulder muscles. These highly specialized locomotor adaptations may be related to feeding behavior while hanging beneath branches. The diet of both gibbons and siamangs is largely composed of fruit. Both (especially the siamang) also eat a variety of leaves, flowers, and insects.

The basic social unit of gibbons and siamangs is the monogamous pair with dependent offspring. As in marmosets and tamarins, male gibbons and siamangs are very much involved in rearing their young. Both males and females are highly territorial and protect their territories with elaborate and siren-like whoops and "songs."

Orangutans   The orangutan (*Pongo pygmaeus*) (Fig. 9–28) is represented by two subspecies found today only in heavily forested areas on the Indonesian islands of Borneo and Sumatra (Fig. 9–26). Due to poaching by humans and continuing habitat loss on both islands, the orangutan faces imminent extinction in the wild.

Orangutans are slow, cautious climbers whose locomotor behavior can best be described as "four-handed," referring to the tendency to use all four limbs for grasping and support. Although they are almost completely arboreal, orangutans

FIGURE 9–27

White-handed gibbon.

FIGURE 9–28
Female orangutan.

do sometimes travel quadrupedally on the ground. Orangutans are also very large animals with pronounced sexual dimorphism (males may weigh 200 pounds or more and females less than 100 pounds).

In the wild, orangutans lead largely solitary lives, although adult females are usually accompanied by one or two dependent offspring. The animals are primarily **frugivorous**, but bark, leaves, insects, and meat (on rare occasions) may also be eaten.

▲ **Frugivorous**
(fru-give´-o-us) Having a diet composed primarily of fruit.

Gorillas   The largest of all living primates, the gorilla (*Gorilla gorilla*) is today confined to forested regions of central Africa (Fig. 9–29). The lowland gorilla is found at lower elevations, while the mountain gorilla (Fig. 9–30) inhabits high-altitude mountainous areas. Gorillas exhibit marked sexual dimorphism, with males weighing up to 400 pounds and females around 200 pounds (Fig. 9–30). Due to their weight, adult gorillas are primarily terrestrial, adopting a semi-quadrupedal (knuckle-walking) posture on the ground.

Gorillas live in family groups consisting of one or more large *silverback* males, a few adult females, and their subadult offspring. The term "silverback" refers to the saddle of white hair across the back of fully adult (at least age 12 or 13 years) male gorillas. Additionally, the silverback may tolerate the presence of a younger adult *blackback* male, probably one of his sons.

Although gorillas have long been considered ferocious wild beasts, they are actually shy and gentle vegetarians (Schaller, 1963; Fossey, 1983). When threatened, males can be provoked to attack, and certainly they will defend their group, but the reputation that gorillas have among humans is little more than myth. Sadly, because of their fierce reputation, the clearing of their habitat for farms, and their targeting by big game hunters, gorillas have been driven to extinction in many areas. Moreover, although there are perhaps 40,000 lowland gorillas remaining in parts of central Africa today, they are endangered, and the mountain gorilla (probably never very numerous) numbers only about 620 (see Issue, p. 236).

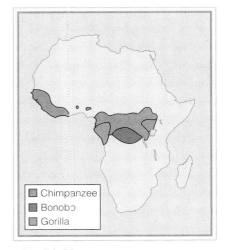

Chimpanzee
Bonobo
Gorilla

FIGURE 9–29
Geographical distribution of modern African apes.

(a) (b)

FIGURE 9–30

Mountain gorilla. (a) Male. (b) Female.

Chimpanzees Probably the best known of all nonhuman primates is the chimpanzee (*Pan troglodytes*) (Fig. 9–31). Often misunderstood because of its displays in zoos, circus acts, and sideshows, the chimpanzee's true nature did not become known until long hours of fieldwork in its natural environment provided a reliable picture. Today, chimpanzees are found in equatorial Africa, distributed in a broad belt from the Atlantic Ocean in the west to Lake Tanganyika in the east (see Fig. 9–29). Their range, however, is patchy within this large geographical area, and with further habitat destruction, it is becoming even more so.

Chimpanzees are in many ways structurally similar to gorillas, with corresponding limb proportions and upper-body shape. This similarity is due to commonalities in locomotion when on the ground (quadrupedal knuckle-walking). Indeed, many authorities (e.g., Tuttle, 1990) consider chimps and gorillas as members of a single genus. However, the ecological adaptations of chimpanzees and gorillas differ, with chimps spending more time in the trees. Moreover, whereas gorillas are typically placid and quiet, chimpanzees are highly excitable, active, and noisy.

FIGURE 9–31

Chimpanzee. (a) Male. (b) Female.

(a) (b)

Chimpanzees are smaller than orangutans and gorillas, and although they are sexually dimorphic, sex differences are not as pronounced as in these other species. While male chimpanzees may weigh over 100 pounds, females may weigh at least 80.

In addition to quadrupedal knuckle-walking, chimpanzees (particularly youngsters) may brachiate while in the trees. When on the ground, they frequently walk bipedally for short distances when carrying food or other objects. Indeed, one adult male at Jane Goodall's study area in Tanzania frequently walked bipedally because one arm was paralyzed by polio (Goodall, 1986).

Chimpanzees eat an amazing variety of items, including fruits, leaves, insects, nuts, birds' eggs, berries, caterpillars, and small mammals. Moreover, both males and females occasionally take part in group hunting efforts to kill such small mammals as red colobus, young baboons, bushpigs, and antelope. When hunts are successful, the prey is shared by the group members.

Chimpanzees live in large, fluid communities of as many as 50 individuals or more. At the core of a chimpanzee community is a group of bonded males. Although relationships between them are not always peaceful or stable, these males nevertheless act as a group to defend their territory and are highly intolerant of unfamiliar chimpanzees, especially nongroup males.

Even though chimpanzees are said to live in communities, there are few times, if any, when all members are together. Indeed, it is the nature of chimpanzees to come and go, so that the individuals they encounter vary from day to day. Moreover, adult females tend to forage either alone or in the company of their offspring (Fig. 9–32). The latter foraging group could comprise several chimps, as females with infants sometimes accompany their own mothers and their younger siblings. A female may also leave her community, either permanently to join another community or temporarily while she is in estrus. This behavioral pattern may serve to reduce the risk of mating with close male relatives, because males apparently never leave the group in which they were born.

Chimpanzee social behavior is complex, and individuals form lifelong attachments with friends and relatives. Indeed, the bond between mothers and infants often remains strong until one or the other dies. This may be a considerable period, because it is not unusual for some chimpanzees to live into their mid-30s and a few into their 40s.

Bonobos Bonobos (*Pan paniscus*) are found only in an area south of the Zaire River in Zaire (Fig. 9–29). Not officially recognized by European scientists until the 1920s, they remain the least studied of the great apes. Although ongoing field studies have produced much information (Susman, 1984; Kano, 1992), research has been periodically hampered by political unrest in Zaire. There are no accurate counts of bonobos, but their numbers are believed to be only in the few thousands, and these are highly threatened by human hunting, warfare, and habitat loss.

Because bonobos bear a strong resemblance to chimpanzees but are somewhat smaller, they have been called "pygmy chimpanzees." However, differences in body size are not sufficient to warrant this designation, and in fact, bonobos exhibit several anatomical and behavioral differences from chimpanzees. Physically, they have a more linear body build, longer legs relative to arms, a relatively smaller head, a dark face from birth, and tufts of hair at the side of the face (Fig. 9–33).

Behaviorally, bonobos are more arboreal than chimpanzees, and they appear to be less excitable and aggressive. While aggression is not unknown, it appears that physical violence both within and between groups is uncommon. Like chimpanzees, bonobos live in geographically based, fluid communities,

FIGURE 9–32
Female chimpanzee with infant and subadult offspring.

FIGURE 9–33
Female bonobos with young.

and they exploit many of the same foods, including occasional meat derived from killing small mammals (Badrian and Malinky, 1984). But bonobo communities are not centered around a group of closely bonded males. Rather, male-female bonding is more important than in chimpanzees (and most other nonhuman primates), and females are not as peripheral to the group (Badrian and Badrian, 1984). This may be related to bonobo sexuality, which differs in expression from that of other nonhuman primates in that copulation is frequent, occurring throughout a female's estrous cycle.

Bonobos are relatively late to arrive on the scene of primate research. But it is crucial that studies of this intriguing species be allowed to progress. Not only do bonobos have the potential of providing information about human behavior and evolution, but also they are of considerable interest in their own right and they are highly endangered. In fact, without research and protection, like so many other nonhuman primates, they are in grave danger of extinction.

Humans   Humans represent the only living species belonging to the family Hominidae (genus *Homo*, species *sapiens*). Our primate heritage is shown again and again in the structure of our body. Our dependence on vision, our lack of reliance on olfactory cues, and our flexible limbs and grasping hands are all long rooted in our primate, arboreal past. Indeed, among the primates, we show in many ways the most developed set of primate characteristics. For example, the development of our cerebral cortex and reliance on learned behavior (with resulting complexity in social behavior) are but elaborations of long-established primate trends.

Several features of humans and our most immediate ancestors distinguish us from other primates. However, probably the most distinctive, and certainly the most observable, difference seen in our earliest (hominid) ancestors is our unique manner of locomotion. The striding bipedal gait, with alternating support placed on one hind limb at a time, has required significant structural modification of the pelvis and lower limbs. By identifying similar structural modifications in the remains of fossil animals, we are able to distinguish our closely related or direct ancestors.

Primate Chromosomes, Proteins, and DNA

The taxonomy presented on page 218 was developed primarily by means of between-species comparisons of numerous anatomical characteristics. But as you know, the goal of taxonomy is to identify biological and evolutionary relationships between groups of organisms. Thus, morphological comparisons, while extremely useful, can sometimes produce misleading results, owing to the effects of parallel evolution. If our goal is the elucidation of biological relationships, then classification schemes must be based on *homologies*, the traits that species share because they inherited them from a common ancestor. (Remember, homologies are contrasted with analogies, which are structural similarities between species that have evolved not because of common ancestry but because of adaptations to similar environments.)

In the past several years, emerging genetic technologies have provided researchers with tools that can help clarify taxonomic relationships. We now have the means to compare directly the DNA and DNA products (i.e., proteins) of species in order to examine relatedness. If two species share similar DNA, that means that both inherited the same blueprint (with minor revisions) from a common ancestor. Thus, we have direct indicators of homologies.

Having stated the major weakness of morphological comparisons, we must make clear that in most cases, genetic data have reaffirmed the taxonomies based on morphology. And when contradictions with traditional taxonomies have appeared, much needed new knowledge has been gained. For example, classifying orangutans with the African great apes seems logical, since they all share marked similarities in form. However, biochemical evidence shows that orangutans are actually quite distinct from gorillas, chimpanzees, and bonobos. Clearly, genetic data have been an extremely important source of information.

Karyotype Comparisons

One way to make genetic comparisons between organisms is to study their karyotypes, identifying similarities and differences in chromosome shape, size, number, and banding patterns. The more closely two species are related, the more alike their karyotypes should be. When we look at the chromosomes of the hominoids, it is readily apparent that humans and the great apes are all quite similar, with gibbons and siamangs having the most distinctive (i.e., derived) pattern (Stanyon and Chiareli, 1982; Mai, 1983).

Among the large-bodied hominoids, the orangutan karyotype is the most conservative, with humans and the African apes displaying more derived features. But within the African hominoids (gorillas, chimpanzees, bonobos, and humans), there is considerable uniformity in the structural arrangement and banding patterns of almost all the chromosomes. Consequently, the chromosomal evidence would support reclassifying orangutans, perhaps by placing them into a separate family from the African apes.

Comparisons of banding patterns of chimpanzee and human chromosomes have revealed a number of highly intriguing results. As you know, humans have 46 chromosomes and chimpanzees have 48. Interestingly, the banding patterns of human chromosome 2 correspond to those of two much smaller chimpanzee chromosomes. This finding has led to speculation that in an ancestral hominoid, these two chromosomes fused to produce what became, in some populations, human chromosome 2 (Fig. 9–34).

The exact sequence of evolutionary relationships among humans and the African great apes is still in some dispute. Some tentative chromosomal data

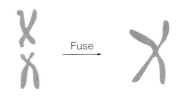

FIGURE 9–34
Fusion of two small chromosomes. This fusion produces one large chromosome (human chromosome 2?).

have suggested that humans and chimpanzees share a more recent ancestry after separating from gorillas (Yunis and Prakash, 1982). A more controlled study, however, with consideration of within-species variation of karyotypes (Stanyon and Chiarelli, 1982), has supported the more traditional branching order, in which the human lineage diverged from the African great ape lineages, which in turn separated later.

Amino Acid Sequencing

Another method of identifying genetic relationships between species is to examine the sequence of amino acids that comprise specific proteins. The more closely related two species are, the more similar their proteins should be. Such comparisons between humans and the African great apes for the approximately half dozen proteins examined show striking similarities. For example, chimpanzees and humans differ with regard to only one amino acid in the series of 146 amino acids that make up the hemoglobin beta chain.

DNA Hybridization

Differences in the DNA strands themselves can be compared using an elaborate technique called DNA hybridization. Scientists have performed some remarkable experiments in which double strands of DNA from two different species are artificially separated and then recombined into a new molecule, a hybrid DNA unlike anything nature ever concocted. The genetic (and evolutionary) similarity of the two species is then calculated by measuring the number of mismatched base pairs along the hybrid sequence (in other words, places where the two sides of the molecule are not complementary: A with T, G with C, etc.).

As in the other techniques, DNA hybridization has reaffirmed most of the basic tenets of primate classification. Indeed, better than any of the other approaches, DNA hybridization has shown how close genetically humans and the African great apes are. The results of this research indicate that, among the major living hominoid groups, the human and chimpanzee lineages were the last to share a common ancestor. That is, humans and chimpanzees (including bonobos) are more closely related to each other than they are to gorillas. The data also suggest that, within the chimpanzee lineage, the split between bonobos (Pan paniscus) and "common" chimpanzees (Pan troglodytes) occurred after the chimpanzee-hominid divergence.

Finally, the revolution in molecular biology brought about by recombinant DNA research has now made it possible to sequence directly the nucleotides of humans and other organisms (Goodman et al., 1983). Once this new technique has been more widely applied, we should be able to ascertain even more unambiguously the precise genetic and evolutionary relationships among the primates.

Summary

In this chapter, we have introduced you to the primates, the mammalian order that includes prosimians, monkeys, apes, and humans. As a group, the primates are generalized in terms of diet and locomotor patterns, and these behavioral generalizations are reflected in the morphology of the teeth and limbs.

We have also discussed some of the anatomical similarities and differences between the major groupings of primates: prosimians, monkeys (New and Old

World), and hominoids. In the next two chapters, we will turn our attention to primate social behavior and cognitive abilities. These are extremely important topics, for it is through better understanding of nonhuman primate behavior that we can make more accurate statements regarding the evolution of human behavior. Moreover, increasing our knowledge is essential if we are to prevent many of these uniquely adapted and marvelous relatives of ours from being lost forever.

Questions for Review

1. Discuss why primates are said to be "generalized mammals."
2. Summarize the major evolutionary trends that characterize the primate order.
3. How does adaptation to an arboreal environment help explain primate evolution?
4. What is the geographical distribution of the nonhuman primates?
5. What are the two major subdivisions of the order Primates?
6. Which major groups of primates are included within the anthropoids?
7. What is a dental formula? What is the dental formula of all the Old World anthropoids?
8. What are quadrupedalism, vertical clinging and leaping, and brachiation? Name at least one primate species that is characterized by each of these.
9. What are the major differences between prosimians and anthropoids?
10. What are at least three anatomical differences between monkeys and apes?
11. Name the two major categories (subfamilies) of Old World monkeys. In general, what is the geographical distribution of each?
12. Explain how a taxonomic classification scheme reflects biological relationships.
13. Where are lemurs and lorises found today?
14. In which taxonomic family are the great apes placed?
15. Define estrus.
16. Describe the type of social organization seen in chimpanzees (*Pan troglodytes*) and gorillas.

Suggested Further Reading

Fleagle, John. 1988. *Primate Adaptation and Evolution* New York: Academic Press.
Jolly, Alison. 1985. *The Evolution of Primate Behavior*. 2nd ed. New York: Macmillan.
Napier, J. R., and P. H. Napier. 1985. *The Natural History of the Primates*. Cambridge, MA: MIT Press.
Mittermeier, Russell A., Ian Tattersall, William R. Konstant, David M. Meyers, and Roderick B. Mast. 1994. *Lemurs of Madagascar*. Washington, D.C.: Conservation International.

Internet Resources

Primate Infonet
http://uakari.primate.wisc.edu/pin
(Includes listings of primate newsletters, meeting calendars, educational resources, information on endangered species, current mountain gorilla projects, taxonomy, and much more.)

Can the Mountain Gorilla Be Saved?

The threatened habitat of the mountain gorilla (*Gorilla gorilla beringei*) is today largely restricted to a series of mostly extinct volcanoes known as the Virungas. These tropical, densely forested mountains, some of which soar to over 14,000 feet, straddle the shared borders of Rwanda, Zaire, and Uganda in central Africa (Fig. 1).

Probably never as numerous as the two subspecies of lowland gorilla, the mountain gorilla currently numbers only about 620 in the wild. There are no captive mountain gorillas. The single most serious threat to their continued existence is habitat loss resulting from forest clearing by a rapidly expanding human population. Illegal hunting of other species, which indirectly affects gorillas, also continues to be a factor; however, until recently, protection was afforded by governmental jurisdiction of the remaining gorilla habitat.

Earlier in this century, almost all the Virunga chain was set aside for preservation, but since human encroachment was not strictly prohibited, protected areas are smaller today than in the past. The 96-square-mile portion in Zaire is called the Parc National des Virungas. The Rwandan section is the Parc National des Volcans (Volcanoes National Park), currently comprising about 54 square miles, or about half of 1 percent of Rwanda's total land area. Approximately 320 gorillas currently live in these two national parks. In

Uganda, the Kigezi Gorilla Sanctuary is home to a few animals, and an additional 300 are found in the Impenetrable Forest, the only known mountain gorilla habitat outside the Virungas.

The mountain gorilla was first recognized and described as a distinct subspecies in 1902, but no behavioral studies were conducted until George Shaller's pioneering work in Zaire in 1959–1960. Following in Shaller's footsteps, Dian Fossey in 1967 established Karisoke, a research station located in the forest between Mt. Karisimbi and Mt. Visoke. In time, she was to become world-famous, not only for field studies, detailed in her popular book, *Gorillas in the Mist*, but also for her efforts to eliminate poaching and restrict human access to park areas. Indeed, her unceasing dedica-

tion to preserving the mountain gorilla led to much conflict and probably contributed to her still unsolved murder on December 26, 1985.

Rwanda, a small country of approximately 10,000 square miles (a bit smaller than the state of Maryland), has faced the same problems seen in most of the world's developing nations (unchecked population growth, poverty, and lack of access to goods and services, to name a few). With a population density of over 700 people per square mile, Rwanda is the most densely inhabited country in Africa. In the spring of 1994, Rwanda's population numbered almost 8 million and was increasing at an annual rate of 3.4 percent. On average, a Rwandan woman gives birth to 8.6 children and efforts to control popu-

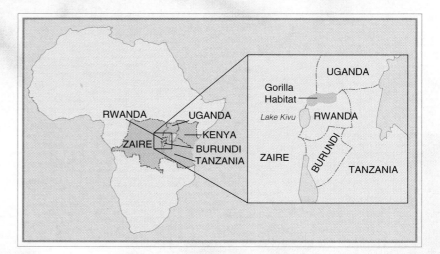

FIGURE 1

Map of central Africa showing Rwanda, Zaire, and Uganda with location of mountain gorilla habitat.

lation increase have not met with success. To make matters even worse, between October 1990 and the summer of 1994, Rwanda suffered from a devastating civil war that largely destroyed tourism. This conflict between the majority tribal group, the Hutu, and the minority Tutsi, culminated in the slaughter of between 500,000 and 1 million Tutsi and Tutsi sympathizers. Moreover, as many as half the total population, or about 4 million, fled the country for refugee camps in neighboring countries.

Prior to the war, the Rwandan countryside was among the most intensively cultivated regions in the world; indeed, terraced fields and grazing lands extended right up to national park boundaries (Fig. 2). Furthermore, poachers constituted an extremely serious threat to wildlife, a threat that has dramatically increased (Fig. 3). The target species of poachers' snares are pri-

marily small antelopes, but more than a few gorillas have also been caught. All too often, this results in the loss of a limb, if not death from infection.

As catastrophic as continued forest clearing, cattle grazing, and poaching are for wildlife in Rwanda, it is important to remember the very real problems faced by an increasingly hard-pressed human population. In 1991, before the most devastating effects of the war had come about, Rwanda's annual gross national product was a mere $310 per capita, compared to $21,000 in the United States. Only 48 percent of Rwandans living in rural areas had access to safe drinking water, and just 55 percent had sanitation facilities.

These few statistics represent the desperate conditions faced by real people. Translated to the local level, where people are attempting simply to "get by," the needs of gorillas, are

of little practical concern. The resulting dilemma, seen throughout developing countries today, is that the demands of ever-growing numbers of humans must always be weighed against those of ever-dwindling numbers of wildlife populations. It is therefore fortunate that through education efforts, an increasing number of Rwandans saw the continued existence of the gorillas and natural areas as beneficial.

One way to protect an endangered species, at least for a while, is to turn it into an economic asset. This approach met (for a time) with considerable success in Rwanda and Zaire, and it is now being tried in Uganda. Until the war, tourism was the third largest source of foreign revenue for Rwanda. Although the lush tropical beauty of Rwanda's terraced hills and forested mountains is certainly appealing, most of this small country's allure for foreign tourists was embodied in the mountain gorilla.

During the fighting and large scale population movements, only two gorillas were known to have died. Additionally, and as a sign of hope, seven new infants were born. However, the crisis for the gorillas is far from over.

Eventually, the Tutsi army claimed victory and restored some degree of order. But over 1 million refugees, fearing reprisals from their new Tutsi-led government, have refused to return to their homes. Consequently, hundreds of people from just one refugee camp go into the park daily to cut trees and set traps for game. Indeed, the people in one camp alone remove in excess of an estimated 400 metric tons of wood from the forest every day! With the refugee situation unresolved and with people entering the forest daily, the research center at

FIGURE 2

Cultivated fields and grazing land encroach upon national park boundaries. Forested slopes are part of the Parc National des Volcans.

ISSUE

FIGURE 3

Tour guides dismantle a poacher's snare encountered while leading tourists through the forest.

Karisoke cannot at present be occupied. In fact, the buildings have been partly dismantled for firewood or use in refugee shelters. Nevertheless, the Karisoke staff still monitor the gorilla study groups as best they can, and they continue to conduct antipoaching patrols. Indeed, the antipoaching patrols are all that remain as protection from snares, not only for gorillas, but for other wildlife as well.

Sadly, antipoaching patrols in Rwanda may not be enough. In August 1995, three gorillas (two silverbacks and one female) were shot and killed in Zaire. These killings followed closely on the heels of reports of four mountain gorillas having been speared to death in Uganda. This terrible news raises fears that, after a hiatus of many years, there has been a resumption of deliberate poaching of mountain gorillas for purposes that are not yet clear.

Amid such human tragedy and suffering, is there hope for the mountain gorillas? The answer is

yes, providing peace can be maintained and protection of the forest is restored. But lasting peace is a tenuous expectation.

Furthermore, if human population growth resumes its former pace, and if current patterns of subsistence and land use continue, Rwandans may have little choice but to clear what forest remnants they possess.

The challenges facing the Rwandans and the mountain gorilla are staggering, and the best solutions are far from perfect. But if mountain gorillas are to be saved, it must be done by means that also help the Rwandan people. The salvation of the gorillas, if indeed it occurs, is likely to be won through their exploitation as economic assets to those countries fortunate enough to have them as residents. We can only hope that the humans who share their world with these extraordinary animals find their association mutually beneficial. Otherwise, it is all too likely that, in the not too distant future, the mists that shroud the

Virunga volcanoes will conceal neither the breathtakingly beautiful forests nor the magnificent mountain gorilla.

Sources

Fossey, Dian. 1983. *Gorillas in the Mist*. Boston: Houghton Mifflin.

Schaller, George B. 1963. *The Mountain Gorilla*. Chicago: University of Chicago Press.

Vedder, Amy. 1989. "In the Hall of the Mountain Gorilla." *Animal Kingdom*. 92(3):30-43.

World Resources Institute. 1992. *The 1992 Information Please Environmental Almanac*. Boston: Houghton Mifflin.

Special appreciation goes to Dieter Steklis, Executive Director, and to Path McGrath, President Emeritus, The Dian Fossey Gorilla Fund, for providing valuable historical details and up-to-date information for this Issue.

Critical Thinking Questions

1. Do you think it important to protect an endangered species such as the mountain gorilla? Why or why not? At what point would you consider it no longer important?

2. How does one weigh the needs of seriously endangered species, such as the mountain gorilla, against the needs of people? Your answer can refer to situations other than those in Rwanda, but various aspects of the Rwandan situation (e.g., overpopulation, war, and the Rwandan attempt to protect gorillas as tourist attractions) should influence your answer.

3. What do you think will be the situation in Rwanda in 30 years? In 75 years? Why?

Fundamentals of Primate Behavior

Introduction

How can we better understand human behavior? Solely observing an urbanized industrialized society such as ours will not tell us very much about our hominid heritage. After all, we have been urbanized for only a few thousand years, and the industrial revolution is not quite two centuries old, barely a flicker in evolutionary time. Consequently, to understand what behavioral components may have shaped our evolution, we need a broader perspective than that which human culture alone provides. Therefore, we study the behavior of contemporary animals adapted to environments similar to those of early hominids in the hope of gaining insight into early hominid evolution.

In this chapter, we place nonhuman primate behavior in the context of its possible relationship to human behavior; that is, we address the question, Does the study of nonhuman primates serve as a model for human behavior, or are nonhuman primates so different in behavior from hominids that the uniqueness of the latter derives little from the former?

Behavior and Human Origins

What does it mean to be human? There are several *physical* characteristics, such as adaptations for bipedal locomotion and an enlarged brain, that characterize humans and—to varying extents—our hominid ancestors. But from a strictly structural point of view, we are not really that unique when compared with other primates, especially when compared with the great apes.

Clearly, it is behavioral attributes that most dramatically set humans apart. Human culture is our strategy for coping with some of life's challenges. No other primate even comes close to the human ability to modify environments. Communication through symbolic language is yet another uniquely human characteristic (see pp. 269–276 for a discussion of cognitive abilities in nonhuman primates). In addition, several other features differentiate humans from the majority of other primates. These are summarized in the following list, but keep in mind that any one of these attributes may be found in one or another primate species. But only humans can claim them all. For example, humans are bipedal; some apes occasionally walk bipedally, but not regularly. All primates learn, as do all mammals, but none has the capacity for learning to the degree shown by humans.

1. Humans are bipedal.
2. Humans live in permanent bisexual social groups with males often bonded to females.
3. Humans have large brains relative to body weight and are capable of complex learning.
4. Partly as a consequence of neurological reorganization, humans make *highly advanced* use of symbolic language.
5. Also related to neurological developments and bipedality, *cultural* response has become the central hominid adaptive strategy.
6. Humans obtain food through some male-female division of labor; moreover, food is actively transported back to a base camp (home) for purposes of sharing.
7. There is a relaxation of the estrous cycle and concealed ovulation in humans, so that females are sexually receptive throughout the year.

These traits are characteristic of all modern humans. Moreover, much of this behavioral complex is thought to be a reasonable theoretical framework within which we can investigate the early stages of hominid emergence. In fact, behavioral reconstructions are often central to theories explaining how hominids came to be hominids in the first place.

Nonhuman Primates

According to most experts, modern African apes and humans last shared a common ancestor somewhere between 8 and 5 m.y.a. Researchers believe that since that time, ape behavior has indeed changed, but that these changes have not been as dramatic as those in hominids, who developed culture as a major strategy of adaptation. Therefore, if we are interested in what hominid behavior might have been like before culture became a significant factor, and if we wish to know what behaviors may have led hominids to become dependent on culture, we may find clues in the behavior of our closest relatives.

Living in social groups (see Box 10–1) is one of the major characteristics of primates, who solve their major adaptive problems within this context (Fig. 10–1). For other animals, "mating, feeding, sleeping, growth of the individual, and protection from predators are usually matters for the solitary individual to solve, but for . . . primates they are most often performed in a social context" (Lancaster, 1975, p. 12).

As you have seen, many different patterns of social groupings exist among the primates. Most typically, primate social groups include members of all ages and of both sexes, a composition that does not vary significantly during the annual cycle. This situation differs from that of most mammals, whose adult males and females associate only during the breeding season and whose young of either sex do not usually remain with the adults after reaching puberty.

FIGURE 10–1
Chimpanzee family grouping, a long-term cohesive unit. These individuals may associate throughout their lives.

BOX 10–1

Types of Nonhuman Primate Social Groups*

1. *One male*. A single adult male, several adult females, and their offspring. This is the most common primate mating structure, in which only one male actively breeds (Jolly, 1985). Usually formed by a male joining a kin group of females. Females usually form the permanent nucleus of the group. Examples: guenons, gorillas, some pottos, some spider monkeys, patas.
2. *Multimale/multifemale*. Several adult males, several adult females, and their young. Several of the males reproduce. The presence of several males in the group may lead to tension and to a dominance hierarchy. Examples: some lemurs, macaques, mangabeys, savanna baboons, vervets, squirrel monkeys, some spider monkeys, chimpanzees.
3. *Monogamous pair*. A mated pair and its young. Usually arboreal, minimal sexual dimorphism, frequently territorial. Adults usually do not tolerate other adults of the same sex. Not found among great apes, and least common of the breeding structures among nonhuman

primates. Examples: gibbons, indris, titis, sakis, owl monkeys, pottos.
4. *Polyandry*. One female and two males. Seen only in some New World monkeys (marmosets and tamarins).
5. *Solitary*. Individual forages for food alone. Seen in some nocturnal prosimians (aye-ayes, lorises, galagos). In some species, adult females may forage in pairs or may be accompanied by offspring. Also seen in orangutans.

Sources

Jolly, 1985; Napier and Napier, 1985.

---

*These are called breeding groups by Jolly and permanent groupings by Napier and Napier. There are also other groupings, such as foraging groups, hunting groups, all female or male groups, and so on. Like humans, nonhuman primates do not always maintain one kind of group; single male groups may sometimes form multimale groups and vice versa. Hamadryas baboons, for example, are described as living in one-male groups but "form herds of 100 or more at night when they move towards the safety of the steep cliffs where they sleep" (Napier and Napier, 1985, p. 61). Also, variability is seen in other forms, for example, red colobus monkeys (see p. 248).

~~~~~~

One important factor that influences the composition of social groups and the interactions within them is *dispersal*. As is true of most mammals (and indeed, most vertebrates) members of one sex leave the group in which they were born (their natal group) about the time they reach puberty. There is considerable variability within and between species regarding which sex leaves, but male dispersal is the most common pattern in primates (e.g., ring-tailed lemurs, vervets and macaques, to name a few). Female dispersal is seen in some colobus species, hamadryas baboons, chimpanzees, and sometimes, in mountain gorillas.

Dispersal may have more than one outcome. Typically, females transfer to another group. Males may do likewise, but in some species they may remain solitary for a time, or they may temporarily join an all male "bachelor" group until they are able to establish a group of their own. But, one common theme that emerges is that those individuals who disperse usually find mates outside their natal group. This commonality has lead primatologists to conclude that the most valid explanations for dispersal are probably related to two major factors: reduced competition for mates (particularly between males); and, perhaps even more importantly, decreased likelihood of close inbreeding.

Members of the **philopatric** sex enjoy certain advantages. Individuals (of either sex) who remain in their natal group are able to establish long-term bonds

▲ **Philopatric**
Remaining in one's natal group or home range as an adult. In most species, members of one sex disperse from their natal group as young adults, and members of the philopatric sex remain. In the majority of nonhuman primate species, the philopatric sex is female.

with relatives and other animals with whom they cooperate to protect resources or enhance their position within the social structure. This is well illustrated by chimpanzee males who permanently reside in their natal groups (see further discussion in chapter 11).

Numerous factors, including mating structure, foraging strategies, and diet influence patterns of dispersal. However, since these patterns sometimes vary even within single species, and since the relationships between various ecological factors and behavior have not been thoroughly elucidated, the highly important roles played by dispersal and philopatry are not yet completely understood.

Because some individuals remain together over a long period of time, members of a primate group learn to know each other well. They learn—as they must—how to respond to a variety of actions that may be threatening, friendly, or neutral. In such social groups, individuals must be able to evaluate a situation before acting. Evolutionarily speaking, this would have placed selective pressure on social intelligence, which in turn, would select for brains that could assess such situations and store the information. One of the results of such selection would be the evolution of proportionately larger and more complex brains, especially among the higher primates (i.e., anthropoids).

Primate Field Studies

While other disciplines, such as psychology and zoology, have long been concerned with nonhuman primates, the study of these animals in their *natural habitats* has primarily become a focus of anthropology. Early work—that done before World War II—was especially stimulated through the influence of the American psychologist Robert Yerkes, who in the late 1920s and 1930s sent students out to the field to study gorillas, chimpanzees, and howler monkeys. It was the last of these studies by Clarence Ray Carpenter (along with his work on gibbons) that stands out particularly as a hallmark of early primate field investigations. Other such studies followed. Japanese scientists began their pioneering work with Japanese macaques in 1948 (Sugiyama, 1965). In 1960, Jane Goodall began her now-famous field study of chimpanzees at Gombe National Park, Tanzania. This project continues today and, along with several others, has provided us with a wealth of information regarding the natural behavior of these remarkable animals. By the early 1960s, field research was in full swing, and since that time, researchers have studied savanna baboons (DeVore and Washburn, 1963; Altmann and Altmann, 1970; Smuts, 1985; Strum 1987), langurs (Dolhinow, 1977; Hrdy, 1977), vervets (Cheney and Seyfarth, 1990), orangutans (Galdikas, 1979, 1981, 1985; Horr, 1975; Rodman, 1973), mountain gorillas (Schaller, 1963; Goodall, 1977; Fossey, 1983), chimpanzees (Nishida, 1968, 1979; Wrangham, 1977, 1986; Goodall, 1986, 1990; McGrew, 1992), and bonobos (Kano, 1980, 1992; Susman, 1984).

The key aspect of these field studies is that researchers attempt to collect information on **free-ranging** animals. Free-ranging animals are not necessarily completely uninfluenced by human activities. With the exception of populations in a recently explored forest in Zaire, it is highly unlikely that there is a single group of nonhuman primates in the world that has not experienced some human interference. Nevertheless, if we are to understand the adaptations and behavior of nonhuman primates, it is necessary to study them in their natural habitats, where human disturbance is reduced and where they feed, travel, mate, and so forth, with minimal human constraints.

▲ **Free-ranging**
Pertaining to noncaptive animals living in their natural habitat, largely free from constraints imposed by humans.

Because of the problems inherent to the study of arboreal primates that move swiftly through dense vegetation (Fig 10–2), the most systematic information thus far collected on free-ranging animals comes from species that spend considerable time on the ground (including langurs, gorillas, and chimps) and most especially those species that travel and feed frequently in open country (e.g., macaques, baboons, vervets, and patas monkeys). Note that the emphasis on certain species in this and the next chapter reflects this research bias.

Another approach taken by some anthropologists involves studying primates in large provisioned colonies, where at least some movement, group dynamics, and so on, are possible. Probably the best example of this type of research is the long-term study of rhesus macaques (Fig 10–3) conducted on Cayo Santiago Island off the coast of Puerto Rico. First established in 1938, the island population now totals close to 1,000 individuals (Richard, 1985).

Despite significant gaps in our knowledge about many aspects of primate behavior, we presently have field data on more than 100 nonhuman primate species. The information from this fascinating and rapidly advancing discipline of primatology forms the remainder of this chapter.

The Ecology of Nonhuman Primates

Scientists who study behavior in free-ranging primates do so within an **ecological** framework, focusing on the relationship between aspects of social behavior and the natural environment. In the 1970s, an emerging perspective called **socioecology** grew out of this approach. One underlying assumption of such an approach is that the various components of ecological systems have evolved together. Therefore, to understand the functioning of one particular component, such as the **social structure** of a given species, it is necessary to determine its relationships with numerous environmental factors, including:

▲ **Ecological**
Pertaining to the relationship between organisms and all aspects of their environment.

▲ **Socioecology**
The study of animals and their habitats; specifically, attempts to find patterns of relationship between the environment and social behavior.

▲ **Social structure**
The composition, size, and sex ratio of a group of animals. Social structures, in part, are the result of natural selection in specific habitats, and they function to guide individual interactions and social relationships.

FIGURE 10–2
Black-and-white colobus monkeys high up in the forest canopy. Can you spot the animals? Imagine trying to recognize them as individuals!

1. Quantity and quality of different kinds of foods (caloric value, digestive energy required, net value to the animal)
2. Distribution of food resources (dense, scattered, clumps, or seasonal availability)
3. Distribution of water
4. Distribution and types of predators
5. Distribution of sleeping sites
6. Activity patterns (nocturnal, diurnal)
7. Relationships with other (nonpredator) species, both primate and non-primate
8. Impact of human activities

A great deal of enthusiasm resulted from the socioecological perspective and led to new research directions as well as attempts to synthesize the information in order to discern broad patterns for the entire primate order. Initially, schemes were relatively simple and attempted to show very general aspects of ecological/behavioral correlations (Crook and Gartlan, 1966; Crook, 1970; Eisenberg et al., 1972). As more data accumulated, however, it became obvious that primates in the wild displayed considerably more variability in social behavior than these simple schemes could accommodate.

As a result, more sophisticated approaches have evolved (Clutton-Brock and Harvey, 1977; Richard, 1985). Primatologists now view ecology, behavior, and biology as complexly interdependent (McKenna, 1982a; 1982b). In addition to the general ecological factors listed above, primatologists must also consider an animal's body size, relative brain size, metabolism, and reproductive physiology, as well as the distribution of food resources into "food patches," and the nutritional value of foods and how they are selected and processed. (See Fleagle, 1988, for a good discussion of these factors.) Moreover, the variability exhibited between closely related species (and even *within* the same species) in ecological adaptations must be understood. Also, the way primates relate to surrounding biological communities, especially to other species of primates, must be described. Indeed, it is a common phenomenon for many prosimian and monkey species to travel and interact with other primate species. (It is important to determine if they eat different foods, or how efficiently they divide their habitat.) Lastly, it is of interest to study why primates select certain foods and avoid others. (What is the nutritional value of insects, fruits, leaves, nuts, gums, small mammals, etc., that are available to them? What toxins exist in certain plant foods that could cause harm?)

Unfortunately, the relationships among ecological variables, social organization, and behavior have not yet been thoroughly worked out, but numerous factors certainly suggest a relationship between, for example group size and problems of obtaining food and avoiding predators. Indeed, average group size and group composition can be viewed as adaptive responses to these problems (Pulliam and Caraco, 1984).

For example, groups composed of several adult males and females (multimale and multifemale groups) have traditionally been viewed as advantageous in areas where predation pressure is high, particularly in mixed woodlands and on open savannas where there are a number of large predators (e.g., hyenas, cheetahs, and lions). Where members of prey species occur in larger groups, there is increased likelihood of early predator detection and thus predator avoidance. Moreover, large-bodied males in such groups are capable of joining forces to chase and even attack predators.

But, as you have already learned, not all primates are found in large groups. Solitary foraging is seen in many species and may be related to diet and distribution

FIGURE 10–3

Rhesus macaques. Part of the large colony on Cayo Santiago Island.

of resources. In the case of the slow-moving, insectivorous loris, for example, solitary feeding reduces competition, which allows for less distance traveled (and thus less expenditure of energy) in the search for prey. Moreover, because insects usually do not appear in dense patches but are scattered, they are more efficiently exploited by widely dispersed individuals rather than by groups. Solitary foraging may also be related to predator avoidance in species that rely chiefly on concealment for protection, rather than on escape. Again, the less-than-agile loris serves as a good example.

Foraging alone or with offspring is also seen in females of some diurnal anthropoid species (e.g., orangutans, chimpanzees). These females, being relatively large-bodied, have little to fear from predators, and by feeding alone or with only one or two youngsters, they maximize their access to food, free from competition with others. In the case of the orangutan, this may be particularly important, as the female is effectively removing herself from competition with males who may be twice her size.

Although the exact relationships between group size and structure and the environment are not well known at this time, it is clear that certain environmental factors, such as resource availability and predation, exert strong influence. The various solutions that primate species have developed to deal with the problems of survival differ in complicated ways. Closely related species living in proximity to one other and exploiting many of the same resources can have very different types of social structure. It is only through continued research that primatologists will be able to sort out the intricate relationships between society and the natural environment.

Environment and Social Behavior

In the remainder of this chapter and in Chapter 11, we will discuss various aspects of nonhuman primate social behavior. An ecological focus can, in many ways, be utilized to illuminate much of primate behavior (see Jolly, 1985, and Richard, 1985, for excellent discussions of this perspective). Here, we cannot adequately discuss all the ways primatologists use ecological, behavioral, and biological data. Nor can we completely summarize the huge amount of information that has accumulated in recent years. What is important, however, is to get a sense of how this approach is used currently by primatologists; hence, we now consider a comprehensive example of primate ecological research.

Five Monkey Species in the Kibale Forest, Uganda   One of the most detailed and controlled studies of primate socioecology has been undertaken in the Kibale Forest (Fig. 10–4) of western Uganda (Struhsaker and Leyland, 1979). The five species thus far studied in detail are all varieties of Old World monkeys and include black-and-white colobus (*Colobus guereza*), red colobus (*Colobus badius*), mangabey (*Cercocebus albigena*), blue monkey (*Cercopithecus mitus*), and the redtail monkey (*Cercopithecus ascanius*). In addition to these five, there are also in the Kibale Forest two other monkey species as well as pottos, two species of galago, and chimpanzees (for a discussion of the latter, see Ghiglieri, 1984). Altogether there are 11 different nonhuman primate species at Kibale, and they display the greatest number of individuals and highest primate biomass for any site yet described (Waser, 1987). In the study under discussion (Struhsaker and Leyland, 1979), comparisons are facilitated as all species were sampled using similar methodologies. This avoids the pitfall of making comparisons between highly variable research strategies, a problem usually unavoidable in making cross-species comparisons. Moreover, the research at Kibale is impor-

FIGURE 10–4
Kibale Forest habitat, Uganda.

tant because this region is probably the least disturbed habitat where primates have been studied long-term.

Although these species are **sympatric**, they differ with regard to anatomy, behavior, and dietary preference. Body weights vary considerably (3 to 4 kg for redtails and up to 7 to 10 kg for the mangabey and colobus species). Diet also differs with the two colobus species primarily eating leaves (i.e., they are folivorous) and the other three species showing more concentration on fruits supplemented by insects.

Several aspects of social organization also vary among the five species. For example, the red colobus and mangabey have several adult males in the group, while only one fully adult male is typically present in the other species. Furthermore, all five species occasionally have solitary males moving independently of the bisexual groups, but bachelor groups do not typically form. Even among the mostly multimale bisexual species, there is a marked difference. In mangabeys, females constitute the permanent core of the group, with males transferring out. In red colobus, it is the females who transfer (with the males remaining the long-term residents) (Struhsaker and Leyland, 1987). Indeed, there is so much variability that Struhsaker and Leyland could find little correlation between social organization and feeding ecology.

More detailed analysis of feeding patterns showed even further differences. For instance, while both colobus species eat mostly leaves, they exploit different resources. Black-and-white colobus eat mature leaf blades, some high in protein. Red colobus, on the other hand, eat a wider variety of leaves, but usually not mature ones, as well as fruits and shoots. Perhaps correlated with these dietary differences are the observations that black-and-white colobus spend less time feeding but more time resting; in contrast, red colobus range further and live in higher density (i.e., higher biomass). In addition, some species show dramatic variability from month to month. Among redtail monkeys, the proportion of fruit in the monthly diet varies from as low as 13 percent to as much as 81 percent (Richard, 1985).

Ecological patterns and social ramifications are unquestionably most complicated. In the same forest at Kibale, the closely related colobus species show

▲ **Sympatric**
Living in the same area; pertaining to two or more species whose habitats partly or largely overlap.

marked differences in social organization. (Black-and-white colobus are found in one-male groups, red colobus in multimale/multifemale groups; see Box 10–1.) Yet in another area (the Tana River Forest of Kenya), red colobus live in one-male groups (like black-and-white colobus at Kibale) and *both* males and females transfer (unlike either colobus species at Kibale)(Richard, 1985). The distinct impression one gathers from attempts to find correlations is that many primate species are exceedingly flexible regarding group composition, a fact that makes generalizing an extremely tentative undertaking at best.

Still, the highly controlled nature of the Kibale study makes some comparisons and provisional generalizations such as the following possible:

1. The omnivores (mangabeys, redtails, blues) move about more than the folivores (the two colobus species).
2. Among the omnivores there is an inverse relationship between body size and group size (i.e., the smaller the body size, the larger the group tends to be); also among the omnivores, there is a direct relationship between body size and **home range**.
3. Omnivores are spatially more dispersed than folivores.
4. Female sexual swelling (see p. 251) is obvious only in those species (red colobus and mangabeys) that live in multimale groups.
5. Feeding, spacing, group residency, dispersal, and reproductive strategies may be very different for males and females of the same species. These considerations have become a central focus of ecological and sociobiological research (see p. 255).

▲ **Home range**
The area exploited by an animal or social group. Usually given for one year—or for the entire lifetime—of an animal.

Because of the complexity of the social relationships among primates, long-term studies are absolutely necessary. As Struhsaker and Leyland conclude from their studies at Kibale, "Meaningful data on group dynamics and probable degree of genetic relatedness among the members can only be collected by observing groups for at least half the adult life span, which for most Old World monkeys means a period of five to six years" (1979, p. 222). Alison Richard (1985) is even more conservative in generalizing about long-term ecological patterns. She suggests that such patterns should be observed at least as long as the periodicity of cycles of critical resources. For Old World monkeys, then, as many as 10 generations might be required—a total of up to 80 years of study!

Clearly, the kinds of data now emerging from primate ecological research (and its manifold social and biological connections) pose tremendous interest and opportunities for primatologists. However, the challenges involved in collecting such data are equally great.

Social Behavior

Since primates solve their major adaptive problems in a social context, we might expect them to participate in a number of activities to reinforce the integrity of the group. The better known of these activities are described in the sections that follow.

Dominance

▲ **Dominance hierarchies**
Systems of social organization wherein individuals within a group are ranked relative to one another. Higher-ranking individuals have greater access to preferred food items and mating partners than lower-ranking individuals. Dominance hierarchies are frequently referred to as "pecking orders."

Most primate societies are organized into **dominance hierarchies**. Dominance hierarchies impose a certain degree of order within groups by establishing parameters of individual behavior. Although aggression is frequently a means of increasing one's status, dominance usually serves to reduce the amount of actual physical violence. Not only are lower-ranking animals unlikely to attack or even threaten a higher-ranking one, but dominant animals are also frequently able to exert control simply by making a threatening gesture.

Individual rank or status may be measured by priority of access to resources, including food items and mating partners. Dominant individuals are given priority by others, and they usually do not give way in confrontations.

Many (but not all) primatologists postulate that the primary benefit of dominance is the increased reproductive success of the individual. This observation would be true if it could be demonstrated that dominant males compete more successfully for mates than do subordinant males. However, there is also good evidence that lower-ranking males of some species successfully mate; they just do so surreptitiously. Likewise, increased reproductive success can be postulated for high-ranking females, who have greater access to food than subordinant females. High-ranking females are provided with more energy for offspring production and care (Fedigan, 1983), and presumably their reproductive success is greater.

An individual's rank is not permanent and changes throughout life. It is influenced by many factors, including sex, age, level of aggression, amount of time spent in the group, intelligence, perhaps motivation, and sometimes, the mother's social position (particularly true of macaques).

In species organized into groups containing a number of females associated with one or several adult males, the males are generally dominant to females. Within such groups, males and females have separate hierarchies, although very high-ranking females can dominate the lowest-ranking males (particularly young males). There are exceptions to this pattern of male dominance. Among all Madagascar lemurs studied, females are the dominant sex. Moreover, among species that form monogamous pairs (e.g., indris, gibbons), males and females seem to be codominant.

All primates *learn* their position in the hierarchy. From birth, an infant is carried by its mother, and it observes how she responds to every member of the group. Just as important, it sees how others react to her. Dominance and subordinance are indicated by gestures and behaviors (see p. 269), some of which are universal throughout the primate order (including humans), and this gestural repertoire is part of every youngster's learning experience.

Young primates also acquire social rank through play with age peers. As they spend more time with play groups, their social interactions widen. Competition and rough-and-tumble play allow them to learn the strengths and weaknesses of peers, and they carry this knowledge with them throughout their lives. Thus, through early contact with the mother and subsequent exposure to peers, young primates learn to negotiate their way through the complex web of social interactions that make up their daily lives.

Grooming

Grooming is seen in most primate species and in part, it reflects the importance of physical contact in primates. Although grooming occurs in other animal species, social grooming is mostly a primate activity, and it plays an important role in day-to-day life (Fig 10–5). Because grooming involves using the fingers to pick through the fur of another individual (or one's own) to remove insects, dirt, and other materials, it serves hygienic functions. But it is much more than that, for it is an immensely pleasurable activity that individuals of some species (especially chimpanzees) engage in for considerable periods of time.

▲ **Grooming**
Picking through fur to remove dirt, parasites, and other materials that may be present. Social grooming is common among primates and reinforces social relationships.

FIGURE 10–5
Grooming primates. (a) Patas monkeys; female grooming male. (b) Longtail macaques. (c) Savanna baboons. (d) Chimpanzees.

(a)

(b)

(c)

(d)

Grooming occurs in a variety of contexts. Mothers groom infants. Males groom sexually receptive females. Subordinant animals groom dominant ones, sometimes to gain favor. Friends groom friends. In general, grooming is comforting. It restores peaceful relationships between animals who have quarreled and provides reassurance during tense situations. In short, grooming reinforces bonds and helps to maintain and strengthen the structure of the group. For this reason, it has been called "the social cement of primates from lemur to chimpanzee" (Jolly, 1985, p. 207).

Reproduction

In most primate species, sexual behavior is tied to the female's reproductive cycle, with females sexually receptive to males only when they are in estrus. Estrus is characterized by behavioral changes that indicate a female is receptive.

In many species, estrus is also accompanied by swelling and changes in color of the skin around the genital area. These changes serve as visual cues of a female's readiness to mate (Fig 10–6).

Bonding between males and females is not common among nonhuman primates. However, male and female savanna baboons sometimes form mating *consortships*. These temporary relationships last while the female is in estrus, and the two spend most of the time together, mating frequently. Moreover, lower-ranking baboon males often form "friendships" (Smuts, 1985) with females and occasionally may mate with them, although they may be driven away by high-ranking males when the female is most receptive.

Mating consortships are sometimes seen in chimpanzees and are particularly common among bonobos. In fact, a male and female bonobo may spend several weeks primarily in each other's company. During this time, they mate often, even when the female is not is estrus. These relationships of longer duration are not typical of chimpanzee (*Pan troglodytes*) males and females.

Such a male-female bond may result in increased reproductive success for both sexes. For the male, there is the increased likelihood that he will be the father of any infant the female conceives. At the same time, the female potentially gains protection from predators or others of her group and perhaps assistance in caring for offspring she may already have.

Mother-Infant Relationships

The basic social unit among all primates is the female and her infants (Fig. 10–7). Except in those species in which monogamy or **polyandry** occurs, males do not participate as members of the mother-infant social unit. Observations both in the field and in captivity suggest that the mother-offspring core provides the social group with its stability.

The mother-infant bond, one of the most basic themes running throughout primate social relations, begins at birth. Although the exact nature of the bonding

▲ **Polyandry**
A mating system wherein a female continuously associates with more than one male (usually two or three) with whom she mates. Among nonhuman primates, this type of pattern is seen only in marmosets and tamarins.

FIGURE 10–6
Estrous swelling of genital tissues in a female chimpanzee.

(a)

(b)

(c)

FIGURE 10–7
Primate mothers with young.
(a) Mongoose lemur.
(b) Chimpanzee. (c) Patas
monkey. (d) Orangutan.
(e) Sykes monkey (a type of
guenon).

(d)

(e)

process is not fully known, there appear to be predisposing innate factors that strongly attract the female to her infant, so long as she herself has had sufficiently normal experience with her own mother. This does not mean that primate mothers possess innate knowledge of how to care for an infant. Indeed, they do not. Monkeys and apes raised in captivity without contact with their own mothers not only do not know how to care for a newborn infant, but may also be afraid of it and attack and kill it. Even if they do not directly attack the infant, they may kill it indirectly through mishandling or improper nursing.

The importance of a normal relationship with the mother has been amply demonstrated by field studies. From birth, infant primates are able to cling to their mother's fur, and they are in more or less constant physical contact with her for several months. During this critical period, the infant develops a closeness with the mother that does not always end with weaning. In species in which females are philopatric this closeness is often maintained throughout life. It is reflected in grooming behavior that continues between mother and offspring, even after the young reach adulthood and have infants of their own.

The crucial role played by primate mothers in their infants' development was clearly demonstrated by the Harlows (1959), who raised infant monkeys with surrogate (substitute) mothers fashioned from cloth and metal. Other monkeys were raised with no mothers at all. In what is probably the most famous experiment, young monkeys were given access to two different surrogates—one made of bare wire, the other covered with soft cloth (Fig 10–8). Without exception, the young animals preferred close contact with the cloth surrogate, even when the wire one provided nourishment (through a bottle with a nipple). The infants transferred to the nourishing wire surrogate solely to feed, spending up to 20 hours per day clinging to the cloth "mother." These results have been generalized to demonstrate the requirement for early attachment for primates in general, including humans. Moreover, the attachment apparently is reinforced through physical contact.

In another experiment (Harlow and Harlow, 1961), monkeys raised without a mother sat passively in their cages and stared vacantly into space. Some chewed their arms until blood flowed. Those raised with a surrogate mother acted similarly, but somewhat less dramatically. None of the males or females raised without real or surrogate mothers ever achieved any semblance of normal sexual behavior. No motherless male ever successfully copulated, and such males often violently assaulted the female with whom they were paired. Among females raised without mothers or with cloth mothers, those that were successfully impregnated paid very little attention to their infants. A mother often brushed away her baby "as if she were brushing off flies" or crushed her infant to the floor, and these mothers rarely held their infants or protected them as normal mothers do. The Harlows concluded, "We only know that these monkeys without normal mothering and without peer affectional relationships have behaved

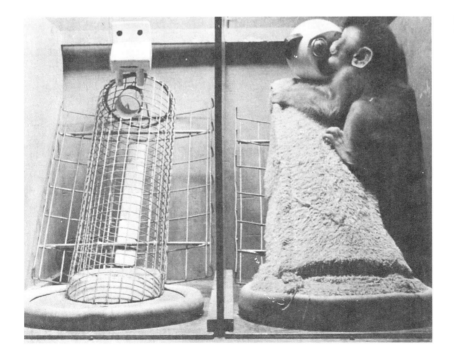

FIGURE 10–8
Wire mother and cloth mother.

toward their infants in a manner completely outside the range of even the least adequate of normal mothers" (1961, p. 55).

In more recent studies, Suomi and colleagues emphasize that social isolation initiated early in life can have devastating effects on subsequent development and behavior for many species of primates. The primate deprivation syndrome that results from early isolation is characterized by displays of abnormal self-directed and stereotypical behavior and by gross deficits in all aspects of social behavior (Suomi et al., 1983, p. 190).

Although infants are mainly cared for by the mother, in some species adult males are also known to take more than a casual interest. This phenomenon has frequently been noted among male hamadryas and savanna baboons (Fig. 10–9). Male gibbons and siamangs are directly involved in the care of offspring, and among marmosets and tamarins, the males provide most of the direct infant care, only transferring them back to their mother for nursing.

What may be an extension of the mother-infant relationship has been called **alloparenting**, or "aunt" behavior. This type of behavior occurs in many animal species but is most richly expressed in primates, and some researchers believe that it is found among all social primates. Usually, alloparents crowd around an infant and attempt to groom, hold, or touch it. Some species, like the common langur, are well known for their aunts, and as many as eight females may hold an infant during its first day of life. Occasionally, rough treatment by inexperienced or aggressive animals can result in injury or death to the infant. For this reason, mothers may attempt to shield infants from overly attentive individuals.

Several functions are suggested for alloparenting. If the mother dies, the infant stands a chance of being adopted by an alloparent or other individual of the group. Moreover, the practice may bind together the adults of the group. Also, it may simply be convenient for the mother to leave her infant occasionally with another female. Finally, the practice of alloparenting may assist in the training of young females for motherhood.

▲ **Alloparenting**

A common behavior in many primate species whereby individuals other than the parent(s) hold, carry, and in general interact with infants.

FIGURE 10–9

Male savanna baboon carrying an infant. An example of alloparenting.

Sociobiology

The sociobiological perspective is an important **paradigm** in primatology today. In the last two decades, this approach has been applied to a wide variety of animals. Indeed, for primatological interpretations, **sociobiology** holds a central position as a theoretical framework for many current researchers and it serves as a theoretical model with which to frame discussion of behavior within an evolutionary context.

Beyond the suppositions concerning nonhuman primates, some contemporary scholars extend this field to the interpretation of *human* primates as well. Naturally, not all primatologists, and certainly not all anthropologists, are sociobiologists. In fact, sociobiology has created and continues to generate a great deal of controversy.

Sociobiological theory postulates that *behavior has evolved through the operation of natural selection.* That is, natural selection is seen to act on behavior in the same way it acts on physical characteristics. Therefore, individuals whose genotypes influence behaviors that lead to higher reproductive success will be more fit and should pass on their genes at a faster rate.

Superficially, such an explanation implies the existence of genes that code for specific behaviors (a gene for aggression, another for cooperation, etc.). Such conclusions have caused a great deal of concern, and rightly so, especially when these principals are applied to humans. If specific human behaviors could be explained in terms of genes, and if populations and sexes varied regarding the frequency of these genes, then such theories could readily be used to support both racism and sexism.

It is true that much behavior in social insects and other invertebrates, as well as in lower vertebrates, is under genetic control. In other words, most behavioral patterns in these forms are *innate*, not learned. However, in many vertebrates, particularly birds and mammals, the proportion of behavior due to *learning* is substantially increased. Accordingly, the proportion that is under genetic influence is reduced. This phenomenon is especially true of primates, and most researchers agree that in humans, who are so much a product of culture, most behavior results from learning.

What sociobiologists are proposing, then, is this: In higher organisms, some behaviors are partly influenced by certain gene products (e.g., hormones). For example, numerous studies have shown that increased levels of testosterone increase aggressive behavior and sexual arousal in many nonhuman species. However, there is current debate over whether this is also true for humans.

A major dispute arises when trying to postulate the actual mechanics of behavioral evolution in complex social animals with flexible neurological responses, such as those seen in primates. Therefore, sociobiologists need to determine which primate behaviors have a genetic basis and how these behaviors influence reproductive success. To accomplish these goals, we must learn considerably more about genotype-phenotype interactions in complex traits, and such an understanding is probably decades away. We also need accurate data on reproductive success in primate groups, and so far, such data are almost completely lacking. Thus, rather than offering precise explanations, sociobiology provides a set of hypotheses for explaining primate behavior, and it remains for these hypotheses to be tested.

Obtaining conclusive data for primates and other mammals is not easy. A good starting point, however, is framing hypotheses concerning behavioral evolution on the basis of the evidence that does exist. A good example of such a perspective is Sarah Blaffer Hrdy's (1977) explanation of infanticide among Hanuman langurs of India (Fig. 10–10). Hanuman langurs typically live in social

▲ **Paradigm**

A cognitive construct or framework within which we explain phenomena. Paradigms shape our world view. They can change as a result of technological and intellectual innovation.

▲ **Sociobiology**

The study of the relationship between behavior and natural selection. Sociobiological theory states that certain behaviors or behavioral patterns have been selected for because they increase reproductive fitness in individuals.

FIGURE 10–10
Hanuman langurs.

groups composed of one adult male, several females, and their offspring. Other males without mates associate in bachelor groups. These peripheral males occasionally attack and defeat the reproductive male and drive him from his group. Sometimes, following such takeovers, the group's infants (fathered by the previous male) are attacked and killed by the new male.

It would seem that such behavior is counterproductive, especially from the species' perspective. However, according to sociobiological principles, individuals act to maximize their *own* reproductive success, no matter what the effect may be on the population or ultimately the species. Ostensibly, that is exactly what the male langur is doing, albeit unknowingly. While a female is *lactating*, she does not come into estrus and therefore she is not sexually available. However, when an infant dies, its mother ceases to lactate, and within two or three months, she resumes cycling and becomes sexually receptive. Therefore, by killing the infants, the male avoids a two- to three-year wait until they are weaned. This could be especially advantageous to him, as chances are quite good that his tenure in the group will not even last two or three years. Moreover, he does not expend energy and put himself at risk defending infants who do not carry his genes.

Hanuman langurs are not the only primates that engage in infanticide. Indeed, infanticide has been observed (or surmised) in several primate species, including redtail monkeys, red colobus, blue monkeys, savanna baboons, howler monkeys, orangutans, gorillas, chimpanzees (Struhsaker and Leyland, 1987), and humans. It also occurs among numerous nonprimate species, such as rodents and cats.

Importantly, in the majority of nonhuman primate cases, infanticide occurs in conjunction with the transfer of a new male into a group or, as in chimpanzees, in an encounter between males and an unfamiliar female and infant. In no case have primatologists shown that a male attacked an infant either known or presumed to be his own offspring.

But numerous objections to the sociobiological explanation (also called the "sexual selection hypothesis") of infanticide have been raised. Alternative explanations have included competition for resources (Rudran, 1973) and aberrant behaviors related to human-induced overcrowding (Curtin and Dohlinow, 1978). Sussman and colleagues (1995), as well as others, have questioned the actual prevalence of the practice arguing that it is not particularly common. These authors have also postulated that if indeed male fitness is increased through the practice, such increases are negligible. Others (Struhsaker and Leyland, 1987; Hrdy, 1995) maintain that the incidence and patterning of infanticide by males are not only significant, but consistent with the assumptions established by sociobiological theory.

Sociobiological interpretations have also been applied to other types of reproductive strategies seen in primates. As you will see in our discussion of the limitations of sociobiological research (p. 258), there are controversies surrounding the issue, and they are not easy to resolve.

Male and Female Reproductive Strategies

The **reproductive strategies** of primates, especially how they differ between the sexes, have been a primary focus of sociobiological research. The goal of such strategies is to produce and successfully rear to adulthood as many offspring as possible.

▲ **Reproductive strategies**
The complex of behavioral patterns that contributes to individual reproductive success. The behaviors need not be deliberate, and they often vary considerably between males and females.

Primates are among the most **K-selected** of mammal species. By this we mean that individuals produce but a few young, in whom they invest a tremendous amount of parental care. Contrast this pattern with that of **r-selected** species, where individuals produce large numbers of offspring but invest little or no energy in parental care. Good examples of r-selected species include insects, most fish, and, among mammals, mice and rabbits.

When we consider the tremendous degree of care required by young, growing primate offspring, it is clear that enormous investment by at least one parent is necessary, and it is usually the mother who carries most of the burden both before and after birth. Primates are totally helpless at birth. They develop slowly and are thus exposed to expanded learning opportunities within a *social* environment. This trend has been elaborated most dramatically in great apes and humans, and most especially in the latter. Thus, what we see in ourselves and our close primate kin (and presumably in our more recent ancestors as well) is a strategy wherein a few "high-quality," slowly maturing offspring are produced through extraordinary investment by the parents, usually the mother.

As a result of the heavy cost of carrying and caring for offspring, females especially are put under physiological stress. For the majority of nonhuman primates, females spend most of their adult lives either pregnant or lactating, and the resulting metabolic demands are enormous. A pregnant or lactating female primate, although perhaps only half the size of her male counterpart, may require about the same number of calories per day as that male. Even then, her physical resources may be drained over the long run. For example, analysis of chimpanzee skeletons from Gombe reveals significant loss of bone and bone mineral in older females (Sumner et al., 1989).

There may be real differences in how male and female primates exploit their environments. Perhaps due to the higher energy/metabolic needs of females, it has been argued (Wrangham, 1980) that they must concentrate their efforts around high-yielding food patches (e.g., particular fruiting trees). Since there is a limited number of such resources, females would tend to defend these areas against other females. However, more than one female may be required to mount a defense. Sociobiological theory predicts that in sharing resources, it would be most advantageous for a female to bond with a close relative (e.g., a sister). In such a situation, not only are her own offspring related to her, but other young in the group (her nieces, nephews, etc.) also share some of her genes as well. Thus, as a result of bonding with relatives, a female's **inclusive fitness** is increased.

Carrying this model further, the pattern of female-female kin-based social bonding may also help explain dispersal patterns among many primates (Pusey and Packer, 1987). Since in most species of Old World monkeys, it is the male who transfers, the long-term social core of the group is composed of females, who are likely to be related. Conversely, males who transfer *into* new groups are unlikely to share much genetic relatedness with other adults.

As we noted in Box 10–1, in several primate groups only one adult male is socially bonded to a group of females. In these cases (e.g., patas monkeys, most groups of red colobus), at least one breeding male is required for reproductive purposes and possibly to aid in defense against predators. But why should females tolerate more than one adult male in their group? Again, sociobiological/socioecological perspectives can possibly explain the evolution of multimale societies among primates. Some resources are harder to defend, so females may, in a sense, tolerate males to help aid in defense of food patches. In addition, for some animals, like savanna baboons, concerted action by numerous adult males apparently is crucial in predator defense.

▲ **K-selected**
Pertaining to an adaptive strategy whereby individuals produce relatively few offspring, in whom they invest increased parental care. Although only a few infants are born, chances of survival are increased for each individual because of parental investments in time and energy. Examples of nonprimate K-selected species are birds and wild canids (e.g., wolves, coyotes, and wild dogs).

▲ **r-selected**
Pertaining to an adaptive strategy that emphasizes relatively large numbers of offspring and reduced parental care (compared to K-selected species). (*K-selection* and *r-selection* are relative terms; e.g., mice are r-selected compared to primates but K-selected compared to insects and many fish species.)

▲ **Inclusive fitness**
The total contribution of an individual's genes to the next generation, including those genes shared by close relatives.

We do not wish to suggest that males are doing next to nothing. In all primate societies, the interplay of behavior is extremely complex for *all* individuals. In fact, there is a marked degree of variability among different species in male parental care, male or female dispersal, and ecological constraints.

Numerous examples of variability in male-female reproductive strategies are known among primates. For example, in gibbons and some cebids (titis and owl monkeys), the typical social group is monogamous. Perhaps even more distinctive, in most callitrichids (marmosets and tamarins), two adult males regularly mate with one adult female (i.e., they are *polyandrous*)(Goldizen, 1987). In all these examples, typically it is the adult males who are most responsible for parental care. In chimps, yet another pattern is seen. Males are the ones who are tightly bonded (presumably for organized defense against other potentially aggressive males—see p. 278), and it is the females who disperse by transferring to a new group, usually when they are young adults.

Thus, as we have said before, there is no simple relationship between biology, ecology, and behavior among primates. Nor, obviously, can simplistic evolutionary scenarios adequately account for the diversity of behavior among primates. What makes sociobiology (and its ecological correlates) so important, however, is that it provides a framework to ask *relevant* questions, thus helping shape future research. Nevertheless, sociobiological interpretation has been subject to considerable criticism by other biologists and social scientists.

Primate Sociobiology— Limitations and Critiques

As we have seen, sociobiological interpretation has had a dramatic impact on the direction of current research—on reproductive strategies, male-female behavioral differences, ecological patterning, and much more. However, sociobiologists have not been without their critics. Indeed, most primatologists who use theoretical models from sociobiology readily admit some of the current methodological shortcomings. For example, Richard and Schulman (1982, pp. 243–244), in a review of primate sociobiological research, list the following central problems for those attempting to apply this approach:

1. The lack of long-term data on the demography and social behavior of large groups of individually known animals
2. The lack of long-term, precise data on the distribution of resources in time and space
3. The nearly complete absence of information on genetic relatedness through the male line
4. The difficulty in assigning reproductive and other costs and benefits to particular behaviors
5. Our almost total ignorance of the genetics of primate social behavior
6. The untestable nature, even under the best of conditions, of many sociobiological models

Some critics have gone even further to question the basic validity of sociobiology as a perspective. Eminent Harvard biologists Stephen Jay Gould and Richard Lewontin (1979) have portrayed sociobiology as a teological (circularly-reasoned) pursuit. In making this point, Gould and Lewontin compare sociobiological adaptive "stories" to the wistful, naive renderings of Candide's sidekick, Dr. Pangloss (from Voltaire's classic satire *Candide*). Even in the most humiliating of circumstances, Pangloss would philosophize that "all is for the best in the best of all possible worlds." In similar fashion, Gould and Lewontin see sociobiologists devising their scenarios to explain perfectly adaptive situations.

Is natural selection indeed such a self-perfecting process? Of course, no one can say for certain, since we see only a small slice of possible evolutionary strategies among living animals; but evidence does suggest that natural selection often works simply "to get by." In this way, a whole host of marginal traits and behaviors could endure for substantial periods of time. The recent lemurs of Madagascar are a case in point. Just a few hundred years ago, the island was inhabited by a host of different lemur species, but human intervention caused rapid extinction of many forms. Consequently, the survivors (like the indri) have probably moved into a variety of habitats from which competitors had once excluded them. Without such competition they now make do, but probably could not be described as particularly well adapted:

> The lemurs alive today inhabit forests from which many species, some of them probably competitors, have vanished. It is not difficult to imagine that the surviving lemurs have expanded their life-style to include foods and perhaps whole habitats from which they were once excluded by competitors. It does not matter that they do not make very good use of these new resources, so long as they do not have to compete with more efficient animals. In short, there is no reason to suppose that the distribution, feeding habits, and social organization of lemurs today are the results of a long, slow evolutionary process, each species finely tuned to make the best of its environment. More likely, what we see are animals getting by and making ecological experiments after two thousand years of rapid evolutionary change. (Richard, 1985, pp. 356–358)

Of course, this is not an evolutionary situation that has had much time to reach equilibrium. But when we look at *any* modern primate population, can we be assured that it is not changing (perhaps rapidly)? Is it showing particularly functional adaptations, and if so, to which circumstances? Is the population in equilibrium? Has it ever been in equilibrium? Beyond these theoretical difficulties, sociobiologists must address the type of information needed to test at least limited hypotheses. Presently, however, it is the lack of long-term precise data that most bedevils attempts to make sociobiology more scientific.

Indeed, among wild primates, the longest-term studies concern Old World monkeys (baboons at Amboseli or Gilgil in Kenya) or chimpanzees in Tanzania (Gombe and Mahale), but still encompass barely two complete generations. Data from captive or heavily provisioned populations (e.g., Japanese macaques) are more complete, but are difficult to interpret, given the potentially large disruption of behavior these animals have experienced.

Behavioral Data and Objectivity in Science   Perhaps an even more nagging problem than lack of long-term data is the very nature of the information itself. Primates are highly complex animals. Their behavior does not reduce down to simple discrete categories that can readily be described. Indeed, for behavioral studies it is often the case that the kinds of data collected and conclusions reached are often the product of the kinds of questions asked, the methodologies employed, and perhaps most importantly (and underlying everything else), the particular training and orientation of the observer.

We want to make it clear that most scientists attempt to be objective and in fact often recognize that they have biases that must be controlled. Moreover, the great majority of scientists are honest in the presentation of research findings. Nevertheless, when dealing with data that are largely subjective, it is often exceedingly difficult to resolve differences of opinion without years of data accumulation and at least some agreement on basic methodologies.

As Hrdy has acknowledged concerning challenges to her interpretation of langur infanticide:

> It has struck me more than once that critics of the sexual selection model sometimes apply a double standard: The criteria for accepting negative evidence appear to be far less stringent than the criteria applied to support the sexual selection model. . . . My own writing errs in the opposite direction, a consequence of the evolutionary bias of my own world view. . . .
>
> When researchers noted for integrity differ so profoundly not only over interpretation of the evidence, but even on the point of what is admissable as evidence, we must look for underlying causes. Inevitably, what researchers see is affected by expectations about their natural world and the way that biological and social systems "ought" to work; the resulting disagreement will not be easily resolved. Often frustrating, invariably time-consuming and inefficient, such debates remain, nevertheless, the best antidote we possess against the biases implicit in every researcher's world view. (1984b, pp. 317)

Summary

In Chapter 9, we saw that structurally the primate order is a most diverse group. In this chapter, we have seen that *socially*, as well, primates are both complex and diverse. Indeed, the myriad demands of primate existence have produced these living forms through an integrated process of *biosocial* evolution.

While the scope of this book does not allow us to touch upon all the fascinating aspects of primatological research, we have introduced some of the more dynamic areas. In particular, we have shown that ecological challenges and how they act to influence primate social relationships are a central concern of current primatology. Another main focus of many contemporary researchers involves evolutionary explanation (through natural selection) of primate behavior. This approach, called sociobiology, is not without its drawbacks and its detractors, both within and outside primatology. Nevertheless, along with ecological considerations, such a perspective has allowed researchers to frame a whole array of new questions concerning primate behavior. We may never have complete answers to these questions, but we can gain useful information only by *attempting* to answer what we consider relevant questions. Such is the nature of science, particularly the science of behavior.

Beyond these methodological considerations, there are specific avenues of research that have been used to provide information on the evolution of human behavior. It is to this information that we turn in the next chapter.

Questions for Review

1. Discuss several reasons for studying nonhuman primates.
2. What features are unique to humans (or at least tend to distinguish humans from other primates)?
3. Why should primates be studied in free-ranging circumstances?

4. What are the primary methodological obstacles to studying free-ranging primates?
5. Given the methodological constraints, which primates are known best in free-ranging circumstances?
6. What major aspects of the environment are thought to influence social behavior of nonhuman primates?
7. Discuss how the study of the five species of primates in the Kibale Forest has contributed to our understanding of primate socioecology.
8. What is a dominance hierarchy? How do dominance hierarchies function within social groups?
9. What are the functions of grooming?
10. Why is the mother-infant bond so crucial for primates?
11. What experimental evidence is there to argue for a strong mother-infant attachment?
12. What is the basic assumption of sociobiology?
13. Discuss the sociobiological explanation for infanticide in langurs.
14. Give examples of how male and female nonhuman primates differ in their adaptive strategies.
15. Discuss some of the major limitations of sociobiological research.
16. Why have primatologists placed so much emphasis on socioecology in recent years?
17. Five types of nonhuman primate groups are mentioned in Box 10–1. Can you give reasons for this variation in social organization in nonhuman primates?

Suggested Further Reading

Bramblett, Claud A. 1994. *Patterns of Primate Behavior*. 2nd ed. Prospect Heights, IL: Waveland Press.

Goodall, Jane. 1986. *The Chimpanzees of Gombe*. Cambridge, MA: The Belknap Press of Harvard University Press.

Kano, Takayoshi. 1992. *The Last Ape. Pygmy Chimpanzee Behavior and Ecology*. Stanford: Stanford University Press.

Quiatt, Duane, and Vernon Reynolds. 1993. *Primate Behavior. Information, Social Knowledge, and the Evolution of Culture*. Cambridge, England: Cambridge University Press.

Smuts, Barbara B., Dorothy L. Cheney, Robert M. Seyfarth, Richard W. Wrangham, and Thomas T. Struhsaker (eds.). 1987. *Primate Societies*. Chicago: University of Chicago Press.

Internet Resources

The African Primates at Home
http://www.indiana.edu/~primate/primates.html
(Visual images and vocalizations of several African apes and monkeys. Links to various related topics, including "East African Research Sites," which gives good descriptions of flora and fauna of localities of current primate research.)

The Primate Info Net
http://uakari.primate.wisc.edu/pin
(Includes listings of primate newsletters, meeting calendars, educational resources, information on endangered species, current research projects, and much more.)

E. Ingmanson

Born in 1957 in Tucson, Arizona, lived in Yellowstone, Iowa, Georgia, and finally, at age 7, moved to Mesa Verde, Colorado. I received my BA from the University of Colorado, Boulder. My MA and Ph.D. (1985) were both from the University of Oregon. I began to observe bonobos in 1986 at the San Diego Zoo, and started my field research on them in 1987, when I joined a Japanese research team at Wamba, Zaire. I am currently just back from my fifth trip to Africa, where I am doing research on Pan troglodytes *in Cameroon. After teaching in a community college in San Diego, then the University of Washington, and NYU, I joined Dickinson College in central Pennsylvania in 1993. I have a house with my own small forest and a puppy named Merlin.*

I cannot imagine having become anything other than an anthropologist. It is often difficult, though, to say how you ended up doing what you do—which events influenced you most. It is rarely a single momentous event, but rather a chain of circumstances, accidents, or even misconceptions that lead us into one career or another. It was for me.

Perhaps part of the key is *enjoyment.* I have always found physical anthropology fun. It is a multimillion year mystery story, with elements of a jigsaw puzzle thrown in. There is so much about the human species we still do not know, and I find it exciting every time a new piece of the puzzle is added.

I don't think it was ever a conscious choice to become an anthropologist. Anthropology has always been part of my life. In many ways my childhood prepared me to think like an anthropologist. The fact that my father was an archeologist, and Mesa Verde, Colorado, was my backyard, probably had some influence. I at least knew what anthropology was—something many entering college students do not. Reading was always encouraged in my home—anything and everything. There were always books, magazines, and newspapers piled around the house. We also travelled around the U.S. a lot—my grandparents lived on opposite coasts. Exchange students lived with our family in high school, and I spent most of my senior year in Japan. I knew at

14 that I would be an anthropologist. But I never considered being an archeologist or a cultural anthropologist. Learning about other peoples and past cultures was interesting, but not the work I wanted to do. It was always physical anthropology that drew me—the discovery, the mystery, and the excitement.

The first course I took in physical anthropology with Dennis Van Gerven at the University of Colorado, confirmed my choice. I loved identifying the skeleton, learning the fossils, and the intricacies of genetics. It was never boring! And the concepts of evolution and natural selection were so logical, they provided the basis for how I would view everything else in life. This course was also my first introduction to primatology, but I did not choose to focus in that area until later.

The decision to focus in primatology was definitely a conscious one. After the usual array of undergraduate courses, I knew I loved both paleoanthropology and primatology, and could see myself doing either. What pushed me into primatology was a practical consideration. I am allergic to the sun. Even a short exposure can be painful and cause me to break out in hives. I knew I would enjoy paleoanthropology, but I also knew I could not walk around in the sun all day looking for fossils. With Donald Johanson's discovery of Lucy occurring just before I entered college, images of the sun pouring down on the Afar were potent. At the time, the green shade of the rainforests seemed a better alternative. And with Jane Goodall's discoveries at Gombe as a guide, there was clearly an exciting world to explore. I began to read everything I could about chimpanzees.

I have often been asked what draws anyone to primatology in the first place, and to what extent the "cute factor" plays a role. To some extent it does. Many nonhuman primates are cute. Few things are as adorable as a baby chimpanzee. But that is only enough to make you stop and take a second look, not spend the rest of your life studying primates. Field primatology is often very difficult, requiring tremendous patience, energy, and time. But I find it immensely interesting—seeing how the small behaviors accumulate over days and weeks to form patterns and how these patterns come together to be a life. And you never know what might happen next.

One of my most exciting days doing fieldwork began as a very frustrating one. The group of bonobos (also called pygmy chimpanzees; *Pan paniscus*) I was observing at Wamba, Zaire, had nested about 10 km from our camp. The truck I often took up the road for the first 7 km or so was not available. If I wanted to observe my group, I would have to walk. I only briefly contemplated not going. Remaining in camp all day was boring. So I set out before dawn (5 A.M.) with my tracker. It took almost two hours of hard

walking to arrive in the area where the pygmy chimpanzees had nested. It was long past dawn and they were no longer in their nests, but fortunately they were still feeding nearby. I had barely caught my breath and pulled out my notebook when a commotion began. It took several moments for me to figure out what was happening. Then I saw—they were chasing something. It was quickly caught by an adult female and killed. It was a flying squirrel. Observing this incident and the next two hours as it was consumed and shared only with other females, made every kilometer walked, every mosquito bite, every frustration that accompanies fieldwork, worthwhile. We knew from fecal remains and a few brief observations of feeding that the pygmy chimpanzees ate squirrels, but no researcher had previously observed the capture and kill. I was the first, and it was an incredibly exciting moment.

Twenty years earlier, Goodall had shocked many when she first described hunting by *Pan troglodytes*. Now we expect to find it, but many questions remain concerning the role and social implications of hunting in the lives of chimpanzees—and in our own evolutionary past. This is the direction my research has taken today—using what we know of primate behavior to help us understand human behavior and evolution.

It took me many years to define more precisely what I actually wanted to focus on in chimpanzee behavior. Everything they

do is interesting. Then I realized that no matter what I observed, I was asking similar questions—what do they know and how did they learn it. In short, I was trying to understand their intelligence. In order to do this, I have examined the who, what, when, and how of communication, tool use, learning, mother-infant relations, and other social interactions. Many of my observations of tool use in pygmy chimpanzees have led me to explore how skills observed in one context are expressed in another environment, and the nature of the skills involved. I want to know how intelligence has evolved, how it differs from one species to another, and what role the environment plays.

One of the most exciting things occurring right now in chimpanzee research is the recognition of diversity. Each group has some unique behaviors, different patterns of interacting with each other and their environment. Is this similar to the beginning of human culture? What does it indicate about the nature of intelligence, the speciation of the apes, or the events that led to humans evolving? These are exciting questions to ponder. Tragically, much of the diversity in chimpanzee behavior is already lost to us. Both species are endangered and only small portions of their habitat are protected. Just as we begin to know some of the questions to ask, the opportunity to answer them is disappearing forever.

Primate Models for Human Evolution

Introduction

As you learned in Chapter 9, one characteristic that distinguishes primates, as a group, from other mammals is increased neurological complexity. Such physiological development is directly reflected in behavioral complexity or, to put it simply, intelligence. The predilection to live in social groups was one of several factors that provided selective pressures favoring intelligence, especially *social* intelligence, as an adaptive strategy for primates.

Primates exhibit a propensity for forming long-term social bonds that frequently include complex alliances and friendships. This predisposition for complex social life provided a foundation for the evolution of the earliest hominids. One of the hallmarks of later hominid evolution is increased relative brain size, but the foundations of neurological complexity were laid long before bipedal hominids made stone tools. Those foundations are still evident today in behavioral patterns shared by human and nonhuman primates.

Within the social sciences, human behavior has traditionally been considered separately from that of all other organisms, even other primates. This perspective has consistently avoided biological explanations for human behavior, emphasizing that most (if not all) of human behavior is *learned.*

Certainly, human behavior *is* predominantly learned. But the *ability to learn* and behave in complex ways is ultimately rooted in biological (genetic) factors, and natural selection has favored increased learning capacities and behavioral modification in the human lineage.

In the last two decades, there has been a growing consensus, particularly among primatologists, that certain human predispositions reflect patterns also seen in other primates (Cartmill, 1990; King, 1994; de Waal, 1996). Moreover, because we do share an evolutionary history with other primates, a useful approach in developing a better understanding of the evolution of human behavior is to identify in other species those factors that also produced specific patterns in humans. This approach places human behavior, although unarguably unique, within a biological and evolutionary context. (*Note:* see the discussion of sociobiology in Chapter 10, pp. 255–260).

A biological perspective does not assume that all human abilities and behavioral patterns are genetically determined or unalterable. Rather, such an approach aids in explaining *how* certain patterns may have come about and what their adaptive significance might be. Within this framework, the plasticity of human behavior is clearly recognized and emphasized.

As Hinde (1987, p. 413) warns, "Attempting to draw parallels in behavior between human and nonhuman species is a dangerous pastime." Hinde proceeds to caution that owing to the number and diversity of primate species and human cultures, it is not difficult to find comparable behaviors in nonhuman and human primates. Once shared behavioral patterns have been identified, it is easy to support almost any hypothesis one develops, regardless of its validity. However, as Hinde further emphasizes, if one recognizes the risks and limitations of drawing comparisons between species, investigations of shared behavioral *patterns* and principles can be a fruitful endeavor.

All the considerations discussed in this chapter regarding the evolution of social behavior in *all* primates (including humans) are ultimately grounded physiologically in the central nervous system. Moreover, the physiological organization of primate neurology is, in turn, directly correlated with growth development, body size, and metabolism, all components of what primatologists have termed **life history**.

▲ **Life history**
Basic components of an animal's development and physiology, viewed from an evolutionary perspective. Such key components include body size, proportional brain size, metabolism, and reproduction.

What follows in this chapter are a few of the many examples of nonhuman primate development and social behavior believed by researchers to have implications for human behavior. Some topics are controversial, and all interpretations are somewhat theoretical. Nevertheless, all the perspectives are significant for achieving the central goal of this book, namely, understanding human evolution.

Aspects of Life History and Body Size

In the last decade, primatologists have become increasingly interested in broad generalizations regarding primate lifestyles, maturation, and reproduction, topics that are all subsumed under the category life history. A crucial factor that cross-cuts all these aspects of life history is body size. By *body size*, we mean some overall measure of body mass, sometimes given as a linear measure, such as stature, or (more critically) some estimate of weight. In modeling significant features of human evolution, a broad comparative perspective using data from other primates can be useful. We can obtain rough estimates of the body size of ancient hominids from preserved skeletal evidence, especially through extrapolation from joint size. In those rare instances where partial (or even mostly complete) skeletons are preserved, details concerning limb proportions, relative brain size, and so forth, can also be tentatively determined. As we will see in succeeding chapters, there are two quite famous partial skeletons (both from East Africa) now available for such reconstruction.

Among living primates, body size is extraordinarily diverse, ranging from the tiny mouse lemur (66 g or 2.4 ounces) to the massive gorilla (117 kg, or 258 pounds). And, of course, there is an array of species in between. Several critical features of primate life history are correlated with variation in adult body size. For example, small-bodied species tend to specialize in insectivorous diets, while only larger-bodied species are leaf eaters (i.e., folivorous). It should be noted that almost *all* species eat some fruit, but how this component is *supplemented* varies considerably and is correlated with body size. Supplementing a diet made up largely of fruits is necessary, for while they are high in calories, fruits lack protein. Primates thus acquire protein from other sources—insects, young buds, leaves, and shoots. In addition, some highly specialized species exploit exudates, that is, tree gums.

Small animals have very high energy needs (per unit of body mass), and for them, insects are an extremely efficient source of calories and protein. However, an animal can capture only so many insects per day, thus placing an upper limit on body size for species that rely heavily on insects to supplement their diet.

On the other hand, to process leaves (especially mature leaves containing cellulose), an animal needs a specialized gut with long intestines and/or multi-chambered stomachs. This physiological adaptation is necessary to digest large amounts of low-energy food, giving microorganisms (bacteria) the opportunity to break down cellulose and neutralize plant toxins. Primates that emphasize leaves in their diets (e.g., colobus monkeys and langurs) have larger overall body size than those that are primarily insectivorous (e.g., tarsiers and lorises).

Tied closely to these dietary factors, body size is also correlated with metabolic rate. The larger an animal is, the more efficient its thermal control will be (see Bergmann's rule, Chapter 6), and consequently, its metabolic rate is lower than that of a smaller animal. "Thus large animals expend less energy and consequently need less food than small animals. Put more simply, two 5-kg

(11-pound) monkeys require more food than a single 10-kg (22-pound) monkey" (Fleagle, 1988, p. 233). The content of the diet also frequently correlates with metabolism (usually measured as basal metabolic rate). On average, folivores have a lower metabolism than other primates—an especially relevant factor when controlling comparisons for animals of roughly equal body size.

Locomotion and habitat preference, too, are partly correlated with overall body size. Most arboreal primates are small and practice some leaping. Larger arboreal primates tend to exhibit more suspensory behavior, and the largest primates of all tend to be at least party terrestrial. Monkeys that weigh over 22 pounds (10 kg) are almost always *primarily* terrestrial in their habitat preference. These relationships, however, are not quite this simple. Adaptive solutions such as locomotor behavior are always compromises among competing requirements. While large size may facilitate a more efficient metabolism, it hinders arboreal locomotion—and might therefore preclude access to some of the most nutritious food items, located at the ends of small terminal branches. On the ground, larger size might, in some cases, discourage predators, but it will also make the animal more conspicuous.

Body Size and Brain Size

Body size is closely correlated with brain size. Clearly, an animal the size of a chimpanzee (100 pounds) has a larger brain than a squirrel monkey (adult weight, 2 pounds). However, in making such a superficial comparison of *absolute* brain size, one is ignoring the more important consideration of *proportional brain size.*

It has been known for some time that in mammals in general, not only is brain size tied directly to body size, but the relationship is not completely linear. In other words, in cross-species comparisons, as body weight increases, brain size does not necessarily increase at the same rate.

The predictable relationship between body and brain size has been called the index of **encephalization** (Jerison, 1973). The degree of encephalization can be a very powerful analytical tool, as it provides a gauge of the expected brain size for any given body size. Most primates fall close to the predicted curve, but there is one notable exception: *Homo sapiens.* Modern humans have a brain size well beyond that expected for a primate of similar body weight. It is this degree of encephalization that must be explained as a unique and central component of recent human evolution. Using these same analytical perspectives as applied to the fossil materials in the next several chapters, you will see that earlier members of genus *Homo* as well as more primitive hominids (*Australopithecus*) are not nearly as encephalized as modern *H. sapiens.*

Timing of growth also provides an interesting contrast. In nonhuman primates, the most rapid period of brain development occurs either before or immediately after birth. In humans, rapid growth occurs prior to and after birth—so that already large-brained neonates continue to show considerable brain expansion for at least the first year after birth. The metabolic costs of such rapid and sustained neurological growth are enormous requiring more than 50 percent of the infant's metabolic output (Aiello, 1992).

Carefully controlled comparisons are essential in making cross-species generalizations regarding animals of differing sizes (a point to keep in mind when we discuss early hominids, most of which varied notably from *Homo sapiens* in body size). Such controls relate to considerations of what is called *scaling,* or (more technically) **allometry**. These allometric comparisons have now become increasingly important in understanding contemporary primate life history vari-

▲ **Encephalization**

The proportional size of the brain relative to some other measure, usually some estimate of overall body size. More precisely, the term refers to increases in brain size beyond that which would be expected given the body size of a particular species.

▲ **Allometry**

Also called "scaling," the differential proportion among various anatomical structures. For example, the relative size of the brain changes during the development of an individual. Moreover, scaling effects must also be considered when comparing species.

ables and adaptations. Moreover, similar approaches, as directly borrowed from these primate models, are now also routinely applied to interpretation of the primate/hominid fossil record.

Communication

Communication is universal among animals and is accomplished by means of an array of scents, behaviors, and **autonomic** responses. Any act that communicates by definition *conveys meaning and influences the behavior of others*; however, communication may or may not be deliberate on the part of the performer.

Largely unintentional behaviors, such as body posture, convey information about an animal's emotional state. For example, a crouched position indicates a certain degree of insecurity or fear, while a purposeful striding gait implies confidence. Likewise, autonomic responses to threatening or novel stimuli, such as raised body hair (in most species) or enhanced body odor (in gorillas), indicate fear or excitement.

Over time, those behaviors and motor patterns that originated in specific contexts have assumed increasing importance as communicatory signals. For example, crouching initially aided in avoiding physical attack. In addition, this behavior conveyed that the individual was fearful, submissive, and nonaggressive. Thus, crouching became valuable not only for its primary function, but for its role in communication as well, and natural selection increasingly favored it for this secondary role. In such a manner, over time, the expressions of specific behaviors may thus become elaborated or exaggerated because of their value in enhancing communication.

Among the more deliberate primate behaviors that serve as communication are a wide variety of gestures, facial expressions, and vocalizations, some of which we humans share. Among many species, a mild threat is indicated by an intense stare. (For this reason, people should avoid eye contact with captive primates.) Humans, too, glare to show disapproval, and certainly we find prolonged eye contact, particularly with strangers, very discomforting. Some other primate threat gestures (not typical of humans) include a quick yawn to expose canine teeth (baboons, macaques) (Fig. 11–1); bobbing back and forth in a crouched position (patas monkeys); and branch shaking (many monkey species and chimpanzees).

There are also behaviors to indicate submission, reassurance, or amicable intentions. In addition to crouching, baboons indicate submission by turning their hindquarters toward another. Chimpanzees may bend at the waist and bob the upper body.

In many species, reassurance takes the form of touching, patting, hugging, or holding hands (Fig. 11–2). As already mentioned in Chapter 10, in addition to hygienic functions, grooming also serves in a number of situations to indicate submission or reassurance.

A wide variety of chimpanzee and bonobo facial expressions indicate emotional states (Fig. 11–3). These include the well-known play face (Fig. 11–3) associated with play behavior (also seen in several other species, including a modified form in humans) and the fear grin (seen in many primates) to indicate fear and submission.

By describing a few communicative behaviors shared by many primates (including humans), we do not intend to convey that these gestures are dictated solely by genetic factors. Indeed, if primates are not reared within a relatively normal social context, such behaviors may not be performed appropriately,

▲ **Communication**
Any act that conveys information, in the form of a message, to another individual. Frequently, the result of communication is a change in the behavior of the recipient. Communication may not be deliberate but may be the result of involuntary processes or a secondary consequence of an intentional action.

▲ **Autonomic**
Pertaining to physiological responses not under voluntary control. An example in chimpanzees would be the erection of body hair during excitement. An example in humans is blushing. Both convey information regarding emotional states, but neither is a deliberate behavior and communication is not intended.

FIGURE 11–1

Adolescent male savanna baboon threatens photographer with a characteristic "yawn" that shows the canine teeth. Note also that the eyes are closed briefly to expose light, cream-colored eyelids. This has been termed the "eyelid flash."

(a)

(b)

FIGURE 11-2

(a) Adolescent male savanna baboons holding hands. (b) Male chimpanzee touches outstretched hand of crouching, submissive female in a gesture of reassurance.

▲ **Displays**
Sequences of repetitious behaviors that serve to communicate emotional states. Nonhuman primate displays are most frequently associated with reproductive or agonistic behavior.

▲ **Ritualized behaviors**
Behaviors removed from their original context and sometimes exaggerated to convey information.

because the contextual manifestations of communicatory actions are *learned*. But the underlying *predisposition* to learn and use them and the motor patterns involved in their execution are genetically influenced, and these factors do have adaptive significance. Therefore, theories about how such expressive patterns evolved focus on motor patterns and the original context in which they occurred.

Primates (and other animals) also use **displays** which are elaborate combinations of gestures and movements used in communication. Moreover, many complex displays incorporate various combinations of **ritualized behaviors**.

Common gorilla displays include chest slapping and the tearing of vegetation to indicate excitement or threat. Likewise, a chimpanzee may threaten an opponent by screaming and waving its arms, sometimes while brandishing sticks and branches (Fig. 11–4). These actions may all be seen as *intention movements* that originated as sequences of motor patterns involved in actual fighting or attack.

Mounting, as seen in baboons, is a good example of a ritualized behavior (Fig. 11–5). Higher-ranking individuals mount the hindquarters of more subordinant animals in the manner of copulation, not to mate, but to express dominance. (It should be noted that when mounting serves a communicatory

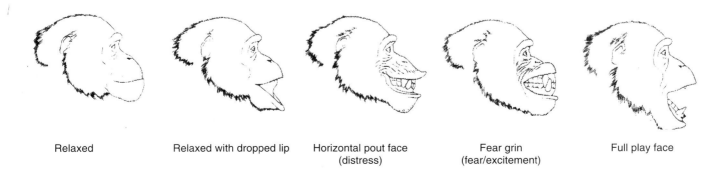

Relaxed   Relaxed with dropped lip   Horizontal pout face (distress)   Fear grin (fear/excitement)   Full play face

FIGURE 11-3

Chimpanzee facial expressions (redrawn from Goodall, 1986).

FIGURE 11–4
Male chimpanzee displays at public at San Francisco zoo.

function, mounters and mountees may be members of the same sex.) In most anthropoid species characterized by one-male or multimale, multifemale groups, males (the mounters in the mating context) are socially dominant to females. Thus, in the context of communication, the mounter assumes the male reproductive role. Likewise, presentation of the hindquarters in solicitation of mounting indicates submission or subordination by the mountee. As communication, these behavior patterns are entirely removed from their original (reproductive) context, and they function instead to reinforce and clarify the respective social roles of individuals in specific interactions.

As already emphasized, group living is crucial to survival for most primates. Living in groups provides better protection from predators and facilitates protection of resources. But social living also has drawbacks, because in groups there is

FIGURE 11-5
One young male savanna baboon mounts another as an expression of dominance.

competition for resources and position within dominance hierarchies (Walters and Seyfarth, 1987). Therefore, the group must maintain a balance between competitive and cooperative behaviors, and these goals are achieved through communication.

Efficient communication facilitates social life and indeed makes social life possible. Therefore, natural selection has favored not only the elaboration and ritualization of many gestures and displays, but also the complexity of the neurological structures that underlie them.

The traditional view held that nonhuman communication consists of mostly involuntary vocalizations and actions that convey information solely about the emotional state of the animal (anger, fear, etc.). Nonhuman animals were not considered capable of communicating about external events, objects, or other animals, either in close proximity or removed in space or time. For example, it was assumed that when a startled baboon barks, its fellow baboons know only that it is startled. What they do not know is what elicited the bark, and this they can only ascertain by looking around. In general, then, it has often been stated that nonhuman animals, including primates, use a *closed system* of communication, where the use of vocalizations and other modalities does not include references to specific external phenomena.

In recent years, these views have been challenged (Steklis, 1985; King, 1994). For example, it is now known that vervet monkeys (Fig. 11–6) use specific vocalizations to refer to particular categories of predators, such as snakes, birds of prey, and leopards (Struhsaker, 1967; Seyfarth, Cheney, and Marler, 1980a, 1980b). When researchers made tape recordings of various vervet alarm calls and played them back within hearing distance of free-ranging vervets, they observed differing responses to various calls. In response to leopard-alarm calls, the monkeys climbed trees; eagle-alarm calls caused them to look upward and run into bushes; and snake-alarm calls elicited visual searching of nearby grass.

These results demonstrate that vervets use distinct vocalizations to refer to specific components of the external environment. These calls are not involuntary, and they do not refer solely to the emotional state (alarm) of the individual, although this information is also conveyed. While these significant findings dis-

FIGURE 11–6
Group of free-ranging vervets.

pel certain long-held misconceptions about nonhuman communication (at least for some species), they also indicate certain limitations. Vervet communication is restricted to the present; as far as we know, no vervet can communicate about a predator it saw yesterday or one it might see in the future.

Other studies have demonstrated that numerous nonhuman primates, including cottontop tamarins (Cleveland and Snowdon, 1982), red colobus (Struhsaker, 1975), and gibbons (Tenaza and Tilson, 1977), produce distinct calls that have specific references. There is also growing evidence that many birds and some nonprimate mammals use specific predator alarm calls (Seyfarth, 1987; Hensen, 1992).

In contrast to that of other species, human communication, or *language*, employs a set of either written or spoken symbols that refer to concepts, other people, objects, and so on. This set of symbols is said to be *arbitrary* in that it has no inherent relationship to whatever it stands for. For example, the English word for *flower* when written or spoken neither looks, smells, nor feels like the thing it represents.

Humans can recombine their linguistic symbols in an infinite variety of ways to create new meanings and can use language to refer to events, places, objects, and people far removed in both space and time. For these reasons, language is described as an *open* system of communication, based on the human ability to think symbolically.

Language, as distinct from other forms of communication, has been considered a uniquely human achievement, setting humans apart from all other species. But work with captive apes has raised doubts about certain aspects of this supposition. While many people remain skeptical about the capacity of nonhuman primates to use language, reports from psychologists (especially those who work with chimpanzees) leave little doubt that apes can learn to interpret visual signs and use them in communication. No mammal other than humans has the ability to speak. However, the fact that apes cannot speak has less to do with lack of intelligence than to differences in the anatomy of the vocal tract and *language-related structures in the brain.*

Because of failed attempts by others to teach young chimpanzees to speak, psychologists Beatrice and Allen Gardner designed a study to test language capabilities in chimpanzees by teaching an infant female named Washoe to use ASL (American Sign Language for the deaf). Beginning in 1966, the Gardners began teaching Washoe signs in the same way parents would instruct a deaf human infant. In just over three years, Washoe acquired at least 132 signs. "She asked for goods and services, and she also asked questions about the world of objects and events around her" (Gardner et al., 1989, p. 6).

Years later, an infant chimpanzee named Loulis was placed in Washoe's care. Researchers wanted to know if Loulis would acquire signing skills from Washoe and other chimpanzees in the study group. Within just eight days, Loulis began to imitate the signs of others. Moreover, Washoe also deliberately *taught* Loulis some signs. For example, instructing him to sit, "Washoe placed a small plastic chair in front of Loulis, and then signed CHAIR/SIT to him several times in succession, watching him closely throughout" (Fouts et al., 1989, p. 290).

There have been other chimpanzee language experiments. The chimp Sara, for instance, was taught by David Premack to recognize plastic chips as symbols for various objects. The chips did not resemble the objects they represented. For example, the chip that represented an apple was neither round nor red. Sara's ability to associate chips with concepts and objects to which they bore no visual similarity implies some degree of symbolic thought.

At the Yerkes Regional Primate Research Center in Atlanta, Georgia, another chimp, Lana, worked with a specially designed computer keyboard with chips attached to keys. After six months, Lana recognized symbols for 30 words and was able to ask for food and answer questions through the machine (Rumbaugh, 1977). Also at Yerkes, two male chimpanzees, Sherman and Austin, have learned to communicate using a series of lexigrams, or geometric symbols, imprinted on a computer keyboard (Savage-Rumbaugh, 1986b).

Francine Patterson, who taught ASL to Koko, a female lowland gorilla, reports that Koko uses more than 500 signs. Furthermore, Michael, an adult male gorilla also involved in the study, has a considerable sign vocabulary, and the two gorillas communicate with each other via signs.

Questions have been raised about this type of experimental work. Do the apes really understand the signs they learn? Are they merely imitating their trainers? Do they learn that a symbol is a name for an object or simply that executing a symbol will produce that object? Other unanswered questions concern the apes' use of grammar, especially when they combine more than just a few "words" to communicate.

Partly in an effort to address some of these questions and criticisms, psychologist Sue Savage-Rumbaugh taught the chimpanzees Sherman and Austin to use symbols to categorize *classes* of objects, such as "food" or "tool." This was done in recognition of the fact that in previous studies, apes had been taught symbols for *specific* items. Savage-Rumbaugh reasoned that simply to use a symbol as a label is not the same thing as understanding the *representational value* of the symbol.

Sherman and Austin were taught to recognize familiar food items, for which they routinely used symbols, as belonging to a broader category referred to by yet another symbol, "food." The chimps were then introduced to unfamiliar food items, for which they had no symbols, in order to see if they would place them in the food category. The fact that both apes had perfect or nearly perfect scores further substantiated that indeed they could categorize unfamiliar objects. More importantly, it was clear that they were capable of assigning to unknown objects symbols that denoted membership in a broad grouping. This ability was a strong indication that the chimpanzees understood that the symbols were being used referentially.

However, subsequent work with Lana, who had different language experiences, did not prove as successful. Although Lana was able to sort actual objects into categories, she was unable to assign generic symbols to novel items (Savage-Rumbaugh and Lewin, 1994). Thus, it became apparent that the manner in which chimpanzees are introduced to language influences their ability to understand the representational value of symbols.

Throughout the relatively brief history of ape language studies, one often repeated assertion was that young chimpanzees must be *taught* to use symbols. This pattern was contrasted with the ability of human children to learn language spontaneously, through exposure, without being deliberately taught. Therefore, it was significant when Savage-Rumbaugh and her colleagues reported that Kanzi, an infant male bonobo Kanzi was *spontaneously* acquiring and using symbols at the age of $2^1/2$ years (Savage-Rumbaugh et al., 1986) (Fig. 11–7). Kanzi's younger half-sister also began to use symbols spontaneously at 11 months of age. Both animals had been exposed to the use of lexigrams when they accompanied their mother to training sessions but neither youngster had received instruction and in fact were not involved in these sessions.

While the abilities shown by Kanzi and his sister reveal a remarkable degree of cognitive complexity, it nevertheless remains evident that apes do not acquire

FIGURE 11–7
The bonobo Kanzi, as a youngster, using lexigrams to communicate with human observers.

and use language in the same way humans do. Moreover, it appears that not all signing apes understand the referential relationship between symbol and object, person, or action. Nonetheless, there is abundant evidence that humans are not the only species capable of some degree of symbolic thought and complex communication.

From an evolutionary perspective, the ape language experiments may suggest clues to the origins of human language. It is quite likely that the last common ancestor hominids shared with the African great apes possessed communication capabilities similar to those we see now in these species. If so, we need to elucidate the factors that enhanced the adaptive significance of these characteristics in our own lineage. It is equally important to explore why these pressures did not operate to the same degree in gorillas, chimpanzees, and bonobos.

For reasons we do not yet fully understand, communication became increasingly important during the course of human evolution, and natural selection favored anatomical and neurological changes that enhanced our ancestors' ability to use spoken language. However, this trend would not have been possible if early hominids had not already been predisposed to language development.

In nonhuman primates, vocalizations are not completely controlled by the **motor cortex**. However, some of the regions of the brain involved in human speech production *are* located in the motor cortex, and they direct movement of the mouth, larynx, and tongue, but *only as those movements pertain to language*. Damage to these neural tracts does not cause paralysis (as damage to other areas will do), but it will disturb speech, demonstrating that these structures are adapted to movements related specifically to speech production. However, human speech involves much more than simply the motor control of specific muscle groups.

In most humans, language function is located primarily in the left hemisphere of the brain, including the left temporal lobe (see Fig. 11–8). In particular,

▲ **Motor cortex**

The *cortex* of the brain, the outer layer, is composed of nerve cells or neurons. The *motor cortex* is that portion pertaining to outgoing signals involved in muscle use.

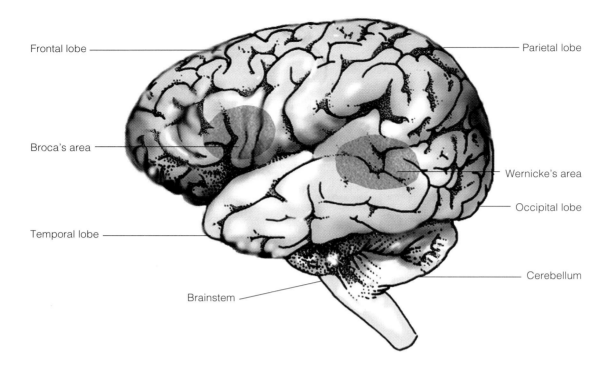

Frontal lobe

Broca's area

Temporal lobe

Brainstem

Parietal lobe

Wernicke's area

Occipital lobe

Cerebellum

FIGURE 11–8

Left lateral view of the human brain, showing major regions and areas involved in speech.

two regions—*Wernicke's area* and *Broca's area*—are directly involved in the perception and production (respectively) of spoken language. But the perception and production of speech involves much more than these two areas, and use of written language requires still other neurological structures.

Association areas, composed of thousands of neural connections, integrate information sent from various parts of the cerebral cortex. Information relating to visual, olfactory, tactile, and auditory stimuli is first combined and then relayed to Broca's area, where it is translated for speech production. This remarkable human ability depends on interconnections between receiving areas for all sensory stimuli. While the brains of other species have such association areas, they do not have the ability to transform this information for the purpose of using language.

In discussions of human evolution, much emphasis is placed on increased brain size, both in relative and absolute terms. While increased brain size is certainly important, it was the *reorganization* of neurological structures that permitted the development of language. Although the study of comparative brain structure is still in its infancy, much current evidence suggests that *new* structures and novel connections have not been the basis for neurological differences among species. Rather, systematic reorganization, elaboration, and/or reduction of existing structures, as well as shifts in the proportions of existing connections, have been far more important (Deacon, 1992).

Some researchers argue that language capabilities appeared late in human evolution (i.e., with the wide dispersal of modern *Homo sapiens* some 100,000 to 30,000 years ago). Others postulate a much earlier origin, possibly with the appearance of the genus *Homo* 2 m.y.a. Whichever scenario is true, language came about as complex and efficient forms of communication gained selective value in our lineage.

Affiliative Behaviors

Within primate societies, there is a constant interplay between **affiliative** behaviors that promote group cohesion, and aggressive behaviors that can lead to group disruption. Conflict within a group frequently develops out of competition for resources, including mating partners and food items. Instead of actual attacks or fighting, most intragroup aggression occurs in the form of various signals and displays, frequently within the context of a dominance hierarchy. Likewise, the majority of such situations are resolved through various submissive and appeasement behaviors.

Although some level of aggression is useful in maintaining order within the group and protecting either individual or group resources, aggression can also be destructive and even result in death. Affiliative or friendly behaviors reduce levels of aggression by defusing potentially dangerous situations, reinforcing bonds between individuals, and promoting group cohesion.

Common affiliative behaviors include reconciliation, consolation, and simple amicable interactions between friends and relatives. Most such behaviors involve physical contact, which, as we have already discussed, is one of the most important factors in primate development and is crucial in promoting peaceful relationships in many primate social groupings.

Following a conflict, chimpanzee opponents frequently move, within minutes, to reconcile (de Waal, 1982). Reconciliation takes many forms, including hugging, kissing, and grooming. Even uninvolved individuals may take part, either grooming one or both participants or forming their own grooming parties. In addition, bonobos are unique in their use of sex to promote group cohesion, restore peace after conflicts, and relieve tension within the group (de Waal, 1987, 1989).

Because relationships are crucial to nonhuman primates, the bonds between individuals can last a lifetime. These relationships serve a variety of functions. Individuals of many species form alliances in which one supports another against a third. Alliances or coalitions, as they are also called, can be used to enhance the status of members. For example, at Gombe, the male chimpanzee Figan achieved alpha status because of support from his brother (Goodall, 1986, p. 424). In fact, chimpanzees so heavily rely on coalitions and are so skillful politically that an entire book, appropriately titled *Chimpanzee Politics* (de Waal, 1982), is devoted to the topic.

▲ **Affiliative**
Pertaining to amicable associations between individuals. Affiliative behaviors, such as grooming, reinforce social bonds and promote group cohesion.

Aggressive Interactions

Interactions *between* groups of **conspecifics** can be just as revealing as those that take place *within* groups. For many primate species, especially those whose ranges are small, contact with one or more other groups of the same species is a daily occurrence, and the form of these encounters can vary from species to species.

Between groups, aggression can be used to protect resources through defense of **territories**. Primate groups are associated with a *home range* where they remain permanently. (Although individuals may leave their home range and join another community, the groups themselves remain in a particular area.) Within the home range is a portion called the **core area**. This area contains the highest concentration of predictable resources and it is where the group most frequently may be found. Although portions of the home range may overlap with

▲ **Conspecifics**
Members of the same species.

▲ **Territories**
Portions of an individual's or group's home range actively defended against intrusion, particularly by conspecifics.

▲ **Core area**
The portion of a home range containing the highest concentration and most reliable supplies of food and water. The core area is frequently the area that will be defended.

the home range of one or more other groups, core areas of adjacent groups do not overlap. The core area can also be said to be a group's territory, and it is the portion of the home range defended against intrusion. However, in some species, other areas of the home range may also be defended. Whatever area is defended is termed the *territory*.

Not all primates are territorial. In general, territoriality is associated with species whose ranges are sufficiently small to permit patrolling and protection (e.g., gibbons and vervets). Among many species (e.g., squirrel monkeys, rhesus macaques, and baboons), group encounters are usually nonaggressive. Nonterritorial tree dwellers use vocalizations to avoid other groups, spacing themselves throughout the forest canopy with minimal contact.

Chimpanzees do not exhibit all the traits typical of true territorial behavior (Goodall, 1986), but males in particular are highly intolerant of unfamiliar chimpanzees, especially other males. Therefore, intergroup interactions are almost always characterized by aggressive displays, chasing, and frequently, actual fighting.

Members of chimpanzee communities frequently travel to areas where their range borders or overlaps that of another community. These peripheral areas are not entirely safe, and before entering them, chimps usually hoot and display to determine if other animals are present. They then remain silent, listening for a response. If members of another community should appear, some form of aggression will ensue until one group retreats.

Male chimpanzees (sometimes accompanied by one or two females) commonly patrol borders. During patrols, party members travel silently in compact groupings. They stop frequently to sniff, look around, or climb tall trees, where they may sit for an hour or more surveying the region. During such times individuals are tense, and a sudden sound, such as a snapping twig, causes them to touch or embrace in reassurance (Goodall, 1986). It is most apparent from their tension and very uncharacteristic silence that the chimpanzees are quite aware that they have ventured into a potentially dangerous situation.

If a border patrol happens upon one or two strangers, the patrollers most surely will attack. However, if they encounter a group larger than their own, they themselves may be attacked, or at least chased.

Recent discussion among primatologists has focused on aggression between groups of the same species and whether the primary motivation is solely territoriality (i.e., protection of resources in a given area) or whether other factors are also involved (Cheney, 1987; Manson and Wrangham, 1991; Nishida, 1991). Much of this discussion has centered on intergroup aggression and lethal raiding in chimpanzees and has emphasized implications for human evolution and behavior as well.

Beginning in 1974, Jane Goodall and her colleagues witnessed at least five unprovoked and extremely brutal attacks by groups of chimpanzees (usually, but not always, males) upon lone individuals. To explain these attacks, it is necessary to point out that by 1973, the original Gombe community had divided into two distinct groups, one located in the north and the other in the south of what had once been the original group's home range. In effect, the southern splinter group had denied the others access to part of their former home range.

By 1977, all seven males and one female of the splinter group were either known or suspected to have been killed. All observed incidents involved several animals, usually adult males, who brutally attacked lone individuals. Although it is not possible to know exactly what motivated the attackers, it was clear that they intended to incapacitate their victims (Goodall, 1986).

Goodall (1986) has suggested that the attacks strongly imply that although chimpanzees do not possess language and do not wage war as we know it, they do exhibit behaviors that, if present in early hominids, could have been precursors to war:

> The chimpanzee, as a result of a unique combination of strong affiliative bonds between adult males on the one hand and an unusually hostile and violently aggressive attitude toward nongroup individuals on the other, has clearly reached a stage where he stands at the very threshold of human achievement in destruction, cruelty, and planned intergroup conflict. If ever he develops the power of language—and, as we have seen, he stands close to that threshold, too—might he not push open the door and wage war with the best of us? (Goodall, 1986, p. 534)

A situation similar to that at Gombe has been reported for a group of chimpanzees in the Mahale Mountains south of Gombe. Over a 17-year period, all the males of a small community disappeared. Although no attacks were actually observed, there was circumstantial evidence that most of these males met the same fate as the Gombe attack victims (Nishida et al., 1985, 1990).

Lethal, unprovoked aggression between groups of conspecifics is *known* to occur in only two mammalian species: humans and chimpanzees. Prior to its discovery in chimpanzees, such lethal aggression was thought to be an exclusively human endeavor, motivated by territoriality. In the past few years, a number of researchers have posed various questions within the theoretical framework that specific aggressive patterns may be explained by similar factors operating in both species. According to Manson and Wrangham (1991, p. 370), "These similarities between chimpanzees and humans suggest a common evolutionary background. Thus, they indicate that lethal male raiding could have had precultural origins and might be elicited by the same set of conditions among humans as among chimpanzees."

In champanzees and most traditional human cultures, males are *philopatric* and form lifelong bonds within their social group. Indeed, the core of a chimpanzee community is a group of closely bonded males who, because of their long-term association, act cooperatively in various endeavors, including hunting and attack. In most other primate species, females are the philopatric sex, and in some species (notably macaques and baboons), females may cooperate in aggressive encounters against females from other groups. (Usually these conflicts develop as contests for resources and they do not result in fatalities.) Generally then, conflicts between groups of conspecifics involve members of the philopatric sex. In fact, Manson and Wrangham (1991) suggest that in chimpanzees, lethal aggression is a male activity *because* males are the philopatric sex.

Efforts to identify the social and ecological factors that predispose human and chimpanzee males to engage in lethal attacks have led to hypotheses that attempt to explain the function and adaptive value of these activities. In this context, the benefits and costs of extreme aggression must be identified. The principal benefit to aggressors is acquisition of mating partners and food. Costs include risk of injury or death and loss of energy expended in performing aggressive acts.

Although the precise motivation of chimpanzee intergroup aggression may never be fully elucidated, it is clear that a number of interrelated factors are involved (Manson and Wrangham, 1991; Goodall, 1986; Nishida et al., 1985, 1990; Nishida, 1991). Moreover, although chimpanzees do not meet all the criteria developed for true territorial behavior (Goodall, 1986), it appears that various aspects of resource acquisition and protection are involved. Through careful examination of shared aspects of human and chimpanzee social life, we can develop hypotheses regarding how intergroup conflict may have arisen in our own lineage.

Cultural anthropologist Napoleon Chagnon (1979, 1988) has argued that among the Yanomamo Indians of Brazil, competition for mates between males is the motivation behind warfare between groups. The Yanomamo are a warlike people with over 30 percent of male deaths attributed to violence. Chagnon believes that the majority of hostilities either *within* or *between* villages (with raids leading to deaths, then revenge raids leading to more fatalities) are caused initially by competition for females. These phenomena are explained as functions of the same sociobiological principles that operate in chimpanzees, in full recognition of the obvious differences between the two species regarding weaponry, language, and mating systems (Manson and Wrangham, 1991). Chagnon (1988, p. 986), using the terminology of sociobiology, states, "Men who demonstrate their willingness to act violently and exact revenge for the deaths of kin may have higher marital and reproductive success."

Early hominids and chimpanzees may well have inherited from a common ancestor the predispositions that have resulted in shared patterns of strife between populations. It is not possible to draw direct comparisons between chimpanzee conflict and human warfare owing to later human elaborations of culture, use of symbols (e.g., national flags), and language. But it is important and intriguing to speculate on the fundamental issues that may have led to the development of similar patterns in both species. And it is equally intriguing to consider why bonobos do not appear to exhibit these behavioral patterns to a similar degree.

Primate Cultural Behavior

One important trait that makes primates, and especially chimpanzees and bonobos, attractive as models for behavior in early hominids may be called *cultural behavior*. Although many cultural anthropologists and others prefer to use the term *culture* to refer specifically to human activities, most biological anthropologists feel that it is appropriate to use the term in discussions of nonhuman primates as well.

Undeniably, there are many aspects of culture that are uniquely human, and one must be cautious in interpreting nonhuman animal behavior. But again, as humans are products of the same evolutionary forces that have produced other species, they can be expected to exhibit some of the same *behavioral patterns* seen in other species, particularly primates. However, because of increased brain size and learning capacities, humans express many characteristics to a greater degree. We would argue that the *aptitude for culture*, as a means of adapting to the natural environment, is one such characteristic.

Among other things, cultural behavior is *learned*, and it is passed from generation to generation—not biologically, but through learning. Whereas humans deliberately teach their young, nonhuman primates (with the exception of a few reports) do not appear to do so. But at the same time, like young nonhuman primates, human children also acquire tremendous knowledge, not from instruction, but through observation.

Just as primate infants, through observing their mothers and others, learn about appropriate behaviors as well as food items, they also learn to use and modify objects to achieve certain ends. In turn, their own offspring will observe their activities. What emerges is a *cultural tradition* that may eventually come to typify an entire group or even a species.

Two famous examples of cultural behavior were seen in a study group of Japanese macaques on Koshima Island. In 1952, Japanese researchers began provisioning the 22-member troop with sweet potatoes. The following year, a young female named Imo began washing her potatoes in a freshwater stream prior to eating them. Within three years, several monkeys had adopted the practice, but they had switched from using the stream to taking their potatoes to the ocean nearby. Perhaps they liked the salt seasoning.

In 1956, the Koshima primatologists began scattering wheat grains onto the sandy beach, and again, Imo introduced a novel behavior. Instead of picking out wheat grains one at a time (as the researchers had expected), Imo picked up handfuls of grain and sand and dropped them together into the water. The sand sank, the wheat kernels floated, and the inventive Imo simply scooped them off the water and ate them. Just as with potato washing, others adopted Imo's technique until the new behavior eventually became common throughout the troop.

The researchers proposed that dietary habits and food preferences are learned and that potato washing and wheat floating were examples of nonhuman culture. Because these practices arose as innovative solutions to problems, and they gradually spread through the troop until they became traditions, they were seen as containing elements of human culture.

Among chimpanzees we see more elaborate examples of cultural behavior in the form of *tool use*. This point is very important, for traditionally, tool use (along with language) was said to set humans apart from other animals.

Chimpanzees insert twigs and grass blades into termite mounds in a practice called "termite fishing" (Fig. 11–9). When termites seize the twig, the chimpanzee withdraws it and eats the attached insects. Chimpanzees modify some of their stems and twigs by stripping the leaves—in effect, manufacturing a tool from the natural material. Chimps can, to some extent, alter objects to a "regular

FIGURE 11-9

(a) Female chimpanzee using a tool to "fish" for termites at Gombe National Park, Tanzania. (b) A chimpanzee at the Sacramento Zoo also uses a tool in the same manner as free-ranging animals.

(a)

(b)

and set pattern" and have been observed preparing objects for later use at an out-of-sight location (Goodall, 1986, p. 535). For example, a chimpanzee will very carefully select a piece of vine, bark, twig, or palm frond and modify it by removing leaves or other extraneous material, then break off portions until it is the proper length. Chimpanzees have also been seen making these tools even before the termite mound is in sight.

All this preparation has several implications. First, the chimpanzees are engaged in an activity that prepares them for a future (not immediate) task at a location spatially removed, which implies planning and forethought. Second, attention to shape and size of raw material indicates that chimpanzee toolmakers have a preconceived idea of what the finished product needs to be in order to be useful. To produce a tool, even a simple tool, based on a concept is an extremely complex behavior. Scientists previously believed that such behavior was the exclusive domain of humans, but now we must question this very basic assumption.

Chimps also crumple and chew handfuls of leaves, which they dip into the hollow of a tree where water has accumulated. Then they suck the water from their newly made "leaf sponges," water that otherwise would have been inaccessible to them. Leaves are also used to wipe substances from fur; twigs are sometimes used as toothpicks; stones may be used as weapons; and various objects, such as branches and stones, may be dragged or rolled to enhance displays. Lastly, sticks or leaves are used as aids in processing mammalian prey, but with one exception these practices appear to be incidental. The one exception, observed in chimpanzees in the Tai forest (Ivory Coast), is the frequent use of sticks to extract marrow from long bones (Boesch and Boesch, 1989).

Chimpanzees in numerous West African study groups use hammerstones with platform stones to crack nuts and hard-shelled fruits (Boesch et al, 1994). Wild capuchin monkeys smash objects against stones (Izawa and Mizuno, 1977), and their use of stones in captivity (both as hammers and *anvils*) has been reported (Visalberghi, 1990). (Stones serve as anvils when fruit or other objects are bashed against the rock surface.) In nature, chimpanzees are the only nonhuman animal to use stones both as hammers and anvils to obtain food. They are the only nonhuman primate that consistently and habitually makes and uses tools (McGrew, 1992).

Chimpanzees exhibit regional variation regarding both the types and methods of tool use. Use of stone hammers and platforms is confined to West African groups. Likewise, at central and eastern African sites, termites are obtained by means of stems and sticks, while at some West African locations, it appears that no tools are used in this context (McGrew, 1992).

Regional dietary preferences are also noted for chimpanzees (Nishida et al., 1983; McGrew, 1992). For example, oil palms are exploited for their fruits and nuts at many locations, including Gombe, but even though they are present in the Mahale Mountains, they are not utilized by chimpanzees. Such regional patterns in tool use and food preferences that are not related to environmental variation are reminiscent of the cultural variations characteristic of humans.

McGrew (1992) presents eight criteria for cultural behaviors in nonhuman species (Table 11–1). Of these, the first six were established by the pioneering cultural anthropologist Alfred Kroeber (1928); the last two were added by McGrew and Tutin (1978). McGrew (1992) demonstrates that Japanese macaques meet the first six criteria. However, all the macaque examples have developed, in some way, from human interference (which is not to say they all resulted directly from human intervention). To avoid this difficulty, the last two criteria were added.

TABLE 11–1	Criteria for Cultural Acts in Other Species
Innovation	New pattern is invented or modified.
Dissemination	Pattern is acquired (through imitation) by another from innovator.
Standardization	Form of pattern is consistent and stylized.
Durability	Pattern is performed without presence of demonstrator.
Diffusion	Pattern spreads from one group to another.
Tradition	Pattern persists from innovator's generation to the next.
Nonsubsistence	Pattern transcends subsistence.
Naturalness	Pattern is shown in absence of direct human influence.

Adapted from Kroeber, 1928, and McGrew and Tutin, 1978. In McGrew, 1992.

Chimpanzees unambiguously meet the first six criteria, although not all groups meet the last two because most study groups have had to be at least minimally provisioned. However, all criteria are met by at least some chimpanzees in some instances (McGrew, 1992). While it is obvious that chimpanzees do not possess human culture, we cannot overlook the implications that tool use and local traditions of learned behavior have for early hominid evolution.

Utilizing sticks, twigs, and stones enhances chimpanzees' ability to exploit resources. Learning these behaviors occurs during infancy and childhood, partly as a function of prolonged contact with the mother. Also important in this regard is the continued exposure to others provided by living in social groupings. These statements also apply to early hominids. While sticks and unmodified stones do not remain to tell tales, surely our early ancestors used these same objects as tools in much the same manner as do chimpanzees.

While chimpanzees in the wild have not been observed modifying the stones they use, the male bonobo Kanzi (see p. 274) has learned to strike two stones together to produce sharp-edged flakes. In a study conducted by Sue Savage-Rumbaugh and archeologist Nicholas Toth, Kanzi was allowed to watch as Toth produced stone flakes, which were then used to open a transparent plastic food container (Savage-Rumbaugh and Lewin, 1994). Although bonobos apparently do not commonly use objects as tools in the wild, Kanzi readily appreciated the utility of the flakes in obtaining foods. Moreover, he was able to master the basic technique of producing flakes without having been taught the various components of the process, but his progress was slow. Eventually Kanzi realized that he could overcome his difficulties by throwing a stone onto a hard floor, causing it to shatter, thus providing an abundance of cutting implements. Although his solution was not necessarily the one that Savage-Rumbaugh and Toth expected, it did serve as an excellent example of bonobo insight and problem-solving capability. Moreover, Kanzi did learn to produce flakes by striking two stones together, and these flakes were then used to obtain food. Not only is this behavior an example of tool manufacture and tool use, albeit in a captive situation, it is also a very sophisticated goal-directed activity.

Human culture has become the environment in which modern *Homo sapiens* lives. Quite clearly, use of sticks in termite fishing and hammerstones to crack nuts is hardly comparable to modern human technology. However, modern human technology had its beginnings in the kinds of cultural behaviors we observe in other primates. This does not mean that nonhuman primates are "on their way" to becoming human. Remember, evolution is not a goal-directed enterprise, and if it were, nothing dictates that modern humans necessarily constitute an evolutionary goal. Such a conclusion is purely a "species-centric" view and has no validity in discussions of evolutionary processes.

Moreover, nonhuman primates have probably been capable of certain cultural behaviors for millions of years. As we have stated, the common ancestor that humans share with chimpanzees undoubtedly used sticks and stones to exploit resources and perhaps as weapons. These behaviors are not newly developed in our close relatives; rather, they have only been recently documented by humans. Further analysis of these capabilities in nonhuman primates in their social and ecological context may elucidate more clearly how cultural traditions emerged in our lineage.

Primate Conservation

Probably the greatest challenge facing primatologists today is the urgent need to preserve in the wild what remains of free-ranging primate species. Without massive changes in public opinion and in the economics of countries with surviving rainforests, it will not be long before there are only a few nonhuman primate species left in the world. Indeed, over half of all living nonhuman primates are now in jeopardy, and some are facing almost immediate extinction in the wild (see Box 11–1).

Population estimates of free-ranging primates are difficult to obtain, but some species (hapalemur, diadem sifaka, aye-aye, lion tamarin, muriqui, red colobus subspecies, lion-tailed macaque, and mountain gorilla) now number only in the hundreds. Others are believed to be represented in the wild by a few thousand (agile mangabey, mentawi langur, red colobus subspecies, moloch gibbon, Kloss' gibbon, orangutan, lowland gorilla, chimpanzee, and bonobo) (Mittermeier and Cheney, 1987).

There are three basic reasons for the worldwide depletion of nonhuman primates: habitat destruction, hunting, and live capture either for export or local trade. Underlying all three causes is one major factor: unprecedented human population growth, which is occurring at a faster rate in developing countries than in the developed world.

Approximately 90 percent of all primates live in the tropical forests of Africa, Asia, and Central and South America, the same areas where most of the world's developing countries are found (Fig. 11–10). Currently, these countries are cutting their forests at a rate of 25 to 50 million acres per year (Mittermeier, 1982). Put another way, worldwide, 1 acre is lost every second! In Brazil, only between 1 and 5 percent of the original Atlantic forest remains, the rest having been destroyed mostly within the last 20 to 30 years (Mittermeier and Cheney, 1987).

Much of the motivation behind the devastation of the rainforests is, of course, economic: the short-term gains from clearing forests to create immediately available (but poor) farmland or ranchland; the use of trees for lumber and paper products; and large-scale mining operations (with their necessary roads, digging, etc., all of which cause habitat destruction). Regionally, the loss of rainforest ranks as a national disaster for some countries. For example, the West African nation Sierra Leone had an estimated 15,000 square miles of rainforest earlier in this century. Today, only 535 square miles remain. At least 70 percent of this destruction has occurred since World War II (Teleki, 1986). People in many developing countries are also short of fuel and frequently use whatever firewood is obtainable; it is estimated that 1.5 billion people in the Third World are

BOX 11–1

Primates in Danger*

About one-fourth of all living primate species live on the African continent; that is 50 to 60 of the world's total of 180 to 200 species. Although Africa is a large continent, nonhuman primates inhabit a relatively small area of it, and much of it is greatly threatened from expanding agriculture and commercial lumbering.

The basic problem in Africa can easily be seen from the following:

1. Forest land is diminishing; for example, of the 49,900 km² of forests in southern Ivory Coast in 1966, only 33,000 km² remained in 1974, a loss of 31 percent in only eight years.
2. The human population rate increased over 3 percent for the 1980–1990 decade.
3. The food supply is decreasing because of environmental factors, inefficient agricultural techniques, and lack of capital resources. From 1970 to 1980, annual food production declined by a rate of 1.1 percent per capita.

As a result of the increase in human population size and lack of a similar increase in the rate of food production, there is agricultural pressure on forests. Where pressures on forest land are not great, monkeys and apes are often hunted for food. It is possible that by the end of the century, numerous nonhuman primate subspecies could be extinct if significant action is not taken to reverse the forces currently acting against them. An informed guess is that in 50 years time, in the absence of major conservation action, about *half the African primate fauna* could be extinct or verging on extinction.

What can be done? Some suggestions: Identify the most urgent conservation priorities; educate all involved as to the meaning, value, and practice of primate (and other resource) conservation; establish more effective wildlife reserves in forest areas; work in close collaboration with African countries; demonstrate to Africans, especially residents of rural Africa, that conservation *can* provide them with tangible benefits.

*Adapted from John Oates.

African Primates in Danger of Extinction

Species/Subspecies Common Name	Location	Estimated Size of Remaining Population	Species/Subspecies Common Name	Location	Estimated Size of Remaining Population
Barbary macaque	North Africa	23,000	Preuss' red colobus	Cameroon	8000
Tana River mangabey	Tana River, Kenya	800–1,100	Bouvier's red colobus	Congo Republic	?
Sanje mangabey	Uzungwa Mts., Tanzania	1,800–3,000	Tana River red colobus	Tana River, Kenya	200–300
Drill	Cameroon, Bioko	?	Uhehe red colobus	Uzungwa Mts., Tanzania	10,000
Preuss' guenon	Cameroon, Bioko	?	Zanzibar red colobus	Zanzibar	1,500
White-throated guenon	Southwest Nigeria	?	Mountain gorilla	Virunga Volcanoes (Rwanda, Uganda, and Zaire) and Impenetrable Forest (Uganda)	550–650
Pennant's red colobus	Bioko	?			

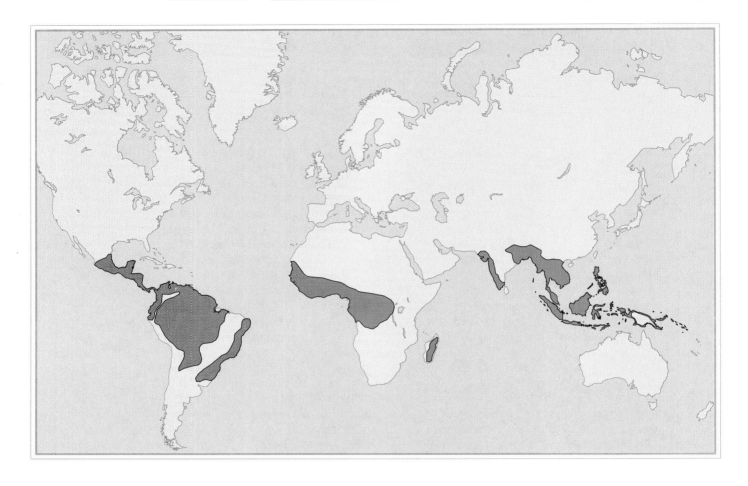

FIGURE 11–10

Tropical rain forests of the world (distribution before recent, massive destruction).

short of fuelwood (Mittermeier and Cheney, 1987). Moreover, we must point out that the demand for tropical hardwoods (e.g., mahogany, teak, and rosewood) in the United States, Europe, and Japan creates a market for rainforest products.

Hunting of primates occurs for numerous reasons. Primates are an important source of food for people in parts of Asia, Africa, and South America, where malnutrition and undernutrition are increasingly serious problems. In these areas, thousands of primates are killed annually to feed growing human populations. (It is sobering to consider that the horrible starvation so well publicized in recent years in Ethiopia and Somalia is increasingly common in many regions of the world.) Primates are also killed for commercial products, such as skins, skulls, and other body parts. Although it is illegal for tourists from the United States and several other countries to return home with such products, the trade flourishes.

Primates have also been captured live for zoos, biomedical research (see Issue, this chapter), and the exotic pet trade. Live capture has declined dramatically since the implementation of the Convention on Trade in Endangered Species of Wild Flora and Fauna (CITES) in 1973. Currently 87 countries have signed this treaty, agreeing not to allow trade in species listed by CITES as being endangered. However, even some CITES members are still occasionally involved in the illegal primate trade (Japan and Belgium, among others).

Fortunately, steps are being taken to ensure the survival of some species. Many developing countries, such as Costa Rica and the Malagasy Republic

(Madagascar), are designating national parks and other reserves for the protection of natural resources, including primates. It is only through such practices and through educational programs that many primate species have a chance of escaping extinction, at least in the immediate future.

If you are in your 20s or 30s, you will probably live to hear of the extinction of some of our marvelously unique and clever cousins. Many more will undoubtedly slip away unnoticed. Tragically, this will occur in most cases, before we have even had the opportunity to get to know them.

Each species on earth is the current result of a unique set of evolutionary events that, over millions of years, has produced a finely adapted component of a diverse ecosystem. When it becomes extinct, that adaptation and that part of biodiversity is lost forever. What a tragedy it will be if, through our own mismanagement and greed, we awaken to a world without chimpanzees, mountain gorillas, or the tiny, exquisite lion tamarin. If and when this day comes, we truly will have lost a part of ourselves, and we will be the poorer for it.

Summary

Various aspects of nonhuman primate behavior and adaptation have been discussed as they pertain to modern humans and to human evolution. Such capacities as efficient communication (including language), affiliation, intergroup aggression, and cultural behavior are explained within an evolutionary framework. Although this does not imply that in mammals, and especially primates, there are genes for specific behaviors, it does suggest that genes may have mediating effects on behavior, perhaps through such products as hormones. Moreover, these capabilities and the similarity of their expression in many primate species argue for their adaptive significance in complex social settings.

Language and tool use, like most human capacities, can be seen as elaborations of patterns observed in many nonhuman primates. Humans reflect their evolutionary heritage as primates and stand as one component of a biological continuum. It is this evolutionary relationship, then, that accounts for many of the behaviors we have in common with prosimians, monkeys, and apes. Finally, we briefly discussed the problems facing nonhuman primates today and some of the steps being taken to protect those populations remaining in the wild.

Questions for Review

1. How can aspects of human behavior be explained in terms of biological evolution without necessarily postulating that complex behaviors are under *strict* genetic control?
2. How is body size in primates related to diet and metabolism?
3. What is meant by encephalization? Give an example of how this concept would be useful in comparing different primate species.
4. What is seen as the basic social unit among all primates? Why is it so important?
5. What are ritualized behaviors? Give an example.
6. Explain how natural selection acts to enhance the communicatory role of some behaviors. Give an example.
7. How does human language differ from most nonhuman communication? What is the evidence to suggest that some nonhuman primates share certain language abilities seen in humans?
8. Briefly discuss neurological changes that occurred in human evolution that relate to language function.

9. Discuss the language acquisition studies using chimpanzees, bonobos, and gorillas. What are the implications of this research?
10. Discuss three ways nonhuman primates can communicate information to other group members. Name at least two "threat gestures."
11. Name two ways in which nonhuman primates communicate reassurance.
12. Discuss an example of between-group aggression. What is thought to have motivated the violence between two groups of chimpanzees at Gombe?
13. Discuss two examples of nonhuman primate cultural behavior. Why is our discovery of these behaviors important to studies of early human evolution?
14. Discuss the major problems facing wild populations of nonhuman primates today.

Suggested Further Reading

Cartmill, Matt. 1990. "Human Uniqueness and Theoretical Content in Paleoanthropology: *International Journal of Primatology* 11(3): 173–192.

Cheney, Dorothy L., and Robert M. Seyfarth. 1990. *How Monkeys See the World*. Chicago: University of Chicago Press.

de Waal, Frans B.M. 1995. "Bonobo Sex and Society." *Scientific American* 272(March): 82–88.

Goodall, Jane. 1986. *The Chimpanzees of Gombe*. Cambridge, MA. The Belknap Press of Harvard University Press.

King, Barbara J. 1994. *The Information Continuum: Social Information Transfer in Monkeys, Apes, and Hominids*. Santa Fe: SAR Press.

McGrew, W. C. 1992. *Chimpanzee Material Culture*. Cambridge, England: Cambridge University Press.

Savage-Rumbaugh, S., and Roger Lewin. 1994. *Kanzi: The Ape at the Brink of the Human Mind*. New York: Wiley.

Smuts, Barbara B., Dorothy L. Cheney, Robert M. Seyfarth, Richard W. Wrangham, and Thomas T. Struhsaker (eds.). 1987. *Primate Societies*. Chicago: University of Chicago Press.

Internet Resources

Laboratory Primate Newsletter
http://www.brown.edu/Research/Primate/current.html
(Excellent quarterly newsletter with articles pertaining to various aspects of research involving captive nonhuman primates. Topics include conservation, enrichment, and funding. Also has listings of current primate research projects. Current and back issues available. Articles are fully reproduced on-line.)

Primate Newsletters
http://night.primate.wisc.edu/pin/newslett.html
(Links to numerous primate newsletters. Fully reproduced articles covering a wide range of topics concerning primate behavior and conservation. Many of these newsletters pertain to particular species only and are very informative.)

Primate Info-Net
http://uakari.primate.wisc.edu:70/1/pin
(Includes listings of primate newsletters, meeting calendars, educational resources, information on endangered species, current research projects, and much more.)

Primates in Biomedical Research: Ethics and Concerns

The use of nonhuman animals for experimentation is an established practice, long recognized for its benefits to human beings as well as to nonhuman animals. Currently, an estimated 17 to 22 million animals are used annually in the United States for the testing of new vaccines and other methods of treating or preventing disease, as well as for the development of innovative surgical procedures. Nonhuman animals are also used in psychological experimentation and in the testing of consumer products.

Because of biological and behavioral similarities shared with humans, nonhuman primates are among those species most desired for biomedical research. According to figures from the United States Department of Agriculture (USDA), 42,620 primates were used in laboratory studies in 1991. On average, about 50,000 are used annually, with approximately 3,000 being involved in more than one study. The most commonly used primates are baboons, vervets, various macaque species, squirrel monkeys, marmosets, and tamarins. Because they are more costly than other species (such as mice, rats, rabbits, cats, and dogs), primates are usually reserved for medical and behavioral studies and not for the testing of consumer goods such as cosmetics or household cleaners. (It should be noted that many cosmetic compa-

nies assert that they no longer perform tests on animals.)

Although work with primates has certainly benefited humankind, these benefits are expensive, not only monetarily but in terms of suffering and animal lives lost. The development of the polio vaccine in the 1950s serves as one example of the costs involved. Prior to the 1950s, polio had killed and crippled millions of people worldwide. Now the disease is almost unheard of, at least in developed nations. But included in the price tag for the polio vaccine were the lives of 1.5 *million* rhesus macaques, mostly imported from India.

Unquestionably, the elimination of polio and other diseases is a boon to humanity, and such achievements are part of the obligation of medical research to promote the health and well-being of humans. But at the same time, serious questions have been raised about medical advances made at the expense of millions of nonhuman animals, many of whom are primates. Indeed, one well-known primatologist, speaking at a conference a few years ago, questioned whether we can morally justify depleting populations of threatened species solely for the benefit of a single, highly overpopulated one.

This question will seem extreme, if not absurd, to many readers, especially in view of the fact that the majority of people would argue that

whatever is necessary to promote human health and longevity is justified.

Leaving the broader ethical issues aside for a moment, one area of controversy regarding laboratory primates is housing. Traditionally, lab animals have been kept in small metal cages, usually one or two per cage. Cages are usually bare, except for food and water and they are frequently stacked one on top of another, so that their inhabitants find themselves in the unnatural situation of having animals above and below them, as well as on each side.

The primary reason for small cage size is simple. Small cages are less expensive than large ones and they require less space (space is also costly). Moreover, sterile, unenriched cages (i.e., lacking objects for manipulation or play) are easier, and therefore cheaper to clean. But for such curious intelligent animals as primates, these easy-to-maintain facilities result in a deprivation that leads to depression, neurosis and psychosis. (The application of these terms to a nonhuman context is criticized as being anthropomorphic by many who believe that nonhuman animals, including primates, cannot be said to have psychological needs.)

Chimpanzees, reserved primarily for AIDS and hepatitis B research, probably suffer more than any other species from inadequate facilities. In 1990, Jane Goodall published a description of conditions she encountered in one lab she visited in Maryland. In this facility, she saw 2- and 3-year-old chimpanzees housed, two together, in cages measuring 22 inches square and 24 inches high. Obviously, movement for these youngsters was virtually impossible, and they had been housed in this manner for over three months. At this same lab and others, adult chimps, infected with HIV or hepatitis, were confined alone for several years in small isolation chambers, where they rocked back and forth, seeing little and hearing nothing of their surroundings.

Fortunately, conditions are improving. There has been increased public awareness of existing conditions; and there is, among some members of the biomedical community, a growing sensitivity toward the special requirements of primates.

In 1991, amendments to the Animal Welfare Act were enacted to require all labs to provide minimum standards for the humane care of all "warm-blooded" animals. (For some reason, this category does not include birds, mice, and rats.) These minimum standards provide specific requirements for cage size based on weight of the animal. For example, primates weighing less than 2.2 pounds must have 1.6 square feet of floor space per animal and the cage must be at least 20 inches high. Those weighing more than 55 pounds are allotted at least

25.1 square feet of floor space per animal and at least 84 inches (7 feet) of vertical space.

Clearly, the enclosures described above are not sufficiently large for normal locomotor activities, and this could certainly contribute to psychological stress. One method of reducing such stress is to provide cages with objects and climbing structures (even part of a dead branch is a considerable improvement and costs nothing). Several facilities are now implementing such procedures. Also, many laboratory staffs are now trained to provide enrichment for the animals in their care. Moreover, the Maryland lab that Dr. Goodall observed no longer maintains chimpanzees in isolation chambers. Rather, they are now housed with other animals in areas measuring 80 cubic feet and are provided with enrichment devices.

Aside from the treatment of captive primates, there continues to be concern over the depletion of wild populations in order to provide research animals. Actually, the number of wild-caught animals used in research today is small compared to the numbers lost to habitat destruction and hunting for food (see p. 284). However, in the past, particularly in the 1950s and 1960s, the numbers of animals captured for research were staggering. In 1968, for example, 113,714 primates were received in the United States alone!

Fortunately, the number of animals imported into the United States has declined dramatically

since the Convention on Trade in Endangered Species (CITES) was ratified in 1973 (see p. 286). In 1984, for example, the United States imported 13,148 primates (Mittermeier and Cheney, 1987). On average, the United States annually imports some 20,000 (some from breeding colonies in the country of origin). Although it would be best if no free-ranging primates were involved, at least these figures represent a substantial improvement since the 1960s.

It is important to note that biomedical research accounts for only a small part of the demand for primates captured in the wild. The exotic pet trade provides a much greater share of the market, both locally and internationally. But even more important is the hunting or live capture of primates for human consumption. This is especially true in parts of West Africa and Asia. Moreover, in several Asian countries there is a growing demand for animal (including primate) products (body parts such as bones or brain tissue) for medicinal purposes.

In response to concerns for diminishing wild populations and regulations to protect them, a number of breeding colonies have been established in the United States and other countries to help meet demands for laboratory animals. Additionally, in 1986, the National Institutes of Health established a National Chimpanzee Breeding Program to provide chimpanzees primarily for AIDS and hepatitis B research.

Furthermore, in 1989, the United States Fish and Wildlife Service upgraded the status of wild chimpanzees from "threatened" to "endangered." The endangered status was not applied to animals born in captivity, but the upgrade was intended to provide additional protection for free-ranging populations. Unfortunately, even with all the policies now in place, there is no guarantee that some wild-born chimps will not find their way into research labs.

The animal rights movement has been described by many in the scientific community as "anti-science," or "anti-intellectual." Certainly, there are extremists in the animal rights movement for whom these labels are appropriate. But to categorize in this manner all who have concern for animals and, in this case, primates, is unjustified. There are many concerned members of the biomedical and scientific communities, including the authors of this text, to whom these labels do not apply.

It is neither anti-science nor anti-intellectual to recognize that humans who derive benefits from the use of nonhuman species have an obligation to reduce suffering and provide adequate facilities for highly intelligent, complex animals. This obligation does not necessitate laboratory break-ins. But improvement does mean that individual members of the biomedical com-

munity must become yet more aware of the requirements of captive primates. Moreover, those involved in primate testing, and the granting agencies that fund them, should be kept well informed as to the status of wild primate populations. Lastly, and perhaps most importantly, existing laws that regulate the capture, treatment, and trade of wild-caught animals *must* be more strictly enforced.

Undoubtedly, humankind has much to gain by using nonhuman primates for experimentation. But we also have a moral obligation to ensure their survival in the wild, as well as to provide them with humane treatment and enriched captive environments. But most of all, we owe them respect as complex, intelligent, and sensitive animals who are not that different from ourselves. If we grant them this, the rest should follow.

Sources

Goodall, Jane. 1990. *Through a Window*. Boston: Houghton-Mifflin.

Holden, Constance. 1988. "Academy Explores Use of Laboratory Animals." *Science*. 242 (October): 185.

Mittermeier, R. A., and D. Cheney. 1987. "Conservation of Primates in their Habitats," in *Primate Societies*, Smuts, B., et al., eds., pp. 477-496. Chicago: University of Chicago Press.

United States Department of Agriculture. Subchapter A—Animal Welfare. Washington, D.C.: U.S.Government Printing Office, Publication Number 311-364/60638, 1992.

Note: We would like to express special appreciation to Dr. Shirley MacGreal, President, International Primate Protection League, and to Dr. Thomas L. Wolfle, Director, Institute of Laboratory Animal Resources, for providing information for this issue.

Critical Thinking Questions

1. What do you see as the benefits derived from using nonhuman primates in biomedical research? Have you personally benefited from this type of research? If so, how?

2. Do you personally have concerns regarding the use of nonhuman primates in biomedical research? Explain your views.

3. Delineate the issues surrounding habitat enrichment for laboratory primates. Do you think enrichment is an important concern? Why or why not? If so, how would you address this issue, bearing in mind that there are constraints on funding?

4. What do you see as solutions to the problem of depletion of wild populations of nonhuman primates? Your answer should be practical and should take into consideration the needs of humans and limited financial resources.

12

Primate Evolution

Introduction

In Chapters 8 through 11, you were introduced to the timescale of evolution and to placental mammals—particularly the primate order. We now turn to the fossil history of primates over the last 60 million years. With what you now know of primate anatomy (teeth, limbs, etc.) and social behavior, you will be able to "flesh out" the bones and teeth that make up the evolutionary record of primate origins. In this way, the ecological adaptations and evolutionary relationships of these fossil forms to each other (and to contemporary primates) will become more meaningful. Note that when we look at primate evolution, we are looking at our own evolution as well.

Timescale

A brief review of the geological timescale will be helpful in understanding primate evolution during the Cenozoic.

Before discussing the fossil primates, we should caution that the formal taxonomic names for the various families and genera are horrendous to pronounce and even harder to remember. Unfortunately, there is no other adequate way to discuss the material. We must make reference to the standard nomenclature. As an aid, we suggest you refer to the margin notes, pronunciation guide, and glossary for those names considered most significant.

Era	Epoch	Approximate Beginning Date (millions of years ago)
Cenozoic	Pleistocene	1.8
	Pliocene	5
	Miocene	22.5
	Oligocene	34
	Eocene	55
	Paleocene	65

Before we go further, we should add a word of caution. In this and subsequent chapters, we trace fossil forms in chronological order and conclude with the appearance of modern humans. However, this chronological sequence is not meant to imply that evolution led to an ultimate goal. Evolution is not a goal-directed process. Nor is there anything in evolution that is analogous to *progress*. More recent organisms are not "better" than more ancient ones. *Homo sapiens* is not inherently superior to other primates or, for that matter to any other organism. Many students think of evolution as having deliberately and inevitably led to *Homo sapiens*. This misconception is a common one and is in part reinforced by the organization of this text and the courses for which it is intended. However, this organization, beginning with earlier forms and concluding with modern humans, is a function of the topical (and unavoidably anthropocentric) nature of anthropology, and it has nothing whatsoever to do with "evolutionary progress." Thus, it is important to remember that the particular series of events (mutations, specific environmental selective factors, the influence of genetic drift, etc.) that resulted in *Homo sapiens* (and all other species) was unique, largely accidental, and obviously, could happen only once.

Early Primate Evolution

The roots of the primate order go back to the base of the rapid placental mammal radiation, circa 65 million years ago. At this time, the earliest primates were diverging from quite early, primitive placental mammals. As discussed in Chapter 9, classifying even the living primates on the basis of clearly defined characteristics is not an easy task. The further back we go in the fossil record, the more primitive and, in many cases, the more generalized the fossil primates become. Such a situation makes classifying very early members of the primate order all the more difficult.

As a case in point, the earliest identifiable primates were long thought to be a Paleocene group known as the plesiadapiforms. Among the best known of this widespread extinct lineage was the genus *Plesiadapis*. However, even for the better known of these fossil forms, the evidence was generally quite fragmentary, based mostly on jaws and teeth. In just the last decade more complete remains of plesiadapiforms have been discovered in Wyoming, including a nearly complete cranium and several elements from the hand and wrist.

As a result of new analyses of this more complete evidence, the plesiadapiforms have been removed from the primate order altogether. From distinctive features (shared derived characteristics) of the cranium and hands, these Paleocene mammals are now thought to be closely related to the colugo. (The colugo is sometimes called a "flying lemur," a name that is an unfortunate misnomer, as this animal is not a lemur and does not fly, but glides.) This group of unusual mammals is probably closely linked to the early roots of primates, but had apparently already diverged by Paleocene times.

Given these new and major reinterpretations, which basically discard everything that had been *assumed* about early primates, we are left with extremely scarce traces of the beginnings of the primate radiation. Some paleontologists have suggested that other recently discovered bits and pieces from the Paleocene of North Africa (Morocco) *may* be that of a primitive, very small primate. Until more evidence is found, and remembering the lesson of the plesiadapiforms, it is best, at present to withhold judgment.

Ancient Landscapes and Early Primate Evolution

The distribution and the eventual fate of early primate forms is understandable only within the context of the environments in which these animals lived. First and foremost, we must remember that 60 m.y.a. landmasses were not arranged as they are today. As we discussed on page 191, the continents have "drifted" to their present position, carried along on the shifting plates of the earth's surface.

During the late Mesozoic, the huge conglomerate landmass called Pangea began to break up into northern and southern continents. To the north, the regions that later became North America, Europe, and Asia formed Laurasia; to the south, Africa, South America, Australia, India, and Antarctica comprised Gondwanaland (see Fig. 8–4a). Throughout the Mesozoic, the two basic landmasses continued to move, with Gondwanaland breaking up into the southern continents. In the north, the continents also were separating, but North America and Europe continued to be connected through Greenland and would remain

close to each other for several million years. As we will see, this "northern connection" had a very significant influence on the geographical distribution of
early primates. In fact, North America and Europe remained in close proximity
until mid-Eocene times (circa 45 m.y.a.) (see Fig. 8–4b).

What makes all this geological activity relevant to primate (and other paleontological) studies is that land-living animals could cross over land bridges, but
were effectively cut off by water barriers. Thus, some species of Paleocene "pri-
matelike" mammals as well as species of early Eocene primates are found in *both*
North America and Europe. As far as primates go, then, from their earliest beginnings (65+ m.y.a.) up until 40 m.y.a., they were mostly limited to North America,
Europe and North Africa, between which some migration was still possible.
With further continental movements, the "New World" and "Old World"
became completely separated, influencing the evolutionary histories of primates
still living today (see p. 227).

As the continents moved, climatic conditions changed dramatically. In the
Mesozoic and into the early Cenozoic, the continental masses were clustered
closer to the equator, and as Laurasia in particular moved north, its climate
cooled. Moreover, the fragmenting of the landmasses and the consequent altering of marine flow patterns (less exchange between northern and southern seas)
caused the climate to cool even further.

Finally, these climatic shifts also heavily affected plant communities. Rather
than the primitive, mostly tropical flora characteristic of the Mesozoic (ferns,
palms, etc.), the Cenozoic was a time of rapid radiation of new varieties of plants,
including flowering plants, deciduous trees, and grasses. Many of these plants
were pollinated by insects. As insects thus became more abundant, so did the
animals who fed on them, including early primates. The world was never to be
the same again.

Clearly, then, it is extremely important to interpret primate evolution within
the context of the earth's changing environments.

Eocene Primates (55–34 m.y.a.)

Prosimian Radiation

The first fossil forms that are clearly identifiable as primates appeared during the
Eocene. A wide variety of primate fossils have been recovered from the early
Eocene, and they all can generally be called "prosimian" (they broadly resemble
lemurs and lorises). Indeed, the Eocene can be viewed as the heyday of prosimians, with more than 60 genera recognized from the 21-million-year span of this
epoch. This time period exhibited the widest geographical distribution and
broadest adaptive radiation ever displayed by prosimians. Indeed, four times as
many prosimian genera have been recognized among the available Eocene sample than are known for the world today (16 living genera, with 10 of these confined to Madagascar).

The best known of the Eocene prosimians are members of the lemurlike family, Adapidae, which includes some 10 genera. The four best known of these are:

Cantius	North America and Europe
Adapis (Ad´-a-pis)	Europe
Notharctus (Noth-ark´-tus)	North America
Smilodectes (Smi-lo-dek´-teese)	North America

Some of these animals have been known from fossil evidence for a remarkably long time. In fact, the initial discovery of *Adapis* was made in France in 1821 and first described by Cuvier (see p. 26).

As mentioned, all these animals are fairly lemurlike in general adaptive level and show distinctive primate tendencies. For example, they all have a complete postorbital bar, larger, rounder braincases, nails instead of claws, and eyes that are rotated forward, allowing overlapping fields of perception and thus binocular vision. In the limb skeleton, further developments in prehensility are suggested, and some evidence points to the presence of an opposable large toe. In all these respects, we see the typical primate adaptive strategies allowing exploitation of an arboreal environment. Whereas these forms resemble lemurs in overall anatomical plan, they do not show the same specializations seen in contemporary lorises and lemurs, such as development of the dental comb (see p. 219).

The separate evolution of the Madagascar (Malagasy) lemurs (see p. 220) may date to late Eocene times, but since this island was already isolated by a deep channel from mainland Africa, they apparently reached their island sanctuary by unintentionally floating over on drifting debris.

The other major group of Eocene prosimians is included in the family **Omomyidae**, known from numerous specimens of jaws and teeth. Omomyids are the most widely distributed of the known Eocene prosimians, with discoveries in North Africa and Europe and a few specimens from Asia as well.

▲ Omomyidae
(oh´-moh-my´-eh-dee)

The earlier members of the family are somewhat more generalized than the later ones and may form an ancestral basis for all later anthropoids—that is, New World monkeys, Old World monkeys, apes, and hominids (Fig. 12–1). Additionally, it has been suggested that some of the omomyids from the late Eocene of Europe are closely related to the tarsier. However, many of the similarities noted are apparently superficial ones, not necessarily indicating any unique (i.e., shared derived) relationship (Fleagle, 1988). Nevertheless, at least one feature, the position of the olfactory portion of the brain, links these Eocene forms with later haplorhines (see p. 217). Also of interest is the fact that from later epochs (the Oligocene in Egypt and the Miocene in Thailand), there are forms that quite clearly share tarsierlike affinities.

In recent years, numerous finds of Eocene prosimians, representing several more genera, have been recovered in North Africa and in the Middle East. Some of these new discoveries are quite distinctive and thus probably belong to still other new families. From some of these remains, E. L. Simons, of Duke University, disputes an omomyid origin of anthropoids, instead suggesting members of the adapid family as more likely candidates. That anthropoids did in fact evolve from *some* prosimian, and that they had already done so in late Eocene times, has become increasingly clear in recent years, largely owing to highly successful excavations led by Simons.

Early Anthropoids

The area where E. L. Simons and his colleagues have had remarkable success for the last three decades is the Fayum Depression in Egypt, 60 miles southwest of Cairo (Fig. 12–2). This site, usually simply called the **Fayum**, is today an extremely arid region 100 miles inland. But in late Eocene and Oligocene times, the Fayum was located closer to the Mediterranean shore and was traversed by meandering streams crisscrossing through areas of tropical rain forest. The relatively speedy sedimentation along the river channels and the subsequent arid conditions have produced highly favorable conditions for the preservation of fossils,

▲ Fayum
(fah-yoom´) A locality in Egypt yielding very abundant fossil primate finds from the late Eocene and early Oligocine (circa 36–33 m.y.a.).

FIGURE 12–1

Summary, early primate evolution.

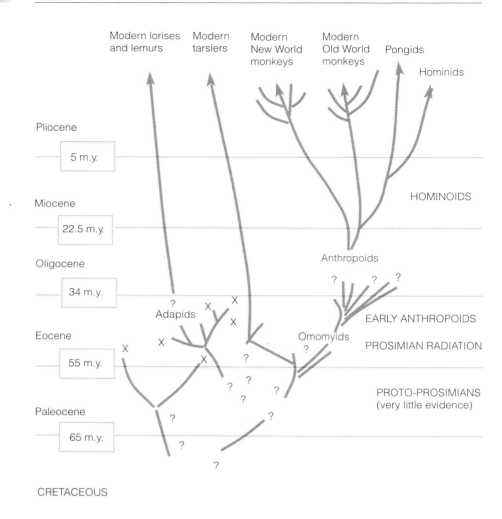

making the Fayum the most productive area anywhere in the world for this time period.

Altogether, thousands of specimens have been recovered from the Fayum, some of the most exciting just since 1988. In a previously unexplored locality, called Quarry L-41, discoveries dated to the late Eocene (circa 36–34 m.y.a.) record an early and surprisingly diverse radiation of early anthropoids. In addition to two new genera of prosimians from Quarry L-41, an additional six new genera of early anthropoids (four from this same locality; two from another Fayum site) have been proposed by Simons and his associate, Tab Rasmussen, of Washington University in St. Louis (Simons and Rasmussen, 1994). With so much material recovered so recently, interpretations are understandably quite provisional. From a general perspective, all the early Fayum anthropoids are thought to have been quite small-bodied and are hypothesized to have eaten a mixed diet of fruits and insects.

The best known of these early anthropoid forms is assigned to the genus *Catopithecus*. This primate is represented at the Fayum by numerous dental remains, a nearly complete cranium (a rare and important find), and two limb bones (the latter provisionally assigned to this genus). From these remains, several of what are thought to be shared derived characteristics linking them with anthropoids are apparent: closure of the back of the orbit, fusion of the midline

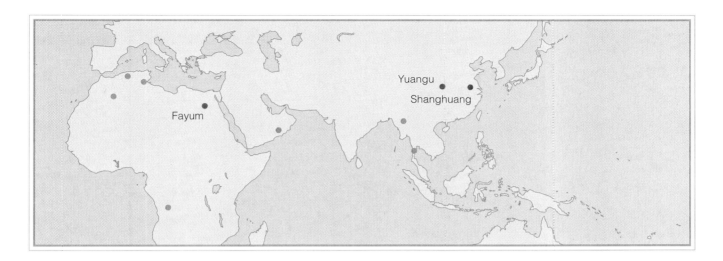

of the frontal into a single bone; anchoring of the eardrum by a bone hoop to the wall of the ear; and rounded cusps on the lower molar teeth. Nevertheless, mixed in with these derived features are other primitive retained characteristics reminiscent of prosimians (including a long snout and a small brain).

Moreover, a number of other recent finds from a variety of widely scattered sites have yielded finds of other potential early anthropoids. These discoveries, in addition to those from Egypt, come from Morocco, Algeria, Tunisia (possibly the earliest of the lot), Angola, Oman, Thailand, Burma (these remains were actually found back in the 1920s), and China (see Fig. 12–2 and Table 12–1). The last of these discoveries, recently announced by Christopher Beard, of the Carnegie Museum of Natural History in Pittsburgh, and his associate Qi Tao, of the Institute of Vertebrate Paleontology and Paleoanthropology in Beijing, is perhaps the most interesting and is certainly the most controversial. First given the name *Eosimias* ("dawn monkey") in 1994, the initial finds from Shanghuang were extremely fragmentary and thus not very convincing to most researchers. However, from sites along central China's Yellow River, much more complete fossils (including the complete upper and lower dentition of an individual) were unearthed in 1995 (Beard et al., 1996). Beard, Tao, and other Chinese scientists are confident that their interpretations of *Eosimias* as an early anthropoid as well as the dating of the sites are correct. Still, many skeptics remain, especially as the new specimens (as of this writing) have not yet become available for critical evaluation. Moreover, the race to find "the earliest anthropoid" still continues, with numerous North African contenders still in the running (remains from Algeria and Tunisia may well be older then *Eosimias*).

New World Monkeys

The center of action for primate evolution after the close of the Eocene is confined largely to the Old World, for only on the continents of Africa and Eurasia can we trace the evolutionary development of apes and hominids. However, the New World, while geographically separated from the Old World, was not completely devoid of anthropoid stock, for here the New World monkeys evolved in their own right.

FIGURE 12–2

Localities of fossil discoveries of possible early anthropoids. (Fossil remains from Fayum and Jiangsu are discussed in the text; for a tabulation of fossils recovered from the other localities, see Table 12–1).

TABLE 12–1	Fossil Discoveries of Potential Eocene Early Anthropoids	
Site	**Genus**	**Comments**
Egypt: Fayum: Quarry L-41	*Catopithecus* *Proteopithecus* *Serapia* *Arsinoea*	Many specimens, including complete cranium
Fayum: Quarry E	*Oligopithecus* *Qatrania*	Many specimens, mostly teeth
Algeria: Gilib Zegdou	*Algeripithecus* *Tabelia*	Isolated teeth
Gour Lazib	*Azilblus*	One jaw fragment
Bir el Ater	*Biretia*	One tooth
Tunisia: Chambri	*Djebelemur*	One jaw fragment; isolated teeth
Angola: Malembe	*Propliopithecus*	One tooth
Oman: Thaytiniti	*Indeterminate*	Two teeth
Burma: Pakokku District	*Amphipithecus* *Pondaungria*	Jaw fragment with teeth Three jaw fragments (first described in 1920s)
Thailand: Krabi Basin	*Indeterminate*	Jaw fragment with two teeth
China: Jiangsu Province (Yuangu and Rencun)	*Eosimias*	Parts of three lower jaws, one almost complete

Any discussion of New World monkey evolution and its relation to Old World anthropoid developments must consider crucial geological events, particularly continental drift. In the late Eocene and early Oligocene, South America was an island continent separate from North America and Africa. In such a geological context, the introduction of monkeys into South America poses a certain problem. As already mentioned, some authorities have postulated that because the distance between South America and Africa was not as great as it is today, monkeys, originating in Africa, could have rafted to the New World (Gavan, 1977; Ciochon and Chiarelli, 1980).

In any case, the likelihood that Old and New World primates shared any evolutionary history after the early Oligocene is minimal. There is no trace of Old World primates anywhere in the New World following this time until fully modern *Homo sapiens* walked into the New World during the late Pleistocene.

While primate fossils abound in the Western Hemisphere (particularly North America) from the Eocene, the record is extremely sparse later on. For the entire span of Oligocene to late Pleistocene, we have only a few bits and pieces—a jaw fragment from Bolivia, a nearly complete skull from Texas, several specimens from southern Argentina, and a few other small fragments from Colombia and Jamaica. Together, all the evidence comprises barely a dozen individuals. Thus, tracing the evolutionary heritage of New World monkeys with any degree of certainty is a difficult task.

Old World Anthropoids

The focus of our attention will henceforth exclusively be the Old World (Europe, Asia, Africa), for this is where our ancestors have lived for the past 34 million years. This evolutionary and geographical fact is reflected in the grouping of Old World anthropoids (Old World monkeys, apes, and humans) into a common infraorder (Catarrhini) separate from the infraorder for New World monkeys (Platyrrhini).

Oligocene (34–22.5 m.y.a.)

From the currently available fossil evidence, it is clear that a great deal of diversification occurred during the Oligocene. By the end of the Oligocene, cercopithecoid and hominoid lineages had diverged from their last common ancestor. No doubt, diverse species of anthropoids were adapting to varied ecological niches in Africa and probably Asia and Europe as well.

Unfortunately, however, for the entire Oligocene epoch, the vast majority of Old World primate fossils comes from just one locality, the Fayum in Egypt—the same area that has yielded abundant late Eocene remains. In fact, since the Fayum deposits (dated 36–33 m.y.a.) straddle the Eocene/Oligocene boundary, it is somewhat arbitrary to separate the fossil finds by epoch (i.e., for practical purposes, just think of all the Fayum primate material as late Eocene/early Oligocene).

For the entire and extremely diverse Fayum primate fossil sample, Simons (1995) and colleagues have named 11 separate genera (with a total of 21 different species). Of these 11 genera, 6 are placed among the anthropoids and 5 are considered prosimians. Altogether, well over a thousand specimens have been retrieved from the Fayum, representing a paleontological record of what was once an extremely rich primate ecosystem (indeed, primates are the most abundant mammals retrieved here). We will now discuss the three best known of the later primate forms (all grouped as anthropoids) that are geologically placed within the early Oligocene (circa 34–33 m.y.a.).

Apidium (Two Species)

The most abundant of the Oligocene fossil forms from the Fayum belong to the genus *Apidium*, represented by about 80 jaws or partial dentitions and over 100 postcranial elements. This animal, about the size of a squirrel, had several anthropoid-like features, but also shows quite unusual aspects in its teeth. *Apidium*'s dental formula (see p. 213) is 2-1-3-3, which indicates a retained third premolar not found in any contemporary Old World anthropoid. For that matter, extremely few fossil anthropoids in the Old World have a third premolar. Some researchers suggest, therefore, that this genus and its close relatives (together

▲ *Apidium*
(a-pid´-ee-um)

called the parapithecids) may have appeared at or even *before* the divergence of Old and New World anthropoids. As noted, *Apidium* is represented by a large array of specimens, both dental and from the limb skeleton. The teeth suggest a diet composed of fruits and probably some seeds. In addition, preserved remains of the limbs indicate that this creature was a small arboreal quadruped, adept at leaping and springing (Table 12–2).

Propliopithecus (Four Species)

Among the first fossils found at the Fayum was an incomplete *Propliopithecus* mandible recovered in 1907. Unfortunately, since detailed geological and pale-ontological methods were not yet developed, the precise geological position of this form is not known.

Morphologically, this fossil represents a quite generalized Old World anthro-poid, displaying a 2-1-2-3 dental formula. In almost every relevant respect, this early *Propliopithecus* form is quite primitive, not showing particular derived ten-dencies in any direction. All *Propliopithecus* species appear small to medium in size (8 to 13 pounds) and were most likely fruit eaters.

Aegyptopithecus (One Species)

Among the most completely represented and significant fossil genera from the Fayum is *Aegyptopithecus*, which is known from several well-preserved crania of differently-aged individuals as well as numerous jaw fragments and several limb bones (most of which have been found quite recently). The largest of the Fayum anthropoids, *Aegyptopithecus* was roughly the size of a modern howler, 13 to 18 pounds (Fleagle, 1983). *Aegyptopithecus* is important because, better than any other fossil primate, it bridges the gap between the Eocene prosimians on the one hand and the Miocene hominoids on the other.

With a dental formula of 2-1-2-3, *Aegyptopithecus* shows the familiar Old World anthropoid pattern. More detailed aspects of the dentition possibly align this Oligocene form with the Miocene hominoids (which we shall discuss shortly), but the evolutionary affinities are not presently well established. In most respects, the dentition is primitive for an Old World anthropoid, without specifi-cally derived features in either the hominoid or Old World monkey direction.

TABLE 12–2 Inferred General Paleobiological Aspects of Fayum Anthropoids				
	Weight Range	**Substratum**	**Locomotion**	**Diet**
Apidium	850–1,600 g* (2–3 lb)	Arboreal	Quadruped; active runner and leaper	Fruit, seeds
Propliopithecus	4,000–5,700 g (8½–9 lb)	Arboreal	Quadruped	Fruit
Aegyptopithecus	6,700 g (15 lb)	Arboreal	Quadruped	Fruit, some leaves?

*g = grams (after Fleagle, 1988; Simons, 1995)

Recently there has been a change in interpreting Old World monkey dental evolution. It was previously believed that the dental patterns (particularly, the molar cusp pattern) seen in Old World monkeys were the more *primitive*, and conversely, the Y-5 seen in hominoids (Fig. 12–3) was more *derived* from the ancestral **catarrhine** condition. Reevaluation of the fossil materials now suggests that the Old Word monkey pattern is more derived, and the hominoid cusp arrangement is the more primitive (Fig. 12–4).

Establishing the "polarities" of primitive versus derived characteristics is crucial to making sound evolutionary interpretations. However, the patterns of evolutionary change are not always easy to ascertain. The determination of the ancestral dental patterns in Old World anthropoids is only one example. In the subsequent section on Miocene hominoids, we will encounter several further dilemmas in sorting out such issues.

Even more primitive than the teeth of *Aegyptopithecus* is the skull, which is small and resembles the skull of a monkey in some details (Fig. 12–5). Brain size and relative proportions can be reconstructed from internal casts of the crania thus far discovered. It appears that the brain was somewhat intermediate between that of prosimians and that of anthropoids. The visual cortex was large compared to prosimians, with concomitant reduction of the olfactory bulbs, but the frontal lobes were not especially expanded. Even considering the relative small size of this animal, the brain—estimated at only 30 to 40 cm^3 (Radinsky, 1973)—was by no means large.

Evidence from the limb skeleton also reveals nothing particularly distinctive. From analysis of limb proportions and muscle insertions, primatologist John Fleagle (1983) has concluded that *Aegyptopithecus* was a short-limbed, heavily muscled, slow-moving arboreal quadruped (see Table 12–2).

Further detailed study of *Aegyptopithecus* anatomy has even allowed primatologists to speculate about the social behavior of this ancient primate. For instance, dental remains from different individuals vary greatly in canine size. This fact implies that male-female differences (sexual dimorphism) were quite marked. Such sexual dimorphism in modern primates is frequently associated with polygynous mating patterns and competition among males for mates. Thus, we may infer that these behaviors were typical of *Aegyptopithecus*.

▲ **Catarrhine**
The group (infraorder) comprising all Old World anthropoids, living and extinct.

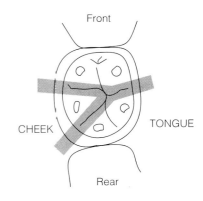

FIGURE 12–3
The Y-5 pattern. A characteristic feature of hominoid lower molars.

FIGURE 12–4
Establishing polarities in character states among Old World anthropoids.

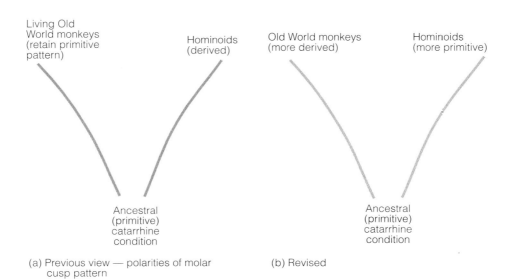

(a) Previous view — polarities of molar cusp pattern

(b) Revised

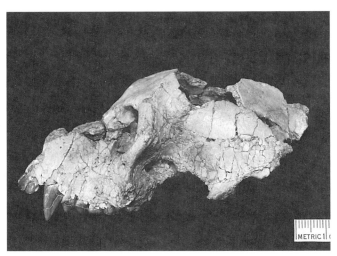

FIGURE 12–5

Aegyptopithecus *skull from the Fayum, Egypt. Oligocene c. 33 m.y.a. Discovered in 1966. (a) Front view. (b) Side view.*

All in all, *Aegyptopithecus* presents a paleontological *mosaic*. In most respects, it is quite primitive as an Old World anthropoid and could potentially be an ancestor of *both* Old World monkeys and hominoids. There are some slight yet suggestive clues in the teeth that have led some researchers (most notably, E. L. Simons) to place *Aegyptopithecus* on the hominoid line. Primarily because of the primitive aspects of this creature, other researchers (Fleagle and Kay, 1983) are not as convinced.

Early Fossil Anthropoids: Summary

The spectacular array of fossils from the Fayum in the period between 36 m.y.a. and 33 m.y.a. demonstrates that anthropoids radiated along several evolutionary lines. As with the earlier primate fossil material from the Eocene, the fragmentary nature of the Oligocene fossil assemblage makes precise reconstruction of these evolutionary lines risky.

Given the primitive nature of these fossil forms, it is wise, for the present, not to conclude specifically how these animals relate to later primates. In earlier primatological studies (as well as earlier editions of this book), such conclusions were made, but reanalysis of the fossil material from the perspective of primitive versus derived evolutionary modifications has cast serious doubt on many of these interpretations. The new interpretations, however, are still far from certain. As we have mentioned, untangling the polarity of primitive versus derived evolutionary states is a most difficult task. Many paleontologists would like to establish a clear link between these Oligocene fossils (particularly *Propliopithecus* and *Aegyptopithecus*) and the unambiguously hominoid forms of the Miocene. Unfortunately, on the basis of current data, this kind of clarity is not yet possible.

As you may recall from the Oligocene fossil anthropoid forms just discussed, *Apidium* and its close relatives may be placed near or even before the split of Old and New World anthropoids. Such circumstance actually accords quite well with an African origin for New World anthropoids and their reaching South America presumably early in the Oligocene (see p. 294). *Aegyptopithecus* and its relatives (including *Propliopithecus*) are seen by most as preceding the major split in catarrhine (Old World anthropoid) evolution, that is, prior to the divergence of Old World monkeys from the ancestral stock of all hominoids. It would appear, then, based on this circumstantial evidence, that this most major of Old World anthropoid evolutionary splits occurred late in the Oligocene or very early in the Miocene.

Hominoids: Large and Small; African and Asian; Fossil and Modern

Before we discuss the complex history of hominoid evolution, a brief review of the basic evolutionary relationships among the hominoids is in order. While not very diverse at all, the living hominoids (which comprise only 6 genera and 14 species) do serve as a model for most of the major radiations that existed in the past. Based on size, the two major subgroupings are termed *small-bodied* and *large-bodied*; small-bodied varieties comprise the gibbon and siamang and would also include all their ancestors and related side branches back to the time they split from the other major hominoid branch, the large-bodied forms (Fig. 12–6).

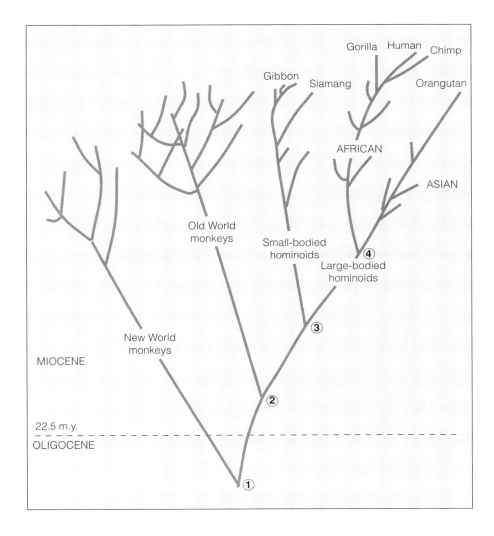

FIGURE 12–6

Major branches in anthropoid evolution.

As we discussed in Chapter 9, there are four genera of large-bodied hominoids living today: *Pongo* (orangutan), *Gorilla, Pan* (chimpanzees and bonobos), and *Homo*. In turn, these four forms can be subdivided into two major subgroups: Asian large-bodied (the orangutan) and African large-bodied (gorillas, chimpanzees, bonobos, and humans). Again, these subgroup designations can be used to denote their respective lineages back to the time when they split from one another.

We can attempt to understand the diversity (and, admittedly, confusing complexity) of the fossil record by reconstructing the fragments and by projecting our conclusions forward to later forms, especially those species living today. Or, we can use the living forms and infer referentially (backward); in so doing, we attempt to highlight the major adaptive radiations that occurred in the past. For example, the increasing refinement of biochemical data obtained from contemporary primates discussed in Chapter 9 is a major advance in the use of such referential models.

One serious drawback exists, however, if we limit ourselves *strictly* to these referential models. Of all the primates that have ever existed, only a small proportion are still living today. As we saw for the Eocene, there were many more varieties of prosimians than survive today. Moreover, during the Miocene, there were many more hominoid species than the few that currently exist. We thus must be very careful not to limit our interpretations to simple models derived from living forms only. Finally, we should not expect all fossil forms to be directly or even particularly closely related to extant varieties. Indeed, we should expect the opposite; that is, most extinct varieties vanish without leaving descendants.

Nevertheless, in combining fossil interpretations (from functional anatomy and ecology) and referential models (especially biochemical data), most primate evolutionists would agree that there have been four major "events" or evolutionary splits in anthropoid evolution prior to the emergence of hominids: (1) between Old World and New World anthropoids; (2) between Old World monkeys and hominoids; (3) between small-bodied and large-bodied hominoids; and (4) between the Asian and African lines of large-bodied hominoids (Fig. 12–6).

Miocene (22.5–5 m.y.a.)— Hominoids Aplenty

If the Eocene was the age of prosimians and the Oligocene the time of great diversity for early anthropoids, the Miocene was certainly the epoch of hominoids.

A great abundance of hominoid fossil material has been found in the Old World from the time period 22–7 m.y.a. The remarkable evolutionary success represented by this adaptive radiation is shown in the geographical range already established for hominoids during this period. Miocene hominoid fossils have been discovered in France, Austria, Spain, the Republic of Slovakia, Germany, Greece, Hungary, China, India, Pakistan, Nepal, Turkey, Saudi Arabia, Uganda, Kenya, and Namibia (Fig. 12–7).

Interpretations of this vast array of fossil material (now including more than 500 individuals and perhaps as many as 1,000) were greatly complicated for several decades owing to inadequate appreciation of the range of biological variation that a single genus or species could represent. As a result, the taxonomic naming of the various fossil finds became a terrible muddle, with close to 30 gen-

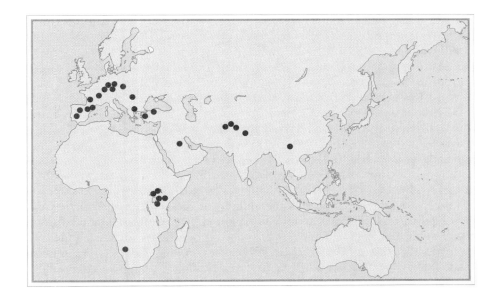

FIGURE 12–7
Miocene hominoid distribution: Fossil sites thus far discovered.

era and over 100 species proposed. The biological implications of such taxonomic enthusiasm were unfortunately not seriously considered. In such an atmosphere, it was possible for two genera to be named—one with only upper jaws represented, the other with only lower jaws, each matching the other!

It is not difficult to understand why such confusion arose if we consider that discoveries of these fossils spanned more than 100 years (the earliest find came from France in 1856) and took place on three continents. Not until the early 1960s did scientists systematically study *all* the material, the result being a considerable simplification of the earlier confusion. As a result of this research, E. L. Simons and David Pilbeam (the latter now at Harvard University) "lumped" the vast majority of Miocene forms into only two genera: one presumably quite "pongid-like" and the other "hominid-like." In just the last few years, however, a tremendous amount of new data has come to light from both new field discoveries and finds in museum collections of previously unrecognized material. Consequently, it is now apparent that the Simons-Pilbeam simplification went too far. Hominoid evolutionary radiation during the Miocene produced a whole array of diverse organisms, many of which have no living descendants (and thus no clear analogue among living higher primates). Indeed, most researchers now recognize again close to 30 genera, but the biological assumptions are much more firmly based (through application of cladistic methods) than was the case earlier in this century. Moreover, there has been a necessary recognition of greater diversity of Miocene forms as a result of the large number of new discoveries.

As these new discoveries are analyzed, many of the perplexing problems concerning Miocene hominoids should be solved. For the moment, it is possible to make only general interpretive statements regarding Miocene hominoid adaptive patterns.

Paleogeography and Miocene Hominoid Evolution

Similar to that of early primate evolution (see p. 295), the factors of changing geography and climates are also crucial to interpretations of the later stages of primate diversification. The Oligocene reveals a proliferation of early Old World anthropoid forms from one area in North Africa. In the early Miocene, the evidence is also restricted to Africa, with fossils coming from rich sites in the eastern part of the continent (Kenya and Uganda). It would thus appear, on the basis of current evidence, that hominoids originated in Africa and experienced a successful adaptive radiation there before dispersing to other parts of the Old World.

The hominoids would maintain this exclusive African foothold for some time. The earliest of these East African hominoid fossils is more than 20 million years old, and later fossil finds extend the time range up to 5 m.y.a. For the first half of this time range, East Africa is thought to have been more heavily forested, with much less woodland and grassland (savanna) than exist today (Pickford, 1983).

As in the earlier Cenozoic, the shifting of the earth's plates during the Miocene played a vital role in primate evolution. Before about 16 m.y.a., Africa was cut off from Eurasia; consequently, once hominoids had originated there in the early Miocene, they were isolated. However, around 16 m.y.a., the African plate "docked" with Eurasia (Bernor, 1983) through the Arabian Peninsula, a contact that was to revolutionize mammalian faunas of the later Miocene. Many forms that originated in Africa, such as elephants, giraffes, and pigs, now migrated into Eurasia (van Couvering and van Couvering, 1976). Apparently, among these mid-Miocene intercontinental pioneers were some hominoids. Since they had evolved in the mainly tropical setting of equatorial Africa, most of the earlier hominoids probably remained primarily arboreal. Accordingly, it has been suggested that to facilitate migration a relatively continuous forest might have been necessary across the Afro-Arabian-Eurasian land bridge.

Ecological changes were, however, already occurring in Africa. By 16 m.y.a., the environment was becoming drier, with less tropical rain forest and more open woodland/bushland and savanna areas emerging (Bernor, 1983; Pickford, 1983). In other words, East African environments were becoming more similar to their current form. With the opportunities thus presented, some African hominoids were almost certainly radiating into these more open niches about 17–16 m.y.a. Part of this adaptation probably involved exploitation of different foods and more ground living than practiced by the arboreal ancestors of these hominoids. Some partly terrestrial, more woodland or mosaic environment–adapted hominoids were probably thus on the scene and fully capable of migrating into Eurasia, even through areas that were not continuously forested.

The environments throughout the Old World were, of course, to alter even more. Later in the Miocene, some of these environmental shifts would further influence hominoid evolution and may have played a part in the origin of our own particular evolutionary lineage, the hominids. More on this later.

Miocene Hominoids—Changing Views and Terminology

Throughout the Miocene, environmental and geographical factors imposed constraints on hominoids as well as opening new opportunities to them. Over a time span of close to 15 million years, hominoids in the middle two-thirds of the Miocene were successful indeed. Once they migrated into Eurasia, they dispersed rapidly and diversified into a variety of species. After 14 m.y.a., we have evidence of widely distributed hominoids from Pakistan, India, Turkey, Greece, Hungary, China, and western Europe. Much of this material has only recently been uncovered and is incredibly abundant. For example, from Lufeng in southern China alone, 5 partial skulls and more than 1,000 teeth have been found in the past 15 years (Wu and Oxnard, 1983). The other areas have also yielded many paleontological treasures in recent years. Moreover, searches through museum collections in East Africa, as well as resurveys of fossil sites, have uncovered yet more fossils (Walker and Teaford, 1989).

Given this abundance of new information, it is not surprising that heretofore existing theories of early hominoid evolution have been reevaluated. In fact, it would not be unfair to describe the last decade as a "revolution" in paleontological views of Miocene hominoid evolution. With a great deal of this recent fossil material still unanalyzed, all the answers are not presently at hand. In fact, the more fossils found, the more complicated the situation seems to become. To simplify matters, we will organize the fossil material primarily on the basis of geography and secondarily on the basis of chronology. Moreover, we will suggest only tentative evolutionary relationships in most cases, as this is the best that can be currently concluded.

African Forms (23–14 m.y.a.)

A wealth of early hominoid fossils has come from the deep and rich stratigraphic layers of Kenya and Uganda. These diverse forms are presently classified within at least two separate families, including perhaps nine different genera (Fleagle, 1988). Indeed, important and mostly new finds (from the 1980s) have been uncovered, suggesting as many as three further hominoid genera in an as-yet-undetermined (and possibly a third) family. In other words, over the 9-million-year period for which we have evidence, as many as 12 different hominoid genera have been sampled from East Africa, with the potential for yet more as the fossil sample accumulates.

Most of the newer material has yet to be described completely, and relationships among specimens are uncertain. The best samples and thus best known forms are those of the genus *Proconsul* (belonging to the proconsulid family) (Fig. 12–8). From the full array of proconsul remains (mostly dental pieces), considerable variation is apparent. Body size estimates range from that of a small monkey (about 10 pounds) to as large as a female gorilla (about 150 to 200 pounds) (Rafferty et al., 1995). Environmental niches were probably also quite varied, for some species were apparently confined to dense rain forests, while others potentially exploited more open woodlands. Some researchers have also suggested considerable diversity of locomotor behaviors, including perhaps some that were at least partly terrestrial (Fleagle, 1988). When on the ground, some of these proconsulids may even have occasionally adopted a bipedal stance (Pilbeam, 1988).

The dentition of all the proconsulid forms is, however, quite uniform, showing the typical Old World anthropoid pattern of 2-1-2-3. Moreover, these forms all display broad upper central incisors and large sexually dimorphic canines. In the molars, the enamel is fairly thick, but the softer dentin below penetrates well into these cusps, so that the enamel wore through fairly quickly with use (Kelly and Pilbeam, 1986). There is also the characteristic hominoid Y-5 pattern of cusps, seen in the lower molars (see Fig. 12–3). We can get some idea of diet from these teeth, which suggest that most forms were probably fruit eaters.

From those well-preserved pieces of crania (representing currently only one species), brain size estimates are at least as large or larger than those for contemporary Old World monkeys (although probably not as large as those for contemporary hominoids). Note, however, that *relative* brain size compared to body size is the crucial feature—a tricky estimate indeed for incomplete fossilized

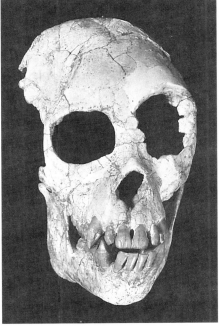

FIGURE 12–3

Proconsul skull, discovered by Mary Leakey in 1948. (From early Miocene deposits on Rusinga Island, Kenya.)

fragments. The surface features of the brain, as inferred from interior surfaces of cranial bones, do not show the derived characteristics of living large-bodied hominoids (Falk, 1983). In fact, they show many primitive hominoid features similar to those seen in gibbon brains (Pilbeam, 1988).

A full understanding of the evolutionary relationships of the East African hominoids has not yet been attained. Indeed, in many cases, the classification still remains a muddle. For example, one fossil (discovered in the 1950s) from Rusinga Island in Kenya has been renamed and reassigned to different evolutionary groups at least six times. Just as paleoanthropologists begin to think that the situation is becoming better defined, new fossil discoveries muddy the waters still further. Some of this new material (discovered in the last decade) may date as early as 18–17 m.y.a., but most of it is in the range 16–14 m.y.a. Thus, for the most part, these finds are *later* than the East African forms just discussed. It is not so surprising, then, to find that the Proconsulids are more primitive hominoids (i.e., less derived). In fact, many primate evolutionists (Andrews, 1985; Pilbeam, 1988) would place these forms before the split of small- and large-bodied hominoids (as shown in Fig. 12–6). Therefore, while some Proconsulid may *not* actually have been the last common ancestor of gibbons as well as all large-bodied hominoids (including ourselves), something resembling it may well have been (Fig. 12–9).

The most important of these somewhat later (Middle Miocene) East African hominoids come from several sites in Kenya dated to approximately 8–7 m.y.a. Several remains of a quite large hominoid, including a partial cranium preserving most of the face, have been assigned to the genus *Afropithecus*. Some features, such as the large central incisors and thick molar enamel, were initially thought to align *Afropithecus* with some of the more derived Asian forms discussed shortly. However, further analysis of the face clearly show that *Afropithecus* shares important anatomical features with the African large-bodied hominoid lineage. Still, there is considerable ambiguity in interpretation that leads to two different hypotheses regarding the evolutionary relationship of this fossil form:

1. These features are shared derived characteristics distinctive of the African large-bodied hominoid lineage. Thus, *Afropithecus* is uniquely related to this group (clade). Furthermore, the evolutionary divergence with the Asian line had *already* occurred (perhaps as early as 18 m.y.a.).
2. These features are primitive characteristics in large-bodied hominoids; thus, *Afropithecus* is an ancestor (or a close relative of such an ancestor) to both later African *and* Asian large-bodied hominoids (and thus the divergence of the two lines could possibly occur well after 18 m.y.a.).

The resolution of these competing interpretations is not yet possible; certainly, further discoveries of better-preserved crania could help. But the real action in contemporary research concerns identification of those derived characteristics that distinguish the various lineages of hominoids from one another and the polarity of these characteristics (as they are transformed between ancestors and potential descendants).

In 1992 and 1993, new finds were announced of a fossil hominoid from an unexpected locale: Namibia, in southwestern Africa. Dated from approximately 13 m.y.a., these new specimens (including a half-portion of a mandible and several postcranial pieces) are just slightly younger than the East African hominoids discussed earlier.

From initial analysis, this specimen clearly appears to be a large-bodied hominoid, perhaps from an animal weighing about 35 pounds. In addition, the

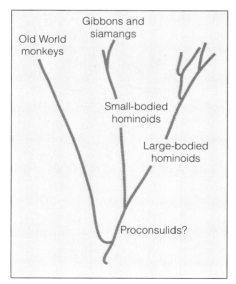

FIGURE 12–9

The probable evolutionary placement of the East African proconsulids prior to the split of small and large-bodied hominoids.

enamel of the molars is quite thin and in this respect quite different from *Afropithecus* (Conroy et al., 1995).

European Forms (13–11 m.y.a.)

Although they are the first of the Miocene hominoids to have been discovered, the European varieties still remain enigmatic. Very few fossils have been discovered, and what has been found consists almost entirely of jaws and lower dentitions. Among the only features that distinguish this varied lot of specimens from France, Spain, Austria (and maybe Hungary, too) is that the molar teeth are thin-enameled (i.e., the dentin penetrates far into the cusps). Most researchers would place all these forms into the genus *Dryopithecus*.

Discovery of similar forms from the Rudabanya Mountains in Hungary during the 1970s has complicated matters further. Initially thought to be similar to the thick-enameled varieties from southern and southwestern Asia (discussed next), the Hungarian fossils are now placed closer to *Dryopithecus* from western Europe. Nevertheless, many researchers still believe that the Rudabanya fossils are probably a distinct genus (*Rudapithecus*) (Kelly and Pilbeam, 1986). It seems unlikely that any of these *Dryopithecus*-group fossils are related closely to any living hominoid.

South/Southwest Asian Forms (16–7 m.y.a.)

Three sites from Turkey have yielded fragmentary fossil hominoid remains dating to the early Middle Miocene (16–14 m.y.a.). As we noted on page 308, following "docking" of the Arabian plate with East Africa about 16 m.y.a., land routes became available for expansion from Africa into Eurasia. It would thus seem, from these Turkish remains, that hominoids quickly took advantage of this route and reached Eurasia by 16 m.y.a. Most researchers would assign these remains to the genus *Sivapithecus*.

Far more complete samples of *Sivapithecus* have been recovered from southern Asia, in the Siwalik Hills of India and Pakistan. Most dramatically, over the last 20 years, paleoanthropologists led by David Pilbeam have recovered numerous excellent specimens from the Potwar Plateau of Pakistan. Included in this superb Pakistani collection is a multitude of mandibles (15 in all, some of which are nearly intact; Fig. 12–10), many postcranial remains (i.e., all skeletal parts except the head), and a partial cranium, including most of the face (Pilbeam, 1982).

Sivapithecus from Turkey and Pakistan was probably a good-sized hominoid, ranging in size from 70 to 150 pounds, and it probably inhabited a mostly arboreal niche. Probably the most characteristic anatomical aspects of *Sivapithecus* are seen in the face, especially the area immediately below the nose (Ward and Kimbel, 1983). Facial remains of *Sivapithecus* from Pakistan and Turkey have concave profiles and projecting incisors (and, overall, remarkably resemble the modern orangutan). In particular, the partial cranium discovered in 1980 at the Potwar Plateau (circa 8 m.y.a.) (Pilbeam, 1982) bears striking similarities to the orangutan (Fig 12–11). The published description of this specimen, with illustrations similar to those shown here, had a tremendous impact on paleoanthropology. As we have seen (p. 234), biochemical evidence demonstrates the distinctiveness of the orangutan from the African apes and humans; here, then, was fossil evidence suggesting some ancient Asian traces of the

FIGURE 12–10

Two Sivapithecus *mandibles from the Potwar Plateau, Pakistan, discovered in 1976 and 1977. Approximate age, 9 million years.*

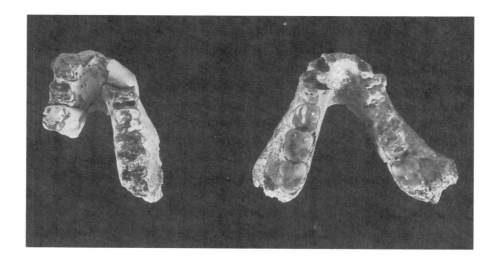

orangutan lineage. As a result, the views of biochemists and paleoanthropologists agree more closely (pp. 316–317).

It must be noted, however, that except for the face and jaw, *Sivapithecus* is *not* like an orangutan. In fact, especially in the postcranium, *Sivapithecus* is distinctively *unlike* an orangutan or any other known hominoid, for that matter. For example, the forelimb suggests a unique mixture of traits, indicating probably some mode of arboreal quadrupedalism but with no suspensory component. In most respects, then, *Sivapithecus* could be described as *highly derived* (Pilbeam, 1986).

FIGURE 12–11

Comparison of a Sivapithecus *cranium (center) with modern chimpanzee (left) and orangutan (right). The* Sivapithecus *fossil is specimen GSP 15000 from the Potwar Plateau, Pakistan, c. 8 m.y.a. (a) Lateral view. (b) Frontal view.*

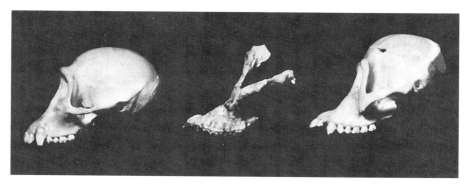

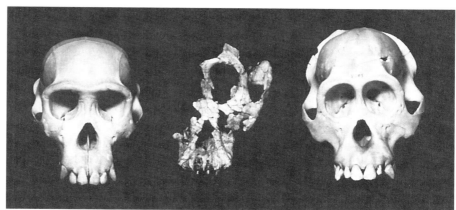

Many earlier fossil-based interpretations of Miocene evolutionary affinities had, of course, to be reevaluated. As we hinted at the beginning of our discussion of Miocene hominoids (p. 307), in the 1960s, E. L. Simons and David Pilbeam suggested a Middle Miocene hominoid as the first hominid (i.e., clearly diverged on the human line and separate from that leading to any extant ape). According to this view, this early hominid was "*Ramapithecus*"*—known at that time mostly from India, with some bits from East Africa.

We have already illustrated some of the dramatic new discoveries of the 1970s and 1980s. As a consequence of these later discoveries, the earlier suggestion that "*Ramapithecus*" was a definite hominid was seriously questioned and has now been rejected altogether. One primary advocate of this revised view is Pilbeam (1982, 1986), an initial architect of the earlier widely accepted theory. Pilbeam, who has led the highly successful paleoanthropological project at the Potwar Plateau, has been swayed by the new fossils recovered there and elsewhere. These more complete specimens (like that shown in Fig. 12–11) are dentally very similar to what had been called "*Ramapithecus*." Researchers now simply lump "*Ramapithecus*" with "*Sivapithecus*."

In summary, then, the fossil remains of *Sivapithecus* from Turkey and India/Pakistan are the most clearly derived large-bodied hominoids we have from the entire Miocene. While some forms (e.g., *Proconsul*) are seemingly quite primitive and others (*Dryopithecus*) are derived in directions quite unlike any living form, *Sivapithecus* has several derived features of the face, linking it evolutionarily with the orangutan. The separation of the Asian large-bodied hominoid line from the African stock (leading ultimately to gorillas, chimps, and humans) thus occurred at least 12 m.y.a. (Pilbeam, 1988) (Figs. 12–12 and 12–13).

Other Miocene Hominoids

Pliopithecus   Another interesting but still not well-understood hominoid is *Pliopithecus*, from the middle and late Miocene of Europe. Since this is a fairly small hominoid (estimated at 11 to 16 pounds; Fleagle, 1988), for several years primatologists suggested that *Pliopithecus* was a gibbon ancestor. Moreover, dental features were also thought to mirror gibbon morphology. However, these similarities are superficial at best. In those respects in which *Pliopithecus* resembles contemporary small-bodied hominoids, the features are all primitive for hominoids in general. In fact, for most relevant anatomical details, *Pliopithecus* is a remarkably primitive hominoid (at least as primitive as *Proconsul*). This is surprising, given its relatively late date and Eurasian distribution (where hominoids are generally more derived than their African cousins). It may be that *Pliopithecus* is a long-surviving descendant of an early Miocene, very primitive ancestor, one that antedated the radiation of major hominoid lineages (Fig. 12–12).

Greece (*Ouranopithecus* 10–9 m.y.a.)   From the Ravin de la Pluie near Salonika, Greece, have come several hominoid specimens (mostly mandibles, but also a partial face) discovered in the 1970s. Because the molar teeth have thick enamel, some researchers initially grouped these finds with *Sivapithecus*. However, analysis of the critical facial anatomy (Kelly and Pilbeam, 1986) has shown that the Greek finds are not similar to *Sivapithecus* (or the orangutan), but

---

*"*Ramapithecus*" is shown in quotes, because the genus is no longer recognized as a legitimate separate entity (i.e., it is not a valid taxon).

FIGURE 12–12

Evolutionary relationships of hominoids.

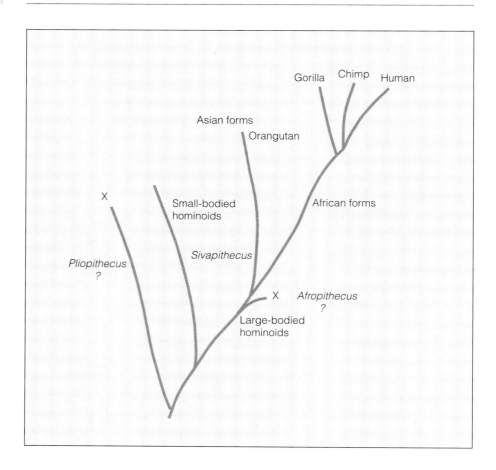

their molar morphology also makes them unlike *Dryopithecus.* The precise evolutionary relationships of this Greek hominoid thus still remain uncertain. Some researchers (de Bonis and Koufos, 1994) have suggested a fairly close link with the hominid line. Others, looking at the same similarities (especially in the face) have hypothesized affinity more generally with the African lineage of large-bodied hominoids.

FIGURE 12–13

Known time ranges of most important miocene hominoid fossil forms*

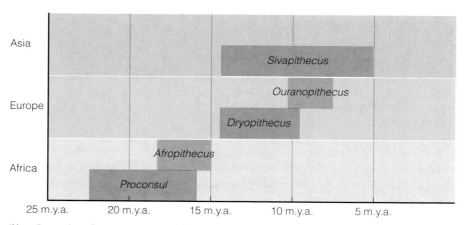

*New discoveries, of course, may extend this range.

Lufeng, Yunnan Province, Southern China (7–6 m.y.a.)   As we mentioned earlier, the recent discoveries from the Lufeng site in southern China have been remarkable, now totaling over 1,000 specimens (including several crania, mostly crushed mandibles, and hundreds of isolated teeth). Since the fossil collection is so large and since the crania are in need of much restoration, most of the material has yet to be fully described. Therefore, conclusions regarding this extremely important fossil collection must remain highly tentative. Indeed, there is still argument concerning how many genera are represented among the Lufeng hominoids, with some experts favoring two, while others see only one. Ongoing interpretation of the dental remains has led some researchers (Kelly and Pilbeam, 1986) to suggest that *only* one species may be represented. If so, this would be an extremely variable species, most likely reflecting extreme sexual dimorphism. In fact, such a degree of sexual dimorphism (at least dentally) would exceed that seen even in the modern orangutan (where males are more than twice the size of females). We have discussed in Chapter 10 (see pp. 256–258) the differing reproductive strategies displayed by contemporary male and female primates. It thus becomes interesting to speculate about the social structure of these apparently highly dimorphic Miocene forms. (*Note*: *Most* Miocene hominoids from East Africa, Europe, and Asia seem to display marked sexual dimorphism.)

Like the relationships among the Greek fossils discussed in the preceding section, the evolutionary relationships of the Chinese specimens are unclear. The Chinese hominoids also do not show the shared derived features of the *Sivapithecus*-orangutan lineage. Determining exactly where they fit thus remains a major challenge for primate evolutionists.

In order to combine all the suggested branching points discussed over the last several pages, we summarize together these suggested evolutionary relationships in Fig. 12–14. The number of question marks indicate continued uncertainty. In other words, treat most of the suggested relationships (all those other than *Sivapithecus*-orangutan) as highly tentative.

The Meaning of Genus and Species

Our discussion of fossil primates has introduced a multitude of cumbersome taxonomic names. We should pause at this point and reasonably ask why we use so many names like *Proconsul*, *Dryopithecus*, and *Sivapithecus*? What does such naming mean in evolutionary terms?

Our goal when applying "genus," "species," or other taxonomic labels to groups of organisms is to make meaningful biological statements about the variation that is present. When looking at populations of living or long extinct animals, we are assuredly going to see variation. This situation is true of *any* sexually reproducing organism owing to the factors of recombination (see Chapter 3) as well as age changes and sexual dimorphism.

Definition of Species

Keeping in mind all the types of variation present within interbreeding groups of organisms, the minimum biological category we would like to define in fossil primate samples is the *species*. As previously defined in Chapter 2, a species is a group of interbreeding or potentially interbreeding organisms that are reproductively

BOX 12–1

Timing the Hominid-Pongid Split

One of the most fundamental of all questions in human evolution is, when did the hominid line originate? Or, to put it another way, when did we last share a common ancestry with our closest living relatives, the African great apes?

Scientists have taken different perspectives in attempting to answer this question. The traditional approach of paleontology is still the most common. Recent years have produced considerably more paleontological sophistication through a vast new array of fossil material, more precise dating, and more rigorous interpretation of primitive and derived characteristics. Still, the fossil record remains incomplete, and significant gaps exist for some of the most crucial intervals. So the question still persists: How old is the hominid line?

Data drawn from a completely different perspective have also been applied to this problem. As advocated by Vincent Sarich and the late Allan Wilson, of the University of California, Berkeley (1967), this perspective utilizes comparisons of living animals. By calibrating the overall immunological reactions of proteins from different species, by sequencing the amino acids within proteins, or by means of DNA hybridization or DNA sequencing (see pp. 233–234), living species can be compared.

Certainly such data are immensely valuable in demonstrating *relative* genetic distances between contemporary organisms (as we discussed in Chapter 9). However, proponents of this view go considerably further and postulate that biochemical distance can be used directly to calculate evolutionary distance. In other words, a "molecular clock" is thought to provide unambiguous divergence dates for a host of evolutionary lineages, including hominids and pongids (Sarich, 1971).

Several hotly disputed assumptions are required, however, to perform this feat. Most important, the rate of molecular evolution must be constant over time. Such regularity could be accomplished if rates of change were constant within a class of proteins or if selection pressures remained constant. Since environmental changes are decidedly not constant through time, the latter assumption is not valid. As for the first point, while neutral mutations certainly do occur (and perhaps do so quite frequently), many researchers are not convinced that most mutations are neutral (e.g., see Livingstone, 1980). Moreover, even if mutations were mostly neutral, major evolutionary shifts may still be quite nongradual in tempo, given the suggested punctuated mode of change (see p. 199).

Another complicating factor concerns generation length. According to strict application of the molecular clock, those species that reproduce in shorter intervals should show, for the same period of time, greater amounts of molecular evolution than more slowly reproducing forms (Vogel et al., 1976). Given the variation in generation lengths, it is not justifiable to make strict linear reconstruction for divergence times among prosimians, monkeys, and hominoids.

In fact, recently collected molecular data (in which DNA sequences are *directly* compared) indicate that the molecular clock does not run constantly with time. Rather, there is a marked *slowdown* in molecular divergence rate among primates, and most especially among the hominoids. Such a

isolated from other such groups. In modern organisms, this concept is theoretically testable by observations of reproductive behavior. In animals long dead, such testing is obviously impossible. Therefore, to get a handle on the interpretation of variation seen in fossil groups like the Miocene hominoids, we must refer to living animals.

The question that must be answered is, What is the biological significance of the variation that is present? Two immediate choices occur: Either the variation is accounted for by individual, age, and sex differences seen within every biological species—**intraspecific**—or the variation represents differences between reproductively isolated groups—**interspecific**. How do we choose between the

▲ **Intraspecific**
Within one species.

▲ **Interspecific**
Between two or more species.

phenomenon is thought to be a function of greater generation length among higher primates when compared to other mammals (Li and Tanimura, 1987).

Another problem is that there is no certain indicator of molecular evolutionary rates; different proteins yield significantly different rates of evolution and thus greatly influence conclusions about divergence times (Corruccini et al., 1980). In fact, the *greatest* margin of error would occur in attempting to calculate relatively recent evolutionary events—for example, the hominid-pongid split.

Analysis of amino acid sequences by another group of biochemists (at Wayne State University in Detroit) has confirmed that, indeed, rates of molecular evolution are not constant, but are instead characterized by periods of acceleration and *deceleration* (the latter being particularly true in the last few million years). Thus, these researchers conclude: "For proteins demonstrating striking shifts in rates of amino acid substitutions over time, it is not possible to calculate accurate divergence dates within Anthropoidea using the molecular clock approach. Our analysis of amino acid sequence data of several proteins by the clock model yields divergence dates, particularly within the Hominoidea, that are far too recent in view of well-established fossil evidence" (Goodman et al., 1983, p. 68).

As a result of such criticisms of the "clock," some paleontologists have been skeptical of its claimed applications. For example, Milford Wolpoff, of the University of Michigan, argues, "Probably the best way to summarize the very disparate points raised is that the 'clock' simply *should not* work" (Wolpoff, 1983b, p. 661).

Naturally, not everyone takes so negative a view of the clock approach. Vincent Sarich continues to believe firmly in its basic accuracy (when applied correctly) and, justifiably, feels vindicated by recent reinterpretations of theories derived from fossil evidence, which bring them closer to the biochemically derived hypotheses.

The fossils themselves are not going to provide the whole answer. The paleontological record is usually too incomplete to provide clear-cut ancestor-descendant associations. More fossils will always help, of course, but the way we think about them (i.e., the questions we raise about them) is also crucial in framing workable theories.

The biochemical perspective has been important in that it has articulated key issues for evolutionary consideration (e.g., the place of the orangutan in relation to other large-bodied hominoids). The interplay between the paleontological and biochemical perspectives has thus been most productive. In fact, these viewpoints agree more now on several aspects of hominoid evolution than they did just a few years ago. The greatest furor has been raised from overly strong claims for the unique validity of either approach. We have shown in this chapter that more fossil evidence *and* more controlled analyses have forced previous views to be reconsidered. Moreover, it is equally unfair to portray the clock approach as a complete answer. As one of the leading advocates of this method has stated, "The clock is one of an approximate, not metronomically perfect nature" (Cronin, 1983, p. 116).

alternatives intra- or interspecific? We clearly must refer to already defined groups where we can observe reproductive behavior—in other words, contemporary species.

If the amount of morphological variation observed in fossil samples is comparable with that seen today *within* contemporary species of closely related forms, then we should not "split" our sample into more than one species. We must, however, be careful in choosing our modern analogues, for rates of morphological evolution vary widely among different groups of mammals. In interpreting past primates, we do best when comparing them with well-known species of modern primates.

FIGURE 12–14
Summary of evolutionary relationships, Miocene hominoids.

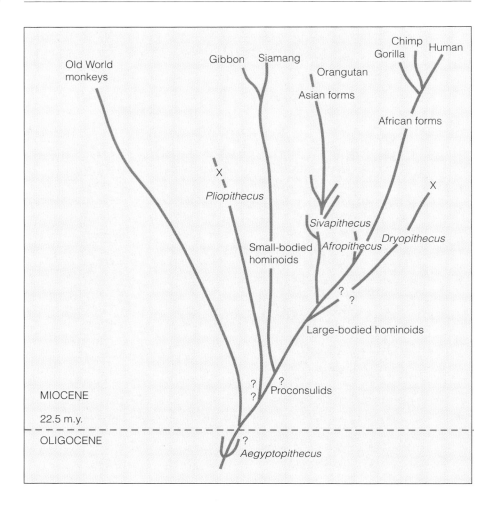

Our evolutionary interpretations of the vast array of variable Miocene hominoids is greatly simplified by adhering to relevant biological criteria:

1. First we must look at *all* relevant material. We are not justified in splitting fossil groups into several species on the basis of only presumed differences in the sample. (Simons' and Pilbeam's contribution was a major step in rectifying this situation for Miocene hominoids.)
2. We must statistically extrapolate the variation observed in our often very small fossil *samples* to realistic dimensions of actual biological *populations*. Every piece of every bone found is part of an individual, who in turn was part of a variable interbreeding population of organisms.
3. We then refer to known dimensions of variation in closely related groups of living primates, keeping in mind expected effects of age, sexual dimorphism, and individual variation.
4. Our next step is to extrapolate the results to the fossil sample and make the judgment: How many species are represented?
5. Since fossil forms are widely scattered in time, we also must place the different species within a firm chronology.
6. Finally, we would like to make interpretations (at least educated guesses) concerning which forms are evolutionarily related to other forms. To do

this, we must pay strict attention to primitive as opposed to derived characteristics.

Following the preceding steps will greatly reduce the kind of confusion that has characterized hominoid studies for so long. We do not, however, wish to convey the impression that the biological interpretation of fossils into taxonomic categories is simple and unambiguous. Far from it! Many complexities must be recognized. Even in living groups, sharp lines between populations representing only one species and populations representing two or more species are difficult to draw. This situation is especially exemplified by the different types of baboons in East Africa. As mentioned in Chapter 9, there are several forms of baboons, two of which, the common baboon and the hamadryas baboon, have partially overlapping ranges. Because there are easily observable physical and behavioral differences between these two types of baboons, they traditionally have been placed in separate species: common baboon (*Papio cynocephalus*) and hamadryas baboon (*Papio hamadryas*). However, numerous examples of hybridization (i.e., mating between the two "species") have been observed. In the wild, interestingly, these *cynocephalus/hamadryas* crosses produce live fertile offspring. Moreover, the behaviors displayed by the hybrids seem to be more similar to the parent they most resemble phenotypically. Thus, what these baboon populations represent is a fluid situation in which some reproductive isolation has begun, but where speciation is not yet complete (see Fig. 8–10 and pp. 198–199). We could then say, regarding these baboons, they represent one species on the verge of becoming two species. But how do we classify animals in such a circumstance? The most conservative approach (especially since the hybrids appear completely fertile) would be simply to group them into one species—a solution, however, that has not been completely implemented by primate researchers.

In contexts dealing with extinct species, the uncertainties are even greater. In addition to the overlapping patterns of variation *over space*, variation also occurs *through time*. In other words, even more variation will be seen in such **paleospecies**, since individuals may be separated by thousands or even millions of years. Applying a strict Linnaean taxonomy to such a situation presents an unavoidable dilemma. Standard Linnaean classification, designed to take account of the variation present at any given time, describes a static situation. But when dealing with paleospecies, we are often involved in great spans of time and thus with much additional variation.

A good example of a paleospecies in the hominid lineage is *Homo erectus*, a fossil form that spans a time period of more than 1 million years. In fact, there are some physical differences between the earlier representatives and those found in more recent contexts (there are also geographical differences to consider). Nevertheless, until recently, most paleoanthropologists have been comfortable grouping all these fossils into one long-lived paleospecies. However, recent analyses are beginning to question this assumption, again illustrating the difficulties involved in this type of study. (We will discuss *Homo erectus* in much more detail later in Chapter 16.) Moreover, the issues raised here regarding classification are fundamental to all the interpretations relating to hominid evolution.

Where do we establish meaningful species boundaries in such a temporally dynamic situation? Often, our task is made easier because of the incompleteness of the fossil record. Quite frequently, fossil samples are separated by great gaps of time (as between A and C in Fig. 12–15), and the morphological differences may also be clear-cut. In such a case, we feel quite comfortable calling these different species. But what about fossil populations (e.g., B) that are intermediate in both time and morphology? This question has no easy answer. Any taxonomic

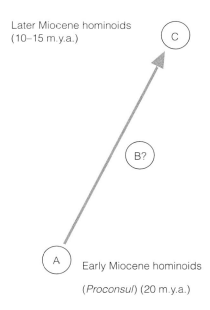

FIGURE 12–15

Evolution in a continuing evolving lineage (an anagenetic line). Where does one designate the different species?

▲ **Paleospecies**

Groups of organisms recognized in the fossil record that are classified within the same species. Their temporal range may extend over a considerable period.

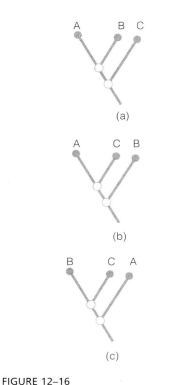

FIGURE 12–16

Cladograms. Three alternative statements representing evolutionary relationships among three taxa. (a) C diverges earliest, with A and B sharing a more recent common ancestor. (b) B diverges earliest, with A and C sharing a more recent common ancestor. (c) A diverges earliest, with B and C sharing a more recent common ancestor.

designation in such a continuously evolving lineage is by necessity going to be arbitrary.

Such a line, which shows no evidence of speciation events, is referred to as anagenetic. For such a lineage, many evolutionary biologists see no point in making separate species designations; that is, the entire line is seen as a single paleospecies (Eldredge and Cracraft, 1980). Many biologists believe, in fact, that long, gradual transformations of this type are not the rule and that branching (i.e., speciation) is much more typical of evolutionary change (once again, a view consistent with punctuated equilibrium; see p. 199).

Moreover, it is imperative in evolutionary interpretation to understand ancestor-descendant relationships. Most paleontologists have traditionally made anatomical comparisons and then immediately constructed evolutionary trees (also called *phylogenies*). Recently, another perspective has been advanced. In this approach a detailed interpretation of primitive versus derived states must first be explicitly stated. Only then can patterns of relationships be shown.

These evolutionary patterns are best interpreted in the form of a *cladogram* (a set of relationships shown as a hypothesis). In fact, several cladograms can usually be constructed from the same set of data (Fig. 12–16). Those seen as most economically explaining the patterns of derived characteristics are then provisionally accepted, while less adequate ones are rejected. Such a perspective has been termed *cladistics* (see p. 188) and has injected a good deal more objectivity into paleontology (Eldredge and Cracraft, 1980). It must be pointed out, however, that not all paleontologists have accepted this approach. A basic assumption of cladistic analysis is that trait *patterns* are developed as the result of ancestor-descendant relationships and that parallelisms (i.e., the *independent* development of similar characteristics in different lineages) are not so common as to be overly confusing, and when they do occur, they should usually be identifiable. In primate evolution, these assumptions may pose some practical difficulties; an analysis of morphological features in lemurs and lorises showed that 80 percent of the traits studied displayed some parallelism (Walker et al., 1981).

Definition of Genus

The next level of formal taxonomic classification, the *genus*, presents another problem. To have more than one genus, we obviously must have at least two species (reproductively isolated groups), and, in addition, the species must differ in a basic way. A genus is therefore defined as a group of species composed of members more closely related to each other than they are to species from another genus.

Grouping contemporary species together into genera is largely a subjective procedure wherein degree of relatedness becomes a mostly relative judgment. One possible test for contemporary animals is to check for results of hybridization between individuals of different species—rare in nature but quite common in captivity. If two normally separate species interbreed and produce live, though *not* necessarily fertile, offspring, this process shows genetically that they are not too distant and that they probably should be classified into a single genus. Well-known examples of such interspecific crosses within one genus are horses with donkeys (*Equus caballus* × *Equus asinus*) and lions with tigers (*Panthera leo* × *Panthera tigris*). In both these cases, the close morphological and evolutionary similarities (as well as similar chromosomal arrangements) between these species are confirmed by their occasional ability to produce live (although usually infertile) hybrids.

As mentioned, we cannot perform breeding experiments with animals that are extinct, but another definition of genus becomes highly relevant. Species that are members of one genus share the same broad adaptive zone, or, in Sewall Wright's terminology (Mayr, 1962), a similar "adaptive plateau." What this represents is a general ecological lifestyle more basic than the particular ecological niches characteristic of species. This ecological definition of genus can be an immense aid in interpreting fossil primates. Teeth are the most often preserved parts, and they are usually excellent general ecological indicators. Therefore, if among the Miocene hominoids some animals appear to inhabit different adaptive/ecological zones (for example *Proconsul* versus *Sivapithecus*), we are justified in postulating more than one genus present.

Operationally, then, categorization at the genus level becomes the most practical biological interpretation of fragmentary extinct forms. While in the past species differences necessarily were also present, these are usually too intricate to recognize in incomplete fossil material.

As a final comment, we should point out that classification by genus is also not always a clear-cut business. Indeed, the ongoing discussion among some primate biologists over whether chimpanzees and gorillas represent one genus (*Pan troglodytes*, *Pan gorilla*) or two different genera (*Pan troglodytes*, *Gorilla gorilla*) demonstrates that even with living animals the choices are not always clear. For that matter, some researchers—pointing to the very close *genetic* similarities between humans and chimps—would place these in the same genus (*Homo sapiens*, *Homo troglodytes*). When it gets this close to home, it gets even more difficult to be objective!

Summary

In this chapter, we have traced the evolutionary history of our primate origins between 60 and 5 m.y.a. Beginning in the late Cretaceous, the earliest primate ancestors were probably little more than arboreally adapted insectivores. In the Paleocene, there are, as yet, still no clearly derived primate forms apparent (despite prior claims to the contrary). In the following epoch, the Eocene, we begin to see an abundant diversification of primates that are readily identifiable. During this epoch, the lemurlike adapids begin their evolutionary radiation. As recent evidence from the Fayum and elsewhere has demonstrated, early anthropoid origins also date to sometime in the late Eocene. In addition, Old and New World primates apparently shared their last common ancestry in the Eocene or early Oligocene and have gone their separate ways ever since.

In the Old World, the Oligocene reveals a large number of possible early anthropoid ancestors again at the Fayum. By and large, all these are primitive Old World anthropoids, and none of the modern lineages (Old World monkeys, gibbons, large-bodied hominoids) can definitely be traced into the Oligocene.

The Miocene reveals an incredibly abundant and highly complex array of hominoid forms, many of large-bodied varieties. More than 10 different genera and probably dozens of species are represented in those remains discovered in Africa, Asia, and Europe. Some early forms from Kenya and Uganda (the Proconsulids) are more primitive than the majority of hominoids from Eurasia. While again there is little firm evidence tying these fossil forms to living apes or to humans, some tentative evidence suggests that *Sivapithecus* is closely related to the ancestors of the orangutan. Where, then, are the ancestors of the African apes or, even more relevant, of ourselves? In the next six chapters, we will seek to answer this question.

Questions for Review

1. Why is it difficult to distinguish the earliest members of the primate order from other placental mammals? If you found a nearly complete skeleton of an early Paleocene mammal, what structural traits might lead you to hypothesize it was a primate?
2. Compare the fossil primates of the Eocene with living members of the primate order.
3. If you (as an expert physical anthropologist) were brought remains of a fossil hominoid from South America purported to be 30 million year old, why might you be skeptical?
4. What kinds of primates were living at the Fayum in Oligocene times? What does it mean to say that they were primitive catarrhines?
5. Compare and contrast the anatomical features of proconsulids with *Sivapithecus*.
6. How did the shifting of the earth's plates, as well as climatic changes, affect hominoid evolution in the Miocene?
7. What is meant by "small-bodied" hominoids compared to "large-bodied" hominoids?
8. If two fossil groups are classified as *Sivapithecus inducus* and *Sivapithecus sivalensis*, at what taxonomic level is the distinction being made? What are the biological implications?

Suggested Further Reading

Conroy, Glenn. 1990. *Primate Evolution*. New York: Norton

Fleagle, John G. 1988. *Primate Adaptation and Evolution*. New York: Academic Press

Simons, E. L., and Tab Rasmussan. 1994. "A Whole New World of Ancestors: Eocene Anthropoideans from Africa." *Evolutionary Anthropology* 4:128–139

Internet Resources

Currently, there are no Internet sites dealing specifically with early primate evolution. For sources dealing generally with paleontology, see Chapter 8, and with living primates, see Chapters 9 through 11.

Dr. David Begun

David Begun has been in the Department of Anthropology at the University of Toronto since 1989. He received his Ph.D. from the University of Pennsylvania in 1987 and has worked at the Smithsonian Institution and Johns Hopkins University. He is currently working on Miocene hominoid functional anatomy and systematics, and has ongoing field projects in Turkey and Hungary.

As passionate as I am about Paleoanthropology, I cannot say exactly what inspired me to pursue the fascinating field of human origins. It is likely, however, that my own origins had an influence. I was born in southwestern France, in the cradle, as it were, of Neandertals and Cro-Magnon. Although I left after three months for my father's native land (New Jersey), I returned frequently to visit my maternal grandparents. My grandfather took me to many of the fossil human localities in the region, including the famous site of Lascaux, though I have to confess that I remember the meals at the many one and two star restaurants of the region more than I do these early paleoanthropological excursions. Nevertheless, I was aware of the existence of fossil humans from an early age.

I did not really know how interested I was In Paleoanthropology until I took a course in Physical Anthropology in the first semester of my first year in college. My enthusiasm for medicine was quickly replaced by a fascination with the science of human origins. Though I remained a "pre-med," I took all the Physical Anthropology and Archeology courses I could, and some courses in Social Anthropology as well. The connection to southwestern France was complete when I returned there in the summer following my second year at college for my first fieldwork experience, at Middle and Upper Paleolithic sites within minutes of the sites I had visited in my youth.

I transferred to the University of Pennsylvania, which had a very strong program in Physical Anthropology, and within a semester, I was dual matriculated in the B.A. and M.A. programs, and gung ho to work on fossils. I though I was interested in archaic *Homo sapiens*, and even spent a summer doing field work at Arago, also in France. I soon realized that I had a good thing going. I was combining the two things I liked most, spending time in France and working on human origins. Although my father nudged me a bit, suggesting that Paleoanthropology was a good hobby for a doctor, I never considered any option other than a Ph.D. program in Paleoanthropology. I remained at Penn, partly because I had already completed much of the course work, and in part because I had become involved in the analysis of fossils arranged by my Masters supervisor.

These fossils were not archaic *Homo sapiens*, but purported fossil apes from a 10 million year old site in Hungary (Rudabánya). The specimens turned out to be Carvivora, more closely related to cats and dogs than to apes and humans, but they taught me not to take anything for granted in Paleoanthropology, and that the older a fossil is, the more different it is from modern forms, and the more mysterious and interesting it is to me. Though I plan to examine other parts of the human fossil record during my career, I embarked on the study of Miocene apes as a Ph.D. student, and have been following that path, with a few side trips, for the past 15 years.

Three experiences remain among the most exciting to me in my career. The first was my initial experience handling fossils. The feel of a bone that has been fossilized and preserved for millions of years still inspires me. The amazing process of fossilization, despite fundamentally transforming a bone, usually preserves minute details of anatomy, and often gives fossils an aesthetic appeal, though I recognize that this can be an acquired taste. The second was my first discovery of a relatively complete fossil, much of the face of the fossil great ape *Dryopithecus laietanus*. The excitement and anticipation of a major discovery is one that I look forward to feeling again. The third experience is related to an unanticipated conclusion of my research. While studying the evolutionary relationships of *Dryopithecus*, I reached the unexpected conclusion

(to me, at least), that gorillas retain more features of their skull anatomy with *Dryopithecus* than do chimps and humans. While the goal of my research had been to understand the evolution of *Dryopithecus*, my focus shifted in a flash to the contentious issue of relations among the African apes and humans, and I found myself nearly alone among researchers on fossils in supporting the conclusions of many molecular systematists that chimps are more closely related to humans than they are to gorillas. Much of my research since then has incorporated this issue as a central concern.

My career this far has been guided by interest, inspiration, and instinct. My continued interest in all things concerning human evolution drives me to work hard in the lab and the field to learn more, and to read and keep up with developments in all areas of Paleoanthropology. I have been inspired by the work of my colleagues and by the fossils them-

selves, which somehow drive me to endure the difficulties of the field, just for a few scraps of fossilized bone. Instinct, combined with luck, has allowed me to take advantage of opportunities as they have presented themselves, and has taken my career path in a direction I would not have anticipated at the beginning.

Despite the job outlook, which has gone from bad when I started out, to dismal today, I would urge any student with the interest and inspiration to follow her/his instinct, seize the opportunity, and pursue a career in Physical Anthropology. It may not end up as expected, but with these ingredients in place, it should be a rewarding experience that will leave you with a keen awareness of the strengths and limitations of Science as a way of understanding the past, and with the skills to address the most complex and multifaceted of research problems.

13

Paleoanthropology

Introduction

In the last four chapters, we have seen how humans are classed as primates, both structurally and behaviorally, and how our evolutionary history coincides with that of other primates. However, we are a unique kind of primate, and our ancestors have been adapted to a particular lifestyle for several million years. Some primitive hominoid may have begun this process more than 10 m.y.a., but there is much more definite hominid fossil evidence from Africa shortly after 5 m.y.a. The hominid nature of these remains is revealed by more than the morphological structure of teeth and bones; we know that these animals are hominids also because of the way they behaved—emphasizing once again the *biocultural* nature of human evolution. In this chapter, we will discuss the methods scientists use to explore the secrets of early hominid behavior, and will demonstrate these methods through the example of the best-known early hominid site in the world: Olduvai Gorge in East Africa.

Definition of Hominid

If any of the Miocene hominoid fossils represent the earliest stages of hominid diversification, our definition of them as hominid must primarily be a *dental* one. Teeth and jaws are most of what we have of these Miocene forms. However, dentition is not the only way to describe the special attributes of our particular evolutionary radiation, and it certainly is not the most distinctive characteristic of later stages. Modern humans and our hominid ancestors are distinguished from our closest living relatives (the great apes) by more obvious features than proportionate tooth and jaw size. For example, various scientists have pointed to such hominid characteristics as large brain size, bipedal locomotion, and toolmaking behavior as being significant (at some stage) in defining what makes a hominid a hominid (as opposed to a pongid or anything else).

It must be emphasized that not all these characteristics developed simultaneously. Quite the opposite, in fact, has been apparent in hominid evolution over the last 5 million years. This pattern, in which different physiological systems (and behavioral correlates) evolve at different rates, is called **mosaic evolution**. As we first pointed out in Chapter 1 and will discuss in more detail in Chapter 14, the most defining characteristic for all of hominid evolution is *bipedal locomotion*. Certainly for the earliest stages of the hominid lineage, skeletal evidence of bipedal locomotion is the only truly reliable indicator of hominid status. However, in later stages of hominid evolution, other features, especially those relating to neurology and behavior, do become highly significant (see Box 13–1).

These behavioral aspects of hominid emergence—particularly toolmaking capacity—is what we wish to emphasize in this chapter. The important structural attributes of the hominid brain, teeth, and especially locomotor apparatus will be discussed in the next two chapters, where we investigate early hominid anatomical adaptations in greater detail.

▲ **Mosaic evolution**
Rates of evolution in one functional system vary from those in other systems. For example, in hominid evolution, the dental system, locomotor system, and neurological system (especially the brain) all evolved at markedly different rates.

Biocultural Evolution: The Human Capacity for Culture

When compared with other animals, the most distinctive behavioral feature of humans is our extraordinary elaboration of and dependence on culture.

Certainly, other primates, and many other animals for that matter, modify their environments. As we saw in Chapter 11, chimpanzees especially are known for such behaviors as using termite sticks and sponges and even transporting rocks to crush nuts. Given such observations, it becomes tenuous to draw sharp lines between hominid toolmaking behavior and that exhibited by other animals.

Another point to remember is that human culture, at least as it is defined in contemporary contexts, involves much more than toolmaking capacity. For humans, culture integrates an entire adaptive strategy involving cognitive, political, social, and economic components. The *material culture*, the tools and other items humans use, is but a small portion of this cultural complex.

Nevertheless, when examining the archeological record of earlier hominids, what is available for study is almost exclusively certain remains of material culture, especially residues of stone tool manufacture. Thus, it is extremely difficult to learn anything about the earliest stages of hominid cultural development prior to the regular manufacture of stone tools. As you will see, this most crucial cultural development has been traced to approximately 2.5 m.y.a. Yet, hominids undoubtedly were using other kinds of tools (such as sticks) and displaying a whole array of other cultural behaviors long before this time. However, without any "hard" evidence preserved in the archeological record, the development of these nonmaterial cultural components remains elusive.

The fundamental basis for human cultural elaboration relates directly to cognitive abilities. Again, we are not dealing with an absolute distinction, but a relative one. As you have learned, some other primates possess some of the symboling capabilities exhibited by humans. Nevertheless, modern humans display these abilities in a complexity several orders of magnitude beyond that of any other animal. Moreover, only humans are so completely dependent on symbolic communication and its cultural by-products—to the point where contemporary *Homo sapiens* could not survive without them.

When did the unique combination of cognitive, social, and material cultural adaptations become prominent in human evolution? We must be careful to recognize the manifold nature of culture and not expect it always to contain the same elements across species (as when compared to nonhuman primates) or through time (when trying to reconstruct ancient hominid behavior). Richard Potts (1993) has critiqued this overly simplistic perspective and suggests a more dynamic approach, one that incorporates many subcomponents (including aspects of behavior, cognition, and social interaction).

We know that the earliest hominids almost certainly did *not* regularly manufacture stone tools (at least, none that has been found!). The earliest members of the hominid lineage, perhaps dating back to approximately 7–5 m.y.a., could be referred to as **protohominids**. These protohominids may have carried objects such as naturally sharp stones or stone flakes, parts of carcasses, and pieces of wood. At minimum, we would expect them to have displayed these behaviors to at least the same degree as living chimpanzees.

Moreover, as you will see in the next Chapter, by at least 4 m.y.a., hominids had developed one crucial advantage: They were bipedal and could therefore much more easily carry all manner of objects from place to place. Ultimately, the efficient exploitation of resources widely distributed in time and space would most likely have led to using "central" spots where key components, especially stone objects, were cached (Potts, 1991).

What is certain is that over a period of several million years, during the formative stages of hominid emergence, numerous components interacted, but not all developed simultaneously. As cognitive abilities developed, more efficient means of communication and learning resulted. Largely as a result of such neural reorganization, more elaborate tools and social relationships also

▲ **Protohominids**
The earliest members of the hominid lineage, as yet basically unrepresented in the fossil record; thus, their structure and behavior are reconstructed hypothetically.

BOX 13-1

Mosaic Evolution of Hominid Characteristics

Locomotion	Brain	Dentition	Tool-making Behavior
Bipedal: shortened pelvis; body size larger; legs longer; fingers and toes not as long	Greatly increased brain size—highly encephalized.	Small incisors; canines further reduced; molar tooth enamel caps thick	Stone tools found after 2.5 m.y.a.; increasing trend of cultural dependency apparent in later hominids
Bipedal: shortened pelvis; some differences from later hominids, showing smaller body size and long arms relative to legs; long fingers and toes; probably capable of considerable climbing	Larger than Miocene forms, but still only moderately encephalized	Moderately large front teeth (incisors); canines somewhat reduced; molar tooth enamel caps very thick	In earliest stages unknown; no stone tool use prior to 2.5 m.y.a.; Probably somewhat more oriented toward tool manufacture and use than chimpanzees
Quadrupedal: long pelvis; some forms capable of considerable arm swinging, suspensory locomotion	Small compared to hominids, but large compared to other primates; a fair degree of encephalization	Large front teeth (including canines); molar teeth variable depending on species; some have thin enamel caps, others thick enamel caps	Unknown—no stone tools; probably had capabilities similar to chimpanzees

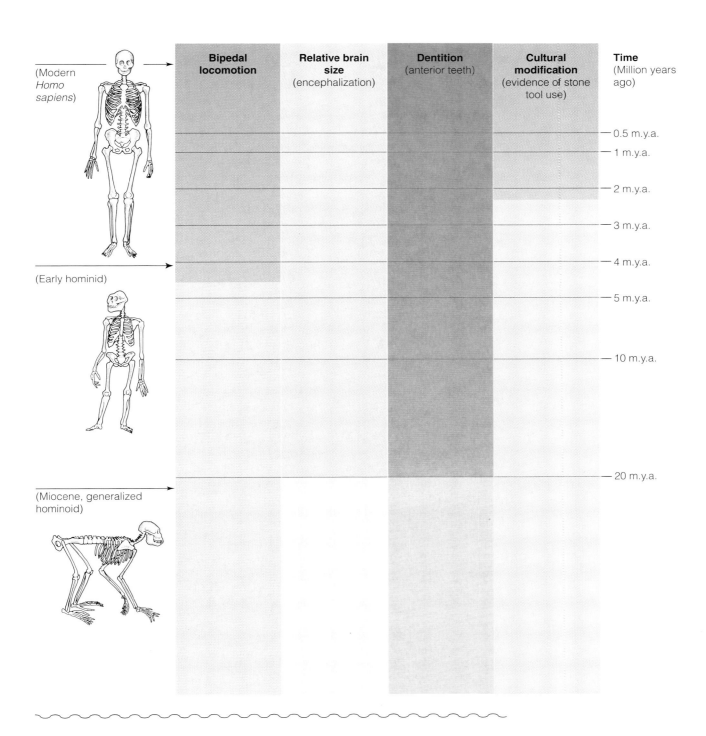

emerged. These, in turn, selected for greater intelligence, which in turn selected for further neural elaboration. Quite clearly, then, these mutual dynamics are at the very heart of what we call hominid *biocultural* evolution.

The Strategy of Paleoanthropology

To understand human evolution adequately, we obviously need a broad base of information. The task of recovering and interpreting all the clues left by early hominids is the work of paleoanthropologists. Paleoanthropology is defined as the study of ancient humans. As such, it is a diverse *multidisciplinary* pursuit seeking to reconstruct every possible bit of information concerning the dating, structure, behavior, and ecology of our hominid ancestors. In just the last few years, the study of early humans has marshaled the specialized skills of many different kinds of scientists. Included primarily in this growing and exciting adventure are geologists, archeologists, physical anthropologists and **paleoecologists** (Table 13–1).

Geologists, usually working with anthropologists, do the initial surveys to locate potential early hominid sites. Many sophisticated techniques can aid in this search, including aerial and satellite photography. Paleontologists are usually involved in this early survey work, for they can help find fossil beds containing faunal remains. Where conditions are favorable for the preservation of bone from such species as pigs and elephants, conditions may also be favorable for the preservation of hominid remains. In addition, paleontologists can (through comparison with known faunal sequences) give fairly quick estimates of the approximate age of fossil sites without having to wait for the more expensive and time-consuming analyses. In this way, fossil beds of appropriate geological ages (i.e., where hominid finds are most likely) can be isolated.

Once potential areas of early hominid sites have been located, much more extensive surveying begins. At this point, at least for some sites postdating 2.5 m.y.a., archeologists take over in the search for hominid "traces." We do not necessarily have to find remains of early hominids themselves to know that they consistently occupied a particular area. Behavioral clues, or **artifacts**, also inform

▲ **Paleoecology**

(*paleo*, meaning "old," and *ecology*, meaning "environmental setting") The study of ancient environments.

▲ **Artifacts**

Traces of hominid behavior; very old ones are usually of stone or, occasionally, of bone.

TABLE 13–1 Subdisciplines of Paleoanthropology		
Physical Sciences	**Biological Sciences**	**Social Sciences**
Geology	Physical anthropology	Archeology
Stratigraphy	Ecology	Ethnoarcheology
Petrology	Paleontology (fossil	Cultural anthropology
(rocks, minerals)	animals)	Ethnography
Pedology (soils)	Palynology (fossil pollen)	Psychology
Geomorphology	Primatology	
Geophysics		
Chemistry		
Taphonomy		

us directly and unambiguously about early hominid activities. Modifying rocks according to a consistent plan or simply carrying them around from one place to another (over fairly long distances) is characteristic of no other animal but a hominid. Therefore, when we see such behavioral evidence at a site, we know absolutely that hominids were present.

Because organic materials such as sticks and bones do not usually preserve in the archeological record, we have no solid evidence of the earliest stages of hominid cultural modifications. On the other hand, our ancestors at some point showed a veritable fascination with stones, for these provided not only easily accessible and transportable materials (to use as convenient projectiles to throw or to hold down objects, such as skins and windbreaks) but also the most durable and sharpest cutting edges available at that time. Luckily for us, stone is almost indestructible, and some early hominid sites are strewn with thousands of stone artifacts. The earliest artifact site now documented is from the Omo region of Ethiopia, dating from at least 2.4 m.y.a. Other contenders for the "earliest" stone assemblage come from the Hadar and Middle Awash areas, farther to the North in Ethiopia, dated 2.5–2 m.y.a.

If an area is clearly demonstrated to be a hominid site, much more concentrated research will then begin. We should point out that a more mundane but very significant aspect of paleoanthropology not shown in Table 13–1 is the financial one. Just the initial survey work in usually remote areas costs many thousands of dollars, and mounting a concentrated research project costs several hundred thousand dollars. Therefore, for such work to go on, massive financial support is required from government agencies and private donations. A significant amount of a paleoanthropologist's efforts and time are necessarily devoted to writing grant proposals or speaking on the lecture circuit to raise the required funds for this work.

Once the financial hurdle has been cleared, a coordinated research project can commence. Usually headed by an archeologist or physical anthropologist, the field crew will continue to survey and map the target area in great detail. In addition, field crew members will begin to search carefully for bones and artifacts eroding out of the soil, take pollen and soil samples for ecological analysis, and carefully recover rock samples for use in various dating techniques. If, in this early stage of exploration, members of the field crew find a fossil hominid, they will feel very lucky indeed. The international press usually considers human fossils the most exciting kind of discovery, a situation that produces wide publicity, often ensuring future financial support. More likely, the crew will accumulate much information on geological setting, ecological data, particularly faunal remains, and, with some luck, archeological traces (hominid artifacts).

After long and arduous research in the field, even more time-consuming and detailed analysis is required back in the laboratory. Archeologists must clean, sort, label, and identify all artifacts, and paleontologists must do the same for all faunal remains. Knowing the kinds of animals represented, whether forest browsers, woodland species, or open-country forms, will greatly help in reconstructing the local *paleoecological* settings in which early hominids lived. In addition, analysis of pollen remains by a palynologist will further aid in a detailed environmental reconstruction. All these paleoecological analyses can assist in reconstructing the diet of early humans (see p. 346). Also, the **taphonomy** of the site must be worked out in order to understand its depositional history—that is, whether the site is of a *primary* or *secondary* **context**.

In the concluding stages of interpretation, the paleoanthropologist will draw together the following essentials:

▲ **Taphonomy**

(*Taphos*: meaning "dead") The study of how bones and other materials came to be buried in the earth and preserved as fossils. A taphonomist studies the processes of sedimentation, the action of streams, preservation properties of bone, and carnivore disturbance factors.

▲ **Context**

The environmental setting where an archeological trace is found. *Primary* context is the setting in which the archeological trace was originally deposited. A *secondary* context is one to which it has been moved (e.g., by the action of a stream).

1. *Dating*
   geological
   paleontological
   geophysical
2. *Paleoecology*
   paleontology
   palynology
   geomorphology
   taphonomy
3. *Archeological traces of behavior*
4. *Anatomical evidence from hominid remains*

From all this information, scientists will try to "flesh out" the kind of animal that may have been our direct ancestor, or at least a very close relative. In this final analysis, still further comparative scientific information may be needed. Primatologists may assist here by showing the detailed relationships between the anatomical structure and behavior of humans and that of contemporary non-human primates (see Chapters 10 through 12). Cultural anthropologists may contribute ethnographic information concerning the varied nature of human behavior, particularly ecological adaptations of those contemporary hunter-gatherer groups exploiting roughly similar environmental settings as those reconstructed for a hominid site.

The end result of years of research by dozens of scientists will (we hope) produce a more complete and accurate understanding of human evolution—how we came to be the way we are. Both biological and cultural aspects of our ancestors pertain to this investigation, each process developing in relation to the other.

Paleoanthropology in Action—Olduvai Gorge

Several paleoanthropological projects of the scope just discussed have recently been pursued in diverse places in the Old World (Fig. 13–1). The most important of these include David Pilbeam's work in the Miocene beds of the Potwar Plateau of western Pakistan (circa 13–7 m.y.a.); Don Johanson's projects at Hadar and other areas of Ethiopia (circa 3.7–1.6 m.y.a.), sponsored by the Institute of Human Origins; a recently intensified effort just south of Hadar in Ethiopia in an area called the Middle Awash (circa 5–4 m.y.a.), led by Berkeley paleoanthropologists Tim White and Desmond Clark; a now completed research project along the Omo River of southern Ethiopia (circa 4–1.5 m.y.a.), directed by F. Clark Howell; Richard and Meave Leakey's fantastically successful research near Lake Turkana (formerly Lake Rudolf) in northern Kenya (circa 4.2–1.5 m.y.a.); Mary Leakey's famous investigations at Olduvai Gorge in northern Tanzania (circa 1.85 m.y.a. to present); and finally the recent exploration by Phillip Tobias of hominid localities in southern Africa (the most important being Swartkrans, discussed in Chapter 14).

Of all these early hominid localities, the one that has yielded the finest quality and greatest abundance of paleoanthropological information concerning the behavior of early hominids has been Olduvai Gorge. First "discovered" in the early twentieth century by a German butterfly collector, Olduvai was soon scientifically surveyed and its wealth of paleontological evidence recognized. In 1931, Louis Leakey made his first trip to Olduvai Gorge and almost immediately realized its significance for studying early humans. From 1935, when she first

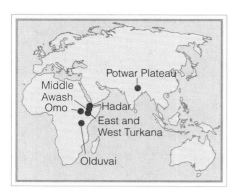

FIGURE 13–1
Major paleoanthropological projects.

worked there, until she retired in 1984, Mary Leakey directed the archeological excavations at Olduvai.

Located in the Serengeti Plain of northern Tanzania, Olduvai is a steep-sided valley resembling a miniature version of the Grand Canyon. A deep ravine cut into an almost mile-high grassland plateau of East Africa, Olduvai extends more than 25 miles in total length. In fact, if one were to include all the side gulleys and ravines, the area of exposures would total more than 70 miles, with potentially hundreds of early hominid sites (Fig. 13–2). Climatically, the semi-arid pattern of present-day Olduvai is believed to be similar to most of the past environments preserved there over the last 2 million years. The surrounding countryside is a grassland savanna broken occasionally by scrub bushes and acacia trees. It is noteworthy that this environment presently (as well as in the past) supports a vast number of mammals (such as zebra, wildebeest, and gazelle), representing an enormous supply of "meat on the hoof."

Geographically, Olduvai is located on the eastern branch of the Great Rift Valley of Africa. The geological processes associated with the formation of the Rift Valley make Olduvai (and other East African sites) extremely important to paleoanthropological investigation. Three results of geological rifting are most significant:

1. Faulting, or earth movement, exposes geological beds near the surface that are normally hidden by hundreds of feet of accumulated overburden.
2. Active volcanic processes cause rapid sedimentation, which often yields excellent preservation of bone and artifacts that normally would be scattered by carnivore activity and erosion forces.
3. Volcanic activity provides a wealth of radiometrically datable material.

FIGURE 13–2
Olduvai Gorge. A sketch map showing positions of the major sites and geological localities.

As a result, Olduvai is the site of superb preservation of ancient hominids and their behavioral patterns in datable contexts, all of which are readily accessible.

The greatest contribution Olduvai has made to paleoanthropological research is the establishment of an extremely well documented and correlated *sequence* of geological, paleontological, archeological, and hominid remains over the last 2 million years. At the very foundation of all paleoanthropological research is a well-established geological context. At Olduvai, the geological and paleogeographical situation is known in minute detail. Olduvai is today a geologist's delight, containing sediments in some places 350 feet thick, accumulated from lava flows (basalts), tuffs (windblown or waterborne fine deposits from nearby volcanoes), sandstones, claystones, and limestone conglomerates, all neatly stratified (Figs. 13–3 and 13–4). A hominid site can therefore be accurately dated relative to other sites in the Olduvai Gorge by cross-correlating known marker beds. At the most general geological level, the stratigraphic sequence at Olduvai is broken down into four major beds (Beds I–IV).

FIGURE 13–3

Aerial view of Olduvai Gorge. Volcanic highlands are visible to the south.

FIGURE 13–4

View of the main gorge at Olduvai. Note the clear sequence of geological beds. The discontinuity to the right is a major fault line.

Louis S. B. Leakey (1903–1972)

Called the "Charles Darwin of prehistory," Louis Leakey was truly a man for all seasons. Blessed with a superior intellect and an almost insatiable curiosity, Leakey untiringly quested after knowledge, which to him included everything there was to know about everything. His interests encompassed not just prehistory, archeology, and paleontology but modern African wildlife and African peoples, including their languages and customs. He once stalked, killed, and butchered a gazelle with just his bare hands and stone tools he had fashioned himself. He had previously attempted to use only his teeth and hands to dismember dead animals, but found it impossible, leading him to the conclusion that early hominids also *must* have used stone tools for butchering. Leakey also was a leading authority on handwriting, a skill he put to good use as the chief of British military intelligence for Africa during World War II.

The child of British missionary parents, Louis was born in a Kikuyu village in 1903—probably one of the first white children born in East Africa. His upbringing was to be as much African as European, and he was actually initiated into the Kikuyu tribe. Sworn to a sacred oath of silence, Louis never revealed the secret rites of initiation, even to his wife, Mary.

Following his early training in the African bush, Louis was dispatched to England for a more formal education, eventually receiving his degree from Cambridge. His consuming interest, however, was focused on Africa, where he returned to begin exploration of prehistoric sites—leading his first expedition in 1926 at the age of 23! In 1931, Leakey made his first trip to Olduvai Gorge with the German paleontologist Hans Reck. Louis liked to relate years later how he found the first stone tool in context at Olduvai within an hour of his arrival there!

In the next 40 years, the fantastic discoveries at Olduvai by Louis and his archeologist wife, Mary, as well as their extensive work at other sites all around the Rift Valley, were to make them famous to professional and layperson alike.

Louis Leakey displaying casts of fossil hominid discoveries from East Africa. To the right is the skull of a male gorilla.

However, perhaps Louis' greatest contribution was not the many discoveries he made himself, but his ability to stimulate and involve others. The definitive research on all the great apes was initiated by Louis Leakey, who personally recruited Jane Goodall to work with chimpanzees, Dian Fossey to investigate the mountain gorilla, and Birute' Galdikas to learn the secrets of the orangutan. Louis' greatest legacy is probably that all these projects continue today.*

---

*The research goes forward on the mountain gorillas, despite the tragic death of Dian Fossey in 1985.

Paleontological evidence of fossilized animal bones also has come from Olduvai in great abundance. More than 150 species of extinct animals have been recognized, including fish, turtles, crocodiles, pigs, giraffes, horses, and many birds, rodents, and antelopes. Careful analysis of such remains has yielded voluminous information concerning the ecological conditions of early human habitats. In addition, the precise analysis of bones directly associated with artifacts can

Mary Leakey (1913–)

Mary Leakey, one of the leading prehistorians of this century, spent most of her professional life living in the shadow of her famous husband. But to a considerable degree, Louis' fame is directly attributable to Mary. Justly known for his extensive fieldwork in Miocene sites along the shores of Lake Victoria in Kenya, Louis Leakey is quite often associated with important hominoid discoveries. However, it was Mary who, in 1948, found the best-preserved *Proconsull* skull ever discovered.

The names Louis Leakey and Olduvai Gorge are almost synonymous, but here, too, it was Mary who made the most significant single discovery—the "Zinj" skull in 1959. Mary had always been the supervisor of archeological work at Olduvai while Louis was busily engaged in traveling, lecturing, or tending to the National Museums in Nairobi.

Mary Leakey did not come upon her archeological career by chance. A direct descendant of John Frere (who, because of his discoveries in 1797, is called the father of Paleolithic archeology), Mary always had a compelling interest in prehistory. Her talent in illustrating stone tools provided her entry into African prehistory and was the reason for her introduction to Louis in 1933. Throughout her career she has done all the tool illustrations for her publications, and has set an extremely high standard of excellence for all would-be illustrators of Paleolithic implements.

A committed, hard-driving woman of almost inexhaustible energy, Mary conducted work at Olduvai, where she spent most of each year. Busily engaged seven days a week, she supervised ongoing excavations, as well as working on the monumental publications detailing the fieldwork already done.

Mary Leakey at the site where she discovered "Zinj" on the thirteenth anniversary of its discovery.

Since Louis' death in 1972, Mary, to some degree, has had to assume the role of traveling lecturer and fund-raiser. Today, she is retired from active fieldwork and lives outside Nairobi, where she continues her research and writing.

---

sometimes tell us about the diets and bone-processing techniques of early hominids. (There are some reservations, however; see Box 13–2.)

The archeological sequence is also well documented for the last 2 million years. Beginning at the earliest hominid site (circa 1.85 m.y.a.), there is already a well-developed stone tool kit, including chopping tools and some small flake tools (Leakey, 1971). Such a tool industry is called *Oldowan* (after Olduvai), and it continues into later beds with some small modifications, where it is called

Developed Oldowan. In addition, around 1.6 m.y.a., the first appearance of a new tool kit, the *Acheulian*, occurs in the Olduvai archeological record. This industry is characterized by large bifacial tools (i.e., flaked on both sides) commonly known as hand axes and cleavers. For several hundred thousand years, Acheulian and Developed Oldowan are *both* found at Olduvai (side by side), and the relationship between these parallel tool kits remains to be determined.

Finally, partial remains of several fossilized hominids have been found at Olduvai, ranging in time from the earliest occupation levels to fairly recent *Homo sapiens*. Of the more than 40 individuals represented, many are quite fragmentary, but a few are excellently preserved. While the center of hominid discoveries has now shifted to other areas of East Africa, it was the initial discovery by Mary Leakey of the *Zinjanthropus* skull at Olduvai in July 1959 that focused the world's attention on this remarkably rich area (Fig. 13–5). "Zinj" provides an excellent example of how financial ramifications directly result from hominid fossil discoveries. Prior to 1959, the Leakeys had worked sporadically at Olduvai on a financial shoestring, making marvelous paleontological and archeological discoveries. Yet, there was little support available for much needed large-scale excavations. However, following the discovery of "Zinj," the National Geographic Society funded the Leakeys' research, and within a year, more than twice as much dirt had been excavated than during the previous 30 years!

Dating Methods

One of the essentials of paleoanthropology is putting sites and fossils into a chronological framework. In other words, we want to know how old they are. How, then are sites dated, or, more precisely, the geological strata in which sites are found? The question is both reasonable and important, so let us examine the dating techniques used by paleontologists, geologists, paleoanthropologists, and archeologists.

Scientists use two kinds of dating for this purpose—relative and **chronometric** (also known as *absolute dating*). Relative dating methods tell you that something is older or younger than something else, but not by how much. If, for example, a cranium were found at a depth of 50 feet, and another cranium at 70 feet at the same site, we would usually assume that the specimen discovered at 70 feet is older. We may not know the date (in years) of either one, but we would know that one is older (or younger) than the other. Although this may not satisfy our curiosity about the actual number of years involved, it would give some idea of the evolutionary changes in cranial morphology (structure), especially if a number of crania at different levels were found and compared.

This method of relative dating is based on **stratigraphy** and was one of the first techniques to be used by scholars working with the vast period of geological time. Stratigraphy, in turn, is based on the law of superposition, which states that a lower stratum (layer) is older than a higher stratum. Given the fact that much of the earth's crust has been laid down by layer after layer of sedimentary rock, much like the layers of a cake, stratigraphy has been a valuable aid in reconstructing the history of the earth and the life upon it.

Stratigraphic dating does, however, have a number of associated problems. Earth disturbances, such as volcanic activity, river activity, and mountain building, may shift strata and the objects within them, and the chronology of the material may be difficult or even impossible to reconstruct. Furthermore, the time period of a particular stratum—that is, the length of time it took to accumulate—is not possible to determine with much accuracy.

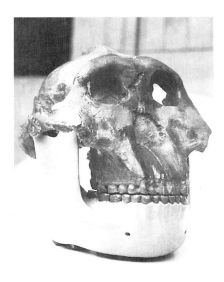

FIGURE 13–5
Zinjanthropus skull, discovered by Mary Leakey at Olduvai Gorge in 1959. The skull and reconstructed jaw depicted here are casts at the National Museums of Kenya, Nairobi. As we will see in Chapter 14, this fossil is now included as part of the genus Australopithecus.

▲ **Chronometric**
(*chrono*, meaning "time," and *metric*, meaning "measure") A dating technique that gives an estimate in actual numbers of years.

▲ **Stratigraphy**
Study of the sequential layering of deposits.

BOX 13–2

Are the Sites at Olduvai Really "Sites"?

The generally agreed-upon interpretation of the bone refuse and stone tools discovered at Olduvai has been that most, if not all, of these materials are the result of hominid activities. More recently, however, a comprehensive reanalysis of the bone remains from Olduvai localities has challenged this view (Binford 1981, 1983). Archeologist Lewis Binford criticizes those drawn too quickly to the conclusion that these bone scatters are the remnants of hominid behavior patterns while simultaneously ignoring the possibility of other explanations. For example, he forcefully states:

> All the facts gleaned from the deposits interpreted as living sites have served as the basis for making up "just-so-stories" about our hominid past. No attention has been given to the possibility that many of the facts may well be referable to the behavior of nonhominids. (Binford, 1981, p. 251)

From information concerning the kinds of animals present, which body parts were found, and the differences in preservation among these skeletal elements, Binford has concluded that much of what is preserved could be explained by carnivore activity. This conclusion has been reinforced by certain details observed by Binford himself in Alaska—details on animal kills, scavenging, the transportation of elements, and preservation as the result of wolf and dog behaviors. Binford describes his approach thus:

> I took as "known," then, the structure of bone assemblages produced in various settings by animal predators and scavengers; and as "unknown" the bone deposits excavated by the Leakeys at Olduvai Gorge. Using mathematical and statistical techniques I considered to what degree the finds from Olduvai Gorge could be accounted for in terms of the results of predator behavior and how much was "left over." (Binford, 1983, pp. 56–57)

In using this uniquely explicit approach, Binford has arrived at quite different conclusions from those previously suggested by other archeologists:

> For instance, the very idea of a site or living floor assumes conditions in the past for which there is no demonstration. In fact, it assumes the very "knowledge" we would like to obtain from the archeological remains. Site and living floor identifications presuppose that concentrations and aggregations of archeological and other materials are only produced by man. Are there not other conditions of deposition that could result in aggregations of considerable density found on old land surfaces? The answer must be a resounding yes. (Binford, 1981, p. 252)

And later he concludes:

Another method of relative dating is *fluorine analysis*, which applies only to bones (Oakley, 1963). Bones in the earth are exposed to the seepage of groundwater that usually contains fluorine. The longer a bone lies in the earth, the more fluorine it will incorporate during the fossilization process. Therefore, bones deposited at the same time in the same location should contain the same amount of fluorine. The use of this technique by Professor Oakley of the British Museum in the early 1950s exposed the Piltdown (England) Hoax by demonstrating that a human skull was considerably older than the jaw (ostensibly also human) found with it (Weiner, 1955). A discrepancy in fluorine content led Oakley and others to a closer examination of the bones, and they found that the

It seems to me that one major conclusion is justi-fied from the foregoing analysis: The large, highly publicized sites as currently analyzed carry little specific information about hominid behavior . . . arguments about base camps, hominid hunt-ing, sharing of food, and so forth are certainly premature and most likely wildly inaccurate. (Binford, 1981, pp. 281–282)

Binford is not arguing that all of the remains found at Olduvai have resulted from nonhominid activity. In fact, he recognizes that "residual material" was consistently found on surfaces with high tool concentration "which could not be explained by what we know about African animals" (Binford 1983).

Support for the idea that at least some of the bone refuse was utilized by early hominids has come from a totally different perspective. Researchers have analyzed (both macroscopically and microscopically) the cut marks left on fossilized bones. By experimenting with modern materials, they have further been able to delineate clearly the differ-ences between marks left by stone tools and those left by animal teeth (or other factors) (Bunn, 1981; Potts and Shipman, 1981). Analysis of bones from several early locali-ties at Olduvai have shown unambiguously that these speci-mens were utilized by hominids, who left telltale cut marks from stone tool usage. The sites thus far investigated reveal a somewhat haphazard cutting and chopping, apparently

unrelated to deliberate disarticulation. It has thus been concluded (Shipman, 1983) that hominids scavenged car-casses (probably of carnivore kills) and did *not* hunt large ani-mals themselves. Materials found at later sites (postdating 1 m.y.a.), on the other hand, do show deliberate disarticula-tion, indicating a more systematic hunting pattern, with pre-sumably meat transport and food sharing as well (Shipman, 1983).

If early hominids (close to 2 m.y.a.) were not hunting consistently, what did they obtain from scavenging the kills of other animals? One obvious answer is, whatever meat was left behind. However, the position of the cut marks suggests that early hominids were often hacking at non meat-bearing portions of the skeletons. Perhaps they were simply after bone marrow, a substance not really being exploited by other predators (Binford, 1981).

The picture that emerges, then, of what hominids were doing at Olduvai around 1.8 m.y.a. hardly suggests consistent big game hunting. In Binford's words:

This is evidence of man eating a little bit of bone marrow, a food source that must have repre-sented an infinitesimally small component of his total diet. The signs seem clear. Earliest man, far from appearing as a mighty hunter of beasts, seems to have been the most marginal of scav-engers. (Binford, 1983, p. 59)

---

jaw was not that of a hominid at all but of a young adult orangutan! (See Issue, p. 349).

Unfortunately, fluorine is useful only with bones found at the same location. Because the amount of fluorine in groundwater is based on local conditions, it varies from place to place. Also, some groundwater may not contain any fluo-rine. For these reasons, comparing bones from different localities by fluorine analysis is impossible.

In both stratigraphy and fluorine analysis, the actual age of the rock stratum and the objects in it are impossible to calculate. To determine the age in years, scientists have developed a variety of chronometric techniques based on the

GREAT MOMENTS IN PREHISTORY

Discovery of Zinjanthropus, July 17, 1959

That morning I work with a headache and a slight fever. Reluctantly I agreed to spend the day in camp.

With one of us out of commission, it was even more vital for the other to continue the work, for our precious seven-week season was running out. So Mary departed for the diggings with Sally and Toots (two of their dalmatians) in the Land-Rover, and I settled back to a restless day off.

Some time later—perhaps I dozed off—I heard the Land-Rover coming up fast to camp. I had a momentary vision of Mary stung by one of our hundreds of resident scorpions or bitten by a snake that had slipped past the dogs.

The Land-Rover rattled to a stop, and I heard Mary's voice calling over and over: "I've got him! I've got him! I've got him!"

Still groggy from the headache, I couldn't make her out. "Got what? Are you hurt?" I asked.

"Him, the man! *Our* man," Mary said. "The one we've been looking for (for 23 years). Come quick, I've found his teeth!"

Magically, the headache departed. I somehow fumbled into my work clothes while Mary waited.

As we bounced down the trail in the car, she described the dramatic moment of discovery. She had been searching the slope where I had found the first Oldowan tools in 1931, when suddenly her eye caught a piece of bone lodged in a rock slide. Instantly, she recognized it as part of a skull— almost certainly not that of an animal.

Her glance wandered higher, and there in the rock were two immense teeth, side by side. This time there was no question: They were undeniably human. Carefully, she marked the spot with a cairn of stones, rushed to the Land-Rover, and sped back to camp with the news.

The gorge trail ended half a mile from the site, and we left the car at a dead run. Mary led the way to the cairn, and we knelt to examine the treasure.

I saw at once that she was right. The teeth were pre-molars, and they had belonged to a human. I was sure they were larger than anything similar ever found, nearly twice the width of modern man's.

I turned to look at Mary, and we almost cried with sheer joy, each seized by that terrific emotion that comes rarely in life. After all our hoping and hardship and sacrifice, at last we had reached our goal—we had discovered the world's earliest known human.

From: "Finding the World's Earliest Man," by L. S. B. Leakey, *National Geographic*, 118 (September 1960);431. Reprinted with permission of the publisher.

---

phenomenon of radioactive decay. The theory is quite simple: Certain radioactive isotopes of elements are unstable, disintegrate, and form an isotopic variation of another element. Since the rate of disintegration follows a definite mathematical pattern, the radioactive material forms an accurate geological time clock. By measuring the amount of disintegration in a particular sample, the number of years it took for the amount of decay may be calculated. Chronometric techniques have been used for dating the immense age of the earth as well as artifacts less than 1,000 years old. Several techniques have been employed for a number of years and are now quite well known.

Uranium 238 (^{238}U) decays with a *half-life* of 4.5 billion years to form lead. That is, one-half of the original amount of ^{238}U is lost in 4.5 billion years and through various processes becomes lead. Therefore, if a sample of rock containing this element is analyzed and one-half of the uranium has been converted to lead, the age of that rock is 4.5 billion years. In another 4.5 billion years, half the remaining ^{238}U will have decayed. The isotope ^{238}U has proved a useful tool in dating the age of the formation of the earth.

Another chronometric technique involves potassium 40 (^{40}K), which has a half-life of 1.3 billion years, and produces argon 40 (^{40}Ar). Known as the K/Ar or potassium-argon method, this procedure has been extensively used by paleoan-thropologists in dating materials in the 1- to 5-million-year range, especially in East Africa. In addition, a variant of this technique (the $^{39}Ar/^{40}Ar$ method) has recently been used to date hominid localities in Java (see Chapter 16). Organic material, such as bone, cannot be measured by these techniques, but the rock matrix in which the bone is found can be. K/Ar was used to provide a minimum date for the deposit containing the *Zinjanthropus* cranium by dating a volcanic layer above the fossil.

Rocks that provide the best samples for K/Ar are those heated to an extremely high temperature, such as that generated by volcanic activity. When the rock is in a molten state, argon, a gas, is driven off. As the rock cools and solidifies, potassium 40 continues to break down to argon, but now the gas is physically trapped in the cooled rock. To obtain the date of the rock, it is reheated and the escaping gas measured.

A well-known radiometric method popular with archeologists makes use of carbon 14 (^{14}C), with a half-life of 5,730 years. Carbon 14 has been used to date material from less than 1,000 years to as old as 75,000 years, although the proba-bility of error rises rapidly after 40,000 years. Since this technique applies to the latter stages of hominid evolution, its applications relate to material discussed in Chapter 17 and 18. In addition, other dating techniques (thermoluminescense and electron spin resonance) that are used for calibrating these latter time peri-ods will be discussed in Chapter 18.

We should stress that none of these methods is precise, and each is beset with problems that must be carefully considered during laboratory measurement and the collection of material to be analyzed. Because the methods are impre-cise, approximate dates are given as probability statements with a plus or minus factor. For example, a date given as 1.75 ± 0.2 million years should be read as having a 67 percent chance that the actual date lies somewhere between 1.55 and 1.95 million years. (see Box 13–3)

There are, then, two ways in which the question of age may be answered. We can say that a particular fossil is *x* number of years old, a date determined usually either by K/Ar or ^{14}C chronometric dating techniques. Or we can say that fossil X lived before or after fossil Y, a relative dating technique.

Application of Dating Methods: Examples from Olduvai

Olduvai has been a rich proving ground for materials datable by numerous tech-niques, and as a result, it has some of the best documented chronology for any hominid site in the Lower or Middle Pleistocene.

Potassium-argon dating had its birth as a paleoanthropological tool in the early 1960s with its application to the dating of the "Zinj" site at Olduvai. To everyone's amazement, including Louis Leakey's, the chronometric age was determined at more than 1.75 million years—more than twice the age depth pre-viously assumed for the *whole* Pleistocene. As a result of this one monumental date (Leakey et al., 1961), the entire history of the Pleistocene and our corre-sponding interpretations of hominid evolution had to be rewritten.

BOX 13–3

Chronometric Dating Estimates

Chronometric dates are usually determined after several geological samples are tested. The dates that result from such testing are combined and expressed statistically. For example, say five different samples were used to give the K/Ar date shown in the text (1.75 ± .20 m.y.) for a particular geological bed. The individual results from each of the five samples are totaled together to give an average date (here, 1.75 m.y.) and also the standard deviation is calculated (here, .20 m.y.; that is, 200,000 years). The dating estimate is then reported as the mean plus or minus (±) one standard deviation. For those of you who have taken statistics, you realize that (assuming a normal distribution) 67 percent of a distribution of dates is included within 1 standard deviation (±) of the mean. Thus, the chronometric results, as shown in the reported range is simply a probability statement that 67 percent of the dates from all the samples tested fell within the range of dates from 1.55 to 1.95 m.y.a. You should carefully read chronometric dates and study the reported ranges: Smaller ranges mean more precise estimates. The smaller the range, probably the more samples that were analyzed; better laboratory controls will also increase precision.

The potassium-argon (K/Ar) method is an extremely valuable tool for dating early hominid sites and has been widely used in areas containing suitable volcanic deposits (mainly in East Africa). At Olduvai, K/Ar has given several reliable dates of the underlying basalt and several tuffs in Bed I, including the one associated with the "Zinj" find (now dated at 1.79 ± .03 m.y.a.). When dating relatively recent samples (from the perspective of a half-life of 1.3 billion years for K/Ar, *all* paleoanthropological material is relatively recent), the amount of radiogenic argon (that argon produced by disintegration of a potassium isotope) is going to be exceedingly small. Experimental errors in measurement can therefore occur as well as the thorny problem of distinguishing the atmospheric argon normally clinging to the outside of the sample from the radiogenic argon. In addition, the initial sample may have been contaminated or argon leakage may have occurred while it lay buried.

Due to the potential sources of error, K/Ar dating must be cross-checked using other independent methods. Once again, the sediments at Olduvai provide some of the best examples of the use of many of these other dating techniques.

Fission-track dating is one of the most important techniques for cross-checking K/Ar determinations. The key to fission-track dating is that uranium 238 (^{238}U) decays regularly by spontaneous fission, so that by counting the fraction of uranium atoms that have fissioned (shown as microscopic tracks caused by explosive fission of ^{238}U nuclei), we can ascertain the age of a mineral or natural glass sample (Fleischer and Hart, 1972). One of the earliest applications of this technique was on volcanic pumice from Olduvai, giving a date of 2.30 (±.28 m.y.a.)—in good accord with K/Ar dates.

Another important means of cross-checking dates is called **paleomagnetism**. This technique is based on the constantly shifting nature of the earth's magnetic pole. Of course, the earth's magnetic pole is now oriented in a northerly

▲ **Paleomagnetism**
Dating method based on shifting magnetic poles.

direction, but this situation has not always been so. In fact, the orientation and intensity of the geomagnetic field have undergone numerous documented changes in the last few million years. From our present point of view, we call a northern orientation "normal" and a southern one "reversed." Major epochs (also called "*chrons*") of recent geomagnetic time are:

0.7 m.y.a.–present	Normal
2.6–0.7 m.y.a.	Reversed
3.4–2.6 m.y.a.	Normal
?–3.4 m.y.a.	Reversed

Paleomagnetic dating is accomplished by carefully taking samples of sediments that contain magnetically charged particles. Since these particles maintain the magnetic orientation they had when they were consolidated into rock (many thousands or millions of years ago), we have a kind of "fossil compass." Then the paleomagnetic *sequence* is compared against the K/Ar dates to check if they agree. Some complications may arise, for during an epoch, a relatively long period of time can occur where the geomagnetic orientation is the opposite of what is expected. For example, during the reversed epoch from 2.6 to 0.7 m.y.a. (the Matuyama epoch), there was an *event* lasting about 210,000 years where orientations were normal (Fig. 13–6). Because this phenomenon was first conclusively demonstrated at Olduvai, it is appropriately called the *Olduvai event*.

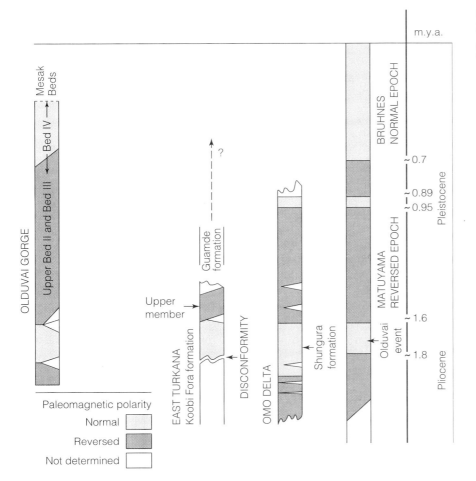

FIGURE 13–6

Paleomagnetic sequences correlated for some East African sites—Olduvai, East Turkana, Omo. (After Isaac, 1975.)

However, once these oscillations in the geomagnetic pole are worked out, the sequence of paleomagnetic orientations can provide a valuable cross-check for K/Ar and fission-track age determinations.

A final dating technique employed in the Lower Pleistocene beds at Olduvai and other African sites is based on the regular evolutionary changes in well known groups of mammals. This technique, called *faunal correlation* or **biostratigraphy**, provides yet another means of cross-checking the other methods. Animals that have been widely used in biostratigraphic analysis in East and South Africa are fossil pigs (suids), elephants (proboscids), antelope (bovids), rodents, and carnivores. From areas where dates are known (by K/Ar, for instance) approximate ages can be extrapolated to other lesser known areas by noting which genera and species are present.

All these methods—potassium-argon, fission-track, paleomagnetism, and biostratigraphy—have been used in dating sites at Olduvai. So many different dating techniques are necessary because no single one is perfectly reliable by itself. Sampling error, contamination, and experimental error can all introduce ambiguities into our so-called "absolute" dates. However, the sources of error are different for each technique; therefore, cross-checking among several independent methods is the most certain way of authenticating the chronology for early hominid sites.

Excavations at Olduvai

Because the vertical cut of the Olduvai Gorge provides a ready cross section of 2 million years of earth history, sites can be excavated by digging "straight in" rather than first having to remove tons of overlying dirt (Fig. 13–7). In fact, sites are usually discovered by merely walking the exposures and observing what bones, stones, etc., are eroding out.

▲ **Biostratigraphy**
Dating method based on evolutionary changes within an evolving lineage.

FIGURE 13–7

Excavations in progress at Olduvai. This site, more than 1 million years old, was located when a hominid ulna (arm bone) was found eroding out of the side of the gorge.

Several dozen hominid sites (at a minimum, they are bone and tool scatters) have been surveyed at Olduvai, and Mary Leakey has extensively excavated close to 20 of these. An incredible amount of paleoanthropological information has come from these excavated areas, data that can be generally grouped into three broad categories of site types, depending on implied function:

1. *"Butchering" localities*, areas containing one or only a few individuals of a single species of large mammal associated with a scatter of archeological traces. Two "butchering" sites, one containing an elephant and another containing a *Deinotherium* (a large extinct relative of the elephant), have been found at levels approximately 1.7 m.y.a. Both sites contain only a single animal, and it is impossible to ascertain whether the hominids actually killed these animals or exploited them (either for meat or, perhaps, to extract marrow) after they were already dead. A third butchering locality dated at approximately 1.2 m.y.a. shows much more consistent and efficient exploitation of large mammals by this time. Remains of 24 *Pelorovis* (a giant extinct relative of the buffalo, with horn spans more than 10 feet across!) have been found here, and Louis Leakey suggested they were driven into a swamp by a band of hominids and then systematically slaughtered (Leakey, 1971).

2. *Quarry localities*, areas where early hominids extracted their stone resources and initially fashioned their tools. At such sites, thousands of small stone fragments of only one type of rock are found, usually associated with no or very little bone refuse. At Olduvai, a 1.6–1.7 million-year-old area was apparently a chert (a rock resembling flint) factory site, where hominids came repeatedly to quarry this material.

3. *Multipurpose localities*, (also called camp sites), general-purpose areas where hominids possibly ate, slept, and put the finishing touches on their tools. The accumulation of living debris, including broken bones of many animals of several different species, and many broken stones (some complete tools, some waste flakes) is a basic human pattern. As Glynn Isaac noted:

    The fact that discarded artifacts tend to be concentrated in restricted areas is itself highly suggestive. It seems likely that such patches of material reflect the organization of movement around a camp or home base, with recurrent dispersal and reuniting of the group at the chosen locality. Among living primates this pattern in its full expression is distinctive of man. The coincidence of bone and food refuse with the artifacts strongly implies that meat was carried back—presumably for sharing (Isaac, 1976, pp. 27–28). [See Box 13–2 for a different interpretation.]

Several such multipurpose areas have been excavated at Olduvai, including one that is over 1.8 million years old. This site has a circle of large stones forming what at one time was thought to be a base for a windbreak; however, this interpretation is now considered unlikely. Whatever its function, without the meticulous excavation and recording of modern archeological techniques, the presence of such an archeological feature would never have been recognized. This point requires further emphasis. Many people assume that archeologists derive their information simply from analysis of objects (stone tools, gold statues, or whatever). However, it is the *context* and **association** of objects (i.e., precisely where the objects are found and what is found associated with them) that give archeologists the data they require to understand the behavioral patterns of ancient human populations. Once pot hunters or looters pilfer a site, proper archeological interpretation is never again possible.

▲ **Association**
What an archeological trace is found with.

The types of activities carried out at these multipurpose sites remain open to speculation (Fig. 13–8). Archeologists had thought, as the quote by Glynn Isaac indicates (and as also argued by Mary Leakey), that the sites functioned as "campsites." Lewis Binford has forcefully critiqued this view and has alternatively suggested that much of the refuse accumulated is the result of nonhominid (i.e., predator) activities (see Box 13–2). Another possibility, suggested by Richards Potts (1984), postulates that these areas served as collecting points (caches) for some tools. This last interpretation has received considerable support from other archeologists in recent years.

Diet of Early Hominids

Paleoanthropological research is concerned with more than the recovery and recording of bones and artifacts. What we are trying to obtain is a reconstruction of the kind of animal our ancestor was. Paleoanthropology must therefore be centrally concerned with interpretation of the behavioral patterns of early hominid populations.

One of the most important questions we would like to answer about early hominids is, What did they eat? Scattered broken bone debris associated with artifacts *may* provide direct evidence concerning one important aspect of early human dietary behavior. However, we must not forget that modern analogues, like the San of South Africa clearly show us that vegetable foods, which usually leave little trace in the archeological record, probably made up a large part (even a majority) of the caloric intake of early hominids. As Glynn Isaac noted, reconstructing dietary behavior is like navigating around an iceberg; four-fifths of what is of interest is not visible (Isaac, 1971, p 280).

Limited by the use of a simple digging stick as a tool, 1–2 m.y.a. hominids were able to exploit a diet that probably included berries, fruits, nuts, buds, shoots,

FIGURE 13–8

A dense scatter of stone and some fossilized animal bone from a site at Olduvai, dated at approximately 1.6 m.y.a. Some of these remains are the result of hominid activities.

shallow-growing roots and tubers, most terrestrial and smaller aquatic reptiles, eggs and nesting birds, some fish, mollusks, insects, and all smaller mammals (Bartholomew and Birdsell, 1953).

Olduvai has shown that a range of postulated meat resources was indeed exploited in earlier beds (1.85–1.0 m.y.a.). Fossils of turtles, rodents, fish, birds, pigs, horses, and small antelope are all fairly common at many Olduvai sites. Of course, exactly how much of these remains were eaten—as opposed to having just died there or having been preyed on by other animals—is still undetermined (see Box 13–2). Evidence for fish eating has also come from a comparably aged site in southern Ethiopia (the Omo), where fish bones have been found in human coprolites (fossilized feces).

Moreover, as the elephant and *Deinotherium* "butchering" sites indicate, occasional exploitation of large mammals also occurred more than 1.5 m.y.a. By 1 m.y.a., some hunting of large mammals may have provided important meat resources, as shown by the *Pelorovis* "butchering" site.

Thanks to the considerable efforts of Louis and Mary Leakey, just one relatively small area of northern Tanzania has provided a continuous record of the development of hominids and their behavior for almost 2 million years. Without their work at Olduvai, which has now stimulated further research at other East African sites, as well as ongoing laboratory analyses by dozens of experts, we would know much less than we do about the emergence of human culture prior to 1 m.y.a.

Summary

The biocultural nature of human evolution requires that any meaningful study of human origins examine both biological and cultural information. The multidisciplinary approach of paleoanthropology is designed to bring together varied scientific specializations in order to reconstruct the anatomy, behavior, and environments of early hominids. Such a task is centered around the skills of the geologist, paleontologist, paleoecologist, archeologist, and physical anthropologist.

Much of what we know about the origins of human culture between 1 and 2 m.y.a. comes from archeological excavations by Mary Leakey at Olduvai Gorge in East Africa. Olduvai's well-documented stratigraphic sequence, its superior preservation of remains, and the varied dating techniques possible there have made it an information bonanza for paleoanthropologists. Excavated sites have yielded a wealth of bones of fossil animals, as well as artifact traces of hominid behavior. Ecological reconstructions of habitat and dietary preferences are thereby possible and inform us in great detail concerning crucial evolutionary processes affecting early hominid populations.

In the next two chapters, we will survey the fossil hominid evidence in South and East Africa that informs us directly about human origins during the Pliocene and Pleistocene.

Questions for Review

1. Why are cultural remains so important in the interpretation of human evolution?
2. How are early hominid sites found, and what kinds of specialist are involved in the excavation and analysis of paleoanthropological data?
3. What kinds of paleoanthropological information have been found at Olduvai Gorge? Why is this particular locality so rich in material?

4. What techniques have been used to date early hominid sites at Olduvai? Why is more than one technique necessary for accurate dating?
5. Why are context and association so important in the interpretation of archeological remains?
6. What different activities can be inferred from the different kinds of sites at Olduvai? Discuss alternative views in the interpretation of these "sites."
7. How do we infer what early hominids were eating? Briefly list the kinds of food that were probably exploited.

Suggested Further Reading

Binford, Lewis. 1981. *Bones: Ancient Men and Myths*. New York: Academic Press.
Leakey, Mary. 1984. *Disclosing the Past. An Autobiography*. Garden City, NJ: Doubleday.
Leakey, Richard. 1981. *The Making of Mankind*. New York: Dutton.
Rasmussen, D. T. (ed.). 1993. *The Origin and Evolution of Humans and Humanness*. Boston: Jones and Bartlett.
Willis, Delta. 1989. *The Hominid Gang: Behind the Scenes in the Search for Human Origins*. New York: Viking.

Internet Resources

Archaeological Resources
http://spirit.lib.uconn.edu/archaelogy.html
(A general listing of many other links to Web servers relating to professional societies, publications, museums, lithics, faunal analysis, method and theory.)
Waikato Home Page
http://www2.waikato.ac.n2./c14/webinfo/index.html
(A very useful introduction to radiocarbon dating with very up-to-date information relating to current applications.)

The Piltdown Caper: Who Dunnit?

When first announced to the world in 1912, *Eoanthropus dawsoni* (Dawson's Dawn Man) created an anthropological sensation. Found during 1911 in Sussex in the south of England by Charles Dawson, a lawyer and amateur geologist, this "fossil" was to bewilder two generations of anthropologists. "Piltdown man," as he popularly came to be called, was composed of a fragmented skull and parts of a lower jaw. The enigma of the fossil from the very beginning was the combination of a large *sapiens*-like partial skull with an apelike lower jaw.

Most tantalizing of all, Piltdown was apparently extremely ancient, associated with long extinct fauna, such as mastodon, hippo, and rhino, all suggesting a date of early Pleistocene. A puzzling feature was the presence of these early fossils mixed in with clearly late Pleistocene fauna. The prevailing consensus, however, was that Piltdown was indeed ancient, "the earliest known representative of man in western Europe."

Despite its seeming incongruities, Piltdown was eagerly accepted by British scientists, including A. Keith, G. Elliot Smith, and A. Smith Woodward (all later knighted). What made the fossil such a delectable treat was that it confirmed just what had been expected, a combination of *modern* ape and *modern* human characteris-

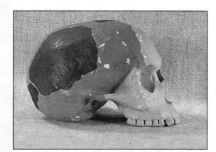

FIGURE 1
The Piltdown skull.

tics—a true "missing link." We, of course, know that no ancestral fossil form is a 50-50 compromise between modern ones, but represents its own unique adaptation. In addition to mistaken enthusiasm for a missing link, the fossil also represented a "true" man as opposed to the obviously primitive beasts (Java man, Neandertals) found elsewhere. Such a fervently biased desire to find an "ancient modern" in the human lineage has obscured evolutionary studies for decades and still causes confusion in some circles.

While generally accepted in England, experts in France, Germany, and the United States felt uneasy about Piltdown. Many critics, however, were silenced when a second fragmentary find was announced in 1917 (actually found in 1915) in an area 2 miles away from the original site. The matter stood in limbo for years, with some

scientists as enthusiastic supporters of the Piltdown man and others remaining uneasy doubters. The uneasiness continued to fester as more hominid material accumulated in Java, China, and (particularly in regard to australopithecines) South Africa. None of these hominids showed the peculiar combination of a human cranium with an apelike jaw seen in Piltdown, but actually indicated the reverse pattern.

The final proof of the true nature of the Dawn Man came in the early 1950s, when British scientists began an intensive reexamination of the Piltdown material. In particular, fluorine analysis performed by Kenneth Oakley showed both the skull and jaw to be relatively recent. Later, more extensive tests showed the jaw to be younger than the skull and *very* recent in date. Now a much more critical eye was turned to all the material. The teeth, looking initially as though they had been worn down flat in the typical hominid fashion, were apparently ape teeth filed down deliberately to give that impression. The mixed bag of fauna was apparently acquired from all manner of places (a fossil elephant came from Tunisia in North Africa), and the fossils were chemically stained so that they were all the same color. Finally, some "tools" found at Piltdown also met the hand of a forger, for the bone implements showed modifications that apparently could have been made only by a metal knife.

The "fossil" itself was probably purchased from local dealers. The skull probably came from a moderately ancient grave (a few thousand years old), and the jaw was a specially broken, filed, and stained mandible of a fairly recently deceased adolescent orangutan! The evidence was indisputable: a deliberate hoax. But who did it?

Just about everyone connected with the "crime" has at one time or another been implicated beginning with Piltdown's discoverer, Charles Dawson. Yet Dawson was an amateur and thus may have lacked the expertise to carry out the admittedly crafty job of anatomical modification.

In addition, at various times, suspicions have been cast toward neuroanatomist Sir Grafton Elliot Smith, geologist W. J. Sollas, anatomist Sir Arthur Keith, and French philosopher and archeologist Father Pierre Teilhard de Chardin.

Until recently, there was not a particularly strong case against Dawson or any of the other "principals." In this kind of uncertain (and suspicious) atmosphere, yet another fanciful but nevertheless intriguing possibility had been raised:

FIGURE 2

The Piltdown committee: the individuals central to the "discovery" and interpretation of the Piltdown "fossil." Back row, standing, left to right: F. O. Barlow (maker of the casts), G. Elliot Smith (anatomist), C. Dawson ("discoverer"), A. Smith Woodward (zoologist). Front row, seated: A. S. Underwood (dental expert), A. Keith (anatomist), W. P. Pycraft (zoologist), Sir Edward Ray Lankester (zoologist). From the painting by John Cook.

There was another, interested figure who haunted the Piltdown site during excavation, a doctor who knew human anatomy and chemistry, someone interested in geology and archeology, and an avid collec- *tor of fossils. He was a man who loved hoaxes, adventure and danger; a writer gifted at manipulating complex plots; and perhaps most important of all, one who bore a grudge against the British science establish-*

ment. He was none other than the creator of Sherlock Holmes, Sir Arthur Conan Doyle. (Winslow and Meyer, 1983, p. 34)

An unsolved mystery is always an irresistible temptation; so the Piltdown "affair" has remained a challenge to three generations of amateur sleuths (especially those otherwise employed as academics). It seemed, however, that there was little hope of solving the mystery, as the forgery had been perpetrated more than 80 years ago (and its demonstration as a hoax had been announced almost 50 years ago). Without some new clues, the case seemed unsolvable and the trail stone cold.

Enter, however, Professor Brian Gardinier of King's College, London, and a startling piece of new evidence. First, the evidence: While literally cleaning the attic at London's Natural History Museum, workers came across a trunk with the initials of Martin Hinton, a curator of zoology at the Museum at the time of the fraud. Contained within the trunk were several pieces of artificially carved and chemically stained fossil bones. The trunk was found in the mid-1970s, but its contents required meticulous analysis and corroboration. Here is where Professor Gardinier comes in. His own investigations had led him to circumstantial evidence implicating Hinton. The contents of the trunk, however, proved to be the final conclusive evidence—as the fossils had been deliberately modified employing exactly the same combination of chemicals as that used on the Piltdown material (it seems that the pieces in the trunk were used in "trial runs" by the forger—Hinton—to practice his technique). Hinton's motives are now difficult to establish, but there is some reason to believe he had a grudge against Smith Woodward, who had been his supervisor at the Museum. If, indeed, the goal was to embarrass Smith Woodward, Hinton did succeed spectacularly—since Smith Woodward spent most of his professional career (he died in 1944) in a spirited defense of the significance and validity of the Piltdown find.

After years of study, Professor Gardinier was prepared to announce his findings—which he did in 1996 to much fanfare and media attention. Has the mystery finally been solved? Since the riddle has survived for more then eight decades, it is difficult now for some to abandon the hunt. There are still a great number of sleuths out there yearning to keep the mystery alive!

Sources

Gee, Henry. 1996. "Box of Bones 'Clinches' Identity of Piltdown Palaeontology Hoaxer." *Nature* 381: 261–262

Spencer, Frank. 1990. *Piltdown: A Scientific Forgery*. New York: Oxford University Press.

Weiner, J. W. 1955. *The Piltdown Forgery*. London: Oxford University Press.

Winslow, John Hathaway, and Alfred Mayer. 1983. "The Perpetrator at Piltdown. *Science* '83. (September): 33–43.

Plio-Pleistocene Hominids

Introduction

In the last two chapters, we have seen that over the years, various researchers have attempted to define hominids (both living *and* extinct) primarily on the basis of either dental traits or presumed toolmaking behavior. As it turns out, neither of these criteria has proved very useful when applied to the *earliest* evidence of the hominid lineage.

In this chapter, we will review the discoveries of what is now a very large collection of early hominids from East and South Africa. Dating to the time period from prior to 4 million years ago to about 1 million years ago, this remarkable group of fossil hominids now consists of several thousand specimens representing several hundred individuals.

Through analysis of these materials paleoanthropologists have concluded that the primary functional adaptation that best distinguishes the hominid lineage is the development of bipedal locomotion. This chapter reviews the history, context, and basic morphology of these discoveries; then in Chapter 15, we take up the varied, and often confusing, interpretation of these finds.

The Bipedal Adaptation

As we discussed in Chapter 9, there is a general tendency in all primates for erect body posture and some bipedalism. However, of all living primates, efficient bipedalism as the primary form of locomotion is seen *only* in hominids. Functionally, the human mode of locomotion is most clearly shown in our striding gate, where weight is alternately placed on a single fully extended hind limb. This specialized form of locomotion has developed to a point where energy levels are used to near peak efficiency. Such is not the case in nonhuman primates, who move bipedally with hips and knees bent and maintain balance in a clumsy and inefficient manner.

From a survey of our close primate relatives, it is apparent that our arboreal ancestors were adapted to frequently assuming an upright upper-body posture. Prosimians, monkeys, and apes all spend considerable time sitting erect while feeding, grooming, or sleeping. Presumably, our early ancestors displayed similar behavior. What caused these forms to come to the ground and embark on the unique way of life that would eventually lead to humans is still a mystery. Perhaps natural selection favored some Miocene hominoid coming occasionally to the ground to forage for food on the forest floor and forest fringe. In any case, once it was on the ground and away from the immediate safety offered by trees, bipedal locomotion became a tremendous advantage.

First of all, bipedal locomotion freed the hands for carrying objects and, initially, for making and using simple tools. Such early cultural developments then had an even more positive effect on speeding the development of yet more efficient bipedalism—once again emphasizing the dual role of biocultural evolution. In addition, standing bipedally provides a broader view of the surrounding area and earlier detection of predators. When on the ground, nonhuman primates, such as baboons and chimpanzees, frequently adopt this posture to "look around" when out in open country. Moreover, bipedal walking is an efficient means of covering long distances, and when large game hunting came into play (several million years after the initial adaptation to ground living), further refinements in the locomotor complex may have been favored. Exactly what initiated the process is difficult to say, but all these factors probably played a role in the adaptation of hominids to their special niche through a unique form of locomotion.

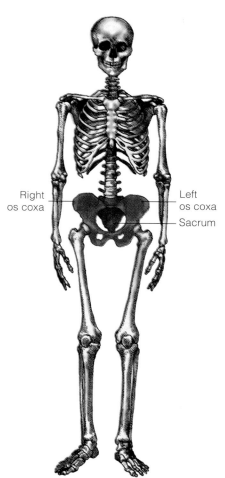

Right os coxa — Left os coxa — Sacrum

FIGURE 14–1

The human pelvis. Various elements shown on a modern skeleton.

Our mode of locomotion is indeed extraordinary, involving as it does an activity in which "the body, step by step, teeters on the edge of catastrophe" (Napier, 1967, p.56). The problem is to maintain balance on the "stance" leg while the "swing" leg is off the ground. In fact, during normal walking, both feet are simultaneously on the ground only about 25 percent of the time, and as speed of locomotion increases, this figure becomes even smaller.

To maintain a stable center of balance in this complex form of locomotion, many drastic structural/anatomical alterations in the basic primate quadrupedal pattern are required. The most dramatic changes are seen in the pelvis. The pelvis is composed of three elements: two *os coxae* joined at the back to the sacrum (Fig. 14–1). In a quadruped, the *os coxae* are elongated bones positioned along each side of the lower portion of the spine and oriented more or less parallel to it. In hominids, the pelvis is comparatively much shorter and broader and extends around to the side (Fig. 14–2). This configuration helps to stabilize the line of weight transmission, in a bipedal posture, from the lower back to the hip joint (Fig. 14–3).

A number of consequences resulted from the remodeling of the pelvis during early hominid evolution. Broadening the two sides and extending them around to the side and front of the body produced a basin-shaped structure that helps support the abdominal organs (indeed, *pelvis* means "basin" in Latin). Moreover, these alterations repositioned the attachments of several key muscles that act on the hip and leg, thus changing their mechanical function. Probably the most important of these altered relationships is that involving *gluteus maximus*, the largest muscle in the body, which in humans forms the bulk of the buttocks. In quadrupeds, the gluteus maximus is positioned to the side of the hip and functions to pull the thigh to the side, away from the body. But in humans, this muscle acts, along with the hamstrings, to extend the thigh, pulling it to the rear during walking and running (Fig 14–4). Indeed, gluteus maximus is a powerful extensor of the thigh and provides additional force, particularly during running and climbing.

Modifications also occurred in other parts of the skeleton as a result of the shift to bipedalism. The most significant of these are summarized in Box 14–1

FIGURE 14–3

Ossa coxae. (*a*) Homo sapiens (*b*) *early hominid* (Australopithecus) *from South Africa* (*c*) *chimpanzee. Note especially the length and breadth of the iliac blade and the line of weight transmission (shown in red).*

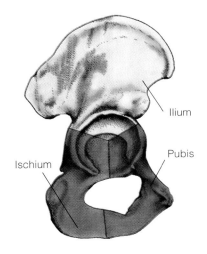

FIGURE 14–2
The human os coxa, composed of three bones (right side shown).

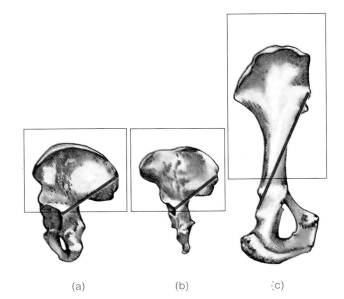

(a)   (b)   (c)

BOX 14–1

Major Features of Hominid Bipedalism

During hominid evolution, several major structural features throughout the body have been reorganized (from that seen in other primates) to facilitate efficient bipedal locomotion. These are illustrated above and listed below, beginning with the head and progressing to the foot: **1** The *foramen magnum* is repositioned further underneath the head, so that the head is more or less balanced on the spine (and thus requires less robust neck muscles to hold the head upright). **2** During locomotion, breathing is no longer tied to movement of the forelimbs. **3** The spine has two distinctive curves—a backward (thoracic) one and a forward (lumbar) one—that keep the trunk (and weight) centered above the pelvis. **4** The pelvis is shaped

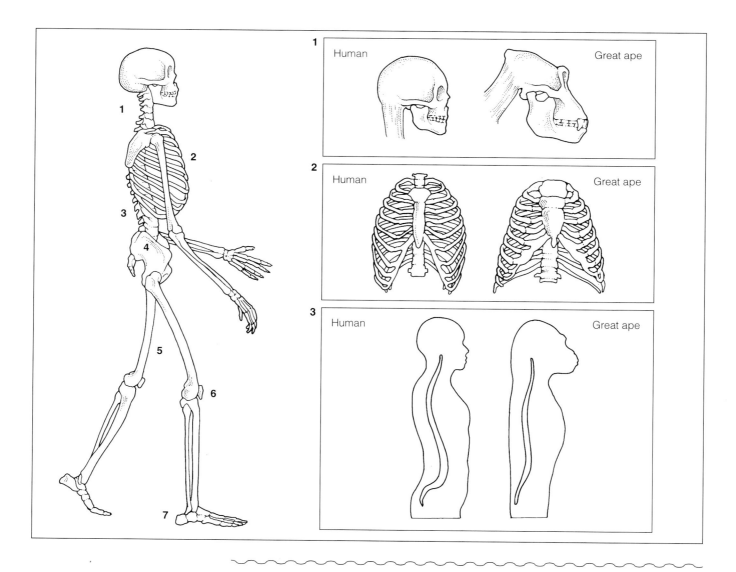

more in the form of a basin to support internal organs; more-over, the os coxae (specifically, iliac blades) are shorter and broader, thus stabilizing weight transmission. **5** Lower limbs are elongated, as shown by the proportional lengths of various body segments (e.g., in humans the thigh comprises 20 percent of body height, while in gorillas it comprises only

11 percent). **6** The femur is angled inward, keeping the legs more directly under the body; modified knee anatomy also permits full extension of this joint. **7** The big toe is enlarged and brought in line with the other toes; in addition, a distinctive longitudinal arch forms, helping absorb shock and adding propulsive spring.

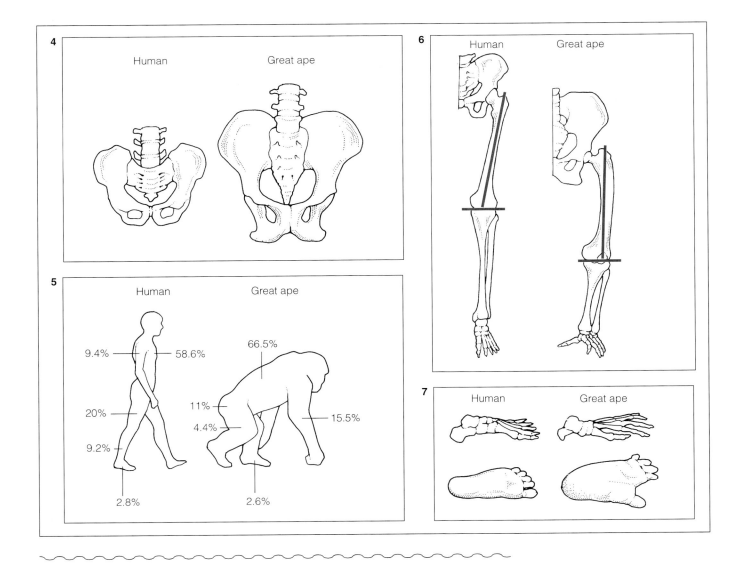

▲ **Foramen magnum**
The opening at the base of the skull through which the spinal cord passes as it enters the body to descend through the vertebral column. In quadrupeds, it is located more to the rear of the skull, while in bipeds, it is located further beneath the skull.

and include (1) repositioning of the **foramen magnum**, the opening at the base of the skull through which the spinal cord emerges; (2) reshaping of the rib cage; (3) the addition of spinal curves that facilitate the transmission of the weight of the upper body to the hips in an upright posture; (4) shortening and broadening of the pelvis and the stabilization of weight transmission (discussed earlier); (5) lengthening of the hind limb, thus increasing stride length; (6) angling of the femur (thighbone) inward to bring the knees and feet closer together under the body; and (7) several structural changes in the foot, including the development of a longitudinal arch and realignment of the big toe in parallel with the other toes (i.e., it was no longer divergent).

As you can appreciate, the evolution of hominid bipedalism required complex anatomical reorganization. For natural selection to produce anatomical change of the magnitude seen in hominids, the benefits of bipedal locomotion must have been significant indeed. We previously mentioned several possible adaptive advantages that bipedal locomotion *may* have conferred upon early hominids. However, these all remain hypotheses (even more accurately, they could be called scenarios), and we lack adequate data with which to test the various proposed alternatives.

Still, given the anatomical alterations that efficient bipedalism necessitated, there must have been some major behavioral stimuli influencing its development. In the interpretation of evolutionary history, biologists are fond of saying that form follows function. In other words, during evolution, organisms do not undergo significant reorganization in structure *unless* these changes (over many generations) assist individuals in some functional capacity (and, in so doing, increase their reproductive success). Such changes did not necessarily occur all at once, but probably evolved over a fairly long period of time. Nevertheless, once behavioral influences initiated certain structural modifications, the process gained momentum and proceeded irreversibly.

We say that hominid bipedalism is *habitual* and *obligate*. By habitual, we mean that hominids, unlike any other primate, move bipedally as their standard and most efficient mode of locomotion. By obligate, we mean that hominids are committed to bipedalism and cannot locomote efficiently in any other manner. For example, the loss of grasping ability in the foot makes climbing much more difficult for humans (although by no means impossible). The central task, then, in trying to understand the earliest members of the hominid family is to identify anatomical features that indicate bipedalism and to interpret to what degree these organisms were committed to this form of locomotion (i.e., was it habitual and was it obligate?).

What structural patterns are observable in early hominids, and what do they imply regarding locomotor function? *All the major structural changes required for bipedalism are seen in early hominids from East and South Africa* (at least insofar as the evidence has thus far been reported). In particular, the pelvis, as clearly documented by several excellently preserved specimens, was dramatically remodeled to support weight in a bipedal stance (Fig. 14–3b).

In addition, other structural changes shown in even the earliest definitive hominid postcranial remains further confirm the pattern seen in the pelvis. For example, the vertebral column (as known from specimens in East and South Africa) shows the same curves as in modern hominids. The lower limbs were also elongated and were apparently proportionately about as long as in modern humans (although the arms were longer). Further, the carrying angle of weight support from the hip to the knee was also very similar to that seen in *Homo sapiens*.

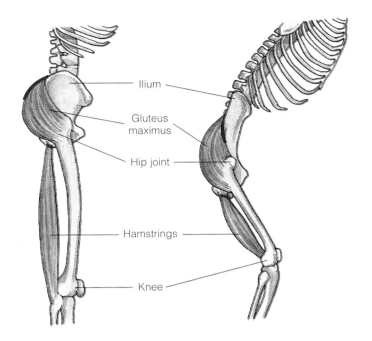

FIGURE 14–4
Comparisons of important muscles that act to extend the hip. Note that the attachment joint (origin, shown in red) of the gluteus maximus in humans is farther in back of the hip bone than in a chimpanzee standing bipedally. Conversely, in chimpanzees, the hamstrings are farther in back of the knee.

Ilium

Gluteus maximus

Hip joint

Hamstrings

Knee

Fossil evidence of early hominid foot structure has come from two sites in South Africa, and especially important are some recently announced new fossils from Sterkfontein (Clarke and Tobias, 1995). These specimens, consisting of four articulating elements from the ankle and big toe, indicate that the heel and longitudinal arch were both well adapted for a bipedal gait. However, the paleoanthropologists (Ron Clarke and Phillip Tobias) also suggest that the large toe was *divergent* unlike the hominid pattern shown in Box 14–1. If the large toe really did possess this (abducted) anatomical position, it most likely would have aided the foot in grasping. In turn, this grasping ability (as in other primates) would have enabled early hominids to more effectively exploit arboreal habitats. Finally, since anatomical remodeling is always constrained by a set of complex functional compromises, a foot highly capable of grasping and climbing is *less* capable as a stable platform during bipedal locomotion. Some researchers therefore see early hominids as not necessarily obligate bipeds.

Further evidence for evolutionary changes in the foot skeleton comes from Olduvai Gorge in Tanzania where a nearly complete hominid foot is preserved, and from Hadar in Ethiopia, where numerous foot elements have been recovered (Fig. 14–5). As in the remains from South Africa, the East African fossils suggest a well-adapted bipedal gait. The arches are developed, but some differences in the ankle also imply that considerable flexibility was possible (again, suggested for continued adaptation to climbing). As we will see, some researchers have recently concluded that many early forms of hominids probably spent considerable time in the trees. Moreover, they may not have been quite as efficient bipeds as has previously been suggested (see p. 371). Nevertheless, to this point, *all* the early hominids that have been identified from Africa are thought by most researchers to have been both habitual and obligate bipeds (notwithstanding the new evidence from South Africa, which will require further study.)

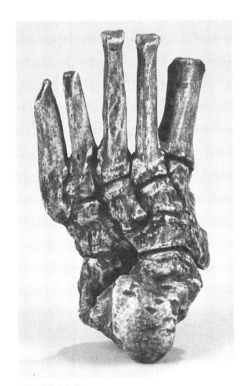

FIGURE 14–5
A nearly complete hominid foot (OH 8) from Olduvai Gorge, Tanzania.

Early Hominids in the Plio-Pleistocene

The beginnings of hominid differentiation almost certainly have their roots in the late Miocene (circa 10–5 m.y.a.). Sometime during the period between 8 and 5 m.y.a., hominids began to adapt more fully to their peculiar ground-living niche, and fossil evidence from this period would be most illuminating, particularly any remains indicating a bipedal adaptation. However, scant information is presently available concerning the course of hominid evolution during this significant 3-million-year gap. But beginning around 4.5 m.y.a., the fossil record picks up considerably. We now have a wealth of fossil hominid material from the Pliocene and the earliest stages of the Pleistocene (5–1 m.y.a.), and this whole span is usually referred to as the Plio-Pleistocene.

The East African Rift Valley

Stretching along a more than 1,200-mile trough extending through Ethiopia, Kenya, and Tanzania from the Red Sea in the north to the Serengeti Plain in the south is the eastern branch of the Great Rift Valley of Africa (Fig. 14–6). This massive geological feature has been associated with active mountain building, faulting, and vulcanism over the last several million years.

Because of these gigantic earth movements, earlier sediments (normally buried under hundreds of feet of earth and rock) were literally thrown to the surface, where they became exposed to the trained eye of the paleoanthropologist.

FIGURE 14–6

The East African Rift Valley system.

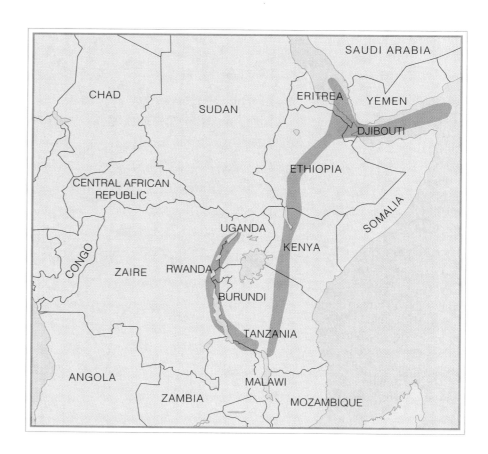

Such earth movements have exposed Miocene beds at sites in Kenya, along the shores of Lake Victoria, where abundant remains of early fossil hominoids have been found. In addition, Plio-Pleistocene sediments are also exposed all along the Rift Valley, and paleoanthropologists in recent years have made the most of this unique opportunity.

More than just exposing normally hidden deposits, rifting has stimulated volcanic activity, which in turn has provided a valuable means of chronometrically dating many sites in East Africa. Unlike the sites in South Africa (see pp. 378–382), those along the Rift Valley are *datable* and have thus yielded much crucial information concerning the precise chronology of early hominid evolution.

The Earliest East African Hominids

The site that focused attention on East Africa as a potential paleoanthropological gold mine was Olduvai Gorge in northern Tanzania. As discussed in great detail in Chapter 13, this site has offered unique opportunities because of the remarkable preservation of geological, paleontological, and archeological records. Following Mary Leakey's discovery of "Zinj" in 1959 (and the subsequent dating of its site at 1.75 m.y.a. by the K/Ar method), numerous other areas in East Africa have been surveyed and several intensively explored. We will briefly review the geological and chronological background of these important sites beginning with the earliest.

Earliest Traces

The oldest specimen discovered to date, which several authorities identify as a *probable* hominid, comes from Lothagam in Northern Kenya (Fig. 14–7). This fossil is very fragmentary and consists of a portion of a lower jaw (mandible). In addition, in the time range 5–4 m.y.a., there are further scattered finds from two other sites in Northern Kenya and from a third locality in northeastern Ethiopia. However, none of this fossil material is very definitive, since, as of yet, only a single (fragmentary) specimen has been recovered from each site (see Table 14–1 for summary of discoveries).

Still, in the last three years, new and much more abundant discoveries have been made at three other localities, two in northern Kenya (Kanapoi and Allia Bay) and the other in Ethiopia (Aramis) (Fig. 14–7). Finds from these three sites have added dramatically to our knowledge of the earliest stages of hominid emergence.

Aramis

One of the most exciting areas for future research in East Africa is the Afar Triangle of northeastern Ethiopia, where the Red Sea, Rift Valley, and Gulf of Aden all intersect. From this area have come many of the most important recent discoveries bearing on human origins. Several areas have yielded fossil remains in recent decades, and many potentially very rich sites are currently being explored. One of these sites just recently discovered, located in the region called the Middle Awash (along the banks of the Awash River), is called Aramis. Initial radiometric dating of the sediments places the hominid remains at 4.4 m.y.a., making this the earliest *collection* of hominids yet discovered.

FIGURE 14–7
Early hominid localities in East and Central Africa.

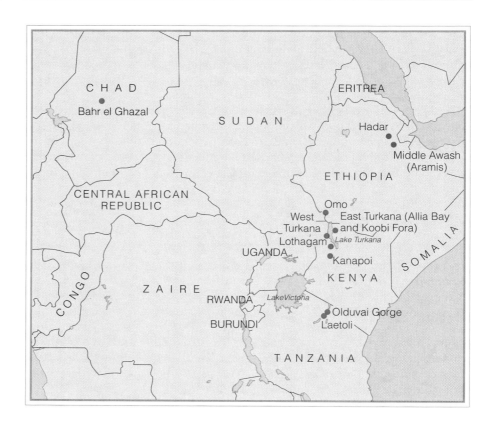

Hominids from Aramis   In 1992 and 1993, up to 17 individuals were discovered at Aramis. First announced in 1994, the remains recovered from the first two field seasons include mostly jaws and teeth, but also represent parts of two crania and some upper limb bones (White et al., 1994). In addition, further important finds were made at Aramis in 1994 and 1995, including isolated teeth and mandibular fragments as well as arm, hand, and foot bones (Figs. 14–8 and

TABLE 14–1 Discoveries of Earliest Hominid* Fossil Remains		
Site	**Dates (m.y.a.)**	**Comments**
Lothagam (Kenya)	5.8–5.6	1 specimen (partial mandible)
Mabaget (Kenya) (Chemeron Beds)	5.1–5.0	1 specimen (partial subadult humerus)
Tabarin (Kenya) (Chemeron Beds)	5.0	1 specimen (partial mandible)
Aramis (Ethiopia)	4.4	More than 40 individuals
Kanapoi (Kenya)	4.2–3.9	12 specimens
Allia Bay (East Turkana) (Kenya)	3.9	9 specimens
Belohdelie (Ethiopia)	3.9–3.8	Pieces of cranium

*Note: In some cases, hominid status is not yet well established.

14–9). With these new finds, Milford Wolpoff (1995) of the University of Michigan suggests that now more than 40 individuals are represented in the growing Aramis collection. And most exciting of all, a 40 percent complete skeleton of an adult hominid, which preserves many cranial and postcranial elements, was partly excavated in late 1994 (Asfaw, 1995).

Since the fossils are so recently discovered and only partially described, only provisional interpretations are possible at this time. However, some general features are apparent. If these forms *are* hominids (and they probably are), then they must be considered quite primitive. The canines are fairly large, and the upper one shears against a cutting surface on the lower first premolar, thus called a *sectorial* tooth (as in apes) (Fig. 14–10). In addition, the base of the cranium is quite apelike (reminiscent of a chimpanzee). With only very incomplete cranial remains available thus far, assessment of cranial capacity is not yet feasible, although the cranial capacity was probably quite small—at least as small as other early hominids. Thus, it might be asked, What makes these forms hominids? The answer lies in anatomical evidence indicative of bipedal locomotion. First, the entrance of the spine into the base of the cranium (the foramen magnum) is positioned further forward than in quadrupeds (see p. 356). Second, features of the humerus suggest that the forelimb was not weight-bearing. And lastly, reports from the field suggest that the morphology of the pelvis (as observed in the partial skeleton) is consistent with bipedalism.

Thus, current conclusions (which will be either unambiguously confirmed or falsified as the skeleton is fully excavated, cleaned, and studied) interpret the Aramis remains as the earliest hominids yet known (the mandible from Lothagam notwithstanding—and it is probably a member of the same species as the individuals from Aramis). These individuals from Aramis, although very primitive hominids, were apparently fully bipedal.

Tim White of the University of California is supervising the excavations, and he and his colleagues have recently argued (White et al., 1995) that the fossil hominids from Aramis are so primitive and so different from other early hominids that they should be assigned to a new genus (and, necessarily, a new

FIGURE 14–8

Excavation of Aramis site. Dr. Gen Suwa is shown in the foreground carefully excavating sediments to uncover new fossils. Team members in the background are screening sediments to make sure even the smallest fragments ae recovered.

©1994 Tim D. White\Brill Atlanta.

FIGURE 14–9

New hominid discoveries from Aramis. Alemayehu Asfaw is holding his discovery of an upper arm bone (humerus). In the background team members search for other fragments; parts of all three bones of the upper appendage of one Ardipithecus ramidus *individual were discovered.*

©1994 Tim D. White\Brill Atlanta

▲ *Australopithecus*
An early hominid genus, known from the Plio-Pleistocene of Africa, characterized by bipedal locomotion, a relatively small brain, and large back teeth.

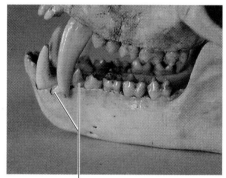
Sectorial lower first premolar

FIGURE 14–10
Left lateral view of the teeth of a male patas monkey. Note how the large upper canine shears against the elongated sur-face of the sectorial *lower first premolar.*

species as well): *Ardipithecus ramidus*. Most especially, the thin enamel caps on the molars are in dramatic contrast to all other early hominids, who show quite thick enamel caps. These other early hominid forms (all somewhat later than *Ardipithecus*) are placed in the genus **Australopithecus**. Moreover, White and his associates have further suggested that as the earliest and most primitive hominid yet discovered, *Ardipithecus* may form the "sister-group" and thus possibly the root species for all later hominids. This interpretation has been tentatively accepted by another major team of researchers (Meave Leakey and colleagues) who are also doing research on the earliest stages of hominid emergence (see next section).

Kanapoi and Allia Bay (East Turkana)

In northernmost Kenya, several important fossil-bearing sites have been explored, making this area the most productive in all of Africa. Two of these localities, Kanapoi (to the west of Lake Turkana) and Allia Bay (on the eastern shore) (see Fig. 14–7) have in the last few years yielded some of the earliest hominid remains yet discovered. Radiometric dates from the two sites place the hominid remains in the time range of 4.2–3.9 m.y.a. Some of the remains (a humerus discovered at Kanapoi in 1965 and a tooth found in 1982 at Allia Bay) have been known for some time, but much more abundant finds were recovered from both localities in 1994 and 1995, and the whole collection was first described in 1995 (Leakey et al., 1995).

Hominids from Kanapoi and Allia Bay   To date, a total of 9 specimens have been recovered from Kanapoi and another 12 specimens have been collected from Allia Bay. Together this collection consists mostly of teeth, but also includes six jaws, the 1965 humerus, a radius, and a partial tibia. The teeth are quite primitive, as are some suggestive facial features. In addition, preliminary analyses suggest that the external ear opening is different from that seen in later hominids. However, unlike the Aramis remains (*Ardipithecus*), the enamel on the molars is thick, and in this respect, the Kanapoi and Allia Bay fossils are like other early hominids (i.e., other members of the genus *Australopithecus*). Finally, anatomical details of the tibia have led researchers to be quite confident that this form was, in fact, bipedal.

From the features that are present, Meave Leakey and her colleagues have assigned the fossil material from Kanapoi and Allia Bay to the genus *Australopithecus*. Moreover, they suggest that these fossils differ significantly enough from later members of *Australopithecus* to warrant their provisional assignment to a separate species, *Australopithecus anamensis*. Whether the distinction (particularly when compared with the slightly later hominid, *Australopithecus afarensis*, discussed below) justifies a separate species designation must await further discoveries and more detailed study. (A consensus will be reached after a number of other researchers have had the opportunity to study the original fossils or cast replicas.)

Laetoli

Thirty miles south of Olduvai Gorge in northern Tanzania lie beds considerably older than those exposed at the gorge. With numerous volcanic sediments in the vicinity, accurate K/Ar testing is possible and provides a date of 3.7–3.5 m.y.a. for this site.

Since systematic fossil recovery began at **Laetoli** (lye´-toll-ee) in 1974, 23 fossil hominid individuals have been found, consisting almost exclusively of jaws and teeth with fragmentary postcranial remains of one immature individual (Johanson and White, 1979; White, 1980). In February 1978, Mary Leakey announced a remarkable discovery at Laetoli: fossilized footprints embossed into an ancient volcanic tuff approximately 3.5 m.y.a! Literally thousands of footprints have been found at this remarkable site, representing more than 20 different kinds of animals (Pliocene elephants, horses, pigs, giraffes, antelope, hyenas, and an abundance of hares). Several hominid footprints have also been found, including a trail more than 75 feet long, made by at least two—and perhaps three—individuals (Leakey and Hay, 1979) (Fig 14–11).

Such discoveries of well-preserved hominid footprints are extremely important in furthering our understanding of human evolution. For the first time, we can make *definite* statements regarding locomotor pattern and stature of early hominids. Initial analysis of these Pliocene footprints compared to modern humans suggests a stature of about 4 feet 9 inches for the larger individual and 4 feet 1 inch for the smaller individual.

Studies of these impression patterns clearly show that the mode of locomotion of these hominids was bipedal (Day and Wickens, 1980). As we have discussed, the development of bipedal locomotion is the most important defining characteristic of early hominid evolution. Some researchers, however, have concluded that these early hominids were not bipedal in quite the same way that modern humans are. From detailed comparisons with modern humans, estimates of stride length, cadence, and speed of walking have been ascertained, indicating that the Laetoli hominids moved in a "strolling" fashion with a rather short stride (Chateris et al., 1981).

Hadar (Afar Triangle)

Also from the Afar Triangle region of Ethiopia, just north of Aramis, is the **Hadar** site (Fig. 14–12). The Hadar area, which has now been investigated for several years (although interrupted for long periods due to warfare), has yielded many of

▲ **Laetoli**
(lye´-toll-ee)

▲ **Hadar**
(had´-are) A very productive fossil hominid site in northeastern Ethiopia, dated 3.9–3.0 m.y.a.

FIGURE 14–11
Hominid footprint from Laetoli, Tanzania. Note the deep impression of the heel and the large toe (arrow) in line (adducted) with the other toes.

FIGURE 14–12

Hadar deposits, northeastern Ethiopia

the best-preserved early hominid fossils. The dates for the Hadar specimens are somewhat later than those from Aramis, Kanapoi, and Allia Bay. Initial K/Ar dating has suggested an age of up to 3.6 m.y.a. for the older Hadar hominid fossils and 2.5 m.y.a. for the upper artifact-bearing beds (Johanson and Edey, 1981). These dates must be considered provisional until systematically corroborated by other laboratories and other dating techniques (Curtis, 1981).

Some of the chronology at Hadar, however, does appear clear cut. For example, there is general agreement that the Lucy skeleton (Fig. 14–13) is about 3 million years old. Analyses of the older beds using a variety of dating techniques have led to some ambiguity regarding their precise dating. Such chronologies often take years of study to sort out. Most crucially, cross-correlations among different dating techniques (K/Ar, biostratigraphy, paleomagnetism, fission-track) must be determined. The most recent calibrations with improved methods of K/Ar dating suggest a range of dates from 3.9–3.0 m.y.a. for the Hadar hominid discoveries.

Owing to the excellent preservation conditions in the once-lakeside environment at Hadar, an extraordinary collection of fossilized bones has been discovered—6,000 specimens in the first two field seasons alone! Among the fossil remains, at least 40 hominid individuals (and perhaps as many as 65) have been discovered (Johanson and Taieb, 1980).

Two extraordinary discoveries at Hadar are most noteworthy. In 1974, a partial skeleton called "Lucy" was found eroding out of a hillside. This fossil is scientifically designated as Afar Locality (AL) 288-1, but is usually just called Lucy (after the Beatles song "Lucy in the Sky with Diamonds"). Representing almost 40 percent of a skeleton, this is one of the two most complete individuals from anywhere in the world for the entire period before about 100,000 years ago.*

The second find, a phenomenal discovery, came to light in 1975 at AL 333. Don Johanson and his amazed crew found dozens of hominid bones scattered along a hillside. These bones represented at least 13 individuals, including 4 infants. Possibly members of one social unit, the members of this group have been argued to have died at about the same time, thus representing a "cata-

---

*The other is a *H. erectus* skeleton from west of Lake Turkana, Kenya (see p. 424).

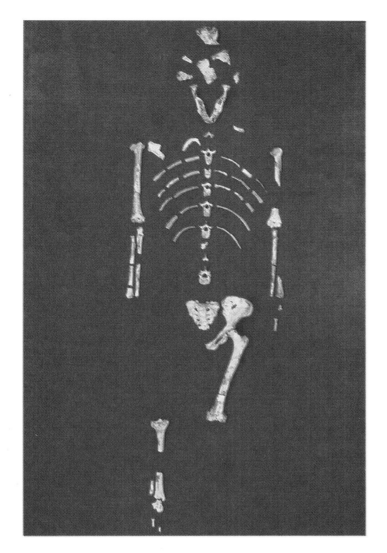

FIGURE 14–13
"Lucy," a partial hominid skeleton, discovered at Hadar in 1974.

strophic" assemblage (White and Johanson, 1989). However, the precise deposition of the site has not been completely explained, so this assertion must be viewed as quite tentative. (In geological time, an "instant" could represent many decades or centuries.) Considerable cultural material has been found in the Hadar area—mostly washed into stream channels, but some stone tools have been reported in context at a site dated at 2.5 m.y.a., potentially making the findings the oldest cultural evidence yet discovered.

Unfortunately, political instability in Ethiopia has caused frequent interruptions of field research at Hadar. However, in the last few years, considerable further surveying has been done in the Afar Triangle (and elsewhere in Ethiopia). Aided by satellite photography (from the space shuttle) that identified those geological exposures most likely to yield fossil discoveries, ground teams have recovered numerous new specimens from the Hadar, including cranial fragments, mandibles, and some post cranial elements (Asfaw, 1992; Wood, 1992a). In addition, in 1992, Yoel Rak, of the Institute of Human Origins and Tel Aviv University, discovered the most complete early hominid cranium yet found at Hadar (Fig. 14–14) (Kimbel et al., 1994).

Hominids from Laetoli and Hadar

Several hundred specimens, representing a minimum of 60 individuals (and perhaps as many as 100) have been removed from Laetoli and Hadar. At present, these materials represent the largest *well-studied* collection of early hominids known. This situation may well change with further discoveries and as analyses are completed for the Aramis, Kanapoi, and Allia Bay localities. Moreover, it has been suggested that fragmentary specimens from other locales in East Africa are remains of the same species as that found at Laetoli and Hadar. Most scholars refer to this species as *Australopithecus afarensis*.

Without question, A. *afarensis* is more primitive than any of the other **australopithecine** fossils from South or East Africa (discussed subsequently), although the recently described materials from Aramis (*Ardipithecus*) and Kanapoi and Allia Bay (*Australopithecus anamensis*) are even more so. By "primitive," we mean that A. *afarensis* is less evolved in any particular direction than are later occurring hominid species. That is, A. *afarensis* shares more primitive features with other early hominoids (such as *Dryopithecus* and *Sivapithecus*) and with living pongids than is true of later hominids, who display more derived characteristics.

For example, the teeth of A. *afarensis* are quite primitive. The canines are often large, pointed teeth that slightly overlap. Moreover, the lower first premolar is semisectorial (i.e., it provides a shearing surface for the upper canine) and the tooth rows are parallel, even converging somewhat toward the back of the mouth (Fig. 14–15).

The cranial portions that are preserved, including the recently discovered specimen (shown in Fig. 14–14), also display several primitive hominoid characteristics, including a compound sagittal/nuchal crest in the back as well as several primitive features of the cranial base. Cranial capacity estimates for A. *afarensis* show a mixed pattern when compared to later hominids. A provisional estimate for the one partially complete cranium—apparently a large individual—gives a figure of 500 cm³, but another, even more fragmentary cranium is apparently quite a bit smaller and has been estimated at about 375 cm³ (Holloway, 1983). Thus, for some individuals (males?), A. *afarensis* is well within the range of other australopithecine species, but others (females?) may have a significantly smaller cranial capacity. However, a detailed depiction of cranial size for A. *afarensis* is not possible at this time; this part of the skeleton is unfortu-

▲ **Australopithecine**
(os-tra-loh-pith´-e-seen) The colloquial name for members of the genus *Australopithecus*. The term was first used as a subfamily designation, but is now most commonly used informally.

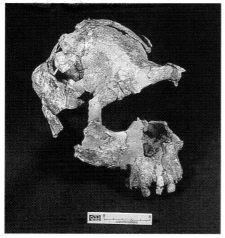

FIGURE 14–14
Australopithecus afarensis *cranium discovered at Hadar in 1992. This is the most complete* A. afarensis *cranium yet found.*

FIGURE 14–15
Jaws of Australopithecus afarensis. *(a) Maxilla, AL 200-1a, from Hadar, Ethiopia. (Note the parallel tooth rows and large canines.) (b) Mandible, LH 4, from Laetoli, Tanzania. This fossil is the type specimen for the species* Australopithecus afarensis.

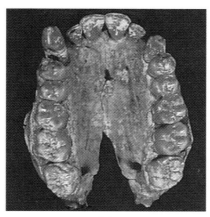

(a)

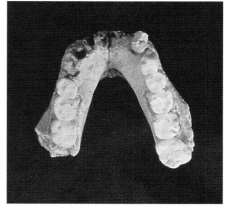

(b)

GREAT MOMENTS IN PREHISTORY

Discovery of the Hadar "Family," November to December, 1975

On November 1, I set out for the new area with photographer David Brill and a visiting scientist, Dr. Becky Sigmon.

Climbing into my Land Rover, David asked, "When do we find our next hominid?"

"Today," I replied.

In less than an hour, anthropology student John Kolar spotted an arm-bone fragment. From some distance away, Mike Bush, a medical student, shouted that he had found something just breaking the ground surface. It was the very first day on survey for Mike.

"Hominid teeth?" he asked, when we ran to him. There was no doubt.

We called that spot Afar Locality 333 and scheduled full excavation for the next day.

Morning found me at 333, lying on my side so that I could wield a dental pick to excavate the upper-jaw fragment Mike had found. Michèle Cavillon of our motion-picture crew called to me to look at some bones higher up the hill.

Two bone fragments lay side by side—one a partial femur and the other a fragmentary heel bone. Both were hominid.

Carefully, we started scouring the hillside. Two more leg bones—fibulae—showed up, but each from the same side. The same side? That could only indicate two individuals.

Then from high on the slope came a cry, "Look at the proximal femur—it's complete!" Turning I saw, outlined against the blue sky, the top end of a thigh bone. Even from a distance I could tell that it was not Lucy-size; it was much larger. Slowly I groped up the hillside and held the femur.

Mike wanted to come look but was distracted by finding two fragments composing a nearly complete lower jaw. The entire hillside was dotted with the bones of what were evidently at least two individuals.

We held a strategy meeting. Maurice (geologist Maurice Taieb) established that the bones we found on the surface had originally been buried several yards up the slope. Mike chose a crew of seven workers to survey carefully every inch of the area and collect all bone material, sifting even the loose soil.

Time was of the essence. Rainstorms during the months of our absence could wash away fragments that would be lost forever down the ravines. I felt I was moving through a dream: Each day produced more remains.

The picture became tangled. Another upper jaw of an adult came to light. The wear pattern on the lower jaw we'd found did not match either of the uppers. At least three individuals had to be represented. More mandible fragments appeared that could not be definitely fitted to either upper jaw. Extraordinary! We had evidence of perhaps as many as five adults of the genus *Homo*.*

Apart from teeth and jaws, we recovered scores of hand and foot bones, leg bones, vertebrae, ribs, even a partial adult skull. A baby tooth turned up, suggesting the presence of a sixth hominid at the site. Then a nearly complete lower jaw of a baby appeared, as well as an almost intact palate with baby teeth. Not heavily worn, the teeth suggested that their possessor was only about 3 years old.

So we had evidence of young adults, old adults, and children—an entire assemblage of early hominids. All of them at one place. Nothing like this had ever been found!

Source: "Ethiopia Yields First 'Family' of Early Man," by Donald C. Johanson, *National Geographic Magazine*, Vol. 150, pp. 790–811, December 1976. Reprinted with permission of the publisher.

---

*Johanson and his colleagues later assigned all this material to *Australopithecus afarensis* (see p. 368).

nately too poorly represented. One thing is clear: A. *afarensis* had a small brain, probably averaging for the whole species not much over 420 cm³.

A host of postcranial pieces has been found at Hadar (mostly from the partial skeleton Lucy and from individuals at AL 333). Initial impressions suggest that, relative to lower limbs, the upper limbs are longer than in modern humans (also a primitive hominoid condition). This statement does not mean that the arms of

BOX 14–2

Cranial Capacity

Cranial capacity, usually reported in cubic centimeters, is a measure of brain size or volume. The brain itself, of course, does not fossilize. However, the space once occupied by brain tissue (the inside of the cranial vault) does sometimes preserve, at least in those cases where fairly complete crania are recovered.

For purposes of comparison it is easy to obtain cranial capacity estimates for contemporary species (including humans) from analyses of skeletonized specimens in museum collections. From studies of this nature, estimated cranial capacities for modern hominoids have been determined as follows (Tobias, 1971, 1983):

	Range (cm³)	Average (cm³)
Human	1150–1750*	1325
Chimpanzee	285–500	395
Gorilla	340–752	506
Orangutan	276–540	411
Bonobo	—	350

These data for living hominoids can then be compared with those obtained from early hominids:

	Averages(s) (cm³)
Ardipithecus	Not presently known
Australopithecus anamensis	Not presently known
Australopithecus afarensis	420
Later australopithecines	410–530
Early members of genus *Homo*	631

As the tabulations indicate, cranial capacity estimates for australopithecines fall within the range of most modern great apes, and gorillas actually average slightly more than *A. afarensis*. It must be remembered, however, that gorillas are very large animals, whereas australopithecines probably weighed on the order of 100 pounds (see Table 14–3, p. 385). Since brain size is partially correlated with body size, comparing such different-sized animals cannot be justified (see Chapter 11, p. 268, for a discussion of such *scaling* considerations). Compared to living chimpanzees (most of which are slightly larger than early hominids) and bonobos (which are somewhat smaller), australopithecines had *proportionately* about 10 percent bigger brains than living apes, and we would therefore say that these early hominids were more *encephalized* (see p. 268).

*The range of cranial capacity for modern humans is very large—in fact, even greater than that shown (which approximates cranial capacity for the *majority* of contemporary *H. sapiens*).

A. afarensis were longer than the legs. In addition, the wrist, hand, and foot bones show several differences from modern humans (Susman et al., 1985). Stature can now be confidently estimated: *A. afarensis* was a short hominid. From her partial skeleton, Lucy is figured to be only 3½ to 4 feet tall. However, Lucy—as demonstrated by her pelvis—was probably a female, and at Hadar and Laetoli there is evidence of larger individuals as well. The most economical hypothesis explaining this variation is that *A. afarensis* was quite sexually dimorphic—the larger individuals are male and the smaller ones, such as Lucy, are female. Estimates of male stature can be approximated from the larger footprints at Laetoli, inferring a height of about 5 feet. If we accept this interpretation, *A. afarensis* was a very sexually dimorphic form. In fact, for overall body size, this species may have been as dimorphic as *any* living primate (i.e., as much as gorillas, orangutans, or baboons).

In a majority of dental and cranial features, A. *afarensis* is clearly more primitive than are later hominids. In fact, from the neck up, A. *afarensis* is so primitive that without any evidence from the limbs, one would be hard-pressed to call it a hominid at all (although the back teeth are large and heavily enameled, unlike pongids, and the position of the foramen magnum indicates an upright posture). In the front teeth, particularly, A *afarensis* is in some ways reminiscent of Miocene hominoids (e.g., *Sivapithecus*) (Greenfield, 1979).

What, then, makes A. *afarensis* a hominid? The answer is revealed by its manner of locomotion. From the abundant limb bones recovered from Hadar and those beautiful footprints from Laetoli, we know unequivocally that A. *afarensis* walked bipedally when on the ground. Whether Lucy and her contemporaries still spent considerable time in the trees, and just how efficiently they walked, have become topics of major dispute.

Locomotion of *Australopithecus afarensis*

A comprehensive analysis of the postcranial anatomy of A. *afarensis* by Jack Stern and Randall Susman of the State University of New York at Stony Brook has challenged the view that this early hominid walked bipedally much as modern humans do (Stern and Susman, 1983). Their interpretation is based on many parts of the skeleton (limbs, hands, feet, pelvis, etc.), which they have compared with other hominids (fossil and modern), as well as with great apes.

Such features as long, curved fingers and toes, long upper limbs but short lower limbs (Jungers, 1982; Susman et al., 1985), the positioning of the hip and knee joints, and pelvic orientation have led these researchers to two conclusions: (1) A. *afarensis* was capable of efficient climbing and probably spent considerable time in the trees (sleeping, feeding, escaping from predators, etc.); and (2) while on the ground, A. *afarensis* was an habitual biped, but walked with a much less efficient bent-hip, bent-knee gait than that seen in modern humans.

As might be expected, these conclusions themselves have been challenged. While pointing out some slight differences from modern humans in postcranial anatomy, Owen Lovejoy (1988) and his associates (e.g., Latimer, 1984) see nothing that suggests that these hominids were arboreal or, conversely, that precluded them from being *very* efficient obligate bipeds. Moreover, Lucy's "little legs" may not really be that short, considering her small body size (Wolpoff, 1983a).

Other researchers have also noted differences between the postcranium of A. *afarensis* and that of later hominids. Interestingly, however, in many respects the hand and pelvis of A. *afarensis* are extremely similar to those seen in some later australopithecines from South Africa (Suzman, 1982; McHenry, 1983).

From all this debate, little has yet emerged in the way of consensus, except that all agree that A. *afarensis* did exhibit some kind of bipedal locomotion while on the ground. In searching for some middle ground between the opposing viewpoints, several researchers have suggested that A. *afarensis* could have been quite at home in the trees *as well* as being an efficient terrestrial biped (McHenry, 1983; Wolpoff, 1983b). As one physical anthropologist has surmised: "One could imagine these diminutive early hominids making maximum use of *both* terrestrial and arboreal resources in spite of their commitment to exclusive bipedalism when on the ground. The contention of a mixed arboreal and terrestrial behavioral repertoire would make adaptive sense of the Hadar australopithecine forelimb, hand, and foot morphology without contradicting the evidence of the pelvis (Wolpoff, 1983b. p. 451)."

Later East African Hominid Sites

An assortment of fossil hominids has been recovered from geological contexts with dates after 3 m.y.a. at several localities in East Africa. Up to 10 different such sites are now known (in the time range of 3–1 m.y.a.), but here we will concentrate on the three most significant ones: East Lake Turkana, West Lake Turkana (both in northern Kenya), and Olduvai Gorge (in northern Tanzania) (Table 14–2).

East Lake Turkana (Koobi Fora)

As noted above, numerous hominids have been discovered in the East Lake Turkana region in recent years. Located very near the considerably older Allia Bay site on the east shore of Lake Turkana is Koobi Fora (Fig. 14–16). This latter locality, with sediments dating to 1.8–1.3 m.y.a., has provided specimens representing at least 100 individuals, and this fine sample includes several complete crania, many jaws, and an assortment of postcranial bones.

Geologically, the situation at East Lake Turkana is exceedingly complex, with deep sections of lake and river deposits crisscrossed by the effects of **tectonic movements**, stream action, and volcanic activity. While the latter is useful in providing material for radiometric dating, the geological complexities have made the precise chronology of the area a matter of dispute.

Next to Olduvai, Koobi Fora has yielded the most information concerning the behavior of early hominids. More than 20 archeological sites have been discovered, and excavation or testing has been done at 10 localities. Two sites are of particular interest and are both directly associated with a volcanic bed dated at 1.8 m.y.a. One is a combination of stone artifacts with the broken bones of several species, whereas the other is the "butchering" site of an extinct form of hippopotamus. The stone tools from these earlier sediments at Koobi Fora are in many ways reminiscent of the Oldowan industry in Bed I at Olduvai (with which they are contemporaneous).

▲ **Tectonic movements**
Movements of the earth's plates that produce mountain building, earthquakes, volcanoes, and rifting.

TABLE 14–2	Summary of Later East African Hominid Discoveries		
Site Name	Location	Age (m.y.a.)	Hominids
Olduvai	N. Tanzania	1.85–1.0	48 specimens; australopithecines; early *Homo*
Turkana	N. Kenya (eastern side of Lake Turkana)	1.9–1.3	More than 150 specimens; many australopithecines; several early *Homo*
	West side of Lake Turkana	2.5–1.6	1 cranium (australopithecine); 1 nearly complete skeleton (*Homo erectus*)
Hadar	N.E. Ethiopia	3.9–3.0	Minimum of 40 individuals (maximum of 65); early australopithecines (*A. afarensis*)
Laetoli	N. Tanzania	3.7–3.5	24 hominids; early australopithecines (*A. afarensis*)

FIGURE 14-16
Excavations in progress at Koobi Fora, in East Lake Turkana, northern Kenya.

West Lake Turkana

Across the lake from the fossil beds discussed above are other deposits that recently have yielded new and very exciting discoveries. In 1984, on the west side of Lake Turkana, a nearly complete skeleton of a 1.6-million-year-old *Homo erectus* adolescent was found (see p. 414), and the following year a well-preserved cranium, 2.5 million years old, was also found. This latter find, "the black skull," is a most important discovery and has caused a major reevaluation of Plio-Pleistocene hominid evolution.

Olduvai Gorge

By now you are no doubt well acquainted with this remarkable site in northern Tanzania, particularly with its clear geological and chronological contributions. Hominid discoveries from Olduvai now total about 50 individuals, ranging in time from 1.85 m.y.a. to Upper Pleistocene times less than 50,000 years ago.

Hominids from Olduvai and Lake Turkana

Most fossil hominids from Olduvai, West Lake Turkana, and especially Koobi Fora are later in time than the *A. afarensis* remains from Laetoli and Hadar (by at least 500,000 years). It is thus not surprising that they are more derived, in some cases dramatically so. Also, these later hominids are considerably more diverse. Most researchers accept the interpretation that all the hominids from Laetoli and Hadar are members of a single taxon, *A. afarensis*. However, it is clear that the remains from the Turkana area and Olduvai collectively represent multiple taxa—two different genera and perhaps up to five or six different species. Current discussion on how best to sort this complex material is among the most vehement in paleoanthropology. Here we summarize the broad patterns of physical

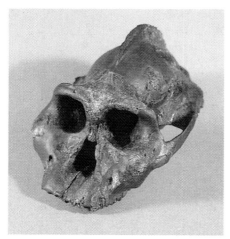

FIGURE 14–17

The "black skull," WT 17,000, discovered at West Lake Turkana in 1985. This specimen is provisionally assigned to Australopithecus aethiopicus.

▲ Sagittal crest
Raised ridge along the midline of the cranium where the temporal muscle (used to move the jaw) is attached.

morphology. In Chapter 15 we will take up the various schemes that attempt to interpret the fossil remains in a broader evolutionary context.

Following 2.5 m.y.a., later (and more derived) representatives of *Australopithecus* are found in East Africa. This is a most distinctive group that has popularly been known for some time as "robust" australopithecines. By "robust" it had generally been meant that these forms—when compared to other australopithecines—were larger in body size. However, recent, more controlled studies (Jungers, 1988; McHenry, 1988; 1992) have shown that all the species of *Australopithecus* overlapped considerably in body size. As you will see shortly, "robust" australopithecines have also been found in South Africa.

As a result of these new weight estimates, many researchers have either dropped the use of the term *robust* (along with its opposite, *gracile*) or present it in quotation marks to emphasize its conditional application. We believe that the term *robust* can be used in this latter sense, as it still emphasizes important differences in the scaling of craniodental traits. In other words, even if they are not larger overall, robust forms are clearly robust in the skull and dentition.

Dating to approximately 2.5 m.y.a., the earliest representative of this robust group comes from northern Kenya on the west side of Lake Turkana. A complete cranium (WT 17,000—"the black skull") was unearthed there in 1985 and has proved to be a most important discovery (Fig. 14–17). This skull, with a cranial capacity of only 410 cm³, has the smallest definitely ascertained brain volume of any hominid yet found and has other primitive traits reminiscent of A. *afarensis*. For example, there is a compound crest in the back of the skull, the upper face projects considerably, the upper dental row converges in back, and the cranial base is extensively pneumatized—that is, it possesses air pockets (Kimbel et al., 1988).

What makes the black skull so fascinating, however, is that mixed with this array of distinctively primitive traits are a host of derived ones linking it to other members of the robust group (including a broad face, a very large palate, and a large area for the back teeth). This mosaic of features seems to place skull WT 17,000 between earlier A. *afarensis* on the one hand and the later robust species on the other. Because of its unique position in hominid evolution, WT 17,000 (and the population it represents) has been placed in a new species, *Australopithecus aethiopicus*.

Around 2 m.y.a., different varieties of even more derived members of the robust lineage were on the scene in East Africa. As well documented by finds at Olduvai and Koobi Fora, robust australopithecines have relatively small cranial capacities (ranging from 510 to 530 cm³) and very large, broad faces with massive back teeth and lower jaws. The larger (probably male) individuals also show a raised ridge, called a **sagittal crest**, along the midline of the cranium. The first find of a recognized Pio-Pleistocene hominid in East Africa, in fact, was of a nearly complete robust australopithecine cranium, discovered in 1959 by Mary Leakey at Olduvai Gorge (see p. 340). As a result of Louis Leakey's original naming of the fossil (as *Zinjanthropus*), this find is still popularly referred to as "Zinj." However, it and other members of the same species in East Africa are now usually classified as *Australopithecus boisei*.

Early Homo

In addition to the robust australopithecine remains in East Africa, there is another Plio-Pleistocene hominid that is quite distinctive. In fact, as best documented by fossil discoveries from Olduvai and Koobi Fora, these materials have been assigned to the genus *Homo*—and thus are different from all species assigned to *Australopithecus*.

The earliest appearance of genus *Homo* in East Africa may be as ancient as that of the robust australopithecines. (As we have discussed, the black skull from West Turkana has been dated to approximately 2.5 m.y.a.) Recent reinterpretations of a temporal fragment from the Lake Baringo region of central Kenya have suggested that early *Homo* may also be close to this same antiquity (estimated age of 2.4 m.y.a) (Hill et al., 1992). Given that the robust australopithecine lineage was probably diverging at this time, it is not surprising to find the earliest representatives of the genus *Homo* also beginning to diversify. Nevertheless, one temporal bone does not provide indisputable proof. Further early remains in well-dated contexts will help provide confirmation.

The presence of a Plio-Pleistocene hominid with a significantly larger brain than seen in *Australopithecus* was first suggested by Louis Leakey in the early 1960s on the basis of fragmentary remains found at Olduvai Gorge. Leakey and his colleagues gave a new species designation to these fossil remains, naming them *Homo habilis*.

The *Homo habilis* material at Olduvai ranges in time from 1.85 m.y.a. for the earliest to about 1.6 m.y.a. for the latest. Due to the fragmentary nature of the fossil remains, interpretations have been difficult and much disputed. The most immediately obvious feature distinguishing the *H. habilis* material from the australopithecines is cranial size. For all the measurable *H. habilis* skulls, the estimated average cranial capacity is 631 cm^3 compared to 520 cm^3 for all measurable robust australopithecines and 442 cm^3 for the less robust species (McHenry, 1988). *Homo habilis*, therefore, shows an increase in cranial size of about 20 percent over the larger of the australopithecines and an even greater increase over some of the smaller-brained forms (from South Africa, discussed shortly). In their initial description of *H. habilis*, Leakey and his associates also pointed to differences from australopithecines in cranial shape and in tooth proportions (larger front teeth relative to back teeth and narrower premolars).

The naming of this fossil material as *Homo habilis* ("handy man") was meaningful from two perspectives. First of all, Leakey inferred that members of this group were the early Olduvai toolmakers. If true, how do we account for a robust australopithecine like "Zinj" lying in the middle of the largest excavated area known at Olduvai? What was he doing there? Leakey suggested he was the remains of a *habilis* meal! Excepting those instances where cut marks are left behind (see pp. 338–339), we must point out again that there is no clear way archeologically to establish the validity of such a claim. However, the debate over this assertion serves to demonstrate that cultural factors as well as physical morphology must be considered in the interpretation of hominids as biocultural organisms. Secondly, and most significantly, by calling this group *Homo*, Leakey was arguing for at least *two separate branches* of hominid evolution in the Plio-Pleistocene. Clearly, only one could be on the main branch eventually leading to *Homo sapiens*. By labeling this new group *Homo* in opposition to *Australopithecus*, Leakey was guessing that he had found our ancestors.

Since the initial evidence was so fragmentary, most paleoanthropologists were reluctant to accept *H. habilis* as a valid taxon distinct from *all* australopithecines. Differences from the hyperrobust East African variety (*A. boisei*) were certainly apparent; the difficulties arose in trying to distinguish *H. habilis* from the more gracile australopithecines from South Africa, particularly regarding dental traits that considerably overlap.

Later discoveries, especially from Lake Turkana, of better-preserved fossil material have shed further light on early *Homo* in the Plio-Pleistocene

(Fig. 14–18). The most important of this additional material is a nearly complete cranium (ER 1470) discovered at Koobi Fora in 1972 (Fig 14–19). With a cranial capacity of 775 cm³, this individual is well outside the known range for australopithecines and actually overlaps the lower boundary for *Homo erectus*. In addition, the shape of the skull vault and face are in many respects unlike those of australopithecines. However, the face is still quite robust (Walker, 1976), and the fragments of tooth crowns that are preserved indicate that the back teeth in this individual were quite large. Dating of the Koobi Fora early *Homo* material places it contemporaneous with the Olduvai remains, that is about 1.8–1.6 m.y.a.

Other Plio-Pleistocene sites also have revealed possible early members of the genus *Homo* (Fig. 14–20). From the Omo in southern Ethiopia, scattered remains of a few teeth and small cranial fragments are similar in pattern to other comparable early *Homo* material. In addition, a newly discovered very partial

FIGURE 14–18

The Kenyan team at East Lake Turkana. Kamoya Kimeu (driving) is the most successful fossil hunter in East Africa. He has been responsible for dozens of important discoveries (see Guest Essay, this chapter).

FIGURE 14–19

A nearly complete "early Homo*" cranium from East Lake Turkana (ER 1470), one of the most important single fossil hominid discoveries from East Africa.*

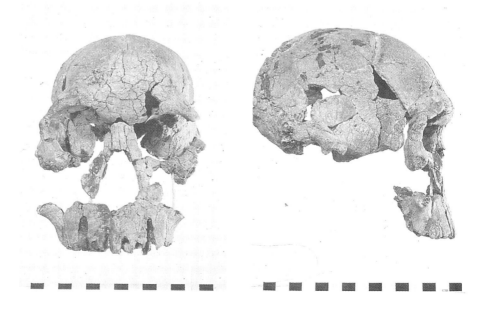

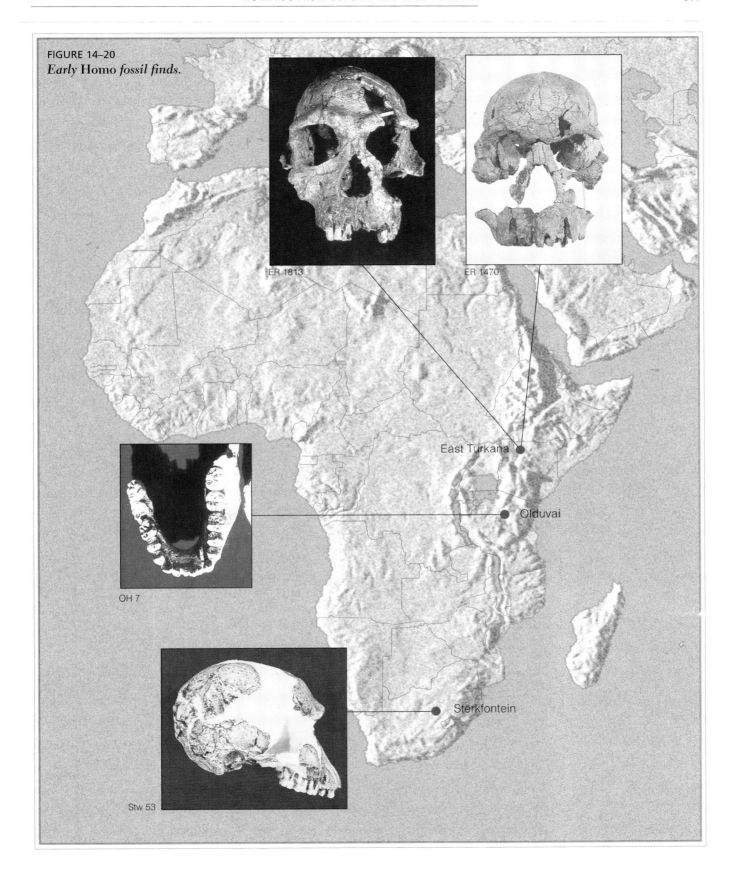

FIGURE 14–20
Early Homo *fossil finds.*

ER 1813

ER 1470

OH 7

East Turkana

Olduvai

Stw 53

Sterkfontein

skeleton from Olduvai Gorge (OH 62) is extremely small-statured (probably less than 4 feet tall) and has several primitive aspects in its limb proportions (Johanson et al., 1987).

On the basis of evidence from Olduvai and particularly from Koobi Fora, we can reasonably postulate that one or more species of early *Homo* was present in East Africa probably by 2.4 m.y.a., developing in parallel with at least one line of australopithecines. These two hominid lines lived contemporaneously for a minimum of 1 million years, after which the australopithecine lineage apparently disappeared forever. At the same time, probably the early *Homo* line was evolving into a later form, *Homo erectus*, which in turn developed into *H. sapiens*.

Central Africa

In 1995, another new early hominid discovery was announced from a rather surprising location—Chad, in central Africa (Brunet et al., 1995) (see Fig. 14–7). From an area called the Bahr el Ghazal (Arabic for "River of the Gazelles"), a partial hominid mandible was discovered in association with faunal remains tentatively dated to 3.5–3.0 m.y.a. (Further confirmation will have to await radiometric dating, assuming that appropriate materials become available.) The preliminary analysis suggests that this fossil is an australopithecine with closest affinities to *A. afarensis*. What makes this find remarkable is its geographical location, more than 1,500 miles west of the previously established range of early hominids!

South Africa: Earliest Discoveries

The first quarter of this century saw the discipline of paleoanthropology in its scientific infancy. Informed opinion considered the likely origins of the human family to be in Asia, where fossil forms of a primitive kind of *Homo* had been found in Indonesia in the 1890s. Europe was also considered a center of hominid evolutionary action, for spectacular discoveries there of early populations of *Homo sapiens* (including the famous Neandertals) and millions of stone tools had come to light, particularly in the early decades of this century.

Few knowledgeable scholars would have given much credence to Darwin's prediction (see Box 14–3) that the most likely place to find early relatives of humans would be Africa. It was in such an atmosphere of preconceived biases that the discoveries of a young Australian-born anatomist were to jolt the foundations of the scientific community in the 1920s. Raymond Dart arrived in South Africa in 1923 at the age of 30 to take up a teaching position in anatomy at the University of Witwatersrand in Johannesburg (Fig 14–21). Fresh from his evolution-oriented training in England under some of the leading scholars of the day (especially Sir Grafton Elliot Smith), Dart had developed a keen interest in human evolution. Consequently, he was well prepared when startling new evidence appeared at his very doorstep.

The first clue came in 1924, when one of Dart's students saw an interesting baboon skull at the home of the director of a commercial quarrying firm. The skull had come from a place called Taung, about 200 miles southwest of

BOX 14–3

Hominid Origins

" In each great region of the world the living mammals are closely related to the extinct species of the same region. It is, therefore, probable that Africa was formerly inhabited by extinct apes closely allied to the gorilla and chimpanzee, and as these two species are now man's nearest allies, it is somewhat more probable that our early progenitors lived on the African continent than elsewhere."

Source: Charles Darwin, *The Descent of Man*, 1871.

Johannesburg. When Dart saw the skull, he quickly recognized it as an extinct form and asked that any other interesting fossil material be sent to him for his inspection.

Soon after, he received two box loads of fossils and immediately recognized something that was quite unusual: a natural **endocast** of the inside of the brain-case of a higher primate, but certainly no baboon. The endocast fit into another limestone block containing the fossilized front portion of a skull, face, and lower jaw. However, these were difficult to see clearly, for the bone was hardened into a cemented limestone matrix called *breccia*. Dart patiently chiseled away for weeks, later describing the task:

> No diamond cutter ever worked more lovingly or with such care on a priceless jewel—nor, I am sure, with such inadequate tools. But on the seventy-third day, December 23, the rock parted. I could view the face from the front, although the right side was still imbedded. . . . What emerged was a baby's face, an infant with a full set of milk teeth and its permanent molars just in the process of erupting. I doubt if there was any parent prouder of his off-spring than I was of my Taung baby on that Christmas. (Dart, 1959, p. 10)

As indicated by the formation and eruption of teeth, the Taung child (Fig. 14–22) was probably about 3 to 4 years of age at death. Interestingly, the rate of development of this and many other Plio-Pleistocene hominids was more like that of apes than of modern *Homo* (Bromage and Dean, 1985; Shipman, 1987). Dart's initial impression that this form was a hominoid was confirmed when he could observe the face and teeth more clearly. However, as it turned out, it took considerably more effort before the teeth could be seen completely, since Dart worked four years just to separate the upper and lower jaws.

But Dart was convinced long before he had an unimpeded view of the dentition that this discovery was a remarkable one, an early hominoid from South Africa. The question was, what kind of hominoid. Dart realized that it was extremely improbable that this specimen could have been a forest ape, for South Africa has had a relatively dry climate for many millions of years. Even though the climate at Taung 3 m.y.a. was not as arid as was previously believed (Butzer, 1974), it was an unlikely place to find an ape!

▲ **Endocast**

A solid (in this case, rock) impression of the inside of the skull, showing the size, shape, and some details of the surface of the brain.

FIGURE 14–21
Raymond Dart, shown working in his laboratory.

FIGURE 14–22
(a) The Taung child discovered in 1924. The endocast is in back, with the fossilized bone mandible and face in front. (b) Taung, location of the initial australopithecine discovery.

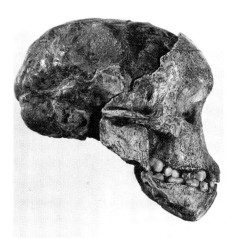

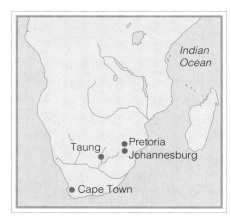

If not an ape, then, what was it? Features of the skull and teeth of this small child held clues that Dart seized on almost immediately. The foramen magnum at the base of the skull was further forward in the Taung child than in modern great apes, though not as much so as in modern humans. From this fact Dart concluded that the head was balanced *above* the spine, indicating erect posture. In addition, the slant of the forehead was not as receding as in apes, the milk canines were exceedingly small, and the newly erupted first molars were large, broad teeth. In all these respects, the Taung fossil looked more like a hominid than a pongid. There was, however, a disturbing feature that was to confuse many scientists for several years: The brain was quite small. Recent studies have estimated the Taung child's brain size at approximately 405 cm^3, which translates to a fully adult size of only 440 cm^3, not very large when compared to modern great apes (see Box 14–2).

Despite the relatively small size of the brain, Dart saw that it was no pongid. Details preserved on the endocast seemed to indicate that the association areas of the parietal lobes were relatively larger than in any known pongid. However, recent reexamination of the Taung specimen has shown that the sulcal (folding) pattern may actually be quite pongidlike (Falk, 1980; 1983).

We must emphasize that any attempt to discern the precise position of the "bumps and folds" in an ancient endocast is no easy feat. The science of "paleoneurology" is thus often marked by sharp differences of opinion. Consequently, it is not surprising that the other leading researcher in this field, Ralph Holloway (1981), disagrees with the conclusion by Falk (just cited) and suggests, alternatively, that the Taung endocast has a more hominid-like sulcal pattern.

Realizing the immense importance of his findings, Dart promptly reported them in the British scientific weekly *Nature* on February 7, 1925. A bold venture, since Dart, only 32, was presumptuously proposing a whole new view of human evolution! The small-brained Taung child was christened by Dart *Australopithecus africanus* (southern ape of Africa), which he saw as a kind of halfway "missing link" between modern apes and humans. The concept of a single "missing link" between modern apes and humans was a fallacious one, but Dart correctly emphasized the hominid-like features of the fossil.

A storm of both popular and scholarly protest greeted Dart's article, for it ran directly counter to prevailing opinion. Despite the numerous hominid fossils already discovered, widespread popular skepticism of evolution still prevailed. The year 1925 was, after all, the year of the Scopes "monkey trial" in Tennessee. However, the biggest fly in the ointment to the leading human evolutionists of

GREAT MOMENTS IN PREHISTORY

Raymond Dart and the Discovery of the Taung Child, November 1924

On his return, Young told me that at Taung he had met an old miner, Mr. M. de Bruyn, who for many years had taken a keen interest in preserving fossils. Only the previous week he had brought quite a number of stone blocks containing bone fragments to Mr. Spiers' office. When Young mentioned my interest to Mr. Spiers, Spiers gave instructions for them to be boxed and railed to me.

I waited anxiously for their arrival, reasoning that if fossilized baboon skulls were such a common feature at Taung, many other, more interesting specimens might be found there. Of course, the packages turned up at the most inappropriate time.

I was standing by the window of my dressing room cursing softly while struggling into an unaccustomed stiff-winged collar when I noticed two men wearing the uniform of the South African Railways staggering along the driveway of our home in Johannesburg with two large wooden boxes.

My Virginia-born wife Dora, who was also donning her most formal outfit, had noticed the men with the boxes and rushed in to me in something of a panic.

"I suppose those are the fossils you've been expecting," she said. "Why on earth did they have to arrive today of all days?" She fixed me with a business-like eye. "Now Raymond," she pleaded, "the guests will start arriving shortly and you can't go delving in all that rubble until the wedding's over and everybody has left. I know how important the fossils are to you, but please leave them until tomorrow."

At the time, however, this seemed of little importance when I considered the exciting anthropological bits and pieces that the boxes from Taung might contain. As soon as my wife had left to complete her dressing I tore the hated collar off and dashed out to take delivery of the boxes which meanwhile obstructed the entrance to the *stoep*. I was too excited to wait until my African servants carried them to the garage, and ordered them to leave the crates under the pergola while I went in search of some tools to open them.

(Later on that momentous day, my wife told me that she had twice remonstrated with me but had been ignored. I had no recollection of any interruptions.)

I wrenched the lid off the first box and my reaction was one of extreme disappointment. . . . In the rocks I could make out traces of fossilized eggshells and turtle shells and a few fragmentary pieces of isolated bone, none of which looked to be of much interest.

Impatiently I wrestled with the lid of the second box, still hopeful but half-expecting it to be a replica of its mate. At most I anticipated baboon skulls, little guessing that from this crate was to emerge a face that would look out on the world after an age-long sleep of nearly a million years.

As soon as I removed the lid a thrill of excitement shot through me. On the very top of the rock heap was what was undoubtedly an endocranial cast or mold of the interior of the skull. Had it been only the fossilized brain cast of any species of ape it would have ranked as a great discovery, for such a thing had never before been reported. But I knew at a glance that what lay in my hands was no ordinary anthropoidal brain. Here in lime-consolidated sand was the replica of a brain three times as large as that of a baboon and considerably bigger than that of any adult chimpanzee. The startling image of the convolutions and furrows of the brain and the blood vessels of the skull was plainly visible.

I stood in the shade holding the brain as greedily as any miser hugs his gold, my mind racing ahead. Here, I was certain, was one of the most significant finds ever made in the history of anthropology.

Source: Adventures with the Missing Link by Raymond Dart, 1959. Reprinted with permission of the author.

the day was the small size of the brain compared to the relatively large proportions of the face and jaws. At that time, anthropologists generally assumed that the primary functional adaptation distinguishing the human family was an immense increase in brain size and that dental and locomotor modifications came later. This view was seemingly confirmed by the Piltdown discovery in 1911, which displayed the combination of a large brain (estimated at 1,400 cm^3,

FIGURE 14–23
Robert Broom

▲ Sterkfontein
(sterk´-fon-tane)

▲ Kromdraai
(kromm´-dry)

▲ Swartkrans
(swart´-kranz)

▲ Makapansgat
(mak-ah-pans´-gat)

well within the range of modern humans) with an apelike jaw (see pp. 349–351). One prominent scientist went so far as to postulate a "cerebral rubicon" of 750 cm³ below which—by definition—no hominid could fall. Most scientists in the 1920s thus regarded this little Taung child as an interesting aberrant form of ape.

Hence, Dart's theories were received with indifference, disbelief, and scorn. Dart realized that more complete remains were needed. The skeptical world would not accept the evidence of one fragmentary, immature individual, no matter how highly suggestive the clues. Clearly, more fossil evidence was required, particularly more complete adult crania. Not an experienced fossil hunter himself, Dart sought further assistance in the search for more australopithecines.

Further Discoveries of South African Hominids

Soon after publication of his controversial theories, Dart found a strong ally in Robert Broom (Fig. 14–23). A Scottish physician and part-time paleontologist, Broom's credentials as a fossil hunter had been established earlier with his highly successful paleontological work on early mammal-like reptiles in South Africa.

Although interested, Broom was unable to participate actively in the search for additional australopithecines until 1936. From two of Dart's students, Broom learned of another commercial limeworks site, called **Sterkfontein**, not far from Johannesburg. Here, as at Taung, the quarrying involved blasting out large sections with dynamite, leaving piles of debris that often contained fossilized remains. Accordingly, Broom asked the quarry manager to keep his eyes open for fossils and when Broom returned to the site in August 1936, the manager asked, "Is this what you are looking for?" Indeed it was, for Broom held in his hand the endocast of an adult australopithecine—exactly what he had set out to find! Looking further over the scattered debris, Broom was able to find most of the rest of the skull of the same individual.

Such remarkable success, just a few months after beginning his search, was not the end of Broom's luck, for his magical touch was to continue unabated for several more years. In 1938, he learned of another australopithecine site at **Kromdraai**, about 1 mile from Sterkfontein, and following World War II (1948), he found yet another, **Swartkrans**, in the same vicinity. A final australopithecine site, **Makapansgat**, was excavated in 1947 by Raymond Dart, who returned to the fossil-discovering stage after an absence of over 20 years.

Numerous extremely important discoveries came from these additional sites, discoveries that would eventually swing the tide of intellectual thought to the views that Dart expressed back in 1925. Particularly important was a nearly complete cranium and pelvis, both found at Sterkfontein in 1947. As the number of discoveries accumulated, it became increasingly difficult to simply write the australopithecines off as aberrant apes.

By 1949, at least 30 hominid individuals were represented from five South African sites, and leading scientists were coming to accept the australopithecines as hominids. With the exposé of the Piltdown forgery in the 1950s (see pp. 349–351), this conversion was complete. With this acceptance also came the necessary recognition that hominid brains had their greatest expansion *after* earlier changes in teeth and locomotor systems. In other words, once again we see that the rate of evolution in one functional system of the body varies from that of other systems, thus displaying the *mosaic* nature of human evolution.

Hominids from South Africa

The Plio-Pleistocene hominid discoveries from South Africa are most significant. First, they were the earliest to be discovered in Africa and helped point the way to later discoveries in East Africa. Second, morphology of the South African hominids shows broad similarities to the forms in East Africa, but with several distinctive features, which argues for separation at least at the species level. Finally, there is a large assemblage of hominid fossils from South Africa, and exciting discoveries are still being made (Fig. 14–24).

Today, the evidence from South Africa continues to accumulate. In the last few years alone, more than 150 *new* specimens have come to light at Sterkfontein. In addition, several important new discoveries have been made at Swartkrans. A truly remarkable collection of early hominids, the remains from South Africa exceed 1,500 (counting all teeth as separate items), and the number of individuals is now more than 200.

From an evolutionary point of view, the most meaningful remains are those of the pelvis, which now include portions of nine os coxae (see p. 355). Remains of the pelvis are so important because, better than any other area of the body, this structure displays the unique requirements of a bipedal animal (as in modern humans *and* in our hominid forebears).

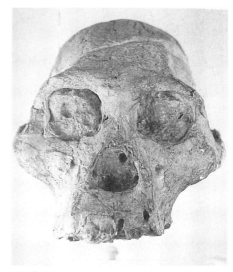

FIGURE 14–24

A gracile australopithecine cranium from Sterkfontein (Sts 5). Discovered in 1947, this specimen is the best-preserved gracile skull yet found in South Africa.

"Robust" Australopithecines

In addition to the discoveries of *A. aethiopicus* and *A. boisei* in East Africa, there are also numerous finds of robust australopithecines in South Africa from sites at Kromdraai and most especially at Swartkrans. Like their East African cousins, the South African robust forms also have small cranial capacities (the only measurable specimen equals 530 cm³), large broad faces, and very large premolars and molars (although not as massive as in East Africa). Owing to the differences in dental proportions, as well as important differences in facial architecture (Rak, 1983), most researchers now agree that there is a species-level difference between the later East African robust variety (*A. boisei*) and the South African group (*A. robustus*).

Despite these differences, all members of the robust lineage appear to be specialized for a diet made up of hard food items, such as seeds and nuts. For many years, paleoanthropologists (e.g., Robinson, 1972) had speculated that robust austrolopithecines concentrated their diet on heavier vegetable foods than are seen in the diet of other early hominids. Recent research that included examining microscopic polishes and scratches on the teeth (Kay and Grine, 1988) has confirmed this view.

"Gracile" Australopithecines

Another variety of australopithecine (also small-brained, but not as large-toothed as the robust varieties) is known from Africa. However, while the robust lineage is represented in both East and South Africa, this other australopithecine (gracile) form is known only from the southern part of the continent. First named *A. africanus* by Dart for the single individual at Taung, this australopithecine is also found at Makapansgat and, especially, at Sterkfontein (Fig. 14–25).

Traditionally, it had been thought that there was a significant variation in body size between the gracile and robust forms. But we mentioned earlier and as

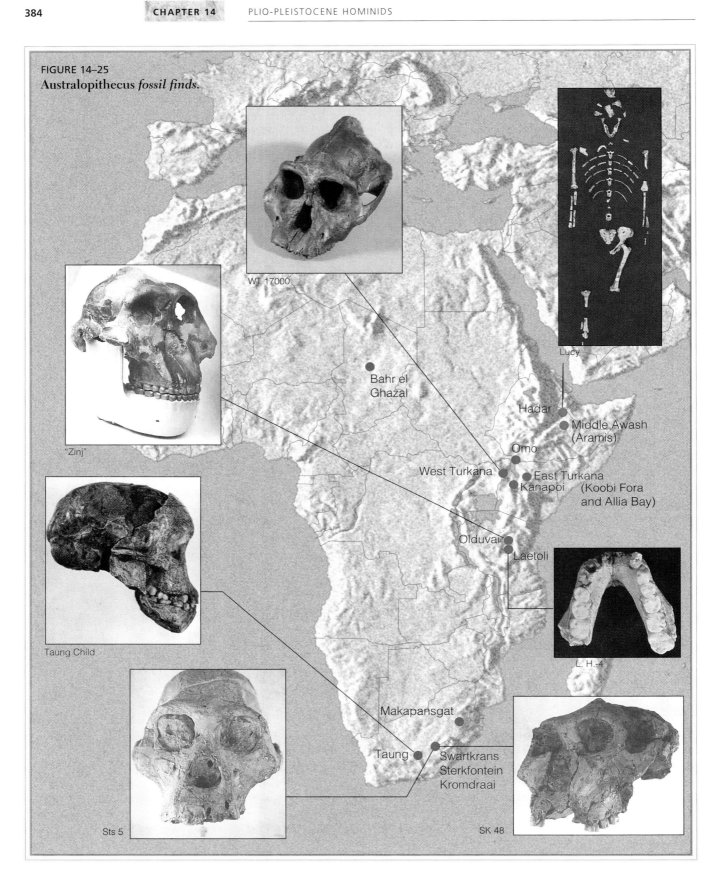

FIGURE 14–25
Australopithecus *fossil finds*.

WT 17000

Lucy

"Zinj"

Bahr el Ghazal

Hadar

Middle Awash (Aramis)

Omo

West Turkana

East Turkana (Koobi Fora and Allia Bay)

Kanapoi

Olduvai

Laetoli

Taung Child

L. H.-4

Makapansgat

Taung

Swartkrans Sterkfontein Kromdraai

Sts 5

SK 48

shown in Table 14–3, there is not much difference in body size among the australopithecines. In fact, most of the differences between the robust and gracile forms are found in the face and dentition.

The face structure of the gracile australopithecines is more lightly built and somewhat dish-shaped compared to the more vertical configuration seen in robust specimens. As we noted earlier, in robust individuals, a raised ridge along the midline of the skull is occasionally observed. Indeed, at Sterkfontein, among the larger individuals (males?), a hint of such a sagittal crest is also seen. This structure provides additional attachment area for the large temporal muscle, which is the primary muscle operating the massive jaw below. Such a structure is also seen in some modern apes, especially male gorillas and orangutans; however, in most australopithecines, the temporal muscle acts most efficiently on the back of the mouth and is therefore not functionally equivalent to the pattern seen in great apes—where the emphasis is more on the front teeth (see Fig 14–26).

The most distinctive difference observed between gracile and robust australopithecines is in the dentition. Compared to modern humans, they both have relatively large teeth, which are, however, definitely hominid in pattern. In fact, more emphasis is on the typical back-tooth grinding complex among these early forms than is seen in modern humans; therefore, if anything, australopithecines are "hyperhominid" in their dentition. Robust forms emphasize this trend to an extreme degree, showing deep jaws and much-enlarged back teeth, particularly the molars, severely crowding the front teeth (incisors and canines) together. Conversely, the gracile australopithecines have proportionately larger front teeth compared to the size of their back teeth. The contrast is seen most clearly in the relative size of the canine compared to the first premolar: In robust individuals, the first premolar is clearly a much larger tooth than the small canine (about twice as large), whereas in gracile specimens, it only averages abut 20 percent larger than the fairly good-sized canine (Howells, 1973).

These differences in the relative proportions of the teeth and jaws best define a gracile, as compared to a robust, australopithecine. In fact, most of the differences in skull shape we have discussed can be directly attributed to contrasting jaw function in the two forms. Both the sagittal crest and broad vertical face of the robust form are related to the muscles and biomechanical requirements of the extremely large-tooth-chewing adaptation of this animal.

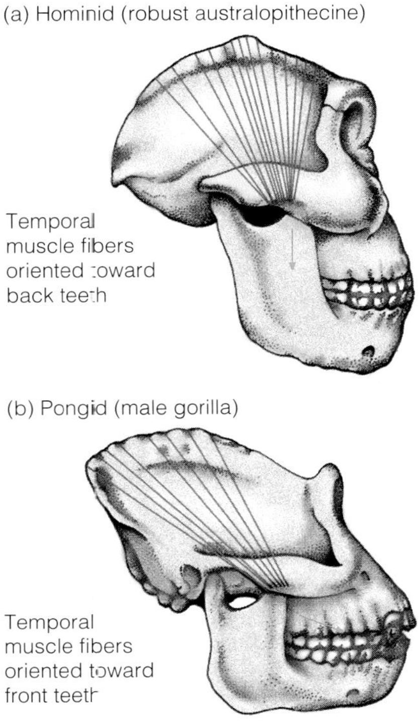

(a) Hominid (robust australopithecine)

Temporal muscle fibers oriented toward back teeth

(b) Pongid (male gorilla)

Temporal muscle fibers oriented toward front teeth

FIGURE 14–26
Sagittal crests and temporal muscle orientations. Hominid compared to pongid.

TABLE 14–3	Estimated Body Weights and Stature in Plio-Pleistocene Hominids			
	Body Weight (kg)		**Stature (cm)**	
	Male	**Female**	**Male**	**Female**
A. afarensis	45 (99 lb)	29 (64 lb)	151 (59 in.)	105 (41 in.)
A. africanus	41 (90 lb)	30 (65 lb)	138 (54 in.)	115 (45 in.)
A. robustus	40 (88 lb)	32 (70 lb)	132 (52 in.)	110 (43 in.)
A. boisei	49 (108 lb)	34 (75 lb)	137 (54 in.)	124 (49 in.)
H. habilis	52 (114 lb)	32 (70 lb)	157 (62 in.)	125 (49 in.)

After McHenry, 1992.

Early *Homo* in South Africa

As in East Africa, early members of the genus *Homo* have also been found in South Africa, apparently living contemporaneously with australopithecines. At both Sterkfontein and Swartkrans, fragmentary remains have been recognized as most likely belonging to *Homo*. In fact, Ron Clarke (1985) has shown that the key fossil of early *Homo* from Sterkfontein (Stw 53) is nearly identical to the OH 24 ***Homo habilis*** cranium from Olduvai.

However, a problem with both OH 24 and Stw 53 is that while most experts agree that they belong to the genus *Homo*, there is considerable disagreement as to whether they should be included in the species *habilis*. The relationships of the Plio-Pleistocene fossil hominids to one another and the difficulties of such genus and species interpretation will be the major topic of Chapter 15.

▲ *Homo habilis*

(hab´-ah-liss) A species of early *Homo*, well known in East Africa, but also perhaps from other regions.

Plio-Pleistocene Hominids Outside Africa

For many years, it had generally been assumed that hominids not only originated in Africa, but also were confined to this continent until about 1 million years ago. As we will discuss in more detail in Chapter 16, this view has had to be substantially modified in recent years. New fossil finds and refined dating tech-

FIGURE 14–27

Timeline of Major Plio-Pleistocene hominid sites. Note that most dates are approximations. Question marks indicate those estimates that are most tentative.

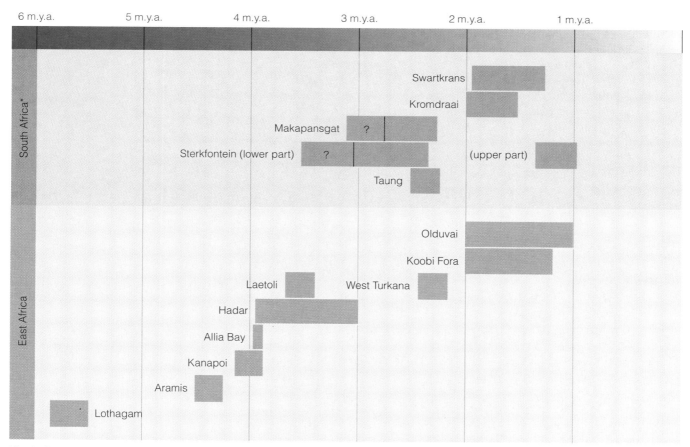

*South African dates are very approximate (see p. 392).

niques have now established that some hominids had already reached Asia by 1.8 m.y.a. and were possibly in Europe prior to 1.5 m.y.a.

As this realization of a fairly early hominid dispersal out of Africa has taken root, it still has been presumed that these first hominid migrants were members of a generally later and more derived member of genus *Homo* (i.e., members of the species *Homo erectus*). Now, even this assumption is being challenged. New finds from Longgupo Cave in central China (first announced in 1995) have been provisionally interpreted by the primary researchers working on the material (Huang Wanpo and Russell Ciochon) as *not* belonging to *Homo erectus*, but as more analogous to early *Homo* from East Africa (Wanpo et al., 1995). Moreover, the estimated age of the site (1.9–1.7 m.y.a.) would also make these Chinese hominids contemporaneous with early *Homo* from East Africa (at Olduvai and Koobi Fora). Thus far, only two specimens have been recovered (a fragmentary mandible and an upper incisor), and more complete remains will prove highly valuable in deciding where these Chinese fossils best fit into the pattern of Plio-Pleistocene hominid evolution (see Fig. 14–27 for a review of the dating of African Plio-Pleistocene sites).

Summary

In East and South Africa during the better part of the twentieth century, a vast collection of early hominids was gathered, a collection totaling more than 500 individuals (and thousands of fossil specimens). While considerable evolution occurred during the Plio-Pleistocene (approximately 3.5 million years are covered in this chapter), all forms are clearly hominid, as shown by their bipedal adaptation. The time range for this hominid material extends back to approximately 4.4 million years in East Africa, with the earliest and most primitive hominid now recognized—*Ardipithecus ramidus*. Two other early hominid forms are also known from East Africa, both members of the genus *Australopithecus*. These two species are *A. anamensis* (4.2–3.9 m.y.a.) and *A. afarensis* (3.9–3.0 m.y.a.).

Later hominids of a robust lineage are also known in East Africa (*A. aethiopicus, A. boisei*) and South Africa (*A. robustus*). These groups seem to have come on the scene about 2.5 m.y.a. and disappeared around 1 m.y.a.

In addition, a smaller-toothed (but not necessarily smaller-bodied) gracile form is known exclusively from South Africa, beginning at a time range estimated at around 2.5 m.y.a.

Finally, best known again in East Africa (but also found in South Africa), a larger-brained and smaller-toothed variety is also present perhaps as early as 2.4 m.y.a. This species, called *Homo habilis*, is thought by most paleoanthropologists to lie closer to our ancestry than the later varieties of australopithecines.

Questions for Review

1. In East Africa, all the early hominid sites are found along the Rift Valley. Why is this significant?
2. Compare the various East African Plio-Pleistocene sites for the kinds of cultural information uncovered.
3. How do the dating problems of the lower beds at Hadar illustrate the necessity of cross-correlation of several dating techniques?
4. Why was Raymond Dart's announcement of a small-brained bipedal hominoid greeted with such skepticism in 1925?
5. What led Dart to suggest that the Taung child was *not* an ape?

6. What was Robert Broom's contribution to revealing the hominid nature of the South African australopithecines?

7. (a) Why is postcranial evidence (particularly the lower limb) so crucial in showing the australopithecines as definite hominids? (b) What particular aspects of the australopithecine pelvis and lower limb are hominid-like?

8. In what ways are the remains of *Ardipithecus ramidus* and *Australopithecus anamensis* primitive? How do we know that these forms are hominids?

9. What hominid sites have yielded remains of *A. afarensis*? In what ways is the fossil material more primitive than that of other hominids from South and East Africa?

10. What kinds of robust australopithecines have been found in East Africa? How do they compare with South African australopithecines?

11. Why are some Plio-Pleistocene hominids from East Africa called "early *Homo*" (or *H. habilis*)? What does this imply for the evolutionary relationships of the australopithecines?

12. What did Louis Leakey mean by using the specific name *habilis* for a fossil hominid from Olduvai?

Suggested Further Reading

Binford, Lewis. 1981. *Bones: Ancient Men and Myths.* New York: Academic Press.

Johanson, Donald, and James Shreeve. 1989. *Lucy's Child: The Discovery of a Human Ancestor.* New York: Morrow.

Lewin, Roger. 1992. *Human Evolution: An Illustrated Introduction* 2d ed. New York: Freeman.

Reader, John. 1988. *Missing Links, The Hunt for Earliest Man.* 2d ed. London: Penguin Books.

Tattersall, Ian. 1995. *The Fossil Trail.* New York: Oxford University Press.

Internet Resources

There are very few Internet sites that focus on hominid evolution. The best currently available is:

Fossil Hominids.

http://earth.ics.uci.edu:8080/faqs/fossilhominids.html

(An excellent review of major hominid species, with good photos and some drawings of key fossils and details of discovery. Much of the discussion focuses on creationist arguments and scientific refutations of these.)

Origins of Humankind.

http://www.dealson.com/origins/

(Resources concerning human evolution. Excellent access to "Bookstore" listing current books, which can be searched by author, title, or key word. Also contains superb links to other web sites dealing with human evolution.)

Kamoya Kimeu*

Kamoya Kimeu is perhaps the best fossil hunter ever to have lived and worked in East Africa, with discoveries that have enhanced the knowledge of fossil ancestors dating from 27 million to around 130,000 years ago. Finding hominids gives him the greatest satisfaction, and his achievements have covered human evolution from the earliest anthropoids through to the later australopithecine and *Homo* lineages.

His introduction into paleontology came not after school or university, but as a result of a rather dramatic ending to his job milking cows at a farm outside Nairobi, Kenya. Caught stealing milk with a group of friends, Kamoya ran away, choosing that option over the choice of 25 strokes or 6 months work without pay. Still on the run from the dairy supervisor, Kamoya was asked by his uncle if he wanted to work for Louis Leakey, then working in Kenya as well as Tanzania and looking for more helpers. When asked what kind of work, his uncle replied simply, "digging up human bones," but even that sombre prospect was better than returning to the cow shed.

Kamoya met Louis Leakey in Nairobi, and for three days Kamoya and other workers camped with tents on the site which was to become the National Museums of Kenya and the base for all future expeditions. Afterwards, Kamoya joined Louis and Mary Leakey's expedition at Olduvai Gorge, Tanzania. After their discovery in 1959 of *Zinjanthropus*, the first

*As told to Simon Milledge.

Australopithecus boisei to be recognized in East Africa, greater funding enabled continuous work to be carried out at Olduvai (see p. 337). Kamoya and many others were recruited to help in the proceeding 18-month excavation. It was after only a few days work that he realized that he was not digging up human bones from graves as he had expected, but bones more like stones. Showing ability and a keen interest, Kamoya was soon moved from carting wheelbarrow loads of sediment to and from the river for washing, to excavating around the site in search of more *Zinjanthropus* skull fragments. An almost complete skull was eventually reconstructed. Once Louis had explained to Kamoya the real purpose for looking for fossils at Olduvai—it is the only way to discover more about our 2 to 1.5 m.y.a. ancestors—he became more and more interested. At that time, Kamoya could not read well, so without the use of textbooks Kamoya rapidly began learning all the different bones from many vertebrates by studying examples of modern specimens. Up until then, Kamoya had thought that finding fossils was beyond him, something only a *mzungu* (white man) could do. Curious and desperate to try, he asked Louis, "Can I find these fossils myself?" Louis replied, "This is luck. You can even find them yourself." Needing no more encouragement, Kamoya soon started finding fossils—at first, carnivores, monkeys, and many other types of fauna.

During 1963–4, Richard Leakey, Louis and Mary's second son, lead an expedition to Lake

Natron in northern Tanzania, and there Kamoya discovered his first hominid fossil, a complete mandible of *Australopithecus boisei*. This was a spectacular find, immensely important as *Zinjanthropus* was missing a mandible. From that day, Kamoya has never looked back. With an uncanny ability to find hominids, Kamoya found them on nearly every expedition. Of course, fossils from a wide variety of other animals were also discovered, but hominids always remained the prize findings. As well as the unique mental templates most paleontologists develop, Kamoya also has a very positive attitude and incredible patience, vital when prospecting in the dry East African heat.

From Tanzania, Richard Leakey's expedition went to Ethiopia where, in 1967, Kamoya found Omo 1, called the Kibish skull, with some associated postcranial material. This distinctively modern looking human was dated at 130,000 years old, pushing back the origin of *Homo sapiens* from 60,000 years ago, when people believed *H. sapiens* evolved from the Neandertals.

After Ethiopia, the expedition moved to Koobi Fora to the east of Lake Turkana in northern Kenya where (in rich deposits) countless hominid skull and limb bones were found between 1968 and 1980. Striking up a strong rapport with Richard Leakey, the two of them developed a formidable partnership and made many important discoveries. The field crew did not have to wait very long before Kamoya found a hominid skull. In 1973, after finding a lot of postcranial material

belonging to *Homo habilis* and *Homo erectus*, he discovered 1813, the skull of a gracile australopithecine. This skull, together with all the other specimens found, cast into doubt the theory that human evolution has involved one single ancestral lineage, but more likely that several hominid lineages occurred (with only one surviving from which modern humans evolved). Kamoya's natural leadership skills encouraged the rest of the team too, important when working in the harshest of environments in Africa, and he, along with Richard, soon became recognized as the leader of the field crew.

In 1980, the prospecting in the Turkana deposits turned to the west side of the lake at Nariokotome. Kamoya became the undisputed number one fossil hunter when, in 1984, he found a fragment of hominid skull not far from camp. After 5 years of excavation, the most complete skeleton ever of *Homo erectus* had been unearthed, now known as the Turkana boy. This was the first time such a skull could be compared with its associated skeleton and determine so much about *H. erectus* 1.6 million years ago, such as height, gait, build, lifestyle, etc. (see p. 414). Staying in west Turkana, the team also worked at the Miocene sites, Losidok and Kalodin, finding early hominoid specimens. Named after its discoverer, *Kamoyapithecus hamiltoni* is the earliest anthropoid species from East Africa, living 27 million years ago. Kamoya also found other hominoid species aged 17 million years old from nearby sediments. *Cercopithecoides kimeui*, a large, ground-living colobine monkey

from the Plio-Pleistocene was also found by and named after Kamoya.

Now 58 years old, Kamoya still continues to find fossils. The current palaeontological research is directed at sediments closer to the theoretical time at which apes and humans split on the evolutionary tree. Led by Meave Leakey, Richard's wife, the field crew from the National Museums of Kenya is currently prospecting at 4 million year old deposits on both sides of Lake Turkana. In 1994, at Kanapoi on the west side, a new species of hominid was discovered, called *Australopithecus anamensis* and dated at 4.1 million years old. This is the earliest *Australopithecus* species, with material showing a primitive skull more like that of an ape, yet human-like postcranial material. True to form, Kamoya contributed, finding a tibia, clearly showing evidence of bipedalism, thus pushing the origin of bipedalism back at least 600,000 years from the date of the Laetoli footprints. The find emphasized the fact that in hominid mosaic evolutionary development, bipedalism occurred before the development and expansion of the skull (see p. 328).

The picture of human evolution is far from complete, with controversies and gaps in the fossil record needing more material. This will come with time, especially with more and more research directed at human origins. The contribution by Kamoya is unmeasurable, with barely a season having gone by without him finding something special. There is no doubt that had he remained at the dairy farm just outside Nairobi, our knowledge of our ancestors would be far less complete.

15

Plio-Pleistocene Hominids: Organization and Interpretation

Introduction

We have seen in the last chapter that a vast and complex array of early hominid material has been discovered in South and East Africa. In just the past few years, particularly in the eastern part of the continent, a great number of new discoveries have been made. We now have Plio-Pleistocene hominid specimens representing close to 200 individuals from South Africa and more than 300 from East Africa. Given the size and often fragmentary nature of the sample, along with the fact that a good deal of it is so recently discovered, we should not be surprised that many complications arise when it comes to interpretation. In addition, both popular enthusiasm and the strong personalities (and strong views) often connected with fossil hominid discoveries have generated even more confusion.

In this chapter, we will look at several hypothetical reconstructions that attempt to organize the huge amount of Plio-Pleistocene hominid material. We ask you to remember that these are hypotheses and must remain so, given the incomplete nature of the fossil record. Even considering the seemingly very large number of fossils, there is a *great* deal of time over which they were distributed. If we estimate about 500 total individuals from all African sites recovered thus far for the period 4.4–1.0 m.y.a., we still are sampling just one individual for every 6,800 years! Until much of the new material from East Africa has been properly analyzed and detailed reports published, we cannot form even reasonably secure hypotheses without extreme difficulty. At the present time, only a few East African hominids have been thoroughly studied; all the rest are thus far described in preliminary reports.

It will no doubt appear that many opposing and conflicting hypotheses attempt to describe exactly what is going on in human evolution during the crucial period between about 4.5 and 1 m.y.a. And, indeed, there are many hypotheses. Hominid fossils are intriguing to both scientists and nonscientists, for some of these ancient bones and teeth are probably those of our direct ancestors. Equally intriguing, some of these fossils are representatives of populations of our close relatives that apparently met with extinction. We would like to know how they lived, what kinds of adaptations (physical and cultural) they displayed, and why some continued to evolve while others died out.

Geology and Dating Problems in South Africa

While, as we saw in the last two chapters, the geological and archeological context in East Africa is often straightforward, the five South African early hominid sites are much more complex geologically. All were discovered by commercial quarrying activity, which greatly disrupted the geological picture and, in the case of Taung, completely destroyed the site.

The hominid remains are found with thousands of other fossilized bones embedded in limestone cliffs, caves, fissures, and sinkholes. The limestone was formed by millions of generations of shells of marine organisms during the Precambrian—more than 2 billion years ago—when South Africa was submerged under a shallow sea. Once deposited, the limestones were cut through by percolating ground water from below and rainwater from above, forming a maze of caves and fissures often connected to the surface by narrow shafts. Through these vertical shafts and horizontal cave openings, bones either fell or were carried in, where they conglomerated with sand, pebbles, and soil into a cementlike matrix call *breccia*.

As the cave fissures filled in, they were constantly subjected to further erosion forces from above and below, so that caves would be partially filled, then closed to the surface for a considerable time, and reopened again to commence accumulation thousands of years later. All this activity yields an incredibly complex geological situation that can be worked out only after the most detailed kind of paleoecological analysis.

Since bones accumulated in these caves and fissures largely by accidental processes, it seems likely that none of the South African australopithecine sites are *primary* hominid localities. In other words, unlike East Africa, these are not areas where hominids organized activities, scavenged food, and so on.

Just how did all the fossilized bone accumulate, and, most particularly, what were the ancient hominids doing there? In the case of Swartkrans, Sterkfontein, and Kromdraai, the bones probably accumulated through the combined activities of carnivorous leopards, saber-toothed cats, and hyenas. However, the unexpectedly high proportion of primate (baboon and hominid) remains suggests that these localities were the location (or very near the location) of primate sleeping sites, thus providing ready prey for the predators (Brain, 1981).

Raymond Dart argued enthusiastically for an alternative explanation, suggesting that the hominids camping at Makapansgat regularly used bone, tooth, and horn remains as tools, which he called the **osteodontokeratic** culture complex. Analogies with the food habits of modern African foragers indicate that the bone accumulation at Makapansgat may be accounted for simply by hominid and carnivore eating practices. More recent paleoecological work at Makapansgat has thrown Dart's assertions into even greater doubt. Apparently, remains accumulated here primarily in a similar fashion to Sterkfontein and Swartkran—through a narrow shaft entrance (Fig. 15–1). Therefore, large animals could have entered but not departed the deep subterranean cavern.

▲ **Osteodontokeratic**
(*osteo*, meaning "bone," *donto*, meaning "*tooth*," and *keratic*, meaning "horn")

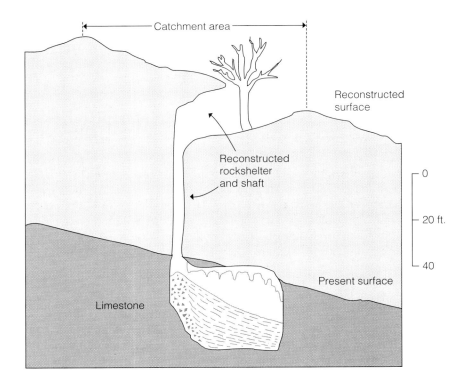

FIGURE 15–1

Swartkrans, geological section. The upper (reconstructed) part has been removed by erosion since the accumulation of the fossil-bearing deposit. (After Brain, 1970.)

Makapansgat, like Sterkfontein and Swartkrans, probably also represents the accumulated debris of carnivore activity (perhaps hyenas) outside the cave entrance. So little is left of the final site, Taung, that accurate paleoanthropological reconstructions are not feasible.

Owing to the complex geological picture, as well as lack of appropriate material such as volcanics for chronometric techniques, dating the South African early hominid sites has posed tremendous problems. Without chronometric dating, the best that can be done is to correlate the faunal sequences in South Africa with areas in East Africa where dates are better known (this approach is called biostratigraphy, see p. 344). Faunal sequencing of this sort on pigs, bovids such as antelope, and Old World monkeys has provided the following tenuous chronology:

Location	Age
	1 m.y.
Swartkrans	
Kromdraai	
	2 m.y.
Makapansgat	
Sterkfontein/Taung	3 m.y.

Attempts at paleomagnetic dating (see p. 342) suggest an age of 3.3–2.8 m.y.a. for Makapansgat (Brock et al., 1977), thus pushing the estimates to the extreme limits of those provided by biostratigraphy. In fact, some researchers believe that the paleomagnetic results are ambiguous and continue to "put their money" on the biostratigraphic data, especially those dates determined by analysis of pig and monkey fossils. From such consideration, they place the South African early hominid sites at perhaps as much as one-half million years later (i.e., for Makapansgat, around 2.5 m.y.a.) (White et al., 1981). This is crucial, since it places *all* the South African hominids after *Australopithecus afarensis* in East Africa (see Fig 15–2). Recent excavations at Sterkfontein have suggested the earliest hominids *may* come from levels as early as 3.5 m.y.a. (Clarke and Tobias, 1995). However, this date, which would be as early as *A. afarensis* in East Africa, has not yet been corroborated.

Interpretations: What Does It All Mean?

By this time, it may seem that anthropologists have an almost perverse fascination in finding small scraps buried in the ground and then assigning them confusing numbers and taxonomic labels impossible to remember. We must realize that the collection of all the basic fossil data is the foundation of human evolutionary research. Without fossils, our speculations would be completely hollow. Several large, ongoing paleoanthropological projects discussed in Chapter 13 are now collecting additional data in an attempt to answer some of the more perplexing questions about our evolutionary history.

The numbering of specimens, which may at times seem somewhat confusing, is an attempt to keep the designations neutral and to make reference to each individual fossil as clear as possible. The formal naming of finds as *Australopithecus, Homo habilis,* or *Homo erectus* should come much later, since it involves a lengthy series of complex interpretations. Assigning generic and specific names to fossil finds is more than just a convenience; when we attach a par-

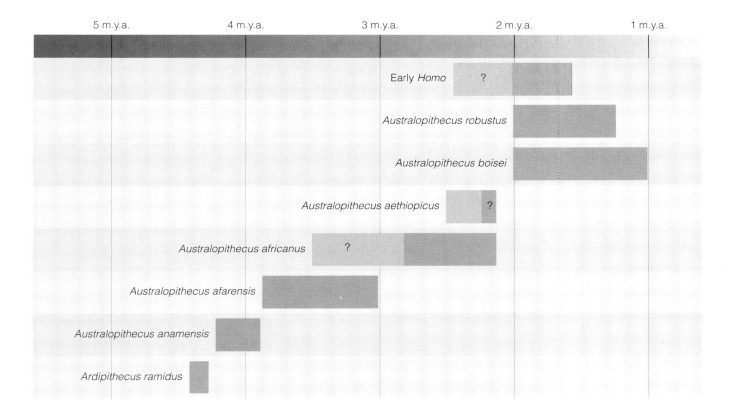

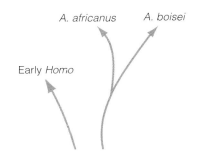

FIGURE 15–2

Time line of Plio-Pleistocene hominids. Note that most dates are approximations. Question marks indicate those estimates that are most tentative.

ticular label, such as A. *boisei*, to a particular fossil, we should be fully aware of the biological implications of such an interpretation (see p. 315).

Even more basic to our understanding of human evolution, the use of taxonomic nomenclature involves interpretations of fossil relationships. For example, both the two fossils "Zinj" and ER 406 (see Fig 15–5) are usually called A. *boisei*. What we are saying here is that they are both members of one interbreeding species. These two fossils can now be compared with others, like Sts 5 (see Fig 14–25) from Sterkfontein, which are usually called A. *africanus*. What we are implying now is that "Zinj" and ER 406 are more closely related to each other than *either* is to Sts 5. Furthermore, that Sts 5 (A. *africanus*) populations were incapable of successfully interbreeding with A. *boisei* populations is a direct biological inference of this nomenclature.

We can carry the level of interpretation even further. For example, fossils such as ER 1470 (see Fig 14–18) are called early *Homo* (*Homo habilis*). We are now making a genus-level distinction, and two basic biological implications are involved:

1. A. *africanus* (Sts 5) and A. *boisei* ("Zinj" and ER 406) are more closely related to each other than either is to ER 1470 (Fig 15–3).
2. The distinction between the groups reflects a basic difference in adaptive level (see Chapter 12).

From the time that fossil sites are first located to the eventual interpretation of hominid evolutionary events, several steps are necessary. Ideally, they should

FIGURE 15–3

Phylogenetic interpretation. Early Homo *generically distinct from australopithecines.*

follow a logical order, for if interpretations are made too hastily, they confuse important issues for many years. Here is a reasonable sequence:

1. Selecting and surveying sites
2. Excavating sites and recovering fossil hominids
3. Designating individual finds with specimen numbers for clear reference
4. Cleaning, preparing, studying, and describing fossils
5. Comparing with other fossil material—in chronological framework if possible
6. Comparing fossil variation with known ranges of variation in closely related groups of living primates
7. Assigning taxonomic names to fossil material

The task of interpretation is still not complete, for what we really want to know in the long run is what happened to the populations represented by the fossil remains. Indeed, in looking at the fossil hominid record, we are looking for our ancestors. In the process of eventually determining those populations that are our most likely antecedents, we may conclude that some hominids are on evolutionary side branches. If this conclusion is accurate, those hominids necessarily must have become extinct. It is both interesting and relevant to us as hominids to try to find out what influenced some earlier members of our family to continue evolving while others died out.

Continuing Uncertainties—Taxonomic Issues

As previously discussed, paleoanthropologists are crucially concerned with making biological interpretations of variation found in the hominid fossil record. Most especially, researchers endeavor to assign extinct forms to particular genera and species. We saw that for the diverse array of Miocene hominoids, the evolutionary picture is exceptionally complex. As new finds accumulate, there is continued uncertainty even as to family assignment, to say nothing of genus and species!

For the Plio-Pleistocene, the situation is considerably clearer. First, there is a larger fossil sample from a more restricted geographical area (South and East Africa) and from a more concentrated time period (spanning 3.4 million years, from 4.4 to 1.0 m.y.a.). Second, more complete specimens exist (e.g., "Lucy"), and we thus have good evidence for most parts of the body. Accordingly, there is considerable consensus on several basic aspects of evolutionary development during the Plio-Pleistocene. Researchers agree unanimously that these forms are hominids (members of the family Hominidae). And as support for this point, all these forms are seen as habitual, well-adapted bipeds, committed at least in part to a terrestrial niche. Moreover, researchers generally agree as to genus-level assignments for most of the forms (although *Ardipithecus* has been so recently named as to not yet be fully evaluated and accepted, and there is also some disagreement regarding how to group the robust australopithecines).

As for species-level designations, little consensus can be found. Indeed, as new fossils have been discovered (e.g., the "black skull"), the picture seems to muddy further. Once again, we are faced with a complex evolutionary process. In attempts to deal with it, we impose varying degrees of simplicity. In so doing, we hope to understand evolutionary developments more clearly—not just for introductory students, but also for professional paleoanthropologists and textbook authors! Nevertheless, evolution is not a simple process, and disputes and disagreements are bound to arise, especially in making such fine-tuned interpretations as species-level designations.

Consider the following ongoing topics of interest and occasional disagreement among paleoanthropologists dealing with Plio-Pleistocene hominids. You should realize, however, that such continued debate is at the heart of scientific endeavor; indeed, it provides a major stimulus for further research. Here, we raise questions regarding five areas of taxonomic interpretation. In general, there is still reasonably strong agreement on these points and we follow, where possible, the current consensus as reflected in recent publications (Fleagle, 1988; Grine, 1988a; Klein, 1989).

1. *Is* Ardipithecus *a hominid? If so, is* Ardipithecus *really generically distinct from* Australopithecus*?*

   Only tentative clues from the cranium and upper limb have thus far suggested that the 4.4-million-year-old fossils from Aramis were bipedal. Descriptions of the more complete skeleton (including a pelvis) have not yet been published. However, from what is known and what has been initially reported, it appears that these forms were bipedal and thus should be classified as hominids. Much more detailed analysis will need to be completed before it can be concluded how habitual and obligate the bipedal adaptation was. Equally uncertain is the genus status of these new finds. Again, from what is known, especially of the dentition (showing thin enamel on the back teeth), the Aramis finds do look quite different from *any* known *Australopithecus* species.

2. *How many species are there at Hadar and Laetoli (i.e., is* Australopithecus afarensis *one species)?*

   Some paleoanthropologists argue that what has been described as a single species (especially regarding the large Hadar sample) actually represents at least two separate species (taxa). However, it is clear that all australopithecines were highly variable, and thus the pattern seen at Hadar might well represent a single, highly dimorphic species. Most scholars accept this interpretation, and it is best, for the moment, to follow this more conservative view. As a matter of good paleontological practice, it is desirable not to overly "split" fossil samples until compelling evidence is presented.

3. *Is* Australopithecus anamensis *(from Allia Bay and Kanapoi) a separate species from* Australopithecus afarensis*?*

   The fossil discoveries of *A. anamensis* have thus far been quite fragmentary. When we compare them with the much better known *A. afarensis* materials, the anatomical differences in the Allia Bay and Kanapoi specimens are by no means striking. Thus, until more complete remains are discovered, it is best to be cautious and regard the new species designation (*Australopithecus anamensis*) as a tentative hypothesis and one requiring further confirmation.

4. *How many genera of* australopithecines *are there?*

   Several years ago, a plethora of genera was suggested by Robert Broom and others. However, in the 1960s and 1970s, most researchers agreed to "lump" all these forms into *Australopithecus.* With the discovery of early members of the genus *Homo* in the 1960s (and its general recognition in the 1970s), most researchers also recognized the presence of our genus in the Plio-Pleistocene as well (Fig. 15–4).

   In the last decade, there has been an increasing tendency to resplit some of the australopithecines. Recognizing that the robust group (*aethiopicus, boisei,* and *robustus*) forms a distinct evolutionary lineage (clade), many researchers (Grine, 1988a; Howell, 1988) have argued that

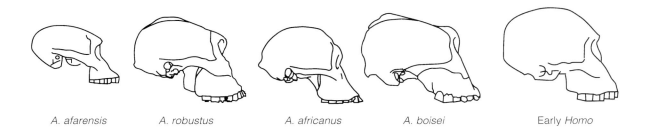

A. afarensis   A. robustus   A. africanus   A. boisei   Early Homo

FIGURE 15–4
Plio-Pleistocene hominids.

the generic term *Paranthropus* should be used to set these robust forms apart from *Australopithecus* (now used in the strict sense). We thus would have *Paranthropus aethiopicus*, *Paranthropus boisei*, and *Paranthropus robustus* in contrast with *Australopithecus afarensis* and *Australopithecus africanus*.

We agree that there are adequate grounds to make a genus-level distinction, given the evolutionary distinctiveness of the robust clade as well as its apparent adaptive uniqueness (as recently further confirmed by microwear studies of teeth) (Fig 15–5). However, for *closely related taxa*, such as we are dealing with here, making this type of interpretation is largely arbitrary. (See discussion, pp. 320–321.) The single genus *Australopithecus* has been used for four decades in the wider sense (to include all robust forms), and because it simplifies terminology, we follow the current consensus and continue the traditional usage—*Australopithecus* for all small-brained Plio-Pleistocene hominids with large thickly enameled teeth (particularly molars) and including all five recognized species: *A. afarensis*, *A. aethiopicus*, *A. africanus*, *A. robustus*, and *A. boisei*.

5. ***How many species of early* Homo *existed?***
Here is another species-level type of interpretation that is unlikely to be resolved soon. Yet, as it strikes closer to home (our own genus) than the issue for robust australopithecines, the current debate is generating more heat.

Whether we find resolution or not, the *form* of the conflicting views is instructive. Of course, the key issue is evaluating variation as *intra-* or *interspecific*. Those who would view all the non-australopithecine African hominids (circa 2.5–1.6 m.y.a.) as one species point out that all Plio-Pleistocene hominid species show extreme intraspecific variation. Much of this variation is assumed to reflect dramatic sexual dimorphism. These scholars are thus reasonably comfortable in referring to all this material as *Homo habilis* (Tobias, 1991). Other researchers, however, see too much variation to accept just one species, even a very dimorphic one. Comparisons with living primates show that the materials called *H. habilis* differ among themselves more than do male and female gorillas (Lieberman et al., 1988) or that the *pattern* of variation does not fit that seen intraspecifically in any extant species (Wood, 1992a). Consequently, we have an added complication: Must we now accept yet another species of early *Homo* in addition to *habilis*? Several researchers believe there is no other alternative, but do not as yet agree on a new name. The recent discovery of the fragmentary partial skeleton at Olduvai Gorge does not help resolve the issue, but actually may cloud it further. This specimen is a very small individual and thus presumably a female. How much sexual dimorphism did *H. habilis* display? Were males (on average) two to three times as large as females? We do not know the answers to these questions;

FIGURE 15–5

Morphology and variation of robust australopithecines. (Note both the typical features and the range of variation as shown in different specimens.)

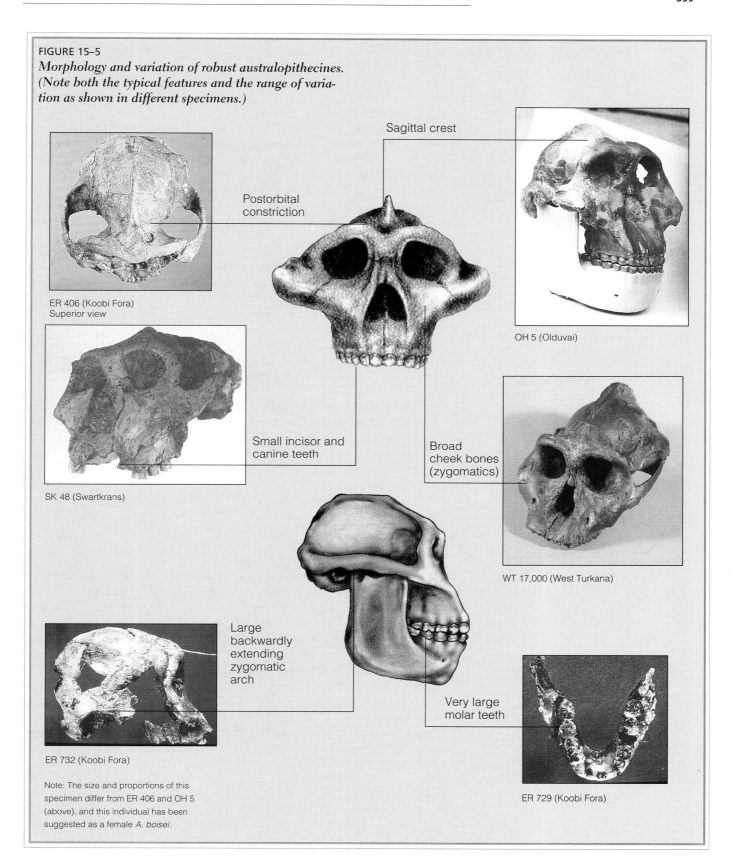

Sagittal crest

Postorbital constriction

ER 406 (Koobi Fora) Superior view

OH 5 (Olduvai)

SK 48 (Swartkrans)

Small incisor and canine teeth

Broad cheek bones (zygomatics)

WT 17,000 (West Turkana)

Large backwardly extending zygomatic arch

Very large molar teeth

ER 732 (Koobi Fora)

Note: The size and proportions of this specimen differ from ER 406 and OH 5 (above), and this individual has been suggested as a female *A. boisei.*

ER 729 (Koobi Fora)

but their framing in biological terms as intra- versus interspecific variation and the use of contemporary primate models demonstrate the basis for ongoing discussion.

For the moment, it is best not to assign formal names to the possible subsets (i.e., "new" species of early *Homo*). There is a growing consensus among paleoanthropologists that more than one species has been subsumed in the grouping called *Homo habilis*. The authors of this text also think that the current evidence argues (at least slightly) in favor of a multiple taxa interpretation. However, it is sufficient, certainly in the context of this textbook, to refer to all these fossils as "early *Homo*" (and thus not worry about subtle, complex species-level interpretations).

Another problem with the so-called "early *Homo*" fossil sample is that it overlaps in time with the earliest appearance of *Homo erectus* (discussed in Chapter 16). As a result, several specimens of what has been labeled "early *Homo*" (or *H. habilis*) may actually belong to *H. erectus*. At about 1.6 m.y.a., *H. erectus* apparently replaced earlier members of the genus *Homo* quite rapidly. At sites (especially East Turkana and Swartkrans) where fragmentary traces of this process are evident, it poses a major challenge to distinguish exactly what is early *Homo* and what is *H. erectus*.

Putting It All Together

▲ **Phylogeny**
A schematic representation showing ancestor-descendant relationships, usually in a chronological framework.

The interpretation of our paleontological past in terms of which fossils are related to other fossils and how they are all related to modern humans is usually shown diagrammatically in the form of a **phylogeny**. Such a diagram is a family tree of fossil evolution. This kind of interpretation is the eventual goal of evolutionary studies, but it is the final goal, only after adequate data are available to understand what is going on.

Another, more basic way to handle these data is to divide the fossil material into subsets. This avoids (for the moment) what are still problematic phylogenetic relationships. Accordingly, for the Plio-Pleistocene hominid material from Africa, we can divide the data into four broad groupings:

Set I. Basal hominids (4.4 m.y.a.)   The earliest (and most primitive) collection of remains that have been classified as hominids are those from Aramis. These fossils have, for the moment, been assigned to *Ardipithecus ramidus* and are hence provisionally interpreted as being generically distinct from all the other Plio-Pleistocene forms (listed in sets II–IV). Analysis thus far indicates that these forms were bipedal, but with a primitive dentition. Brain size of *A. ramidus* is not yet known, but was almost certainly quite small.

Set II. Early, primitive *Australopithecus* (4.2–3.0 m.y.a.)   This grouping comprises one well-known species, *A. afarensis*, especially well documented at Laetoli and Hadar. Sightly earlier, closely related forms (perhaps representing a distinct second species) come from Allia Bay (East Turkana) and Kanapoi and are provisionally called "*Australopithecus anamensis*." Best known from analysis of the *A. afarensis* material, these hominids are characterized by a small brain, large teeth (front and back), and a bipedal gait (probably still allowing for considerable climbing).

Set III. Later, more derived *Australopithecus* (2.5–1.0 m.y.a.; possibly as early as 3.5 m.y.a.)   This group is composed of numerous species (most experts recognize at least three; some subdivide this material into five or more species). Remains have come from several sites in both South and East Africa. All of these forms have very large back teeth and do not show appreciable brain enlargement (i.e., encephalization) compared to A. *afarensis*.

Set IV. Early *Homo* (2.4–1.8 m.y.a.) The best known specimens are from East Africa (East Turkana and Olduvai), but early remains of *Homo* have also been found in South Africa (Sterkfontein and possibly Swartkrans). This group is composed of possibly just one, but probably more than one, species. Early *Homo* is characterized (compared to *Australopithecus*) by greater encephalization, altered cranial shape, and smaller (especially molars) and narrower (especially premolars) teeth.

Although hominid fossil evidence has accumulated in great abundance, the fact that so much of the material has been discovered so recently makes any firm judgments concerning the route of human evolution premature. However, paleoanthropologists are certainly not deterred from making their "best guesses," and diverse hypotheses have abounded in recent years. The vast majority of more than 300 fossils from East Africa is still in the descriptive and early analytical stages. At this time, the construction of phylogenies of human evolution is analogous to building a house with only a partial blueprint. We are not even sure how many rooms there are! Until the existing fossil evidence has been adequately studied, to say nothing about possible new finds, speculative hypotheses must be viewed with a critical eye.

In Figure 15–6, we present several phylogenies representing different and opposing views of hominid evolution. We suggest that you not attempt to memorize them, for they *all* could be out of date by the time you read this book. It will prove more profitable to look at each one and assess the biological implications involved. Also, note which groups are on the "main line" of human evolution (the one including *Homo sapiens*) and which are placed on extinct side branches.

Interpreting the Interpretations

All the schemes in Figure 15–6 postdate 1979, when A. *afarensis* was first suggested as the most likely common ancestor of all later hominids (Johanson and White, 1979). Since the early 1980s, most paleoanthropologists have accepted this view. One exception is shown in phylogeny B (after Senut and Tardieu, 1985), but this position—based on the premise that A. *afarensis* is actually more than one species—has not been generally supported.

We have not included evolutionary schemes prior to 1979, as they do not account for the crucial discoveries at Hadar and Laetoli of *Australopithecus afarensis*. These now-outdated models frequently postulated A. *africanus* as the common ancestor of later *Australopithecus* (robust varieties) and early *Homo*. In modified form, this view is still continued in some respects (see phylogeny C).

Indeed, probably the most intractable problems for interpretation of early hominid evolution involve what to do with A. *aethiopicus* and A. *africanus*. Carefully look at the different evolutionary reconstructions to see how various researchers deal with these complicated issues. Finally, the newest finds from Aramis (*Ardipithecus*) and from Allia Bay and Kanapoi (*Australopithecus anamensis*) will need to be incorporated into these schemes. Phylogeny E is an initial attempt to do so, but only points up how frequently hominid evolutionary interpretations need to be reevaluated and substantially revised.

PHYLOGENY A
A. afarensis common ancestor theory
(after Johanson and White, 1979)

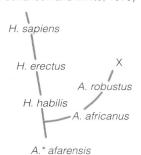

Note: Afarensis postulated as common ancestor to all Plio-Pleistocene hominids

PHYLOGENY B
Multiple lineage early divergence
(after Senut and Tardieu, 1985)

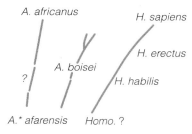

Note: Major split occurs before *A. afarensis*. Possible multiple lineages in Plio-Pleistocene.

PHYLOGENY C
A. africanus common ancestor theory
(after Skelton et al., 1986)

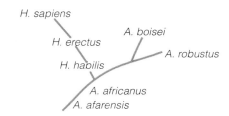

Note: Major split occurs after *A. africanus*. Therefore, *A. africanus* is seen as still in our lineage as well as that of more derived australopithecines.

PHYLOGENY D
Early robust lineage
(after Delson, 1986, 1987; Grine, 1993)

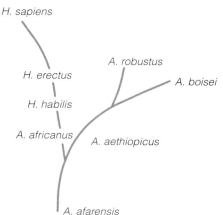

PHYLOGENY E
Ardipithecus as probable root species for later hominids (and also incorporating other recent modifications) (after Skelton and McHenry, 1992; Wolpoff, 1995)

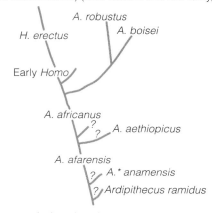

* For genus designation, the "*A*" in all phylogenies refers to *Australopithecus*.

FIGURE 15–6

Phylogenies of hominid evolution.

Summary

After two chapters detailing hominid evolution in the Plio-Pleistocene, you may feel frustrated by what must seem to be endlessly changing and conflicting interpretations. However, after 75 years of discoveries of early hominids in Africa, there are several general points on which most researchers agree:

1. A. *afarensis* is the earliest hominid, at present with substantial definite supporting evidence. We can anticipate, however, that *Ardipithecus* will soon supplant A. *afarensis* for this status of earliest definite (and widely accepted) hominid.
2. A. *afarensis*, as defined, probably represents only one species.
3. A. *afarensis* is probably ancestral to all later hominids (or is very closely related to the species that is).
4. A. *aethiopicus* is ancestral solely to the "robust" group (clade), linking it with earlier *afarensis* as well as with one (or both) later robust species.
5. All robust australopithecines were extinct by 1 m.y.a. (or shortly thereafter).

6. All australopithecine species (presumably early *Homo* as well) were highly variable, showing extreme sexual dimorphism.
7. Since there is so much intraspecific variation, on average there was not much difference in body size among australopithecine species.
8. *A. africanus* was probably not the last common ancestor of the robust lineage *and* genus *Homo* (that is, phylogeny C is probably not entirely correct. Indeed, the robust "lineage" may actually be more than one group, or clade; as phylogeny E suggests, *A. aethiopicus* may have diverged earlier, prior to *A. africanus*).
9. All forms (*Australopithecus* and early *Homo*) were small brained (as compared to later species of the genus *Homo*); nevertheless, all early hominids are more encephalized than apes of comparable body size.
10. Most forms (including some members of early *Homo*) had large back teeth.
11. There was substantial parallelism in physical traits among early hominid lineages.
12. Given the current state of knowledge, there are several equally supportable phylogenies. In fact, in a recent publication, three leading researchers (Bill Kimbel, Tim White, and Don Johanson, 1988) make this point; moreover, they note that of four possible phylogenetic reconstructions they present (various modifications of phylogenies D and E), they have not reached agreement among themselves as to which is the most likely.

As points 1 through 11 make clear, we have come a long way in reaching an understanding of Plio-Pleistocene hominid evolution. Nevertheless, a truly complete understanding is not at hand. Such is the stuff of science!

Questions for Review

1. What kinds of dating techniques have been used in South Africa?
2. Why is the dating control better in East Africa than in South Africa?
3. Discuss the first thing you would do if you found an early hominid and were responsible for its formal description and publication. What would you include in your publication?
4. Discuss two current disputes regarding taxonomic issues concerning early hominids. Try to give support for alternative positions.
5. Why would one use the taxonomic term *Paranthropus* in contrast to *Australopithecus*?
6. What is a phylogeny? Construct one for early hominids (4.4–1 m.y.a.). Make sure you can describe what conclusions your scheme makes. Also, try to defend it.
7. Discuss at least two alternative ways that *A. africanus* is currently incorporated into phylogenetic schemes.
8. What are the most recently discovered of the Plio-Pleistocene hominid materials, and how are they, for the moment, incorporated into a phylogenetic scheme? How secure do you think this interpretation is?

Suggested Further Reading

Corruccini, Robert S., and Russel L. Ciochon (eds.). 1994. *Integrative Paths to the Past: Paleoanthropology Advances in Honor of F. Clark Howell.* Englewood Cliffs, NJ: Prentice Hall.

Delson, Eric (ed.). 1985. *Ancestors: The Hard Evidence.* New York: Liss.

Grine, Fred (ed.). 1988. *Evolutionary History of the Robust Australopithecines*. New York: de Gruyter.

Rak, Yoel. 1983. *The Australopithecine Face*. New York: Academic Press.

Internet Resources

See listings, Chapter 14.

Henry M. McHenry

Henry M. McHenry received his Ph.D. from Harvard University and is currently Professor in the Department of Anthropology, University of California, Davis. He has studied fossil hominids from many parts of the world and has written extensively on the functional anatomy and phylogeny of Miocene apes and early hominids.

The theme of this text might be thought of as probing the question "Who are we?" The answer is usually addressed from the point of view of cultural traditions that go back to folktales and myths. But in physical anthropology, we take the historical perspective. We are the products of our history. And how do we come to know about our history? By observation of the material world—not the intuition of wise teachers or insights that our own minds might bring us. For the last few thousand years, this hard evidence is often in the form of written documents. But before that, it is taken from the earth as fossilized bones or tools or refuse left by our ancestors.

This approach may seem narrow; after all, the question of "who are we?" is usually addressed from grand theories of philosophy, religion, or psychology. But my experience has shown that one can derive a great deal of satisfaction from this historical approach. For one thing, it is self correcting—that is, self correcting in the sense that new material evidence or new interpretation of old evidence continually checks the accuracy of our understanding of history. It does not get stuck in dogma. And for another thing, when we look up from the details of the material evidence, we can experience the magnificence of the universe and of life on earth, and especially of our own lives.

The patterns of professional careers are somewhat like the patterns of history: They appear to have direction and purpose in hindsight, but chance plays a major role.

Career opportunities often arise out of unpredictable circumstances. It is essential to recognize these opportunities and pursue them with delight and effort. I was blessed by having an undergraduate advisor, Warren Kinzey, whose enthusiasm and encouragement kept me on track. It was just good luck that I met Dr. Kinzey. I am happy that I saw clearly enough to take advantage of my good fortune. He and his colleague, Martin Baumhoff, started me on research. My topic was the scars of childhood trauma left as thickened lines in the interior structure of long bones. It was their idea. I provided the energy, persistence, and, eventually, the skill to carry it out. I was able to show that the sequence of early, middle, and late people of prehistoric California showed increasingly less childhood traumas as they adapted to the natural resources of California with increasing sophistication. These childhood scars were well known to radiologists from the X rays of children. I was in the fortunate position of being able to compare the X rays directly with the internal architecture of the bones.

Unexpected opportunities pop up occasionally that change one's direction substantially. For me it was a semester visit by Bernard Campbell while I was searching for graduate research topics. He had just come from a research trip in Africa working on the 2 to 3 million year old fossil hominids. He encouraged me to apply the methods of multivariate statistical techniques to the interpretation of these fossils. These methods had been successfully applied by my Ph.D. mentor, William Howells. With their help, I changed my research focus to the interpretation of fossil hominid postcranial anatomy. That was more than a quarter of a century ago. It was a time when very little was known about the posture, body size, or locomotion of *Australopithecus*. Thanks to the extraordinary efforts of fossil collecting teams led by Louis, Mary, Richard, and Meave Leakey, Clark Howell, Don Johanson, Tim White, Phillip Tobias, Bob Brain, and many others, the sample size of fossil specimens has grown enormously.

The expanded sample of the postcranium of early hominids has led to the exploration of many interesting questions. One central concern stems from estimates of body weight. It is the size of the hip, knee, and ankle joints that best reflect a biped's body weight. By relating the dimensions of these

joints to body weight in apes and humans of known body weight, I was able to predict the body sizes of species of early hominid. From those estimates, it was possible to compare relative brain size, tooth size, and male/female size in early hominids with living species of primates including humans. From these comparisons one can approach an understanding of our ancestors' adaptations.

What emerges from these studies is a picture of the mosaic pattern of human evolution. The postcranial anatomy of the earliest hominids was clearly adapted to bipedality, but our unique craniodental morphology evolved later. The dentition in our earliest ancestors was much like that seen in modern apes except for reduced canines. The brain was quite ape-like in size relative to scaled body weight. Our ancestor's cheek teeth appear to have expanded through time from 4.4 million years ago

(when they were quite ape-like) to 2.5 million years ago when they were enormous relative to modern species of Hominoidea. By at least 2 million years ago, at least one lineage diverged from this track of ever increasing cheek-tooth size. This event is accompanied by the appearance in the archeological record of stone tools which might be associated with a change in diet or at least how food was processed.

Two of the most interesting questions that will likely be resolved in the very near future due to recent discoveries of fossil hominids are when did our lineage diverge and how diverse was the early radiation of our late Miocene/early Pliocene ancestors?

Palaeoanthropology cannot be stuck in dogma. It is, in many respects, a wide open field. Its vitality relies on open-mindedness. But speculation is bound to the apparent reality of the hard evidence buried in the crust of the earth.

16

Homo erectus

Introduction

In Chapters 13, 14, and 15, we traced the earliest evidence of hominid evolution by reviewing the abundant fossil material from Africa that documents the origins of *Australopithecus* and *Homo* during the Pliocene and early Pleistocene. In this chapter, we take up what might be called the next stage of hominid evolution, the appearance and dispersal of *Homo erectus* (Fig. 16–1).

Homo erectus was a widely distributed species that also had a long temporal record spanning over 1 million years. Our discussion focuses on the defining physical characteristics of *Homo erectus* compared to what came immediately before (early *Homo*) and what came immediately after (*Homo sapiens*). As we have emphasized, hominid evolution has long been characterized by a biocultural interaction. Thus, it is only through explaining the behavioral capacities of *Homo erectus* (in concert with morphological change) that we can understand the success of this hominid species. For this reason, we also highlight some of the abundant archeological evidence and related biocultural reconstructions that have so long occupied and fascinated paleoanthropologists.

Homo erectus—
Terminology and Geographical Distribution

The discoveries of fossils now referred to as *H. erectus* go back to the nineteenth century. Later on in this chapter, we will discuss in some detail the historical background of these earliest discoveries in Java and the somewhat later discoveries in China. From this work, as well as presumably related finds in Europe and North Africa, a variety of taxonomic names were suggested. The most significant of these earlier terms were *Pithecanthropus* (for the Javanese remains) and *Sinanthropus* (for the fossils from northern China). In fact, you may still see these terms in older sources or occasionally used colloquially and thus placed in quotation marks (e.g., "Pithecanthropus").

It is important to realize that taxonomic *splitting* (which this terminology reflects) was quite common in the early years of paleoanthropology. Only after World War II and with the incorporation of the Modern Synthesis (see p. 87) into paleontology did more systematic biological thinking come to the fore. Following this trend, in the early 1950s all the material previously referred to as "Pithecanthropus," "Sinanthropus," and so forth, was included in a single species of genus *Homo*—*H. erectus*. This reclassification proved to be a most significant development on two counts:

1. It reflected the incorporation of modern evolutionary thinking into hominid paleontology.
2. The simplification in terminology, based as it was on sound biological principles, refocused research away from endless arguments regarding classification to broader populational, behavioral, and ecological considerations.

Discoveries in the last few decades have established *well-dated* finds of *H. erectus* in East Africa from geological contexts radiometrically dated as old as 1.8 m.y.a. In addition, new dates first published in 1994 by geologists from the

Berkeley Geochronology Laboratory (Swisher et al., 1994) have suggested that two localities in Java are as old as those in East Africa (with dates of 1.8 and 1.6 m.y.a.). These early dates have come as somewhat of a surprise to many paleoanthropologists, but as you will see, there is now growing evidence for an early dispersal of hominids outside of Africa—that is, one *well before* 1 m.y.a. Moreover, there are some newly discovered tantalizing clues from China suggesting that members of the genus *Homo* may have emigrated from Africa *prior* to the appearance of *H. erectus*. As we discussed on page 387, the fragmentary finds from Longgupo Cave have been interpreted by some researchers as likely belonging to a species of early *Homo*.

Thus, current interpretations view the first hominid dispersal out of Africa as occurring between 1.5 and 2 m.y.a. A likely route would have taken these hominids through southwestern Asia, and there are some intriguing hints from the Ubeidiya site in Israel that this route was indeed exploited quite early on. The most conclusive evidence from Ubeidiya is archeological, including a number of stone tools dated (by paleomagnetism and faunal correlation) to 1.4–1.3 m.y.a. In addition, there are some fragmentary hominid remains, including cranial pieces and two teeth. Unfortunately, however, the association of these hominid remains with the tools at a date prior to 1 m.y.a. is uncertain. Consequently, there is not yet *definitive* fossil evidence of *H. erectus* (or a close relative) from Southwest Asia. Nevertheless, the Ubeidiya archeological discoveries are highly suggestive and fit with the overall emerging pattern of an early hominid dispersal from Africa.

More than likely, these first continental migrants were members of *H. erectus* or a group very closely related to *H. erectus* (although an earlier dispersal of a more primitive member of genus *Homo* cannot be ruled out). What the current evidence most economically suggests is that *Homo erectus* migrated out of East Africa, eventually to occupy South and North Africa, southern and northeastern Asia, and perhaps Europe as well. A recent, not yet fully described hominid mandible from the Dmanisi site in the Republic of Georgia has been provisionally dated at 1.5 m.y.a. Another new find pushing back the antiquity of hominids in Europe has come from the 500,000-year-old Boxgrove site in southern England, where a hominid tibia (shinbone) was unearthed in 1994.

Finally, some other fossil remains from Spain, also discovered in 1994 and announced in 1995, may well be the oldest hominids yet found in western Europe (see Fig. 16–1 for locations of these hominid sites). From the Gran Dolina site in the highly productive Atapuerca region of northern Spain, where numerous, somewhat more recent hominid fossils have also been discovered (discussed in Chapter 17), several fragments of at least four individuals have been found (Carbonell et al., 1995). The dating, based on paleomagnetic determinations (see p. 342), places the Gran Dolina hominids at approximately 780,000 y.a.* (Parés and Pérez-González, 1995). If this dating is further corroborated, these early Spanish finds would be *at least* 250,000 years older than any other hominid yet discovered in western Europe. Because all the 36 pieces thus far identified are quite fragmentary, the taxonomic assignment of these fossils still remains problematic. Initial analysis, however, suggests that they probably are *not H. erectus*. Whether any of these early European hominids belong within the species *Homo erectus* still remains to be determined.

The dispersal of *Homo erectus* from Africa was influenced by climate, topography, water boundaries, and access to food and other resources. Paleoenvironmental reconstructions are thus of crucial importance in understanding

---

*y.a. stands for "years ago."

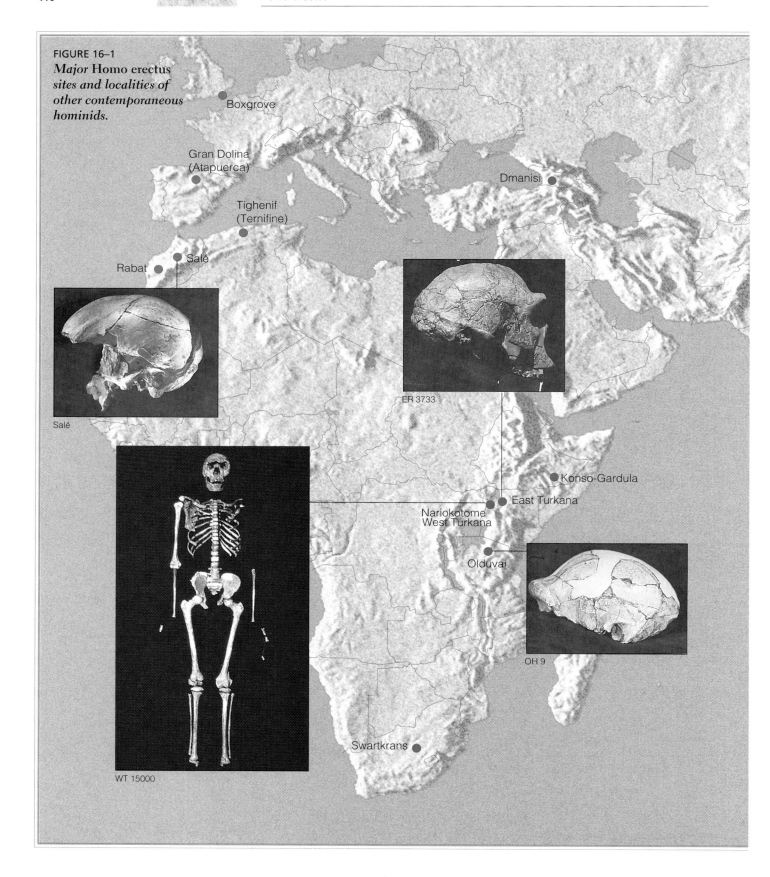

FIGURE 16–1
Major Homo erectus *sites and localities of other contemporaneous hominids.*

Boxgrove

Gran Dolina (Atapuerca)

Dmanisi

Tighenif (Ternifine)

Rabat

Salé

Salé

ER 3733

Konso-Gardula

East Turkana

Nariokotome
West Turkana

Olduvai

OH 9

WT 15000

Swartkrans

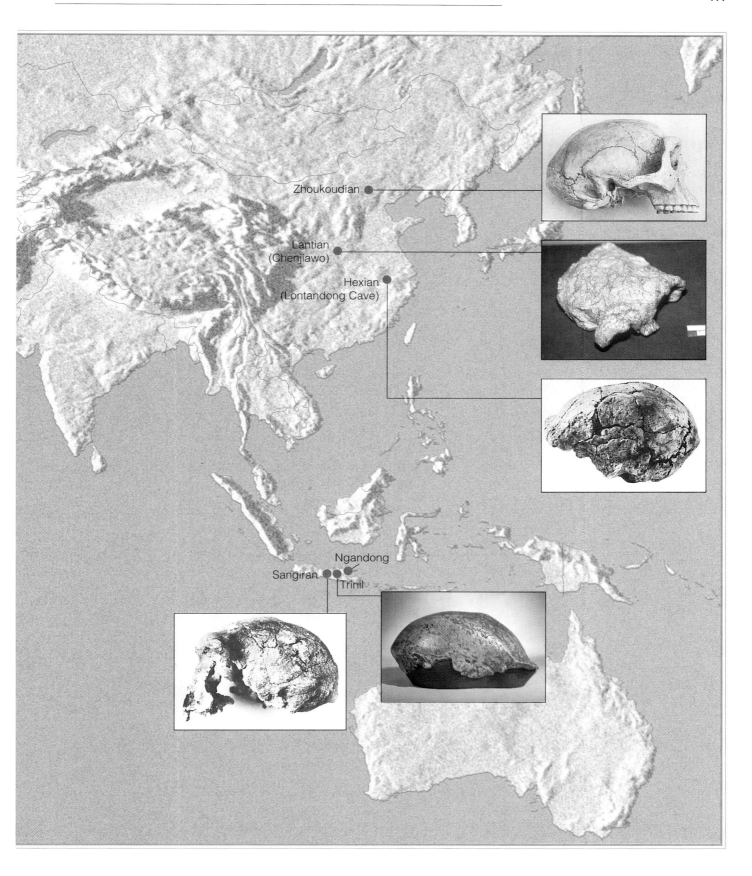

Zhoukoudian

Lantian
(Chenjiawo)

Hexian
(Lontandong Cave)

Ngandong

Sangiran

Trinil

▲ **Pleistocene**
The epoch of the Cenozoic from
1.8 m.y.a. until 10,000 y.a. Frequently
referred to as the Ice Age, this epoch is
associated with continental glaciations
in northern latitudes.

the expansion of *H. erectus* to so many parts of the Old World. The long temporal span of *H. erectus* begins very early in the **Pleistocene** and extends to fairly late in that geological epoch. To comprehend the world of *Homo erectus*, we must understand how environments shifted during the Pleistocene.

The Pleistocene (1.8 m.y.a.–10,000 y.a.)

During much of the Pleistocene (also known as the Age of Glaciers or Ice Age), large areas of the Northern Hemisphere were covered with enormous masses of ice, which advanced and retreated as the temperature fell and rose. An early classification of glacial (and interglacial) Europe divided the Pleistocene into four major glacial periods. However, climatic conditions varied in different areas of Europe, and distinctive glacial periods are also now known from the North Sea, England, and eastern Europe, not to mention Asia and North America. New dating techniques have revealed a much more complex account of glacial advance and retreat, and the many oscillations of cold and warm temperatures during the Pleistocene affected both plants and animals: "The Pleistocene record shows that there were about 15 major cold periods and 50 minor advances during its 1.5-m.y. duration, or one major cold period every 100,000 years" (Tattersal et al., 1988, p. 230).

The Pleistocene, which lasted more than 1.75 million years, was a significant period in hominid evolutionary history and encompassed the appearance and disappearance of *Homo erectus*. By the end of the Pleistocene, modern humans had already appeared, dependence on culture had dramatically increased, and domestication of plants and animals—one of the great cultural revolutions of human history—was either about to commence or had already begun. Given this background on the time span in which *H. erectus* evolved and lived, let us examine more closely this predecessor of *H. sapiens*.

The Morphology of *Homo erectus*

Brain Size

Homo erectus differs in several respects from both early *Homo* and *Homo sapiens*. The most obvious feature is cranial size (which, of course, is closely related to brain size) (see p. 268). Early *Homo* had cranial capacities ranging from as small as 500 cm³ to as large as 800 cm³. *H. erectus*, on the other hand, shows considerable brain enlargement with a cranial capacity of 750 to 1,250 cm³ (with a mean slightly greater than 1,000 cm³). However, in making such comparisons, we must bear in mind two key questions: What is the comparative sample, and what were the overall body sizes of the species being compared?

In relation to the first question, you should recall that many scholars are now convinced that there was more than one species of early *Homo* in East Africa around 2 m.y.a. If so, only one of these could have been ancestral to *H. erectus*. (Indeed, it is possible that neither species gave rise to *H. erectus* and that perhaps we have yet to find direct evidence of the ancestral species.) Taking a more optimistic view that at least one of these fossil groups is a likely ancestor of later hominids, the question still remains—"which one?" If we choose the smaller-bodied sample of early *Homo* as our presumed ancestral group, then *H. erectus* shows as much as a 40 percent increase in cranial capacity. However, if the comparative sample is the larger-bodied group of early *Homo* (as exemplified by ER 1470), then *H. erectus* shows a 25 percent increase in cranial capacity.

As we previously discussed in Chapter 11, brain size is closely tied to overall body size (a relationship termed *encephalization*). We have made a point of the *increase* in *H. erectus* brain size; however, it must be realized that *H. erectus* was also considerably larger overall than earlier members of the genus *Homo*. In fact, when *H. erectus* is compared to the larger-bodied early *Homo* sample, *relative* brain size is about the same (Walker, 1991). But *absolute* brain size in *Homo erectus* is approximately 30 percent less than the average for *H. sapiens*. Moreover, when one considers relative brain/body proportions, *H. erectus* was notably less encephalized than modern *H. sapiens* (although the difference would not be as dramatic in comparison with archaic forms of *sapiens*; see Chapter 17).

Body Size

As we have just mentioned, another feature displayed by *H. erectus*, compared to earlier hominids, is a dramatic increase in body size. For several decades, little was known of the postcranial skeleton of *H. erectus*. However, with the discovery of a nearly complete skeleton in 1984 from **Nariokotome** (on the west side of Lake Turkana in Kenya) and its recent detailed analysis (Walker and Leakey, 1993), the data base is now much improved (see Box 16–1). From this specimen (and from less complete individuals at other sites), some *Homo erectus* adults are estimated to have weighed well over 100 pounds, with a mean adult stature of about 5 feet 6 inches (McHenry, 1992; Ruff and Walker, 1993). Another point to keep in mind is that *Homo erectus* was quite sexually dimorphic—at least as indicated by the East African specimens. Thus, for male adult body size, weight and stature in some individuals may have been considerably greater than the average figures just mentioned. In fact, it is estimated that if the Nariokotome boy had survived, he would have attained an adult stature of over 6 feet (Walker, 1993). Females were probably considerably smaller, but may still have been as large, on average, as the presumptive males of even the bigger-bodied early *Homo* individuals (Walker, 1993).

Associated with the large stature (and explaining the significant increase in body weight) is also a dramatic increase in robusticity. In fact, this characteristic of very heavy body build was to dominate hominid evolution not just during *H. erectus* times, but through the long transitional era of archaic *Homo sapiens* as well. Only with the appearance of anatomically modern *H. sapiens* do we see a more gracile skeletal structure, which is still characteristic of most modern populations.

Cranial Shape

The cranium of *Homo erectus* displays a highly distinctive shape, partly as the result of increased brain size, but probably more correlated with significant body size (robusticity). The ramifications of this heavily built cranium are reflected in thick cranial bone (most notably in Asian specimens) and large browridges (supraorbital tori) in the front of the skull and a projecting nuchal torus at the rear (Fig. 16–2).

▲ **Nariokotome**
(nar´-ee-oh-ko´-tow-may)

FIGURE 16–2
Morphology and variation in
Homo erectus

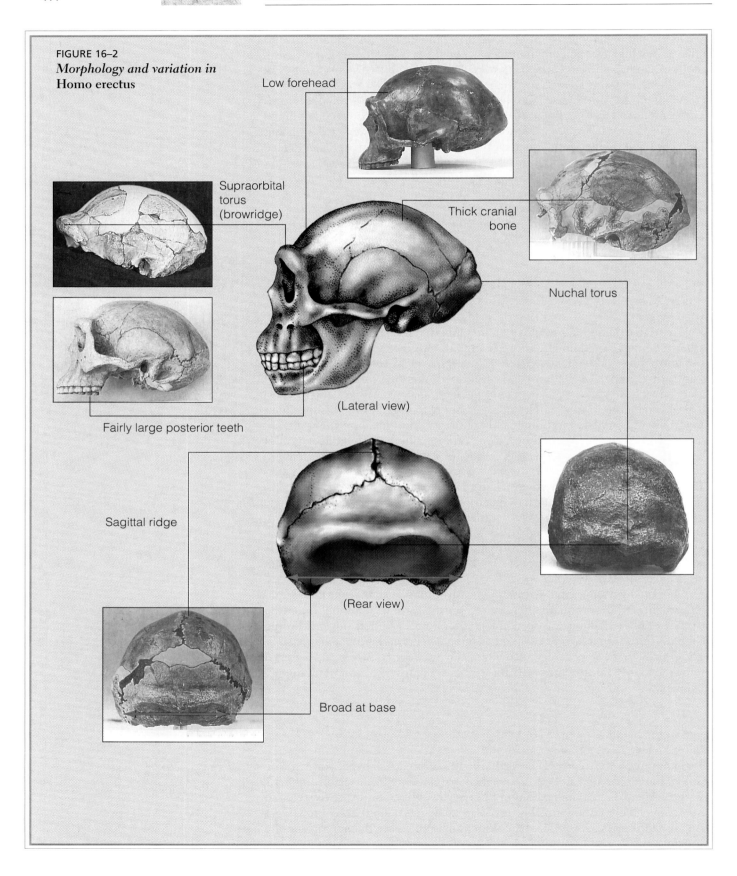

Low forehead

Supraorbital
torus
(browridge)

Thick cranial
bone

Nuchal torus

Fairly large posterior teeth

(Lateral view)

Sagittal ridge

(Rear view)

Broad at base

The vault is long and low, receding back from the large browridges with little forehead development. Moreover, the cranium is wider at the base compared to earlier *or* later species of genus *Homo*. The maximum breadth is below the ear opening, giving a pentagonal contour to the cranium (when viewed from behind). In contrast, both early *Homo* crania and *H. sapiens* crania have more vertical sides, and the maximum width is *above* the ear openings.

Dentition

The dentition of *Homo erectus* is much like that of *Homo sapiens*, but the earlier species exhibits somewhat larger teeth. However, compared to early *Homo*, *H. erectus* does show some dental reduction.

Another interesting feature of the dentition of some *H. erectus* specimens is seen in the incisor teeth. On the back (distal) surfaces, the teeth are scooped out in appearance, forming a surface reminiscent of a shovel. Accordingly, such teeth are referred to as "shovel-shaped" incisors (Fig. 16–3). It has been suggested that teeth shaped in this manner are an adaptation in hunter-gatherers for processing foods, a contention not yet proved (or really even framed in a testable manner). One thing does seem likely: Shovel-shaped incisors are probably a primitive feature of the species *H. erectus*, as the phenomenon has been found not just in the Chinese specimens but also in the early individual from Nariokotome.

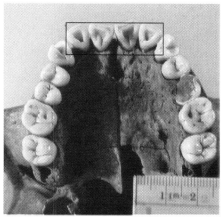

FIGURE 16–3
Shovel-shaped incisors.

Historical Overview of Homo erectus Discoveries

In our discussion of Plio-Pleistocene hominids, we traced the evolutionary developments in *chronological* order, that is, discussing the oldest specimens first. Here we take a different approach and discuss the finds in the order in which they were discovered. We believe that this approach is useful, as the discoveries cover a broad range of time—indeed, almost the entire history of paleoanthropology. Given this relatively long history of scientific discovery, the later finds were assessed in the light of earlier ones (and thus can still be best understood within an historical context).

Java

Dutch anatomist Eugene Dubois (1858–1940) (Fig. 16–4) was the first scientist to deliberately design a research plan that would take him from his anatomy lab to where fossil bones might be buried. Up until this time, embryology and comparative anatomy were considered the proper methods of studying humans and their ancestry, and the research was done in the laboratory. Dubois changed all this.

The latter half of the nineteenth century was a period of intellectual excitement. In Europe, Darwin's *Origin of Species* (published in 1859) provoked scientists as well as educated laypeople to take opposing sides, often with heated emotion. In 1856, an unusual skull had been recovered near Düsseldorf,

FIGURE 16–4
Eugene Dubois, discoverer of the first H. erectus *fossil to be found.*

BOX 16–1

The Nariokotome Skeleton— A Boy for All Seasons

The discovery of the spectacularly well-preserved skeleton from Nariokotome on the west side of Lake Turkana has allowed considerable new insight into key anatomical features of *Homo erectus*. Since its recovery in 1984 and 1985, detailed studies have been undertaken, and recent publication of the results (Walker, 1993; Walker and Leakey, 1993) allows some initial conclusions to be drawn. Moreover, the extraordinary quality of the remains has also allowed anthropologists to speculate on some major behavioral traits of *H. erectus* in Africa (and, more generally, of the entire species).

The remains comprise an almost complete skeleton, lacking only most of the small bones of the hands and feet and the unfused ends of long bones. This degree of preservation is remarkable, and this individual is the most complete skeleton of *any* fossil hominid yet found from before about 100,000 y.a. (after which deliberate burial facilitated much improved preservation). This superior preservation may well have been aided by rapid sedimentation in what is thought to have been an ancient shallow swamp. Once the individual died, his skeleton would have been quickly covered up, but some disturbance and breakage nevertheless did occur—from chewing by catfish, but most especially from trampling by large animals wading in the swamp 1.6 m.y.a.

As we have discussed, the individual was not fully grown when he died. His age (11 to 13 years—Walker, 1993) is determined by the stage of dental eruption (his permanent canines are not yet erupted) and by union of the ends of long bones (see p. 157). Moreover, as we have noted, this young *Homo erectus* male was quite tall (5 feet 3 inches), and using modern growth curve approximations, his adult stature would have been over 6 feet had he lived to full maturity.

More than simply tall, the body proportions of this boy's skeleton are intriguing. Reconstructions suggest that he had a linear build with long appendages, thus conforming to predictions of *Allen's rule* for inhabitants of hot climates (see p. 143). Further extrapolating from this observation, Alan Walker also suggests that *H. erectus* must have had a high sweating capacity to dissipate heat (in the modern human fashion). (See pp. 142–144 for a discussion of heat adaptation in humans.)

Germany. This specimen is now known as Neandertal, but when a description of it was published, scientific opinion was again divided, and feelings ran high.

This stimulating intellectual climate surrounded the youthful Eugene Dubois, who left Holland for Sumatra in 1887 to search for, as he phrased it, "the missing link." Dubois went to work immediately and soon unearthed a variety of animal bones, including orangutan, gibbon, and several other mammalian species. However, his successes soon diminished, and in 1890 he switched his fieldwork to the banks of the Solo River near the town of Trinil, on the neighboring island of Java.

In October 1891, the field crew unearthed a skullcap that was to become internationally famous. The following year, a human femur was recovered about 15 yards upstream in what Dubois claimed was the same level as the skullcap. Dubois assumed that the skullcap (with a cranial capacity of over 900 cm³) and the femur belonged to the same individual.

After studying these discoveries for a few years, Dubois startled the world in 1894 with a paper provocatively titled "*Pithecanthropus erectus*, A Manlike Species of Transitional Anthropoid from Java." In 1895, Dubois returned to

The boy's limb proportions suggest a quite warm mean annual temperature (90°F/30°C) in East Africa 1.6 m.y.a. Paleoecological reconstructions confirm this estimate of tropical conditions (much like the climate today in northern Kenya).

Another fascinating anatomical clue is seen in the beautifully preserved vertebrae. The opening through which the spinal cord passes (the neural canal; see Appendix A) is quite small in the thoracic elements. The possible behavioral corollaries of this reduced canal (as compared to modern *H. sapiens*) are also intriguing. Ann MacLarnan (1993) has proposed that the reduced canal argues for reduced size of the spinal cord, which in turn may suggest less control of the muscles between the ribs (the intercostals). One major function of these muscles is the precise control of breathing during human speech. From these data and inferences, Alan Walker has concluded that the Nariokotome youth (and *H. erectus* in general) was not fully capable of human articulate speech. (As an argument regarding language potential, this conclusion will no doubt spark considerable debate).

A final interesting feature can be seen in the pelvis of this adolescent skeleton. It is very narrow and is thus correlated with a narrow bony birth canal. Walker (1993) again draws a behavioral inference from this anatomical feature. He estimates that a newborn with a cranial capacity no greater than a mere 200 cm³ could have passed through this pelvis. As we showed elsewhere, the adult cranial capacity estimate for this individual was slightly greater than 900 cm³—thus arguing for significant postnatal growth of the brain (exceeding 75 percent of its eventual size, again mirroring the modern human pattern). Walker speculates that this slow neural expansion (compared to other primates) leads to delayed development of motor skills and thus a prolonged period of infant/child dependency (what Walker terms "secondary altriciality"). (See p. 159 for a discussion of brain growth and development in modern humans.) Of course, as with other speculative behavioral scenarios, critics will no doubt find holes in this reconstruction as well. One point you should immediately note is that this specimen is the immature pelvis of a male. Thus, the crucial dimensions of an adult female *H. erectus* pelvis remain unknown. Nevertheless, they could not have departed too dramatically from the dimensions seen at Nariokotome—unless one accepts an extreme degree of sexual dimorphism in this species.

Europe, where his paper had received strong criticism. He countered the criticism by elaborating the points briefly covered in his original paper. He also brought along the actual fossil material, which gave scientists an opportunity to examine the evidence. As a result, many opponents became more sympathetic to his views.

However, to this day, questions about the finds remain: Does the femur really belong with the skullcap? Did the field crew dig through several layers, thus mixing the remains? Moreover, many anthropologists believe the Trinil femur to be relatively recent and representative of modern *H. sapiens*, not *H. erectus*.

Despite the still-unanswered questions, there is general acceptance that Dubois was correct in identifying the skull as representing a previously undescribed species; that his estimates of cranial capacity were reasonably accurate; that "*Pithecanthropus erectus*," or *H. erectus* as we call it today, is the ancestor of *H. sapiens*; and that bipedalism preceded enlargement of the brain.

By 1930, the controversy had faded, especially in the light of important new discoveries near Peking (Beijing), China, in the late 1920s (discussed shortly). Similarities between the Beijing skulls and Dubois' "*Pithecanthropus*" were obvious, and scientists pointed out that the Java form was not an "apeman," as Dubois contended, but rather was closely related to modern *Homo sapiens*.

One might expect that Dubois would welcome the finds from China and the support they provided for the human status of "*Pithecanthropus*," but Dubois would have none of it. He refused to recognize any connection between Beijing and Java and described the Beijing fossils as "a degenerate Neanderthaler" (von Koenigswald, 1956, p. 55). He also refused to accept the classification of "*Pithecanthropus*" in the same species with von Koenigswald's later Java finds.*

Homo erectus from Java

Six sites in eastern Java have yielded all the *H. erectus* fossil remains found to date on that island. The dating of these fossils has been hampered by the complex nature of Javanese geology. It has been generally accepted that most of the fossils belong in the Middle Pleistocene and are less than 800,000 years old. However, as we noted earlier, new dating estimates have suggested one find (from Modjokerto) to be close to 1.8 m.y.a. and another fossil from the main site of Sangiran to be approximately 1.6 m.y.a.

At Sangiran, where the remains of at least five individuals have been excavated, the cranial capacities of the fossils range from 813 cm³ to 1,059 cm³. Like Sangiran, another site called Ngandong has also been fruitful, yielding the remains of 12 crania (Fig. 16–5). The dating here is also confusing, but the Upper Pleistocene has been suggested, which may explain the larger cranial measurements of the Ngandong individuals as well as features that are more modern than those found on other Javanese crania. Ngandong 6, for example, has a cranial capacity of 1,251 cm³, a measurement well within the range of *H. sapiens*.

We cannot say much about the *H. erectus* way of life in Java. Very few artifacts have been found, and those have come mainly from river terraces, not from primary sites: "On Java there is still not a single site where artifacts can be associated with *H. erectus*" (Bartstra, 1982, p. 319).

Peking (Beijing)

The story of Peking *H. erectus* is another saga filled with excitement, hard work, luck, and misfortune. Europeans had known for a long time that "dragon bones," used by the Chinese as medicine and aphrodisiacs, were actually ancient mammal bones. In 1917, the Geological Survey of China decided to find the sites where these dragon bones were collected by local inhabitants and sold to apothecary shops. In 1921 a Swedish geologist, J. Gunnar Andersson, was told of a potentially fruitful fossil site in an abandoned quarry near the village of **Zhoukoudian**. A villager showed Andersson's team a fissure in the limestone wall, and within a few minutes they found the jaw of a pig: "That evening we went home with rosy dreams of great discoveries" (Andersson, 1934, pp. 97–98).

A young Chinese geologist, Pei Wenshong, took over the excavation in 1929 and began digging out the sediment in one branch of the lower cave, where he found one of the most remarkable fossil skulls to be recovered up to that time. One of the Chinese workers tells the story:

FIGURE 16–5

Rear view of a Ngandong skull. Note that the cranial walls slope downward and outward (or upward and inward), with the widest breadth low on the cranium, giving it a pentagonal form.

▲ Zhoukoudian
(zhoh´-koh-dee´-en)

---

*G. H. R. von Koenigswald worked in Java in the early 1930s and was a friend of Dubois'.

We had got down about 30 meters deep. . . . It was there the skull-cap was sighted, half of it embedded in loose earth, the other in hard clay. The sun had almost set . . . . The team debated whether to take it out right away or to wait until the next day when they could see better. The agonizing suspense of a whole day was felt to be too much to bear, so they decided to go on (Jia, 1975, pp. 12–13).

Pei brought the skull to anatomist Davidson Black (Fig 16–6). Because the fossil was embedded in hard limestone, it took Black four months of hard, steady work to free it from its tough matrix. The result was worth the labor. The skull, that of a juvenile, was thick, low, and relatively small, but in Black's mind there was no doubt it belonged to an early hominid. The response to this discovery, quite unlike that which greeted Dubois almost 40 years earlier, was immediate and enthusiastically favorable.

Franz Weidenreich (Fig 16–7), a distinguished anatomist and well known for his work on European fossil hominids, succeeded Black. After Japan invaded China in 1933, Weidenreich decided to move the fossils from Beijing to prevent them from falling into the hands of the Japanese. Weidenreich left China in 1941, taking excellent prepared casts, photographs, and drawings of the Peking material with him. After he left, the bones were packed, and arrangements were made for the U.S. Marine Corps in Beijing to take them to the United States. The bones never reached the United States and they have never been found. To this day, no one knows what happened to them, and their location remains a mystery.

FIGURE 16–6
Davidson Black, responsible for the study of the Zhoukoudian fossils.

Zhoukoudian *Homo erectus*

In their recent book (1990), Jia and Huang list the total fossil remains of *H. erectus* unearthed at the Zhoukoudian Cave as of 1982 (Fig. 16–8):

14 skullcaps (only 6 relatively complete) (Fig. 16–9)
6 facial bones (including maxillae, palates, and zygomatic bone fragments)
15 mandibles (mostly one side, only one nearly complete, many fragments)
122 isolated teeth
38 teeth rooted in jaws
3 humeri (upper arm bones, only 1 well preserved, the rest in fragments)
1 clavicle (both ends absent)
1 lunate (wrist bone)
7 femurs (only 1 well preserved)
1 tibia (shinbone, fragmentary)
(and over 100,000 artifacts)

FIGURE 16–7
Franz Weidenreich.

These remains belong to upward of 40 male and female adults and children and constitute a considerable amount of evidence, the largest number of *H. erectus* specimens found at any one site. With the meticulous work by Weidenreich, the Zhoukoudian fossils have led to a good overall picture of the eastern *H. erectus* of China.

Peking *H. erectus*, like those from Java, possess typical *H. erectus* features, including the supraorbital torus in front and the nuchal torus behind; also, the skull is keeled by a sagittal ridge, the face protrudes, the incisors are shoveled, and the molars contain large pulp cavities. Again, like the Javanese forms, the

FIGURE 16–8

Zhoukoudian Cave. The grid on the wall was drawn for purposes of excavation. The entrance to the cave can be seen near the grid.

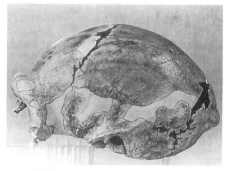

FIGURE 16–9

H. erectus *(specimen from Zhoukoudian). From this view, the supra-orbital torus, low vault of the skull, and angled occiput can clearly be seen.*

skull shows the greatest breadth near the bottom. (These similarities were recognized long ago by Black and Weidenreich.)

Cultural Remains   More than 100,000 artifacts have been recovered from this vast site that was occupied intermittently for almost 250,000 years. According to the Chinese (Wu and Lin, 1983, p.86), Zhoukoudian "is one of the sites with the longest history of habitation by man or his ancestors." The occupation of the site has been divided into three cultural stages:

Earliest Stage (460,000–420,000 y.a.)*   The tools are large, close to a pound in weight, and made of soft stone, such as sandstone.
Middle Stage (370,000–350,000 y.a.)   Tools become smaller and lighter (under a pound), and these smaller tools comprise approximately two-thirds of the sample.
Final Stage (300,000–230,000 y.a.)   Tools are still small, and the tool materials are of better quality. The coarse quartz of the earlier periods is replaced by a finer quartz, sandstone tools have almost disappeared, and flint tools increase in frequency by as much as 30 percent.

The early tools are crude and shapeless but become more refined over time. Common tools at the site are choppers and chopping tools, but retouched flakes were fashioned into scrapers, points, burins, and awls (Fig 16–10).

Stone was not the only material used by *H. erectus* at Zhoukoudian; these hominids also utilized bone and probably horn. Found in the cave were antler fragments, which had been hacked into pieces. Antler bases might have served as hammers and the sharp tines as digging sticks. Also found in abundance were many deer skulls lacking facial bones as well as antlers, thus leaving only the braincases intact. Jia suggests that because the skulls show evidence of repeated whittling and over 100 specimens were discovered, all similarly shaped, "it is reasonable to infer they served as 'drinking bowls.'" He goes on to conjecture that the braincases of the Beijing *H. erectus* fossils "retain similar characteristics and probably served the same purpose."

---

*These dates should be considered tentative until more precise chronometric techniques are available.

Quartzite chopper

Flint point

Flint awl

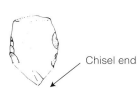
Chisel end

Graver or burin

FIGURE 16–10
Chinese tools from Middle Pleistocene sites. (Adapted from Wu and Olsen, 1985.)

The way of life at Zhoukoudian has traditionally been described as that of hunter-gatherers who killed deer and horses as well as other animals and gathered fruits, berries, and ostrich eggs. Fragments of charred ostrich eggshells, the copious deposits of hackberry seeds unearthed in the cave, and the flourishing plant growth surrounding the cave all suggest that meat was supplemented by the gathering of herbs, wild fruits, tubers, and eggs. Layers of ash in the cave, over 18 feet deep at one point, suggest fire and hearths, but whether Beijing hominids could actually *make* fire is unknown (see Issue, pp. 431–433). Wu and Lin (1983, p. 94) state that "Peking Man was a cave dweller, a fire user, a deer hunter, a seed gatherer and a maker of specialized tools," but several questions about Zhoukoudian *H. erectus* remain unanswered.

Did *H. erectus* at Zhoukoudian use language? If by language we mean articulate speech, it is unlikely. Nevertheless, some scholars believe that speech originated early in hominid evolution; others argue that speech did not originate until up to 200,000 years later in the Upper Paleolithic, with the origin of anatomically modern humans (see Chapter 18). We agree with Dean Falk when she writes, "Unfortunately, what it is going to take to *settle* the debate about when language originated in hominids is a time machine. Until one becomes available, we can only speculate about this fascinating and important question" (1989, p. 141).

Did these hominids wear clothes? Almost surely clothing of some type, probably in the form of animal skins, was worn. Winters in Beijing are harsh today and appear to have been bitter during the Middle Pleistocene as well. Moreover, awls were found at Zhoukoudian, and one of the probable bone tools may be a needle.

What was the life span of *H. erectus* at Zhoukoudian? Apparently, not very long, and infant and childhood mortality was probably very high. Studies of the fossil remains reveal that almost 40 percent of the bones belong to individuals under the age of 14, and only 2.6 percent are estimated to be in the 50- to 60-year age group (Jia, 1975).

This picture of Zhoukoudian life has been challenged by archeologist Lewis Binford and colleagues (Binford and Ho, 1985; Binford and Stone, 1986a, 1986b). Binford and his colleagues reject the description of Beijing *H. erectus* as hunters and believe that the evidence clearly points to them as scavengers. As we saw in Chapter 13, the controversy of early hominids as hunters or scavengers has engaged the attention of paleoanthropologists, and the matter is not yet settled. Binford and his colleagues also do not believe that the Beijing hominids were clearly associated with fire, except in the later phases of occupation (about 250,000 y.a.). Jia and Huang insist that the Beijing hominids *did* use and control fire: "Peking Man certainly used fire. . . . The fact that some ash substances are found in piles shows that Peking Man knew how to control fire" (Jia and Huang, 1990, p. 79).

Other Chinese Sites

More work has been done at Zhoukoudian than at any other Chinese site. Nevertheless, there are other hominid sites worth noting. Three of the more important sites, besides Zhoukoudian, are Chenjiawo and Gongwangling (both in Lantian County and sometimes referred to as Lantian) and Lontandong Cave in Hexian County (often referred to as the Hexian find) (see Table 16–1).

At Chenjiawo an almost complete mandible containing several teeth was found in 1963. It is quite similar to those from Zhoukoudian but has been provisionally dated at about 600,000–500,000 y.a. If the dating is correct, this specimen would be older than the Beijing material. The following year, a partial cranium was discovered at Gongwangling, not far from Chenjiawo. Provisionally dated to about 1.15 m.y.a. (Etler and Tianyuan, 1994), Gongwangling may be the oldest Chinese *Homo erectus* fossil yet known.

Perhaps the most significant find was made in 1980 at Lontandong Cave, where remains of several individuals were recovered. One of the specimens is a well-preserved cranium (with a cranial capacity of about 1,025 cm³) lacking much of its base. Dated roughly at 250,000 y.a., it is not surprising that this Hexian cranium displays several advanced features. The postorbital constriction, for example, is not as pronounced as in earlier forms, and certain temporal and occipital characteristics are "best compared with the later forms of *H. erectus* at Zhoukoudian" (Wu and Dong, 1985, p. 87).

TABLE 16–1 *H. erectus* Fossils of China

Designation	Site	Age* (Years Ago)	Material	Cranial Capacity (cm³)	Year Found	Remarks
Hexian	Longtandong Cave, Anhui	250,000	Calvarium, skull fragments, mandible fragments, isolated teeth	1,025	1980–81	First skull found in southern or southwest China
Zhoukoudian (Peking)	Zhoukoudian Cave, Beijing	500,000–200,000	5 adult crania, skull fragments, facial bones, isolated teeth, postcranial pieces 40+ individuals	850–1,225; avg: 1,010	1927–ongoing	Most famous fossils in China and some of the most famous in the world
Yunxian	Longgudong Cave, Hubei	?500,000	Isolated teeth		1976–82	
Yunxian	Quyuanhekou	350,000	2 mostly complete (but crushed) crania	undetermined	1989	The most complete crania from China, but still requiring much restoration
Lantian	Chenjiawo, Lantian	650,000	Mandible		1963	Old female
Lantian	Gongwangling, Lantian	800,000	Calvarium, facial bones	780	1964	Female over 30; oldest *H. erectus* found so far in China

Sources: Atlas of Primitive Man in China (1980); Lisowski 1984; Pope, 1984; Wu and Dong 1985.

*These are best estimates—authorities differ.

In June 1993, Li Tianyuan and Dennis Etler reported that two relatively complete skulls were discovered in 1989 at a hominid site in Yunxian County. The date given for the site is 350,000 y.a., which, if correct, would make these the most complete crania of this great antiquity in China (Fig 16–11).

The Yunxian crania are both large and robust, considerably exceeding in size those from Zhoukoudian. In general, the Yunxian individuals fit within *Homo erectus*, but in the facial region especially they also show some interesting advanced features. A few of these features suggest to some scholars "a mid-facial morphology similar to that of modern Asians" (Etler and Tianyuan, 1994, p. 668).

Unfortunately, both skulls are still covered with a hard calcareous matrix, and critics argue that until the skulls are cleaned and the crushed parts properly put together, it is too early to make accurate assessments. In any case, these Yunxian crania will ultimately provide considerable data to help clarify hominid evolution in China and perhaps elsewhere in the Old World as well.

A number of archeological sites have been excavated in China, and early Paleolithic stone tools have been found in numerous locations in widely separated areas. At present, there is little reason to believe that *H. erectus* culture in these provinces differed much from that described at Zhoukoudian.

The Asian crania from both Java and China are mainly Middle Pleistocene fossils and share many similar features, which may be explained by *H. erectus* migration from Java to China about 800,000 y.a. African *H. erectus* forms are generally older than most Asian forms and are not as similar to them as Asian forms (i.e., from Java and China) are to each other.

East Africa

Olduvai   Back in 1960, Louis Leakey unearthed a fossil skull at Olduvai (OH 9) that he identified as *H. erectus*. Skull OH 9 from Upper Bed II is dated at 1.4 m.y.a. and preserves a massive cranium but is faceless except for a bit of nose below the supraorbital torus. Estimated at 1,067 cm³, the cranial capacity of OH 9 is the largest of all the African *Homo erectus* specimens. The browridge is huge, the largest known for any hominid in both thickness and projection, but the vault walls are thin.

East Turkana   Some 400 miles north of Olduvai Gorge, on the northern boundary of Kenya, is Lake Turkana. Explored by Richard Leakey and colleagues since 1969, the eastern shore of the lake has been a virtual gold mine for australopithecine, early *Homo*, and *H. erectus* fossil remains.

The most significant *H. erectus* discovery from East Turkana is ER 3733, an almost complete skull lacking a mandible (Fig. 16–12). Discovered in 1974, the specimen has been given a firm date of close to 1.8 m.y.a. The cranial capacity is estimated at 848 cm³, at the lower end of the range for *H. erectus*, but this is not surprising considering its early date. The cranium resembles Asian *H. erectus* in most features.

Not many tools have been found at *H. erectus* sites in East Turkana. Oldowan types of flakes, cobbles, and core tools have been found, and the introduction of **Acheulian** tools about 1.4 m.y.a. replaced the Oldowan tradition.

West Turkana*   In August 1984, Kamoya Kimeu (see Guest Essay, pp. 389–390), a member of Richard Leakey's team, lived up to his reputation as an outstanding fossil hunter and discovered a small piece of skull near the base camp on the west

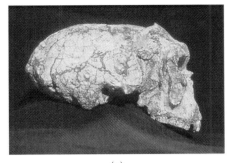

(a)

(b)

FIGURE 16–11
(a) EV 9002 (Yunxian, China). The skull is in better shape than its companion, and its lateral view clearly displays features characteristic of H. erectus: *flattened vault, receding forehead (frontal bone), angulated occiput, and supraorbital torus. (b) EV 9001 (Yunxian). Unfortunately, the skull was crushed, but it preserves some lateral facial structures absent in EV 9002.*

▲ **Acheulian**
(ash´-oo-lay-en)
Pertaining to a stone tool industry of the Lower and Middle Pleistocene characterized by a large proportion of bifacial tools (flaked on both sides). Acheulian tool kits are very common in Africa, Southwest Asia, and western Europe, but are nearly absent elsewhere. (Also spelled "Acheulean.")

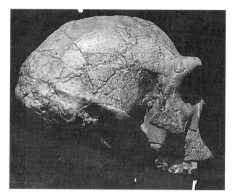

FIGURE 16–12
ER 3733, the most complete East Turkana H. erectus *cranium.*

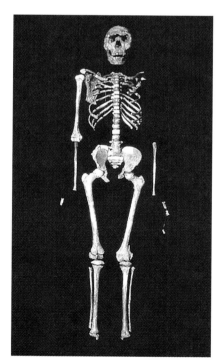

FIGURE 16–13
WT 15,000 from Nariokotome, Kenya: the most complete H. erectus *specimen yet found.*

side of Lake Turkana. Leakey and his colleague, Alan Walker of Pennsylvania State University, excavated the site known as Nariokotome in 1984 and again in 1985 (discussed above on p. 413).

The dig was a resounding success. The workers unearthed the most complete *H. erectus* skeleton yet found (Fig. 16–13). Known properly as WT 15,000, the all but complete skeleton includes facial bones and most of the postcranial bones, a rare event indeed for *H. erectus*, since these particular elements are scarce at other *H. erectus* sites. The completeness of the skeleton is helping to resolve some of the riddles associated with *H. erectus* (see Box 16–1).

Another remarkable feature of the find is its age. Its dating is based on the chronometric dates of the geological formation in which the site is located and is set at about 1.6 million years. The skeleton is that of a boy about 12 years of age and 5 feet 3 inches tall. Had he grown to maturity, his height, it is estimated, would have been more than 6 feet, taller than *H. erectus* was heretofore thought to have been. The postcranial bones appear to be quite similar, though not identical, to those of modern humans. The cranial capacity of WT 15,000 is estimated at 880 cm³; brain growth was nearly complete, and it is estimated that the boy's adult cranial capacity would have been approximately 909 cm³ (Begun and Walker, 1993).

Ethiopia   In southern Ethiopia, the 1991 Paleoanthropological Inventory of Ethiopia team of international scientists discovered a site, Konso-Gardula (KGA), containing a remarkable abundance of Acheulian tools, a hominid upper third molar, and an almost complete mandible with several cheek teeth. Both specimens are attributed to *H. erectus* "because they lack specialized characteristics of robust *Australopithecus*" (Asfaw et al., 1992).

The mandible is robust and is dated to about 1.3 m.y.a. The Acheulian stone tools, mainly bifaces and picks, are made of quartz, quartzite, and volcanic rock, from cobbles, blocks, cores, and flakes.

The *Homo erectus* remains from East Africa show several differences from the fossil samples from Java and China. The African specimens (as exemplified by ER 3733, presumably a female, and WT 15,000, presumably a male) are not as strongly buttressed in the cranium (by supraorbital or nuchal tori) and do not have such thick cranial bones as seen in Asian representatives of *H. erectus*. These differences, as well as others observed in the postcranial skeleton, have so impressed some researchers that they in fact argue for a *separate* species status for the African *H. erectus* remains (as distinct from the Asian samples). Bernard Wood, the leading proponent of this multiple-species solution, has suggested that the name *Homo ergaster* be used for the African remains. (*H. erectus* would then be reserved solely for the Asian material) (Wood, 1991). In addition, the very early dates now postulated for the dispersal of *H. erectus* into Asia (Java) would argue for a more than 1-million-year separate history for Asian as compared to African populations. Furthermore, the possible concurrent evolutionary development of early *Homo* in China (see p. 387) also suggests an even longer and potentially quite distinct evolutionary history of Asian as compared to African hominids. Such a long and potentially distinct period of isolation might well further argue the case for two separate species.

Nevertheless, this taxonomic division has not been generally accepted, and the current consensus (reflected in this text) is to continue to refer to all these hominids as *Homo erectus*. As with the Plio-Pleistocene samples, we accordingly will have to accommodate a considerable degree of intraspecific variation within

---

*WT is the symbol for West Turkana, that is, the west side of Lake Turkana. The east side is designated by ER—East Rudolf. Rudolf was the former name of the lake (see p. 372).

this species. Wood has concluded, regarding variation within such a broadly defined *H. erectus* species, "It is a species which manifestly embraces an unusually wide degree of variation in both the cranium and postcranial skeleton" (Wood, 1992a, p. 329).

South Africa

A mandible was found among fossil remains collected at Swartkrans in South Africa in the 1940s and 1950s. This specimen, SK 15, was originally assigned to *"Telanthropus capensis,"* but is now placed within the genus *Homo* (there is, however, disagreement about its species designation). Rightmire (1990) believes that it may be linked with *Homo erectus*, but others are not certain. If it is *H. erectus*, it would demonstrate that *H. erectus* inhabited South Africa as well as the other regions documented by other more complete fossil finds.

North Africa

With evidence from China and Java, it appears clear that *H. erectus* populations, with superior tools and weapons and presumably greater intelligence than their predecessors, had expanded their habitat beyond that of early hominids. The earliest evidence for *H. erectus*, 1.6–1.8 m.y.a., comes from East Africa and Java and about 1 million years later in China. It is not surprising, therefore, that *H. erectus* migrations would have taken them to northwest Africa as well.

North African remains, consisting almost entirely of mandibles or mandible fragments and a partial parietal bone, have been found at Ternifine (now Tighenif), Algeria, and in Morocco, at Sidi Abderrahman and Thomas Quarries. The three Ternifine mandibles and the parietal fragment are quite robust and have been dated to about 700,000 y.a. The Moroccan material is not as robust as Ternifine and may be a bit younger, at 500,000 years. In addition, an interesting cranium was found in a quarry north of Salé, in Morocco. The walls of the skull vault are thick, and several other features resemble those of *H. erectus*. Some features suggest that Salé is *H. sapiens*, but a date of 400,000 y.a. and an estimated cranial capacity of about 900 cm^3 appear to nullify that possibility.

Europe presents a similar situation. At present, many paleoanthropologists argue that early European inhabitants, once assigned to *H. erectus*, should now be reassigned to early *H. sapiens* status, known as "archaic *H. sapiens*." Needless to say, not everyone agrees. These enigmatic archaic *H. sapiens* are discussed in Chapter 17. A time line for the *H. erectus* discoveries discussed in this chapter as well as other finds of more uncertain status is shown in Figure 16–14.

Technological and Social Trends in the Middle Pleistocene

Technological Trends

Scholars have noted the remarkable stasis of the physical and cultural characteristics of *Homo erectus* populations, which seemed to change so little in the more than 1.5 million years of their existence. There is, however, dispute on this point.

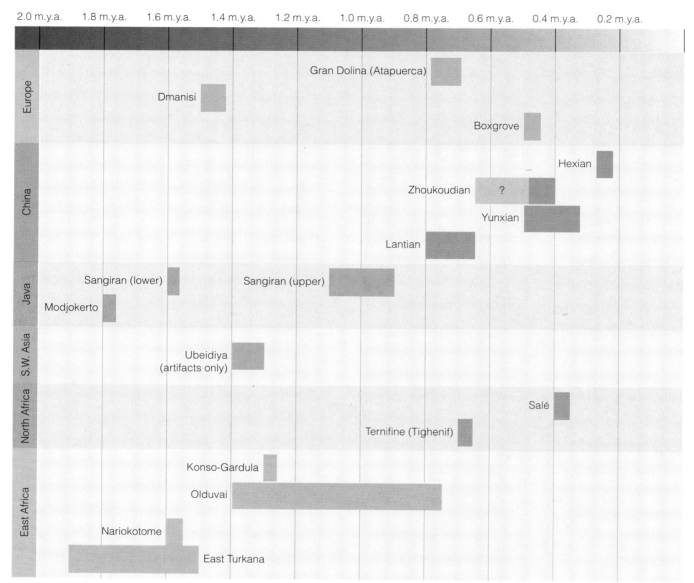

*Note: Most dates are only imprecise estimates. However, the dates from East African sites are radiometrically determined and are thus much more secure. In addition, the early dates from Java are also radiometric and are gaining wide acceptance, although some researchers (e.g., Wolpoff, 1995) suggest that they may be as much as .50 to .75 m.y. later than shown.

FIGURE 16–14

Time line for Homo erectus *discoveries and of other contemporary hominids. Note that most dates are approximations. Question marks indicate those estimates that are most tentative.*

Some scholars (Rightmire, 1981) see almost no detectable changes in cranial dimensions over more than 1 million years of *H. erectus* evolution. Other researchers (e.g., Wolpoff, 1984), who use different methodologies to date and subdivide their samples, draw a different conclusion, seeing some significant long-term morphological trends. Accepting a moderate position, we can postulate that there were some changes: The brain of later *H. erectus* was somewhat larger, the nose more protrusive, and the body not as robust as in earlier forms. Moreover, there were modifications in stone tool technology.

Expansion of the brain presumably enabled *H. erectus* to develop a more sophisticated tool kit than seen in earlier hominids. The important change in this kit was a core worked on both sides, called a *biface* (known widely as hand axes and cleavers; Fig 16–15). The biface had a flatter core than the roundish earlier Oldowan pebble tool. And, probably even more important, this *core* tool was obviously a target design, that is, the main goal of the toolmaker. This greater focus and increased control enabled the stoneknapper to produce sharper, straighter edges, resulting in a more efficient implement. This *Acheulian* stone tool became standardized as the basic *H. erectus* all-purpose tool (with only minor modification) for more than a million years. It served to cut, scrape, pound, dig, and more—a most useful tool that has been found in Africa, parts of Asia, and later in western Europe. Like populations elsewhere, *H. erectus* in China manufactured choppers and chopping tools as their core tools, and like other *H. erectus* toolmakers, fashioned scrapers and other small tools, but they did not regularly manufacture bifaces (Fig. 16–16). Interestingly, while the Acheulian is known from Africa as early as 1.4 m.y.a. and persisted there and in western Europe and southwestern Asia for over 1 million years, this industry has *never* been found in eastern Europe or East Asia. Why there was such a long period of cultural distinctiveness has never been completely explained. It has been thought that other kinds of raw materials for tools were employed (bamboo, perhaps, in China). Another possibility suggested by the redating of the early Java sites is that *H. erectus* left Africa *prior* to the development of the Acheulian, and after reaching Asia, some groups continued to remain culturally isolated in certain regions.

In early days, toolmakers employed a stone hammer (simply an ovoid-shaped stone about the size of an egg or a bit larger) to remove flakes from the core, thus leaving deep scars. Later, they used other materials, such as wood and bone. They learned to use these new materials as soft hammers, which gave them more control over flaking, thus leaving shallow scars, sharper edges, and a more symmetrical form. Toward the end of the Acheulian industry, toolmakers blocked out a core with stone hammers and then switched to wood or bone for refining the edges. This technique produced more elegant-appearing and pear-shaped implements.

Evidence of butchering is widespread at *H. erectus* sites, and in the past, such evidence has been cited in arguments for consistent hunting. For example, at the Olorgesailie site in Kenya (Fig. 16–17), dated at approximately 800,000 y.a., thousands of Acheulian hand axes have been recovered in association with remains of large animals, including giant baboons (now extinct). However, the assumption of consistent hunting has been challenged, especially by archeologists who believe that the evidence does not prove the hunting hypothesis. Instead, they believe that *H. erectus* was primarily a scavenger, a hypothesis that also has not yet been proved conclusively. We thus discuss *H. erectus* as a potential hunter *and* scavenger. It is also crucial to remember that *gathering* of wild plant foods was also practiced by *H. erectus* groups (as evidenced by the seeds at Zhoukoudian). Indeed, probably a majority of the calories they consumed came from such gathering activities.

Moreover, as we have seen, the mere *presence* of animal bones at archeological sites does not prove that hominids were killing animals or even necessarily exploiting meat. Thus, in making interpretations of early hominid sites, we must consider a variety of alternatives. As Stanford University archeologist Richard Klein has concluded regarding Middle Pleistocene sites, the interpretations are far from clear: "In sum, the available data do not allow us to isolate the relative roles of humans, carnivores, and factors such as starvation, accidents, and stream action in creating bone assemblages. . . . Certainly, as presently understood, the sites do not tell us how successful or effective *Homo erectus* was at obtaining meat" (1989, p. 221).

FIGURE 16–15
Acheulian biface ("hand axe"), a basic tool of the Acheulian tradition.

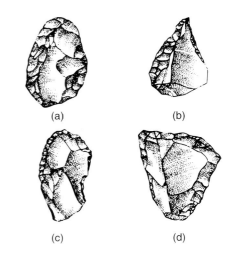

FIGURE 16–16
Small tools of the Acheulian industry. (a) Side scraper. (b) Point. (c) End scraper. (d) Burin.

FIGURE 16–17
(a) A Middle Pleistocene butchering site at Olorgesailie, Kenya, excavated by Louis and Mary Leakey, who had the catwalk built for observers. (b) A close-up of the Acheulian tools, mainly hand axes, found at the site.

Social Trends

One of the fascinating qualities of *H. erectus* was a penchant for travel. From the relatively close confines of East Africa, *H. erectus* dispersed widely in the Old World. By the time *H. sapiens* appeared a million or more years later, *H. erectus* had migrated to South and North Africa, and even earlier, perhaps some groups had moved from Africa to Asia.

The life of hunter-scavengers (and still, no doubt, *primarily* gatherers) was nomadic, and the woodland and savanna that covered the southern tier of Asia would have been an excellent environment for *H. erectus* (as it was similar to the econiche of their African ancestors). As the population grew, small groups budded off and moved on to find their own resource areas. This process, repeated again and again, led *H. erectus* east, crossing to Java, arriving there, it seems, as early as the most ancient known sites in East Africa itself.

Once in Java, it would have been impossible to venture further east, since there was no land bridge joining Australia to Java. It was possible, however, to travel north, and by 700,000 y.a., *H. erectus* had also reached China. (Earlier *Homo* may have already reached China, perhaps as much as 1 million years prior.)

When we look back at the evolution of *H. erectus*, we realize how significant this early human's achievements were. It was *H. erectus* who increased in body size with more efficient bipedalism; who embraced culture wholeheartedly as a strategy of adaptation; whose brain was reshaped and increased in size to within *H. sapiens* range; who became a more efficient scavenger and likely hunter with greater dependence on meat; who apparently established more permanent bases; and who probably used fire and may have also controlled it. In short, it was *H. erectus*, committed to a cultural way of life, who transformed hominid evolution to human evolution, or as Foley states: "The appearance and expansion of *H. erectus* represented a major change in adaptive strategy that influenced the subsequent process and pattern of human evolution" (1991, p. 425).

Summary

Homo erectus remains are found in geological contexts dating from about 1.8 million to about 200,000 years ago, a period of more than 1.5 million years. The first finds were made by Dubois in Java, and later discoveries came from China and Africa. Differences from early *Homo* are notable in *H. erectus*' larger brain, taller stature, robust build, and changes in facial structure and cranial buttressing.

The long period of *H. erectus*' existence was marked by a remarkably uniform technology over space and time. Nevertheless, compared to earlier hominids, *H. erectus* introduced more sophisticated tools and probably ate novel and/or differently processed foods, using these new tools and probably fire as well. They were also able to move into different environments and successfully adapt to new conditions.

Originating in East Africa, *H. erectus* migrated in several directions: south and northwest in Africa and east to Java and China. The evidence from China, especially Zhoukoudian, supports a *H. erectus* way of life that included gathering, scavenging, hunting, and controlled use of fire (but note that there is not complete agreement about this archeological reconstruction).

It is generally assumed that some *H. erectus* populations evolved to *H. sapiens*, since many fossils, such as Ngandong (and others discussed in Chapter 17), display both *H. erectus* and *H. sapiens* features. There remain questions about *H. erectus*' behavior (e.g., did they hunt?) and about evolution to *H. sapiens* (was it gradual or rapid, and which *H. erectus* populations contributed genes to *H. sapiens*?). The search for answers continues.

Questions for Review

1. Describe the Pleistocene in terms of (a) temperature and (b) the dating of fossil hominids.
2. Describe *Homo erectus*. How is *H. erectus* anatomically different from early *Homo*? From *H. sapiens*?
3. In what areas of the world have *Homo erectus* fossils been found?

4. In comparing *H. erectus* with earlier hominids, why is it important to specify which comparative sample is being used?
5. What was the intellectual climate in Europe in the latter half of the nineteenth century, especially concerning human evolution?
6. Why do you think there was so much opposition to Dubois' interpretation of the hominid fossils he found in Java?
7. Why do you think Zhoukoudian *H. erectus* was enthusiastically accepted, whereas the Javanese fossils were not?
8. What questions are still being asked about Dubois' finds? Explain.
9. Describe the way of life of *H. erectus* at Zhoukoudian as suggested in the text. What disagreements have been voiced about this conjecture?
10. *H. erectus* has been called the first human. Why?
11. What is the *H. erectus* evidence from Africa, and what questions of human evolution does the evidence raise?
12. Can you suggest any reason why the earliest remains of *H. erectus* have come from East Africa?
13. *H. erectus* migrated to various points in Africa and vast distances to eastern Asia. What does this tell you about the species?
14. What kinds of stone tools have been found at *H. erectus* sites?

Suggested Further Reading

Day, Michael. 1986. *Guide to Fossil Man*. Chicago: University of Chicago Press.

Rightmire, G.P. 1990. *The Evolution of* Homo erectus. New York: Cambridge University Press.

Shapiro, Harry L. 1980. *Peking Man*. New York: Simon & Schuster.

Walker, Alan, and Richard Leakey (eds). 1993. *The Nariokotome* Homo erectus *Skeleton*. Cambridge: Harvard University Press.

Wolpoff, Milford. 1984. "Evolution in *Homo erectus*: The Question of Stasis." *Paleobiology* **10**:389–406.

Internet Resources

See list in Chapters 13 and 14.

The Control of Fire

After a brush fire, some animals take advantage of the available food, such as carcasses of burnt animals, fallen bees' nests, and roasted plants. "Bush fires in Africa and probably elsewhere," writes archeologist John Gowlett, "are used by intelligent predators as a means of trapping prey. Animals such as the cheetah will position themselves so as to pounce on animals fleeing from the flames, and hawks will do the same" (1984, p. 56). Gowlett repeats a traveler's story that apes, probably gorillas, would warm themselves around an abandoned fire until the fire burned out. It follows that if nonhuman animals are intelligent enough to make use of fire, it is quite likely that early hominids did so as well. As Henry Lewis, of the University of Alberta, puts it:

It is difficult to accept that an animal with the mental capacity and physical dexterity to make even the simplest stone tools would not have recognized the advantages of using fire—to heat and illuminate caves or open sites, not to mention cooking food or affecting plants and animals—and been able to maintain it and move it from place to place. (1989, p. 14)

An important distinction exists between the *making* of fire and the *use* of fire captured from natural sources. Some very ancient methods that could have been used deliberately to make fire might have

included striking hard rocks together or rubbing wood together to create sparks through friction. Without such technological innovations, earlier hominids would have been limited to obtaining and transporting fire from natural sources, such as lightning strikes and geothermal localities.

The archeological evidence, however, may never be sufficiently complete to allow this distinction to be made with much precision. Nevertheless, *at minimum*, the consistent use of fire would have been a major technological breakthrough and could have had potentially marked influence on hominid biological evolution as well. For example, as a result of cooking, food items would have been more tender; thus, chewing stresses would have been reduced, perhaps leading also to selection for reduced size of the dentition.

It is possible that australopithecines took advantage of and used naturally occurring fire, but the evidence relating to the use of fire is not always easy to interpret. At open-air sites, for example, remains suggesting an association between hominids and burning may be found. However, ashes may already have been blown away, and stones and bones blackened by fire could be the result of a natural brush fire, as could charcoal and baked earth. Furthermore, remains found on the surface of a site might be the result of a natural fire that occurred long after the hominids had left. Another

problem is that at many sites, the burned material is too scanty to serve as causal evidence of fire. (Indeed, this should remind you of the critical thinking dictum that correlation does not necessarily equal causation.)

The difficulties of working with evidence at "use" sites (where fire was probably not deliberately made) also apply to sites where hominids may have ignited the fires. These are often referred to as controlled fires, and it is the earliest makers (or at least *systematic* users) of fire that interest us in this Issue. Some sort of regular *control* of this important resource is the real key here. We cite Gowlett once again:

The control of fire is of critical importance to humanity; it provides warmth, protection and a means of cooking. For early man it was also a technological catalyst—with the aid of fire numerous processes became easier—wooden objects could be shaped and flint could be heated so that it flaked more easily . . . [It] is so rooted in culture that it has a symbolic significance; religion has its fire-gods and innumerable habits and rites connected with fire have been recorded, revealing its deep spiritual importance. The ability to control and use fire sets man apart from the rest of the natural world. (1984, p. 56)

The preceding quotes have suggested several possible advantages that controlled use of fire may have provided to earlier hominids, including:

1. Warmth
2. Cooking meat and/or plant foods, thus breaking down fibers and, in the case of many plants, neutralizing toxins
3. Fire-hardening wood, such as the end of a spear
4. Facilitating the predictable flaking of certain stone materials, thus aiding in the production of stone tools
5. Chasing competing predators (such as bears) from caves and keeping dangerous animals at bay
6. Providing illumination in caves and, more fundamentally, extending usable light into the night

This last implication of human control of fire may have had a profound effect on human sleep cycles and with it alterations in activity patterns, neurological functioning, and hormonal balance. In fact, recent experiments have suggested that humans still today can readily (and comfortably) adjust to "natural" light/dark cycles with periods of inactivity of up to 14 hours (thus

simulating winter conditions *prior* to the systematic control of fire).

Since controlling fire is so important to humans, it would be useful to know who tamed the wild flames and when, where, and how they did it. With that knowledge we could learn much more about the culture of our ancient ancestors and their evolution. Archeologists are not certain who the first fire makers were. Some believe that *Homo erectus* may have been the first, but the evidence has been questioned; others believe it was archaic *H. sapiens* (discussed in Chapter 17) who invented the earliest method of making fire. Two of the earliest presumed examples of fire use come from Africa, and both have been suggested as indicating deliberate hominid pyrotechnics *prior* to 1 m.y.a. First, at Chesowanja in southern Kenya, patches of burned clay dated at 1.4 m.y.a. were found in association with stone tools. John Gowlett (quoted earlier) and his colleague, Jack Harris, have suggested

---

*Swartkrans was not a cave during the time of hominid archeological accumulation, but has been shown to have been a natural fissure into which animals and other objects fell.

that the burned clay is the residue of ancient campfires. Second, recent excavations from upper levels at Swartkrans in South Africa by C. K. Brain and Andrew Sillen have recovered many pieces of burnt bone, again in association with stone tools dated at 1.3–1.0 m.y.a. (For a further discussion of Swartkrans see pp. 382–386.) Both of these possible occurrences of hominid control of fire in Africa are thought to be associated with *Homo erectus*. However, neither of the early African contexts has yet to fully convince experts.

True caves* may be a more probable source for finding human-made fire, because caves, except at the entrance, are damp, very dark, and impossible for habitation without light. Also, by the time humans began to occupy caves, they may have invented a method of making fire. It is possible, of course, to carry a natural fire into a cave, which is another snag in determining whether the fire was deliberately made or natural.

Probably the cave best known to paleoanthropologists is Zhoukoudian (discussed in this chapter), not far from Beijing, China, where both Chinese and

Western archeologists have been working for more than 60 years. Evidence of fire is abundant, but the evidence (such as charred animal bones, layers of ash, charcoal, and burned stone artifacts) has led to differing interpretations by archeologists. The Chinese scholars and many of their colleagues who have worked at Zhoukoudian are convinced that *H. erectus*, who inhabited the cave, made and controlled fire, perhaps as much as half a million years ago. Other archeologists, led by Lewis Binford of Southern Methodist University, doubt this and believe that the layers of "ash" are not really ash and that other evidence of burning in the cave was most likely due to natural causes.

At certain open *H. erectus* sites in China, there appears to be evidence for deliberately made fires, and several caves in Europe, provisionally dated to about 300,000 years ago, have yielded evidence of fire possibly made by archaic *H. sapiens*. But, again, not all archeologists are persuaded that humans were responsible.

Other prehistorians are sure that Neandertals (discussed in Chapter 17), who built hearths, were the first to make fire—toward the end of the Middle Pleistocene (circa 125,000 years ago). A deliberately built hearth is probably the best evidence for human-controlled fire. Ancient hearths are usually built with stone cobbles, arranged in a circular or oval shape to constrain the fire within the stone boundaries. The presence of numerous hearths at a site (like finding a box of matches near a fire) tends to serve as proof that the fires were probably started by humans. It is the absence of hearths that is so troublesome at the older sites and which immediately signals a doubt that the fire was made (or even systematically used) by hominids. It will take the development of carefully constructed interpretive techniques to overcome the difficulties of solving the case of the first significant controllers of fire.

Critical Thinking Questions

1. What types of evidence have been used to assess whether early hominids were either making or using fire?
2. Given the nature of the evidence, what are the problems in distinguishing the actual *making* of fire from the simple *use* of fire?
3. If you read a report that burnt bone and burnt rock found at a site were being interpreted as evidence of deliberate control of fire, what procedure would you follow to attempt to *falsify* this claim?
4. Why is it good scientific procedure to attempt to falsify hypotheses like the one in question 3? If there is no clear method to falsify the hypothesis, what does it tell you of its scientific utility?

Sources

Binford, Lewis P., and Chuan Kuntto. 1985. "Taphonomy at a Distance: Zhoukoudian, the Cave Home of Beijing Man." *Current Anthropology* 26:413–442.

Gowlett, John. 1984. *Ascent to Civilization*. New York: Alfred A. Knopf.

Lewis, Henry. 1984. "Comments." *Current Anthropology* 30:14–15.

17

Neandertals and Other Archaic *Homo sapiens*

Introduction

In Chapter 16, we saw that *H. erectus* was present in Africa approximately 1.8 m.y.a. and also in Java at about this same time. Except for the new find at Dmanisi, in the Republic of Georgia, we also noted that *H. erectus* fossils thus far have not been found in Europe, although several routes could easily have provided access. A major difficulty in accurately assessing finds is that a number of fossils from Europe—as well as Africa, China, and Java—display *both H. erectus* and *H. sapiens* features.

These particular forms, possibly representing some of the earliest members of our species, fall into the latter half of the Middle Pleistocene, from about 400,000 to 130,000 years ago, and are often referred to as **archaic *H. sapiens*** (Fig. 17–1). The designation *H. sapiens* is used because the appearance of some derived sapiens traits suggests that these hominids are transitional forms. In most cases, these early archaic *H. sapiens* also retain some *H. erectus* features mixed with those derived features that distinguish them as *H. sapiens*. However, as they do not possess the full suite of derived characteristics diagnostic of **anatomically modern *H. sapiens***, we classify them as archaic forms of our species. In general, we see in several different areas of the Old World through time a morphological trend from groups with more obvious *H. erectus* features to later populations displaying more diagnostic *H. sapiens* features.

When we speak of evolutionary trends and transitions from one species to another—for example, from *H. erectus* to *H. sapiens*—we do not wish to imply that such changes were in any way inevitable. In fact, most *H. erectus* populations never evolved into anything else. *Some* populations of *H. erectus* did apparently undergo slow evolutionary changes, and thus, some populations of what we call archaic *H. sapiens* emerge as transitional forms. In turn, *some* of these archaic *H. sapiens* populations suggest evolutionary change in the direction of anatomically modern *H. sapiens*.

In this chapter and the next, we attempt, where the data permit, to focus on those populations that provide clues regarding patterns of hominid evolutionary change. We would like to ascertain *where* such transformations took place, *when* they occurred, and *what* the adaptive stimuli were (both cultural and biological) that urged the process along.

There are still significant gaps in the fossil data, and we certainly do not have a complete record of all the transitional stages; nor are we ever likely to possess anything approaching such a complete record. What we will do in this and the next chapter is to paint the evolution of later hominids in fairly broad strokes to show the general trends.

Early Archaic *H. sapiens*

In many cases, early archaic forms show morphological changes compared to *H. erectus*. These derived changes are reflected in brain expansion; increased parietal breadth (the basal portion of the skull is no longer the widest area, and therefore, the shape of the skull as seen from the rear is no longer pentagonal); some decrease in the size of the molars; and general decrease in cranial and postcranial robusticity.

Archaic *H. sapiens* fossils have been found on the three continents of Africa, Asia, and Europe (Fig. 17–2). In Europe, the well-known Neandertals are

▲ **Archaic *H. sapiens*** Earlier forms of *Homo sapiens* (including Neandertals) from the Old World that differ from *H. erectus* but lack the full set of characteristics diagnostic of modern *H. sapiens*.

▲ **Anatomically modern *H. sapiens*** All modern humans and some fossil forms, perhaps dating as early as 200,000 y.a.; defined by a set of derived characteristics, including cranial architecture and lack of skeletal robusticity; usually classified at the subspecies level as *Homo sapiens sapiens* (see Chapter 18).

included in this category. (Neandertals are not found anywhere *except* Europe and western Asia.)

Africa

In Africa, archaic *H. sapiens* fossils have been found at several sites (see Fig. 17–2). One of the best known is Broken Hill (Kabwe) (Fig. 17–1). At this site in Zambia, a complete cranium and other cranial and postcranial material belonging to several individuals were discovered.

In this and other African early archaic specimens, a mixture of older and more recent traits can be seen. The skull's massive supraorbital torus (one of the largest of any hominid), low vault, and prominent occipital torus recall those of *H. erectus*. On the other hand, the occipital region is less angulated, the cranial vault bones are thinner, and the cranial base is essentially modern. Dating estimates of Broken Hill and most of the other early archaic *H. sapiens* from Africa have ranged throughout the Middle and Upper Pleistocene, but recent estimates have given dates for most of the localities in the range of 150,000–125,000 y.a.

A total of eight other archaic *H. sapiens* crania from South and East Africa also show a combination of *H. erectus* and *H. sapiens* characteristics, and they are all mentioned in the literature as being similar to Broken Hill. The most important of these African finds come from the sites of Florisbad and Elandsfontein in South Africa, Laetoli in Tanzania, and Bodo in Ethiopia (see Fig. 17–1 and Table 17–1). The general similarities in all these African archaic *H. sapiens* may signify a fairly close genetic relationship of hominids from East and South Africa. It is also possible—although it seems less likely—that several populations were evolving in a somewhat similar way from *H. erectus* to a more *H. sapiens*-looking morphology.

We should point out that the evolutionary path of these hominids did not take a Neandertal turn. It seems that there were no Neandertals in Africa—nor were there any in the Far East.

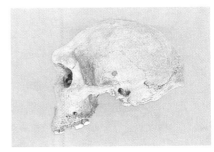

FIGURE 17–1
Broken Hill (Kabwe). Note the very heavy supraorbital torus.

Asia

China   Like their counterparts in Europe and Africa, Chinese archaic *H. sapiens** also display both older and later characteristics. Chinese paleoanthropologists believe that archaic *H. sapiens* traits, such as a sagittal ridge (see p. 416) and flattened nasal bones, are shared with *H. erectus*, especially those specimens from Zhoukoudian. They also point out that some of these features can be found in modern *H. sapiens* in China today, indicating substantial genetic continuity. That is, Chinese researchers suggest that anatomically modern Chinese did not evolve from *H. sapiens* in either Europe or Africa, evolving instead specifically in China from a separate *H. erectus* lineage.

That such regional evolution occurred in many areas of the world or, alternatively, that anatomically modern migrants from Africa displaced local populations is the subject of a major ongoing debate in paleoanthropology. This important controversy will be discussed in Chapter 18.

Dali, the most complete skull of the late Middle or early Upper Pleistocene fossils in China, displays *H. erectus* and *H. sapiens* traits, but it is clearly classified

---

*Chinese anthropologists prefer the term "early *Homo sapiens*" instead of "archaic *H. sapiens*."

FIGURE 17–2
Fossil discoveries of archaic Homo
sapiens.

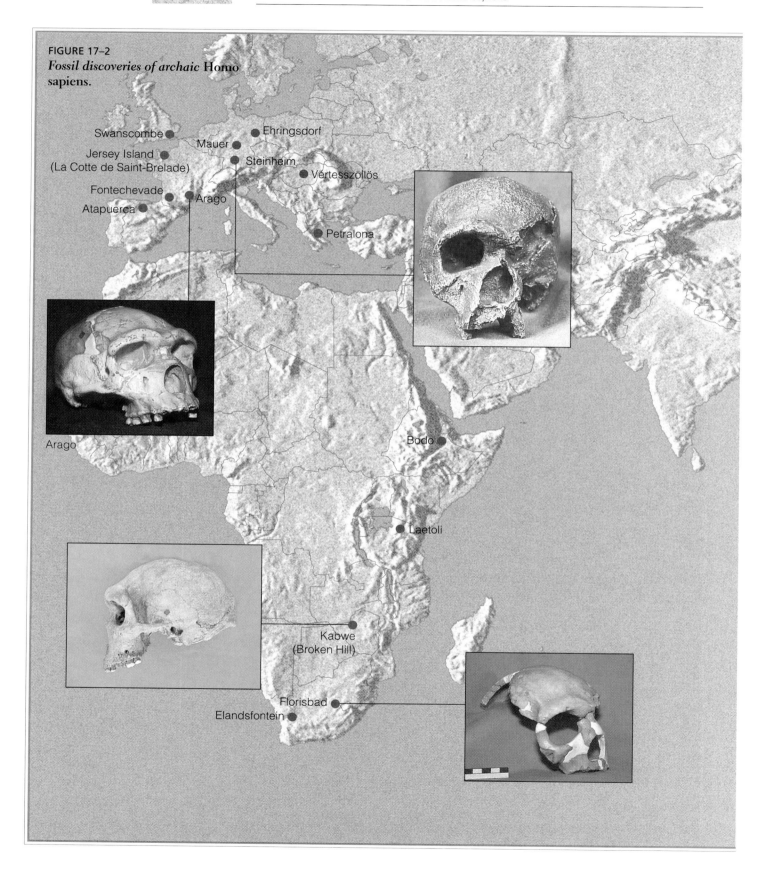

Swanscombe
Ehringsdorf
Mauer
Jersey Island
(La Cotte de Saint-Brelade)
Steinheim
Vértesszöllös
Fontechevade
Arago
Atapuerca
Petralona

Arago

Bodo

Laetoli

Kabwe
(Broken Hill)

Florisbad
Elandsfontein

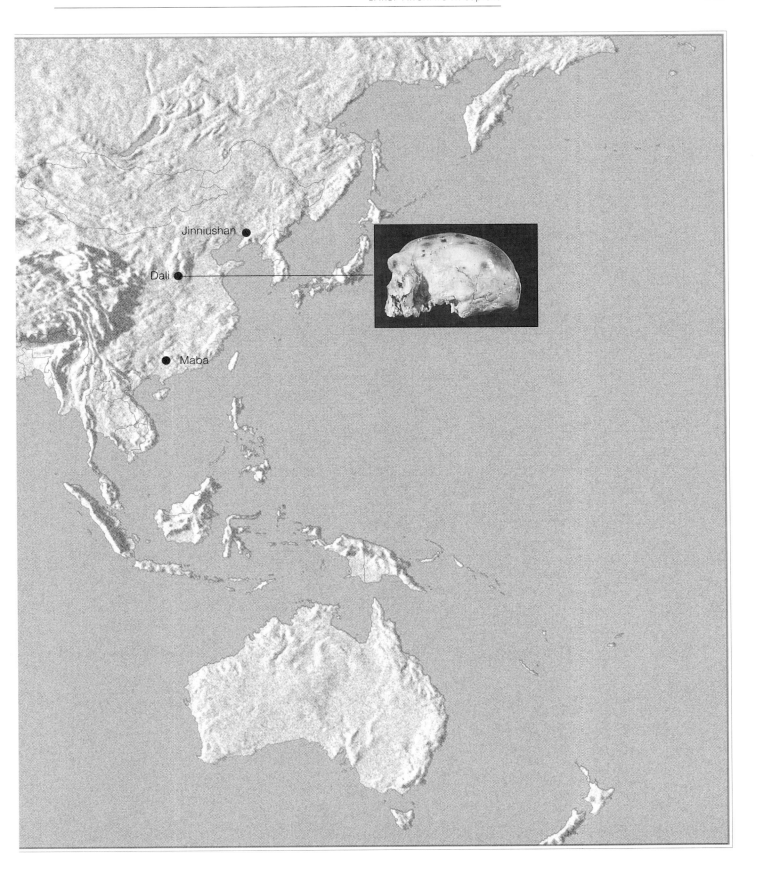

Jinniushan

Dali

Maba

as early *H. sapiens* (despite its relatively small cranial capacity of 1,120 cm³). Several other Chinese specimens also reflect both earlier and later traits and are placed in the same category as Dali. In addition, the recently discovered (1984) partial skeleton from Jinniushan, in northeast China, has been given a provisional date of 200,000 y.a. (Tiemel et al., 1994). The cranial capacity is fairly large (approximately 1,260 cm³), and the walls of the braincase are thin—both modern features and quite unexpected in an individual this ancient (if the dating estimate does indeed hold up).

India   In 1982, a partial skull was discovered in the Narmada Valley, in central India. Associated with this fossil were various hand axes, cleavers, flakes, and choppers. This Narmada specimen has been dated as Middle Pleistocene with a probable cranial capacity within the range of 1,155 to 1,421 cm³. K. A. R. Kennedy (1991), who made a recent study of the fossil, believes that Narmada should be viewed as an early example of *H. sapiens*.

Table 17–1   A Partial List of Archaic *Homo sapiens* (Outside of Europe)

Name	Site	Date*	Human Remains	Associated Finds	Cranial Capacity (cm³)	Comments
AFRICA Bodo	Awash River Valley, Ethiopia	Middle Pleistocene (600,000 y.a.?)	Incomplete skull, part of braincase	Acheulian artifacts, animal bones	Insufficient remains for measurement	Resembles Broken Hill; first evidence of scalping
Broken Hill (Kabwe)	Cave deposits near Kabwe, Zambia	Late Middle Pleistocene; (130,000 y.a. or older)	Nearly complete cranium, cranial fragments of second individual, miscellaneous postcranial bones	Animal bones and artifacts in cave, but relationship to human remains unknown	1,280	Massive browridge, low vault, prominent occipital torus; cranial capacity within range of modern *H. sapiens*
CHINA Dali	Shaanxi Province, north China	Late Middle Pleistocene (230,000–180,000 y.a.)	Nearly complete skull	Flake tools, animal bones	1,120–1,200	Robust supra-orbital ridge, low vault, retreating forehead, canine fossa
Jinniushan	Liaoning Province, northeast China	Late Middle Pleistocene (200,000 y.a.)	Partial skeleton, including a cranium	Flake tools	1,260	Thin cranial bones
Maba	Cave near Maba village, Guangdong Province, south China	Early Upper Pleistocene (140,000–120,000 y.a.)	Incomplete skull of middle-aged male	Animal bones	Insufficient remains for measurement	Receding forehead, modest keel on frontal bone

*Also see Figure 17–3.

Europe

Various attempts have been made to organize European archaic *H. sapiens* of the Middle and early Upper Pleistocene in the time range of 250,000–105,000 y.a. (Fig. 17–3). Because in many cases definite dates or adequate remains (or both) are lacking, it is difficult to be certain which fossils belong where in the evolutionary sequence. *H. erectus* may once have roamed the plains of Central and Western Europe, but there are no fossils that unequivocally prove it. As already noted, what we find in Europe are fossils, such as those in Africa and China, whose features resemble both *H. erectus* and *H. sapiens*. You should further note that the earliest fossil finds from Europe (including those from Boxgrove in England and Atapuerca in Spain, discussed in Chapter 16) already show some of these transitional features.

The earliest archaic *H. sapiens* representatives from Europe show some resemblances to *H. erectus* in the robusticity of the mandible, thick cranial bones, pronounced occipital torus, heavy supraorbital torus, receding frontal bone, greatest parietal breadth near base of the skull, and large teeth. (They, of course, also have one or more *H. sapiens* characteristics.) Examples of these early archaic forms from Europe include fossils from Steinheim, Swanscombe, and Vértesszöllös (see Fig. 17–1). Later European archaic representatives also possess some *H. erectus* characteristics, but they also have one or more of the following traits: larger cranial capacity, more rounded occipital area, parietal expansion, and reduced tooth size (see Table 17–2).

FIGURE 17–3

Time line of early archaic Homo sapiens. *Note that most dates are approximations. Question marks indicate those estimates that are most tentative.*

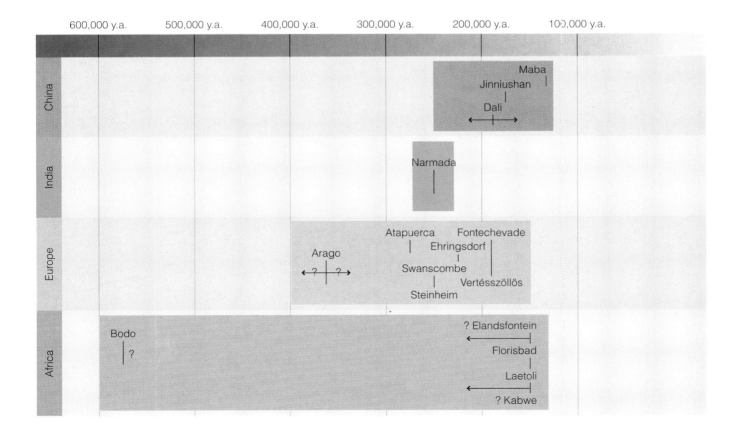

Table 17–2   Archaic *Homo sapiens* in Europe*

Name	Site	Date*	Human Remains	Associated Finds	Cranial Capacity (cm³)	Comments
Arago (Tautavel)	Cave site near Tautavel, Verdouble Valley, Pyrenees, southeastern France	400,000–300,000 y.a.; date uncertain	Face; parietal perhaps from same person; many cranial fragments; up to 23 individuals represented	Upper Acheulian artifacts, animal bones	1,150	Thick supraorbital torus, pronounced alveolar prognathism; parietal resembles Swanscombe
Bilzingsleben	Quarry at Bilzingsleben, near Erfurt, Germany	425,000–200,000 y.a., probably 280,000 y.a.	Skull fragments and teeth	Flake industry, plant and animal remains	Insufficient material	Resembles *H. erectus* in some features
La Chaise	Caves of Bourgeois-DeLauny, near La Chaise, Charente, western France	200,000–150,000 y.a.	Cranial fragments, fragmentary postcranial bones, teeth	None	Insufficient material	Mandible resembles Neandertal
Petralona	Cave near Petralona, Khalkidhiki, northeastern Greece	300,000–200,000 y.a.; date uncertain	Nearly complete skull	None	1,190–1,220	Mosaic; some bones resemble Neandertal, Broken Hill, and *H. erectus*
Steinheim	Gravel pit at Steinheim, Germany	Mindel-Riss Interglacial—300,000–250,000 y.a.; date uncertain	Nearly complete skull, lacking mandible	No artifacts, some animal bones	1,100	Pronounced supraorbital torus, frontal low, occipital rounded
Swanscombe	Swanscombe, Kent, England	Mindel-Riss Interglacial—300,000–250,000 y.a.; date uncertain	Occipital and parietals	Middle Acheulian artifacts, animal bones	1,325 (estimate)	Bones thick like *H. erectus*; occipital resembles Neandertal
Vértesszöllös	Near village of Vértesszöllös, 30 miles west of Budapest, Hungary	210,000–160,000 y.a.; date uncertain	Adult occipital bone, fragments of infant teeth	Flake and pebble tools, animal bones	1,115–1,434 (estimate)	Occipital thick (*H. erectus* trait), but size and angulation suggest *H. sapiens*

*Also see Figure 17–3.

The later group, essentially from the later half of the Middle Pleistocene, overlaps to some extent with the earlier group. From an evolutionary point of view, this later group may have evolved from the earlier one, and since many of these display traits unique to Neandertals, they may in turn have given rise to the Neandertals. Examples of this somewhat later European transitional group include specimens from Fontechevade (France) and Ehringsdorf (Germany), as well as recent discoveries from Atapuerca, in northern Spain, in the same region as the newly discovered more ancient remains discussed in Chapter 16. This last site, dated to approximately 300,000 y.a., has yielded the largest sample yet of archaic *Homo sapiens* and includes the remains of at least 29 individuals (among which are several excellently preserved crania) (Arsuaga et al., 1993). Excavations continue at this remarkable site, where bones have somehow accumulated within a deep chamber inside a cave. Only provisional descriptions have thus far been completed, but the morphology has been interpreted as showing several indications of an early Neandertal-like pattern (arching browridges, projecting midface, and other features).

A Review of Middle Pleistocene Evolution (Circa 400,000–125,000 y.a.)

Like the *erectus/sapiens* mix in Africa and China, the fossils from Europe also exhibit a mosaic of traits from both species (Fig. 17–4). However, it is important to note that the fossils from each continent differ; that is, the mosaic Chinese forms are not the same as those from Africa or Europe. Some European fossils, assumed to be earlier, are more robust and possess more similarities to *H. erectus* than to *H. sapiens*. The later Middle Pleistocene European fossils appear to be more Neandertal-like, but the uncertainty of dates prevents a clear scenario of the Middle Pleistocene evolutionary sequence.

The physical differences from *H. erectus* are not extraordinary. Bones remain thick, the supraorbital torus is prominent, and vault height shows little increase. There is, however, a definite increase in brain size and a change in the shape of the skull from pentagonal to globular as seen from the rear. There is also a trend, especially with the later Middle Pleistocene forms, toward less occipital angulation. It is interesting to note that in Europe, the changes move toward a Neandertal *H. sapiens* pattern, but in Africa and Asia, toward modern *H. sapiens*.

FIGURE 17–4

Cast of an archaic Homo sapiens *skull from Germany (Steinheim). (a) Frontal view showing damaged skull. (b) Basal view, showing how the foramen magnum was enlarged, apparently for removal of the brain, for dietary or ritualistic purposes.*

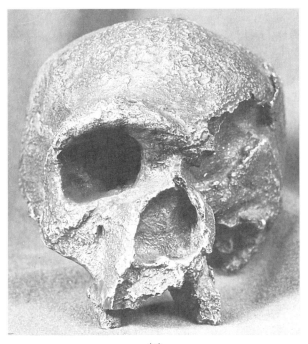

(a)

(b)

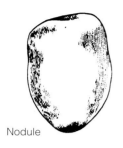

Nodule

The nodule is chipped
on the perimeter.

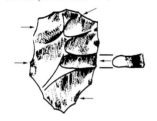

Flakes are radially
removed from top surface.

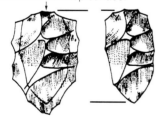

A final blow at one end
removes a large flake.

FIGURE 17–5
The Levallois technique.

Middle Pleistocene Culture

The Acheulian technology of *H. erectus* persevered in the Middle Pleistocene with relatively little change until near the end of the period, when it became slightly more sophisticated. The hand axe, almost entirely absent in China in the Lower Pleistocene, remains rare in the Middle Pleistocene, and choppers and chopping tools continue to be the basic tools. Bone, a very useful tool material, apparently went practically unused by archaic *H. sapiens*. Stone flake tools similar to those of the earlier era persisted, perhaps in greater variety. Archaic *H. sapiens* in Africa and Europe invented a method—the Levallois technique (Fig. 17–5)—for controlling flake size and shape (Klein, 1989). Requiring several coordinated steps, this was no mean feat and suggests to many scholars increased cognitive abilities in late archaic *H. sapiens* compared to earlier archaic forms.

Interpretation of the distribution of artifacts during the later Middle Pleistocene has generated considerable discussion among archeologists. We have noted (in Chapter 16) that there is a *general* geographical distribution characteristic throughout most of the Lower Pleistocene with bifaces (mostly hand axes) found quite commonly in sites in Africa, but only very rarely at sites in most of Asia, and not at all among the rich assemblage at Zhoukoudian (see p. 420). Moreover, where hand axes proliferate, the stone tool industry is referred to as Acheulian, while at localities without hand axes, various other terms are used (e.g., "chopper/chopping tool"—a misnomer, since most of the tools are actually flakes).

Acheulian assemblages have been found at many African sites as well as numerous European ones (e.g., Swanscombe in England and Arago in France). Nevertheless, the broad geographical distribution of what we call Acheulian should not blind us to the considerable intra-regional diversity in stone tool industries. For example, while a variety of European sites do show a typical Acheulian complex, rich in bifacial hand axes and cleavers, other contemporaneous ones (e.g., Bilzingsleben in Germany and Vértesszöllös in Hungary) do not. At these latter two sites, a variety of small retouched flake tools and flaked pebbles of various sizes were found, but no hand axes.

It thus appears that different stone tool industries coexisted in some areas for long periods. Various explanations (Villa, 1983) have been offered to account for this apparent diversity: (1) The tool industries were produced by different peoples (i.e., different cultures, perhaps hominids that also differed biologically); (2) the tool industries represent different types of activities carried out at separate locales; (3) the presence (or absence) of specific tool types—bifaces—represents the availability (or unavailability) of appropriate local stone resources.

Archaic *H. sapiens* continued to live both in caves and in open-air sites, but may have increased their use of caves. Did archaic *H. sapiens* control fire? Klein (1989, p. 255) suggests they did. He writes that there was a "concentration of burnt bones in depressions 50–60 cm across at Vértesszöllös," and "fossil hearths have also been identified at Bilzingsleben and in several French caves that were probably occupied by early *H. sapiens*." Chinese archeologists insist that many Middle Pleistocene sites in China contain evidence of human-controlled fire. However, not everyone is convinced.

That archaic *H. sapiens* built temporary structures is revealed by concentrations of bones, stones, and artifacts at several sites. Here, they manufactured artifacts and exploited the area for food. The stones may have been used to support the sides of a shelter.

In the Lazaret Cave in the city of Nice, in southern France, a shelter about 36 feet by 11 feet was built against the cave wall, and skins probably were hung over a framework of poles as walls for the shelter. The base was supported by rocks and large bones, and inside the shelter were two hearths. The hearth charcoal suggests that the hominid occupants used slow-burning oak and boxwood, which produced easy-to-rekindle embers. Very little stone waste was found inside the shelter, suggesting that they manufactured tools outside, perhaps because there was more light.

Archeological evidence clearly alludes to the utilization of many different food sources, such as fruits, vegetables, seeds, nuts, and bird eggs, each in its own season. Marine life was also exploited. From Lazaret and Orgnac (southern France) comes evidence of freshwater fishing for trout, perch, and carp. The most detailed reconstruction of Middle Pleistocene life in Europe, however, comes from evidence at Terra Amata, on the southern coast of France (de Lumley and de Lumley, 1973; Villa, 1983). From this site has come fascinating evidence relating to short-term, seasonal visits by archaic *H. sapiens* who built flimsy shelters (Fig. 17–6), gathered plants, exploited marine resources, and possibly hunted medium-size and large mammals.

The hunting capabilities of these early members of *H. sapiens*, as for earlier hominids, remains open to dispute. What seems clear is that the evidence does not yet unambiguously establish any advanced abilities. In earlier professional discussions (as well as in earlier editions of this text), archeological evidence from Terra Amata (in France) and Torralba and Ambrona (in Spain) was used to argue for significantly advanced hunting skills for archaic *H. sapiens* in Europe. However, reconstruction of these sites by Richard Klein and others has now cast doubt on those prior conclusions. Once again, we see that application of scientific rigor (which is simply good critical thinking) makes us question assumptions. And in so doing, we frequently must conclude that other less dramatic (and less romantic) explanations fit the evidence as well as or better than those based on initial imaginative scenarios.

A possible exception to the current, much more conservative view of archaic *H. sapiens* hunting skills comes from an archeological site excavated on the Channel Island of Jersey off the west coast of France (see map, p. 438). In a cave site called La Cotte de Saint-Brelade, many bone remains of large mammals

FIGURE 17–6
Cutaway of Terra Amata hut (reconstruction). Note the hearth, the stone scatters where people sat making tools, the poles that supported the roof, and the stones at the base of the hut supporting the sides. (Adapted from De Lumley, 1969).

(mammoth and woolly rhinoceros) were found in association with stone flakes. Unlike the remains from the sites mentioned earlier, the animals sampled at La Cotte de Saint-Brelade represent primarily subadults and adults in prime age (*not* what one would expect in naturally occurring accumulations). Moreover, the preserved elements also exhibit the kind of damage that further suggests hominid activities. Directly killing such large animals may not have been within the capabilities of the hominids (archaic *H. sapiens?*) who occupied this site. Thus, K. Scott, who led the excavations, has suggested that these early hominids may have driven their prey off a nearby cliff, bringing certain prized parts back to the cave for further butchering (1980).

As documented by the fossil hominid remains as well as artifactual evidence from archeological sites, the long period of transitional hominids in Europe was to continue well into the Upper Pleistocene (after 125,000 y.a.). However, the evolution of archaic *H. sapiens* was to take a unique turn with the appearance and expansion of the Neandertals.

Neandertals: Late Archaic *H. sapiens* (130,000–35,000 y.a.)

Since their discovery more than a century ago, the Neandertals have haunted the best-laid theories of paloanthropologists. They fit into the general scheme of human evolution, and yet they are misfits. Classified as *H. sapiens*, they are like us and yet different. It is not an easy task to put them in their place.*

While Neandertal fossil remains have been found at dates approaching 130,000 y.a., in the following discussion of Neandertals, we refer to those populations that lived especially during the last glaciation, which began about 75,000 y.a. and ended about 10,000 y.a. (Fig. 17–7). The majority of fossils have been found in Europe, where they have been most studied. Our description of Neandertals, therefore, is based primarily on those specimens from western Europe, who are usually called *classic* Neandertals or late archaic *H. sapiens*. Not all Neandertals—including others from eastern Europe and western Asia and those from the interglacial that preceded the last glacial—entirely conform to our description of the classic morphology. They tend to be less robust, perhaps because the climate in which they lived was not as cold as western Europe during the last glaciation.

One striking feature of Neandertals is brain size, which in these hominids actually was larger than that of *H. sapiens* today. The average for contemporary *H. sapiens* centers around 1,400 cm^3, while for Neandertals it was 1,520 cm^3. The larger size may be associated with the metabolic efficiency of a larger brain in cold weather. The Inuit (Eskimo) brain also averages larger than that of other modern human populations (about the size of the Neandertal brain). It should also be pointed out that the larger brain size in both archaic and contemporary *Homo sapiens* in populations adapted to *cold* climates is partially correlated with larger body size, which has also evolved among these groups (see Chapter 6).

Homo sapiens neanderthalensis is the subspecific designation for Neandertals, although not all paleoanthropologists agree with this terminology. (The subspecies for anatomically modern *H. sapiens* is designated as *Homo sapiens sapiens*.) *Thal*, meaning "valley," is the old spelling and is kept in the species designation (the "h" was always silent and not pronounced). The modern spelling is *tal* and is now used this way in Germany; we shall adhere to contemporary usage in the text with the spelling *Neandertal*.

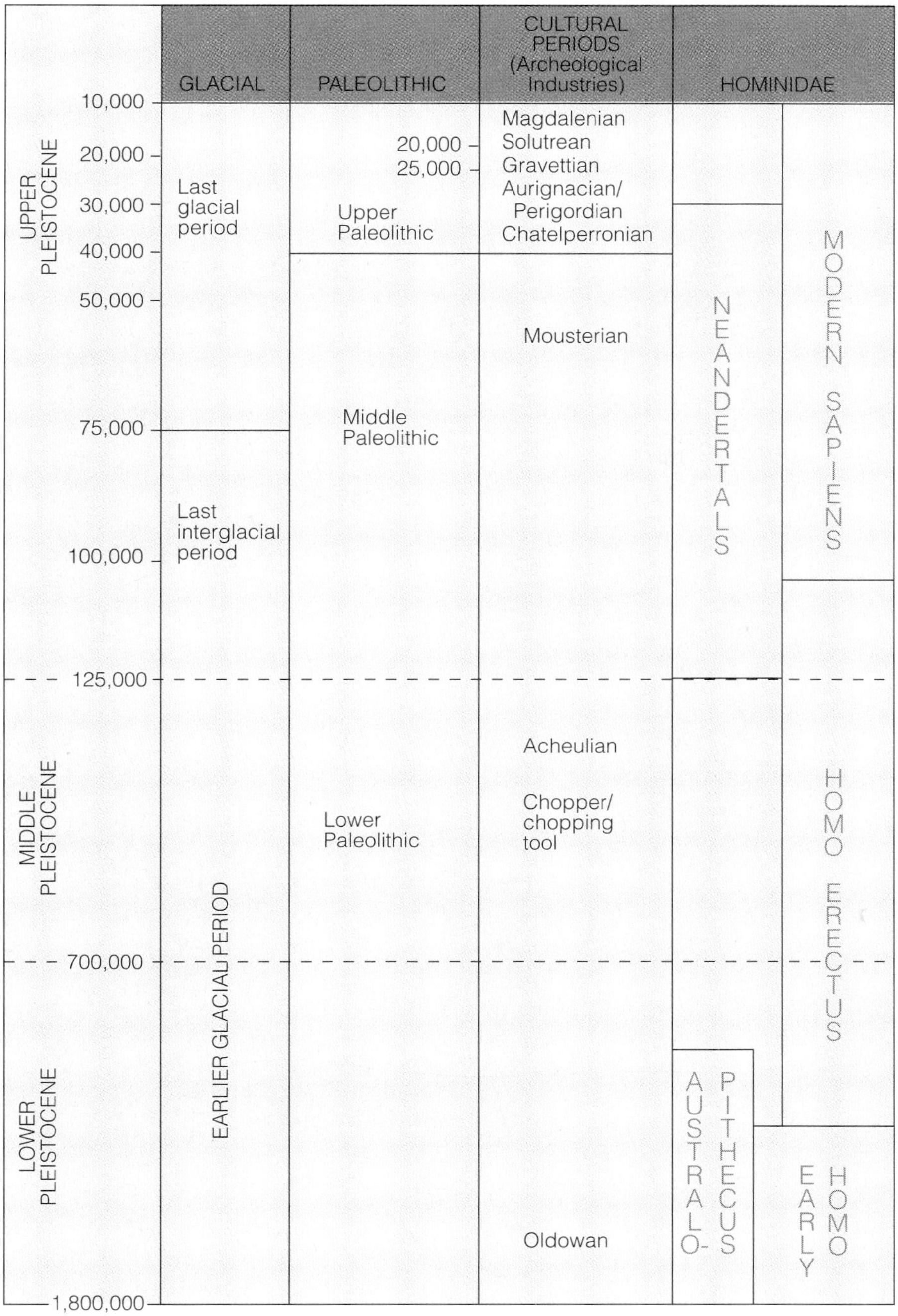

(Years)	GLACIAL	PALEOLITHIC	CULTURAL PERIODS (Archeological Industries)	HOMINIDAE
10,000				
20,000	Last glacial period	Upper Paleolithic (20,000 – / 25,000 –)	Magdalenian / Solutrean / Gravettian / Aurignacian/Perigordian / Chatelperronian	NEANDERTALS / MODERN SAPIENS
30,000				
40,000				
50,000		Middle Paleolithic	Mousterian	
75,000				
100,000	Last interglacial period			
125,000				
		Lower Paleolithic	Acheulian	HOMO ERECTUS
700,000	EARLIER GLACIAL PERIOD		Chopper/chopping tool	
				AUSTRALO-PITHECUS / EARLY HOMO
			Oldowan	
1,800,000				

(Left axis: UPPER PLEISTOCENE, MIDDLE PLEISTOCENE, LOWER PLEISTOCENE)

FIGURE 17–7

Correlation of Pleistocene subdivisions with archeological industries and hominids. Note that the geological divisions are separate and different from the archeological stages (e.g., Upper Pleistocene is not synonymous with Upper Paleolithic).

The classic Neandertal cranium is large, long, low, and bulging at the sides. Viewed from the side, the posterior portion of the occipital bone is somewhat bun-shaped, but the marked occipital angle typical of many *H. erectus* crania is absent. The forehead rises more vertically than that of *H. erectus*, and the browridges arch over the orbits instead of forming a straight bar (Fig. 17–8).

Compared to anatomically modern humans, the Neandertal face stands out. It projects almost as if it were pulled forward. This feature can be seen when the

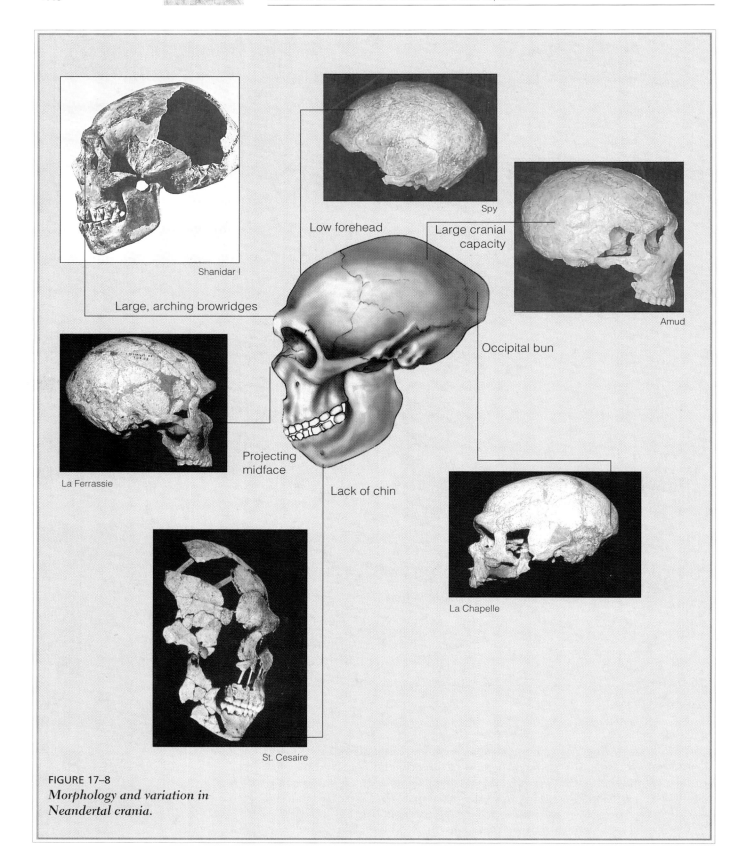

Shanidar I

Spy

Amud

Low forehead

Large cranial capacity

Large, arching browridges

Occipital bun

Projecting midface

La Ferrassie

Lack of chin

La Chapelle

St. Cesaire

FIGURE 17–8
Morphology and variation in Neandertal crania.

distance of the nose and teeth from the eye orbits is compared with that of modern H. *sapiens*. Postcranially, Neandertals were very robust, barrel-chested, and powerfully muscled. This robust skeletal structure, in fact, dominates hominid evolution from *H. erectus* through archaic *H. sapiens*.

For about 100,000 years, Neandertals lived in Europe and western Asia (Fig. 17–9), and their coming and going has raised more questions and controversies than perhaps any other hominid group. Neandertal forebears date back to the later archaic *H. sapiens*. But these were transitional forms, and it is not until the last interglacial that Neandertals were fully recognizable.

Neandertal takes its name from the Neander Valley, near Düsseldorf, Germany. In 1856, workmen quarrying limestone caves in the valley came across some fossilized bones. The owner of the quarry believed them to be bear and gave them to a natural science teacher who realized they were not the remains of a cave bear, but rather, the remains of an ancient human. Exactly what the bones represented became a *cause célébre* for many years, and the fate of "Neandertal Man," as the bones were named, hung in the balance until later finds provided more evidence.

What swung the balance in favor of accepting the Neander Valley specimen as a genuine hominid fossil were other nineteenth-century finds similar to it. What is more important, the additional fossil remains brought home the realization that a form of human different from nineteenth-century Europeans had in fact once existed.

France and Spain

One of the most important Neandertal discoveries was made in 1908 at La Chapelle-aux-Saints in southwestern France. A nearly complete skeleton was found buried in a shallow grave in a flexed position, with several fragments of nonhuman long bones placed over the head, and over them, a bison leg. Around the body were flint tools and broken animal bones.

The skeleton was turned over for study to a well-known French paleontologist, Marcellin Boule, who published his analysis in three copious volumes. Boule depicted the La Chapelle Neandertal as a brutish, bent-kneed, not fully erect biped. As a result of this exaggerated interpretation, some scholars, and certainly the general public, concluded that all Neandertals were highly primitive creatures.

Why did Boule draw these conclusions from the La Chapelle skeleton? Apparently, he misconstrued Neandertal posture owing to the presence of spinal osteoarthritis in this older male. In addition, and probably more important, Boule and his contemporaries found it difficult to accept fully as a human ancestor an individual who appeared to depart, however slightly, from the modern pattern. "With the over-emphasis of the nonmodern features of the La Chapelle-aux-Saints skeleton, it became a much less likely candidate for the forefather of the succeeding Upper Paleolithic forms" (Brace and Montagu, 1977, p. 219).

The skull of this male, who was at least 40 years of age when he died, is very large, with a cranial capacity of 1,620 cm³. As is typical for western European "classic" forms, the vault is low and long, the supraorbital ridges are immense, with the typical Neandertal arched shape, the forehead is low and retreating, and the face is long and projecting. The back of the skull is protuberant and bun-shaped (Figs. 17–8 and 17–10).

La Chapelle, however, is not a typical Neandertal, but an unusually robust male that "evidently represents an extreme in the Neandertal range of variation"

FIGURE 17–9

Fossil discoveries of Neandertals.

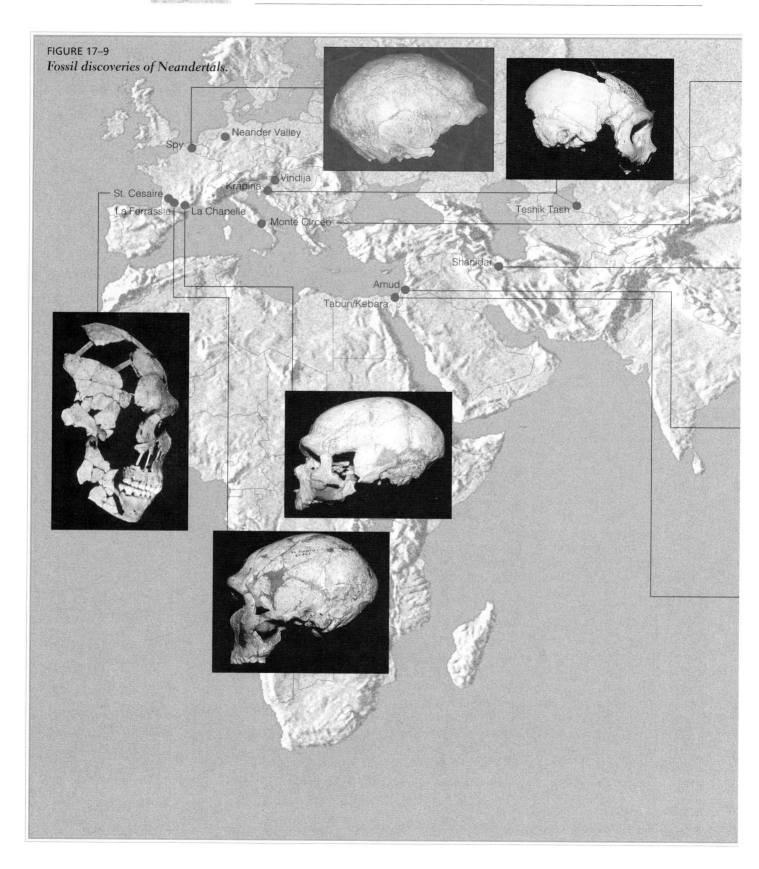

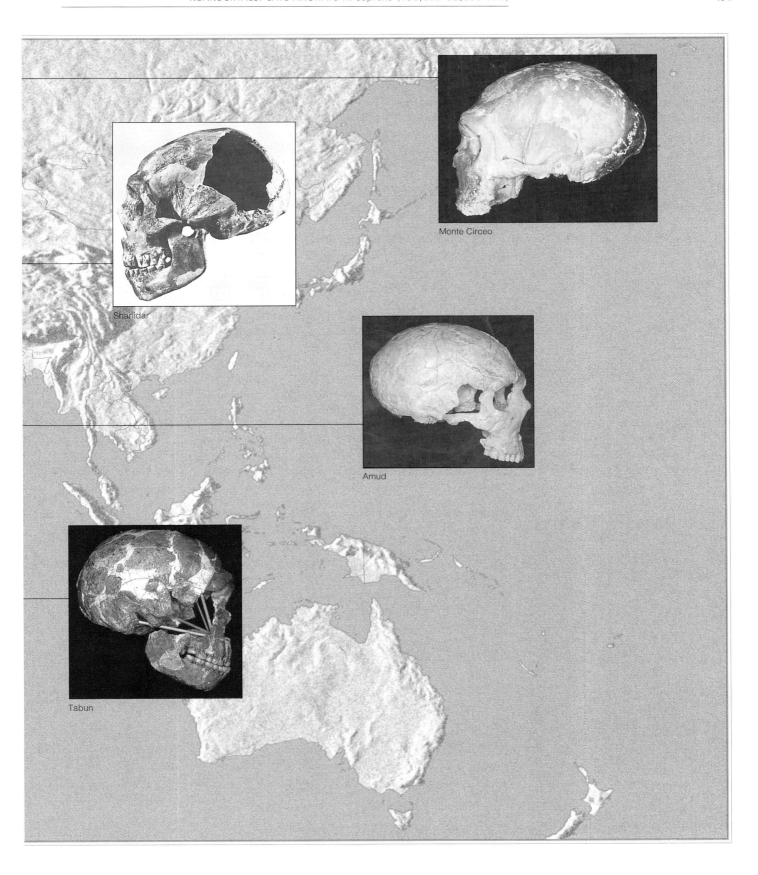

Shanidar

Monte Circeo

Amud

Tabun

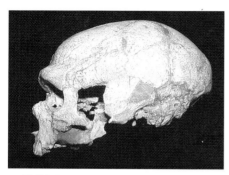

FIGURE 17–10
La Chapelle-aux-Saints. Note the occipital bun, projecting face, and low vault.

▲ **Chatelperronian**
Pertaining to an Upper Paleolithic tool industry containing blade tools found in France and Spain and associated with Neandertals.

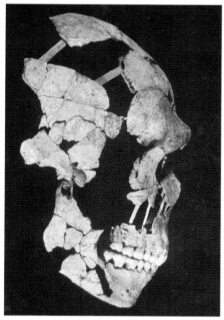

FIGURE 17–11
St. Cesaire, the "last" Neandertal.

(Brace et al., 1979, p. 117). Unfortunately, this skeleton, which Boule claimed did not even walk completely erect, was widely accepted as "Mr. Neandertal." But not all Neandertal materials express the suite of "classic Neandertal" traits to the degree seen in La Chapelle.

Some of the most recent of the western European Neandertals come from St. Cesaire, in southwestern France, and are dated at about 35,000 y.a. (Figs. 17–11 and 17–12). The bones were recovered from a bed including discarded chipped blades, hand axes, and other stone tools of an Upper Paleolithic tool industry associated with Neandertals. Another site, Zafarraya Cave in southern Spain, may provide yet a more recent time range for Neandertal occupation in Europe. During the 1980s and 1990s, a few pieces of hominid individuals have been found at Zafarraya that have been interpreted as Neandertal in morphology. What is most interesting, however, is the *date* (as determined by radiocarbon dating) suggested for the site. French archeologist Jean-Jacques Hublin, who has excavated the site, asserts that the date is close to 29,000 y.a.—a full 6,000 years later than St. Cesaire. Thus, if this date is confirmed, the Zafarraya hominids would gain the distinction of being the most recent Neandertals thus far discovered.

The St. Cesaire and Zafarraya sites are fascinating for several reasons. Anatomically modern humans were living in western Europe by about 35,000 y.a. or a bit earlier. Therefore, it is possible that Neandertals and modern *H. sapiens* were living in close proximity for several thousand years. How did these two groups interact? Evidence from a number of French sites (Harrold, 1989) indicates that Neandertals borrowed technological methods and tools (such as blades) from the anatomically modern populations and thereby modified their own tools, creating a new industry, the **Chatelperronian**. However, such an example of cultural diffusion does not specify *how* the diffusion took place. Did the Neandertals become assimilated into modern populations? Did the two groups interbreed? It would also be interesting to know more precisely how long the coexistence of Neandertals and modern *H. sapiens* lasted.* No one knows the answers to these questions, but it has been suggested that an average annual difference of 2 percent mortality between the two populations (i.e., modern *H. sapiens* lived longer than Neandertals) would have resulted in the extinction of the Neandertals in approximately 1,000 years (Zubrow, 1989).

It should be noted that not all paleoanthropologists agree with the notion of the coexistence of Neandertals and Upper Paleolithic modern humans. For example, in a recent paper, David Frayer of the University of Kansas states: "There is still *no human fossil evidence* which supports the coexistence of Neanderthal and Upper Paleolithic forms in Europe" (emphasis added) (1992, p. 9) That is, despite the indications of cultural diffusion noted above, no European site has yet produced directly associated remains of *both* types of humans.

Central Europe

There are quite a few other European classic Neandertals, including significant finds in central Europe. At Krapina, Croatia, an abundance of bones—almost 1,000 fragments—add up to 70 individuals and 1,000 stone tools or flakes (Trinkaus and Shipman, 1992). Krapina is an old site, perhaps the earliest show-

---

*For a fictionalized account of the confrontation of Neandertals and anatomically modern humans, read Nobel Prize winner William Golding's excellent novel *The Inheritors*. Another novel on the subject is Jean M. Auel's *Clan of the Cave Bear*. Several movies have also been made on this theme.

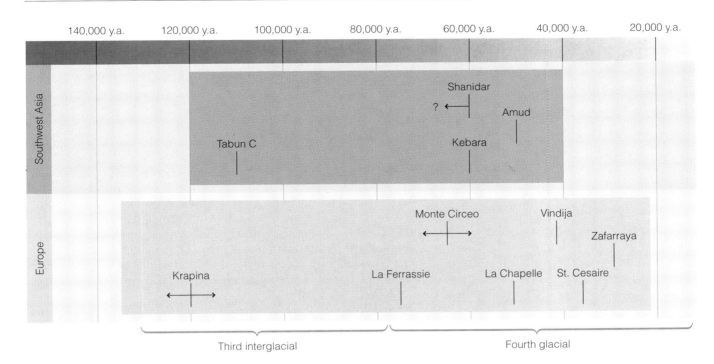

ing the full "classic" Neandertal morphology, dating back to the third inter-glacial (estimated at 130,000–110,000 y.a.). Moreover, despite the relatively early date, the characteristic Neandertal features of the Krapina specimens (although less robust) are similar to the western European finds (Fig. 17–13). Krapina is also important as an intentional burial site, one of the oldest on record.

Another interesting site in central Europe is Vindija, about 30 miles from Krapina. The site is an excellent source of faunal, cultural, and hominid materials stratified in *sequence* throughout much of the Upper Pleistocene. Neandertal fossils, consisting of some 35 specimens, are tentatively dated at about 42,000 y.a. Even though some of their features approach the morphology of early modern south-central European *H. sapiens*, the overall pattern is definitely Neandertal. However, these modified Neandertal features, such as smaller browridges and slight chin development, may also be seen as an evolutionary trend toward modern *H. sapiens*.

Fred Smith, at Northern Illinois University, takes the view that variation in Vindija cranial features points to a trend continuing on to the later anatomically modern specimens found in the upper levels of the cave. Does Vindija support the proposition that the origin of *H. sapiens* could have occurred here in central

FIGURE 17–12

*Time line for Neandertal (*Homo sapiens neanderthalensis*) fossil discoveries. Note that most dates are approximations. Question marks indicate those estimates that are most tentative.*

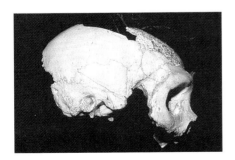 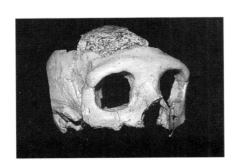

FIGURE 17–13

Krapina C. (a) Lateral view showing characteristic Neandertal traits. (b) Three-quarters view.

Europe? Smith does not insist on this interpretation and suggests that anatomically modern *Homo sapiens* could have come from elsewhere. But he does believe that there is at least some morphological and genetic continuity between the lower and upper levels of the cave.

Western Asia

Israel   In addition to European Neandertals, there are numerous important discoveries from southwest Asia. Several specimens from Israel display modern features and are less robust than the classic Neandertals of Europe, but again the overall pattern is Neandertal. The best known of these discoveries is from Tabun (Mugharet-et-Tabun, "Cave of the Oven") at Mt. Carmel, a short drive south from Haifa (Fig. 17–14). Tabun, excavated in the early 1930s, yielded a female skeleton, recently dated by thermoluminescence (TL) at about 110,000 y.a. If this dating proves accurate, it places that Tabun find as clearly contemporary with early modern *H. sapiens* found in nearby caves (TL dating is discussed in Chapter 18, p. 476).

A more recent Neandertal burial, a male discovered in 1983, comes from Kebara, a neighbor cave of Tabun at Mt. Carmel. Although the skeleton is incomplete—the cranium and much of the lower limbs are missing—the pelvis, dated to 60,000 y.a., is the most complete Neandertal pelvis so far recovered. Also recovered at Kebara is a hyoid bone, the first from a Neandertal, and this find is especially important from the point of view of reconstructing language capabilities (see Issue, p. 464).

Iraq   A most remarkable site is Shanidar, in the Zagros Mountains of northeastern Iraq, where partial skeletons of nine individuals—males and females, seven adults and two infants—were found, four of them deliberately buried. One of the

FIGURE 17–14

Excavation of the Tabun Cave, Mt. Carmel, Israel.

more interesting individuals is Shanidar 1, a male who lived to be approximately 30 to 45 years old, a considerable age for a prehistoric human (Fig. 17–15). His stature is estimated at 5 feet 7 inches, with a cranial capacity of 1,600 cm³. This individual shows several fascinating features:

> There had been a crushing blow to the left side of the head, fracturing the eye socket, displacing the left eye, and probably causing blindness on that side. He also sustained a massive blow to the right side of the body that so badly damaged the right arm that it became withered and useless; the bones of the shoulder blade, collar bone, and upper arm are much smaller and thinner than those on the left. The right lower arm and hand are missing, probably not because of poor preservation . . . but because they either atrophied and dropped off or because they were amputated. (Trinkaus and Shipman, 1992, p. 340)

In addition to these injuries, there was damage to the lower right leg (including a healed fracture of a foot bone). The right knee and left leg show signs of pathological involvement, and these changes to the limbs and foot may have left this man with a limping gait.

How such a person could perform normal obligations and customs is difficult to imagine. However, both Ralph Solecki, who supervised the work at Shanidar Cave, and Erik Trinkaus, who has carefully studied the Shanidar remains, believe that in order to survive, he must have been helped by others: "A one-armed, partially blind, crippled man could have made no pretense of hunting or gathering his own food. That he survived for years after his trauma was a testament to Neandertal compassion and humanity" (Trinkaus and Shipman, 1992, p. 341).*

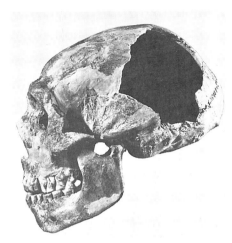

FIGURE 17–15
Shanidar 1. Does he represent an example of Neandertal compassion for the handicapped?

Central Asia

Uzbekistan   About 1,600 miles east of Shanidar in Uzbekistan, in a cave at Teshik-Tash, is the easternmost Neandertal discovery. The skeleton is that of a 9-year-old boy who appears to have been deliberately buried. It was reported that he was surrounded by five pairs of wild goat horns, suggesting a burial ritual or perhaps a religious cult, but owing to inadequate published documentation of the excavation, this interpretation has been seriously questioned. The Teshik-Tash individual, like the specimens from Croatia and southwest Asia, also shows a mixture of Neandertal traits (heavy browridges and occipital bun) and modern traits (high vault and definite signs of a chin).

As noted, the Teshik-Tash site represents the easternmost location presently established for Neandertals. Thus, based on current evidence, it is clear that the geographical distribution of the Neandertals extended from France eastward to central Asia, a distance of about 4,000 miles.

Culture of Neandertals

Neandertals, who lived in the cultural period known as the Middle Paleolithic, are usually associated with the **Mousterian** industry (although the Mousterian

▲ **Mousterian**
Pertaining to the stone tool industry associated with Neandertals and some modern *H. sapiens* groups. This industry is characterized by a larger proportion of flake tools than is found in Acheulian tool kits. Also called Middle Paleolithic.

---

*K. A. Dettwyler (1991) believes that Shanidar I could have survived without assistance and that there is no solid evidence that compassion explains this individual's survival.

industry is not always associated with Neandertals). In the early Würm, Mousterian culture extended across Europe and North Africa into the former Soviet Union, Israel, Iran, and as far east as Uzbekistan and perhaps even China. Moreover, in Africa the contemporaneous Middle Stone Age industry is broadly similar to the Mousterian.

Technology

Neandertals improved on previous prepared-core techniques (i.e., the Levallois) by inventing a new variation. They trimmed a flint nodule around the edges to form a disk-shaped core. Each time they struck the edge, they produced a flake, continuing this way until the core became too small and was discarded. Thus, the Neandertals were able to obtain more flakes per core than their predecessors. They then trimmed (retouched) the flakes into various forms, such as scrapers, points, and knives (Fig.17–16).

Neandertal craftspeople elaborated and diversified traditional methods, and there is some indication of development in the specialization of tools used in skin and meat preparation, hunting, woodworking, and hafting. There is, however, still nearly a complete absence of bone tools, in strong contrast to the succeeding cultural period, the Upper Paleolithic. Nevertheless, Neandertals advanced their technology, which tended to be similar in basic tool types over considerable geographical distances, far beyond that of *H. erectus*. It is quite possible that their modifications in technology helped provide a basis for the remarkable changes of the Upper Paleolithic (discussed in Chapter 18).

Settlements

People of the Mousterian culture lived in a variety of open sites, caves, and rock shelters. Living in the open on the cold tundra suggests the building of structures, and there is some evidence of such structures (although the last glaciation must have destroyed many open sites). At the site of Moldova, in the Ukraine (now an independent state and neighbor of Russia), archeologists found traces of an oval ring of mammoth bones enclosing an area of about 26 by 16 feet and which may have been used to weigh down the skin walls of a temporary hut or tent. Inside the ring are traces of a number of hearths, hundreds of tools, thousands of waste flakes, and many bone fragments, quite possibly derived from animals brought back for consumption.

FIGURE 17–16

Mousterian tools. (After Bordes.)

Convex side scraper   Point   Convergent scraper   Levallois flake

Evidence of life in caves is abundant. Windbreaks of poles and skin were probably erected at the cave mouth for protection against severe weather. Fire was in general use by this time and was no doubt used for cooking, warmth, light, and keeping predators at bay.

How large were Neandertal settlements, and were they permanent or temporary? These questions are not yet answered, but Binford (1981) believes that the settlements were used repeatedly for short-term occupation.

Subsistence

Neandertals were successful hunters, as the abundant remains of animal bones at their sites demonstrate. But while it is clear that Neandertals could hunt large mammals, they may not have been as efficient at this task as were Upper Paleolithic hunters. Inferring from his detailed work in the Middle East, Harvard anthropologist Offer Bar-Yosef has suggested (1994) that only after the beginning of the Upper Paleolithic was the spearthrower, or atlatl (see p. 483), invented. Moreover, shortly thereafter, the bow and arrow may have greatly facilitated efficiency (and safety) in hunting large mammals. Lacking such long-distance weaponry, and thus mostly limited to close-proximity spears, Neandertals may have been more prone to serious injury—a hypothesis recently given some intriguing support by University of New Mexico scholars Thomas Berger and Erik Trinkaus. Berger and Trinkaus (1995) analyzed the pattern of trauma (particularly fractures) in Neandertals and compared it to that seen in contemporary human samples. Interestingly, the pattern in Neandertals—especially the relatively high proportion of head and neck injuries—matched most closely to that seen in contemporary rodeo performers. Berger and Trinkaus thus conclude, "The similarity to the rodeo distribution suggests frequent close encounters with large ungulates unkindly disposed to the humans involved." (Berger and Trinkaus, 1995, p. 841)

Meat was, of course, not the only component of Neandertal diet. Evidence (from Shanidar, for example) indicates that Neandertals gathered as well, consuming berries, nuts, and other plants.

It is assumed that in the bitter cold of the fourth glacial period, Neandertals wore clothing, and they probably had developed methods of curing skins. But since there is no evidence of sewing equipment, the clothing was probably of simple design, perhaps something like a poncho.

We know much more of European Middle Paleolithic culture than of any prior period, as it has been studied longer by more scholars. In recent years, however, Africa has been a target not only of physical anthropologists (as we have seen copiously documented in earlier chapters), but also of archeologists, who have added considerably to our knowledge of African Pleistocene hominid history. In many instances, the technology and assumed cultural adaptations were similar in Africa to those in Europe and southwest Asia. We will see in the next chapter that the African technological achievements also kept pace with (or even preceded) those in western Europe.

Symbolic Behavior

In the Issue at the end of this chapter (pp. 464–466), we discuss various hypotheses concerning the speech capacities of Neandertals. As we will show, the broad current consensus is that Neandertals were *capable* of articulate speech, even perhaps fully competent in the range of sounds produced by modern humans. However, this conclusion is not to argue that because Neandertals *could* speak, they necessarily had the same language capacities as modern *Homo sapiens*. A major contemporary focus among paleoanthropologists is the apparently sudden expansion of modern *H. sapiens* (discussed in Chapter 18) and various explanations for their success. Moreover, at the same time we are explaining how and why *H. sapiens sapiens* expanded their geographic range, we are left with the further problem of explaining what happened to the Neandertals. In making these types of interpretations, a growing number of paleoanthropologists suggest that *behavioral* differences are the key.

Upper Paleolithic *H. sapiens* is hypothesized to have possessed some significant behavioral advantage(s) that Neandertals (and other archaic *H. sapiens*) lacked. Was it some kind of new and expanded ability to symbolize, communicate, organize social activities, elaborate technology, obtain a wider range of food resources, care for the sick or injured, or was it some other factor? Were there, compared to *H. sapiens sapiens*, neurological differences that limited the Neandertals and thus contributed to their demise?

The direct anatomical evidence derived from Neandertal fossils is not especially helpful in specifically answering these questions. In the Issue at the end of this chapter, Ralph Holloway is quoted as maintaining that Neandertal brains (at least as far as the fossil evidence suggests) do not differ significantly from that of modern *H. sapiens*. Moreover, Neandertal vocal tracts and other morphological features, compared to our own, do not appear seriously to have limited them. Most of the doubts about advanced cognitive abilities thus come from archeological data. Interpretation of Neandertal sites, when compared to succeeding Upper Paleolithic sites (especially as documented in western Europe), have led to several intriguing contrasts as shown in Table 17–3.

On the basis of this type of behavioral evidence, Neandertals in recent years have increasingly been viewed as an evolutionary dead end. Whether their disappearance and ultimate replacement by anatomically modern Upper Paleolithic peoples (with their presumably "superior" culture) was solely the result of cultural differences or was also influenced by biological variation cannot at present be determined. An intriguing possibility for future research exists: Some Neandertal bones are not completely mineralized, nor are those from some Upper Paleolithic burials; thus, there is a good chance that ancient DNA can someday be obtained and compared.

Burials

It has been known for some time that Neandertals deliberately buried their dead. Indeed, the spectacular discoveries at La Chapelle, Shanidar, and elsewhere were the direct results of ancient burial, thus facilitating much more complete preservation. Such deliberate burial treatment extends back at least 90,000 years at Tabun. Moreover, some form of consistent "disposal" of the dead (but not necessarily below-ground burial) is evidenced at Atapuerca, Spain, where at least 29 individuals comprising more than 700 fossilized elements were found in a cave at the blind end of a deep vertical shaft (Bermudez de Castro and Nicolas, 1995).

The provisional 300,000-year-old age for Atapuerca suggests that Neandertals (more precisely, their immediate precursors) were, by the Middle Pleistocene, handling their dead in special ways, a behavior thought previously to have emerged only much later (in the Upper Pleistocene). And, apparently as far as current data indicate, this practice is seen in western European contexts well before it appears in Africa or in eastern Asia. For example, in the archaic *H. sapi-*

Table 17–3	Cultural Contrasts* Between Neandertals and Upper Paleolithic *Homo sapiens sapiens*	

Neandertals	Upper Paleolithic *H. sapiens sapiens*
Tool Technology	
Numerous flake tools; few, however, apparently for highly specialized functions; use of bone, antler, or ivory very rare; relatively few tools with more than one or two parts	Many more varieties of stone tools; many apparently for specialized functions; frequent use of bone, antler, and ivory; many more tools comprised of two or more component parts
Hunting Efficiency and Weapons	
No long-distance hunting weapons; close-proximity weapons use and thus more likelihood of injury	Use of spear thrower and bow and arrow; wider range of social contacts, perhaps permitting larger, more organized hunting parties (including game drives)
Stone Material Transport	
Stone materials transported only short distances (just "a few kilometers") (Klein, 1989)	Stone tool raw materials transported over much longer distances, implying wider social networks and perhaps trade
Art	
Artwork uncommon; usually small; probably mostly of a personal nature; some items perhaps misinterpreted as "art"; others may be intrusive from overlying Upper Paleolithic contexts; cave art absent	Artwork much more common, including transportable objects as well as elaborate cave art; well executed, using a variety of materials and techniques; stylistic sophistication
Burial	
Deliberate burial at several sites, graves unelaborated; graves frequently lack artifacts	Burials much more complex, frequently including both tools and remains of animals

*The contrasts shown are more apparent in some areas (particularly western Europe) than others (eastern Europe, Near East). Elsewhere (Africa, eastern Asia), where there were no Neandertals, the cultural situation is quite different (see p. 488). Moreover, even in western Europe, the cultural transformations were not necessarily abrupt, but may have developed more gradually from Mousterian to Upper Paleolithic times. For example, Straus (1995) argues that many of the Upper Paleolithic features were not consistently manifested until after 20,000 y.a.

ens sites at Laetoli, Kabwe, and Forisbad (discussed earlier), deliberate disposal of the dead is not documented. Nor is it seen in African early modern sites either (e.g., Klasies River Mouth, dated at 120,000–100,000 y.a.; see Chapter 18).

Nevertheless, in later contexts (after 35,000 y.a.) in Europe, where anatomically modern *H. sapiens* (*H. sapiens sapiens*) remains are found in clear burial contexts, their treatment is considerably more complex than is seen in Neandertal burials. In these later (Upper Paleolithic) sites, grave goods, including bone and stone tools as well as animal bones, are found more consistently and in greater concentrations. Because many Neandertal sites were excavated in the nineteenth or early twentieth century, before the development of more rigorous archeological methods, there are questions regarding numerous purported burials. Nevertheless, the evidence seems quite clear that deliberate burial was practiced at La Chapelle, La Ferrassie (eight graves), Tabun, Amud, Kebara, Shanidar, and Teshik-Tash (as well as at several other localities, especially in France). Moreover,

▲ **Flexed**

The position of the body in a bent orientation, with the arms and legs drawn up to the chest.

in many instances, the *position* of the body was deliberately modified and placed in the grave in a **flexed** posture. Such a flexed position has been found in 16 of the 20 best documented Neandertal burial contexts (Klein, 1989).

Finally, the placement of supposed grave goods in burials, including stone tools, animal bones (such as cave bear), and even arrangements of flowers, together with stone slabs on top of the burials, have all been postulated as further evidence of Neandertal symbolic behavior. However, in many instances, again due to poor excavation documentation, these assertions are questionable. Placement of stone tools, for example, is occasionally seen, but apparently was not done consistently. In those 33 Neandertal burials for which adequate data exist, only 14 show definite association of stone tools and/or animal bones with the deceased (Klein, 1989).

It is not until the next cultural period, the Upper Paleolithic, that we see a major behavioral shift, as demonstrated in more elaborate burials and development of art. It is to this remarkable period and its people that we turn in the next chapter.

Conclusion: Evolutionary Trends in the Genus *Homo*

To understand the evolution of the various forms of *Homo sapiens* discussed in this chapter, it is useful to briefly review general trends of evolution in the genus *Homo* over the last two million years. In doing so, we see that at least three major *transitions* have taken place. Paleoanthropologists are keenly interested in interpreting the nature of these transitions, as they inform us directly regarding human origins. In addition, such investigations contribute to a broader understanding of the mechanics of the evolutionary process—at both the micro- and macroevolutionary levels.

The first transition of note was from that of early *Homo* to *Homo erectus*. This transition was apparently geographically restricted to Africa and appears to have been quite rapid (lasting 200,000 years at most, perhaps considerably less). It is important to recall that such a transition by no means implies that all early *Homo* groups actually evolved into *H. erectus*. In fact, many paleoanthropologists (part of a growing consensus) suggest that there were more than one species of early *Homo*. Clearly, only one could be ancestral to *H. erectus*. Even more to the point, only *some* populations of this one species would have been part of the genetic transformation (speciation) that produced *Homo erectus*.

The second transition is more complex and is the main topic of this chapter. It is the gradual change in populations of *H. erectus* grading into early *H. sapiens* forms—what we have termed archaic *H. sapiens*. This transition was not geographically restricted, as there is evidence of archaic *H. sapiens* widespread in the Old World (in East and South Africa, in China and Java, and in Europe). Moreover, the transition appears not to have been rapid, but rather quite slow and uneven in pace from area to area. The complexity of this evolutionary transition creates ambiguities for our interpretations and resulting classifications.

For example, in Chapter 16, we included the Ngandong (Solo) material from Java within *Homo erectus*. However, there are several derived features in many of these specimens that suggest, alternatively, that they could be assigned to *Homo sapiens*. The dating (a rough estimate only) of 130,000 y.a. would argue that if this *is* a *H. erectus* group, it is a very late remnant, probably isolated, *H. erectus* population surviving in southern Asia at the same time that archaic

H. sapiens populations were expanding elsewhere. Whatever the interpretation of Ngandong—either as a late *H. erectus* or as a quite primitive (i.e., not particularly derived) archaic *H. sapiens*—the conclusion is actually quite arbitrary (after all, the evolutionary process is continuous). We, by the nature of our classifications, have to draw the line *somewhere*. (As a further aside, these largely arbitrary lines determine which specimens are discussed in which chapters!)

Another important ramification of such considerations relates to understanding the nature of the *erectus/sapiens* transition itself. In Java, the transition (with late-persisting *H. erectus* genetic components) appears to have been slower than, for example, in southern Africa or in Europe. Nowhere, however, does this transition appear to have been as rapid as that which originally produced *H. erectus*. Why should this be so? To answer this question, we must refer back to basic evolutionary mechanisms (discussed in Chapters 4 and 5). First, the environments certainly differed from one region of the Old World to another during the time period 350,000–100,000 y.a. And recall that by the beginning of this time period, *H. erectus* populations had been long established in eastern and southern Asia and North and East Africa. Moreover, by 250,000 years ago, *H. erectus* groups or their immediate descendants had already reached Europe—or soon would do so. Clearly, we would not expect the same environmental conditions in northeast China as we would in Indonesia. Accordingly, natural selection could well have played a *differential* role, influencing the frequencies of alternative alleles in different populations in a pattern similar (but more intensive) to that seen in environmental adaptations of contemporary populations (see Chapter 6).

Second, many of these populations (in Java, southernmost Africa, and glacial Europe) could have been isolated and thus probably quite small. Genetic drift, therefore, also would have played a role in influencing the pace of evolutionary change. Third, advance or retreat of barriers, such as water boundaries or glacial ice sheets, would dramatically have affected migration routes.

Thus, it should hardly come as a surprise that some populations of *H. erectus* evolved at different rates and in slightly different directions from others. Some limited migration almost certainly occurred among the various populations. With sufficient gene flow, the spread of those few genetic modifications that distinguish the earliest *H. sapiens* eventually did become incorporated into widely separated populations. This, however, was a long, slow, inherently uneven process.

What, then, of the third transition within the genus *Homo*? This is the transition from archaic *H. sapiens* to anatomically modern *H. sapiens*—and it was considerably *faster* than the transition we have just discussed. How quickly anatomically modern forms evolved and exactly *where* this happened is a subject of much contemporary debate—and is the main topic of our next chapter.

Summary

During the Middle Pleistocene, significant changes occurred in *H. erectus* morphology. The changes, especially in cranial traits, led scientists to assign a new species designation to these forms (*Homo sapiens*). Because they exhibited a mosaic of *H. erectus* and *H. sapiens* characteristics, the name archaic *H. sapiens* is used to indicate that they were forms transitional between *H. erectus* and anatomically modern humans. Some archaic *H. sapiens* possessed more derived modern traits than others, and these populations are sometimes referred to as later archaic *H. sapiens* or early *H. sapiens sapiens*. It has been suggested that some later European archaic forms were directly ancestral to Neandertals.

In addition to morphological changes among archaic forms, there were cultural developments as well. Archaic *H. sapiens* invented new kinds of tools and toolmaking techniques, exploited new foods, built more complex shelters, probably controlled fire, and may have used some form of speech.

In western Europe, archaic *H. sapiens* developed into a unique form—classic Neandertals—who apparently migrated from Europe to the Near East, and then even further into Asia. Neandertals were physically robust and muscular, different from both early archaic forms and modern *H. sapiens*. Their culture was more complex than earlier archaic cultures, and it appears that in Europe and the Near East, they lived in areas also inhabited by modern *H. sapiens*. Whether modern forms in these areas evolved directly from Neandertals or migrated from Africa (or the Near East) and ultimately replaced Neandertals is one of the important issues currently being debated by paleoanthropologists.

Finally, we would emphasize that Neandertals and all humans on earth today belong to the same species, *H. sapiens*. There are physical differences between these forms, of course, and for that reason Neandertals are assigned to the subspecies *H. sapiens neanderthalensis* and anatomically modern forms to the subspecies *H. sapiens sapiens*.

We should point out that this assignment of a *separate* subspecies for the Neandertals emphasizes some notable degrees of variation; that is, Neandertals are viewed as more different from *any* modern group of *H. sapiens* than these groups differ from one another. Some scholars (still representing a minority view) would even more dramatically emphasize this variation and thus assign Neandertals to a separate species from *Homo sapiens*. In this view, Neandertals would be placed in the separate species, *Homo neanderthalensis*. The behavioral differences between Neandertals and anatomically modern *H. sapiens*, as interpreted from the archeological record, are also discussed. These differences are emphasized by those scholars who view Neandertals as an evolutionary dead end.

Questions for Review

1. In what respect do *H. sapiens* (broadly defined) contrast with *H. erectus*?
2. What is meant by "archaic" *H. sapiens*?
3. How do archaic *H. sapiens* contrast with anatomically modern *H. sapiens*?
4. In what areas of the world have archaic *H. sapiens* been discovered? Compare and contrast the finds from two separate areas.
5. What do we mean when we say archaic *H. sapiens* specimens are transitional?
6. Why have Neandertals been depicted (by the popular press and others) as being primitive? Do you agree with this interpretation? Why or why not?
7. In what general areas of the world have Neandertal fossil remains been discovered?
8. What evidence suggests that Neandertals deliberately buried their dead? What interpretations do such treatment of the dead suggest to you?
9. What physical characteristics distinguish the Neandertals from anatomically modern *Homo sapiens*?
10. What behavioral characteristics distinguish Neandertal culture from that of the Upper Paleolithic?
11. What two major transitions within the genus *Homo* have been discussed in this chapter and in Chapter 16? Compare these transitions for geographical distribution as well as for aspects of evolutionary pace.

Suggested Further Reading

Mellars, Paul. 1995. *The Neanderthal Legacy. An Archaeological Perspective from Western Europe*. Princeton, NJ: Princeton University Press.

Shreeve, James. 1995. *The Neandertal Enigma*. New York: Morrow.

Stiner, Mary C. 1995. *Honor Among Thieves. A Zooarchaeological Study of Neandertal Ecology*. Princeton, NJ: Princeton University Press.

Stringer, Christopher and Clive Gamble. 1993. *In Search of the Neanderthals*. New York: Thames and Hudson.

Trinkaus, Erik and Pat Shipman. 1993. *The Neandertals: Changing the Image of Mankind*. New York: Knopf.

Internet Resources

See list in Chapters 13 and 14.

Did Neandertals Speak?

Actually, no one denies the Neandertal ability to speak. The real question is, Were Neandertals able to use all the vowels and consonants of modern human languages, or were they somehow compromised in their ability to communicate? As with determining the date hominids first controlled fire (Issue, Chapter 16), the pros and cons of this question have been argued for years, and the end is not in sight.

Ralph Holloway, a specialist in the study of fossil brains,* maintains that the Neandertal brain was similar to our own and, on average, slightly larger. Holloway writes, "I believe the Neandertal brain was fully *Homo*, with no essential differences in its organization compared to our own. . . . Neandertals did have language" (1985, p.320).

Philip Lieberman (1992), a linguist, argues that the Neandertal larynx was located high in the vocal tract, a position closer in form to *nonhuman* primates than to modern humans. In modern humans, Lieberman states, the larynx is positioned further down in the throat. Furthermore, the size of the

Neandertal oral cavity (the distance from the teeth to the back of the mouth) was greater than ours. Following the logic of this reconstruction, had the tongue and vocal tract been configured as in modern humans, the larynx, because of the oral cavity's large size, would have been located in the chest! Such a position is unknown in any animal species. Therefore, concludes Lieberman, Neandertals could not have had the same positioning of the tongue and other structures of the vocal tract as seen in modern humans, and this differently arranged vocal tract could not have formed the vowels [i], as in tea; [u], as in too; and [a], as in tall; or the consonants [k] and [g], as in Kate and gate.

Lieberman points out that the skeletal structure of the basicranium (the base of the cranium, especially the portion between the back of the palate and the front of the foramen magnum, which is preserved sometimes in fossils) is a clue to the positioning of the supralaryngeal vocal tract (which does not fossilize): "In brief, flexed basicrania are associated with modern human supralaryngeal vocal tracts, in which the larynx is positioned low in the neck" (Lieberman, 1994, p. 173). Flat basicrania, he contends, are associated with the larynx positioned high in

the neck, resulting in limited speech.†

Lieberman claims that the La Chapelle-aux-Saints Neandertal had a flat basicranium, which made for a highly positioned larynx, and that this individual accordingly

---

*Fossils do not possess brains, of course, since the soft tissue has long since decomposed. It is the landscape of the inside surface of the cranium that is studied for clues to the structure of the brain.

---

†It has been suggested that this communication handicap may have affected Neandertals' ability to survive and led to their extinction. In fact, Lieberman argues, "the extinction of Neandertal hominids was due to the competition of modern human beings who were better adapted for speech and language" (cited in Trinkaus and Shipman, 1992, p. 391). This argument has been used by some paleoanthropologists who believe that Neandertals were not the ancestors of anatomically modern humans in Europe and the Near East, thus supporting the notion that they (and other archaic *H. sapiens*) were replaced by populations presumably migrating out of Africa (this and alternative theories will be discussed in Chapter 18).

With reference to the demise of the Neandertals, John Fremlen of the University of Birmingham, England, wrote the following letter to *Science* (1975, 187, p. 600), wittily demonstrating that even if Neandertals could not use the three vowels noted above, they could, nevertheless, successfully communicate.

> Et seems quete prebable thet the Ne'enderthals ked speke less well then ther seccessers, end thet thes wes the resen fer ther demese. But even if we beleve the kempeter reselts it seems emprebeble thet ther speech was enedeqwete bekes of the leck of the three vewels seggested. The kemplexete of speech depends en the kensenents, net en the vewels, es ken be seen frem the general kemprehensebelete of thes letter.

would have had a vocal tract unable to produce full articulation.

Lieberman initially collaborated with Edmund Crelin at Yale University. More recently, his ideas have also been supported by another anatomist, Jeffrey Laitman of Mount Sinai School of Medicine in New York City. In fact, Laitman has further argued that Neandertal cranio-facial morphology (including aspects of the basicranium, nasal area, and sinuses) was specialized for respiration in a cold climate. As a result, Laitman hypothesizes, these upper respiratory specializations "would have placed limitations on Neandertal vocal modification mechanisms as compared to ours" (Laitman et al., 1993, p. 129).

Are Lieberman and colleagues correct in their interpretations? Perhaps. But then again, perhaps not. From the earliest publications (1971, 1972), the hypotheses have been vigorously challenged by other anatomists and have been especially strongly critiqued by anthropologists.

The proposed high location of the larynx is criticized by anatomist Dean Falk, who points out that this position is not found in newborn humans, adult humans, or for that matter, chimpanzees. She con-

cludes that "the statement that Neandertal was less than fully articulate remains unsubstantiated because it rests on a questionable reconstruction of the larynx" (1975, p. 123). In fact, other anatomists have shown that in the initial reconstruction as proposed by Lieberman and associates, Neandertals would not only have been unable to speak fully, but also would have been unable to swallow or open their mouths!

David Frayer, a paleoanthropologist, notes (1993) that the La Chapelle cranium was recently reconstructed, and the basicranium in the newly constructed version is *flexed*, not flat. La Chapelle's larynx, then, according to Lieberman's own hypothesis, should have been positioned low in the throat, like that of modern humans, and be capable of complete articulation. Lieberman's response was that the recent reconstruction of the La Chapelle skull may not have been correct, and he still maintains that Neandertals were probably limited in speech.

Frayer also measured the angle of flexion of the basicrania of skulls from the Upper Paleolithic, the Mesolithic (about 15,000–10,000 y.a.), and from a collection of human remains from medieval Hungary, all of whom presumably

possessed modern human speech capabilities. Comparing his results with measurements from a number of Neandertal crania, Frayer found some of the Neandertal basicrania were just as, or even more, flexed than those of anatomically modern humans (i.e., some of the modern crania were *flatter* than those of Neandertals). He points out that even if Neandertal basicrania were *flat*, Neandertals would have been as capable of unlimited speech as were the modern humans from the three time periods mentioned above.

The matter of Neandertal language capability is not settled. The hypotheses presented by Lieberman and Frayer cannot both be correct, although it must be admitted that most professionals strongly disagree with Lieberman. A recent discovery from the Kebara Cave site in Israel of a Neandertal hyoid bone (a bone found in the neck that helps support the larynx) further questions Lieberman's conclusions. This bone, the first Neandertal hyoid ever discovered, is modern in all major details and thus in no way provides evidence of differing speech capabilities. Further research may (or may not) provide confirmation of one or the other hypothesis, or a new one may even be suggested, which is the nature of the scientific process.

Sources

Falk, Dean. 1975. "Comparative Anatomy of the Larynx in Man and the Chimpanzee: Implications for Language in Neandertal." *American Journal of Physical Anthropology* 43:123–132.

Frayer, D. W. 1993. "On Neanderthal Crania and Speech: Response to Lieberman." *Current Anthropology* 34:721.

Holloway, Ralph L. 1985. "The Poor Brain of *Homo sapiens neanderthalensis.*" In: *Ancestors, the Hard Evidence*, Eric Delson (ed.), New York: Alan R. Liss, pp. 319–324.

Laitman, J. T., J. S. Reidenberg, D. R. Friedland, et al. 1993. "Neandertal Upper Respiratory Specializations and Their Effect Upon Respiration and Speech." *American Journal of Physical Anthropology* Supplement 16:129.

Lieberman, Phillip. 1992. "On Neanderthal Speech and Neanderthal Extinction," *Current Anthropology*. 33:409–410.

____. 1994. "On the Kebara 2 Hyoid and Neanderthal Speech." *Current Anthropology* 34:172–175.

Lieberman, P., and E. S. Crelin. 1971. "On the Speech of Neanderthal Man." *Linguistic Inquiries* 2:203–222.

Lieberman, P., E. S. Crelin, and D. H. Klatt. 1972. "Phonetic Ability and Related Anatomy of the Newborn and Adult Human, Neanderthal Man, and the Chimpanzee." *American Anthropologist* 74:287–307.

Critical Thinking Questions

1. Milford Wolpoff (1995, p. 706) has noted: "Science advances by trying to disprove null hypotheses. The simplest hypothesis supported by known observations made on Neandertals is that their ability to speak cannot be distinguished from living humans." Try to phrase this null hypothesis in slightly different words.

2. Why is it useful in science to *start* with a null hypothesis and then evaluate whether available evidence can or cannot disprove it?

3. A reviewer of this text has stated: "As argued by Lieberman, Laitman, etc., the Neandertal speech problem isn't testable. No matter what contrary evidence comes in (e.g., the Kebara Hyoid), they still argue that Neandertal speech was probably nonmodern." Do you agree or disagree with this statement? What kind of evidence would you accept as definitive to falsify the hypothesis proposed by Lieberman and Laitman?

18

$\mathcal{H}omo\ sapiens\ sapiens$

Introduction

In this chapter, we come to anatomically modern humans, taxonomically known as *Homo sapiens sapiens*. As we discussed in Chapter 17, in some areas evolutionary developments produced early archaic *H. sapiens* populations exhibiting a mosaic of *H. erectus* and *H. sapiens* traits. In some regions, the trend emphasizing *H. sapiens* characteristics continued, and possibly as early as 200,000 y.a., transitional forms (between early archaic and anatomically modern forms) appeared in Africa. Given the nature of the evidence and ongoing ambiguities in dating, it is not possible to say exactly when anatomically modern *H. sapiens* first appeared. However, the transition and certainly the wide dispersal of *H. sapiens sapiens* in the Old World appear to have been relatively rapid evolutionary events. Thus, we can ask several basic questions:

1. *When* (approximately) did *H. sapiens sapiens* first appear?
2. *Where* did the transition take place? Did it occur in just one region, or in several?
3. *What* was the pace of evolutionary change? How quickly did the transition occur?
4. *How* did the dispersal of *H. sapiens sapiens* to other areas of the Old World (outside that of origin) take place?

In a recent paper, evidence was presented that anatomically modern forms first evolved in Africa about 130,000 y.a. (Foley and Lahr, 1992), but whether such humans evolved *solely* in Africa or also evolved from archaic *H. sapiens* in other regions has been a matter of considerable debate for most of the last decade. Disagreeing with those who believe that modern *H. sapiens* originated solely in Africa are the regional continuity advocates. As we shall see, there is at present insufficient evidence to prove either case.

We will take up these varied hypotheses in this chapter and trace the evolution of anatomically modern human populations. We will also discuss the culture of the people who lived mainly during the **Upper Paleolithic**, a time of extraordinary technological change and artistic development.

▲ **Upper Paleolithic**
Pertaining to a cultural period associated with early modern humans and distinguished by technological innovation in various stone tool industries. Best known from western Europe, similar industries are also known from central and eastern Europe and Africa.

The Origin and Dispersal of *Homo sapiens sapiens* (Anatomically Modern Human Beings)

One of the most puzzling questions debated in paleoanthropology today is the origin of modern humans. There are three basic hypotheses: (1) the complete replacement model, (2) the partial replacement model, and (3) the regional continuity model.

The Complete Replacement Model (Recent African Evolution)

The complete replacement model, developed by Stringer and Andrews (1988), is based on the origin of modern humans in Africa and later replacement of populations in Europe and Asia (Fig. 18–1). In brief, this theory proposes that

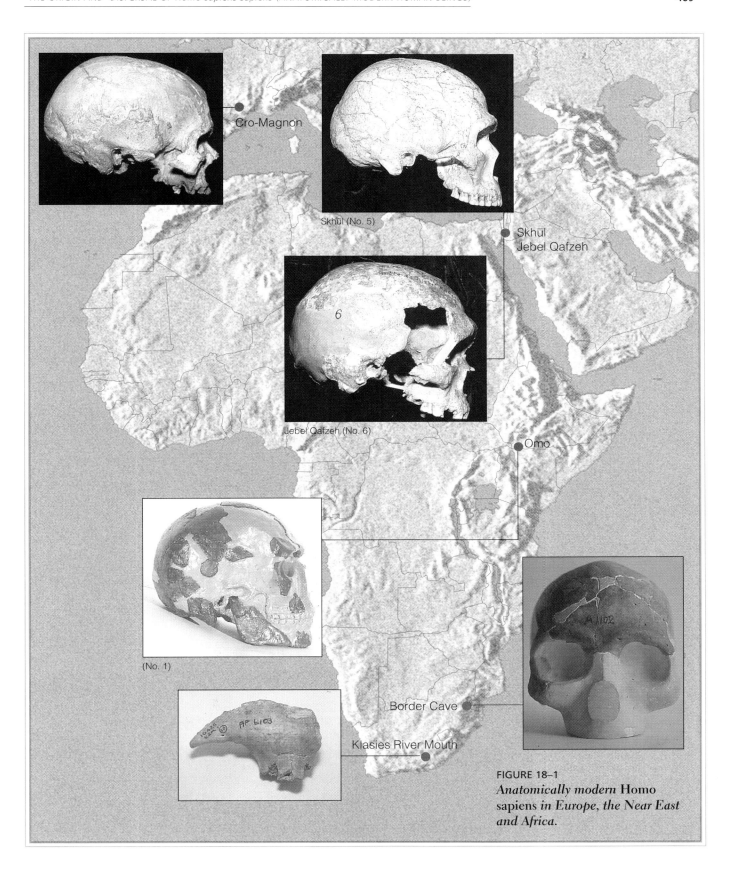

FIGURE 18–1
Anatomically modern Homo sapiens *in Europe, the Near East and Africa.*

anatomically modern populations arose in Africa within the last 200,000 years, then migrated from Africa, completely *replacing* populations in Europe and Asia. This model does not take into account any transition from archaic *H. sapiens* to modern *H. sapiens* anywhere in the world except Africa. A critical deduction of the Stringer and Andrews theory is that it considers the appearance of anatomically modern humans as a biological speciation event. Thus, in this view there could be no admixture of migrating African modern *H. sapiens* with local populations; it would have been impossible, because the African modern humans were a *biologically* different species. While this speciation explanation fits nicely with, and in fact helps explain, *complete* replacement, Stringer has more recently stated that he is not dogmatic regarding this issue. Thus, he suggests that there may have been potential for interbreeding, but he argues that very little apparently took place.

A crucial source of supporting evidence for the African origin hypothesis (and complete replacement elsewhere) has come from genetic data obtained from living peoples. Underlying this approach is the assumption that genetic patterning seen in contemporary populations will provide clues to relationships and origins of ancient *Homo sapiens*. However, as with numerous prior attempts to evaluate such patterning from data on human polymorphisms (e.g., ABO, HLA—see Chapter 5), the obstacles are enormous.

A recent innovation uses genetic sequencing data derived directly from DNA. The most promising application has come not from the DNA within the nucleus, but from DNA found in the cytoplasm, that is, mitochondrial DNA (mtDNA). Mitochondria are organelles found in the cell, outside the nucleus. They contain a set of DNA, dissimilar from nuclear DNA, inherited only through the mother. Thus, mtDNA does not undergo the genetic recombination that occurs in nuclear DNA during meiosis.

Using mtDNA gathered from a number of different populations, scientists at the University of California, Berkeley, constructed "trees" (something like a family tree) that, they claimed, demonstrated that the entire population of the world today descended from a single African lineage. However, the methodology of these molecular biologists has been faulted. Using the same mtDNA material, other scientists constructed many trees that differed from those of the Berkeley group, and some of them are *without African roots*.

This question of the applicability of the mtDNA evidence continues to generate considerable disagreement. Paleoanthropologist Robert Corruccini of Southern Illinois University has been unimpressed with the entire approach, stating that "critical shortcomings of molecular population genetic assumptions and of analysis . . . render any mtDNA conclusions virtually useless to ruminations about human evolution" (Corruccini, 1994, p. 698). However, molecular anthropologist Mark Stoneking of Pennsylvania State University (and one of the founders of this approach) remains much more confident in the general reliability of the mtDNA results, especially as they show a much greater diversity among contemporary African groups as compared to other world populations. Stoneking thus concludes: "Because non-African populations that predate the mtDNA ancestor apparently did not contribute mtDNAs to contemporary human populations, it follows that the spread of modern populations was accomplished with little or no admixture with resident non-African populations. If it were otherwise, there should be evidence of much more divergent mtDNA types in contemporary human populations" (Stoneking, 1993, pp. 66–67).

Recently, some further genetic data have helped bolster some of the main tenets of the complete replacement model. A team of Yale, Harvard, and

University of Chicago researchers (Dorit et al., 1995) have investigated variation in the Y chromosome, finding *much* less variation in humans than in other primates. And, another group of Yale researchers (Tishkoff et al., 1996), looking at DNA sequences on chromosome 12, again found much more variation among contemporary Africans than is seen in all the remainder of the world combined. Nevertheless, some geneticists find the results unconvincing (e.g., Ayala, 1995; Templeton, 1996), and as you will see shortly, many paleoanthropologists (agreeing with the views expressed by Corruccini) are extremely skeptical of the main conclusions derived from the genetic data (see Box 18–1 for further discussion).

The Partial Replacement Model (African–European *sapiens* Hypothesis)

The partial replacement model also begins with African early archaic *H. sapiens*, from which emerged a late archaic stage. Later, also in Africa, anatomically modern *H. sapiens* populations first evolved. This theory, proposed by Gunter Bräuer of the University of Hamburg, postulates the earliest dates for African modern *Homo sapiens* at over 100,000 y.a. Bräuer sees the initial dispersal of *H. sapiens sapiens* out of South Africa as a result of climatic and environmental conditions and thus as a gradual process. Moving into Eurasia, modern humans hybridized, probably to a limited degree, with resident archaic groups, thereby eventually replacing them. The disappearance of archaic humans was therefore due to both hybridization and replacement and was a gradual and complex process. This model includes components of regional continuity, hybridization, and replacement, with the emphasis on replacement.

The Regional Continuity Model (Multiregional Evolution)

The regional continuity model is most closely associated with paleoanthropologist Milford Wolpoff of the University of Michigan and his associates (Thorne and Wolpoff, 1992; Wolpoff et al., 1994). These researchers suggest that local populations (not all, of course) in Europe, Asia, and Africa continued their indigenous evolutionary development from archaic *H. sapiens* to anatomically modern humans. A question immediately arises: How is it possible for different local populations around the globe to evolve with such similar morphology? The multiregional model explains this phenomenon by (1) denying that the earliest modern *H. sapiens* populations originated *exclusively* in Africa and challenging the notion of complete replacement and (2) asserting that some gene flow (migration) between archaic populations was extremely likely, and consequently, modern humans cannot be considered a species separate from archaic forms.

Through gene flow and local selection, according to the multiregional hypothesis, local populations would *not* have evolved totally independently from one another, and such mixing would have "prevented speciation between the regional lineages and thus maintained human beings as a *single*, although obviously polytypic, species throughout the Pleistocene" (Smith et al., 1989).

BOX 18–1

The Garden of Eden Hypothesis

Gathering samples of mtDNA from placentas of women whose ancestors lived in Africa, Asia, Europe, Australia, and New Guinea, biologists Allan Wilson, Rebecca Cann, and Mark Stoneking, from the University of California, Berkeley, postulated a distinctive genetic pattern for each area. They then compared the diversity of the various patterns (Cann et al., 1987).

They found the greatest variation among Africans and therefore postulated Africa to have been the home of the oldest human populations (the assumption is that the longer the time, the greater the accumulation of genetic variation). They also found that the African variants contained only African mtDNA, whereas those from other areas all included at least one African component. Therefore, the biologists concluded, there must have been a migration initially from Africa, ultimately to all other inhabited areas of the world. By counting the number of genetic mutations and applying the *rate* of mutation, Rebecca Cann and her associates calculated a date for the origin of anatomically modern humans: between 285,000 and 143,000 years ago—in other words, an average estimate of about 200,000 years ago. Indeed, a further contention of the mtDNA researchers is that the pattern of variation argues that all modern humans shared in common a single African female lineage that lived sometime during this time range. Thus was born the popularized concept of "mitochondrial Eve."

Not all scientists, by any means, agree with this scenario. The estimated rate of mutations may be incorrect, and therefore, the proposed date of migration out of Africa would also be in error. Secondly, differing population size in Africa, compared to elsewhere, would complicate interpretations (Relethford and Harpending, 1994). Also, secondary migration, outside Africa, could disrupt the direct inheritance of the African maternal line. Even more troubling are the inher-

ent biases in the statistical technique used to identify the primary population relationships ("trees"). Recent reanalyses of the data suggest that the situation is not nearly as clear-cut as originally believed.

Scrutiny of the mitochondrial DNA–based model of modern human origins came when the approach was attempted by other laboratories using similar techniques and statistical treatments. In February 1992, three different papers were published by different teams of researchers, all of which severely challenged the main tenets of the hypotheses as proposed by Wilson, Cann, and Stoneking. The most serious error was a failure to recognize how many *equally valid* results could be deduced statistically from the *same set* of original data. In science, as we have remarked before, beyond the data themselves, the methodological treatments (especially statistical models) greatly influence both the nature and *confidence limits* of the results.

The central conclusion that Africa alone was the *sole* source of modern humans could still be correct. Yet, now it had to be admitted that dozens (indeed, thousands) of other equally probable renditions could be derived from the supposedly unambiguous mitochondrial data. Thus, barely a few months after the original researchers had proposed their most systematic statement of their hypotheses, the entire perspective (especially its statistical implications) was shaken to its very foundations—and, in many people's eyes, falsified altogether.

An interesting twist regarding this entire reassessment is that the team from Pennsylvania State University that challenged the initial results was joined in its critique by Mark Stoneking, one of the original formulators of the now-questioned hypothesis. A viable scientific perspective, so well illustrated here, is that new approaches (or refined applications) often necessitate reevaluation of prior hypotheses. It takes both objectivity and courage to admit miscalculations.

The Earliest *Homo sapiens sapiens* Discoveries

Current evidence strongly indicates that the earliest modern *H. sapiens* fossils come from Africa, but not everyone agrees on the dates or designations or precisely which specimens are the modern and which are the archaic forms. With this cautionary note, we continue our discussion, but there undoubtedly will be corrections as more evidence is gathered.

By so doing, an even more permanent and positive legacy helps contain the inherent personal biases that sometimes have so divided the study of human origins.

On the basis of these new studies, many have proclaimed that mitochondrial Eve is dead—and perhaps the complete replacement hypothesis with her. As could be expected, the proponents of the African origin view are not yet ready to bury Eve or significantly alter their confidence in the complete replacement hypothesis.

As the debate continues, new lines of evidence and new techniques are being pursued: more ways to sequence both mitochondrial and nuclear DNA; more complete evidence of human polymorphisms; genetic sequence data for the Y chromosome; and, it is hoped, more reliable statistical techniques to interpret these complex data. The new data for the Y chromosome are particularly interesting. Since the Y chromosome is inherited *paternally* (and thus also is *not* recombined), its pattern of genetic diversity makes for an excellent complement to the maternally inherited mtDNA. Biologist Robert Dorit of Yale University, along with his team of researchers, sequenced a portion of the Y chromosome. Surprisingly, they found absolutely *no* variation in this region, but did see much more Y chromosome variation in great apes (chimpanzees, gorillas, orangutans). Dorit suggests that this lack of variation indicates a recent origin for *Homo sapiens*. He notes at the same time, however, that "the lack of variation in the Y chromosome regions we examined also makes it impossible for us to reconstruct the geographic location of the last common ancestor" (Henahan, 1995).

Further evidence along these lines has come from another group of Yale biologists led by Sarah Tishkoff (Tishkoff et al., 1996). Tishkoff and her colleagues have been investigating genetic patterns within nuclear DNA (their research target is a region on chromosome 12). Assembling a very large sample of data (1,600 individuals from 42 populations), Tishkoff and her team found by far the most variation among contemporary Africans. (Of 24 possible variants, 21 of these were found in Africa; Europe and the Middle East displayed only 3; Asia, the Pacific Islands, and the New World together displayed a mere 2.) Tishkoff draws the same conclusion as that proposed by both the mtDNA and the Y chromosome researchers—that all modern humans are the result of a single recent evolutionary event. (Tishkoff, in fact, places the date at 100,000–70,000 y.a., even more recent than that suggested by the mtDNA evidence.) Moreover, the results from the chromosome 12 DNA polymorphisms, like those relating to mtDNA, suggest that Africa was the geographical source for all modern humans.

What can we then conclude? Results are still tentative, but various studies are now corroborating one another. First, we can conclude that *Homo sapiens* is not a very genetically variable species; indeed, genetically, we are quite a homogeneous lot (a point we emphasized in Chapter 5). By some estimates, comparisons with other primates suggest that human mtDNA is only about 1/40th to 1/50th as variable as the mtDNA of chimpanzees (Cann et al., 1994)! Does human genetic homogeneity imply a *recent* origin for all *H. sapiens sapiens*? Perhaps. At the least, these increasingly consistent genetic data argue that it is unlikely that the present genetic patterning in *H. sapiens* can be traced back to the early dispersal of *H. erectus* out of Africa (circa 1.8 m.y.a.). It would appear that there must have been one or more later dispersals as well. But, how much later? The broadest time limits so far reasonably indicated by various genetic techniques would suggest a time frame in the range of 440,000–100,000 y.a. If you were inclined to make a wager on the probabilities of the time of the last major dispersal of hominids, somewhere in this range looks like a good bet.

Africa

In Africa, several early fossil finds have been interpreted as fully anatomically modern forms (see Fig. 18–1). These specimens come from the Klasies River Mouth on the south coast (which could be the earliest find), Border Cave slightly to the north, and Omo Kibish 1 in southern Ethiopia. With the use of relatively new techniques, all three sites have been dated to about

▲ **Provenience**
In archeology, the specific location of a
discovery, including its geological context.

120,000–80,000 y.a. **Provenience** at Border Cave is uncertain, and the fossils
may be younger than at the other two sites (See Box 18–2 and Fig. 18–5). Some
paleoanthropologists consider these fossils to be the earliest known anatomically
modern humans. Problems with dating, provenience, and differing interpretations of the evidence have led other paleoanthropologists to question whether
the *earliest* modern forms (Fig. 18–2) really did evolve in Africa. Other modern
H. sapiens, possibly older than these Africans, have been found in the Near East.

The Near East

In Israel, early modern *H. sapiens* fossils (the remains of at least 10 individuals)
were found in the Skhūl Cave at Mt. Carmel (Figs. 18–3 and 18–4a), very near
the Neandertal site of Tabun. Also from Israel, the Qafzeh Cave has yielded the
remains of at least 20 individuals (Fig. 18–4b). Although their overall configuration is definitely modern, some specimens show certain archaic (i.e., Neandertal)
features. Skhūl has been dated to about 115,000 y.a., and Qafzeh has been placed
around 100,000 y.a. (Bar-Yosef, 1993; 1994) (Fig. 18–5).

Such early dates for modern specimens pose some problems for those advo-
cating local replacement (the multiregional model). How early do archaic
H. sapiens (Neandertals) appear in the Near East? A recent chronometric cali-
bration for the Tabun Cave suggests a date as early as 120,000 y.a. Neandertals
thus may *slightly* precede modern forms in the Near East, but there would
appear to be considerable overlap in the timing of occupation by these different
H. sapiens forms. And recall, the modern site at Mt. Carmel (Skhūl) is very near
the Neandertal site (Tabun). Clearly, the dynamics of *Homo sapiens* evolution in
the Near East are highly complex, and no simple model may explain later
hominid evolution adequately.

Central Europe

Central Europe has been a source of many fossil finds, including numerous
fairly early anatomically modern *H. sapiens*. At several sites, it appears that some
fossils display both Neandertal and modern features, which supports the regional
continuity hypothesis (from Neandertal to modern). Such continuity apparently
was the case at Vindija in Croatia, where typical Neandertals were found in earlier contexts (see p. 453).

Smith (1984) offers another example of local continuity from Mladeč, in the
Czech Republic. Among the earlier European modern *H. sapiens*, dated to
about 33,000 y.a., the Mladeč crania display a great deal of variation, partly due
to sexual dimorphism. Although each of the crania (except for one of the
females) displays a prominent supraorbital torus, it is reduced from the typical
Neandertal pattern. Even though there is some suggestion of continuity from
Neandertals to modern humans, Smith is certain that the Mladeč remains are
H. sapiens sapiens. Reduced midfacial projection, a higher forehead, and postcranial elements "are clearly modern *H. sapiens* in morphology and not specifically Neandertal-like in a single feature" (Smith, 1984, p. 174).

Western Europe

This area of the world and its fossils have received the greatest paleoanthropological attention for several reasons, one of which is probably serendipity. Over the

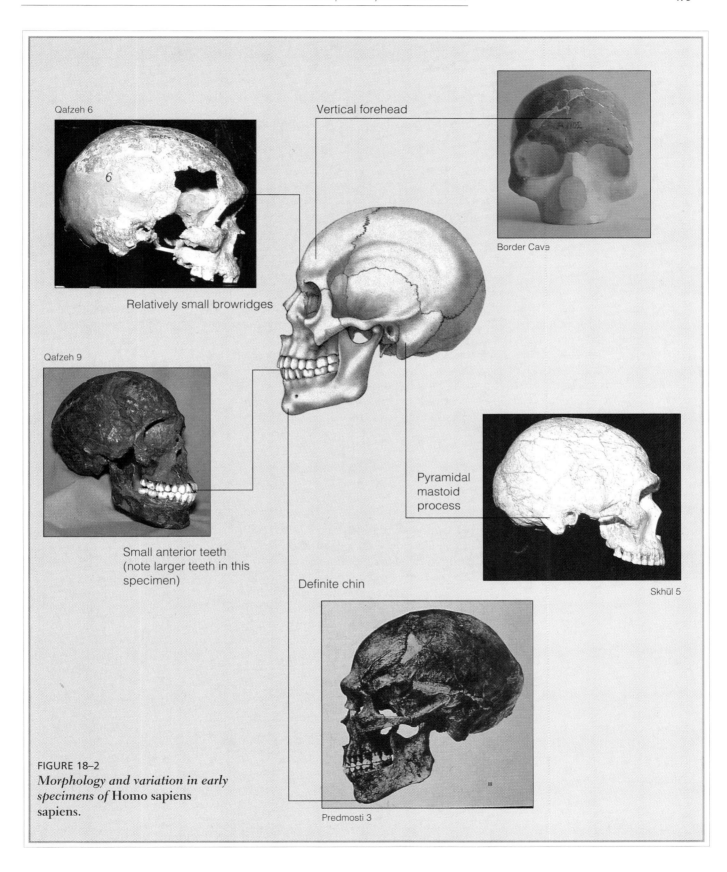

Qafzeh 6

Vertical forehead

Border Cave

Relatively small browridges

Qafzeh 9

Small anterior teeth
(note larger teeth in this
specimen)

Pyramidal
mastoid
process

Skhūl 5

Definite chin

Predmosti 3

FIGURE 18–2
*Morphology and variation in early
specimens of* Homo sapiens
sapiens.

Additional Techniques for Dating Middle and Upper Pleistocene Sites

In addition to the paleoanthropological dating methods discussed in Chapter 13, three other techniques have important applications for dating sites in the 500,000–50,000 y.a. range:

1. *Uranium series dating,* based on radioactive decay of short-lived uranium isotopes. This technique is used to date limestone formations, such as stalagmites, and has recently been attempted on ancient ostrich eggshells. Uranium series dating has been used to estimate the age of the Jinniushan site in China, which has been further corroborated by ESR dates (see below).
2. *Thermoluminescence dating (TL),* based on the accumulation of trapped electrons within certain crystals

released during heating. This technique has been used on ancient flint tools (either accidentally or deliberately heated) and has recently provided key dates for the Qafzeh site.
3. *Electron spin resonance dating (ESR),* based on the measurement (actually the counting) of accumulated trapped electrons. This technique has been used on dental enamel and has further corroborated the dating of the Qafzeh, Skhūl, and Tabun sites in Israel as well as the Klasies River Mouth and Border Cave sites in South Africa.

For further information, see Cook et al., 1984; Aiken et al., 1993.

---

last century and a half, many of the scholars interested in this kind of research happened to live in western Europe, and the southern region of France happened to be a fossil cornucopia. Also, early on, discovering and learning about human ancestors caught the curiosity and pride of the local population.

Because of this scholarly interest beginning back in the nineteenth century, a great deal of data accumulated, with little reliable comparative information available from elsewhere in the world. Consequently, theories of human evolution were based almost exclusively on the western European material. It has only been in recent years, with growing evidence from other areas of the world and with the application of new dating techniques, that recent human evolutionary dynamics have been seriously considered on a worldwide basis.

There are many anatomically modern human fossils from western Europe going back 40,000 years or more, but by far the best-known western European *H. sapiens* is from the **Cro-Magnon** site. A total of eight individuals were discovered in 1868 in a rock shelter in the village of Les Eyzies, in the Dordogne region of southern France (Gambier, 1989).

Associated with an **Aurignacian** tool assemblage, an Upper Paleolithic industry, the Cro-Magnon materials, dated at 30,000 y.a., represent the earliest of France's anatomically modern humans. The so-called "Old Man" (Cro-Magnon I) became the archetype for what was once termed the Cro-Magnon, or Upper Paleolithic, "race" of Europe (Fig.18–6). Actually, of course, there is no such race, and Cro-Magnon I is not typical of Upper Paleolithic western

▲ **Cro-Magnon**
(crow mah´yon)

▲ **Aurignacian**
Pertaining to an Upper Paleolithic stone tool industry in Europe beginning at about 40,000 y.a.

(a)

(b)

Europeans, and not even all that similar to the other two male skulls that were found at the site.

Considered together, the male crania reflect a mixture of modern and archaic traits. Cro-Magnon I is the most gracile of the three—the supraorbital tori of the other two males, for example, are more robust. The most modern-looking is the female cranium, the appearance of which may be a function of sexual dimorphism.

The question of whether continuous local evolution produced anatomically modern groups directly from Neandertals in some regions of Eurasia is far from settled. Variation seen in the Mladeč and Vindija fossils indicate a combination of both Neandertal and modern characteristics and may suggest gene flow between the two different *H. sapiens* groups. However, tracing such relatively

FIGURE 18–3

(a) Mt. Carmel, studded with caves, was home to H. sapiens sapiens *at Skhūl (and to Neandertals at Tabun and Kebara). (b) Skhūl Cave.*

FIGURE 18–4

(a) Skhūl 5 (b) Qafzeh 6. These specimens from Israel are thought to be representatives of early modern Homo sapiens. *The vault height, forehead, and lack of prognathism are modern traits.*

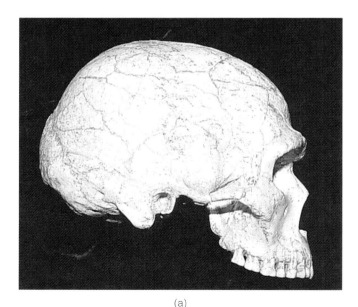

(a)

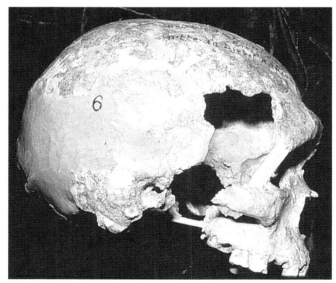

(b)

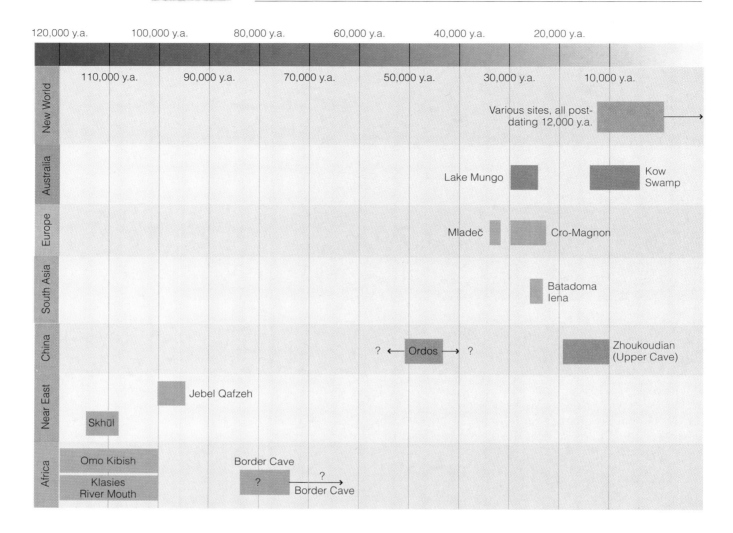

FIGURE 18–5

Time line of Homo sapiens sapiens *discoveries. Note that most dates are approximations. Question marks indicate those estimates that are most tentative.*

minor genetic changes—considering the ever-present problems of dating, lack of fossils, and fragmented fossil finds—may well prove impossible.

Asia

There are six early anatomically modern human localities in China, the most significant of which are Upper Cave at Zhoukoudian and Ordos. The fossils from these sites are all fully modern, and most are considered to be of quite late Upper Pleistocene age. Upper Cave at Zhoukoudian has been dated to between 18,000 and 10,000 y.a. The Ordos find was discovered at Dagouwan, Inner Mongolia, and may be the oldest anatomically modern material from China, perhaps dating to 50,000 y.a. or more (Etler, personal communication).

In addition, the Jinniushan skeleton discussed in Chapter 17 (see p. 000) has been suggested by some researchers (Tiemel et al., 1994) as hinting at modern features in China as early as 200,000 y.a. If this date (as early as that proposed for direct antecedents of modern *H. sapiens* in Africa) should prove accurate, it would cast doubt on the complete replacement model. Indeed, quite opposed to the complete replacement model and more in support of regional continuity, Chinese paleoanthropologists see a continuous evolution from Chinese *H. erec-*

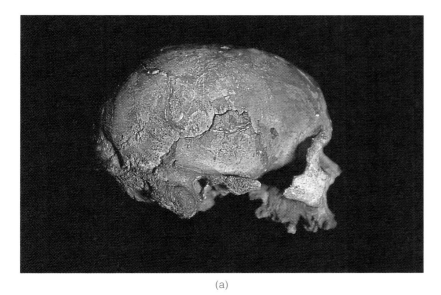

(a)

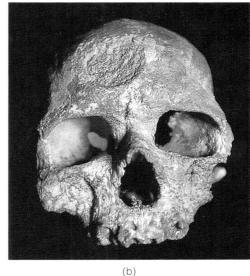

(b)

tus to archaic *H. sapiens* to anatomically modern humans. This view is supported by Wolpoff, who mentions that materials from Upper Cave at Zhoukoudian "have a number of features that are characteristically regional" and that these features are definitely not African (1989, p. 83).*

In addition to the well-known finds from China, anatomically modern remains have also been discovered in southern Asia. At Batadomba Iena, in southern Sri Lanka, modern *Homo sapiens* have been dated to 25,500 y.a. (Kennedy and Deraniyagala, 1989).

Australia

During glacial times, the Indonesian islands were joined to the Asian mainland, but Australia was not. It is likely that by 40,000 y.a., Sahul—the area including New Guinea and Australia—was inhabited by modern humans. Bamboo rafts may have been the means of crossing the sea between islands, which would not have been a simple exercise. Just where the future Australians came from is unknown, but Borneo, Java, and New Guinea have all been suggested.

Archeological sites in Australia have been dated to at least 55,000 y.a. (Roberts et al., 1990), but the oldest human fossils themselves have been dated to about 30,000 y.a. These oldest Australians are from Lake Mungo, where the remains of two burials (one individual was first cremated) date to 25,000 y.a. and at least 30,000 y.a., respectively (Fig. 18–7). The crania are rather gracile with, for example, only moderate development of the supraorbital torus.

Unlike these more gracile early Australian forms are the Kow Swamp people, who are believed to have lived between about 14,000 and 9,000 years ago (Fig. 18–8). The presence of certain archaic traits, such as receding foreheads, heavy supraorbital tori, and thick bones, are difficult to explain, since these features contrast with the postcranial anatomy, which matches that of recent native Australians.

FIGURE 18–6

Cro-Magnon 1 (France). In this specimen, modern traits are quite clear. (a) Lateral view. (b) Frontal view. (Courtesy of David Frayer.)

---

*Wolpoff's statement supports his belief in regional continuity. His reference to Africa is a criticism of the complete replacement hypothesis.

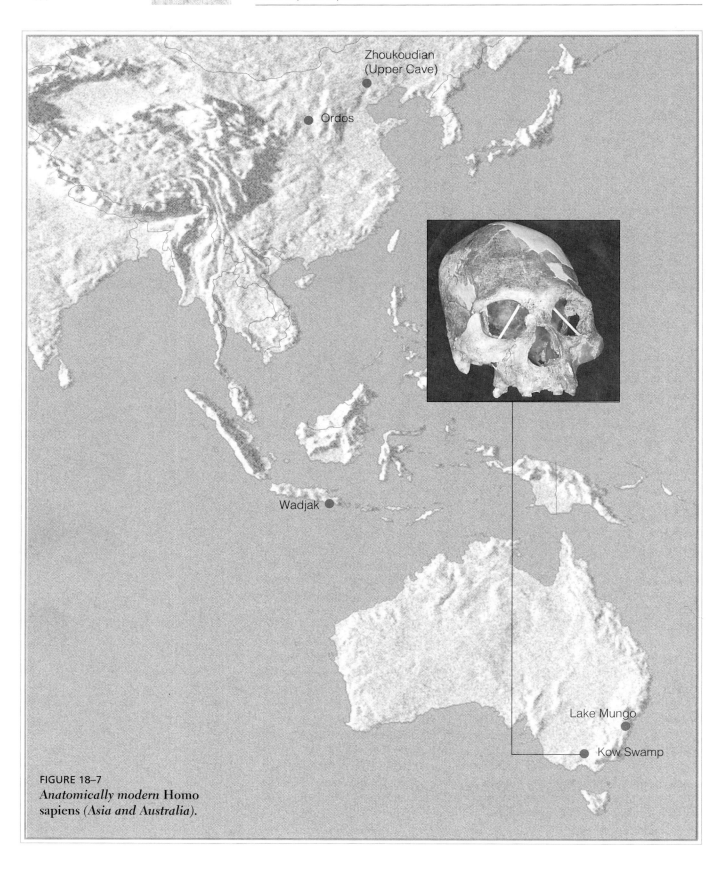

FIGURE 18–7
Anatomically modern Homo
sapiens *(Asia and Australia).*

The New World

There have been considerable, and often heated, arguments regarding the *earliest* entry of humans into the New World. It must be remembered that the ancestors of Native Americans reached the New World through multiple migrations over the Bering Land Bridge over many millennia. Regarding the first migration, all claims of great antiquity (prior to 30,000 y.a.) have now been refuted. Nevertheless, there are still varied claims that archeological materials (i.e., evidence of artifacts) put the date of the initial migration at prior to 15,000 y.a. Such claims have come from evidence excavated at widely scattered locales (e.g., from the Yukon, Pennsylvania, and Peru). Because of concerns about accurate dating or the nature of the artifacts (were they actually made by humans?), these reports, too, have been subjected to rigorous scrutiny. As a result, these claims are not considered well established at this time.

The most indisputable proof would, of course, be actual hominid finds in clear, datable contexts. As with the earliest confirmed archeological discoveries, direct evidence indicating the greatest antiquity for hominids anywhere in the New World goes back only about 12,000 years. From the broader perspective of human evolution, we must emphasize that all the hominid material found thus far is obviously fully modern *Homo sapiens*. This fact should come as no surprise, given the relatively late entry of *Homo sapiens* into the Americas, perhaps as much as 40,000 years after hominids had reached Australia.

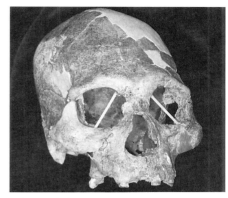

FIGURE 18–8

Kow Swamp (Australia). Note the considerable robusticity in this relatively late Australian Homo sapiens sapiens *cranium.*

Technology and Art in the Upper Paleolithic

Europe

The cultural period known as the Upper Paleolithic began in western Europe approximately 40,000 years ago (Fig. 18–9). Upper Paleolithic cultures are usually divided into five different industries based on stone tool technologies: (1) Chatelperronian, (2) Aurignacian, (3) Gravettian, (4) Solutrean, and (5) Magdalenian. Major environmental shifts were also apparent during this period. During the last glacial period, at about 30,000 y.a., a warming trend lasting several thousand years partially melted the glacial ice. The result was that much of Eurasia was covered by tundra and steppe, a vast area of treeless country dotted with lakes and marshes. In many areas in the north permafrost prevented

GLACIAL	UPPER PALEOLITHIC (beginnings)	CULTURAL PERIODS
W Ü R M	17,000 –	Magdalenian
	21,000 –	Solutrean
	27,000 –	Gravettian
	33,000 –	Aurignacian Chatelperronian
	Middle Paleolithic	Mousterian

FIGURE 18–9

Cultural periods of the European Upper Paleolithic and their approximate beginning dates.

the growth of trees but permitted the growth, in the short summers, of flowering plants, mosses, and other kinds of vegetation. This vegetation served as an enormous pasture for herbivorous animals, large and small, and carnivorous animals fed off the herbivores. It was a hunter's paradise, with millions of animals dispersed across expanses of tundra and grassland, from Spain through Europe and into the Russian steppes.

Large herds of reindeer roamed the tundra and steppes along with mammoths, bison, horses, and a host of smaller animals that served as a bountiful source of food. In addition, humans exploited fish and fowl systematically for the first time, especially along the southern tier of Europe. It was a time of relative affluence, and ultimately Upper Paleolithic people spread out over Europe, living in caves and open-air camps and building large shelters. Large dwellings with storage pits have been excavated in the former Soviet Union, with archeological evidence of social status distinctions (Soffer, 1985). During this period, either western Europe or perhaps portions of Africa achieved the highest population density in human history up to that time.

In Eurasia, cultural innovations allowed humans for the first time to occupy easternmost Europe and northern Asia. In these areas, even during glacial warming stages, winters would have been long and harsh. Human groups were able to tolerate these environments probably because of better constructed structures as well as warmer, better fitting *sewn* clothing. The evidence for wide use of such tailored clothing comes from many sites and includes pointed stone tools such as awls and (by at least 19,000 y.a.) bone needles as well. Especially noteworthy is the clear evidence of the residues of clothing (including what has been interpreted as a cap, a shirt, a jacket, trousers, and moccasins) in graves at the 22,000-year-old Sungir site, located not far from Moscow (Klein, 1989).

Humans and other animals in the mid-latitudes of Eurasia had to cope with shifts in climatic conditions, some of which were quite rapid. For example, at 20,000 y.a. another climatic "pulse" caused the weather to become noticeably colder in Europe and Asia as the continental glaciations reached their maximum extent for this entire glacial period (called the Würm in Eurasia). Meanwhile, the southern continents, too, experienced widespread climatic effects. Notably, in Africa around 20,000 y.a. it became significantly wetter, thus permitting reoccupation of areas in the north and south that had previously been abandoned.

As a variety of organisms attempted to adapt to these changing conditions, *Homo sapiens* had a major advantage: the elaboration of an increasingly sophisticated technology (and probably other components of culture as well). Indeed, probably one of the greatest challenges facing numerous late Pleistocene mammals was the ever more dangerously equipped humans—a trend that has continued to modern times.

The Upper Paleolithic was an age of technological innovation and can be compared to the past few hundred years in our recent history of amazing technological change after centuries of relative inertia. Anatomically modern humans of the Upper Paleolithic not only invented new and specialized tools (Fig. 18–10), but, as we have seen, also greatly increased the use of, and probably experimented with, new materials, such as bone, ivory, and antler.

Solutrean tools are good examples of Upper Paleolithic skill and perhaps esthetic appreciation as well (Fig. 18–10b). In this lithic (stone) tradition, stone-knapping developed to the finest degree ever known. Using a pressure-flaking technique (see p. 484), the artist/technicians made beautiful parallel-sided lance heads, expertly flaked on both surfaces, with such delicate points that they can be considered works of art that quite possibly never served, or were intended to serve, a utilitarian purpose.

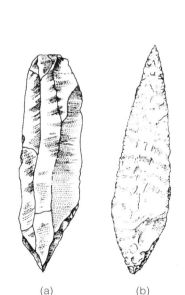

(a)   (b)

FIGURE 18–10

(a) Burin. A very common Upper Paleolithic tool. (b) Solutrean blade. This is the best-known work of the Solutrean tradition. Solutrean stonework is considered the most highly developed of any Upper Paleolithic industry.

The last stage of the Upper Paleolithic, known as the **Magdalenian**, saw even more advances in technology. The spear thrower (Fig. 18–11), a wooden or bone hooked rod (called an *atlatl*), acted to extend the hunter's arm, thus enhancing the force and distance of a spear throw. For catching salmon and other fish, the barbed harpoon is a clever example of the craftsperson's skill. There is also evidence that the bow and arrow may have been used for the first time during this period. The introduction of the punch technique (Fig. 18–12) provided an abundance of standardized blank stone flakes that could be fashioned into: **burins** (Fig. 18–10a) for working wood, bone, and antler; borers for drilling holes in skins, bones, and shells; and blades for knives with serrated or notched edges for scraping wooden shafts into a variety of tools.

The elaboration of many more specialized tools by Upper Paleolithic peoples probably made more resources available to them and may also have had an impact on the biology of these populations. C. Loring Brace, of the University of Michigan, has suggested that with more efficient tools used for food processing, anatomically modern *H. sapiens* would not have required the large front teeth (incisors) seen in earlier populations. With relaxed selection pressures (no longer favoring large anterior teeth), incorporation of random mutations would through time lead to reduction of dental size and accompanying facial features. In particular, the lower face became less prognathic (as compared to archaic specimens) and thus produced the concavity of the cheekbones called a *canine fossa*. Moreover, as the dental-bearing portion of the lower jaw regressed, the buttressing below would have become modified into a *chin*, that distinctive feature seen in anatomically modern *H. sapiens* (see Fig. 18–2).

In addition to their reputation as hunters, western Europeans of the Upper Paleolithic are even better known for their symbolic representation, what has commonly been called "art." Certainly, in the famous caves of France and Spain (discussed below), we easily relate to an aesthetic property of the images—one that *may* have been intended by the people who created them. But here we cannot be certain. Our own cultural perspectives create labels (and categories) such as "art," which in itself *assumes* aesthetic intent. While such a cultural orientation is obviously a recognizable part of Western culture, many other contemporary peoples would not relate to this concept within their own cultural context. Furthermore, prehistoric peoples during the Upper Paleolithic did not necessarily create their symbols as true artistic representations. Rather, these representations may have served a variety of quite utilitarian and/or social functions—as do contemporary highway signs or logos on a company's letterhead. Would we call these symbols art?

Given these uncertainties, archeologist Margaret Conkey, of the University of California, Berkeley (see p. 492), refers to Upper Paleolithic cave paintings, sculptures, engravings, and so forth, as "visual and material imagery" (Conkey,

▲ **Magdalenian**
Pertaining to the final phase (stone tool industry) of the Upper Paleolithic in Europe.

▲ **Burins**
Small, chisel-like tools (with a pointed end) thought to have been used to engrave bone, antler, ivory, or wood.

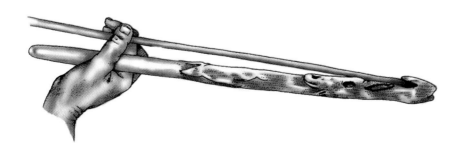

FIGURE 18–11
Spear thrower (atlatl). Note the carving.

(a) A large core is selected and the top portion is removed by use of a hammerstone.

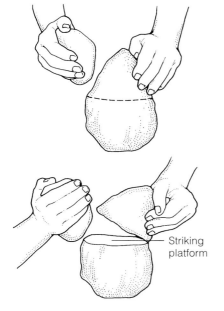

(b) The objective is to create a flat surface called a striking platform.

Striking platform

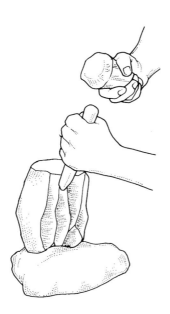

(c) Next, the core is struck by use of a hammer and punch (made of bone or antler) to remove the long narrow flakes (called blades).

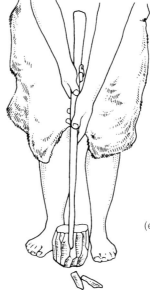

(d) Or the blades can be removed by pressure flaking.

(e) The result is the production of highly consistent sharp blades, which can be used, as is, as knives; or they can be further modified (retouched) to make a variety of other tools (such as burins, scrapers, and awls).

FIGURE 18–12

The punch blade technique.

1987, p. 423). We will continue to use the term *art* to describe many of these prehistoric representations, but you should recognize that we do so mainly as a cultural convention—and perhaps a limiting one.

Moreover, the time depth for these prehistoric forms of symbolic imagery is quite long, encompassing the entire Upper Paleolithic (from at least 35,000—10,000 y.a.). Over this time span there is considerable variability in style, medium, content, and no doubt, meaning as well. In addition, there is an extremely wide geographical distribution of symbolic images, best known from many parts of Europe, but now also well documented from Siberia, North Africa, South Africa, and Australia. Given the 25,000-year time depth of what we call "Paleolithic art" and its nearly worldwide distribution, there is indeed marked variability in expression.

In addition to cave art, there are numerous examples of small sculptures excavated from sites in western, central, and eastern Europe. Beyond these quite well known figurines, there are numerous other examples of what is frequently termed "portable art," including elaborate engravings on tools and tool handles (Fig. 18–13). Such symbolism can be found in many parts of Europe and was already well established early in the Aurignacian (by 35,000 y.a.). Innovations in symbolic representations also benefited from, and probably further stimulated, technological advances. New methods of mixing pigments and applying them were important in rendering painted or drawn images. Bone and ivory carving and engraving were made easier with the use of special stone tools (see Fig. 18–10). At two sites in the Czech Republic, Dolni Vestonice and Predmosti (both dated at 27,000 y.a.), small animal figures were fashioned from fired clay—

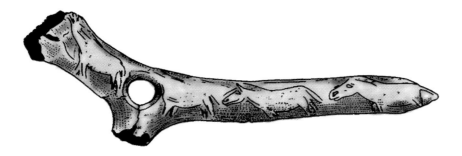

FIGURE 18–13

Magdalenian bone artifact. Note the realistic animal engraving on this object, the precise function of which is unknown.

the first documented use of ceramic technology anywhere (and preceding later pottery invention by more than 15,000 years!).

Female figurines, popularly know as Venuses, were sculpted not only in western Europe, but in central and eastern Europe and Siberia as well. Some of these figures were realistically carved, and the faces appear to be modeled after actual women (Fig. 18–14). Other figurines may seem grotesque, with sexual characteristics exaggerated, perhaps for fertility or ritual purposes (Fig. 18–15).

It is, however, during the final phases of the Upper Paleolithic, particularly during the Magdalenian, that European prehistoric art reached its climax. Cave art is now known from more than 150 separate sites, the vast majority from southwestern France and northern Spain. Apparently, in other areas the rendering of such images did not take place in deep caves. Peoples in central Europe, China, Africa, and elsewhere certainly may have painted or carved representations on rockfaces in the open, but these images long since would have eroded. Thus, it is fortuitous that the people of at least one of the many sophisticated cultures of the Upper Paleolithic chose to journey below ground to create their artwork, preserving it not just for their immediate descendants, but for us as well.

In Lascaux Cave of southern France, immense wild bulls dominate what is called the Great Hall of Bulls, and horses, deer, and other animals adorn the walls in black, red, and yellow, drawn with remarkable skill. In addition to the famous cave of Lascaux, there is equally exemplary art from Altamira Cave in

(a) (b)

FIGURE 18–14

Venus of Brassempouy. Upper Paleolithic artists were capable of portraying human realism (shown here) as well as symbolism (depicted in Fig 18–15).
(a) Frontal view.
(b) Lateral view.

FIGURE 18–15
Venus of Willendorf, Austria.

FIGURE 18–16
Cave art. (a) Bear. Grotte Chauvet, France (b) Aurochs and rhinoceros, Grotte Chauvet.

Spain. Indeed, discovered in 1879, Altamira was the first example of advanced cave art recorded in Europe. Filling the walls and ceiling of the cave are superb portrayals of bison in red and black, the "artist" taking advantage of bulges to give a sense of relief to the paintings. The cave is a treasure of beautiful art whose meaning has never been satisfactorily explained. It could have been religious or magical, a form of visual communication, or art for the sake of beauty.

Yet another spectacular example of cave art from western Europe was discovered in late 1994. On December 24, a team of three French cave explorers chanced upon a fabulous discovery in the valley of the Ardeche at Combe d'Arc (see map, p. 489). Inside the cave, called the Grotte Chauvet after one of its discoverers, preserved unseen for perhaps 20,000 years, are many hundreds of images, including stylized dots, stenciled human handprints, and most dramatically, hundreds of animal representations. Included are depictions of such typical Paleolithic subjects as bison, horse, ibex, auroch, deer, and mammoth. But quite surprisingly, there are also numerous images of animals rarely portrayed elsewhere—such as rhino, lion, and bear. Three animals seen at Grotte Chauvet—a panther, a hyena, and an owl—have never before been documented at cave sites (Fig. 18–16). The artwork, at least after provisional study, seems to consistently repeat several stylistic conventions, causing French researchers to suggest that the images all may have been produced by the same artist. Dating, also provisional as of this writing, has been attributed to the Solutrean (21,000–17,000 y.a.), and thus Grotte Chauvet may be somewhat earlier than the Magdalenian sites of Lascaux and Altamira. The cave was found as Paleolithic peoples had left it, and the initial discoverers, as well as archeologists, have been careful not to disturb the remains. Among the archeological traces already noted are dozens of footprints on the cave floor, produced by bears as well as by humans. We do not know yet how far the cave extends or what crucial artifactual remains lie along the floor.

A familiar motif seen at Grotte Chauvet and elsewhere is the representation of human hands, usually in the form of outlines. Apparently, the technique used was to liquefy the pigment and blow it onto a hand held flat against the cave wall. At one site in France, at least 159 such hand outlines were found (Leroi-

(a)

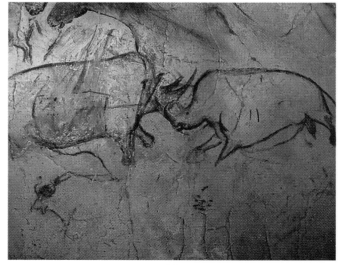

(b)

Gourhan, 1986). Another stylistic innovation was the partial sculpting of a rock face—in what is called bas-relief (a technique used much later, for example, by the ancient Greeks at the Parthenon). Attaining depths up to 6 inches, some of the Paleolithic sculptures were quite dramatic and were attempted on a fairly grand scale. In one rock shelter in southwest France, several animals (including mountain goats, bison, reindeer, and horses) and one human figure were depicted in bas-relief. Interestingly, these representations were carved in an area also used as a living site—quite distinct from the special-purpose contexts in the deep cave locations. These bas-reliefs were executed throughout the Magdalenian, always in areas immediately adjacent to those of human habitation.

Strikingly, subject matter seems to differ by location and type of art motif. In portable art, common themes are horses and reindeer as well as stylized human figures; rarely are bison represented. However, in cave contexts, bison and horses are frequently seen, but almost never do we see reindeer (although in Europe, reindeer were probably the most common meat source). Cave artists were thought heretofore to have depicted carnivores only rarely, but the new finds at Grotte Chauvet give us a further perspective on the richness *and* diversity of Paleolithic art.

Ever since ancient art was discovered, attempts have been made to interpret the sculptures, paintings, and other graphic material found in caves or on rocks and tools at open-air archeological sites. One of the early explanations of Upper Paleolithic art emphasized the relationship of paintings to hunting. Hunting rituals were viewed as a kind of imitative magic that would increase prey animal populations or help hunters successfully find and kill their quarry. As new hypotheses were published, their applicability and deficiencies were discussed. When many of these new hypotheses faded, others were expounded, and the cycle of new hypotheses followed by critiques continued.

Among these hypotheses, the association of religious ritual and magic is still considered viable because of the importance of hunting in the Upper Paleolithic. Nevertheless, other ideas about these graphics have been widely discussed, including the viewing of Upper Paleolithic art from a male/female perspective and the consideration of a prevalent dots-and-lines motif as a notational system associated with language, writing, or a calendar (Marshack, 1972). Other perspectives and ongoing questions include why certain areas of caves were used for painting, but not other, similar areas; why certain animals were painted, but not others; why males were painted singly or in groups, but women only in groups; why males were painted near animals, but women never were; and why groups of animals were painted in the most acoustically resonant areas. (Were rituals perhaps performed in areas of the cave with the best acoustic properties?) It should be noted that given the time depth, different contexts, and variable styles of symbolic representations, no *single* explanation regarding their meaning is likely to prove adequate. As one expert has concluded, "it is clear that there can no longer be a single 'meaning' to account for the thousands of images, media, contexts, and uses of what we lump under the term 'paleolithic art'" (Conkey, 1987, p. 414).

A recent explanation for the florescence of cave art in certain areas has been suggested by archeologists Clive Gamble (1991) and Lawrence Straus (1993), who point to the severe climatic conditions during the maximum (coldest interval) of the last glacial, around 20,000–18,000 y.a. It was during this period in southwestern France and northern Spain that most of the cave art was created. Straus notes that wherever there are clusters of living sites, there are cave art sanctuaries and residential sites with abundant mobile art objects. The caves could have been meeting places for local bands of people and locations for group activities. Bands could share hunting techniques and knowledge, and paintings and engravings served as "encoded information" that could be passed on across generations. Such information, Straus argues, would have been crucial for dealing with the severe conditions of the last glacial period.

Africa

Early accomplishments in rock art, perhaps as early as in Europe, are seen in southern Africa (Namibia), where a site containing such art is dated between 28,000 and 19,000 y.a. In addition, evidence of portable personal adornment is seen as early as 38,000 y.a. in the form of beads fashioned from ostrich eggshells.

In terms of stone tool technology, microliths (thumbnail-sized stone flakes hafted to make knives, saws, etc.) and blades characterize Late Stone Age* African industries. There was also considerable use of bone and antler in central Africa, perhaps some of it quite early. Recent excavations in the Katanda area of eastern Zaire have shown remarkable development of bone craftsmanship. In fact, preliminary reports by Alison Brooks, of George Washington University, and John Yellen, of the National Science Foundation, have demonstrated that these technological achievements rival those of the more renowned European Upper Paleolithic (Yellen et al., 1995).

The most important artifacts discovered at Katanda are a dozen intricately made bone tools excavated from three sites along the Semiliki River (not far from Lake Rutanzige—formerly, Lake Edward) (Fig. 18–17). These tools, made from the ribs or long bone splinters of large mammals, apparently were first ground to flatten and sharpen them, and then some were apparently precisely pressure-flaked (see p. 484) to produce a row of barbs. In form these tools are similar to what have been called "harpoons" from the later Upper Paleolithic of Europe (Magdalenian, circa 15,000 y.a.). Their function in Africa, as well, is thought to have been for spearing fish, which archeological remains indicate were quite large (catfish weighing up to 150 pounds!). In addition, a few carved bone rings with no barbs were also discovered, but their intended function (if indeed they were meant to have a utilitarian function at all) remains elusive.

The dating of the Katanda sites is crucial for drawing useful comparisons with the European Upper Paleolithic. However, the bone used for the tools retained no measurable nitrogen and thus proved unsuitable for radiocarbon dating (perhaps it was too old and beyond the range of this technique). As a result, the other techniques now used for this time range—thermoluminescence, electron spin resonance, and uranium series dating (see p. 476)—were all applied. Among these techniques, the results proved consistent, indicating dates between 180,000 and 75,000 y.a.[†]

However, there remain some difficulties in establishing the clear association of the bone implements with the materials that have supplied the chronometric age estimates. Indeed, Richard Klein, a coauthor of one of the initial reports (Brooks et al., 1995), does not accept the suggested great antiquity for these finds and believes they may be much younger. Nevertheless, if the early age estimates should hold up, we once again will look *first* to Africa as the crucial source area for human origins—not just for biological aspects, but for cultural aspects as well.

---

*The Late Stone Age in Africa is equivalent to the Upper Paleolithic in Eurasia.

†If these dates prove accurate, Katanda woulds actually be earlier than Late Stone Age (and thus be referrable to the Middle Stone Age).

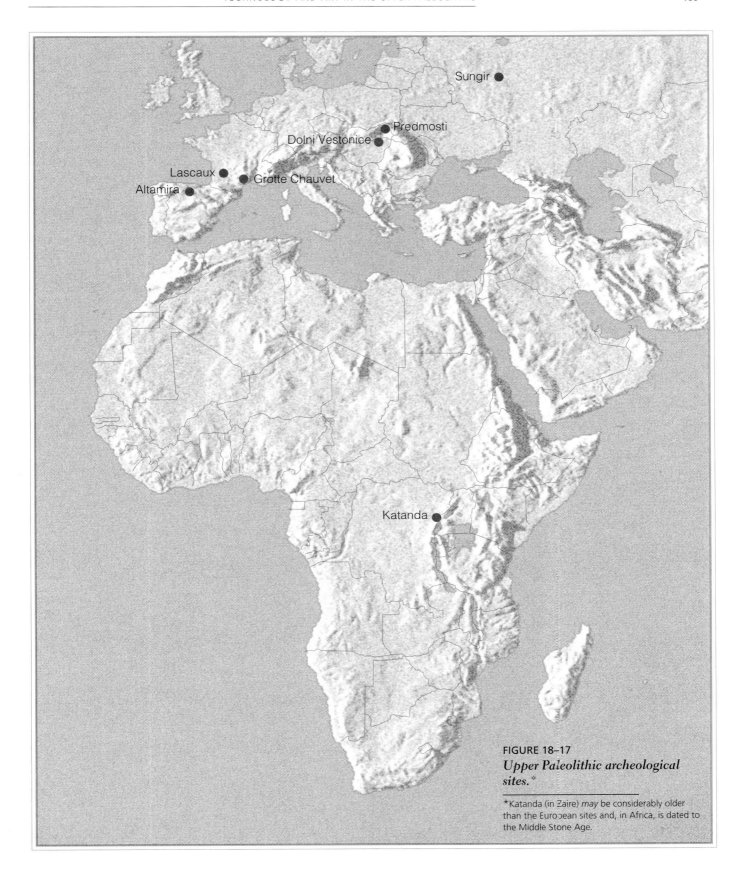

FIGURE 18–17
*Upper Paleolithic archeological sites.**

*Katanda (in Zaire) *may* be considerably older than the European sites and, in Africa, is dated to the Middle Stone Age.

Summary of Upper Paleolithic Culture

As we look back at the Upper Paleolithic, we can see it as the culmination of 2 million years of cultural development. Change proceeded incredibly slowly for most of the Pleistocene, but as cultural traditions and materials accumulated, and the brain (and, we assume, intelligence) expanded and reorganized, the rate of change quickened.

Cultural evolution continued with the appearance of early archaic *H. sapiens* and moved a bit faster with later archaic *H. sapiens*. Neandertals in Eurasia and their contemporaries elsewhere added deliberate burials, technological innovations, and much more.

Building on existing cultures, late Pleistocene populations attained sophisticated cultural and material heights in a seemingly short (by previous standards) burst of exciting activity. In Europe and central Africa particularly, there seem to have been dramatic cultural innovations that saw big game hunting, potent new weapons (including harpoons, spear throwers, and possibly the bow and arrow), body ornaments, needles, "tailored" clothing, and burials with elaborate grave goods (the latter might indicate some sort of status hierarchy).

This dynamic age was doomed, or so it appears, by the climatic changes of about 10,000 y.a. As the temperature slowly rose and the glaciers retreated, animal and plant species were seriously impacted, and humans were thus affected as well. As traditional prey animals were depleted or disappeared altogether, other means of obtaining food were sought.

Grinding hard seeds or roots became important, and as familiarity with plant propagation increased, domestication of plants and animals developed. Dependence on domestication became critical, and with it came permanent settlements, new technology, and more complex social organization.

The long road from hominid origins, from those remarkable footprints engraved into the African savanna, has now led by millions of chance evolutionary turnings to ourselves, anatomically modern human beings. But this road is not yet finished. We are the inheritors, both biologically and culturally, of our hominid forebears. Now, for the first time in human evolution, perhaps we have some choice in the direction our species may take. Knowledge of the past—of human potentials and of human limitations—might well be our best guide in making intelligent choices as individuals and most especially as a species. Evolution has endowed us with a marvelous brain and with it the capacity for great intelligence, artistic achievement, and much more. However, wisdom is a hard-won treasure to be learned anew every generation.

Summary

The date and location of the origin of anatomically modern human beings have been the subject of a fierce debate for the past decade, and the end is not in sight. One hypothesis (complete replacement) claims that anatomically modern forms first evolved in Africa more than 100,000 y.a. and then, migrating out of Africa, completely replaced archaic *H. sapiens* in the rest of the world. Another school (regional continuity) takes a diametrically different view and maintains that in various geographical regions of the world, local groups of archaic *H. sapiens* evolved directly to anatomically modern humans. A third hypothesis (partial replacement) takes a somewhat middle position, suggesting an African origin but also accepting some later hybridization outside of Africa.

The Upper Paleolithic was an age of extraordinary innovation and achievement in technology and art. Many new and complex tools were introduced, and their production indicates fine skill in working wood, bone, and antler. It was a period that might be compared, for its time, to the past few hundred years of our own technological advances.

Cave art in France and Spain displays the masterful ability of Upper Paleo-lithic painters, and beautiful sculptures have been found at many European sites. Art has also been found in Africa and elsewhere. Upper Paleolithic *Homo sapiens* displayed amazing development in a relatively short period of time. The culture produced during this period led the way to still newer and more complex cultural techniques and methods.

Questions for Review

1. What characteristics define anatomically modern *H. sapiens*?
2. How do the characteristics of modern *H. sapiens* compare with those of archaic *H. sapiens*?
3. What are the three major theories that seek to explain the origin and dispersal of *Homo sapiens sapiens*? Compare and critically discuss these three views.
4. How have data from mitochondrial DNA been used to support an African origin of *H. sapiens sapiens*? What other genetic data have recently been analyzed, and how do they accord with the mtDNA results?
5. Discuss (and compare) the early evidence of anatomically modern humans from two different regions.
6. It is said that the Upper Paleolithic was a time of technological innovation. Support this statement with specific evidence, and compare the Upper Paleolithic with cultural data from earlier in the Pleistocene.
7. From which regions has cave art, dating to the Upper Pleistocene, been discovered? Particularly for the cave art of Europe, what explanations of its meaning have been proposed?

Suggested Further Reading

Aitken, M. J., C. B. Stringer, and P. A. Mellars (eds.). 1993. *The Origin of Modern Humans and the Impact of Chronometric Dating.* Princeton, NJ: Princeton University Press.

Klein, Richard. 1989. *The Human Career: Human Biological and Cultural Origins.* Chicago: University of Chicago Press.

Nitecki, Matthew H., and Doris V. Nitecki (eds.). 1994. *Origins of Anatomically Modern Humans.* New York: Plenum.

Smith, Fred, and Frank Spencer (eds.). 1984. *The Origin of Modern Humans.* New York: Liss.

Wolpoff, Milford. 1995. *Human Evolution.* New York: McGraw-Hill, College Custom Series.

Internet Resources

Footsteps of Man
http://www.geocities.com/Tokyo/2384/links.html
A central website providing access to petroglyph and rock art links worldwide. Includes access to over 600 links in the form of a hypertextual encyclopedia (including text and pictures).

Grotte Chauvet
http://web/culture.fr/culture/gvpda-en.html
A description of finds at Grotte Chauvet plus five excellent photographs.

Margaret W. Conkey

I was educated at Mt. Holyoke College and the University of Chicago, in Ancient History, Art History, and Anthropology. I have taught in Environmental Studies and primarily in Anthropology departments—at San Jose State University, at the State University of New York, Binghamton, and at the University of California at Berkeley, where I currently direct the Archaeological Research Facility. I am the President-Elect of the Association for Feminist Anthropology, and am carrying out fieldwork in the Midi-Pyrénées of France.

When I meet a class for the first time, I usually ask them to fill out an index card with all sorts of information; I am especially interested to know why they have signed up for the class. Inevitably, there are at least several students who say that they have always wanted to be an archeologist, that they have always wanted to study the mysteries of human evolution. I was not one of those who "knew" since my youth that I wanted to be an archeologist; my mother always thought I ought to be a librarian, but perhaps my interests in classifying things is a common aspect to both professions! However, a chance opportunity to participate in an archeological excavation in the Middle East as a college junior was the event that turned me toward archeology, although my path to studying the early humans—those of the Ice Age—was not direct. When I was in graduate school (at the University of Chicago), I was informed that before I could begin the work on the Paleolithic of Europe (an area that I had come to identify as a potential speciality) I should go off and do archeology in other settings and that sought to explore other problems. One reason for this, I was told, was that once I did begin my special research, which I hoped would be in Spain or France, I may "stay" there for my professional career. Consequently, I should get some other perspectives before I dug in to a speciality.

I have long been convinced that my advisors were right about this; I have increasingly valued my early opportunities to do fieldwork in the Valley of certain questions about ancient humans, questions that only lead to more questions!

When I decided to pursue research about the Upper Paleolithic period of southwestern Europe, I was convinced that I would try to use other lines of evidence than the stone tools or lithics that were certainly the center stage of research attention. Of course, they were abundantly preserved, richly and intriguingly varied, and a crucial data set for understanding some of the aspects of prehistoric life that archeologists preferred to concentrate on—technology and economy. I was not convinced by fellow archeologists of the Upper Paleolithic period—the period of *Homo sapiens sapiens*—that the "art" on cave walls or what we would take to be artistic material culture (such as the little sculptures out of ivory or antler) of this period was not very useable in interpreting this period. To some, it was useful as a decoration for the covers of their books, but a humanistic distraction from what many thought was the real business of Paleolithic archeology, which was excavation of deeply stratified sites, improved chronological controls, increasing samples of fauna and lithics in stratified contexts. Nonetheless, I ventured into how we might analyze such things as the decorations of engraved bones and antlers to make inferences about social groups. I have continued to be an avid follower of the work done by colleagues in interpreting and in studying the cave art. But the ultimate irony of my early stand to try, if possible, and avoid stone tools, is that my current research project is completely dependent upon them, as I explain below. But what are the wider issues that keep me going? Why am I now excited even by stone tools?

Several years ago, I became enchanted with a phrase used by a South African colleague who has revolutionized the study of rock art on an international scale, Professor David Lewis-Williams of the University of the Witwatersrand. In demonstrating the complex symbolism and rich meanings that lie behind the rock paintings of southern Africa, long dismissed as the naive doodles of denigrated "bushman" peoples, Lewis-Williams came to present these new interpretations as part of South Africa's place in the "archeology of human understanding." To me, this was an eloquent way of capturing what I think has been motivating me for many years. How did the image-making in Paleolithic caves come about as a means for expressing important cultural issues? What were the social contexts within which late Paleolithic peoples across Eurasia made a symbolic and material repertoire of objects—out of bone, antler, ivory, baked clay, steatite, and so forth? How did these material and presumably symbolic forms "work" in their daily lives?

For the last several years, with assistance from numerous granting agencies, we have been trying to understand some of these ambitious questions in what may appear to be an indirect way. Rather than concentrating on the well-known and abundant cave sites of southwestern Europe, where there is rich preservation and stratigraphy (albeit never easy to decode), and which are being investigated with an increasing sophistication by many colleagues, we have decided to see if we might shed some light on the wider social, ritual, and everyday landscapes within which the mobile hunter-gatherers moved about; that is, we are investigating what lies "between the caves." We have focused on the area called the Midi-Pyrénées in France, just north of the tiny principality of Andorra. This is an area rich in caves, in cave art, and in innovative cave research, but it is an area where no systematic research has been done to look for traces of Paleolithic peoples across the landscape and between the caves. And thus, as we begin, we find that to do the first round of documenting these movements of people, we are doing archeological surveys in plowed fields, finding thousands of stone tools, characteristically Paleolithic. And so, even as I begin to pursue the question of "why art?", I am back to stone tools! Thus, if you choose to pursue any of the questions and issues in understanding human evolution, you will find that all evidence is relevant, all questions must be chased down, and each new door onto the past leads in many directions. If only we had enough lifetimes to follow each clue!

Appendix A
Atlas of Primate
Skeletal Anatomy

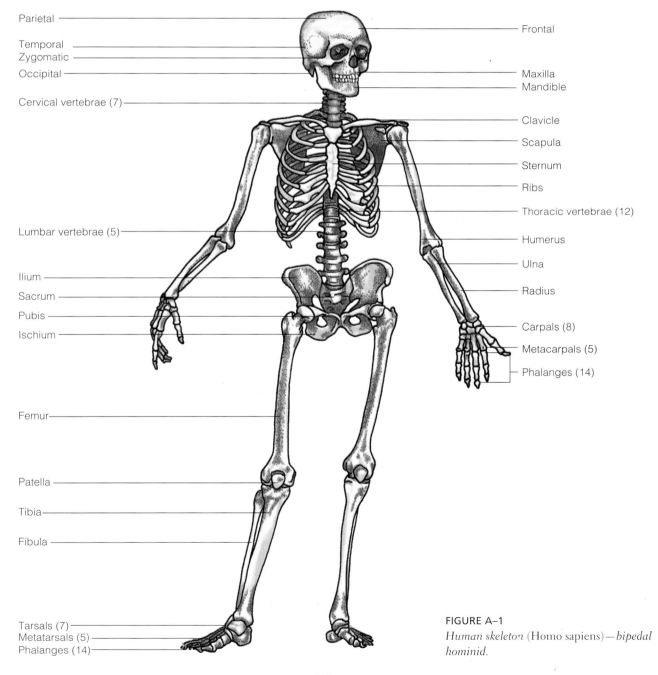

Parietal

Temporal
Zygomatic

Occipital

Cervical vertebrae (7)

Lumbar vertebrae (5)

Ilium

Sacrum

Pubis

Ischium

Femur

Patella

Tibia

Fibula

Tarsals (7)
Metatarsals (5)
Phalanges (14)

Frontal

Maxilla
Mandible

Clavicle

Scapula

Sternum

Ribs

Thoracic vertebrae (12)

Humerus

Ulna

Radius

Carpals (8)

Metacarpals (5)

Phalanges (14)

FIGURE A–1

Human skeleton (Homo sapiens)—*bipedal hominid.*

FIGURE A–2
Chimpanzee skeleton (Pan troglodyes)—
knuckle-walking pongid.

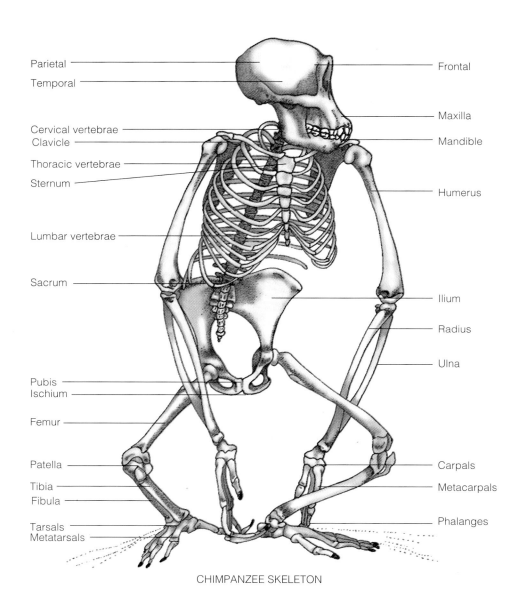

Parietal

Temporal

Cervical vertebrae

Clavicle

Thoracic vertebrae

Sternum

Lumbar vertebrae

Sacrum

Pubis

Ischium

Femur

Patella

Tibia

Fibula

Tarsals

Metatarsals

Frontal

Maxilla

Mandible

Humerus

Ilium

Radius

Ulna

Carpals

Metacarpals

Phalanges

CHIMPANZEE SKELETON

FIGURE A–3
*Monkey skeleton (rhesus macaque;
Macaca mulatta)—A typical
quadrupedal primate.*

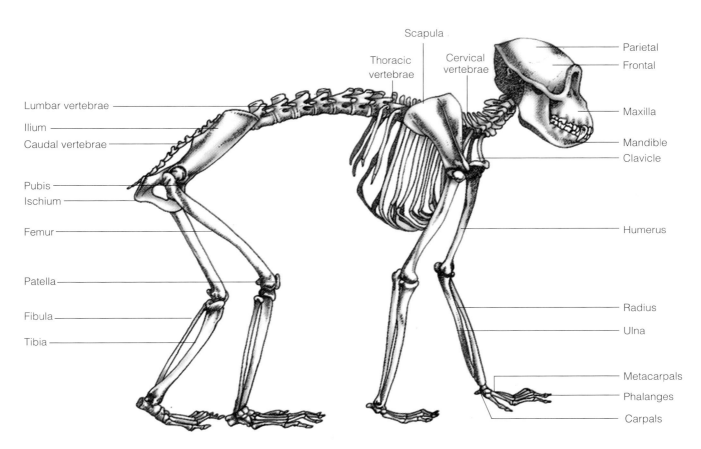

Scapula

Thoracic
vertebrae

Cervical
vertebrae

Parietal

Frontal

Lumbar vertebrae

Ilium

Caudal vertebrae

Maxilla

Mandible

Clavicle

Pubis

Ischium

Femur

Humerus

Patella

Fibula

Tibia

Radius

Ulna

Metacarpals

Phalanges

Carpals

MONKEY SKELETON

FIGURE A–4

Human cranium.

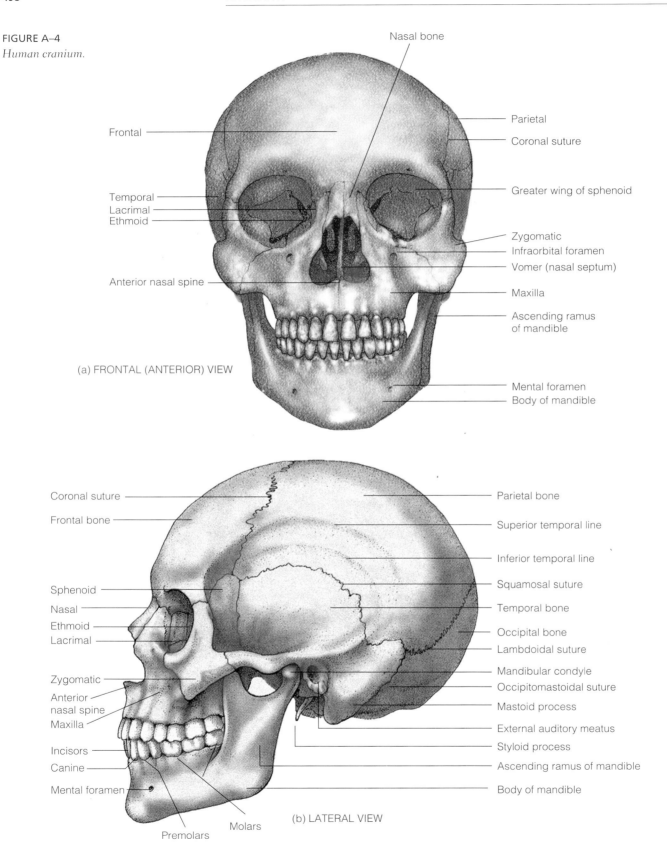

Nasal bone

Frontal

Parietal

Coronal suture

Greater wing of sphenoid

Temporal
Lacrimal
Ethmoid

Zygomatic

Infraorbital foramen

Vomer (nasal septum)

Anterior nasal spine

Maxilla

Ascending ramus
of mandible

(a) FRONTAL (ANTERIOR) VIEW

Mental foramen
Body of mandible

Coronal suture

Parietal bone

Frontal bone

Superior temporal line

Inferior temporal line

Sphenoid

Squamosal suture

Nasal

Temporal bone

Ethmoid

Lacrimal

Occipital bone

Lambdoidal suture

Zygomatic

Mandibular condyle

Anterior
nasal spine

Occipitomastoidal suture

Maxilla

Mastoid process

External auditory meatus

Incisors

Styloid process

Canine

Ascending ramus of mandible

Mental foramen

Body of mandible

(b) LATERAL VIEW

Molars

Premolars

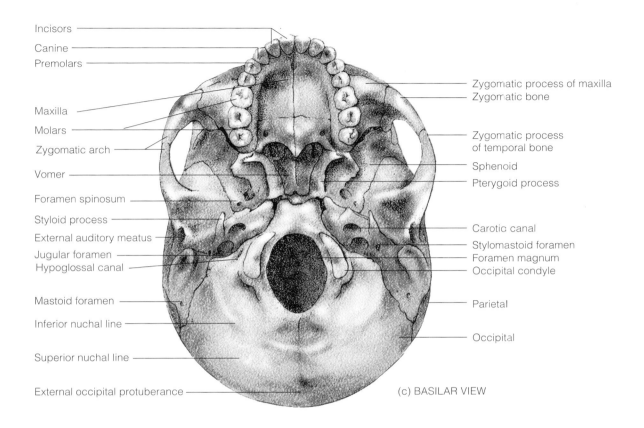

Incisors
Canine
Premolars

Maxilla
Molars
Zygomatic arch
Vomer
Foramen spinosum
Styloid process
External auditory meatus
Jugular foramen
Hypoglossal canal

Mastoid foramen
Inferior nuchal line

Superior nuchal line

External occipital protuberance

Zygomatic process of maxilla
Zygomatic bone
Zygomatic process of temporal bone
Sphenoid
Pterygoid process

Carotic canal
Stylomastoid foramen
Foramen magnum
Occipital condyle

Parietal

Occipital

(c) BASILAR VIEW

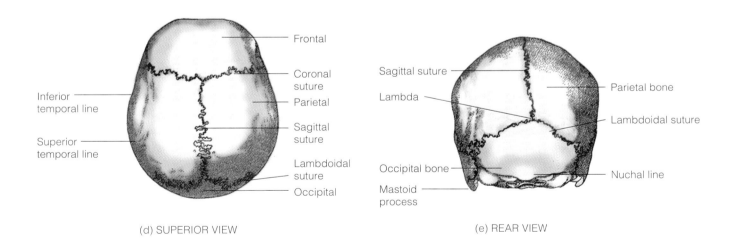

Frontal
Coronal suture
Parietal
Sagittal suture
Lambdoidal suture
Occipital

Inferior temporal line
Superior temporal line

(d) SUPERIOR VIEW

Sagittal suture
Lambda
Occipital bone
Mastoid process

Parietal bone
Lambdoidal suture
Nuchal line

(e) REAR VIEW

FIGURE A–5

Human vertebral column (lateral view) and representative cervical, thoracic, and lumbar vertebrae (superior views).

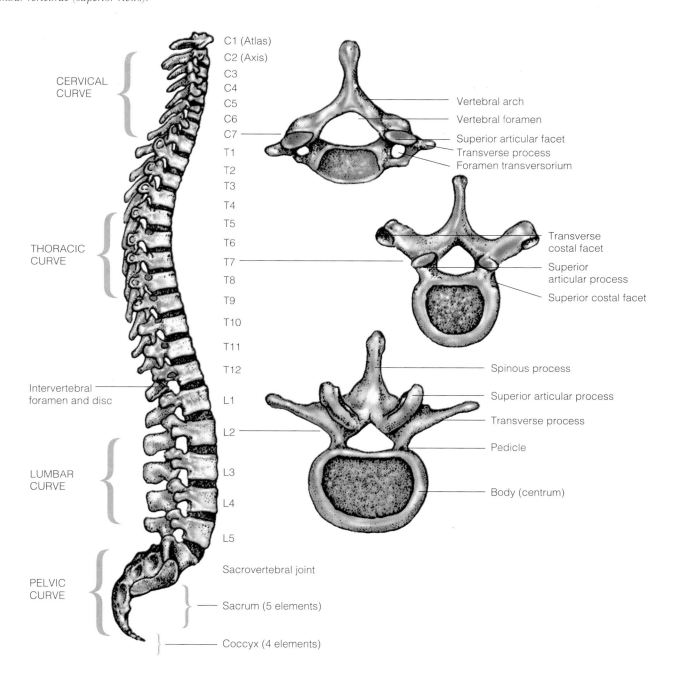

CERVICAL CURVE

THORACIC CURVE

Intervertebral foramen and disc

LUMBAR CURVE

PELVIC CURVE

C1 (Atlas)
C2 (Axis)
C3
C4
C5
C6
C7
T1
T2
T3
T4
T5
T6
T7
T8
T9
T10
T11
T12
L1
L2
L3
L4
L5
Sacrovertebral joint
Sacrum (5 elements)
Coccyx (4 elements)

Vertebral arch
Vertebral foramen
Superior articular facet
Transverse process
Foramen transversorium

Transverse costal facet
Superior articular process
Superior costal facet

Spinous process
Superior articular process
Transverse process
Pedicle
Body (centrum)

FIGURE A–6
Pelvic girdles.

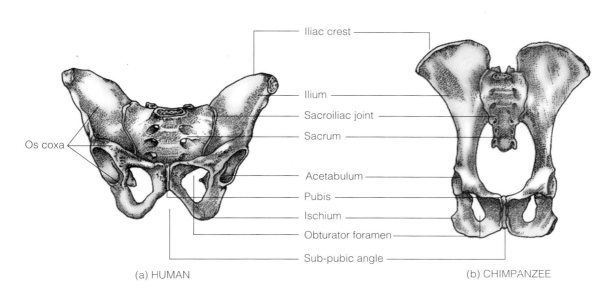

Iliac crest

Ilium

Sacroiliac joint

Sacrum

Os coxa

Acetabulum

Pubis

Ischium

Obturator foramen

Sub-pubic angle

(a) HUMAN   (b) CHIMPANZEE

FIGURE A–7
Hand anatomy.

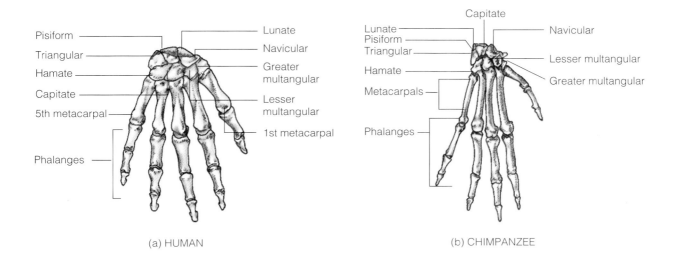

Pisiform   Lunate
Triangular   Navicular
Hamate   Greater
                            multangular
Capitate   Lesser
5th metacarpal   multangular
                            1st metacarpal
Phalanges

(a) HUMAN

Capitate
Lunate   Navicular
Pisiform
Triangular   Lesser multangular
Hamate   Greater multangular
Metacarpals

Phalanges

(b) CHIMPANZEE

FIGURE A–8

Foot (pedal) anatomy.

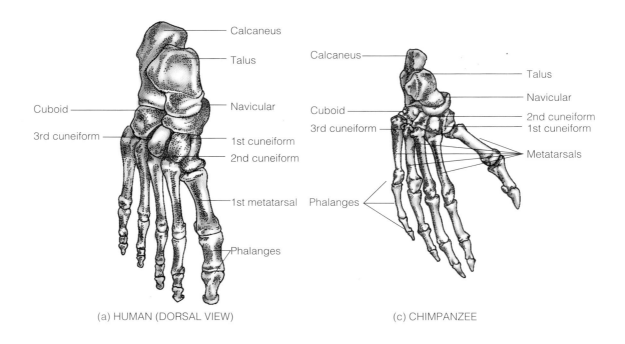

Calcaneus

Talus

Navicular

Cuboid

3rd cuneiform

1st cuneiform

2nd cuneiform

1st metatarsal

Phalanges

(a) HUMAN (DORSAL VIEW)

Calcaneus

Cuboid

3rd cuneiform

Talus

Navicular

2nd cuneiform

1st cuneiform

Metatarsals

Phalanges

(c) CHIMPANZEE

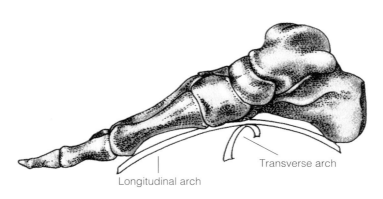

Longitudinal arch

Transverse arch

(b) HUMAN (MEDIAL VIEW)

MAJOR FOSSIL
HOMINID SIRES

WORLD POLITICAL MAP

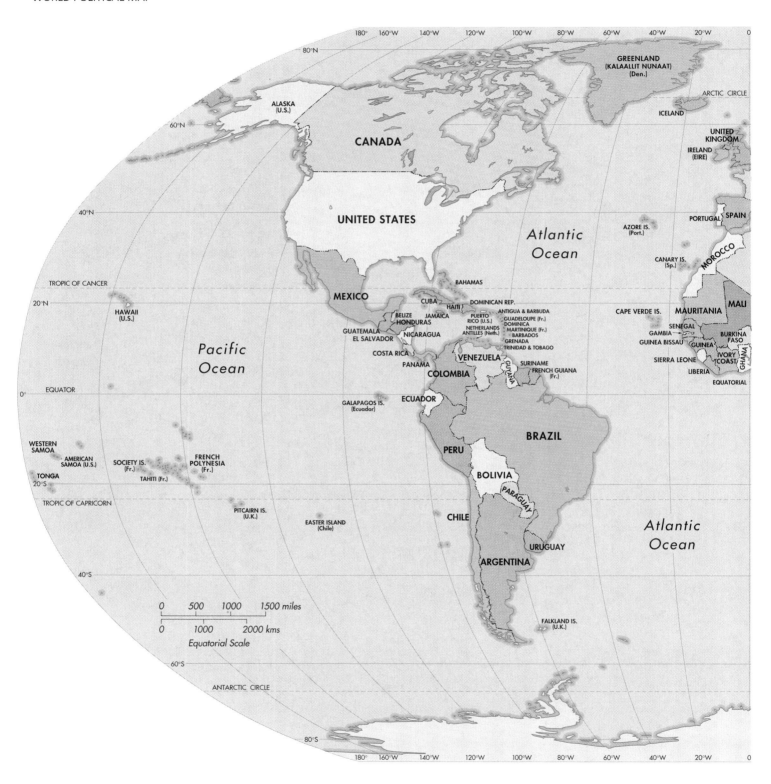

ARCTIC CIRCLE

GREENLAND
(KALAALLIT NUNAAT)
(Den.)

ICELAND

UNITED
KINGDOM

IRELAND
(EIRE)

ALASKA
(U.S.)

CANADA

PORTUGAL SPAIN

AZORE IS.
(Port.)

MOROCCO

UNITED STATES

Atlantic
Ocean

CANARY IS.
(Sp.)

TROPIC OF CANCER

MAURITANIA MALI

CAPE VERDE IS.

MEXICO

CUBA
HAITI
DOMINICAN REP.

BAHAMAS

HAWAII
(U.S.)

BELIZE
HONDURAS

JAMAICA

ANTIGUA & BARBUDA
GUADELOUPE (Fr.)
DOMINICA
MARTINIQUE (Fr.)
BARBADOS

SENEGAL
GAMBIA
GUINEA BISSAU

BURKINA
FASO

GUINEA

PUERTO
RICO (U.S.)

Pacific
Ocean

GUATEMALA
EL SALVADOR

NICARAGUA

NETHERLANDS
ANTILLES (Neth.)

GRENADA
TRINIDAD & TOBAGO

SIERRA LEONE

IVORY
(COAST)

GHANA

COSTA RICA

LIBERIA

VENEZUELA

PANAMA

GALAPAGOS IS.
(Ecuador)

COLOMBIA

ECUADOR

GUYANA

SURINAME
FRENCH GUIANA
(Fr.)

EQUATORIAL

EQUATOR

WESTERN
SAMOA

AMERICAN
SAMOA (U.S.)

TONGA

SOCIETY IS.
(Fr.)

TAHITI (Fr.)

FRENCH
POLYNESIA
(Fr.)

PERU

BRAZIL

BOLIVIA

PARAGUAY

TROPIC OF CAPRICORN

PITCAIRN IS.
(U.K.)

EASTER ISLAND
(Chile)

CHILE

URUGUAY

Atlantic
Ocean

0   500   1000   1500 miles

ARGENTINA

0   1000   2000 kms

Equatorial Scale

FALKLAND IS.
(U.K.)

ANTARCTIC CIRCLE

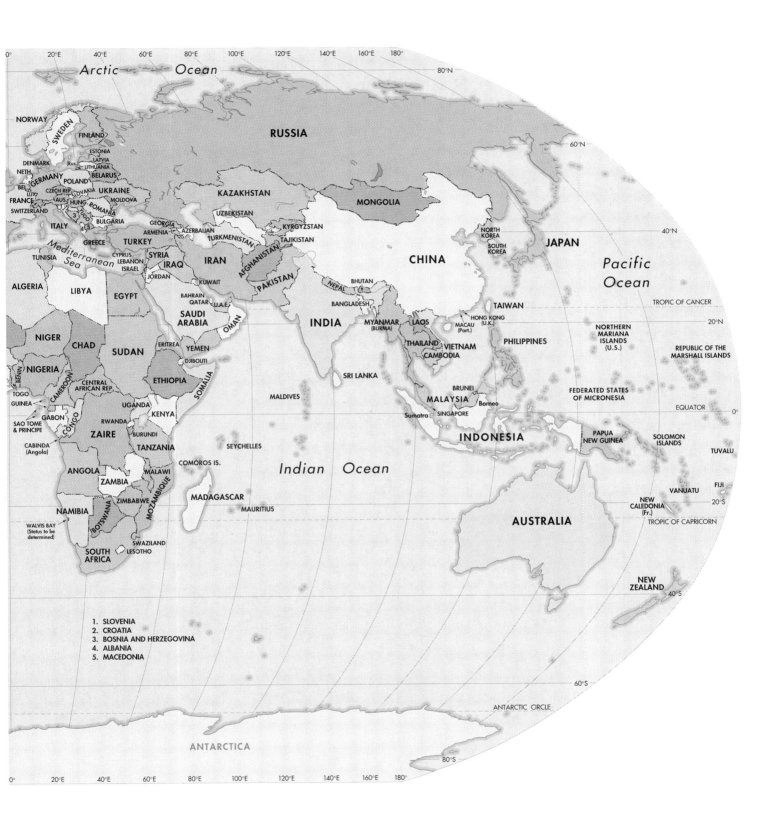

1. SLOVENIA
2. CROATIA
3. BOSNIA AND HERZEGOVINA
4. ALBANIA
5. MACEDONIA

Glossary

Acclimatization Physiological response to changes in the environment that occurs during an individual's lifetime. Such responses may be short-term. The capacity for acclimatization may typify an entire population or species. This capacity is under genetic influence and thus is subject to evolutionary factors such as natural selection.

Acheulian (ash´-oo-lay-en) Pertaining to a stone tool industry of the Lower and Middle Pleistocene characterized by a large proportion of bifacial tools (flaked on both sides). Acheulian tool kits are very common in Africa, Southwest Asia, and western Europe, but are nearly absent elsewhere. (Also spelled "Acheulean.")

Adaptation Functional response of organisms or populations to the environment. Adaptation results from evolutionary change (specifically, as a result of natural selection).

Adaptive niche The entire way of life of an organism: where it lives, what it eats, how it gets food, etc. (see also, Ecological Niche).

Adaptive radiation The relatively rapid expansion and diversification of an evolving group of organisms as they adapt to new niches.

Adolescent growth spurt The period during adolescence in which well-nourished teens typically increase in stature at greater rates than at other points in the life cycle.

Affiliative Pertaining to amicable associations between individuals. Affiliative behaviors, such as grooming, reinforce social bonds and promote group cohesion.

Allele frequency The proportion of one allele among all the alleles that occur at a given locus in a population.

Alleles Alternate forms of a gene. Alleles occur at the same locus on homologous chromosomes and thus govern the same trait. However, because they are different, their action may result in different expressions of that trait. The term is often used synonymously with *gene*.

Allometry Also called "scaling," the differential proportion among various anatomical structures. For example, the relative size of the brain changes during the development of an individual. Moreover, scaling effects must also be considered when comparing species.

Alloparenting A common behavior in many primate species whereby individuals other than the parent(s) hold, carry, and in general interact with infants.

Amino acids Small molecules that are the components of proteins.

Analogies Similarities between organisms based strictly on common function with no assumed common evolutionary descent.

Anatomically modern *H. sapiens* All modern humans and some fossil forms, perhaps dating as early as 200,000 y.a.; defined by a set of derived characteristics, including cranial architecture and lack of skeletal robusticity; usually classified at the subspecies level as *Homo sapiens sapiens*.

Antigens Large molecules found on the surface of cells. Several different loci governing antigens on red and white blood cells are known. (Foreign antigens provoke an immune response in individuals.)

Anthropoids Members of a suborder of Primates, the *Anthropoidea* (pronounced "an-throw-poid´-ee-uh"). Traditionally, the suborder includes monkeys, apes, and humans.

Anthropology The field of inquiry that studies human culture and evolutionary aspects of human biology; includes cultural anthropology, archeology, linguistics, and physical anthropology.

Anthropometry Measurement of human body parts. When osteologists measure skeletal elements, the term *osteometry* is often used.

Apidium (a-pid´-ee-um) An Oligocene anthropoid.

Arboreal   Tree-living; adapted to life in the trees.

Arboreal hypothesis   The traditional view that primate characteristics can be explained as a consequence of primate diversification into arboreal habitats.

Archaic *H. sapiens*   Earlier forms of *Homo sapiens* (including Neandertals) from the Old World that differ from *H. erectus* but lack the full set of characteristics diagnostic of modern *H. sapiens*.

Artifacts   Objects or materials made or modified for use by hominids. The earliest artifacts tend to be tools made of stone or, occasionally, bone.

Association   What an archeological trace is found with.

Aurignacian   Pertaining to an Upper Paleolithic stone tool industry in Europe beginning about 40,000 y.a.

Australopithecine (os-tra-loh-pith´-e-seen)   The colloquial name for members of the genus *Australopithecus*. The term was first used as a subfamily designation, but is now most commonly used informally.

Australopithecus   An early hominid genus, known from the Plio-Pleistocene of Africa, characterized by bipedal locomotion, a relatively small brain, and large back teeth.

Autonomic   Pertaining to physiological responses not under voluntary control. An example in chimpanzees would be the erection of body hair during excitement. An example in humans is blushing. Both convey information regarding emotional states, but neither is a deliberate behavior and communication is not intended.

Autosomes   All chromosomes except the sex chromosomes.

Balanced polymorphism   The maintenance of two or more alleles in a population due to the selective advantage of the heterozygote.

Beriberi   Disease resulting from a dietary deficiency of thiamine (vitamin B$_1$). Symptoms include nerve damage and cardiovascular problems.

Binocular vision   Vision characterized by overlapping visual fields provided by forward-facing eyes; essential to depth perception.

Binomial nomenclature (*Binomial* means "two names")   In taxonomy, the convention established by Carolus Linnaeus whereby genus and species names are used to refer to species. For example, *Homo sapiens* refers to human beings.

Biocultural evolution   The mutual, interactive evolution of human biological structure and human culture. The concept that biology makes culture possible and that developing culture further influences the direction of biological evolution; a basic concept in understanding the unique components of human evolution.

Biological determinism   The concept that phenomena, including various aspects of behavior (e.g., intelligence, values, morals) are governed by biological (genetic) factors; the inaccurate association of various behavioral attributes with certain biological traits, such as skin color.

Biostratigraphy   Dating method based on evolutionary changes within an evolving lineage.

Bipedally   On two feet. Walking habitually on two legs is the single most distinctive feature of the Hominidae.

Brachiation   A form of suspensory locomotion in which the support is alternated from one forelimb to the other.

Brachycephalic   Having a broad head in which the width measures more than 80 percent of the length.

Breeding isolates   Populations that are clearly isolated geographically and/or socially from other breeding groups.

Burins   Small, chisel-like tools (with a pointed end) thought to have been used to engrave bone, antler, ivory, or wood.

Callitrichidae (kal-eh-trick´-eh-dee)   Family of New World monkeys that includes marmosets and tamarins.

Catarrhine   The group (infraorder) comprising all Old World anthropoids, living and extinct.

Catastrophism   The view that the earth's geological landscape is the result of violent cataclysmic events. This view was promoted by Cuvier, especially in opposition to Lamarck.

Catch-up period   A period of time during which a child who has experienced delayed growth because of malnutrition, undernutrition, or disease can increase in height to the point of his or her genetic potential.

Cebidae (see´-bid-ee)   Family of New World monkeys that includes cebus monkeys, howler monkeys, and squirrel monkeys.

Centromere   The constricted portion of a chromosome. After replication, the two strands of a double-stranded chromosome are joined at the centromere.

Cercopithecidae (serk-oh-pith´-eh-sid-ee)   Family that includes all Old World monkeys.

Cercopithecines (serk-oh-pith´-eh-seens)   The subfamily of Old World monkeys that includes baboons, macaques, and guenons.

Chatelperronian   Pertaining to an Upper Paleolithic tool industry containing blade tools found in France and Spain and associated with Neandertals.

Chordata (Chordates)   The phylum of the animal kingdom that includes vertebrates.

Chromatin   The loose, diffuse form of DNA seen during interphase. When condensed, chromatin forms into chromosomes.

Chromosomes   Discrete structures composed of DNA and protein found only in the nuclei of cells. Chromosomes are only visible under magnification during certain phases of cell division.

Chronometric (*chrono*, meaning "time," and *metric*, meaning "measure")   A dating technique that gives an estimate in actual numbers of years.

Cladistics The approach to taxonomy that groups species (as well as other levels of classification) on the basis of shared derived characteristics. In this way, organisms are classified solely on the basis of presumed closeness of evolutionary relationship.

Classification In biology, the ordering of organisms into categories, such as phyla, orders, and families, to show evolutionary relationship.

Cline A gradient of genotypes (usually measured as allele frequencies) over geographical space; more exactly, the depiction of allele distribution produced by connecting points of equal frequency (as on a temperature map).

Codominance The expression of two alleles in heterozygotes. In this situation, neither allele is dominant or recessive, so that both influence the phenotype.

Codons The triplets of messenger RNA bases that refer to a specific amino acid during protein synthesis.

Colobines (kole´-uh-beans) The subfamily of Old World monkeys that includes the African colobus monkeys and Asian langurs.

Communication Any act that conveys information, in the form of a message, to another individual. Frequently, the result of communication is a change in the behavior of the recipient. Communication may not be deliberate but may be the result of involuntary processes or a secondary consequence of an intentional action.

Complementary Referring to the fact that DNA bases form base pairs in a precise manner. For example, adenine can bond only to thymine. These two bases thus are *complementary* because one requires the other to form a complete DNA base pair.

Conspecifics Members of the same species.

Context The environmental setting where an archeological trace is found. *Primary* context is the setting in which the archeological trace was originally deposited. A *secondary* context is one to which it has been moved (e.g., by the action of a stream).

Continental drift The movement of continents on sliding plates of the earth's surface. As a result, the position of large landmasses has shifted dramatically during earth's history.

Continuum A set of relationships in which all components fall along a single integrated spectrum. All life reflects a single *biological* continuum.

Core area The portion of a home range containing the highest concentration and most reliable supplies of food and water. The core area is frequently the area that will be defended.

Cretinism Mental and growth retardation in infants resulting from iodine deficiency in the mother during pregnancy.

Culture All aspects of human adaptation, including technology, traditions, language, and social roles. Culture is learned and transmitted from one generation to the next by nonbiological means.

Cusps The elevated portions (bumps) on the chewing surfaces of premolar and molar teeth.

Cytoplasm The portion of the cell contained within the cell membrane, excluding the nucleus. The cytoplasm consists of a semifluid material and contains numerous structures involved with cell function.

Deoxyribonucleic acid (DNA) The double-stranded molecule that contains the genetic code. DNA is a main component of chromosomes.

Derived Relating to a character state that is modified from the ancestral condition and reflects a more specific evolutionary line and thus is more informative of precise evolutionary relationships.

Development Differentiation of cells into different types of tissues and their maturation.

Diploid Referring to the full complement of chromosomes in a somatic cell—two of each pair.

Displays Sequences of repetitious behaviors that serve to communicate emotional states. Nonhuman primate displays are most frequently associated with reproductive or agonistic behavior.

Distal The end of a bone that is farthest from the point at which the bone attaches to the body. For example, the elbow is at the distal end of the humerus.

Diurnal Active during the day.

Dolichocephalic Having a long, narrow head in which the width measures less than 75 percent of the length.

Dominance hierarchies Systems of social organization wherein individuals within a group are ranked relative to one another. Higher-ranking individuals have greater access to preferred food items and mating partners than lower-ranking individuals. Dominance hierarchies are frequently referred to as "pecking orders."

Dominant Describing a trait governed by an allele that can be expressed in the presence of another, different allele (i.e., in heterozygotes). Dominant alleles prevent the expression of recessive alleles in heterozygotes.

Ecological Pertaining to the relationship between organisms and all aspects of their environment.

Ecological niches The positions of species within their physical and biological environments, together making up the *ecosystem*. A species' ecological niche is defined by such components as diet, terrain, vegetation, type of predators, relationships with other species, and activity patterns, and each niche is unique to a given species.

Encephalization The proportional size of the brain relative to some other measure, usually some estimate of overall body size. More precisely, the term refers to increases in brain size beyond that which would be expected given the body size of a particular species.

Endemic   Continuously present in a population. In regard to disease, refers to populations in which there will always be some infected individuals.

Endocast   A solid (in this case, rock) impression of the inside of the skull, showing the size, shape, and some details of the surface of the brain.

Endogamy   Mating with individuals from the same group.

Endothermic (*endo*, meaning "within" or "internal")   Able to maintain internal body temperature through the production of energy by means of metabolic processes within cells; characteristic feature of mammals, birds, and probably some dinosaurs.

Enzymes   Specialized proteins that initiate and direct chemical reactions in the body.

Epochs   Categories of the geological timescale; subdivisions of periods. In the Cenozoic, epochs include Paleocene, Eocene, Oligocene, Miocene, Pliocene (from the Tertiary), and the Pleistocene and Holocene (from the Quaternary).

Essential amino acids   The eight (nine for infants) amino acids that must be ingested by humans for normal growth and body maintenance; includes tryptophan, leucine, lysine, methionine, phenylalanine, isoleucine, valine, and threonine (histidine for infants).

Estrus (ess´-truss)   Period of sexual receptivity in female mammals (except humans) correlated with ovulation. When used as an adjective, the word is spelled "estrous."

Ethnocentric   Viewing other cultures from the inherently biased perspective of one's own culture. Ethnocentrism often results in cultures being seen as inferior to one's own.

Ethnographies   Detailed descriptive studies of human societies. In cultural anthropology, an ethnography is traditionally the study of a non-Western society.

Eugenics   The philosophy of "race improvement" through forced sterilization of members of some groups and encouraged reproduction among others; an overly simplified, often racist view that is now discredited.

Evolution   A change in the genetic structure of a population. The term is also frequently used to refer to the appearance of a new species.

Evolutionary trends   Overall characteristics of an evolving lineage, such as the primates. Such trends are useful in helping to categorize the lineage as compared to other lineages (i.e., other placental mammals).

Exogamous   Referring to a mating system whereby individuals find mating partners from outside their natal group. When applied to humans, the term may refer to marriage rules that dictate marriage with partners from another social grouping (e.g., village, kinship group, or clan).

Exogamy   Mating with individuals from other groups.

Fayum (fah-yoom´)   A locality in Egypt yielding very abundant fossil primate finds from the late Eocene and early Oligocene (circa 36–33 m.y.a.).

Fertility   Production of offspring; distinguished from *fecundity*, which is the ability to produce children. For example, a woman in her early 20s is probably fecund, but she is not actually fertile unless she has had children.

Fitness   Pertaining to natural selection, a measure of *relative* reproductive success of individuals. Fitness can be measured by an individual's genetic contribution to the next generation compared to that of others.

Fixity of species   The notion that species, once created, can never change; an idea diametrically opposed to theories of biological evolution.

Flexed   The position of the body in a bent orientation, with the arms and legs drawn up to the chest.

Foramen magnum   The opening at the base of the skull through which the spinal cord passes as it enters the body to descend through the vertebral column. In quadrupeds, it is located more to the rear of the skull, while in bipeds, it is located further beneath the skull.

Forensic anthropology   An applied anthropological approach dealing with matters of law. Forensic anthropologists use their expertise to assist coroners and others in the analysis and interpretation of human remains.

Founder effect   Also called the *Sewall Wright effect*, a type of genetic drift in which allele frequencies are altered in small populations that are taken from, or are remnants of, larger populations.

Free-ranging   Pertaining to noncaptive animals living in their natural habitat, largely free from constraints imposed by humans.

Frugivorous (fru-give´-or-us)   Having a diet composed primarily of fruit.

Gametes   Reproductive cells (eggs and sperm in animals) developed from precursor cells in ovaries and testes.

Gene   A sequence of DNA bases that specifies the order of amino acids in an entire protein or, in some cases, a portion of a protein. A gene may be made up of hundreds or thousands of DNA bases.

Gene flow   Movement of genes between populations.

Gene pool   The total complement of genes shared by reproductive members of a population.

Genetic drift   Evolutionary changes—that is, changes in allele frequencies—produced by random factors. Genetic drift is a result of small population size.

Genetics   The study of gene structure and action and the patterns of inheritance of traits from parent to offspring. Genetic mechanisms are the underlying foundation for evolutionary change.

Genome The full genetic complement of an individual (or of a species). In humans, it is estimated that each individual possesses approximately 3 billion nucleotides in his or her nuclear DNA.

Genotype The genetic makeup of an individual. *Genotype* can refer to an organism's entire genetic makeup or to the alleles at a particular locus.

Geological timescale The organization of earth history into eras, periods, and epochs commonly used by geologists and paleoanthropologists.

Goiter Enlargement of the thyroid gland resulting from a dietary deficiency of iodine.

Grooming Picking through fur to remove dirt, parasites, and other materials that may be present. Social grooming is common among primates and reinforces social relationships.

Growth Increase in mass or number of cells.

Hadar (had´-ar) A very productive fossil hominid site in northeastern Ethiopia, dated 3.9–3.0 m.y.a.

Haploid Referring to a half set of chromosomes, one member of each pair. Haploid sets are found in gametes.

Hardy-Weinberg theory of genetic equilibrium The mathematical relationship expressing—under ideal conditions—the predicted distribution of genes in populations; the central theorem of population genetics.

Hemizygous (*hemi* means "half") Having only one member of a pair of alleles. Because males have only one X chromosome, all their X-linked alleles are hemizygous. All recessive alleles on a male's X chromosome are expressed in the phenotype.

Heterodont Having different kinds of teeth; characteristic of mammals, whose teeth consist of incisors, canines, premolars, and molars.

Heterozygous Having different alleles at the same locus on members of a pair of homologous chromosomes.

Home range The area exploited by an animal or social group. Usually given for one year—or for the entire lifetime—of an animal.

Homeostasis A condition of balance, or stability, within a biological system, maintained by the interaction of physiological mechanisms that compensate for changes (both external and internal).

Hominidae The taxonomic family to which humans belong; also includes other, now extinct, bipedal relatives.

Hominids Members of the family Hominidae.

Hominoidea The formal designation for the superfamily of anthropoids that includes apes and humans.

Hominoids Members of the superfamily Hominoidea. The group includes apes and humans.

Homo habilis (hab´-ah-liss) A species of early *Homo*, well known in East Africa, but also perhaps from other regions.

Homologies Similarities between organisms based on descent from a common ancestor.

Homologous Referring to members of chromosome pairs. Homologous chromosomes carry loci that govern the same traits. During meiosis, homologous chromosomes pair and exchange segments of DNA. They are alike with regard to size, position of centromere, and banding pattern.

Homoplasy (*homo*, meaning "same," and *plasy*, meaning "growth") The separate evolutionary development of similar characteristics in different groups of organisms.

Homozygous Having the same allele at the same locus on both members of a pair of homologous chromosomes.

Hormones Substances (usually proteins) that are produced by specialized cells and that travel to other parts of the body, where they influence chemical reactions and regulate various cellular functions.

Human Genome Project A multinational effort designed to map (and ultimately sequence) the complete genetic complement of *Homo sapiens*.

Hybrids Offspring of parents who are in some ways genetically dissimilar. The term can also refer to heterozygotes.

Hylobatidea (high-lo-baht´-id-ee) Family of small-bodied apes, including gibbons and siamangs.

Hypoxia Lack of oxygen. Hypoxia can refer to reduced amounts of available oxygen in the atmosphere (due to lowered barometric pressure) or to insufficient amounts of oxygen in the body.

Inbreeding A type of nonrandom mating in which relatives mate more often than predicted under random mating conditions.

Inclusive fitness The total contribution of an individual's genes to the next generation, including those genes shared by close relatives.

Intelligence Mental capacity; ability to learn, reason, or comprehend and interpret information, facts, relationships, meanings, etc.; the capacity to solve problems, whether through the application of previously acquired knowledge or through insight.

Interphase The portion of a cell's cycle during which metabolic processes and other cellular activities occur. Chromosomes are not visible as discrete structures at this time. DNA replication occurs during interphase.

Interspecific Between two or more species.

Intraspecific Within one species.

Ischial callosities Patches of tough, hard skin on the buttocks of Old World monkeys and chimpanzees.

Karyotype The chromosomal complement of an individual or that which is typical for a species. Usually displayed in a photomicrograph, the chromosomes are arranged in pairs and according to size and position of the centromere.

K-selected   Pertaining to an adaptive strategy whereby individuals produce relatively few offspring, in whom they invest increased parental care. Although only a few infants are born, chances of survival are increased for each individual because of parental investments in time and energy. Examples of nonprimate K-selected species are birds and wild canids (e.g., wolves, coyotes, and wild dogs).

Kromdraai (kromm´-dry)   A fossil hominid site in South Africa.

Lactation   The production of milk in mammals.

Lactose intolerance   The inability to digest fresh milk products; caused by the discontinued production of *lactase*, the enzyme that breaks down lactose, or milk sugar.

Laetoli (lye´-toll-ee)   A fossil hominid site in East Africa.

Life history   Basic components of an animal's development and physiology, viewed from an evolutionary perspective. Such key components include body size, proportional brain size, metabolism, and reproduction.

Locus (*pl.,* **loci**) (pronounced, lo´-kus and lo-sigh´)   The position on a chromosome where a given gene occurs. The term is used interchangeably with *gene,* and when used in this manner, it refers to the DNA segment that codes for the production of a polypeptide chain.

Macaques (muh-kaks´)   Group of Old World monkeys made up of several species, including the rhesus monkey.

Macroevolution   Changes produced only after many generations, such as the appearance of a new species.

Magdalenian   Pertaining to the final phase (stone tool industry) of the Upper Paleolithic in Europe.

Makapansgat (mak-ah-pans´-gat)   A fossil hominid site in South Africa.

Malnutrition   A diet insufficient in quality (i.e., lacking some essential component) to support normal health.

Material culture   The physical manifestations of human activities; includes tools, art, and structures. As the most durable aspects of culture, material remains make up the majority of archeological evidence of past societies.

Meiosis   Cell division in specialized cells in ovaries and testes. Meiosis involves two divisions and results in four daughter cells, each containing only half the original number of chromosomes. These cells can develop into gametes.

Mendelian traits   Characteristics that are influenced by alleles at only one genetic locus. Examples include many blood types, such as ABO, and many genetic disorders, including sickle-cell anemia and Tay-Sachs disease.

Messenger RNA (mRNA)   A form of RNA that is assembled on one sequence (one strand) of DNA bases. It carries the DNA code to the ribosome during protein synthesis.

Metazoa   Multicellular animals; a major division of the animal kingdom.

Microevolution   Small changes occurring within species, such as a change in allele frequencies.

Mitochondria (*sing.,* mitochondrion) Organelles that are found in the cytoplasm of cells and that are responsible for producing energy for cellular functions.

Mitochondrial DNA (mtDNA)   DNA found in the mitochondria (structures found within the cytoplasm of the cell) and inherited through the maternal line.

Mitosis   Simple cell division; the process by which somatic cells divide to produce two identical daughter cells.

Molecules   Structures made up of two or more atoms. Molecules can combine with other molecules to form more complex structures.

Monogenism   The theory that all human "races" are descended from one pair (Adam and Eve), but they differ from one another because they have occupied different habitats. This concept was an attempt to explain phenotypic variation between populations, but did not imply evolutionary change.

Morphology   The form (shape, size) of anatomical structures; can also refer to the entire organism.

Mosaic evolution   Rates of evolution in one functional system vary from those in other systems. For example, in hominid evolution, the dental system, locomotor system, and neurological system (especially the brain) all evolved at markedly different rates.

Motor cortex   The *cortex* of the brain, the outer layer, is composed of nerve cells or neurons. The *motor cortex* is that portion pertaining to outgoing signals involved in muscle use.

Mousterian   Pertaining to the stone tool industry associated with Neandertals and some modern *H. sapiens* groups. This industry is characterized by a larger proportion of flake tools than is found in Acheulian tool kits. Also called Middle Paleolithic.

Mutation   A change in DNA. Technically, mutation refers to changes in DNA bases as well as changes in chromosome number and/or structure.

Nariokotome (nar´-ee-oh-ko´-tow-may) A fossil hominid site in East Africa containing the mostly complete skeleton of an adolescent *H. erectus.*

Natural selection   The mechanism of evolutionary change first articulated by Charles Darwin. Refers to genetic change or changes in the frequencies of certain traits in populations due to differential reproductive success between individuals.

Negative assortative mating   A type of nonrandom mating in which individuals of unlike phenotype mate more often than predicted under random mating conditions.

Nocturnal   Active during the night.

Nondisjunction   The failure of homologous chromosomes or chromosome strands to separate during cell division.

Nonrandom mating   Patterns of mating in a population in which individuals choose mates preferentially.

Nucleotides   Basic units of the DNA molecule, composed of a sugar, a phosphate, and one of four DNA bases.

Nucleus A structure (organelle) found in all eukaryotic cells. The nucleus contains chromosomes (nuclear DNA).

Ossification Process by which cartilage cells are broken down and replaced by bone cells.

Osteodontokeratic (*osteo*, meaning "bone," *donto*, meaning "*tooth*," and *keratic*, meaning "horn")

Osteology The study of skeletons. Human osteology focuses on the interpretation of the skeletal remains of past groups. The same techniques are used in paleoanthropology to study early hominids.

Paleoanthropology The interdisciplinary approach to the study of earlier hominids—their chronology, physical structure, archeological remains, habitats, etc.

Paleoecology (*paleo*, meaning "old," and *ecology*, meaning "environmental setting") The study of ancient environments.

Paleomagnetism Dating method based on shifting magnetic poles.

Paleopathology The branch of osteology that studies the traces of disease and injury in human skeletal (or, occasionally, mummified) remains.

Paleospecies Groups of organisms recognized in the fossil record which are classified within the same species. Their temporal range may extend over a considerable period.

Pandemic An extensive outbreak of disease affecting large numbers of people over a wide area; potentially, a worldwide phenomenon.

Paradigm A cognitive construct or framework within which we explain phenomena. Paradigms shape our world view. They can change as a result of technological and intellectual innovation.

Parallel evolution The independent evolution of similarities in structure in distantly related (or nonrelated) lineages. Morphological similarities result from adaptation to similar selective pressures.

Pathogens Substances or microorganisms, such as bacteria or viruses, that cause disease.

Pedigree chart A diagram showing family relationships in order to trace the hereditary pattern of particular genetic (usually Mendelian) traits.

Pellegra Disease resulting from a dietary deficiency of niacin (vitamin B_3). Symptoms include dermatitis, diarrhea, dementia, and death (the "four Ds").

Phenotypes The observable or detectable physical characteristics of an organism; the detectable expressions of the genotype.

Phenotypic ratio The proportion of one phenotype to other phenotypes in a group of organisms. For example, Mendel observed that there were approximately three tall plants for every short plant in the F_2 generation. This is expressed as a phenotypic ratio of 3:1.

Philopatric Remaining in one's natal group or home range as an adult. In most species, members of one sex disperse from their natal group as young adults, and members of the philopatric sex remain. In the majority of nonhuman primate species, the philopatric sex is female.

Phylogeny A schematic representation showing ancestor-descendant relationships, usually in a chronological framework.

Plasticity The capacity to change; in a physiological context, the ability of systems or organisms to make alterations in order to respond to differing conditions.

Pleistocene The epoch of the Cenozoic from 1.8 m.y.a. until 10,000 y.a. Frequently referred to as the Ice Age, this epoch is associated with continental glaciations in northern latitudes.

Point mutation The change in a single base of a DNA sequence.

Polar body A nonviable product of female meiosis, as it contains minimal cytoplasm.

Polyandry A mating system wherein a female continuously associates with more than one male (usually two or three) with whom she mates. Among nonhuman primates, this type of pattern is seen only in marmosets and tamarins.

Polygenic Referring to traits that are influenced by genes at two or more loci. Examples of such traits are stature, skin color, and eye color. Many polygenic traits are also influenced by environmental factors.

Polygenism A theory, opposed to monogenism, that states that human "races" are not all descended from Adam and Eve. Instead, there had been several original human pairs, each giving rise to a different racial group. Thus, human "races" were considered to be separate species.

Polymorphism A genetic trait governed by a locus with more than one allele in appreciable frequency. That is, the locus has two or more alleles, each with a frequency of at least 1 percent.

Polypeptide chain A sequence of amino acids that may act alone or in combination as a functional protein.

Polytypic Referring to species composed of populations that differ with regard to the expression of one or more traits.

Pongidae (ponj´-id-ee) The family of great apes.

Population Within a species, a community of individuals where mates are usually found.

Positive assortative mating A type of nonrandom mating in which individuals of like phenotype mate more often than predicted under random mating conditions.

Prehensility Grasping, as by the hands and feet of primates.

Primates Members of the mammalian order Primates (pronounced "pry-may´-tees"), which includes prosimians, monkeys, apes, and humans. When the term is used colloquially, it is pronounced "pry´-mates."

Primatologists Scientists who study the evolution, anatomy, and behavior of nonhuman primates. Those who study primate behavior in non-captive animals are usually trained as anthropologists.

Primatology The study of the biology and behavior of nonhuman primates (prosimians, monkeys, and apes).

Primitive Relating to a character state that reflects an ancestral condition and thus not diagnostic of those derived lineages usually branching later.

Principle of independent assortment The distribution of one pair of alleles into gametes does not influence the distribution of another pair. The genes controlling different traits are inherited independently of one another.

Principle of segregation Genes (alleles) occur in pairs (because chromosomes occur in pairs). During gamete production, the members of each pair of alleles separate, so that each gamete contains one member of each pair. During fertilization, the full number of chromosomes is restored, and members of gene or allele pairs are reunited.

Prosimians Members of a suborder of Primates, the *Prosimii* (pronounced "pro-sim´-ee-eye"). Traditionally, the suborder includes lemurs, lorises, and tarsiers.

Protein synthesis The assembly of chains of amino acids into functional protein molecules. The process is directed by DNA.

Proteins Three-dimensional molecules that serve a wide variety of functions through their ability to bind to other molecules.

Protohominids The earliest members of the hominid lineage, as yet basically unrepresented in the fossil record; thus, their structure and behavior are reconstructed hypothetically.

Provenience In archeology, the specific location of a discovery, including its geological context.

Proximal The end of a bone that is closest to the point at which the bone attaches to the body. For example, the head of the humerus is on the proximal end.

Punctuated equilibrium The concept that evolutionary change proceeds through long periods of stasis, punctuated by rapid periods of change.

Quadrupedal Using all four limbs to support the body during locomotion. The basic mammalian (and primate) form of locomotion.

r-selected Pertaining to an adaptive strategy that emphasizes relatively large numbers of offspring and reduced parental care (compared to K-selected species). (*K-selection* and *r-selection* are relative terms; e.g., mice are r-selected compared to primates but K-selected compared to insects and many fish species.)

Racial In biology, pertaining to populations of a species that differ from other populations of the same species with regard to some aspects of outwardly expressed phenotype. Such phenotypic variation within a species is usually associated with differences in geographical location.

Random assortment The random distribution of chromosomes to daughter cells during meiosis; along with recombination, the source of variation resulting from meiosis.

Recessive Describing a trait that is not expressed in heterozygotes; also refers to the allele that governs the trait. For a recessive allele to be expressed, there must be two copies of the allele (i.e., the individual must be homozygous).

Recombination (crossing over) The exchange of genetic material between homologous chromosomes during meiosis.

Replicate To duplicate. The DNA molecule is able to make exact copies of itself.

Reproductive strategies The complex of behavioral patterns that contributes to individual reproductive success. The behaviors need not be deliberate, and they often vary considerably between males and females.

Reproductive success The number of offspring an individual produces and rears to reproductive age. An individual's genetic contribution to the next generation, as compared to the contributions of other individuals.

Restriction fragment length polymorphisms (RFLPs) Variation among individuals in the length of DNA fragments produced by enzymes that break the DNA at specific sites.

Rhinarium (rine-air´-ee-um) The moist, hairless pad at the end of the nose seen in most mammalian species. The rhinarium enhances an animal's sense of smell.

Ribonucleic acid (RNA) A single-stranded molecule, similar in structure to DNA. The three forms of RNA are essential to protein synthesis.

Ribosomes Structures that are found in the cytoplasm and that are essential to the manufacture of proteins.

Ritualized behaviors Behaviors removed from their original context and sometimes exaggerated to convey information.

Sagittal crest Raised ridge along the midline of the cranium where the temporal muscle (used to move the jaw) is attached.

Scurvy Disease resulting from a dietary deficiency of vitamin C. It may result in anemia, poor bone growth, abnormal bleeding and bruising, and muscle pain.

Selective pressures Forces in the environment that influence reproductive success in individuals. In the example of the peppered moth, birds applied the selective pressure.

Sex chromosomes In mammals, the X and Y chromosomes.

Sexual dimorphism Differences in physical characteristics between males and females of the same species. For example, humans are slightly sexually dimorphic for body size, with males being taller, on average, than females of the same population.

Shared derived Relating to specific character states shared in common between two forms and considered the most useful for making evolutionary interpretations.

Sickle-cell anemia A severe inherited disease that results from inheriting two copies of a mutant allele. This allele results from a single base substitution at the DNA level.

Slash-and-burn agriculture A traditional land-clearing practice whereby trees and vegetation are cut and burned. In many areas, fields were abandoned after a few years and clearing occurred elsewhere.

Social structure The composition, size, and sex ratio of a group of animals. Social structures, in part, are the result of natural selection in specific habitats, and they function to guide individual interactions and social relationships.

Sociobiology The study of the relationship between behavior and natural selection. Sociobiological theory states that certain behaviors or behavioral patterns have been selected for because they increase reproductive fitness in individuals.

Socioecology The study of animals and their habitats; specifically, attempts to find patterns of relationship between the environment and social behavior.

Somatic cells Basically, all the cells in the body except those involved with reproduction.

Specialized Evolved for a particular function. The term *specialized* usually refers to a specific trait (e.g., incisor teeth), but may also refer to the entire way of life of an organism.

Speciation The process by which new species are produced from earlier ones; the most important mechanism of macroevolutionary change.

Species A group of organisms that can interbreed to produce fertile offspring. Members of one species are reproductively isolated from members of all other species (i.e., they cannot mate with them to produce fertile offspring).

Stereoscopic vision The condition whereby visual images are, to varying degrees, superimposed on one another. This provides for depth perception, or the perception of the external environment in three dimensions. Stereoscopic vision is a function of structures in the brain.

Sterkfontein (sterk´-fon-tane) A fossil hominid site in South Africa.

Stratigraphy Study of the sequential layering of deposits.

Stress In a physiological context, any factor that acts to disrupt homeostasis; more precisely, the body's response to any factor that threatens its ability to maintain homeostasis.

Swartkrans (swart´-kranz) A fossil hominid site in South Africa.

Sympatric Living in the same area; pertaining to two or more species whose habitats partly or largely overlap.

Taphonomy (*taphos:* meaning "dead") The study of how bones and other materials came to be buried in the earth and preserved as fossils. A taphonomist studies the processes of sedimentation, the action of streams, preservation properties of bone, and carnivore disturbance factors.

Taxonomy The branch of science concerned with the rules of classifying organisms on the basis of evolutionary relationships.

Tectonic movements Movements of the earth's plates that produce mountains, earthquakes, volcanoes, and rifting.

Territories Portions of an individual's or group's home range actively defended against intrusion, particularly by conspecifics.

Transmutation The change of one species to another. The term *evolution* did not assume its current meaning until the late nineteenth century.

Transfer RNA (tRNA) The type of RNA that binds to specific amino acids and transports them to the ribosome during protein synthesis.

Undernutrition A diet insufficient in quantity (calories) to support normal health.

Uniformitarianism The theory that the Earth's features are the result of long-term processes that continue to operate in the present as they did in the past. Elaborated on by Lyell, this theory opposed catastrophism and provided for immense geological time.

Upper Paleolithic Pertaining to a cultural period associated with early modern humans and distinguished by technological innovation in various stone tool industries. Best known from western Europe, similar industries are also known from central and eastern Europe and Africa.

Variation (genetic) Inherited differences between individuals; the basis of all evolutionary change.

Vasoconstriction Narrowing of blood vessels to reduce blood flow to the skin. Vasoconstriction is an involuntary response to cold and reduces heat loss at the skin's surface.

Vasodilation Expansion of blood vessels, permitting increased blood flow to the skin. Vasodilation permits warming of the skin and also facilitates radiation of warmth as a means of cooling. Vasodilation is an involuntary response to warm temperatures, various drugs, and even emotional states (blushing).

Vectors Agents that serve to transmit disease from one carrier to another. Mosquitoes are vectors for malaria, just as fleas are vectors for bubonic plague.

Vertebrates Animals with bony backbones. Includes fishes, amphibians, reptiles, birds, and mammals.

Viviparous Giving birth to live young.

World view General cultural orientation or perspective shared by members of a society.

Zhoukoudian (zhoh´-koh-dee´-en) A fossil hominid site in China.

Zygote A cell formed by the union of an egg and a sperm cell. It contains the full complement of chromosomes (in humans, 46) and has the potential of developing into an entire organism.

Bibliography

Aiello, L. C.
  1992 "Body Size and Energy Requirements." *In: The Cambridge Encyclopedia of Human Evolution,* J. Jones, R. Martin, and D. Pilbeam (eds.), Cambridge, England: Cambridge University Press, pp. 41–45.
Aitken, M. J., C. B. Stringer, and P. A. Mellars (eds.)
  1993 *The Origin of Modern Humans and the Impact of Chronometric Dating.* Princeton, N.J.: Princeton University Press.
Alland Jr., Alexander
  1971 *Human Diversity.* New York: Anchor Press/Doubleday.
Altmann, Jeanne
  1981 *Baboon Mothers and Infants.* Cambridge: Harvard University Press.
Altmann, Stuart A. and Jeanne Altmann
  1970 *Baboon Ecology.* Chicago: University of Chicago Press.
Anderson, J. Gunnar
  1934 *Children of the Yellow Earth.* New York: Macmillan.
Andrews, Peter
  1985 "Family Group Systematics and Evolution among Catarrhine Primates." *In: Ancestors: The Hard Evidence,* E. Delson (ed.), New York: Alan R. Liss, pp. 14–22.

  ———

  1992 "Evolution and Environment in Miocene Hominoids." *Nature,* **360**:641–646.
Andrews, Peter and Jens Lorenz Franzen (eds.)
  1984 *The Early Evolution of Man.* Frankfurt: Cour. Forsch.-Inst. Seckenberg.
Andrews, Peter and David Pilbeam
  1996 "The Nature of the Evidence," News and Views. *Nature,* **379**:123–124.
Ardrey, Robert
  1976 *The Hunting Hypothesis.* New York: Atheneum.

Arensburg, B., L. A. Schepartz, et al.
  1990 "A Reappraisal of the Anatomical Basis for Speech in Middle Paleolithic Hominids." *American Journal of Physical Anthropology,* **83**(2):137–146.
Arensburg, B., A. M. Tillier, et al.
  1989 "A Middle Paleolithic Human Hyoid Bone." *Nature,* **338**:758–760.
Aronson, J. L., R. C. Walter, and M. Taieb
  1983 "Correlation of Tulu Bor Tuff at Koobi Fora with the Sidi Hakoma Tuff at Hadar." *Nature,* **306**:209–210.
Arsuga, Juan-Luis et al.
  1993 "Three New Human Skulls from the Sima de los Huesos Middle Pleistocene Site in Sierra de Atapuerca, Spain." *Nature,* **362**:534–537.
Asfaw, Berhane
  1992 "New Fossil Hominids from the Ethiopian Rift Valley and the Afar." Paper presented at the Annual Meeting, American Association of Physical Anthropologists.
Asfaw, Berhane et al.
  1992 "The Earliest Acheulian from Konso-Gardula." *Nature,* **360**:732–735.

  ———

  1995 Three Seasons of Hominid Paleontology at Aramis, Ethiopia. Paper presented at Paleoanthropology Society meetings, Oakland, Ca., March 1995.
Avery, O. T., C. M. MacLeod, and M. McCarty
  1944 "Studies on the Chemical Nature of the Substances Inducing Transformation in Pneumoccal Types." *Journal of Experimental Medicine,* **79**:137–158.
Ayala, Francisco
  1995 "The Myth of Eve: Molecular Biology and Human Origins." *Science,* **270**:1930–1936.
Badrian, Alison and Noel Badrian
  1984 "Social Organization of *Pan paniscus* in the Lomako Forest, Zaire." *In: The Pygmy Chimpanzee,* Randall L. Susman (ed.), New York: Plenum Press, pp. 325–346.

Badrian, Noel and Richard K. Malenky
1984 "Feeding Ecology of *Pan paniscus* in the Lomako Forest, Zaire." *In: The Pygmy Chimpanzee*, Randall L. Susman (ed.), New York: Plenum Press, pp. 275–299.

Baker, Paul T. and Michael A. Little
1976 "The Environmental Adaptations and Perspectives." *In: Man in the Andes*, P. T. Baker and M. A. Little (eds.), Stroudsburg, Penn.: Dowden, Hutchinson, and Ross, pp. 405–428.

Barash, David
1982 *Sociobiology and Behavior.* (2nd Ed.) New York: Elsevier.

Bartholomew, C. A. and J. B. Birdsell
1953 "Ecology and the Protohominids." *American Anthropologist*, **55**:481–498.

Bartstra, Gert-Jan
1982 "*Homo erectus erectus*: The Search for Artifacts." *Current Anthropology*, **23**(3):318–320.

Bar-Yosef, Ofer
1993 "The Role of Western Asia in Modern Human Origins." *In*: M. J. Aitken et al. (eds.), q.v., pp. 132–147.

_____
1994 "The Contributions of Southwest Asia to the Study of the Origin of Modern Humans." *In: Origins of Anatomically Modern Humans*, M. H. Nitecki and D. V. Nitecki (eds.), New York: Plenum Press, pp. 23–66.

Barzun, Jacques
1965 *Race: A Study in Superstition.* New York: Harper & Row.

Bass, W. M.
1987 *Human Osteology: A Laboratory and Field Manual* (3rd Ed.). Columbia, Mo.: Missouri Archaeological Society Special Publication No. 2.

Beard, K. Christopher, Yong Shenj Tong, Mary R. Dawson, Jingwen Wang, and Xueshi Huang
1996 "Earliest Complete Dentition of an Anthropoid Primate from the Late Middle Eocene of Shanxi Province, China." *Science*, **272**:82–85.

Bearder, Simon K.
1987 "Lorises, Bushbabies and Tarsiers: Diverse Societies in Solitary Foragers." *In*: Smuts et al., q.v., pp. 11–24.

Begun, David R.
1992 "Phyletic Diversity and Locomotion in Primitive European Hominoids." *American Journal of Physical Anthropology*, 87:311–340.

_____
1994 "Relations Among the Great Apes and Humans: New Interpretations Based on the Fossil Great Ape *Dryopithecus*." *Yearbook of Physical Anthropology*, 37:11–63.

Begun, D. and A. Walker
1993 "The Endocast." *In*: A. Walker and R. E. Leakey (eds.), q.v., pp. 326–358.

Behrensmeyer, Anna K. and Andrew P. Hill
1980 *Fossils in the Making: Vertebrate Taphonomy and Paleoecology.* Chicago: University of Chicago Press.

Berger, Thomas and Erik Trinkaus
1995 "Patterns of Trauma Among the Neandertals." *Journal of Archaeological Science*, **22**:841–852.

Bernor, R. L.
1983 "Geochronology and Zoogeographic Relationships of Miocene Hominoidea." *In*: R. L. Ciochon and R. S. Corruccini (eds.), q.v., pp. 21–66.

Binford, Lewis R.
1981 *Bones. Ancient Men and Modern Myths.* New York: Academic Press.

_____
1983 *In Pursuit of the Past.* New York: Thames and Hudson.

_____
1985 "Ancestral Lifeways: The Faunal Record." AnthroQuest, **32**, Summer 1985.

Binford, Lewis R. and Chuan Kun Ho
1985 "Taphonomy at a Distance: Zhoukoudian, 'The Cave Home of Beijing Man'?" *Current Anthropology*, **26**:413–442.

Binford, Lewis R. and Nancy M. Stone
1986a "The Chinese Paleolithic: An Outsider's View." *AnthroQuest*, Fall 1986(1):14–20.

_____
1986b "Zhoukoudian: A Closer Look." *Current Anthropology*, **27**(5):453–475.

Birdsell, Joseph B.
1981 *Human Evolution.* (3rd Ed.). Boston: Houghton Mifflin.

Boas, F.
1910 "Changes in the Bodily Form of Descendants of Immigrants." *American Anthropologist*, **14**:530–562.

Boaz, N. T., F. C. Howell, and M. L. McCrossin
1982 "Faunal Age of the Usno, Shungura B and Hadar Formation, Ethiopia." *Nature*, **300**:633–635.

Bodmer, W. F. and L. L. Cavalli-Sforza
1976 *Genetics, Evolution, and Man.* San Francisco: W. H. Freeman and Company.

Boesch, Christophe and H. Boesch
1989 "Hunting Behavior of Wild Chimpanzees in the Tai National Park." *American Journal of Physical Anthropology*, **78**:547–573.

Boesch, Christophe, Paul Marchesi, Nathalie Marchesi, Barbara Fruth, and Frédéric Joulian
1994 "Is Nut Cracking in Wild Chimpanzees a Cultural Behaviour?" *Journal of Human Evolution*, **26**:325–338.

Boggess, Jane
1984 "Infant Killing and Male Reproductive Strategies in Langurs (*Presbytis entellus*)." *In*: G. Hausfater and S. B. Hrdy (eds.), q.v., pp. 280–310.

Bogin, Barry
1988 *Patterns of Human Growth.* Cambridge: Cambridge University Press.

Bongaarts, John
1980 Does Malnutrition Affect Fecundity? A Summary of Evidence. *Science*, **208**:564–569.

Bordes, François
1968   *The Old Stone Age.* New York: McGraw-Hill Book Co.
Bowler, Peter J.
1983, 1989   *Evolution: The History of an Idea.* Berkeley: University of California Press.

_____
1988   The *Non-Darwinian Evolution: Reinterpreting a Historical Myth.* Baltimore: Johns Hopkins University Press.
Brace, C. L. and Ashley Montagu
1977   *Human Evolution* (2nd Ed.). New York: Macmillan.
Brace, C. Loring, H. Nelson, and N. Korn
1979   *Atlas of Human Evolution* (2nd Ed.). New York: Holt, Rinehart & Winston.
Brain, C. K.
1970   "New Finds at the Swartkrans Australopithecine Site." *Nature,* **225**:1112–1119.

_____
1981   *The Hunters or the Hunted? An Introduction to African Cave Taphonomy.* Chicago: University of Chicago Press.
Bramblett, Claud A.
1994   *Patterns of Primate Behavior* (2nd Ed.). Prospect Heights, Ill.: Waveland Press.
Bräuer, Gunter
1984   "A Craniological Approach to the Origin of Anatomically Modern *Homo sapiens* in Africa and Implications for the Appearance of Modern Europeans." *In:* F. H. Smith and F. Spencer (eds.), q.v., pp. 327–410.

_____
1989   "The Evolution of Modern Humans: A Comparison of the African and Non-African Evidence." *In:* Mellars and Stringer (eds.), q.v.
Brock, A., P. L. McFadden, and T. C. Partridge
1977   "Preliminary Paleomagnetic Results from Makapansgat and Swartkrans." *Nature,* **266**:249–250.
Bromage, Timothy G. and Christopher Dean
1985   "Re-evaluation of the Age at Death of Immature Fossil Hominids." *Nature,* **317**:525–527.
Brooks, Alison et al.
1995   "Dating and Context of Three Middle Stone Age Sites with Bone Points in the Upper Semliki Valley, Zaire." *Science,* **268**:548–553.
Brose, David and Milford H. Wolpoff
1971   "Early Upper Paleolithic Man and Late Middle Paleolithic Tools." *American Anthropologist,* **73**:1156–1194.
Brown, B, A. Walker, C. V. Ward, and R. E. Leakey
1993   "New *Australopithecus boisei*: Calvaria from East Lake Turkana, Kenya." *American Journal of Physical Anthropology,* **91**:137–159.
Brown, F. H.
1982   "Tulu Bor Tuff at Koobi Fora Correlated with the Sidi Hakoma Tuff at Hadar." *Nature,* **300**:631–632.

Brown, T. M. and K. D. Rose
1987   "Patterns of Dental Evolution in Early Eocene Anaptomorphine Primates Comomyidael from the Bighorn Basin, Wyoming." *Journal of Paleontology,* **61**:1–62.
Brues, Alice M.
1959   "The Spearman and the Archer." *American Anthropologist,* **61**:457–469.

_____
1990   *People and Races* (2nd Ed.). Prospect Heights, Ill.: Waveland Press.

_____
1991   "The Objective View of Race." Paper presented at American Anthropological Association 90th Annual Meeting, Chicago, Nov.
Brunet, Michel et al.
1995   "The First Australopithecine 2,500 Kilometers West of the Rift Valley (Chad)." *Nature,* **378**:273–274.
Buffon, George Louis Leclerc, Compte de
1860   "*Histoire Naturelle Generale et Particuliere.*" Translated by Wm. Smellie. *In: The Idea of Racism,* Louis L. Snyder, New York: Van Nostrand Reinhold, 1962.
Bunn, Henry T.
1981   "Archaeological Evidence for Meat-eating by Plio-Pleistocene Hominids from Koobi Fora and Olduvai Gorge." *Nature,* **291**:574–577.
Burkhardt, Richard W., Jr.
1984   "The Zoological Philosophy of J. B. Lamarck." (Introduction) *In:* Lamarck, q.v.
Butzer, Karl W.
1974   "Paleoecology of South African Australopithecines: Taung Revisited." *Current Anthropology,* **15**:367–382.
Cann, R. L., M. Stoneking, and A. C. Wilson
1987   "Mitochondrial DNA and Human Evolution." *Nature,* **325**:31–36.
Cann, Rebecca L., Olga Rickards, and J. Koji Lum
1994   "Mitochondrial DNA and Human Evolution: Our One Lucky Mother." *In:* M H. Nitecki and D. V. Nitecki (eds.), q.v., pp. 135–148.
Carbonell, E. et al.
1995   Lower Pleistocene Hominids and Artifacts from Atapuerca-TDG (Spain)." *Science,* **269**:826–830.
Carrol, Robert L.
1988   *Vertebrate Paleontology and Evolution.* New York: W. H. Freeman and Co.
Cartmill, Matt
1972   "Arboreal Adaptations and the Origin of the Order Primates." *In: The Functional and Evolutionary Biology of Primates,* R. H. Tuttle (ed.), Chicago: Aldine-Atherton, pp. 97–122.

_____
1990   "Human Uniqueness and Theoretical Content in Paleoanthropology." *International Journal of Primatology,* **11**(3):173–192.

_____
1992   "New Views on Primate Origins." *Evolutionary Anthropology,* **1**:105–111.

Cavalli-Sforza, L. L., A. Piazza, P. Menozzi, and J. Mountain
  1988   "Reconstruction of Human Evolution: Bringing
          Together Genetic, Archaeological, and Linguistic
          Data." *Proceedings of the National Academy of
          Sciences*, **85**:6002–6006.
Chagnon, N. A.
  1979   "Mate Competition Favoring Close Kin and Village
          Fissioning among the Yanomamo Indians." *In:
          Evolutionary Biology and Human Social Behavior: An
          Anthropological Perspective*, N. Chagnon and W. Irons
          (eds.), North Scituak, Mass.: Duxbury Press,
          pp. 86–132.

  1988   "Life Histories, Blood Revenge, and Warfare in a
          Tribal Population." *Science*, **239**:985–992.
Chard, Chester S.
  1975   *Man in Prehistory*. New York: McGraw-Hill.
Charteris, J., J. C. Wali, and J. W. Nottrodt
  1981   "Functional Reconstruction of Gait from Pliocene
          Hominid Footprints at Laetoli, Northern Tanzania."
          Nature, **290**:496–498.
Cheney, Dorothy L.
  1987   "Interaction and Relationships Between Groups." *In:*
          B. Smuts et al. (eds.), q.v., pp. 267–281.
Cheney, D. L. and R. M. Seyfarth
  1990   *How Monkeys See the World*. Chicago: Chicago
          University Press.
Ciochon, R. L. and A. B. Chiarelli (eds.)
  1980   *Evolutionary Biology of the New World Monkeys and
          Continental Drift*. New York: Plenum Press.
Ciochon, Russel L. and Robert S. Corruccini (eds.)
  1983   *New Interpretations of Ape and Human Ancestry*. New
          York: Plenum Press.
Clark, W. E. LeGros
  1967   *Man-apes or Ape-men?* New York: Holt, Rinehart &
          Winston.
  1971   New York Times Books (3rd Ed.).
Clarke, R. J.
  1985   "*Australopithecus* and Early *Homo* in Southern
          Africa." *In: Ancestors: The Hard Evidence*, E. Delson
          (ed.), New York: Alan R. Liss, pp. 171–177.
Clarke, Ronald J. and Phillip V. Tobias
  1995   "Sterkfontein Member 2 Foot Bones of the Oldest
          South African Hominid." *Science*, **269**:521–524.
Cleveland, J. and C. T. Snowdon
  1982   "The Complex Vocal Repertoire of the Adult Cotton-
          top Tamarin (*Saguinus oedipus oedipus*)." *Zeitschrift
          Tierpsychologie*, **58**:231–270.
Clutton-Brock, T. H. and Paul H. Harvey
  1977   "Primate Ecology and Social Organization." *Journal
          of Zoological Society of London*, **183**:1–39.
Conkey, M.
  1987   New Approaches in the Search for Meaning? A
          Review of the Research in "Paleolithic Art." *Journal
          of Field Archaeology*, **14**:413–430.
Conroy, G., C. J. Jolly, D. Cramer, and J. E. Kalb
  1978   "Newly Discovered Fossil Hominid Skull from the
          Afar Depression." *Nature*, **272**:67–70.

Conroy, G. C., M. Pickford, B. Senut, J. van Couvering, and
P. Mein
  1992   "*Otavipithecus namibiensis*, First Miocene Hominoid
          from Southern Africa." *Nature*, **356**:144–148.
Conroy, Glenn C., Jeff W. Lichtman, and Lawrence B. Martin
  1995   "Brief Communication: Some Observations on
          Enamel Thickness and Enamel Prism Packing in
          Miocene Hominoid *Otavipithecus namibiensis*."
          American Journal of Physical Anthropology,
          98:595–600.
Coon, C. S., S. M. Garn, and J. B. Birdsell
  1950   *Races—A Study of the Problems of Race Formation in
          Man*. Springfield, Ill.: Charles C. Thomas.
Corruccini, R. S., M. Baba, M. Goodman, et al.
  1980   "Non-Linear Macromolecular Evolution and the
          Moleculer Clock." *Evolution*, **34**:1216–1219.
Corruccini, R. S. and H. M. McHenry
  1980   "Cladometric Analysis of Pliocene Hominids."
          Journal of Human Evolution, **9**:209–221.
Corruccini, Robert S.
  1994   "Reaganomics and the Fate of the Progressive
          Neandertals." *In:* R. S. Corruccini and R. I. Ciochon
          (eds.), q.v., pp. 697–708.
Crapo, Lawrence
  1985   *Hormones: The Messengers of Life*. New York: W. H.
          Freeman and Company.
Cronin, J. E.
  1983   "Apes, Humans, and Molecular Clocks. A
          Reappraisal." *In:* R. L. Ciochon and R. S. Corruccini
          (eds.), q.v., pp. 115–150.
Crook, J. H.
  1970   "Social Organization and Environment: Aspects of
          Contemporary Social Ethology." *Animal Behavior*,
          18:197–209.
Crook, J. H. and J. S. Gartlan
  1966   "Evolution of Primate Societies." *Nature*,
          210:1200–1203.
Culotta, Elizabeth
  1995   "Asian Anthropoids Strike Back." *Science*, **270**:918.
Cummings, Michael
  1994   *Human Heredity. Principles and Issues* (3rd Ed.).
          St. Paul: West Publishing Co.
Curtin, R. and P. Dolhinow
  1978   "Primate Social Behavior in a Changing World."
          American Scientist, **66**:468–475.
Curtis, Garniss
  1981   "A Matter of Time: Dating Techniques and Geology
          of Hominid Sites." Symposium Paper, Davis, Ca.,
          May 10, 1981.
Dalrymple, G. B.
  1972   "Geomagnetic Reversals and North American
          Glaciations." *In: Calibration of Hominoid Evolution*,
          W. W. Bishop and J. A. Miller (eds.), Edinburgh:
          Scottish Academic Press, pp. 303–329.
Dart, Raymond
  1959   *Adventures with the Missing Link*. New York: Harper
          & Brothers.

Darwin, Charles
1859 *On the Origin of Species.* A Facsimile of the First Edition, Cambridge, Mass.: Harvard University Press (1964).

Darwin, Francis (ed.)
1950 *The Life and Letters of Charles Darwin.* New York: Henry Schuman.

Day, M. H. and E. H. Wickens
1980 "Laetoli Pliocene Hominid Footprints and Bipedalism." *Nature,* **286**:385–387.

Day, Michael
1986 *Guide to Fossil Man* (4th Ed.), Chicago: University of Chicago Press.

Deacon, T. W.
1992 "The Human Brain." *In: The Cambridge Encyclopedia of Human Evolution,* S. Jones, R. Martin, and D. Pilbeam (eds.), Cambridge, England: Cambridge University Press, pp. 115–123.

Dean, M., M. Carring, C. Winkler, et al.
1996 "Genetic Restriction of HIV-1 Infection and Progression to AIDS by a Deletion Allele of the CKR5 Structural Gene." *Science,* **273**:1856–1862.

de Bonis, Louis and George D. Koufos
1994 "Our Ancestors' Ancestor: *Ouranopithecus* Is a Greek Link in Human Ancestry." *Evolutionary Anthropology,***3**:75–83.

de Lumley, Henry and M. de Lumley
1973 "Pre-Neanderthal Human Remains from Arago Cave in Southeastern France." *Yearbook of Physical Anthropology,* **16**:162–168.

Delson, Eric (ed.)
1985 *Ancestors: The Hard Evidence.* New York: Alan R. Liss.

_____
1987 "Evolution and Paleobiology of Robust Australopithecus." *Nature,* **327**:654–655.

Dene, H. T., M. Goodman, and W. Prychodko
1976 "Immunodiffusion Evidence on the Phylogeny of the Primates." *In: Molecular Anthropology,* M. Goodman, R. E. Tashian, and J. H. Tashian (eds.), New York: Plenum Press, pp. 171–195.

Desmond, Adrian and James Moore
1991 *Darwin.* New York: Warner Books.

Dettwyler, K. A.
1991 "Can Paleopathology Provide Evidence for Compassion?" *American Journal of Physical Anthropology,* **84**:375–384.

DeVore, I. and S. L. Washburn
1963 "Baboon Ecology and Human Evolution." *In: African Ecology and Human Evolution,* F. C. Howell and F. Bourliére (eds.), New York: Viking Fund Publication, No. 36, pp. 335–367.

De Vos, J.
1985 "Faunal Stratigraphy and Correlation of the Indonesian Hominid Sites." *In: Ancestors: The Hard Evidence,* E. Delson (ed.), New York: Alan R. Liss, pp. 215–220.

de Waal, Frans
1982 *Chimpanzee Politics.* London: Jonathan Cape.

_____
1987 "Tension Regulation and Nonreproductive Functions of Sex in Captive Bonobos (*Pan paniscus*)." *National Geographic Research,* **3**:318–335.

_____
1989 *Peacemaking among Primates.* Cambridge: Harvard University Press.

_____
1996 *Good Natured. The Origins of Right and Wrong in Humans and Other Animals,* Cambridge, Mass.: Harvard University Press.

Dolhinow, P.
1978 "A Behavior Repertoire for the Indian Langur Monkey (*Presbytis entellus*)." *Primates,* **19**:449–472.

Dorit, R. L., H. Akashi, and W. Gilbert
1995 Absence of Polymorphism at the Zfy Locus on the Human Y Chromosome. *Science,* **268**:1183–1185.

Duchin, Linda E.
1990 "The Evolution of Articulate Speech." *Journal of Human Evolution,* **19**:687–697.

Dumont, R. and B. Rosier
1969 *The Hungry Future.* New York: Praeger.

Dunbar, I. M.
1988 *Primate Social Systems.* Ithaca: Cornell University Press.

Durham, William
1981 Paper presented to the Annual Meeting of the American Anthropological Association, Washington, D.C., Dec. 1980. Reported in *Science,* **211**:40.

Eaton, S. Boyd, Marjorie Shostak, and Melvin Konner.
1988 *The Paleolithic Prescription.* New York: Harper and Row.

Eaton, S. Boyd and Melvin Konner
1985 Paleolithic Nutrition: A Consideration of Its Nature and Current Implications. *New England Journal of Medicine,* **312**:283–289.

Eaton, S. Boyd, Malcolm C. Pike, Roger V. Short, et al.
1994 Women's Reproductive Cancers in Evolutionary Context. *The Quarterly Review of Biology,* **69**:353–367.

Eiseley, Loren
1961 *Darwin's Century.* New York: Anchor Books.

Eisenberg, J. F., N. A. Muckenhirn, and R. Rudran
1972 "The Relation Between Ecology and Social Structure in Primates." *Science,* **176**:863–874.

Eldredge, Niles and Joel Cracraft
1980 *Phylogenetic Patterns and the Evolutionary Process.* New York: Columbia University Press.

Etler, Denis
1992 Personal communication.

Etler, Dennis A. and Li-Tianyuan
1994 "New Archaic Human Fossil Discoveries in China and Their Bearing on Hominid Species Definition During the Middle Pleistocene." *In:* R. Corruccini and R. Ciochon (eds.), q.v., pp. 639–675.

Falk, Dean
   1980   "A Reanalysis of the South African Australopithecine
           Natural Endocasts." *American Journal of Physical
           Anthropology*, **53**:525–539.

   1983   "The Taung Endocast: A Reply to Holloway."
           American Journal of Physical Anthropology,
           60:479–489.

   1987   "Brain Lateralization in Primates and Its Evolution in
           Hominids." *Yearbook of Physical Anthropology*,
           30:107–125.

   1989   "Comments." *Current Anthropology*, **30**:141.
Fedigan, Linda M.
   1982   *Primate Paradigms*. Montreal: Eden Press.

   1983   "Dominance and Reproductive Success in Primates."
           Yearbook of Physical Anthropology, **26**:91–129.

   1986   "The Changing Role of Women in Models of
           Human Evolution." *Annual Review of Anthropology*,
           15:25–66.
Fisher, R. A.
   1930   *The Genetical Theory of Natural Selection*. Oxford:
           Clarendon.
Fleagle, J. G.
   1983   "Locomotor Adaptations of Oligocene and Miocene
           Hominoids and Their Phyletic Implications." *In:*
           R. L. Ciochon and R. S. Corruccini (eds.), q.v.,
           pp. 301–324.

   1988   *Primate Adaptation and Evolution*. New York:
           Academic Press.
Fleagle, J. G. and R. F. Kay
   1983   "New Interpretations of the Phyletic Position of
           Oligocene Hominoids." *In:* R. L. Ciochon and R. S.
           Corruccini (eds.), q.v., pp. 181–210.
Fleischer, R. C. and H. R. Hart, Jr.
   1972   "Fission Track Dating, Techniques and Problems."
           In: Calibration of Hominoid Evolution, W. W. Bishop
           and J. A. Miller (eds.), Edinburgh: Scottish Academic
           Press, pp. 135–170.
Foley, R. A.
   1991   "How Many Species of Hominid Should There Be?"
           Journal of Human Evolution, **30**:413–427.
Foley, R. A. and M. M. Lahr
   1992   "Beyond 'Out of Africa.'" *Journal of Human
           Evolution*, **22**:523–529.
Fossey, Dian
   1983   *Gorillas in the Mist*. Boston: Houghton Mifflin.
Fouts, Roger S., D. H. Fouts, and T. T. van Cantfort
   1989   "The Infant Loulis Learns Signs from Cross-Fostered
           Chimpanzees." *In:* R. A. Gardner et al., q.v., pp.
           280–292.
Francoeuer, Robert T.
   1965   *Perspectives in Evolution*. Baltimore: Helicon.

Frayer, David
   1980   "Sexual Dimorphism and Cultural Evolution in the
           Late Pleistocene and Holocene of Europe." *Journal of
           Human Evolution*, **9**:399–415.

   1992   "Evolution at the European Edge: Neanderthal and
           Upper Paleolithic Relationships." *Prehistoire
           Europeenne*, **2**:9–69.

   n.d.   "Language Capacity in European Neanderthals."
Friedman, Milton J. and William Trager
   1981   "The Biochemistry of Resistance to Malaria."
           Scientific American, **244**:154–164.
Frisancho, A. Roberto
   1978   "Nutritional Influences on Human Growth and
           Maturation." *Yearbook of Physical Anthropology*,
           21:174–191.
Frisancho, A. Roberto
   1993   *Human Adaptation and Accommodation*. Ann Arbor:
           University of Michigan Press.
Frisch, Rose E.
   1988   Fatness and Fertility. *Scientific American*, **258**:88–95.
Froelich, J. W.
   1970   "Migration and Plasticity Physique in the Japanese-
           Americans of Hawaii." *American Journal of Physical
           Anthropology*, **32**:429.
Galdikas, Biruté M.
   1979   "Orangutan Adaptation at Tanjung Puting Reserve:
           Mating and Ecology." *In: The Great Apes*, D. A.
           Hamburg and E. R. McCown (eds.), Menlo Park,
           Ca.: Benjamin/Cummings Publishing Co., pp.
           195–233.
Gambier, Dominique
   1989   "Fossil Hominids from the Early Upper Palaeolithic
           (Aurignacian) of France." *In:* Mellars and Stringer
           (eds.), q.v., pp. 194–211.
Gamble, C.
   1991   "The Social Context for European Palaeolithic Art."
           Proceedings of the Prehistoric Society, **57**:3–15.
Gardner, R. Allen, B. T. Gardner, and T. T. van Cantfort (eds.)
   1989   *Teaching Sign Language to Chimpanzees*. Albany:
           State University of New York Press.
Garn, Stanley M.
   1965, 1969   *Human Races*. Springfield, Ill.: Charles C.
           Thomas.
Gates, R. R.
   1948   *Human Ancestry*. Cambridge: Harvard University
           Press.
Gavan, James
   1977   *Paleoanthropology and Primate Evolution*. Dubuque,
           Ia.: Wm. C. Brown Co.
Ghiselin, Michael T.
   1969   *The Triumph of the Darwinian Method*. Chicago:
           University of Chicago Press.
Gibbons, Ann
   1992   "Mitochondrial Eve, Wounded but Not Dead Yet."
           Science, **257**:873–875.

Gighlieri, Michael P.
  1984   *The Chimpanzees of Kibale Forest.* New York: Columbia University Press.
Gingerich, Phillip D.
  1985   "Species in the Fossil Record: Concepts, Trends, and Transitions." *Paleobiology*, **11**:27–41.
Goldizen, Anne Wilson
  1987   "Tamarins and Marmosets: Communal Care of Offspring." *In:* Smuts et al. (eds.), q.v., pp. 34–43.
Goldstein, M., P. Tsarong, and C. M. Beall
  1983   "High Altitude Hypoxia, Culture, and Human Fecundity/Fertility: A Comparative Study." *American Anthropologist*, **85**:28–49.
Goodall, A. G.
  1977   "Feeding and Ranging Behaviour of a Mountain Gorilla Group, *Gorilla gorilla beringei* in the Tshibinda-Kahuze Region (Zaire)." *In: Primate Ecology.* T. H. Clutton-Brock (ed.). London: Academic Press, pp. 450–479.
Goodall, Jane
  1968   "The Behavior of Free Living Chimpanzees in the Gombe Stream Reserve." *Animal Behavior Monographs*, **1**:(3).

  1986   *The Chimpanzees of Gombe.* Cambridge, Mass.: Harvard University Press.

  1990   *Through a Window.* Boston: Houghton Mifflin.
Goodman, M., M. L. Baba, and L. L. Darga
  1983   "The Bearing of Molecular Data on the Cladogenesis and Times of Divergence of Hominoid Lineages." *In:* R. L. Ciochon and R. S. Corruccini (eds.), q.v., pp. 67–86.
Gossett, Thomas F.
  1963   *Race, the History of an Idea in America.* Dallas: Southern Methodist University Press.
Gould, Stephen Jay
  1977   *Ontogeny and Phylogeny.* Cambridge, Mass.: Harvard University Press.

  1981   *The Mismeasures of Man.* New York: W. W. Norton.

  1985   "Darwin at Sea—and the Virtues of Port." *In:* Stephen Jay Gould, *The Flamingo's Smile. Reflections in Natural History.* New York: W. W. Norton, pp. 347–359.

  1987   *Time's Arrow Time's Cycle.* Cambridge: Harvard University Press.
Gould, S. J. and N. Eldredge
  1977   "Punctuated Equilibria: The Tempo and Mode of Evolution Reconsidered." *Paleobiology*, **3**:115–151.
Gould, S. J. and R. Lewontin
  1979   "The Spandrels of San Marco and the Panglossian Paradigm: A Critique of the Adaptionist Programme." *Proceedings of the Royal Society of London*, **205**:581–598.

Gowlett, John
  1984   *Ascent to Civilization.* New York: Alfred A. Knopf.
Greenberg, Joel
  1977   "Who Loves You?" *Science News*, **112** (August 27):139–141.
Greene, John C.
  1981   *Science, Ideology, and World View.* Berkeley: University of California Press.
Greenfield, L. O.
  1979   "On the Adaptive Pattern of *Ramapithecus*." *American Journal of Physical Anthropology*, **50**:527–548.
Grine, F. E.
  1993   "Australopithecine Taxonomy and Phylogeny: Historical Background and Recent Interpretation." *In: The Human Evolution Source Book*, R. L. Ciochon and J. G. Fleagle (eds.), Englewood Cliffs, N.J.: Prentice Hall, pp. 198–210.
Grine, Frederick E. (ed.)
  1988a *Evolutionary History of the "Robust" Australopithecines.* New York: Aldine de Gruyter.

  1988b "New Craniodental Fossils of *Paranthropus* from the Swartkrans Formation and Their Significance in "Robust" Australopithecine Evolution." *In:* F. E. Grine (ed.), q.v., pp. 223–243.
Haldane, J.B.S.
  1932   *The Causes of Evolution.* London: Longmans, Green (reprinted as paperback, Cornell University Press, 1966).
Hamilton, W. D.
  1964   "The Genetical Theory of Social Behavior. I and II." *Journal of Theoretical Biology*, **7**:1–52.
Hanna, Joel M. and Daniel A. Brown
  1979   "Human Heat Tolerance: Biological and Cultural Adaptations." *Yearbook of Physical Anthropology*, 1979, **22**:163–186.
Harlow, Harry F.
  1959   "Love in Infant Monkeys." *Scientific American*, **200**:68–74.
Harlow, Harry F. and Margaret K. Harlow
  1961   "A Study of Animal Affection." *Natural History*, **70**:48–55.
Harrold, Francis R.
  1989   "Mousterian, Chatelperronian and Early Aurignacian in Western Europe: Continuity or Discontinuity." *In: The Human Revolution*, P. Mellars and C. Stringer (eds.), Princeton, N.J.: Princeton University Press, pp. 212–231.
Hartl, Daniel
  1983   *Human Genetics.* New York: Harper & Row.
Harvey, Paul H., R. D. Martin, and T. H. Clutton-Brock
  1987   "Life Histories in Comparative Perspective." *In:* Smuts et al. (eds.), q.v., pp. 181–196.
Hass, J. D., E. A. Frongillo, Jr., C. D. Stepick, J. L. Beard, and G. Hurtado
  1980   Altitude, Ethnic and Sex Difference in Birth Weight and Length in Bolivia. *Human Biology*, **52**:459–477.

Hausfater, Glenn
1984 "Infanticide in Langurs: Strategies, Counter Strategies, and Parameter Values." *In:* G. Hausfater and S. B. Hrdy, (eds.), q.v., pp. 257–281.

Hausfater, Glenn and Sarah Blaffer Hrdy (eds.)
1984 *Infanticide. Comparative and Evolutionary Perspectives.* Hawthorne, New York: Aldine de Gruyter.

Hayden, Brian
1993 "The Cultural Capacities of Neandertals: A Review and Reevaluation." *Journal of Human Evolution,* **24**:113–146.

Henahan, Sean
1995 Men haven't changed in 270,000 years. Access Excellence, Genentech Inc., Worldwide Web Source.

Hiernaux, Jean
1968 *La Diversité Humaine en Afrique subsahariénne.* Bruxelles: L'Institut de Sociologie, Université Libre de Bruxelles.

Hill, A., S. Ward, A. Deino, G. Curtis, and R. Drake
1992 "Earliest *Homo.*" *Nature,* **355**:719–722.

Hill, Andrew and Steven Ward
1988 "Origin of the Hominidae: The Record of African Large Hominoid Evolution Between 14 my and 4 my." *Yearbook of Physical Anthropology,* 1988, **31**:49–83.

Hinde, Robert A.
1987 "Can Nonhuman Primates Help Us Understand Human Behavior?" *In:* B. Smuts et al. (eds.), q.v., pp. 413–420.

Hoffstetter, R.
1972 "Relationships, Origins, and History of the Ceboid Monkeys and the Caviomorph Rodents: A Modern Reinterpretation." *In: Evolutionary Biology* (Vol. 6), T. Dobzhansky, T. M. K. Hecht, and W. C. Steere (eds.), New York: Appleton-Century-Crofts, pp. 323–347.

Holloway, Ralph L.
1969 "Culture: A Human Domain." *Current Anthropology,* **10**:395–407.

_____
1981 "Revisiting the South African Taung Australopithecine Endocast: The Position of the Lunate Sulcus as Determined by the Stereoplotting Technique." *American Journal of Physical Anthropology,* **56**:43–58.

_____
1983 "Cerebral Brain Endocast Pattern of *Australopithecus afarensis* Hominid." *Nature,* **303**:420–422.

Hooton, E. A.
1926 "Methods of Racial Analysis." *Science,* **63**:75–81.

Horr, D. A.
1975 "The Bornean Orangutan: Population Structure and Dynamics in Relationship to Ecology and Reproductive Strategy." *In: Primate Behavior: Developments in Field and Laboratory Research,* vol. 4, L. A. Rosenblum (ed.), New York: Academic Press.

Howell, F. Clark
1978 "Hominidae." *In: Evolution of African Mammals,* V. J. Maglio and H.B.S. Cooke (eds.), Cambridge: Harvard University Press, pp. 154–248.

_____
1988 "Foreword." *In:* Grine (ed.), q.v., pp. xi–xv.

Howells, W. W.
1973 *Evolution of the Genus* Homo. Reading, Mass.: Addison-Wesley.

_____
1980 "*Homo erectus*—Who, When, Where: A Survey. *Yearbook of Physical Anthropology,* **23**:1–23.

Hrdy, Sarah Blaffer
1977 *The Langurs of Abu.* Cambridge, Mass.: Harvard University Press.

_____
1984a "Assumptions and Evidence Regarding the Sexual Selection Hypothesis: A Reply to Boggess." *In:* G. Hausfater and S. B. Hrdy (eds.), q.v., pp. 315–319.

_____
1984b "Female Reproductive Strategies." *In:* M. Small (ed.), q.v., pp. 103–109.

_____
1995 "Infanticide: Let's Not Throw Out the Baby with the Bath Water." *Evolutionary Anthropology,* **3**(5):151–154.

Hu, Dale J., Timothy J. Dondero, Mark A. Rayfield, et al.
1996 "The Emerging Genetic Diversity of HIV. The Importance of Global Surveillance, for Diagnostics, Research, and Prevention." *Journal of the American Medical Association,* **275**(3):210–216.

Hull, David L.
1973 *Darwin and His Critics.* Chicago: University of Chicago Press.

Humphries, Rolfe
1955 *Ovid Metamorphoses.* Bloomington: Indiana University Press.

The Institute of Vertebrate Paleontology and Paleoanthropology, Chinese Academy of Sciences
1980 *Atlas of Primitive Man in China.* Beijing: Science Press (Distributed by Van Nostrand, New York).

Isaac, G. L.
1971 "The Diet of Early Man." *World Archaeology,* **2**:278–299.

_____
1975 "Stratigraphy and Cultural Patterns in East Africa During the Middle Ranges of Pleistocene Time." *In: After the Australopithecines,* K. W. Butzer and G. L. Isaac (eds.), Chicago: Aldine Publishing Co., pp. 495–542.

_____
1976 "Early Hominids in Action: A Commentary on the Contribution of Archeology to Understanding the Fossil Record in East Africa." *Yearbook of Physical Anthropology,* 1975, **19**:19–35.

Izawa, K. and A. Mizuno
1977   "Palm-Fruit Cracking Behaviour of Wild Black-Capped Capuchin (*Cebus apella*)." *Primates*, 18:773–793.

Jensen, Arthur
1969   *Environment, Heredity, and Intelligence*. Cambridge, Mass.: Harvard Educational Review.

Jerison, H. J.
1973   *Evolution of the Brain and Behavior*. New York: Academic Press.

Jia, L. and Huang Weiwen
1990   *The Story of Peking Man*. New York: Oxford University Press.

Jia, Lan-po
1975   *The Cave Home of Peking Man*. Peking: Foreign Language Press.

Johanson, D. C. and T. D. White
1979   "A Systematic Assessment of Early African Hominids." *Science*, 203:321–330.

Johanson, Donald and Maitland Edey
1981   *Lucy: The Beginnings of Humankind*. New York: Simon & Schuster.

Johanson, Donald, F. T. Masao, et al.
1987   "New Partial Skeleton of *Homo habilis* from Olduvai Gorge, Tanzania." *Nature*, 327:205–209.

Johanson, Donald C. and Maurice Taieb
1976   "Plio-Pleistocene Hominad Discoveries in Hadar, Ethiopia." *Nature*, 260:293–297.

————
1980   "New Discoveries of Pliocene Hominids and Artifacts in Hadar." International Afar Research Expedition to Ethiopia (Fourth and Fifth Field Seasons, 1975–77). *Journal of Human Evolution*, 9:582.

Jolly, Alison
1984   "The Puzzle of Female Feeding Priority." *In*: M. F. Small (ed.), q.v., pp. 197–215.

————
1985   *The Evolution of Primate Behavior* (2nd Ed.), New York: Macmillan.

Jones, Rhys
1990   East of Wallace's Line: Issues and Problems in the Colonization of the Australian Continent." *In: The Human Revolution*, P. Mellars and C. Stringer (eds.), Princeton, N.J.: Princeton University Press, pp. 743–782.

Jungers, W. L.
1982   "Lucy's Limbs: Skeletal Allometry and Locomotion in *Australopithecus afarensis*." *Nature*, 297:676–678.

————
1988   "New Estimates of Body Size in Australopithecines." *In*: F. E. Grine (ed.), q.v., pp. 115–125.

Kano, T.
1980   The Social Behavior of Wild Pygmy Chimpanzees (*Pan Paniscus*) of Wamba: A Preliminary Report. *Journal of Human Evolution*, 9:243–260.

————
1992   *The Last Ape. Pygmy Chimpanzee Behavior and Ecology*. Stanford: Stanford University Press.

Katz, S. H., M. L. Hediger, and L. A. Valleroy
1974   Traditional Maize Processing Techniques in the New World. *Science*, 184:765–773.

Kay, R. F., J. G. Fleagle, and E. L. Simons
1981   "A Revision of the Oligocene Apes of the Fayum Province, Egypt." *American Journal of Physical Anthropology*, 55:293–322.

Kay, Richard and Frederick E. Grine
1988   "Tooth Morphology, Wear and Diet in *Australopithecus* and *Paranthropus, In*: F. Grine (ed.), q.v., pp. 427–447.

Kelly, Mark and David Pilbeam
1986   "The Dryopithecines: Taxonomy, Comparative Anatomy, and Phylogeny of Miocene Large Hominoids." *In: Comparative Primate Biology*. Vol. 1, *Systematics, Evolution, and Anatomy*, D. R. Swindler and J. Erwin (eds.), New York: Alan R. Liss, pp. 361–411.

Kennedy, G. E.
1983   "A Morphometric and Taxonomic Assessment of a Hominid Femur from the Lower Member, Koobi Fora, Lake Turkana." *American Journal of Physical Anthropology*, 61:429–436.

Kennedy, K. A. R.
1991   "Is the Narmada Hominid an Indian *Homo erectus*?" *American Journal of Physical Anthropology*, 86:475–496.

Kennedy, Kenneth A. R. and S. U. Deraniyagala
1989   "Fossil Remains of 28,000-Year-Old Hominids from Sri Lanka." *Current Anthropology*, 30:397–399.

Kimbel, William H.
1988   "Identification of a Partial Cranium of *Australopithecus afarensis* from the Koobi Fora Formation, Kenya." *Journal of Human Evolution*, 17:647–656.

Kimbel, William H., Donald C. Johanson, and Yoel Rak
1994   "The First Skull and Other New Discoveries of *Australopithecus afarensis* at Hadar, Ethiopia." *Nature*, 368:449–451.

Kimbel, William H., Tim D. White, and Donald C. Johanson
1988   "Implications of KNM-WT-17000 for the Evolution of 'Robust' *Australopithecus*." *In*: F. E. Grine (ed.), q.v., pp. 259–268.

King, Barbara J.
1994   *The Information Continuum*. Santa Fe: School of American Research Press.

Klein, R. G.
1989   *The Human Career. Human Biological and Cultural Origins*. Chicago: University of Chicago Press.

————
1992   "The Archeology of Modern Human Origins." *Evolutionary Anthropology*, 1:5–14.

Konner, Melvin and Carol Worthman
1980   Nursing Frequency, Gonadal Function, and Birth Spacing among !Kung Hunter-Gatherers. *Science*, 207:788–791.

Kramer, Andrew
1986   "Hominid-Pongid Distinctiveness in the Miocene-
        Pliocene Fossil Record: The Lothagam Mandible."
        American Journal of Physical Anthropology,
        70:457–473.

_____
1993   "Human Taxonomic Diversity in the Pleistocene:
        Does *Homo erectus* Represent Multiple Hominid
        Species?" *American Journal of Physical Anthropology*,
        91:161–171.

Kroeber, A. L.
1928   "Sub-human Cultural Beginning." *Quarterly Review
        of Biology*, **3**:325–342.

Krogman, W. M.
1962   *The Human Skeleton in Forensic Medicine.*
        Springfield: C. C. Thomas.

Krummer, Hans
1971   *Primate Societies.* Chicago: Aldine-Atherton, Inc.

Lack, David
1966   *Population Studies of Birds.* Oxford: Clarendon.

Lamarck, Jean Baptiste
1809, 1984   *Zoological Philosophy.* Chicago: University of
        Chicago Press.

Lancaster, Jane B.
1975   *Primate Behavior and the Emergence of Human
        Culture.* New York: Holt, Rinehart & Winston.

Lancaster, Jane B. and C. S. Lancaster
1983   Parental Investment: The Hominid Adaptation. *In:
        How Humans Adapt: A Biocultural Odyssey*, D. J.
        Ortner (ed.), Washington, D.C.: Smithsonian
        Institution Press.

Landau, M.
1984   "Human Evolution as Narrative." *American Scientist*,
        72:262–268.

Lasker, Gabriel W.
1969   "Human Biological Adaptability: The Ecological
        Approach in Physical Anthropology." *Science*,
        166:1480–1486.

Latimer, Bruce
1984   "The Pedal Skeleton of *Australopithecus afarensis.*"
        American Journal of Physical Anthropology, **63**:182.

Leakey, L. S. B., J. F. Everden, and G. H. Curtis
1961   "Age of Bed I, Olduvai Gorge, Tanganyika." *Nature*,
        191:478–479.

Leakey, L. S. B., P. V. Tobias, and J. R. Napier
1964   "A New Species of the Genus Homo from Olduvai
        Gorge." *Nature*, **202**:7–10.

Leakey, M. D.
1971   "Remains of *Homo erectus* and Associated Artifacts in
        Bed IV at Olduvai Gorge, Tanzania." *Nature*,
        232:380–383.

Leakey, M. D. and R. L. Hay
1979   "Pliocene Footprints in Laetoli Beds at Laetoli,
        Northern Tanzania." *Nature*, **278**:317–323.

Leakey, Meave G. et al.
1995   "New Four-Million-Year-Old Hominid Species from
        Kanapoi: and Allia Bay, Kenya." *Nature*,
        376:565–571.

Leakey, R. E. F. and M. D. Leakey
1986   "A New Miocene Hominoid from Kenya." *Nature*,
        324:143–146.

Lederberg, J.
1996   "Infection Emergent" (editorial). *Journal of the
        American Medical Association*, **275**(3):243–245.

Lerner, I. M. and W. J. Libby
1976   *Heredity, Evolution, and Society.* San Francisco:
        W. H. Freeman and Company.

Leroi-Gourhan, André
1986   "The Hands of Gargas." *October* **37**:18–34.

Lewontin, R. C.
1972   "The Apportionment of Human Diversity." *In:
        Evolutionary Biology* (Vol. 6), T. Dobzhansky et al.
        (eds.), New York: Plenum, pp. 381–398.

Li, Wen-Hsiung and Masako Tanimura
1987   "The Molecular Clock Runs More Slowly in Man
        than in Apes and Monkeys." *Nature*, **326**:93–96.

Lieberman, Daniel, David R. Pilbeam, and Bernard A. Wood
1988   "A Probalistic Approach to the Problem of Sexual
        Dimorphism in *Homo habilis*: A Comparison of
        KNM-ER-1470 and KNM-ER-1813." *Journal of
        Human Evolution*, **17**:503–511.

Linnaeus, C.
1758   *Systema Naturae.*

Lisowski, F. P.
1984   "Introduction." *In: The Evolution of the East African
        Environment.* Centre of Asian Studies Occasional
        Papers and Monographs, No. 59, R. O. Whyte (ed.),
        Hong Kong: University of Hong Kong, pp. 777–786.

Livingstone, Frank B.
1964   "On the Nonexistence of Human Races." *In: Concept
        of Race*, A. Montagu (ed.), New York: The Free Press,
        pp. 46–60.

_____
1969   "Polygenic Models for the Evolution of Human Skin
        Color Differences." *Human Biology*, **41**:480–493.

_____
1980   "Natural Selection and the Origin and Maintenance
        of Standard Genetic Marker Systems." *Yearbook of
        Physical Anthropology*, 1980, **23**:25–42.

Lovejoy, C. O.
1988   "Evolution of Human Walking." *Scientific American*,
        259(Nov.):118–125.

Lovejoy, C. O., G. Kingsbury, G. Heiple, and A. H. Burstein
1973   "The Gait of *Australopithecus.*" *American Journal of
        Physical Anthropology*, **38**:757–780.

Lovejoy, Thomas E.
1982   "The Tropical Forest—Greatest Expression of Life on
        Earth." *In: Primates and the Tropical Forest*,
        Proceedings, California Institute of Technology and
        World Wildlife Fund—U.S., pp. 45–48.

MacKinnon, J. and K. MacKinnon
1980   "The Behavior of Wild Spectral Tarsiers."
        International Journal of Primatology, **1**:361–379.

MacLarnon, Ann
1993 "The Vertebral Canal of KNM-WT 1500 and the Evolution of the Spinal Cord and Other Canal Contents." *In:* A. Walker and R. E. Leakey (eds.), q.v., pp. 359–390.

Mai, L. L.
1983 "A Model of Chromosome Evolution and Its Bearing on Cladogenesis in the Hominoidea." *In:* R. Ciochon and R. Corruccini (eds.), q.v., pp. 87–114.

Manson, J. H. and R. Wrangham
1991 "Intergroup Aggression in Chimpanzees and Humans." *Current Anthropology,* **32**:369–390.

Marshack, A.
1972 *The Roots of Civilization.* New York: McGraw-Hill Publishing Co.

———
1989 "Evolution of the Human Capacity: The Symbolic Evidence." *Yearbook of Physical Anthropology,* 1989, **32**:1–34.

Masserman, J., S. Wechkin, and W. Terris
1964 "'Altruistic' Behavior in Rhesus Monkeys." *American Journal of Physical Anthropology,* **121**:584–585.

Mayer, Peter J.
1982 Evolutionary Advantages of Menopause. *Human Ecology,* **10**:477–494.

Mayr, Ernst
1962 "Taxonomic Categories in Fossil Hominids." *In: Ideas on Human Evolution,* W. W. Howells (ed.), New York: Atheneum, pp. 242–256.

———
1970 *Population, Species, and Evolution.* Cambridge: Harvard University Press.

———
1991 *One Long Argument.* Cambridge: Harvard University Press.

McGrew, W. C.
1992 *Chimpanzee Material Culture. Implications for Human Evolution.* Cambridge: Cambridge University Press.

McGrew, W. C. and E. G. Tutin
1978 "Evidence for a Social Custom in Wild Chimpanzees?" *Man,* **13**:234–251.

McHenry, Henry
1983 "The Capitate of *Australopithecus afarensis* and *A. africanus.*" *American Journal of Physical Anthropology,* **62**:187–198.

———
1988 "New Estimates of Body Weight in Early Hominids and Their Significance to Encephalization and Megadontia in 'Robust' Australopithecines." *In:* F. E. Grine (ed.), q.v., pp. 133–148.

———
1992 "Body Size and Proportions in Early Hominids." *American Journal of Physical Anthropology,* 87:407–431.

McKenna, James J.
1982a "Primate Field Studies: The Evolution of Behavior and Its Socioecology." *In: Primate Behavior.* James L. Fobes and James E. King (eds.). New York: Academic Press, pp. 53–83.

———
1982b "The Evolution of Primate Societies, Reproduction, and Parenting." *In: Primate Behavior.* James L. Fobes and James E. King (eds.). New York: Academic Press, pp. 87–133.

McKusick, Victor
1990 *Mendelian Inheritance in Man.* (9th Ed.) Baltimore: Johns Hopkins Press.

Mellars, P. and C. Stringer (eds.)
1989 *The Human Revolution.* Princeton, N.J.: Princeton University Press.

Mittermeir, R. A.
1982 "The World's Endangered Primates: An Introduction and a Case Study—The Monkeys of Brazil's Atlantic Forests." *In: Primates and the Tropical Rain Forest,* Proceedings, California Institute of Technology, and World Wildlife Fund—U.S., pp. 11–22.

Mittermeir, R. A. and D. Cheney
1987 "Conservation of Primates in Their Habitats." *In:* B. B. Smuts et al., q.v., pp. 477–496.

Montagu, A.
1961 Neonatal and Infant Immaturity in Man. *Journal of the American Medical Association,* **178**:56–57.

Molnar, Stephen
1983 *Human Variation. Races, Types, and Ethnic Groups* (2nd Ed.). Englewood Cliffs: Prentice Hall.

Moore, Lorna G. et al.
1994 Genetic Adaptation to High Altitude. *In: Sports and Exercise Medicine,* Stephen C. Wood and Robert C. Roach (eds.), New York: Marcel Dekker, Inc., pp. 225–262.

Moore, Lorna G. and Judith G. Regensteiner
1983 "Adaptation to High Altitude." *Annual Reviews of Anthropology,* **12**:285–304.

Morbeck, M. E.
1975 "*Dryopithecus africanus* Forelimb." *Journal of Human Evolution,* **4**:39–46.

———
1983 "Miocene Hominoid Discoveries from Rudabánya. Implications from the Postcranial Skeleton." *In:* R. L. Ciochon and R. S. Corruccini (eds.), q.v., pp. 369–404.

Morgan, Elaine
1972 *The Descent of Women.* New York: Stein and Day.

Morris, Desmond
1967 *The Naked Ape.* New York: McGraw-Hill.

Mountain, Joanna L., Alice A. Lin, Anne M. Bowcock, and L. L. Cavalli-Sforza
1993 "Evolution of Modern Humans: Evidence from Nuclear DNA Polymorphisms." *In:* M. J. Aitken et al. (eds.), q.v., pp. 69–83.

Mourant, A. E., A. C. Kopec, and K. Sobczak
  1976   *The Distribution of the Human Blood Groups.*
          Oxford: Oxford University Press.
Moyá-Solà, Salvador and Meike Köhler
  1996   "A *Dryopithecus* Skelton and the Origins of Great-ape
          Locomotion. *Nature*, 379:156–159.
Mueller, William H. et al.
  1979   "A Multinational Andean Genetic and Health
          Program. VIII. Lung Function Changes with
          Migration between Altitudes." *American Journal of
          Physical Anthropology*, 51:183–196.
Murray, R. D.
  1980   "The Evolution and Functional Significance of
          Incest Avoidence." *Journal of Human Evolution*,
          9:173–178.
Nabhan, G. P.
  1991   Desert Legumes as a Nutritional Intervention for
          Diabetic Indigenous Dwellers of Arid Lands. *Arid
          Lands Newsletter*, 31:11–13.
Napier, J. R. and P. H. Napier
  1967   *A Handbook of Living Primates.* New York: Academic
          Press.

_____
  1985   *The Natural History of the Primates.* Cambridge,
          Mass.: The MIT Press.
Napier, John
  1967   "The Antiquity of Human Walking." *Scientific
          American*, 216:56–66.
Nature
  1986   "Chernobyl Report." *Nature*, 323:26–30.
Neel, J. V.
  1962   Diabetes Mellitus: A "Thrifty" Genotype Rendered
          Detrimental by "Progress"? *American Journal of
          Human Genetics*, 61:1099–1102.
Newman, Marshall T.
  1975   "Nutritional Adaptation in Man." *In: Physiological
          Anthropology*, Albert Damon (ed.), New York: Oxford
          University Press, pp. 210–259.
Newman, Russell W.
  1970   "Why Man Is Such a Sweaty and Thirsty Naked
          Animal: A Speculative Review." *Human Biology*,
          42:12–27.
Newman, Russell W. and Ella H. Munro
  1955   "The Relation of Climate and Body Size in U.S.
          Males." *American Journal of Physical Anthropology*,
          13:1–17.
Nishida, T.
  1968   "The Social Group of Wild Chimpanzees in the
          Mahale Mountains." *Primates*, 9:167–224.

_____
  1979   "The Social Structure of Chimpanzees of the Mahale
          Mountains." *In: The Great Apes*, D. A. Hamburg and
          E. R. McCown (eds.), Menlo Park: Benjamin
          Cummings, pp. 73–122.

_____
  1991   Comments. *In:* J. H. Manson and R. Wrangham, q.v.,
          pp. 381–382.

Nishida, T., M. Hiraiwa-Hasegawa, T. Hasegawa, and Y. Takahata
  1985   "Group Extinction and Female Transfer in Wild
          Chimpanzees in the Mahale National Park,
          Tanzania." *Zeitschrift Tierpsychologie*, 67:284–301.
Nishida, T., H. Takasaki, and Y. Takahata
  1990   "Demography and Reproductive Profiles." *In: The
          Chimpanzees of the Mahale Mountains*, T. Nishida
          (ed.), Tokyo: University of Tokyo Press, pp. 63–97.
Nishida, T., R. W. Wrangham, J. Goodall, and S. Uehara
  1983   "Local Differences in Plant-feeding Habits of
          Chimpanzees between the Mahale Mountains and
          Gombe National Park, Tanzania." *Journal of Human
          Evolution*, 12:467–480.
Novitski, Edward
  1977   *Human Genetics.* New York: Macmillan.
Oakley, Kenneth
  1963   "Analytical Methods of Dating Bones." *In: Science in
          Archaelogy*, D. Brothwell and E. Higgs (eds.), New
          York: Basic Books, Inc.
Olliaro, Piero, Jackqueline Cattani, and Dyann Wirth
  1996   "Malaria, the Submerged Disease." *In: Journal of the
          American Medical Association*, 275(3):230–233.
Olson, John W. and R. Ciochon
  1990   "A Review of the Evidence for Postulated Middle
          Pleistocene Occupation in Viet Nam." *Journal of
          Human Evolution*, 19:761–788.
Ortner, Donald J.
  1981   "Biocultural Interaction in Human Adaptation." *In:
          How Humans Adapt.* Donald J. Ortner (ed.),
          Washington, D.C.: Smithsonian Institution Press.
Parés, Josef M. and Alfredo Pérez-González
  1995   "Paleomagnetic Age for Hominid Fossils at Atapuerca
          Archaeological Site, Spain." *Science*, 269:830–832.
Parker, Seymour
  1976   "The Precultural Basis of the Incest Taboo: Toward a
          Biosocial Theory." *American Anthropologist*,
          78:285–305.
Pickford, M.
  1983   "Sequence and Environments of the Lower and
          Middle Miocene Hominoids of Western Kenya." *In:*
          R. L. Ciochon and R. S. Corruccini (eds.), q.v., pp.
          421–439.
Pilbeam, David
  1972   *The Ascent of Man.* New York: Macmillan.

_____
  1977   "Beyond the Apes: Pre-*Homo* Hominids: The
          Ramapithecines of Africa, Asia, and Europe."
          Symposium Lecture, March 5, 1977, Davis, Ca.

_____
  1982   "New Hominoid Skull Material from the Miocene of
          Pakistan." *Nature*, 295:232–234.

_____
  1986   "Distinguished Lecture: Hominoid Evolution and
          Hominoid Origins." *American Anthropologist*,
          88:295–312.

1988 "Primate Evolution." *In: Human Biology*, G. A. Harrison et al., (eds.), New York: Oxford University Press, pp. 76–103.

Pope, G. G.
1984 "The Antiquity and Paleoenvironment of the Asian Hominidae." *In: The Evolution of the East Asian Environment*. Center of Asian Studies Occasional Papers and Monographs, No. 59, R. O. Whyte (ed.), Hong Kong: University of Hong Kong, pp. 822–847.

1992 "Craniofacial Evidence for the Origin of Modern Humans in China." *Yearbook of Physical Anthropology*, 1992, **35**:243–298.

Popp, Joseph L. and Irven DeVore
1979 "Aggressive Competition and Social Dominance Theory." *In: The Great Apes*, D. A. Hamburg and E. R. McCown (eds.), Menlo Park, Ca.: Benjamin/ Cummings Publishing Co., pp. 317–318.

Post, Peter W., Farrington Daniels, Jr., and Robert T. Binford, Jr.
1975 "Cold Injury and the Evolution of 'White' Skin." *Human Biology*, **47**:65–80.

Potts, R.
1984 "Home Bases and Early Hominids." *American Scientist*, **72**:338–347.

Potts, Richard
1991 "Why the Oldowan? Plio-Pleistocene Toolmaking and the Transport of Resources." *Journal of Anthropological Research*, **47**:153–176.

1993 "Archeological Interpretations of Early Hominid Behavior and Ecology." *In:* D. T. Rasmussen (ed.), q.v., pp. 49–74.

Potts, Richard and Pat Shipman
1981 Cutmarks Made by Stone Tools from Olduvai Gorge, Tanzania." *Nature*, **291**:577–580.

Proctor, Robert
1988 "From Anthropologie to Rassenkunde." *In: Bones, Bodies, Behavior. History of Anthropology* (Vol. 5), 6. W. Stocking, Jr. (ed.), Madison: University of Wisconsin Press, pp. 138–179.

Profet, M.
1988 The Evolution of Pregnancy Sickness as a Protection to the Embryo Against Pleistocene Teratogens. *Evolutionary Theory*, **8**:177–190.

Pulliam, H. R. and T. Caraco
1984 "Living in groups: Is There an Optimal Size?" *In: Behavioral Ecology: An Evolutionary Approach* (2nd ed.), J. R. Krebs and N. B. Davies (eds.), Sunderland, Mass.: Sinauer Associates.

Pusey, Anne E. and Craig Packer
1987 "Dispersal and Philopatry." *In:* B. B. Smuts et al. (eds.), q.v., pp. 250–266.

Radinsky, Leonard
1973 "*Aegyptopithecus* Endocasts: Oldest Record of a Pongid Brain." *American Journal of Physical Anthropology*, **39**:239–248.

Rafferty, Katherine L. et al.
1995 "Postcranial Estimates of Body Weight, with a note on a Distal Tibia of *P. major* from Napak, Uganda. *American Journal of Physical Anthropology*, **97**:391–402.

Rak, Y.
1983 *The Australopithecine Face*. New York: Academic Press.

Relethford, John H. and Henry C. Harpending
1994 "Craniometric Variation, Genetic Theory, and Modern Human Origins." *American Journal of Physical Anthropology*, **95**:249–270.

Richard, A. F.
1985 *Primates in Nature*. New York: W. H. Freeman and Co.

Richard, A. F. and S. R. Schulman
1982 "Sociobiology: Primate Field Studies." *Annual Reviews of Anthropology*, **11**:231–255.

Rightmire, G. P.
1981 "Patterns in the Evolution of *Homo erectus*." *Paleobiology*, **7**:241–246.

1990 *The Evolution of* Homo erectus. New York: Cambridge University Press.

Roberts, D. F.
1973 *Climate and Human Variability*. An Addison-Wesley Module in Anthropology, No. 34. Reading, Mass.: Addison-Wesley.

Roberts, Richard, Rhys Jones, and M. A. Smith
1990 "Thermoluminescence Dating of a 50,000-Year-Old Human Occupation Site in Northern Australia," *Nature*, **345**:153–156.

Robinson, J. T.
1972 *Early Hominid Posture and Locomotion*. Chicago: University of Chicago Press.

Rodman, P. S.
1973 "Population Composition and Adaptive Organisation among Orangutans of the Kutai Reserve." *In: Comparative Ecology and Behaviour of Primates*, R. P. Michael and J. H. Crook (eds.), London: Academic Press, pp. 171–209.

Rose, M. D.
1991 "Species Recognition in Eocene Primates." *American Journal of Physical Anthropology*, Supplement 12, p. 153.

Rudran, R.
1973 Adult Male Replacement in One-Male Troops of Purple-Faced Langurs (*Presbytis senex senex*) and its Effect on Population Structure. *Folia Primatologica*, **19**:166–192.

Ruff, C. B. and Alan Walker
1993 "The Body Size and Shape of KNM-WT 15000." *In:* A. Walker and R. Leakey (eds.), q.v., pp. 234–265.

Rumbaugh, D. M.
1977 *Language Learning by a Chimpanzee: The Lana Project*. New York: Academic Press.

Sachick, Kathy B. and Dong Zhuan
1991 "Early Paleolithic of China and Eastern Asia." *Evolutionary Anthropology*, **2**(1):22–35.

Samson, M., F. Libert, B. J. Doranz, et al.
1996 Resistance to HIV-1 Infection in Caucasian Individuals Bearing Mutant Alleles of the CCR-5 Chemokine Receptor Gene. *Nature* **382**(22): 722–725.

Sarich, V. M. and A. C. Wilson
1967 "Rules of Albumen Evolution in Primates." *Proceedings, National Academy of Science,* **58**:142–148.

Sarich, Vincent
1971 "A Molecular Approach to the Question of Human Origins." *In: Background for Man,* P. Dolhinow and V. Sarich (eds.), Boston: Little, Brown & Co., pp. 60–81.

Savage-Rumbaugh, E. S.
1986 *Ape Language: From Conditioned Responses to Symbols.* New York: Columbia University Press.

Savage-Rumbaugh, S., K. McDonald, R. A. Sevic, W. D. Hopkins, and E. Rupert
1986 "Spontaneous Symbol Acquisition and Communicative Use by Pygmy Chimpanzees (*Pan paniscus*)." *Journal of Experimental Psychology: General,* **115**(3):211–235.

Savage-Rumbaugh, S. and R. Lewin
1994 *Kanzi. The Ape at the Brink of the Human Mind.* New York: John Wiley and Sons.

Schaller, George B.
1963 *The Mountain Gorilla.* Chicago: University of Chicago Press.

Scheller, Richard H. and Richard Axel
1984 "How Genes Control Innate Behavior." *Scientific American,* **250**:54–63.

Scott, K.
1980 "Two Hunting Episodes of Middle Paleolithic Age at La Cotte Sainte-Brelade, Jersey (Channel Islands)." *World Archaeology,* **12**:137–152.

Senut, Brigette and Christine Tardieu
1985 "Functional Aspects of Plio-Pleistocene Hominid Limb Bones: Implications for Taxonomy and Phylogeny." *In: Ancestors: The Hard Evidence,* E. Delson (ed.), New York: Alan R. Liss, pp. 193–201.

Seyfarth, Robert M., Dorothy L. Cheney, and Peter Marler
1980a "Monkey Responses to Three Different Alarm Calls." *Science,* **210**:801–803.

1980b "Ververt Monkey Alarm Calls." *Animal Behavior,* **28**:1070–1094.

Shipman, P. L.
1983 "Early Hominid Lifestyle. Hunting and Gathering or Foraging and Scavenging?" Paper presented at 52nd Annual Meeting, American Association of Physical Anthropologists, Indianapolis, April.

1987 "An Age-Old Question: Why Did the Human Lineage Survive?" *Discover,* **8**:60–64.

Sibley, Charles and Jon E. Ahlquist
1984 "The Phylogeny of the Hominoid Primates as Indicated by DNA-DNA Hybridization." *Journal of Molecular Evolution,* **20**:2–15.

Simons, E. L.
1969 "The Origin and Radiation of the Primates." *Annals of the New York Academy of Sciences,* **167**:319–331.

1972 *Primate Evolution.* New York: Macmillan.

1985 "African Origin, Characteristics and Context of Earliest Higher Primates." *In: Hominid Evolution: Past, Present, and Future.* P. Tobias (ed.), New York: Alan R. Liss, pp. 101–106.

1995 "Egyptian Oligocene Primates: A Review." *Yearbook of Physical Anthropology,* **38**:199–238.

Simons, Elwyn L. and Tab Rasmussen
1994 "A Whole New World of Ancestors: Eocene Anthropoideans from Africa." *Evolutionary Anthropology,* **3**:128–139.

Simpson, G. G.
1945 "The Principles of Classification and a Classification of Mammals." *Bulletin of the American Museum of Natural History,* **85**:1–350.

Simpson, G. G., C. S. Pittendright, and L H. Tiffany
1957 *Life.* New York: Harcourt, Brace and Co., Inc.

Skelton, R. R., H. M. McHenry, and G. M. Drawhorn
1986 "Phylogenetic Analysis of Early Hominids." *Current Anthropology,* **27**:1–43; 361–365.

Skelton, Randall R. and Henry M. McHenry
1992 "Evolutionary Relationships among Early Hominids." *Journal of Human Evolution,* **23**:309–349.

Small, Meredith F. (ed.)
1984 *Female Primates. Studies by Women Primatologists.* Monographs in Primatology, Vol. 4. New York: Alan R. Liss.

Smith, Fred H.
1984 "Fossil Hominids from the Upper Pleistocene of Central Europe and the Origin of Modern Europeans." *In:* F. H. Smith and F. Spencer (eds.), q.v., pp. 187–209.

Smith, Fred H., A. B. Falsetti, and S. M. Donnelly
1989 "Modern Human Origins." *Yearbook of Physical Anthropology,* **32**:35–68.

Smith, Fred H. and Frank, Spencer (eds.)
1984 *The Origins of Modern Humans.* New York: Alan R. Liss, Inc.

Smuts, Barbara
1985 *Sex and Friendship in Baboons.* Hawthorne, N.Y.: Aldine de Gruyter.

Smuts, Barbara B. et al. (eds.)
1987 *Primate Societies.* Chicago: University of Chicago Press.

Snowdon, Charles T.
1990 "Language Capacities of 'Nonhuman Animals.'" *Yearbook of Physical Anthropology,* **33**:215–243.

Soffer, Olga
1985 *The Upper Paleolithic of the Central Russian Plain.* New York: Academic Press.
Solecki, Ralph
1971 *Shanidar, The First Flower People.* New York: Alfred A. Knopf.
Stanyon, Roscoe and Brunetto Chiarelli
1982 "Phylogeny of the Hominoidea: The Chromosome Evidence." *Journal of Human Evolution,* **11**:493–504.
Steegman, A. T., Jr.
1970 "Cold Adaptation and the Human Face." *American Journal of Physical Anthropology,* **32**:243–250.

1975 "Human Adaptation to Cold." *In: Physiological Anthropology,* A. Damon (ed.), New York: Oxford University Press, pp. 130–166.
Steklis, Horst D.
1985 "Primate Communicatioan, Comparative Neurology, and the Origin of Language Re-examined." *Journal of Human Evolution,* **14**:157–173.
Stern, Curt
1973 *Principles of Human Genetics,* 3rd ed. San Francisco: W. H. Freeman.
Stern, Jack T. and Randall L. Susman
1983 "The Locomotor Anatomy of *Australopithecus afarensis.*" *American Journal of Physical Anthropology,* **60**:279–317.
Stewart, T. D.
1979 *Essentials of Forensic Anthropology: Especially as Developed in the United States.* Springfield: C. C. Thomas.
Stiner, Mary C.
1991 "The Faunal Remains from Grotta Guatari." *Current Anthropology,* **32**(2)April:103–117.
Stoneking, Mark
1993 "DNA and Recent Human Evolution." *Evolutionary Anthropology,* **2**:60–73.
Straus, Lawrence Guy
1993 "Southwestern Europe at the Last Glacial Maximum." *Current Anthropology,* **32**:189–199.

1995 "The Upper Paleolithic of Europe: An Overview." *Evolutionary Anthropology,* **4**:4–16.
Stringer, C. B. (ed.).
1985 "Middle Pleistocene Hominid Variability and the Origin of Late Pleistocene Humans." *In: Ancestors: The Hard Evidence,* E. Delson (ed.), New York: Alan R. Liss, pp. 289–295.

1993 "Secrets of the Pit of the Bones." *Nature,* **362**:501–502.
Stringer, C. B. and P. Andrews
1988 "Genetic and Fossil Evidence for the Origin of Modern Humans." *Science,* **239**:1263–1268.

Struhsaker, T. T.
1967 "Auditory Communication among Vervet Monkeys (*Cercopithecus aethiops*)." *In: Social Communication Among Primates,* S. A. Altmann (ed.), Chicago: University of Chicago Press.

1975 *The Red Colobus Monkey.* Chicago: University of Chicago Press.
Struhsaker, Thomas T. and Lysa Leland
1979 "Socioecology of Five Sympatric Monkey Species in the Kibale Forest, Uganda." *Advances in the Study of Behavior,* Vol. 9, New York: Academic Press, pp. 159–229.

1987 "Colobines: Infanticide by Adult Males." *In:* B. B. Smuts et al. (eds.), q.v., pp. 83–97.
Strum, S. C.
1987 *Almost Human. A Journey into the World of Baboons.* New York: W. W. Norton.
Sugiyama, Y.
1965 "Short History of the Ecological and Sociological Studies on Non-Human Primates in Japan." *Primates,* **6**:457–460.
Sumner, D. R., M. E. Morbeck, and J. Lobick
1989 "Age-Related Bone Loss in Female Gombe Chimpanzees." *American Journal of Physical Anthropology,* **72**:259.
Suomi, Stephen J., Susan Mineka, and Roberta D. DeLizio
1983 "Short- and Long-Term Effects of Repetitive Mother-Infant Separation on Social Development in Rhesus Monkeys." *Developmental Psychology,* **19**(5):710–786.
Susman, Randall L. (ed.)
1984 *The Pygmy Chimpanzee: Evolutionary Biology and Behavior.* New York: Plenum Press.
Susman, Randall L.
1988 "New Postcranial Remains from Swartkrans and Their Bearing on the Functional Morphology and Behavior of *Paranthropus robustus.*" *In:* F. E. Grine (ed.), q.v., pp. 149–172.
Susman, Randall L., Jack T. Stern, and William L. Jungers
1985 "Locomotor Adaptations in the Hadar Hominids." *In: Ancestors: The Hard Evidence,* E. Delson (ed.), New York: Alan R. Liss, pp. 184–192.
Sussman, Robert W., James M. Cheverud and Thad Q. Bartlett
1995 Infant Killing as an Evolutionary Strategy: Reality or Myth? *Evolutionary Anthropology,* **3**(5):149–151.
Suzman, I. M.
1982 "A Comparative Study of the Hadar and Sterkfontein Australopithecine Innominates." *American Journal of Physical Anthropology,* **57**:235.
Swisher, C. C. III, G. H. Curtis, T. Jacob, et al.
1994 "Age of the Earliest Known Hominids in Java, Indonesia." *Science,* **263**:1118–1121.
Szalay, Frederick S. and Eric Delson
1979 *Evolutionary History of the Primates.* New York: Academic Press.

Tattersal, Ian, Eric Delson, and John Van Couvering
  1988   *Encyclopedia of Human Evolution and Prehistory.*
          New York: Garland Publishing.
Teleki, G.
  1986   "Chimpanzee Conservation in Sierra Leone—A
          Case Study of a Continent-wide Problem." Paper pre-
          sented at Understanding Chimpanzees Symposium,
          Chicago Academy of Sciences, Chicago, Nov. 7–10,
          1987.
Templeton, Alan R.
  1996   "Gene Lineages and Human Evolution." *Science,*
          272:1363–1364.
Tenaza, R. and R. Tilson
  1977   "Evolution of Long-Distance Alarm Calls in Kloss'
          Gibbon." *Nature,* **268**:233–235.
Thorne, A. G. and M. H. Wolpoff
  1992   "The Multiregional Evolution of Humans." *Scientific
          American,* **266**:76–83.
Tiemel, Chen, Yang Quan, and Wu En
  1994   "Antiquity of *Homo sapiens* in China." *Nature,*
          368:55–56.
Tishkoft, S. A., E. Dietzsch, W. Speed, et al.
  1996   "Global Patterns of Linkage Disequilibrium at the
          CD4 Locus and Modern Human Origins." *Science,*
          271:1380–1387.
Tobias, Phillip
  1971   *The Brain in Hominid Evolution.* New York:
          Columbia University Press.

  1983   "Recent Advances in the Evolution of the Hominids
          with Especial Reference to Brain and Speech."
          Pontifical Academy of Sciences, *Scrita Varia,*
          50:85–140.

  1991   *Olduvai Gorge, Volume IV. The Skulls, Endocasts and
          Teeth of* Homo habilis. Cambridge: Cambridge
          University Press.
Trevathan, Wenda R.
  1987   *Human Birth: An Evolutionary Perspective.*
          Hawthorne, NY: Aldine de Gruyter.
Trinkaus, E.
  1983   *The Shanidar Neandertals.* New York: Academic
          Press.

  1984   "Western Asia." *In:* F. H. Smith and F. Spencer (eds.),
          q.v., pp. 251–293.
Trinkaus, E. and W. W. Howells
  1979   "The Neandertals." *Scientific American,*
          241(6):118–133.
Trinkaus, Erik and Pat Shipman
  1992   *The Neandertals.* New York: Alfred A. Knopf.
Trivers, R. L.
  1971   "The Evolution of Reciprocal Altruism." *Quarterly
          Review of Biology,* **46**:35–57.

  1972   "Parental Investment and Sexual Selection." *In:
          Sexual Selection and the Descent of Man,* B.
          Campbell (ed.), Chicago: Aldine, pp. 136–179.

Tuttle, Russell H.
  1990   "Apes of the World." *American Scientist,* **78**:115–125.
Van Couvering, A. H. and J. A. Van Covering
  1976   "Early Miocene Mammal Fossils From East Africa."
          In: Human Origins, G. Isaac and E. R. McCown
          (eds.), Menlo Park, CA.: Benjamin/Cummings,
          pp. 155–207.
Villa, Paola
  1983   *Terra Amata and the Middle Pleistocene
          Archaeological Record of Southern France.* University
          of California Publications in Anthropology, Vol. 13.
          Berkeley: University of California Press.
Visalberghi, E.
  1990   "Tool Use in Cebus." *Folia Primatologica,*
          54:146–154.
Vogel, F.
  1970   "ABO Blood Groups and Disease." *American Journal
          of Human Genetics,* **22**:464–475.
Vogel, F., M. Kopun, and R. Rathenberg
  1976   "Mutation and Molecular Evolution." *In: Molecular
          Anthropology,* M. Goodman et al. (eds.), New York:
          Plenum Press, pp. 13–33.
Von Koenigswald, G. H. R.
  1956   *Meeting Prehistoric Man.* New York: Harper &
          Brothers.
Vrba, E. S.
  1988   "Late Pliocene Climatic Events and Hominid
          Evolution." *In:* F. Grine (ed.), q.v., pp. 405–426.
Walker, A.
  1976   "Remains Attributable to *Australopithecus* from East
          Rudolf." *In: Earliest Man and Environments in the
          Lake Rudolf Basin,* Y. Coppens et al. (eds.), Chicago:
          University of Chicago Press, pp. 484–489.

  1991   "The Origin of the Genus *Homo.*" *In:* S. Osawa and
          T. Honjo (eds.), *Evolution of Life.* Tokyo: Springer-
          Verlag, pp. 379–389.

  1993   "The Origin of the Genus *Homo*" *In:* D. T.
          Rasmussen (ed.), *The Origin and Evolution of
          Humans and Humanness.* Boston: Jones and Bartlett,
          pp. 29–47.
Walker, A., D. Pilbeam, and M. Cartmill
  1981   "Changing Views and Interpretations of Primate
          Evolution." Paper presented to the Annual Meetings,
          American Association of Physical Anthropologists.
          Detroit, Mich.
Walker, Alan and R. E. Leakey (eds.)
  1993   *The Nariokotome* Homo erectus *Skeleton.*
          Cambridge: Harvard University Press.
Walker, Alan and Mark Teaford
  1989   "The Hunt for *Proconsul.*" *Scientific American,*
          260(Jan):76–82.
Walters, Jeffrey and Robert Seyfarth
  1987   "Conflict and Cooperation." *In:* B. B. Smuts et al.
          (eds.), q.v., pp. 306–317.
Wanpo, Huang, Russell Ciochon, et al.
  1995   "Early *Homo* and Associated Artifacts from Asia."
          Nature, **378**:275–278.

Ward, S. C. and D. R. Pilbeam
1983   Maxillofacial Morphology of Miocene Hominoids from Africa and Indo-Pakistan." *In:* R. L. Ciochon and R. S. Corruccini (eds.), q.v., pp. 211–238.

Ward, Steven and William H. Kimbel
1983   "Subnasal Alveolar Morphology and the Systematic Position of *Sivapithecus*." *American Journal of Physical Anthropology*, 61:157–171.

Waser, Peter M.
1987   "Interactions among Primate Species." *In:* B. B. Smuts et al. (eds.), q.v., pp. 210–226.

Washburn, S. L.
1963   "The Study of Race." *American Anthropologist*, 65:521–531.

_____
1971   "The Study of Human Evolution." *In:* P. Dolhinow and V. Sarich (eds.), *Background for Man: Readings in Physical Anthropology*, Boston: Little, Brown, pp. 82–121.

Watson, J. B. and F. H. C. Crick
1953a   "Genetical Implications of the Structure of the Deoxyribonucleic Acid." *Nature*, 171:964–967.

_____
1953b   "A Structure for Deoxyribonucleic Acid." *Nature*, 171:737–738.

Weiner, J. S.
1955   *The Piltdown Forgery.* London: Oxford University Press.

Weiss, K. M., K. K. Kidd, and J. R. Kidd
1992   "A Human Genome Diversity Project." *Evolutionary Anthropology*, 1:80–82.

Weiss, Mark L. and Alan E. Mann
1981   *Human Biology and Behavior*, 3rd ed. Boston: Little Brown.

White, T. D.
1980   "Evolutionary Implications of Pliocene Hominid Footprints." *Science*, 208:175–176.

_____
1983   Comment Made at Institute of Human Origins Conference on the Evolution of Human Locomotion (Berkeley, Ca.).

White, T. D. and J. M. Harris
1977   "Suid Evolution and Correlation of African Hominid Localities." *Science*, 198:13–21.

White, T. D., G. Suwa, and B. Asfaw
1995   Corrigendum (White et al., 1994). *Nature*, 375:88.

White, T. D., D. C. Johanson, and W. H. Kimbel
1981   "*Australopithecus africanus*: Its Phyletic Position Reconsidered." *South African Journal of Science*, 77:445–470.

White, Tim D. and Donald C. Johanson
1989   "The Hominid Composition of Afar Locality 333: Some Preliminary Observations." *Hominidae*, Proceedings of the 2nd International Congress of Human Paleontology, Milan: Editoriale Jaca Book, pp. 97–101.

White, Tim D., Gen Suwa, and Berhane Asfaw
1994   *Australopithecus ramidus*, A New Species of Early Hominid from Aramis, Ethiopia. *Nature*, 371:306–312.

Whyte, Robert Orr (ed.)
1984   "The Evolution of the East Asian Environment." Centre of Asian Studies Occasional Papers and Monographs, No. 59. Hong Kong: University of Hong Kong.

Williams, George C.
1966   *Adaptation and Natural Selection: A Critique of Some Current Evolutionary Thought.* Princeton: Princeton University Press.

Williams, George C. and Randolph M. Nesse
1991   The Dawn of Darwinian Medicine. *The Quarterly Review of Biology*, 66:1–22.

Williams, Robert C.
1985   "HLA II: The Emergence of the Molecular Model for the Major Histocompatibility Complex." *Yearbook of Physical Anthropology*, 1985, 28:79–95.

Wilson, E. O.
1975   *Sociobiology. The New Synthesis.* Cambridge: Harvard University Press.

Wolf, Katherine and Steven Robert Schulman
1984   "Male Response to 'Stranger' Females as a Function of Female Reproduction Value among Chimpanzees." *The American Naturalist*, 123:163–174.

Wolpoff, Milford H.
1983a   "Lucy's Little Legs." *Journal of Human Evolution*, 12:443–453.

_____
1983b   "*Ramapithecus* and Human Origins. An Anthropologist's Perspective of Changing Interpretations." *In:* R. L. Ciochon and R. S. Corruccini (eds.), q.v., pp. 651–676.

_____
1984   "Evolution in *Homo erectus:* The Question of Stasis." *Paleobiology*, 10:389–406.

_____
1989   "Multiregional Evolution: The Fossil Alternative to Eden." *In:* P. Mellars and C. Stringer, q.v., pp. 62–108.

_____
1995   *Human Evolution* 1996 Edition. New York: McGraw-Hill Inc, College Custom Series.

Wolpoff, Milford H. et al.
1981   "Upper Pleistocene Human Remains from Vindija Cave, Croatia, Yugoslavia." *American Journal of Physical Anthropology*, 54:499–545.

_____
1994   "Multiregional Evolutions: A World-Wide Source for Modern Human Population." *In:* M. H. Nitecki and D. V. Nitecki (eds.), q.v., pp. 175–199.

Wolpoff, M., Wu Xin Chi, and Alan G. Thorne
1984   "Modern *Homo sapiens* Origins." *In:* Smith and Spencer (eds.), q.v., pp. 411–483.

Wood, Bernard
1991   *Koobi Fora Research Project IV: Hominid Cranial Remains from Koobi Fora.* Oxford: Clarendon Press.

_____
1992a   "Origin and Evolution of the Genus *Homo.*" *Nature,* **355**:783–790.

_____
1992b   "A Remote Sense for Fossils." *Nature,* **355**:397–398.

Wood, C. S., G. A. Harrison, C. Dove, and J. S. Weiner
1972   "Selection Feeding of *Anopheles gambiae* According to ABO Blood Group Status." *Nature,* **239**:165.

Wrangham, R. W.
1977   "Feeding Behaviour of Chimpanzees in Gombe National Park, Tanzania." *In: Primate Ecology,* T. H. Clutton-Brock (ed.). New York: Academic Press, pp. 503–538.

_____
1986   "Ecology and Social Relationships in Two Species of Chimpanzees." *In: Ecology and Social Evolution: Birds and Mammals,* D. I. Rubenstein and R. W. Wrangham (eds.), Princeton: Princeton University Press, pp. 352–378.

Wrangham, Richard
1980   "An Ecological Model of Female-Bonded Primate Groups." *Behavior,* **75**:262–300.

Wu, Rukang and S. Lin
1983   "Peking Man." *Scientific American,* **248**(6):86–94.

Wu, Rukang and C. E. Oxnard
1983   "Ramapithecines from China: Evidence from Tooth Dimensions." *Nature,* **306**:258–260.

Wu, Rukang and John W. Olsen (eds.)
1985   *Paleoanthropology and Palaeolithic Archaeology in the People's Republic of China.* New York: Academic Press.

Wu, Rukang and Xingren Dong
1985   "*Homo erectus* in China." *In: Palaeoanthropology and Palaeolithic Archaeology in the People's Republic of China,* R. Wu and J. W. Olsen (eds.), New York: Academic Press, pp. 79–89.

Yellen, John E. et al.
1995   "A Middle Stone Age Worked Bone Industry from Katanda, Upper Semliki Valley, Zaire." *Science,* **268**:553–556.

Yi, Seonbok and G. A. Clark
1983   "Observations on the Lower Palaeolithic of Northeast Asia." *Current Anthropology,* **24**:181–202.

Young, David.
1992   *The Discovery of Evolution.* Cambridge: Natural History Museum Publications, Cambridge University Press.

Yunis, Jorge J. and Om Prakesh
1982   "The Origin of Man: A Chromosomal Pictorial Legacy." *Science,* **215**:1525–1530.

Zhou Min Zhen and Wang Yuan Quing
1989   "Paleoenvironmental Contexts of Hominid Evolution in China." *Circum-Pacific Prehistory Conference,* Seattle: University of Washington Press.

Zubrow, Ezra
1989   "The Demographic Modeling of Neanderthal Extinction." *In: The Human Revolution,* P. Mellars and C. Stringer, Princeton, N.J.: Princeton University Press, pp. 212–231.

Index

A

ABO blood group system
  allele frequencies
    dominance and, 79
    evolutionary changes in, 88–89
    variations among populations, 111–114
  as Mendelian trait, 75, 77, 110
  mother-fetus incompatibilities, 116–117
abortion, therapeutic, 100–101
acclimatization
  defined, **139**
  to high altitude, 145
  as short-term response to environmental
    change, 139
Acheulian (glossary term), **423**
Acheulian tool kit
  archaic *Homo sapiens*, 444
  East Turkana site, 423
  Homo erectus, 426–427
  Olduvai Gorge site, 337
achondroplasia, 78
acquired characteristics, theory of inheritance
  of, 26
adaptation
  as addressed by anthropology, 6
  anthropological perspective in examining,
    15–16
  bipedalism as, 354–359
  environment as agent of. *See* environment,
    as agent of adaptation
  environmental stressors and
    high altitude, 145–146
    infectious disease, 146–151
    solar radiation, vitamin D, and skin
      color, 139–142
    thermal environment, 142–145
    types of responses to environmental
      change, 139
  generalized and specialized characteristics
    in, 193

genetic variation
    as essential to, 61
    selective pressures in natural selection,
      93–94
  of primates to arboreal living, 209–212
adaptive niche
  defined, **209**
  for primates, trees as, 209
adaptive radiation
  of Cenozoic mammals, 191
  defined, **191**
  described, 193
  Eocene prosimian, 296–297
  of Mesozoic reptiles, 191, 193
  of Miocene hominoids, 305–306
adenine, 44
adenosine triphosphate. *See* ATP (adenosine
  triphosphate)
adolescence, as life cycle stage, 177–178
adolescent growth spurt, **159**
adult acclimatizations to high altitude, 145
adulthood
  as life cycle stage, 178–180
  social recognition of onset of, 178
Aegyptopithecus, 302–304
affiliative behaviors, 277
affiliative (glossary term), **277**
Africa
  archaic *Homo sapiens* fossils, 437
  Central
    australopithecine, possible, 378
    early hominid localities, 362
  deforestation and primate endangerment
    in, 284–286
  first hominid dispersal from, 409
  Great Rift Valley. *See* geological rifting
  H. sapiens sapiens fossil finds, as earliest
    known, disputed, 473–474
  HIV origin in, possible, 149–150
  hominoid evolution

evidence for origins in, 308
  Miocene fossil forms, 309–311
as origin of *H. sapiens sapiens*
  complete replacement model, 468–471
  disputed, 468, 472–473
slash-and-burn agriculture, malaria and,
  119
Upper Paleolithic technology and art, 488
See also Central Africa; East African
    hominids; North African hominids;
    South African hominids
African populations
  body shape and stature, 143
  lactose tolerance distribution in, 121
  Rh negative percentage, 114
African-American populations
  racial purity theories directed against, 154
  rickets, nineteenth century incidence of,
    141
Afropithecus, 310
age
  attitudes toward advanced, U. S., 178, 179
  of death for female primates, 179
  maternal, trisomy 21 vs., 63
age spans, primate, 174
aggression
  affiliative behaviors as reducing level of,
    277
  dominance hierarchies and, 249
  interactions based on, 277–280
aging
  as addressed by cultural anthropology, 7
  as life cycle stage, 178–179
agriculture
  adoption of, dietary changes after, 166–167
  slash-and-burn, **119**
  See also preagricultural period
AIDS (acquired immunodeficiency
  syndrome)
  adaptive significance, 148–150

Photo credits

Chapter 1
p. 2   Fig. 1–1 . . . . Courtesy Peter Jones
p. 3   Fig. 1–2 . . . . Bettmann Archive
p. 5   Fig. 1–3(a) . . . . Institute of Human Origins
p. 5   Fig. 1–3(b) . . . . Lynn Kilgore
p. 5   Fig. 1–3(c) . . . . Lynn Kilgore
p. 5   Fig. 1–3(d) . . . . R. Jurmain
p. 10   Fig. 1–4 . . . . Institute of Human Origins
p. 11   Fig. 1–5 . . . . R. Jurmain
p. 11   Fig. 1–6 . . . . Courtesy Judith
                                      Regensteiner/Michael Whitney
p. 12   Fig. 1–7(a) . . . . Bonnie Pedersen/Arlene Kruse
p. 12   Fig. 1–7(b) . . . . R. Jurmain
p. 13   Fig. 1–8(a) . . . . Lynn Kilgore
p. 13   Fig. 1–8(b) . . . . R. Jurmain
p. 14   Fig. 1–9 . . . . Courtesy Lorna Pierce/Judy
                                      Suchey

Chapter 2
p. 24   Fig. 2–1 . . . . Bancroft Library, University of
                                      California
p. 25   Fig. 2–2 . . . . American Museum of Natural
                                      History
p. 25   Fig. 2–3 . . . . American Museum of Natural
                                      History
p. 26   Fig. 2–4 . . . . Bettmann Archive
p. 26   Fig. 2–5 . . . . Bettmann Archive
p. 27   Fig. 2–6 . . . . Reprinted by permission from
                                      p. 115, 118 of Historical Geology:
                                      Evolution of the Earth and Life
                                      Through Time, by Reed Wicander
                                      and James S. Monroe, copyright ©
                                      1989 by West Publishing
                                      Company. All rights reserved
p. 27   Fig. 2–7 . . . . American Museum of Natural
                                      History
p. 28   Fig. 2–8 . . . . American Museum of Natural
                                      History
p. 28   Fig. 2–9 . . . . American Museum of Natural
                                      History
p. 29   Fig. 2–10 . . . . American Museum of Natural
                                      History
p. 31   Fig. 2–13 . . . . Lynn Kilgore
p. 32   Fig. 2–14 . . . . Library, N.Y. Academy of Medicine
p. 34   Fig. 2–15(a) . . . . Michael Tweedie/Photo
                                      Researchers
p. 34   Fig. 2–15(b) . . . . Breck P. Kent/Animals, Animals

Chapter 3
p. 54   Fig. 3–7 . . . . From: Harrison, C. et al., 1983.
                                      Cytogen. Cell Genet 35: 21–27. S.
                                      Karger, A. G., Basel
p. 56   Fig. 3–9 . . . . University of California Medical
                                      Center

Chapter 4
p. 70   Fig. 4–1 . . . . American Museum of Natural
                                      History

Chapter 5
p. 122 Fig. 5–3 . . . . Fr. Peter Weigand, O.S.B.

Chapter 6
p. 141 Fig. 6–2 . . . . Norman Lightfoot/Photo
                                      Researchers
p. 143 Fig. 6–3(a) . . . . Renee Lynn/Photo Researchers
p. 143 Fig. 6–3(b) . . . . George Holton/Photo Researchers
p. 146 Fig. 6–4(a) . . . . William Pratt
p. 146 Fig. 6–4(b) . . . . L. G. Moore

Chapter 7
p. 157 Fig. 7–1 . . . . Courtesy of Dr. Mushtaq A. Khan,
                                      Pakistan Institute of Medical
                                      Sciences, Islambad
p. 182 Guest Essay . . . . Courtesy James J. McKenna

Chapter 8
p. 195 Fig. 8–8 . . . . Hansejudy Beste/Animals, Animals
p. 195 Fig. 8–9 . . . . J. C. Stevenson/Animals, Animals

Chapter 9
p. 210 Fig. 1 in Box 9–1 . . . . . . Lynn Kilgore
p. 211 Fig. 2 in Box 9–1 . . . . . . Lynn Kilgore
p. 211 Fig. 3 in Box 9–1 . . . . . . Lynn Kilgore
p. 211 Fig. 4 in Box 9–1 . . . . . . Lynn Kilgore
p. 219 Fig. 9–11 . . . . Courtesy Fred Jacobs
p. 219 Fig. 9–12 . . . . Courtesy Fred Jacobs
p. 219 Fig. 9–13 . . . . Courtesy San Francisco Zoo
p. 219 Fig. 9–14 . . . . Courtesy Bonnie Pedersen/Arlene
                                      Kruse
p. 220 Fig. 9–16 . . . . David Haring, Duke University
                                      Primate Center
p. 221 Fig. 9–18 . . . . © Zoological Society of San Diego,
                                      photo by Ron Garrison
p. 221 Fig. 9–19 . . . . Raymond Mendez/Animals,
                                      Animals
p. 224 Fig. 9–21 . . . . Robert L. Lubeck/Animals,
                                      Animals
p. 225 Fig. 9–23 . . . . R. Jurmain
p. 226 Fig. 9–24(a) . . . . Lynn Kilgore
p. 226 Fig. 9–24(b) . . . . Courtesy Bonnie Pedersen/Arlene
                                      Kruse
p. 226 Fig. 9–25 . . . . R. Jurmain
p. 228 Fig. 9–27 . . . . Lynn Kilgore
p. 229 Fig. 9–28 . . . . R. Jurmain, Photo by Jill
                                      Matsumoto/Jim Anderson
p. 230 Fig. 9–30(a) . . . . Lynn Kilgore
p. 230 Fig. 9–31(b) . . . . Lynn Kilgore
p. 230 Fig. 9–31(a) . . . . R. Jurmain, Photo by Jill
                                      Matsumoto/Jim Anderson
p. 230 Fig. 9–31(b) . . . . R. Jurmain, Photo by Jill
                                      Matsumoto/Jim Anderson
p. 231 Fig. 9–32 . . . . Arlene Kruse/Bonnie Pedersen
p. 232 Fig. 9–33 . . . . Courtesy, Ellen Ingmanson
p. 237 Fig. 2 Issue . . . . Lynn Kilgore
p. 238 Fig. 3 Issue . . . . R. Jurmain

Chapter 10
p. 241 Fig. 10–1 . . . . Bonnie Pedersen
p. 244 Fig. 10-2 . . . . Courtesy John Oates
p. 245 Fig. 10-3 . . . . Courtesy Jean De Rousseau
p. 247 Fig. 10-4 . . . . Courtesy John Oates
p. 250 Fig. 10-5(a) . . . . R. Jurmain
p. 250 Fig. 10-5(b) . . . . Meredith Small
p. 250 Fig. 10-5(c) . . . . Lynn Kilgore

559

FINAL

WED   DEC 10   8-10 AM
FRI   DEC 12   10¹⁵-12¹⁵
NO TUES   DEC 16   10¹⁵-12¹⁵
WED   DEC 17   10¹⁵-12¹⁵
THURS DEC 11   8-10 PM

QUIZ
4-2 DEC 2ND
4-3 DEC 9TH
4-4 thru 4-7 DUE at FINAL

484-8467